Welcome to

McGraw-Hill Education
United States History

How to Use This Book

*S*AT Subject Test: United States History contains test-taking strategies and a review of the topics you will need to know for the SAT United States History Test. This book provides six full-length practice tests to help you sharpen your skills in preparation for taking the test, as well as test-taking tips and a study plan to help you maximize your preparation time.

1 Take the Diagnostic Test

The Diagnostic Test at the beginning of this workbook will give you an idea of where your strengths and weaknesses lie. It will help you to decide which chapters of the Topic Review will be most valuable to you. The diagnostic test also will help you to become familiar with the question formats that appear on the actual exam. Take the Diagnostic Test in a controlled environment, with as few distractions as possible. In order to closely simulate testing conditions, limit yourself to 60 minutes, and use the answer sheet provided.

When you are done, or when time is up, check your answers in the Answer Key. Explanations of the correct response to each question follow the Answer Key. Be sure to review any questions you missed so that you can learn from your mistakes and can identify the Topic Review chapters on which you most need to concentrate. Calculate your score on the Diagnostic Test using the chart at the end of the test.

2 Prepare for Each Topic Tested

The Topic Review is divided into 33 chapters, each of which is devoted to a specific area of United States history. These chapters will give you an idea of the content of the United States History SAT Subject Test and the types of questions you may be asked. The questions also have been carefully designed to match the test content and format specified by the test makers. Answers and explanations for the practice questions in each chapter are located at the end of each chapter.

3 Practice Your Test-Taking Skills

At the end of the Topic Review, there are six more full-length practice tests in Part III of this book. These tests can help you to reevaluate yourself after you have worked through each chapter in the Topic Review. These practice tests also can help you to identify any areas in which you need further study or review as you prepare. Since there are six full-length practice tests in Part III of this book, you can repeat this process many times until you feel comfortable with your performance on the United States History SAT Subject Test. Answers to each practice test are located at the end of the test, and explanations are provided.

The Top 30 Topics You Need to Study for the United States History SAT Subject Test

Here is a checklist of 30 topics that are very likely to appear on the United States History SAT Subject Test. Use this list for a last-minute review before your exam. See the Test-Taking Strategies section of this book for specific types of questions and how to approach each type.

1 Settlement of North America
Know the various Native American nations that first settled North America and which nations lived in which regions. See Chapter 1.

2 European Exploration and Settlement
Know the areas that Spain, France, and Great Britain explored and settled, and recognize the names of the major explorers. See Chapters 1 and 2.

3 British Settlement of the Atlantic Coast
Know the names of the 13 colonies that became the first 13 states. Have a basic idea of when they were settled, by whom, and with what motive (e.g., economics, religion, etc.). See Chapters 1–3.

4 The French and Indian War
Know why the war was fought, who fought on each side, and the most important effects of the war's outcome. Identify the key names of people and places. You should be able to identify the Albany Plan of Union and understand its importance. See Chapter 5.

5 The American Revolution
Know the following about the American Revolution:

- The factors that led up to it (effects of the French and Indian War and parliamentary legislation such as the Stamp Act)
- Colonial protests against new British taxes and British responses (e.g., the Boston Tea Party, the Intolerable Acts, and the formation of the Continental Congress)
- The main ideas and the authors of *Common Sense* and the Declaration of Independence
- Major names in the American army, its allies, and the Continental Congress
- Major battles (e.g., Bunker Hill, Trenton, New York, and Saratoga)

See Chapters 4–6.

6 Founding Documents of the United States of America
These include the Articles of Confederation, the Constitution, and the Bill of Rights. You should know the most important authors and the main ideas of each. You also should be familiar with the authors, purpose, and main ideas of *The Federalist Papers*. See Chapters 7 and 8.

7 Early Administrations
Identify the most important acts and events of the first few presidential administrations. Know the names of the presidents. Be able to identify each of the following and briefly explain its

causes and effects: the Louisiana Purchase, the XYZ Affair, the Lewis and Clark Expedition, the War of 1812, and the Monroe Doctrine. See Chapters 9 and 10.

8   Westward Expansion

Know the causes and effects of westward expansion into land populated by Native Americans and the resulting clashes. Identify the Trail of Tears and which Indian nations were affected. Trace the growing tension over the expansion of slavery as the nation added more states. Know the key figures in the political battles on this issue. Understand the reasons why the United States became more politically divided as it grew in size. Identify the concept of Manifest Destiny and the Compromise of 1850. See Chapters 10 and 13.

9   The Nineteenth Century: Changes In Society

Identify the Seneca Falls Convention, and trace the rise of women's rights. Know when and how labor unions began to form and gain power. Name the major technological inventions and their creators. Identify major artistic, literary, and cultural figures such as Edgar Allan Poe. See Chapters 11 and 12.

10   The Mexican War

Identify the causes of the Mexican War and who fought on which side. Know the key names in the military on both sides. Identify the Alamo. Know the results of the war and its effect on the size of the United States. See Chapter 13.

11   The Civil War

Know the events that led up to the Civil War (e.g., Missouri Compromise, *Dred Scott* decision, John Brown, and Harpers Ferry). Be able to discuss the development of the Republican Party, the Lincoln–Douglas debates, and the election of Abraham Lincoln. Understand what prompted the secession of South Carolina, and be able to list the states that joined the Confederacy. Understand the development and effects of the Emancipation Proclamation. Know the major names in the Union and Confederate armies and the major battles, especially Gettysburg. See Chapters 14 and 15.

12   Reconstruction

Know the important results of the Civil War for African Americans. Be familiar with the provisions of the 13th, 14th, and 15th Amendments. Understand the effect of Lincoln's assassination on reconstruction. Be able to explain how reconstruction gave way to the Jim Crow laws of the 1870s and another century of oppression of African Americans. See Chapter 16.

13   Postwar Westward Expansion

Know the causes of westward expansion after the Civil War (such as the building of the national railroad). Identify the Homestead Act and the effect of expansion on the Plains Indians. Describe clashes between Native Americans and the U.S. Army and their outcomes. See Chapter 17.

14   Rise of Big Business

Know the key figures in the rise of big business, trusts, and monopolies. Identify the major inventions that ushered in the era of mass production, and know the names of the inventors. Identify the effect of the rise of big business on the economy, on workers, and on society as a whole. See Chapter 18.

15   Rise of Big Cities

Know the causes of the rise of big cities. Describe the pre–World War I wave of immigration, and identify the major nationalities who emigrated to the United States and their ports of entry.

Know the basic story of big-city politics and major names, such as William Marcy Tweed. Know the connection between the influx of immigrants and the rise of big business. See Chapter 19.

16   The Age of Reform
Identify the key reforms undertaken by Roosevelt, Taft, and Wilson. Know the names of the key muckraking journalists and what they accomplished. See Chapter 20.

17   Foreign Affairs at the Start of the Twentieth Century
Identify the importance of the following in U.S. foreign policy, and know the key figures involved in each event or issue: the acquisition of Alaska and Hawaii, the opening of trade with Japan, the Spanish-American War, and the Panama Canal. See Chapter 21.

18   World War I
Know the reasons the United States entered World War I and which nations it was allied with. Know the U.S. involvement in the Treaty of Versailles, the treaty's provisions, and its effects. Identify the League of Nations and the 14 Points. See Chapter 22.

19   The Jazz Age
Know the key cultural figures. Know the cause of Prohibition and its repeal and the connection between Prohibition and organized crime. Understand the sweeping changes in society with the rise of the flapper and the passage of the 19th Amendment. See Chapter 23.

20   The Great Depression
Know the major causes and effects of the stock market crash and the Great Depression. You should have a basic knowledge of the New Deal programs of the Roosevelt administration and know what acronyms such as WPA stand for. See Chapter 24.

21   World War II
Know when and why the United States declared war and on whom. Be able to give a basic overview of the war in Europe and the Pacific. Know which nations were U.S. allies and what pacts and treaties were made between the United States and other nations during the war. Understand the effects of the war on the home front and the outcome of the war, including formation of the United Nations and the U.S. occupation of Germany. See Chapters 25 and 26.

22   The Cold War Abroad
Know the following about the Cold War era that lasted from 1945 to 1989:

- The division of Germany and Berlin and its effect on U.S. policy
- The Truman Doctrine
- U.S. attacks on Cuba, Vietnam, and Laos
- The Korean War
- The Iron Curtain: where it was, what it was, and how it affected the United States
- The Cuban Missile Crisis

See Chapters 27 and 28.

23   The Cold War at Home
Know what McCarthyism was, and know the causes and effects of anticommunist hysteria. Identify the House Un-American Activities Committee. Know the basic ideas behind the New

Frontier of the Kennedy administration and the space race between the United States and the Soviet Union. See Chapters 27 and 28.

24 Civil Rights and the Great Society

Identify the civil rights and antipoverty programs of the Kennedy and Johnson administrations. Identify key individuals in the Civil Rights Movement, such as Rosa Parks and Martin Luther King, Jr. Know the basic facts of desegregation and extension of voting rights. Know the causes, effects, and key players of the Black Power Movement. See Chapter 29.

25 The Vietnam War

Know the causes and effects of the Vietnam War. Know the basic chronology of the war, including major events such as the Tet Offensive. Know the Gulf of Tonkin Resolution. Know the basic story of the nationwide protests against the war and their effects, such as the lowering of the voting age to 18. Know the outcome of the war and its effect on the United States. See Chapter 30.

26 Watergate

Know the basic history of crime and corruption in the Nixon administration, including the Watergate burglary, the press coverage, the Saturday Night Massacre, the special prosecutor's investigation, and Nixon's resignation from office. Understand the major effects this scandal had on U.S. society. See Chapter 31.

27 Recent History

Be familiar with the history of the 1980s to the present. Know the main events of the Reagan, Bush, Clinton, Bush II, and Obama administrations. Understand the effect of the end of the Cold War on U.S. foreign policy. See Chapters 32–34.

28 Presidents of the United States

Given the name of any president of the United States, know roughly when he was in office, and identify the key events and issues of his presidency.

29 The Map of the United States

Be able to locate the following on a map of the United States:

- The 13 original colonies
- The Northwest Territory
- The Louisiana Purchase
- The route of the Lewis and Clark Expedition
- The Confederate States of America
- The Oregon Trail
- The Gadsden Purchase

30 Causes and Effects

All of history is made of a long chain of causes and effects. Many SAT Subject Test: United States History questions will ask about the cause(s) or effect(s) of a certain event, speech, or act. As you review U.S. history, keep in mind the causes and effects that connect the events to one another.

Eight-Week Study Plan*

Week 1 (8 weeks before your test date):

- Register for your test.
- Review the front pages of this book, including this study plan.
- Read *Part I*, up to the Diagnostic Exam.
- Take the *Diagnostic Exam*.
- Schedule your study time on your calendar so that you do not let other things push it aside.
- Make flash cards for the U.S. presidents, listing their names, terms of office, and major events during their presidencies.

Week 2 (7 weeks before your test date):

- Read and work through Chapters 1–6.

Week 3 (6 weeks before your test date):

- Read and work through Chapters 7–11.
- Take *Practice Test 1*, and review any questions that relate to American history up to the mid-nineteenth century.

Week 4 (5 weeks before your test date):

- Read and work through Chapters 12–16.
- Take *Practice Test 2*, and review any questions that relate to American history up to the end of Reconstruction.

Week 5 (4 weeks before your test date):

- Read and work through Chapters 17–20.
- Take *Practice Test 3*, and review any questions that relate to American history up to 1920.
- Review all your flash cards, and mark any that you do not know well.

Week 6 (3 weeks before your test date):

- Read and work through Chapters 21–24.
- Take *Practice Test 4*, and review any questions that relate to American history up to 1940.

Week 7 (2 weeks before your test date):

- Read and work through Chapters 25–30.
- Take *Practice Test 5*, and review any questions that relate to American history up to the end of the Vietnam War.

Week 8 (the week leading up to your test):

- Read and work through Chapters 31–33.

- Take *Practice Test 6*, and review it thoroughly. Do some extra work on any topic areas with which you still struggle.
- Find your testing center, and be sure that you know how to get there and how long it will take you on the morning of the test.

The day before your test:

- Organize your ID and supplies. Gather your Admission Ticket, your photo ID, your pencils (two no. 2 pencils with erasers), a watch (without any beeping alarm), a snack for any breaks you have between multiple subject tests, and a sweater or light jacket.
- Do *not* try to study the night before the test. Cramming does not work well. You have studied already, and your brain needs a break. Do something relaxing, such as watching a movie or playing a game.
- Get plenty of sleep.

Test day:

- Get up early.
- Flip through the book to warm up your brain. Do not redo practice questions; just read a bit about each topic.
- Eat breakfast, but nothing too heavy that will make you sluggish.
- Double-check your supplies.
- Arrive early at the testing center. Be there by 7:45 AM for an 8:00 AM testing time.

If you have fewer than eight weeks to study, you can modify this plan to speed things up.

McGRAW-HILL EDUCATION

SAT
SUBJECT TEST
UNITED STATES HISTORY

SAT
SUBJECT TEST
UNITED STATES HISTORY

Fourth Edition

Daniel Farabaugh, Editor
Stephanie Muntone
T.R. Teti

New York | Chicago | San Francisco | Athens | London | Madrid
Mexico City | Milan | New Delhi | Singapore | Sydney | Toronto

1 2 3 4 5 6 7 8 9 10   RHR/RHR   1 2 1 0 9 8 7 6 5

ISBN   978-1-259-58409-1
MHID   1-259-58409-7

e-ISBN   978-1-259-58410-7
e-MHID   1-259-58410-0

SAT is a registered trademark of the College Board, which was not involved in the production of, and does not endorse, this product.

McGraw-Hill Education products are available at special quantity discounts to use as premiums and sales promotions or for use in corporate training programs. To contact a representative, please visit the Contact Us pages at www.mhprofessional.com.

CONTENTS

McGRAW-HILL EDUCATION

SAT
SUBJECT TEST
UNITED STATES HISTORY

PART I

INTRODUCTION TO THE SAT SUBJECT TEST: U.S. HISTORY

All About the SAT Subject Test: U.S. History Test

THE SAT SUBJECT TESTS

What are the SAT Subject Tests?

The SAT Subject Tests (formerly called the SAT II Tests and the Achievement Tests) are a series of college entrance tests that cover specific academic subject areas. Like the better-known SAT test, which measures general verbal and mathematical skills, the SAT Subject tests are given by the College Entrance Examination Board. Colleges and universities often require applicants to take one or more SAT Subject tests along with the SAT.

SAT Subject tests are generally not as difficult as advanced placement tests, but they may cover more than is taught in basic high school courses. Students usually take an SAT Subject test after completing an advanced placement course or an honors course in the subject area.

How Do I Know If I Need to Take SAT Subject Tests?

Review the admissions requirements of the colleges to which you plan to apply. Each college will have its own requirements. Many colleges require that you take a minimum number of SAT Subject tests—usually one or two. Some require that you take SAT Subject tests in specific subjects. Some may not require SAT Subject scores at all.

When are SAT Subject Tests Given, and How Do I Register for Them?

SAT Subject tests usually are given on six weekend dates spread throughout the academic year. These dates are usually the same ones on which the SAT is given. To find out the test dates, visit the College Board Web site at www.collegeboard.com. You also can register for a test at the Web site. Click on the tab marked "students" and follow the directions you are given by creating your own account. You will need to use a credit card if you register online. As an alternative, you can register for SAT Subject tests by mail, using the registration form in the SAT Registration Bulletin, which should be available from your high school guidance counselor.

How Many SAT Subject Tests Should I Take?

You can take as many SAT Subject tests as you wish. According to the College Board, more than one-half of all SAT takers take three tests and about one-quarter take four or more. Keep in mind, though, that you can take only three tests on a single day. If you want to take more than three tests, you will have to take the others on a different testing date. When deciding how many SAT Subject tests to take, base your decision on the requirements of the colleges to which you plan to apply. It is probably not a good idea to take many more SAT Subject tests than you need. You probably will do better by focusing only on the ones that your preferred colleges require.

Which SAT Subject Tests Should I Take?

If a college to which you are applying requires one or more specific SAT Subject tests, then of course you must take those particular tests. If the college simply requires that you take a minimum number of SAT Subject tests, choose the test or tests for which you think you are best prepared and are likely to get the best score. If you have taken an advanced placement course or an honors course in a particular subject and have done well in that course, you probably should consider taking an SAT Subject test in that subject.

When Should I Take SAT Subject Tests?

Timing is important. It is a good idea to take an SAT Subject test as soon as possible after completing a course in the test subject, while the course material is still fresh in your mind. If you plan to take an SAT Subject test in a subject you have not studied recently, make sure to leave yourself enough time to review the course material before taking the test.

What Do I Need on the Day of the Test?

To take an SAT Subject test, you will need an admission ticket to enter the examination room and acceptable forms of photo identification. You also will need two number 2 pencils. Be sure that the erasers work well at erasing without leaving smudge marks. The tests are scored by machine, and scoring can be inaccurate if there are smudges or other stray marks on the answer sheet.

Any devices that can make noise, such as cell phones and wristwatch alarms, should be turned off during the test. Study aids such as dictionaries and review books, as well as food and beverages, are barred from the test room.

THE SAT U.S. HISTORY TEST

What is the Format of the SAT U.S. History Test?

The SAT U.S. History test is a one-hour examination consisting of 90 to 95 multiple-choice questions. The questions deal with historical events, developments, trends, and concepts, as well as with social science concepts and methods as they are used in the study of history. According to the College Board, the test measures the following knowledge and skills:

- Familiarity with historical concepts, cause-and-effect relationships, geography, and other data necessary for understanding major historical developments
- Grasp of concepts essential to historical analysis
- Ability to use historical knowledge in interpreting data in maps, graphs, charts, and cartoons

The test covers U.S. history from pre-Columbian times to the present. It covers not just political history and foreign policy but also economic, social, intellectual, and cultural history. The following chart shows the general test subject areas, as well as the approximate portion of the test devoted to each subject.

SAT U.S. History Questions by Subject Area

Subject Area	Approximate Percentage of Exam
Political History	32–36%
Economic History	18–20%
Social History	18–22%
Intellectual and Cultural History	10–12%
Foreign Policy	13–17%

This next chart shows the breakdown of test questions by historical period.

SAT U.S. History Questions by Historical Period

Historical Period	Approximate Percentage of Exam
Pre-Columbian Era to 1789	20%
1790 to 1898	40%
1899 to the present	40%

What School Background Do I Need for the SAT U.S. History Test?

The College Board recommends that you have at least the following experience before taking the SAT U.S. History test:

- One-year comprehensive course in U.S. history at the college preparatory level
- Social studies courses and outside reading
- Familiarity with "periodization," the trends within major historical periods

How is the SAT U.S. History Test Scored?

On the SAT U.S. History test, your "raw score" is calculated as follows: You receive one point for each question you answer correctly, but you lose one-quarter point for each question you answer incorrectly. You do not gain or lose any points for questions you do not answer at all. Your raw score then is converted into a scaled score by a statistical method that takes into account how well you did compared with others who took the same test. Scaled scores range from 200 to 800 points. Your scaled score will be reported to you, to your high school, and to the colleges and universities you designate to receive it.

When Will I Receive My Score?

You can view your scores by logging into our My SAT account approximately three weeks after the test. Refer to the College Board Web site to see what date your score will become available. Scores are also mailed to students for free by accessing the College Board Web site, or you can get your score for an additional fee by calling (866) 756-7346.

How Do I Submit My Score to Colleges and Universities?

When you register to take the SAT or SAT Subject test, your fee includes free reporting of your scores to up to four colleges and universities. To have your scores reported to additional schools, visit the College Board Web site or call (866) 756-7346. You will have to pay an additional fee.

TEST-TAKING STRATEGIES FOR THE U.S. HISTORY TEST

The SAT U.S. History test covers a huge number of topics, and there's no avoiding the fact that the best way to get a high score is to study, study, study. However, because it is a multiple-choice test and because it includes particular types of questions, there are some specific test-taking strategies that you should know to get your best score. This chapter will explain some of those strategies and provide examples to show you how to use them when test day comes.

STRATEGY: Make sure you know what the question is asking.

1. Watch for key words such as not, except, *and* most often.

It is important to make sure you know exactly what the question is asking. A single word such as *not* or *except* can change the whole meaning, and if you miss it when you read the question, you'll never pick the correct answer. Therefore, make sure to read very carefully. If you come to a word such as *not* or *except*, it's a good idea to underline it so that you keep it in mind as you read through the answer choices.

Example:

32. Which of the following was NOT a primary aim of the Progressive movement of the early 1900s?

    (A) Passing laws that would improve slum conditions in large cities
    (B) Teaching immigrants to read, write, and speak English
    (C) Supporting legislation that would make the workplace safer
    (D) Creating public baths, parks, and playgrounds in urban areas
    (E) Making English the official language of the United States

If you do not read this question correctly and miss the word *not*, you could spend your time trying to decide if A, B, C, or D was the best answer. But because of the word *not*, the only choice that could possibly be correct is choice E. You may think that reading questions correctly is a simple matter that you don't have to worry about, but remember how stressed you're likely to be on test day. Make sure you read carefully and accurately. It's better to be safe than sorry!

2. Watch for key words that summarize the question.

In each question there is usually one key word that summarizes what the question is about. That word may be the name of a person, a place, a historical era, or a political doctrine or party. When you find that word, underline or circle it. Then, after choosing the answer you think is correct, go back and look at your underlined or circled word to make sure it agrees with your choice.

Example:

19. Which of the following quotations best explains the concept of Manifest Destiny?

    (A) "Our fathers brought forth on this continent, a new nation, dedicated to the prospect that all men are created equal."
    (B) "We have it in our power to begin the world over again."
    (C) "We hold these truths to be self-evident: that all men are created equal. . . ."
    (D) "The American colonies stand no longer in need of England's protection."
    (E) "The American claim is . . . to overspread and possess the whole of the continent which Providence has given us. . . ."

This question is asking about the concept known as Manifest Destiny, a very important idea in U.S. history. Underline the words "Manifest Destiny" so that your mind focuses on what you know about that particular idea. Now the question looks like this:

19. Which of the following quotations best explains the concept of <u>Manifest Destiny</u>?

Now it is easier to go through the distracters and pick out the correct answer.

    (A) "Our fathers brought forth on this continent, a new nation, dedicated to the prospect that all men are created equal." (*Wrong*)
    (B) "We have it in our power to begin the world over again." (*Wrong*)
    (C) "We hold these truths to be self-evident: that all men are created equal. . . ." (*Wrong*)
    (D) "The American colonies stand no longer in need of England's protection." (*Wrong*)
    (E) "The American claim is . . . to overspread and possess the whole of the continent which Providence has given us. . . ." (*Correct*)

3. Summarize lengthy or confusing distracters.

If you don't know the correct answer and find the distracters lengthy and confusing, try to summarize the idea in each distracter in just a few words. That way, you can compare the different answer choices quickly and easily and try to decide which one is correct. This technique also can be helpful if you decide to skip a question and come back to it later. Study the following example to see how this works.

Example:

60. As the Constitutional Convention ended, Benjamin Franklin commented about a half-sun with its rays painted on George Washington's chair that "now at length I have the happiness to know that it is <u>a rising and not a setting sun</u>." Franklin meant these words as

    (A) a <u>criticism</u> of the delegates in the Convention who did not share his faith in the Constitution
    (B) an indication that he knew the <u>fight</u> for the ratification of the Constitution would be <u>difficult</u>
    (C) a <u>joke</u> about the poor quality of the furniture in Independence Hall
    (D) an <u>expression of hope</u> and optimism for the new government he had helped design
    (E) a <u>criticism</u> of the painter of the chair

Several of the distracters in this question are lengthy and confusing. To make it easier to understand them and compare them with each other, each one has been summarized by having a key word or phrase underlined. The summaries make it clear that you are comparing a few simple alternatives: "a criticism," an indication of a "difficult fight," a "joke," an "expression of hope," and another "criticism." Choice C can be eliminated because it is highly unlikely that a joke would have historical significance. Choices A and E can be eliminated because a "rising sun" is not an image used to express criticism. It is also not an image that evokes the idea of a "difficult fight" (choice B). The only answer choice that makes sense is choice D: a rising sun often is used as an image of hope and optimism.

STRATEGY: Look for clues in the distracters.

1. Look in the distracters for terms that are synonyms for words in the question.

Many important events and ideas in U.S. history can be referred to by several different names. Often a question will use one name in the question stem but use the synonymous term for the same idea in the correct answer. By doing this, the test makers are trying to hide the correct answer, but their words can give you the clue for which you are looking. To see how this works, study the following example.

Example:

28. "The <u>survival of the fittest</u> is simply the survival of the strong, which implies and would better be called the destruction of the weak. If nature progresses through the destruction of the weak, man progresses through the protection of the weak."

The speaker of the above quotation most likely opposed

    (A) Progressivism
    (B) Social Darwinism
    (C) Prohibition
    (D) labor unions
    (E) woman suffrage

The key term in the question is underlined for you. The term *survival of the fittest* derives from Charles Darwin's theory of natural selection. Some thinkers, especially in the late nineteenth century and early twentieth century, believed that the principle of natural section applies to human society as well and that unfettered economic competition is the best way of organizing human relations because it will produce a society dominated by the "fittest." If you are familiar with Darwin's theory, the name "Social Darwinism" in choice B should be an immediate tip-off that this is the correct answer. You should still read the other distracters and eliminate them, but recognizing that "Darwinism" is a synonym for "survival of the fittest" is the clue you are looking for.

2. When two distracters say the same thing in different words, you can rule out both of them.

In some questions you will find two distracters that say essentially the same or almost the same thing but in different words. Remember: A question cannot have two correct answers! That means that both of these distracters must be incorrect and you can rule them out immediately. Here is an example.

Example:

32. Between 1891 and 1910, millions of immigrants came to the United States for all the following reasons EXCEPT:

    (A) to seek economic opportunity
    (B) to escape poverty at home
    (C) to escape religious or political persecution at home
    (D) to earn enough money to return home and live well there
    (E) to lose their cultural identities as soon as possible

Choices A and B say pretty much the same thing: people who want to "escape poverty" also want to "seek economic opportunity." Both of these choices are essentially the same answer, and so both must be incorrect. Furthermore, choice D is not too different from choices A and B, and so you can rule it out as well. That means that you need to deal only with choices C and E, and if you have studied immigration, you should be able to pick choice E as the correct answer.

3. When two distracters contradict each other, you can rule out one of them.

In some questions you will find distracters that express opposite or nearly opposite ideas. Only one of them can be correct, and so one of the two can be ruled out. Of course, you will need to have some knowledge of the topic or find some other hints in the question before you can choose which one to rule out, but it can be helpful to recognize that one of two contradictory distracters is sure to be wrong.

Example:

15. The Jim Crow laws were

    (A) Southern state laws designed to enforce racial segregation
    (B) laws supported by civil rights activists of the 1960s
    (C) proposals for liquor taxes made by Senator James Crow of Missouri
    (D) regulations that provoked the Whiskey Rebellion
    (E) tariffs imposed on the colonies by Great Britain

Distracters A and B express directly contradictory ideas (segregation laws versus civil rights laws), and so one of the two must be incorrect. If you have studied the history of racial segregation in the South, you should know that choice B is incorrect. The Jim Crow laws were the laws enacted in Southern states in the late nineteenth century and early twentieth century to enforce racial segregation.

STRATEGY: Use the process of elimination to narrow down your choices.

1. Rule out any distracters that you know are wrong.

When you cannot pick the answer to a question immediately, the best strategy is to use the process of elimination to narrow down your choices. Start by reading over the distracters and ruling out any that you know for certain are not the correct answer. Don't be shy about marking up the test booklet! Use your pencil to cross out incorrect distracters. That way you will remove them from your field of vision and be able to concentrate on the remaining choices.

Example:

3. The earliest people to arrive in the Americas probably followed animal herds over a wide land bridge that connected

   (A) Siberia to Greenland
   (B) Siberia to North America
   (C) Europe to Iceland
   (D) North America to Cuba
   (E) Europe to Canada

If you know your geography, you can quickly cross out choices A and C. Choice A must be incorrect because Greenland and Siberia are nowhere near each other and could not possibly be connected by a land bridge. Choice C must be incorrect because people crossing a land bridge from Europe to Iceland still would not yet have arrived in North America. Now the question looks like this:

3. The earliest people to arrive in the Americas probably followed animal herds over a wide land bridge that connected

   (A) Siberia to Greenland
   (B) Siberia to North America
   (C) Europe to Iceland
   (D) Cuba to North America
   (E) Europe to Canada

This makes the question much easier to deal with, and if you have to guess, your odds of picking the right answer are one in three. Suppose, though, that instead of guessing you decide to move on and come back to this question later. In that case, the fact that you have crossed out two distracters will make the question that much easier to deal with when you return. (The correct answer to this question is choice B.)

    Crossing out distracters is especially important in longer, wordier items. Look at the following example. Try to choose the correct answer without crossing out distracters and see how many times you have to reread the question and the distracters. If you find yourself rereading something that you already know is wrong, you'll understand why crossing out is a useful strategy.

Example:

32. All the following suggest that President Theodore Roosevelt did not support the interests of large corporations EXCEPT:

   (A) He signed laws that broke up monopolies into smaller businesses.
   (B) He ordered an investigation into the practices of the food-processing and food-manufacturing industry.
   (C) He set aside nearly 150 million acres of land for national parks.
   (D) He signed laws that gave the government the authority to regulate the railroads.
   (E) He encouraged arbitration of labor disputes.

It is hard to keep straight what each of these distracters says. To do so, you have to go back and look at each one again and again. Furthermore, the use of the word *except* makes the question even more confusing. Keep in mind that you are looking for an answer choice that does *not* reflect a policy that was against the interests of big business. In other words, you can eliminate any choice that *does* reflect an antibusiness policy. Choice A is clearly a policy that was against big business, and so it can be eliminated. Choice B also can be eliminated; an investigation into industrial practices is definitely not likely to be favored by big business. Now the question looks like this:

32. All the following suggest that President Theodore Roosevelt did not support the interests of large corporations EXCEPT:

   (A) He signed laws that broke up monopolies into smaller businesses.
   (B) He ordered an investigation into the practices of the food-processing and food-manufacturing industry.
   (C) He set aside nearly 150 million acres of land for national parks.
   (D) He signed laws that gave the government the authority to regulate the railroads.
   (E) He encouraged arbitration of labor disputes.

Now you can focus on figuring out the meaning of distracters C, D, and E. Choice D can be eliminated because the railroads were among the biggest corporations in Roosevelt's day, and laws designed to impose government regulation would not have been in the railroads' interest. Choice E also can be eliminated; the big corporations in Roosevelt's day strongly resisted arbitration of labor disputes. That leaves choice C, which is the correct answer; creating national parks was not necessarily against the interests of large corporations.

2. If you can rule out one or more distracters, make an educated guess.

It's true that on the SAT U.S. History test you will lose a fraction of a point for a wrong answer and that it is a bad idea to guess if you are completely stumped and cannot rule out even one distracter. The reason is that if you cannot rule out any distracters, your chances of guessing the correct answer are very slim. However, if you can rule out one or two or more distracters, the odds start to improve in your favor. If you have to choose among only three distracters, you have a one in three chance of picking the correct answer. If you have to choose between only two distracters, your chances are one in two. Guessing when you can eliminate one or more distracters is called educated guessing. If you can make an educated guess, go ahead and do so. You have more to gain than you have to lose.

STRATEGY: Use what you know about time periods to rule out wrong answers.

One of the most important things to look for in a question is the time period. If you know the time period the question relates to, you can rule out any distracters that do not fall into that period. Ruling out distracters is your key goal. If the question asks about a war, a presidential term, a particular era, or the like, you can exclude anything that is not in the same period.

Example:

11. The Fourteen Points, presented in January 1918, were

   (A) Winston Churchill's plans for dealing with Hitler
   (B) American suffragists' demands for women's rights

    (C) Woodrow Wilson's plan for building peace in the post–World War I world

    (D) sections of the income tax amendment to the Constitution

    (E) the Socialist Party's proposal for economic fairness

Use the time period to exclude distracters that do not belong. Choice A can be eliminated because Hitler did not come to power in Germany until 1933, long after 1918. Choice D can be eliminated because the constitutional amendment authorizing the income tax was ratified in 1913. Now the question looks like this:

11. The Fourteen Points, presented in January 1918, were

    (A) Winston Churchill's plans for dealing with Hitler

    (B) American suffragists' demands for women's rights

    (C) Woodrow Wilson's plan for building peace in the post–World War I world

    (D) sections of the income-tax amendment to the Constitution

    (E) the Socialist Party's proposal for economic fairness

Now your chance of picking the correct answer is one in three. Look again at the question. What was going on in January 1918? If you have studied the period, you know that that the United States had entered World War I in April 1917 and that the war would come to an end in November 1918. Therefore, it makes sense to infer that in January 1918 leaders such as Woodrow Wilson were concerned with planning the postwar world. That would make choice C the most likely answer, and it is indeed correct.

STRATEGY: Learn how to answer quotation questions.

One special kind of question that appears commonly on the SAT U.S. History test is the quotation question. In this kind of question you are presented with a quotation from some era in U.S. history. You then may be asked to decide who said the quoted words. The choices may be famous people in history, or they may be unnamed persons such as "a former slave" or "a factory worker" who would be likely to have said the words in question. Other variations of this kind of question might ask, "The speaker quoted above would most likely agree with which of the following statements?" or "This statement [or question] was used by [a particular historical figure] to justify which of the following?" or "The sentiments in this quotation are most characteristic of which of the following?"

    Quotation questions can be daunting. The first thing to realize is that even though you sometimes are told who is speaking, often you are not given that information, and in fact, you do not always have to know the name of the individual. Usually it is more important to be able to place the quote within its historical background, that is, what event or historical development it refers to, what historical era it most likely dates from, what ideas or opinions it expresses, and who or what sorts of people might have held those ideas or opinions. To figure this out, start by examining the words in the quote. What clues do you see? What ideas does the speaker emphasize? What references are there, if any, to people, places, and events? Who in history—individuals or groups—might have emphasized those ideas or made those references, and why? Then read through the answer choices. If you can't pick the correct answer immediately, try finding it through the process of elimination.

Example:

1. "Slavery now stands erect, clanking its chains on the territory of Kansas, surrounded by a code of death and trampling upon all cherished liberties."

This statement was most likely made by a(n)

   (A) Whig
   (B) "muckraker"
   (C) plantation owner
   (D) Democrat
   (E) abolitionist

Examine the words of the quote. The speaker is describing slavery in the harshest terms, as "clanking its chains" and "surrounded by a code of death." There is also another clue: Kansas is described as a territory, which means that the quote dates from the pre–Civil War era. Now you can start eliminating choices. Choice B can be eliminated because "muckraker" is a term used to describe crusading journalists in the Progressive Era of the early twentieth century, long after the end of the Civil War. Choice C can be eliminated because plantation owners in the old South probably would have been supporters, not opponents, of slavery. Now the question looks like this:

1. "Slavery now stands erect, clanking its chains on the territory of Kansas, surrounded by a code of death and trampling upon all cherished liberties."

This statement was most likely made by a(n)

   (A) Whig
   (B) "muckraker"
   (C) plantation owner
   (D) Democrat
   (E) abolitionist

If you have studied this era, you know that "abolitionist" is a term used to describe those who, in the pre–Civil War era, vigorously opposed slavery and called for its abolition. That matches the ideas presented in the quote, and so choice E must be the correct answer.

STRATEGY: Learn how to answer "cartoon" questions.

Political cartoons have a long and lively history in the United States, and the SAT U.S. History test usually includes a question about a political cartoon. The cartoons that appear on the test often are taken from nineteenth-century or early twentieth-century newspapers. They satirize political figures and events of the day, usually expressing strong positive or negative opinions. You may be asked to tell who or what is being satirized in the cartoon, what point of view is being expressed, or even what other persons might agree or disagree with that point of view.

To interpret political cartoons, keep the following suggestions in mind. First, the people and objects in the cartoons often are labeled to tell readers who or what they are. Look for those labels if you need help understanding what is being represented. Second, the people in cartoons often are shown in situations that parody the ones that actually took place. The parody is the source of the cartoon humor. Third, many cartoons use symbols to stand for political parties, social groups, political ideas, and the like. These symbols are fairly standard, and so it pays to get to know them. Here is a list of some of the most common symbols used in political cartoons:

Well-dressed portly man = businessman or powerful politician
Skinny beggar = the poor
Donkey = Democrat or Democratic Party
Elephant = Republican or Republican Party
Blindfolded woman or scales = justice
Statue of Liberty = liberty or freedom
Uncle Sam = United States
Young African-American man or woman = slave or slavery in general
Eagle = United States
Dove = person who wishes for peace
Hawk = person who wishes for war

Cartoons also frequently deal in stereotypes and caricatures. Although many of them are offensive today, they have been common throughout U.S. history. African Americans, Asians, and other minority groups often have been portrayed negatively in propaganda and cartoons. For the U.S. History test, you need to be able to recognize these various stereotypes.

Cartoons from two particular periods are especially common on the test. The first period is the antebellum period, when cartoons frequently used caricatures and stereotypes to depict Northerners, Southerners, and slaves. The second period is the post–Civil War "Gilded Age," when the artist Thomas Nast drew many cartoons satirizing contemporary political figures, especially the notoriously corrupt "Boss" William Tweed and his associates in New York City's Tammany Hall Democratic political machine. Nast has a very distinctive style that is easily recognized. His cartoons appear very frequently on the SAT U.S. History test. The following are two typical Nast cartoons.

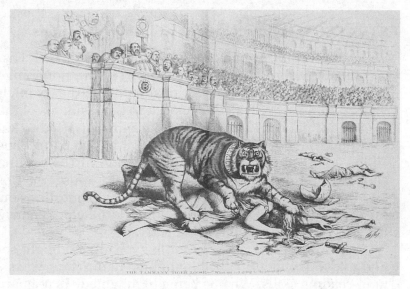

http://cartoons.osu.edu/nast/tammany_tiger.htm

"THAT'S WHAT'S THE MATTER."

Boss Tweed. "As long as I count the Votes, what are you going to do about it? say?"

© 1999 HarpWeek

http://www2.truman.edu/parker/research/cartoons.html

Nast often symbolizes the corruption and venality of Tammany Hall by picturing it as a ferocious-looking tiger. He likewise often portrays Boss Tweed as an overweight, unkempt ruffian with an air of violence about him. He also almost invariably portrays Tweed in the act of destroying the public trust by ravaging symbolic figures of common people or justice or by using intimidation to steal public funds or bully voters. These are quite standard depictions, and they appear over and over in SAT Subject test items.

STRATEGY: Learn how to answer map questions.

First and foremost, map questions on the SAT U.S. History test refer to a significant event in American history. You are not going to get a map question that asks about the establishment of the municipal boundaries of Peoria, Illinois. With all due respect to the residents of that city, that is not a significant national event. The geography you need to know for the test has to do with major national events. You will need to know the states of the Union and the Confederacy, the location of the original 13 colonies, the Northwest Ordinance, the Missouri Compromise, the Compromise of 1850, and the various additions to the Union. Map questions on these topics come up again and again, and there's no trick to help you answer them. You just have to know these subjects by heart.

SAT Subject test map questions typically highlight something on a map and ask you to identify the highlighted item. Thus, you should sharpen your map-reading skills. What is being highlighted? Is it a particular state? Is it a specific historical dividing line? If you encounter this kind of question, do not be intimidated just because there is a map. All you have to do is identify what the map represents and nothing more.

Example:

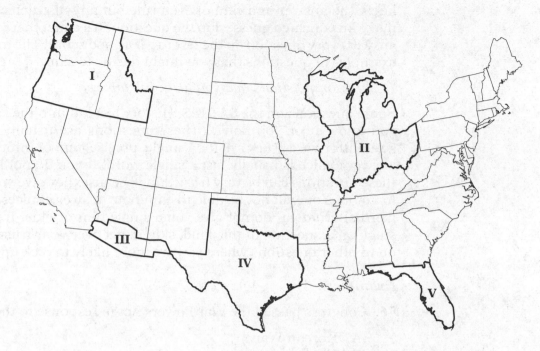

23. Which number on the map marks the Northwest Territory?

    (A) I
    (B) II
    (C) III
    (D) IV
    (E) V

This question is asking you only to identify what the map represents. As is usually the case with map questions, it is no more complex than that. There is no reason to be daunted just because a map is involved.

You are asked to identify the Northwest Territory. Even if you don't know what that term signifies, the name itself is a clue: it must be located either "northwest of something" or "in the Northwest." You can rule out choice D because area IV is neither of those things; it is Texas. You also can rule out choice E because area V is located in the Southwest; it is in fact the state of Florida. You can also rule out choice C because it is in the Southwest.

That leaves choices A and B. Area I is what we now call the Northwest; today it consists of the states of Oregon and Washington. However, that is different from the Northwest Territory, and so choice A is not the correct answer. You should know from your studies that the Northwest Territory included those areas to the northwest of the original 13 states that became part of the United States after the Revolutionary War. Today they make up the states of Ohio, Michigan, Illinois, Indiana, and Wisconsin. Thus, the correct answer is choice B.

STRATEGY: If you don't know the answer and cannot even make an educated guess, skip the question.

Remember: On the SAT Subject tests, you get one point for each question you answer correctly, but if your answer is incorrect, you *lose* a fraction of a point.

In other words, wrong answers can hurt you. Therefore, if you really do not know the answer and cannot even rule out any distracters so that you can make an educated guess, skip the question. It's a fact that you do not have to answer every question on the test to get a good score! The following are some examples of questions that you might decide to skip.

1. Either/or questions that you just can't answer

Some questions on the SAT U.S. History test fall into the category of "either you know it or you don't." These questions are usually very simple and straightforward. They ask for a single, precise item of information, and each answer choice is usually just a single word. If you do not know the answer, these questions can be very frustrating because they give you almost nothing to go on. You will not be able to eliminate answer choices because the one-word alternatives do not give you a single hint or clue. If you find yourself stuck on a question of this kind, skip it, get over your frustration, and move on to other questions where you are more likely to pick up points.

Example:

76. Congress passed the War Powers Act in response to the

    (A) Korean War
    (B) Vietnam War
    (C) Persian Gulf War
    (D) War of 1812
    (E) Iraq War

Now, if you happen to know that the War Powers Act was passed in response to the Vietnam War, you are in luck. Mark your answer and get the credit. But if you do not know that vital piece of information, the question gives you absolutely nothing more to go on than the name of the act. If you do not know the answer to a question like this, skip it and go on to other questions where you are more likely to pick up points.

2. Questions about totally unfamiliar people or events

You may be unlucky enough to come across a question that asks about some-one or something that is totally unfamiliar to you. The problem here is not that there is nothing in the question stem or the distracters that might give you a hint or a clue; it is simply that you have no information on which to base a decision. Here is an example.

Example:

14. The United States became involved in the affairs of Indochina because of the departure from that area of which colonial power?

    (A) France
    (B) Great Britain
    (C) the Netherlands
    (D) Spain
    (E) Germany

If you do not know the answer to this question, any one of the answer choices might seem plausible. Do you have any idea which areas were included in the British and French empires? Do you know which areas were colonized by the

Netherlands, Spain, or Germany? This information could help you rule out answer choices and at least make an educated guess. But if you recall nothing at all about which European country ruled Indochina, you have nothing to gain by staring at this question. Do not try to spin an answer out of nothing. Skip the question and move on to other questions where you are more likely to pick up points.

3. Questions that leave you confused even after a second reading

Some SAT U.S. History questions are very long and intricate. They take time to read and are filled with extremely detailed information. Some may be so lengthy and complicated that even after you read them over twice, you still have no idea what is being asked. If that happens, do not pause to fret and worry as you try to decipher the meaning. Your time is precious! It is better spent going on to questions that are easy for you to answer and that will add quick points to your score. Skip the very lengthy and complex question for now. Star it or circle it so that you can find it again easily. Then, if you have time at the end of the test, you can come back to the question and try to figure it out. Here is an example of this kind of question.

Example:

41. The Antifederalists opposed the original Constitution for all the following reasons EXCEPT:

    (A) Delegates had conspired under a "veil of mystery" to create a new government beyond what they had been charged to do.
    (B) A strong central government would destroy states' rights.
    (C) The new system of government resembled a monarchy and thus violated the principle of liberty for all citizens.
    (D) The system of the electoral college was undemocratic.
    (E) The Constitution included a bill of rights that specified the privileges of all citizens.

This question requires you to know a lot of information. You need to know about the politics of the early Federal period, the political ideas of the Federalists and the Antifederalists, and the provisions of the original Constitution. The Federalists were proponents of a strong central government. The Antifederalists, in contrast, were proponents of states' rights and were fearful of the power of a strong central government. The Antifederalists opposed the original Constitution because they thought it gave too much power to the federal government and did not reserve enough power to the individual states. This matches choice B, which is the correct answer.

Note that it took a full paragraph just to tell what you have to know to answer this question. If you are not very familiar with this era, you are going to have a hard time figuring out the correct answer. Since there is a lot of information in the question, you may be able to work it out eventually, but is it worth the time that would take? In a case like this, if you cannot spot the correct answer immediately, you might be better off skipping this question and moving on to others that you can answer much more rapidly.

DIAGNOSTIC TEST

U.S. HISTORY

The following Diagnostic Test is designed to be just like the real SAT U.S. History test in content coverage and level of difficulty. However, it is only half as long as the real examination.

When you are finished with the test, determine your score and carefully read the answer explanations for the questions you answered incorrectly. Identify any weak areas by determining the areas in which you made the most errors. Review those chapters of the book first. Then, as time permits, go back and review your stronger areas.

Allow 30 minutes to take the test. Time yourself and work uninterrupted. If you run out of time, take note of where you ended when time ran out. Remember that you lose $\frac{1}{4}$ of a point for each incorrect answer. Because of this penalty, do not guess on a question unless you can eliminate one or more of the answers. Your score is calculated by using the following formula:

Number of correct answers $- \frac{1}{4}$(Number of incorrect answers)

This Practice Test will be an accurate reflection of how you'll do on test day if you treat it as the real examination. Here are some hints on how to take the test under conditions similar to those of the actual exam.

- Complete the test in one sitting.
- Time yourself.
- Tear out your Answer Sheet and fill in the ovals just as you would on the actual test day.
- Become familiar with the directions to the test and the reference information provided. You'll save time on the actual test day by already being familiar with this information.

DIAGNOSTIC TEST
U.S. HISTORY

ANSWER SHEET

Tear out this answer sheet and use it to mark your answers.

There are 100 lines of numbered ovals on this answer sheet. If there are more lines than you need, leave the remainder blank.

1. (A) (B) (C) (D) (E)	26. (A) (B) (C) (D) (E)	51. (A) (B) (C) (D) (E)	76. (A) (B) (C) (D) (E)
2. (A) (B) (C) (D) (E)	27. (A) (B) (C) (D) (E)	52. (A) (B) (C) (D) (E)	77. (A) (B) (C) (D) (E)
3. (A) (B) (C) (D) (E)	28. (A) (B) (C) (D) (E)	53. (A) (B) (C) (D) (E)	78. (A) (B) (C) (D) (E)
4. (A) (B) (C) (D) (E)	29. (A) (B) (C) (D) (E)	54. (A) (B) (C) (D) (E)	79. (A) (B) (C) (D) (E)
5. (A) (B) (C) (D) (E)	30. (A) (B) (C) (D) (E)	55. (A) (B) (C) (D) (E)	80. (A) (B) (C) (D) (E)
6. (A) (B) (C) (D) (E)	31. (A) (B) (C) (D) (E)	56. (A) (B) (C) (D) (E)	81. (A) (B) (C) (D) (E)
7. (A) (B) (C) (D) (E)	32. (A) (B) (C) (D) (E)	57. (A) (B) (C) (D) (E)	82. (A) (B) (C) (D) (E)
8. (A) (B) (C) (D) (E)	33. (A) (B) (C) (D) (E)	58. (A) (B) (C) (D) (E)	83. (A) (B) (C) (D) (E)
9. (A) (B) (C) (D) (E)	34. (A) (B) (C) (D) (E)	59. (A) (B) (C) (D) (E)	84. (A) (B) (C) (D) (E)
10. (A) (B) (C) (D) (E)	35. (A) (B) (C) (D) (E)	60. (A) (B) (C) (D) (E)	85. (A) (B) (C) (D) (E)
11. (A) (B) (C) (D) (E)	36. (A) (B) (C) (D) (E)	61. (A) (B) (C) (D) (E)	86. (A) (B) (C) (D) (E)
12. (A) (B) (C) (D) (E)	37. (A) (B) (C) (D) (E)	62. (A) (B) (C) (D) (E)	87. (A) (B) (C) (D) (E)
13. (A) (B) (C) (D) (E)	38. (A) (B) (C) (D) (E)	63. (A) (B) (C) (D) (E)	88. (A) (B) (C) (D) (E)
14. (A) (B) (C) (D) (E)	39. (A) (B) (C) (D) (E)	64. (A) (B) (C) (D) (E)	89. (A) (B) (C) (D) (E)
15. (A) (B) (C) (D) (E)	40. (A) (B) (C) (D) (E)	65. (A) (B) (C) (D) (E)	90. (A) (B) (C) (D) (E)
16. (A) (B) (C) (D) (E)	41. (A) (B) (C) (D) (E)	66. (A) (B) (C) (D) (E)	91. (A) (B) (C) (D) (E)
17. (A) (B) (C) (D) (E)	42. (A) (B) (C) (D) (E)	67. (A) (B) (C) (D) (E)	92. (A) (B) (C) (D) (E)
18. (A) (B) (C) (D) (E)	43. (A) (B) (C) (D) (E)	68. (A) (B) (C) (D) (E)	93. (A) (B) (C) (D) (E)
19. (A) (B) (C) (D) (E)	44. (A) (B) (C) (D) (E)	69. (A) (B) (C) (D) (E)	94. (A) (B) (C) (D) (E)
20. (A) (B) (C) (D) (E)	45. (A) (B) (C) (D) (E)	70. (A) (B) (C) (D) (E)	95. (A) (B) (C) (D) (E)
21. (A) (B) (C) (D) (E)	46. (A) (B) (C) (D) (E)	71. (A) (B) (C) (D) (E)	96. (A) (B) (C) (D) (E)
22. (A) (B) (C) (D) (E)	47. (A) (B) (C) (D) (E)	72. (A) (B) (C) (D) (E)	97. (A) (B) (C) (D) (E)
23. (A) (B) (C) (D) (E)	48. (A) (B) (C) (D) (E)	73. (A) (B) (C) (D) (E)	98. (A) (B) (C) (D) (E)
24. (A) (B) (C) (D) (E)	49. (A) (B) (C) (D) (E)	74. (A) (B) (C) (D) (E)	99. (A) (B) (C) (D) (E)
25. (A) (B) (C) (D) (E)	50. (A) (B) (C) (D) (E)	75. (A) (B) (C) (D) (E)	100. (A) (B) (C) (D) (E)

DIAGNOSTIC TEST
Time: 30 Minutes

1. Which of the following early cultures was centered in the eastern and southeastern part of what is now the United States?

    (A) The Olmec
    (B) The Toltec
    (C) The Mound Builders
    (D) The Anasazi
    (E) The Inca

2. "The only safety of man is to cultivate reason and extend his knowledge so that he will be sure to understand life and as many mysteries of the universe as he can possibly solve."

    These sentiments are most characteristic of

    (A) secular humanism
    (B) creationism
    (C) progressivism
    (D) imperialism
    (E) socialism

3. The earliest people to arrive in the Americas probably followed animal herds over a wide land bridge that connected

    (A) Siberia to Greenland
    (B) Siberia to North America
    (C) Europe to Iceland
    (D) Cuba to North America
    (E) Europe to Canada

4. The Bay of Pigs invasion was a low point of which U.S. president's administration?

    (A) Franklin D. Roosevelt
    (B) Harry S. Truman
    (C) Dwight D. Eisenhower
    (D) John F. Kennedy
    (E) Lyndon B. Johnson

5. The map above suggests that the reason the Continental Congress chose to meet in Philadelphia was that

    (A) it was the home of Benjamin Franklin
    (B) it was in the heart of the Southern colonies
    (C) its central location afforded the best access to the greatest number of delegates
    (D) it was not on the Atlantic coast
    (E) it was the capital of a Quaker colony

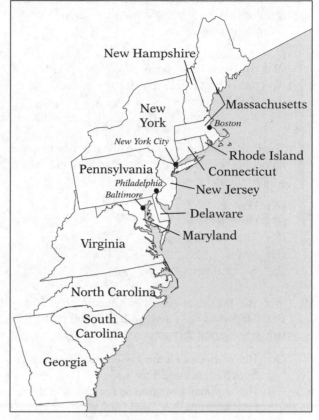

The 13 Colonies

6. The Constitution states that the president of the United States is to be elected by

    (A) popular vote
    (B) the Supreme Court
    (C) the Congress
    (D) the electors of all the states
    (E) the governors of all the states

7. Which of the following served as president of the United States without being elected to that office?

    (A) William Henry Harrison
    (B) Grover Cleveland
    (C) Abraham Lincoln
    (D) Chester A. Arthur
    (E) Warren G. Harding

GO ON TO THE NEXT PAGE ➡

DIAGNOSTIC TEST—*Continued*

8. Economic troubles in the years after World War I, unequal distribution of income in the United States, and consumer spending during the 1920s were all contributing causes of

   (A) the Jazz Age
   (B) the Great Depression
   (C) the Teapot Dome scandal
   (D) the New Frontier
   (E) Reconstruction

9. The United States became involved in the affairs of Indochina because of the departure from that area of which colonial power?

   (A) France
   (B) Great Britain
   (C) The Netherlands
   (D) Spain
   (E) Switzerland

10. Why did President Abraham Lincoln greet Harriet Beecher Stowe with the words "So you're the little lady who started this great war"?

    (A) Her work as a Union spy behind Confederate lines had shortened the war.
    (B) Her sons had been among the troops that fired on Fort Sumter in April 1861.
    (C) Her request to see him had started a quarrel between Lincoln and his wife.
    (D) Her novel *Uncle Tom's Cabin* had been burned in the Confederate capital city.
    (E) Her novel *Uncle Tom's Cabin* had turned many people against slavery.

11. The American Federation of Labor was founded in 1886 primarily as a result of

    (A) strikes in the workplace across the country
    (B) the desire of midwives to organize a union
    (C) congressional action
    (D) Theodore Roosevelt's push for social and economic reforms
    (E) the breakup of the railroad monopoly

12. Who was the winner of the first presidential election in which the voters, not the state legislatures, chose the slate of presidential electors?

    (A) John Quincy Adams
    (B) Martin Van Buren
    (C) Abraham Lincoln
    (D) James Madison
    (E) Andrew Jackson

13. "The great security against a gradual concentration of the several powers in the same department consists in giving to those who administer each department the necessary constitutional means . . . to resist encroachments of the others."

    This quotation by James Madison from the *Federalist Papers,* Number 10, most aptly argues for

    (A) rule by a constitutional monarchy
    (B) a system of checks and balances
    (C) the Monroe Doctrine
    (D) the creation of a national treasury
    (E) the creation of a bill of citizens' rights

14. What is the significance of the shadows behind the five men gesturing toward the immigrant in the cartoon opposite?

    (A) They show that the immigrant will prosper through hard work.
    (B) They show that the men welcome the immigrant because he reminds them of their past.
    (C) They show that the men were once immigrants or the children of immigrants.
    (D) They show that the men do not want the immigrant to cross the bridge.
    (E) They show that the men will hire thugs to kill the immigrant if he crosses the bridge.

15. The Jim Crow laws were

    (A) Southern state laws designed to enforce racial segregation
    (B) laws supported by civil rights activists of the 1960s
    (C) proposals for liquor taxes made by Senator James Crow of Missouri
    (D) regulations that provoked the Whiskey Rebellion
    (E) tariffs imposed on the colonies by Great Britain

16. What is the significance of the title "Move On" of the cartoon from 1867 on the opposite page?

    (A) The men in the cartoon want to sell their votes.
    (B) The men are gambling at the polling place.
    (C) Black and white men are voting together.
    (D) Native Americans are denied the right to vote.
    (E) The Native American was not dressed properly and therefore could not vote.

GO ON TO THE NEXT PAGE

DIAGNOSTIC TEST—*Continued*

Looking Backward

Move On

GO ON TO THE NEXT PAGE ➤

DIAGNOSTIC TEST—*Continued*

17. The first U.S. astronaut to orbit the earth in a space capsule was

    (A) Alan Shepard
    (B) John Glenn
    (C) M. Scott Carpenter
    (D) Chuck Yeager
    (E) Virgil Grissom

18. England passed the Navigation Acts of the 1650s primarily to

    (A) expand and enlarge its financial profits from the American colonies
    (B) ensure that the American colonies imported more goods than they exported
    (C) force Catholics to flee Great Britain or face religious persecution
    (D) encourage trade between Holland and the colonies
    (E) encourage smuggling among the colonies

19. Which of the following quotations best explains the concept of Manifest Destiny?

    (A) "Our fathers brought forth on this continent, a new nation, dedicated to the prospect that all men are created equal."
    (B) "We have it in our power to begin the world over again."
    (C) "We hold these truths to be self-evident: that all men are created equal. . . ."
    (D) "The American colonies stand no longer in need of England's protection."
    (E) "The American claim is . . . to overspread and possess the whole of the continent which Providence has given us. . . ."

20. The 38th parallel was an important boundary established by the United States after World War II in which of the following countries?

    (A) Japan
    (B) Korea
    (C) Hungary
    (D) Burma
    (E) Germany

21. President Lyndon B. Johnson's program to expand the welfare system, promote civil rights legislation, and increase spending on social programs was termed

    (A) the New Deal
    (B) the Lend-Lease Act
    (C) the Great Society
    (D) the Poor People's Campaign
    (E) Reaganomics

22. "At the time I established myself in Pennsylvania there was not a good bookseller's shop . . . to the southward of Boston."

    Which of the following is most likely to have expressed this sentiment?

    (A) Edward Rendell
    (B) Henry David Thoreau
    (C) Thomas Jefferson
    (D) Benjamin Franklin
    (E) Abigail Adams

23. Langston Hughes, Jean Toomer, and Zora Neale Hurston were all

    (A) nineteenth-century carpetbaggers
    (B) literary figures of the Harlem Renaissance
    (C) competitors in the 1948 Olympic Games
    (D) post–World War II philanthropists
    (E) civil rights leaders

24. Many people opposed the Kansas-Nebraska Act of 1854 because they feared that it would

    (A) expand slavery and thus rob white farmers of their ability to compete in the West
    (B) take away people's right to vote in the territories
    (C) reinforce the provisions of the Missouri Compromise
    (D) expand federal law over the concept of states' rights
    (E) discourage settlers from moving to Kansas and Nebraska

25. "Give me your tired, your poor,
    Your huddled masses yearning to breathe free
    Send these, the homeless, tempest-tossed, to me.
    I lift my lamp beside the golden door."

    This excerpt from a sonnet by Emma Lazarus refers to

    (A) shiploads of European immigrants sailing into New York Harbor
    (B) American colonists fighting for independence in the Revolutionary War
    (C) Southern slaves freed by the Emancipation Proclamation of 1863
    (D) sinners who repented and pleaded for salvation during the Great Awakening
    (E) suffragists fighting and demonstrating for the right to vote

GO ON TO THE NEXT PAGE

DIAGNOSTIC TEST—*Continued*

26. In which of the following wars was the U.S. military involved for less than two years?

    (A) Revolutionary War
    (B) War of 1812
    (C) Civil War
    (D) World War I
    (E) World War II

27. Between 1828 and 1860, congressional debate over applications for statehood centered primarily on which of the following issues?

    (A) Land grants to farmers
    (B) Temperance
    (C) Woman suffrage
    (D) Slavery
    (E) Free public education

28. At the start of the French and Indian War, all the land west of the Appalachians not under British or Spanish control was called

    (A) the Great Northwest
    (B) Kaskaskia
    (C) the Indiana Terriotory
    (D) the Louisiana Purchase
    (E) New France

29. President Bill Clinton was impeached primarily because

    (A) he used the Oval Office for illegal purposes
    (B) he was sued by a private citizen
    (C) he allegedly perjured himself in grand jury testimony
    (D) he was involved in a questionable real estate deal known as Whitewater
    (E) his close friend Vincent Foster committed suicide

30. Which of the following was the best-known center of the hippie counterculture of the late 1960s?

    (A) the Beacon Hill neighborhood of Boston
    (B) the Soho neighborhood of New York City
    (C) the Wilshire district of Los Angeles
    (D) the Haight-Ashbury neighborhood of San Francisco
    (E) the Garden District of New Orleans

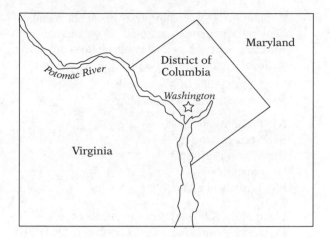

31. Look at the map above. President Lincoln used the army to keep Maryland from seceding in the 1860s in order to

    (A) warn the rest of the states that he would not tolerate further secession
    (B) prevent the Union's capital from being surrounded by Confederate states
    (C) keep the support and loyalty of Maryland voters
    (D) maintain Union access to the Atlantic Coast
    (E) prove to the Confederacy that the Union Army was too strong to lose the war

32. Between 1891 and 1910, millions of immigrants came to the United States for all the following reasons EXCEPT:

    (A) to seek economic opportunity
    (B) to escape poverty at home
    (C) to escape religious or political persecution at home
    (D) to earn enough money to return home and live well there
    (E) to lose their cultural identities as soon as possible

33. Which of the following people would have been LEAST likely to support the Progressive movement of the early twentieth century?

    (A) a native-born U.S. citizen
    (B) a person with a college degree
    (C) the owner of a small business
    (D) the owner of a large corporation
    (E) a middle-class woman

GO ON TO THE NEXT PAGE

DIAGNOSTIC TEST—*Continued*

34. "A just social order promotes in all its members habits of criticizing its attained goods and habits of projecting schemes of new goods. It does not aim at intellectual and moral subordination."

    Which of the following would the speaker of the above quotation most likely support?

    (A) Prohibition
    (B) Segregation
    (C) Woman suffrage
    (D) Anarchy
    (E) Trusts and monopolies

35. Which of the following was the primary cause of the skyscraper boom in New York City during the 1920s?

    (A) The patenting of the Bessemer converter
    (B) The Great Migration
    (C) Passage of the Nineteenth Amendment
    (D) The Harlem Renaissance
    (E) Economic prosperity

36. A woman living in one of the 13 original British colonies in North America might have any of the following occupations EXCEPT:

    (A) Seamstress
    (B) Judge
    (C) Midwife
    (D) Minister or religious leader
    (E) Serving maid

37. John D. Rockefeller ordered the destruction of a Rockefeller Center lobby mural glorifying the Soviet leader Vladimir Lenin primarily because Lenin

    (A) was opposed to the capitalist system that had made Rockefeller rich
    (B) had never held political office
    (C) had been immortalized in George Orwell's novel *1984*
    (D) had never fought in a war
    (E) believed that the United States was a good model for the Soviet Union to copy

38. Which of the following documents would give a historian the most accurate and detailed understanding of elegant New York City society in the 1890s?

    (A) A novel by Willa Cather
    (B) A copy of New York City's *Social Register* for 1892
    (C) A concert program from Carnegie Hall from 1895
    (D) The diary of a society matron
    (E) A week's worth of issues of the *New York*

    Times from 1899

39. Which was the most important result of the 1978 Camp David peace talks attended by President Jimmy Carter, Anwar Sadat, and Menachem Begin?

    (A) Agreeing on a framework for peace between Israel and the Palestinians
    (B) Winning the Nobel Peace Prize
    (C) Bringing an end to war in the Middle East
    (D) Signing a peace treaty between Egypt and Israel one year later
    (E) Proving to the world that conflicts could be resolved peacefully

40. The surge of women in the workforce during the first half of the 1940s was caused primarily by

    (A) policies of the Roosevelt administration
    (B) economic recovery from the Great Depression
    (C) the departure to war of millions of men
    (D) the relaxation of segregationist laws in the South
    (E) the migration of millions of African Americans to the North

41. The Antifederalists opposed the original Constitution for all the following reasons EXCEPT:

    (A) Delegates had conspired under a "veil of mystery" to create a new government beyond what they had been charged to do.
    (B) A strong central government would destroy states' rights.
    (C) The new system of government resembled a monarchy and thus violated the principle of liberty for all citizens.
    (D) The system of the electoral college was undemocratic.
    (E) The Constitution included a bill of rights that specified the privileges of all citizens.

42. The McKinley Tariff of 1890 resulted primarily in

    (A) hard economic times in Hawaii
    (B) the blowing up of the USS *Maine*
    (C) the acquisition of vast tracts of land in Alaska
    (D) a deadlock between the two major political parties in Congress
    (E) the reelection of William McKinley in 1896

GO ON TO THE NEXT PAGE ➤

DIAGNOSTIC TEST—*Continued*

43. Which of the following positions did the Know-Nothing Party support?

(A) Immigration from Catholic nations should be encouraged.

(B) Immigrants' right to vote should be restricted.

(C) Voters should not take a candidate's religion into account when making a choice.

(D) The waiting period for naturalization should be shortened.

(E) Immigrants should be encouraged to run for political office.

44. Between 1960 and 1964, defense spending rose by more than $6 billion. What effect did this increase in spending most likely have on the economy?

(A) It created more jobs in the defense industries.

(B) It threw millions of people out of work.

(C) It made it easy for Congress to balance the budget.

(D) It caused a decline in the prices of consumer goods.

(E) It led the nation to the brink of a second Great Depression.

45. The main purpose of the Alien and Sedition Acts of 1797 was to

(A) gain support for a potential war against France

(B) maintain the peace and safety of the United States

(C) ensure that the Democratic-Republicans would remain in office

(D) establish states' rights to challenge the federal government

(E) demonstrate that the Bill of Rights applied to U.S. citizens only

S T O P

IF YOU FINISH BEFORE TIME RUNS OUT, GO BACK AND CHECK YOUR WORK.

ANSWER KEY

1. C	11. A	21. C	31. B	41. E
2. A	12. E	22. D	32. E	42. A
3. B	13. B	23. B	33. D	43. B
4. D	14. C	24. A	34. C	44. A
5. C	15. A	25. A	35. E	45. B
6. D	16. D	26. D	36. B	
7. D	17. B	27. D	37. A	
8. B	18. A	28. E	38. D	
9. A	19. E	29. C	39. D	
10. E	20. B	30. D	40. C	

ANSWERS AND EXPLANATIONS

1. **C** The Inca were in South America, the Anasazi in the Southwest, the Olmec on the coast of the Gulf of Mexico, and the Toltec in central Mexico.

2. **A** The speaker (Clarence Darrow) states that reason is the highest goal of man. This was the belief of the Renaissance humanists and the Enlightenment philosophers who influenced the founding fathers of the United States.

3. **B** The land bridge connected Asia to North America; the portion of Asia closest to North America is Siberia.

4. **D** The Bay of Pigs invasion of Cuba by Cuban exiles armed and trained by the United States occurred in the first year of Kennedy's presidency.

5. **C** Philadelphia is more or less centrally located. Since travel was a slow and arduous undertaking in the 1770s, it made sense to choose a central location so that all delegates would have the shortest journeys possible.

6. **D** The president is chosen by the electors of each state. Congress, the Supreme Court, and the governors of the states do not vote for president except as private individuals. Individual voters do not choose the president; they choose the slate of electors for their state.

7. **D** Arthur was vice president when President James A Garfield was shot. When Garfield died, Arthur became president. The other four were elected.

8. **B** Choices A, C, and E list events that took place before or during the 1920s. Choice D lists a government program of the 1960s.

9. **A** The other four powers listed had not colonized what is now known as Vietnam.

10. **E** Stowe's novel was published before the war began and was so popular that it may well have constituted a cause for the war. None of the other choices is a true statement.

11. **A** The other four choices did not lead directly to the founding of the AFL.

12. **E** 1828 was the first year in which the voters, not the state legislatures, chose the electors. Andrew Jackson defeated John Quincy Adams in the 1828 election.

13. **B** The language in the statement clearly addresses concerns about one branch of the government becoming too powerful.

14. **C** The shadows are there to show what these five men were like in the past. They used to be just like the immigrant who wants to cross the bridge. Ironically, they have forgotten that now that they are wealthy and respectable.

15. **A** "Jim Crow" was a character from a minstrel show who became, among Southern whites, a symbol for supposed black inferiority. The civil rights era came much later, and the other choices do not address racial segregation.

16. **D** The man with the club is making the Native American "move on" rather than allowing him to vote.

17. **B** The people listed in other four choices were noted for aeronautical achievements that do not include being the first U.S. astronaut to orbit the earth in a space capsule.

18. **A** Britain's main motive was to expand its own profits from colonial trade.

19. **E** The principle of Manifest Destiny stated that U.S. settlers had the right and duty to settle the entire North American continent between Canada and Mexico.

20. **B** The 38th parallel is the Demilitarized Zone dividing North Korea and South Korea.

21. **C** The other choices relate to programs in other administrations.

22. **D** The language in the quotation makes it clear that it comes from the early modern period, not the present day. Franklin settled in Pennsylvania as a young man, but the other three colonial era choices were from Massachusetts or Virginia.

23. **B** These are three African American writers who flourished in the 1920s and 1930s, during the period known as the Harlem Renaissance.

24. **A** It was commonly believed that this was a likely economic effect of the act. The other four choices do not agree with what the act states.

25. **A** The internal reference to "tempest-tossed" indicates sea travel. "I lift my lamp" is a direct reference to the Statue of Liberty, the character who speaks the poem. The Statue of Liberty is famous worldwide for welcoming immigrants to New York Harbor.

26. **D** The United States entered World War I in April 1917 and the war ended in November 1918. The United States was involved in all the other wars for two years or more.

27. **D** The great question facing Congress was whether the United States as a whole should be a slaveholding or a free nation. Congress was divided geographically over the issue of how each new state, as a slaveholding or a free state, would affect the national balance.

28. **E** The land was not called the Louisiana Purchase until after 1800, when Thomas Jefferson bought it from the French. Before that, the land was held by the French, who called it New France.

29. **C** Perjury is a crime, and a president can be impeached only for "high crimes and misdemeanors."

30. **D** In the late 1960s the Haight-Ashbury neighborhood of San Francisco became the leading center of the so-called hippie counterculture.

31. **B** As the map shows, Washington, D.C., is bordered on three sides by Maryland and on one side by Virginia. Virginia had already seceded. Lincoln could not allow the capital to be surrounded and have any hope of winning the war.

32. **E** Immigrants clung to their cultural identities as comforts in a strange new land. All the other choices are reasons why many people came to the United States.

33. **D** Although many large corporation owners supported Progressive legislation as a way to destroy their smaller competition, the owner of a large corporation was still the least likely choice in this group to support the Progressive movement. The other four choices describe people who made up the backbone of the Progressive movement.

34. **C** The speaker would not want women to be subordinated intellectually or morally.

35. **E** The economic prosperity of the era allowed clients to commission and pay for skyscrapers of unprecedented height.

36. **B** Only men were allowed to be judges. Anne Hutchinson is an example of a religious leader; Quakers also allowed women to preach. The other three choices are traditional female jobs.

37. **A** Rockefeller's main objection to Lenin in particular and to communism in general was on economic grounds.

38. **D** The society matron's diary would have the greatest wealth of detail about the society events she hosted and attended. Some of the other choices would be useful, but choice D would give the most accurate details.

39. **D** This is the result that was of the greatest importance to the greatest number of people.

40. **C** When men went overseas to fight in World War II, women often replaced them in the factories and offices where they had worked.

41. **E** The original Constitution contained no bill of rights. The Federalists agreed to one because the Antifederalists demanded it.

42. **A** The McKinley Tariff drove down the price of sugar, which was the mainstay of the Hawaiian economy.

43. **B** The other four choices all state positions the Know-Nothings opposed.

44. **A** It follows from a rise in defense spending that there will be more defense jobs. The other choices do not follow logically from a rise in defense spending.

45. **B** This was the stated intention of the acts.

PART II
TOPIC REVIEW FOR THE U.S. HISTORY TEST

CHAPTER 1

PRE-COLUMBIAN AMERICA AND THE AGE OF EXPLORATION

INTRODUCTION

Historians believe that the first human inhabitants of North and South America were people who originally came from Asia. Thousands of years ago, during the last ice age, they crossed a land bridge that linked Asia and North America. These people are called "American Indians" or "Native Americans." This is a misnomer, since archaeological evidence strongly suggests that humans are not native to the Americas.

Some Native Americans settled in the harsh, frozen Northwest, where they first crossed into America. Many others moved on, spreading out to the south and east until they eventually settled all the habitable parts of the Americas, including the Caribbean islands. The wide variety of climates and types of soil in the Americas led to a great diversity of culture among the various tribes that were formed. Some were farmers, some were hunters, and some were gatherers. Some were warlike; others were peaceful. Some developed trade networks with nearby tribes; others were isolated and did not seek outside connections.

The Native American way of life held undisputed sway in the Americas until the late 1400s. After the arrival of the Spanish explorers, Native Americans were conquered and displaced by a people who had powerful weapons and would take whatever they wanted by force. When the Spaniards discovered stupendous wealth in the South American empires, French- and English-sponsored explorers went west on voyages of their own. By the 1600s all three nations were seizing land, building towns and forts, and establishing colonies of their mother countries. Native Americans resisted fiercely, but with no guns and no immunity to European diseases such as smallpox, they had no chance. The newcomers subjugated and enslaved them.

TIMELINE

circa 50,000–15,000 BC Land bridge across Bering Strait links Asia and North America, making human migration possible.

circa 35,000–25,000 BC Age of the oldest human remains discovered in North America.

circa 11,000–9000 BC Land bridge disappears permanently under water.

1500 BC Corn, native to Mexico and South America, is grown in the north.

circa 100 BC Anasazi culture takes shape at present-day "Four Corners" in the Southwest.

circa 1450 Iroquois Confederacy founded in the Northeast.

1492 Christopher Columbus and his party are first Europeans to land in Caribbean.

1516 Smallpox epidemic decimates Native American population.

1539 Hernando de Soto explores the Southeast; has many hostile encounters with Indian tribes.

1565 Pedro Menendez de Áviles founds St. Augustine on Florida coast.

KEY TERMS

adobe a type of brick made of mud; used in construction by Native Americans in the Southwest

archaeological having to do with the study of ancient artifacts

cultural exchange exchange among distinct peoples of their customs, habits, foods, art forms, languages, religions, and so on

immigrants those who move to and settle in a land other than the one where they were born

Iroquois Confederacy a council of elders of five (later six) tribes of the Iroquois nation that met to settle differences peacefully

missionaries religious officials who attempt to convert others to their faith

nation group of tribes related by language and customs

Northwest Passage a water route that connects the Atlantic and Pacific oceans

pre-Columbian the era before the 1492 voyage of Christopher Columbus

tribe a group of people related by blood, culture, language, religion, and customs

The First Americans

The term "Native Americans" is actually a misnomer. **Archaeological** evidence suggests that human beings are not native to the Americas but came there from somewhere else. During the last ice age, the levels of the world's oceans dropped by hundreds of feet, temporarily exposing certain landforms. Historians believe that the first Americans were Asian nomads who crossed a land bridge between Siberia and Alaska in the wake of the herds of animals on which they depended for food.

Some of those long-ago **immigrants** settled in the harsh, frozen north. Others continued to travel south and east in search of more comfortable climates. Eventually, they settled all the habitable regions of North and South America and the Caribbean islands. Those widespread groups soon developed tribal identities. They developed their own languages and cultures. The map below shows the diversity of Native American peoples and the places where they settled.

Unlike the Europeans who would follow them west, the Native Americans adapted their habits to the climate and the available natural resources.

Native American Tribes before the Arrival of the Europeans

The Aleut and Inuit of the far north dressed in heavy layers of clothing and built houses made of snow and ice. The Anasazi and Zuñi of the southwestern deserts built thick-walled **adobe** structures that kept out the intense heat. The Iroquois of the northeastern forests built wooden houses a few feet off the ground so that animals could not enter. Native Americans fished and hunted in areas where there was game; gathered edible plants, fruits, and vegetables in the areas where they grew naturally; and farmed in areas where the soil was rich and arable. When a Native American killed an animal, no part of it was wasted. The flesh was cooked and eaten; the bones and teeth were used to make weapons, tools, jewelry, and musical instruments; and the hide was used to make clothing and shoes. Although Native Americans often are lumped together into one group, their diversity is more consistent with a collection of nations.

The early American culture has two major characteristics: diversity and unity. Both characteristics are related to the land, the climate, and natural forces. A **tribe** developed its culture in accordance with the climate and natural resources where the people settled. A **nation** was a group of tribes that settled close to one another and had languages and customs that did not diverge widely. Although tribes that lived near one another communicated regularly for economic and social reasons, tribes that lived far apart had no contact. This meant that **cultural exchange** among Native Americans remained at a minimum and tribal identities remained distinct and individual.

However, *most* Native American cultures are united by certain shared characteristics. Because Native Americans depended entirely on the land for food, clothing, and shelter, they all treated it with respect. Native American religious rituals across many tribes involve prayer for good weather, harvests, and hunting. Native Americans believe that nature is not to be mastered but to be served and maintained.

Compared with Europeans, Native Americans were not technologically advanced. They made everything they needed, but they did not invent machines. Without the population pressure necessary for development, they did not advance out of the stone and iron ages for the most part in terms of tool creation. They made pottery and woven baskets that remain beautiful and functional to this day.

Politically, most North American Native American tribes were democratic. Because tribes were small groups of people, it was easy to get everyone's opinion and consider it in making decisions. The town meetings that would later develop in New England villages were much the same. Most Native American cultures were matriarchal; the women of the tribes held important positions as heads of families. However, chiefs were male, and in theory if not in fact, councils of men made most tribal decisions.

Democracy in **pre-Columbian** America reached its most sophisticated form among the Iroquois tribes of the Northeast. The Seneca, Cayuga, Oneida, Onondaga, and Mohawk, all members of the Iroquois nation, were prone to quarrel. During the 1400s tribal leaders agreed that it was time to form a regular council in which conflicts could be settled peacefully. They agreed to form a confederacy. Elders and chiefs chosen by popular vote from each of the five tribes would meet to discuss issues of importance to their people. The founders of the council agreed that all decisions were to be based on the welfare of the people. Chiefs could be removed from the council for committing crimes.

A sixth nation, the Tuscarora, joined the **Iroquois Confederacy** during the 1700s. In the colonial period, the confederacy provided a powerful bulwark against colonial and British expansion. The confederacy remained powerful until after the American Revolution. It continues to meet to this day.

European Voyages of Discovery in the New World

The first Europeans to reach the Americas were Norsemen. Around the year AD 982, Erik the Red discovered Greenland and soon afterward established a Viking settlement there. In the year 1000 his son Leif Erikson landed on the eastern coast of Canada. However, the Norsemen did not pursue their ventures into the western hemisphere.

Spanish Exploration

The first European voyager to affect American history arrived in the Caribbean in 1492. This was the Spanish-sponsored Italian adventurer Christopher Columbus, who arrived in a fleet of three ships. Columbus's goal had been to find a trade route to the Far East. Europeans had developed a taste for the spices and fabrics of China and India, but the trade routes were overland, long, and difficult. As a result of a mistake in navigation, Columbus reasoned that there might be an easier approach; since the world was spherical, one should be able to reach the east by sailing west. However, neither Columbus nor any other European knew of the existence of two continents and another ocean between Europe and Asia.

Columbus did not "discover America." He never set foot on the mainland of the present-day United States. His first voyage is important because it marked the beginning of the cultural exchange between the Americas and Europe and because he proved that it was possible to cross the Atlantic Ocean and return safely. In a total of four voyages to the Caribbean, Columbus claimed various islands for Spain, establishing a base of operations for the many Spanish explorers who followed him. Columbus's belief that he had reached India is responsible for the name "Indians" that has stuck to Native Americans ever since. To this day the Caribbean islands are called "the West Indies."

When Columbus returned safely to Spain, bringing with him several Taino people he had enslaved and examples of Caribbean plants and gold nuggets, word spread throughout Europe. Many other explorers were curious to see the "New World," and monarchs realized that by sponsoring explorers, they could establish colonies and expand their power bases abroad. **Missionaries** of the Catholic Church were pleased at the discovery that there were whole societies of people to convert to their faith.

It was not long before Spain sponsored more voyages to the West. Columbus crossed the Atlantic again almost immediately. In 1513, Vasco Nunez de Balboa sailed to Panama, crossed the isthmus of land, and became the first European to see the Pacific Ocean. In 1519, the Portuguese explorer Ferdinand Magellan sailed all the way around South America. Magellan died in the Philippincs, but 35 of his crew returned safely to Spain, having circled the globe. They established beyond doubt that it was possible to reach the East by sailing west.

The Spanish conquests were marked by brutality and violence. The conquistadors were driven by an all-consuming desire to obtain gold. Columbus instituted a policy in which Native Americans who did not bring him gold had their hands chopped off. Between 1519 and 1531, the Spaniards defeated and conquered the mighty Aztec and Inca armies of Mexico and Peru. The subjugated Native Americans were forced to work in deadly slave mines and plantations. The great wealth the Spaniards seized fired the imaginations of explorers such as Juan Ponce de León and Hernando de Soto, who sailed to North American in search of similar wealth. Ponce de León led the first party of explorers to reach the mainland. They landed near present-day Tampa Bay, Florida, in 1513. Hernando de Soto followed Ponce de León in 1539. He and his party penetrated deep into the heart of what is now the southeastern United States, killing, kidnapping, and robbing the numerous Native American tribes they encountered. In 1541, De Soto and his party became the first Europeans to see and cross the Mississippi River. At the same time, Francisco Vasquez de Coronado, Gárcia López de Cárdenas, and Juan Rodriguez Cabrillo were exploring the Southwest and the California coast.

In 1565, Pedro Menendez de Áviles finally established the first Spanish colony in North America. He and his party founded the city of St. Augustine, Florida. The Spaniards began to settle in Texas in the late 1600s and in California in the mid-1700s. Their influence can still be seen in the Spanish place names, the architectural styles, and the predominance of Catholic churches in those areas.

French Exploration

Whereas the Spaniards had sought fairy-tale riches in the New World, the French were interested at first solely in expanding the fur trade. Giovanni da Verrazano in 1524 and Jacques Cartier in 1535 were the first Frenchmen to explore any part of North America. However, the French did not attempt to establish American colonies until 1603, when a party of fur traders traveled west to Canada. Samuel de Champlain went with the party as their mapmaker. He mapped the St. Lawrence River and the northern Atlantic coast. Champlain founded the towns of Port Royal and Quebec. He established friendly relations with the Huron and Algonquin tribes, which repaid him by allying themselves with the French during the French and Indian War.

In 1615, Champlain became the first European to see the Great Lakes. That area became the hub of the French fur-trading industry. As the French prospered, they began exploring farther to the south. They settled in parts of what is now Ohio and sailed all the way down the Mississippi River to the Gulf of Mexico, where Robert Cavalier de la Salle founded the colony of Louisiana.

The French fur traders explored as far west as present-day South Dakota. They built forts and trading posts along the rivers but did not try to set up permanent governments or colonies beyond those they had established in the East. Instead, they tried to cooperate with the local Native Americans, who were able to provide guidance and advice.

English Exploration

The British were not in search of gold or furs. Their original interest in North America was the same as Columbus's: they wanted to find a way to sail west to Asia. The search for this elusive "**Northwest Passage**" was the motive for their early explorations. In 1497, John Cabot landed on the coast of Maine, becoming the first European since Leif Erikson to see North America. Cabot never returned from a second voyage. His son Sebastian followed him in 1508 and reached the entrance to Hudson Bay. In 1609 Henry Hudson found the mouth of the Hudson River and followed it north to Albany before he and his crew realized it would not lead them west. On a second voyage, Hudson drove his crew farther and farther west through the network of islands north of Canada; finally, terrified for their lives in the frigid unknown waters, his crew marooned Hudson and turned the ship back toward the east and safety.

In the end, England realized that Spain and France were establishing a foothold in the Americas and that it should join in the competition for colonies. In 1584, Sir Walter Raleigh claimed the territory of Virginia. About 500 people sailed west to settle the colony. When more sailed west to join them in 1590, the colony had vanished without a trace.

The British persevered nonetheless. By 1638, they had founded seven colonies along the Atlantic coast. As the population grew, the colonies began to carry out the commands of their royal charters to continue exploring and expanding their territory westward.

The following chart shows the names of some of the explorers of the era, along with the nations that sponsored their voyages and the important discoveries they made.

Date	Name	Nation	Discoveries/Accomplishments
1492–1502	Christopher Columbus	Spain	First European to discover Caribbean islands; claims many of them for Spain, establishing a base of operations for future Spanish explorers
1496	John Cabot	England	First European to land on North America since Leif Erikson; lands in northern Maine or Canada; Europeans now know for sure that the Americas are a new continent, not Asia
1508	Sebastian Cabot	England	Discovers entrance to Hudson Bay
1513	Juan Ponce de León	Spain	Lands on Atlantic coast of North America; names it Florida; sails around peninsula; maps Florida coast and keys.
1520	Ponce de León	Spain	Second voyage to Florida; entire landing party killed/chased away in an ambush
1528	Alvar Nuñez Cabeza de Vaca; Panfilo de Narvaez	Spain	Party lands at Tampa Bay and splits up; Cabeza de Vaca and land party enslaved by Karankawa tribe; Vaca and three other survivors live by wits, assimilate into Native American culture; meet other Spaniards in Texas in 1536
1539–1542	Hernando de Soto	Spain	Lands near Tampa Bay; explores Southeast; first Europeans to see and cross Mississippi River
1540	Francisco Vasquez de Coronado; Gárcia López de Cárdenas	Spain	Explores Southwest; meets Pueblo Indians; Cardenas and some of his men first Europeans to see the Grand Canyon
1541	Coronado	Spain	Explores what is now Texas, Oklahoma, Kansas
1542	Juan Rodriguez Cabrillo	Spain	Lands in California at San Diego Bay; explores Pacific Coast to Oregon
1565	Pedro Menendez de Áviles	Spain	Founds St. Augustine on Florida coast
1594–1590	Sir Walter Raleigh	England	Claims territory of Virginia; founds colony; by 1590 colony has vanished
1598	Samuel de Champlain	France	Sees Central America and conceives idea of a canal through Panama
1603–1609	Champlain	France	Sails up St. Lawrence River to Lachine Rapids; makes maps of North Atlantic coast; founds Port Royal in Nova Scotia; founds Quebec; forms alliances with Algonquin
1609	Henry Hudson	England	Sails to Virginia; heads north; finds entrance to Hudson River; sails upriver as far as Albany
1615	Champlain	France	First European to see Great Lakes

Clashes between Native Americans and Europeans

Clashes between Native Americans and Europeans were inevitable. The two groups of people were different in every possible way. The Native Americans had settled the land thousands of years before the arrival of the Europeans and naturally considered that it belonged to them. They did not keep written records; their culture was oral. They respected the land and adapted their needs and lives to suit what it could provide. They were not technologically advanced. They did not share language, religion, or any social customs with the Europeans who invaded their lands in the Age of Exploration.

The various groups of Europeans had some common religious, linguistic, and cultural traits. They had developed sophisticated weapons. They had a conquering mentality that differed greatly from that of the Native American tribes, which had found that there was room enough for all to settle, with fights over territory being very rare.

The Europeans looked at the primitive Native American architecture, clothing, and weapons; noted the lack of written records; noted the Native Americans' dark skin and physical characteristics, which were different from their own; and observed that the Native Americans were not Christians. For all these reasons, the Europeans believed themselves racially superior to the Native Americans. They felt that this gave them the right to enslave them, convert them to European faiths, and take control of their lands.

The Native Americans were friendly at first. They were unimpressed with the Europeans and helped them at what they saw as small trading posts. When the Native Americans realized that the Europeans intended to steal their lands and their liberty, they fought fiercely. However, Native American bows and arrows could do little against European guns. Native Americans also had no defenses against European diseases such as smallpox; the germs traveled west with explorers, and with no immunity to a disease to which their population had never been exposed, the Native Americans died by the millions.

When the Europeans began to establish colonies, more clashes arose. Native Americans and Europeans now were fighting for possession of land. Despite the tenacity of their struggles, the Native Americans eventually gave way slowly to the superior weapons of the Europeans. The Europeans also saw no necessity to uphold the treaties they signed or general rules of combat. The Native Americans slowly but surely were driven away from their ancestral lands. A pattern of encroachment and violent skirmishes followed by extermination campaigns became the normal pattern of interaction.

REVIEW QUESTIONS

1. The term "American Indians" is a misnomer because the people it designates

   (A) are not native to the Americas
   (B) originally came from Asia
   (C) did not inhabit the East Indies
   (D) did not speak any European languages
   (E) first settled the Americas during the 1400s

2. Which of the following contributed the most to the founding and success of the Iroquois Confederacy?

   (A) The small size of the Iroquois tribes
   (B) The fact that the tribes all belonged to the same nation
   (C) The popular election of the council members
   (D) The constant conflicts among the Iroquois tribes
   (E) The example of the New England town meeting

3. Which nation has had the greatest influence on modern American culture?

   (A) Asia
   (B) England
   (C) France
   (D) Italy
   (E) Spain

4. A major reason that the Europeans succeeded in dominating the Native Americans and gradually taking over their land because

   (A) their religion was more compelling
   (B) their respect for the land was greater
   (C) they were better farmers than the Native Americans
   (D) their weapons were more sophisticated and deadly
   (E) they arrived in America before the Native Americans

Answers and Explanations

1. **C** Choice C is correct because the name "American Indians" is due to Christopher Columbus's error in believing that he had reached the East Indies. He called the people of the Caribbean "Indians," and the name has stuck to Native Americans ever since.

2. **B** The fact that the Iroquois tribes all belonged to the same nation meant that they had a common heritage. Their languages and customs were quite similar. This meant that communication and understanding were easy. This ability to understand one another was clearly the most crucial factor in establishing the Iroquois Confederacy.

3. **B** The English colonies along the Atlantic coast were the original United States of America. English is the dominant language in the United States. American schools are taught in English, and the government and businesses conduct their affairs in English. The media broadcast largely in English.

4. **D** European guns were much more efficient and deadly weapons than Native American spears or bows and arrows. In addition, catastrophic epidemics, especially smallpox, reduced native populations by two-thirds. None of the other four choices is true.

CHAPTER 2

ENGLISH COLONIAL SETTLEMENTS

INTRODUCTION

Because England soon became the dominant force in North America, this chapter will concentrate on how the English established a foothold on the Atlantic Coast.

Before the late 1500s England had shown little interest in the western hemisphere. However, once Spain and France began to show enormous profits from trade with the Americas, the English did not want to be left out. They began with acts of piracy and then serious exploration. The first attempt at an English colony came in 1588. That attempt and a few more failed, but the English did not give up, and they finally established the colony of Jamestown near Chesapeake Bay in 1607. Thirteen years later, the famous *Mayflower* and its load of Pilgrims arrived in Massachusetts.

The Pilgrims were religious dissenters who had left England because they felt that the Protestant Reformation did not take things far enough. Their radical ideas about how church services should be conducted found little favor at home, and they were eager to establish a religious colony in the New World. It soon appeared that the Pilgrims intended religious freedom only for themselves; they resisted any attempt on anyone else's part to dissent. Those who disagreed with the Pilgrims soon moved elsewhere along the rivers and the coast of New England, starting their own colonies.

Meanwhile, the English settlers began to cultivate tobacco and build towns. This led to conflicts with the Indian tribes on whose lands they were encroaching.

TIMELINE

1583 Sir Humphrey Gilbert attempts to establish an English colony in Newfoundland, but he and his ships are lost at sea on the return voyage.

1584 Sir Walter Raleigh explores Atlantic coast and claims Virginia territory for England.

1585–1590 Establishment and disappearance of colony on Roanoke Island.

1588 English Navy defeats Spanish Armada, revealing that Spain is too weak to maintain its interests in the Americas for long.

1607 London Company establishes colony of Jamestown near Chesapeake Bay.

1619 Twenty African slaves brought to the Chesapeake colony become the first Africans to come to North America.

1620 *Mayflower* reaches Cape Cod Bay; Pilgrims, religious separatists, settle Plymouth Colony; sign Mayflower Compact.

1629 Puritans found Massachusetts Bay Colony by royal charter.

1632 Lord Baltimore establishes colony on the Chesapeake; named Maryland in 1632 by his son on his death.

1636 Roger Williams establishes the colony of Providence, Rhode Island.

1638 Religious dissenters found colony of Connecticut.

1700s African slave trade is established.

KEY TERMS

galleon ship used for trade or war during and after the Age of Exploration

joint-stock company a group of people who invest money in a venture, agreeing to share the profits or losses equally

Mayflower Compact an agreement that Plymouth would govern itself by majority rule of male church members

Pilgrims first major puritan sect to leave England for the Americas

plantation a large farm usually concentrating on only one crop, such as rice, cotton, or tobacco

Protestant Reformation a widespread sixteenth-century protest against and departure from the Catholic Church sparked by Martin Luther; led to the establishment of various rival Christian churches

Puritans Protestants who felt that the Reformation did not go far enough in correcting and eliminating the abuses of Catholic tradition

republican form of government in which citizens elect representatives who make the laws

Spanish Armada name for the naval fleet of Spain or for the 1588 naval battle in which England defeated Spain

theocracy political rule by a church

English Expansion in the New World

During the 1500s, the English realized that Spain was bringing home huge profits and great treasures from its empire in the New World. This led to the beginnings of piracy on the high seas. An English ship would attack a home-bound Spanish **galleon,** murder or capture its crew, and commandeer its treasure for the queen. Francis Drake was an especially fearless pirate captain. When Elizabeth I knighted Drake for his courage, Philip II of Spain was furious. He saw Drake as a common thief and the queen's gesture as an insult. Philip decided it was time to assert the supremacy of Spain once and for all.

In 1588 the **Spanish Armada** sailed toward the English Channel. The Armada was a fleet of 130 ships manned by thousands of sailors. Philip intended to invade England with his navy. The Armada looked intimidating and impressive, but the English navy was craftier and more maneuverable. English sailors set their own small ships on fire and steered them toward the Spaniards, who panicked at the sight of the burning boats. The formation of the Armada broke into disorder as each ship tried to avoid attack. When a fierce storm came up, the English knew they had won the battle.

This was the last time Spain would make a serious attack on England. The small island nation had proved its superiority on the high seas with its pirates and in an all-out naval battle. Having exploited and exposed Spain's weaknesses, England was ready to establish American colonies of its own.

Early Attempts: Roanoke and Jamestown

In 1583, Sir Humphrey Gilbert sailed west to establish a colony on Newfoundland. He never returned to England; historians believe that his ship went down with all hands on the return voyage. Gilbert's half brother Sir Walter Raleigh made the next attempt. Raleigh explored the Atlantic Coast and claimed the territory of Virginia, named in honor of Elizabeth, the "Virgin Queen." This territory was much larger than the present-day state of Virginia; it included West Virginia, Maryland, and the Carolinas.

Raleigh felt that the Virginia territory was ideal for a colony. The climate was mild, rivers and game were plentiful, and the soil was fertile. His enthusiastic reports aroused enough enthusiasm that he was able to return to Virginia in 1585 with a small group of people who were prepared to settle the new colony. They landed on the island of Roanoke, off present-day North Carolina. However, few were able to manage in what to them was an uncivilized wilderness. They gave up the attempt after struggling for a year. Raleigh, however, was too stubborn to accept defeat. He recruited about 100 people to make another attempt and put John White in command of the group. White saw his charges settled on Roanoke and then returned to England for supplies. He was unable to return to Virginia until 1590. When he did return, there was no trace of the colony he had left. To this day historians do not know what became of the settlers of Roanoke.

The British were still convinced that they would succeed in settling America. King James I issued the Charter of 1606, licensing the Plymouth Company to settle the coast from Maine to Virginia and the London Company to do the same from New York to South Carolina. Those **joint-stock companies** were formed by investors who agreed to share in the expenses of the voyages in return for equal shares of the profits (if any). The London Company lost no time sending its first shipload of willing men to America. They settled on a river leading to the Chesapeake Bay and named their colony Jamestown, in honor of the king. The colony initially suffered greatly, going through a period named the "starving time." The colonists were unwilling to work until John Smith, a strong-willed and capable man who had been by turns an adventurer, a murderer, a soldier, and a pirate, became their leader. He instituted harsh discipline that made the colony self-sustaining.

The Jamestown colonists were fortunate to find the local Algonquin tribes friendly and helpful. The Algonquin introduced them to corn, which the settlers had never seen before as it was native to the Americas and unknown in Europe. They showed the English how to grow their own corn and how to find other food. The Algonquin chief Wahunsonacock (called Powhatan by the English) had a daughter age 10 or 12 called Pocahontas. Her friendliness to the settlers helped maintain good relations between the Indians and the English. Both sides trusted her, and she argued for the release of English prisoners of the Algonquin (although many historians doubt the story that she threw herself across John Smith's body to save him from being killed).

Smith returned to England, and as time passed, Pocahontas's visits to Jamestown became less frequent. The winter months of 1609–1610 proved bitterly cold, and the English were still unable to fend for themselves in the strange new country. They felt no scruples about raiding Algonquin villages for food and supplies. Hostilities between the two groups continued more or less constantly from that time on.

Plymouth and Massachusetts Bay

The settlers of Jamestown had been practical people. They had traveled west in search of financial opportunity and adventure. The groups that settled Plymouth and the Massachusetts Bay Colony had entirely different motives for sailing west.

The **Protestant Reformation** had splintered the religious unity that had characterized Western Europe for centuries. The Catholic Church had ruled supreme. When Henry VIII defied the Pope's authority and established the Church of England (Anglican Church) and when Martin Luther founded the Lutheran faith, that unity was broken. Long years of religious strife lay ahead.

Many British citizens did not feel that the Church of England went far enough. They insisted that it maintained many of the most objectionable Catholic customs, such as the elaborate robes worn by priests. Those separatists met in groups and celebrated religion as they saw fit—no works of art, no incense, and no use of Latin. The most extreme of the Protestants were called **Puritans** because they wanted to purify the Church of England. The most zealous of the Puritans were called **Pilgrims.** They wanted a society separate from the corrupting influences of the Anglican Church.

English society was strictly conformist and did not welcome religious separatism. Many Pilgrims fled to Holland, where their habits of worship were tolerated. However, they did not like the Dutch culture and customs and cast about for a better solution. The New World provided them with an answer.

In 1620, the *Mayflower* set sail from Holland with a full company of Pilgrims aboard. Virginia was their goal, but they chose to land in Cape Cod Bay, outside the dictates of the Jamestown charter. Fearful that the non-Pilgrims would refuse to work together, they agreed that their first priority was to set up a government by which all could agree to be ruled. The result of this was the **Mayflower Compact,** which called for majority rule of male church members. It stated in part:

> We, whose names are underwritten . . . do by these Presents solemnly and mutually promise in the presence of God, and one of another, covenant and combine ourselves into a civil Body Politik, for our better ordering and preservation and furtherance of the ends aforesaid; and by Virtue hereof, to enact, constitute, and frame such just and equal Laws, ordinances, acts, constitutions, and offices from time to time, as shall be thought most meet and convenient for the Good of the Colony unto which we promise all due submission and obedience.

The settlers named their colony Plymouth. They had much to endure from the unforgiving Massachusetts climate. During the first winter after the colony was established, nearly half the settlers died of disease, extreme cold, and a poor diet.

The local Wampanoag tribes came to the colonists' rescue. One Wampanoag in particular, Squanto, became a liaison between Native Americans and colonists. Because Squanto had lived in Spain and England, he was able to make himself understood, and the English settlers trusted him. With Squanto's help, the two groups signed a peace treaty and celebrated the first English harvest together.

In 1629 a group of English Puritans formed the Massachusetts Bay Company and sailed to America, intending to settle near Plymouth. Among the settlements they founded in Massachusetts, Boston soon became the most important. Unlike the Pilgrims, the Puritans did not scorn Anglicanism. They wished to establish a "city on a hill," as the Bible described it—a moral Christian community in which every member would contribute his or her best efforts for the good of the whole population.

Like Plymouth, the Puritan colony of Massachusetts Bay practiced a limited form of **republican** government. All adult men who were church members and property owners had the right to vote for representatives to the General Court, a body that made the colony's laws. John Winthrop was chosen the first governor of the Massachusetts Bay Colony. Instead of the modern separation between church and state, the Puritans believed in making them work together. This was symbolized by the fact that the same building did duty as both a church and a town-meeting hall.

One of the first issues the voters discussed was a school system. Puritans believed that Christians should devote their lives to God, and to do that they had to be able to read and understand the Bible. Therefore, it was important that all children be taught to read and that young men should be educated to become preachers. In 1636, the General Court founded Harvard College as a school for would-be clergy.

Work was very important to the Puritans, as they believed that every person had a calling before God. It glorified God to work and profit. That belief would help make the colony self-sufficient and profitable very quickly.

Connecticut and Rhode Island

It soon became clear that although the Puritans insisted on religious freedom for themselves, they would not allow it for anyone else. Dissenting colonists found that their lives were made very uncomfortable. The interconnection between church and politics in early Massachusetts meant that this was not only a religious issue but a social and political one as well. In addition, the population was growing steadily and good farmland was becoming scarce.

In 1639 a minister named Thomas Hooker had had enough of the Puritans' rigid theology. He and a group of like-minded colonists moved south and founded the colony of New Haven on the southern coast of Connecticut. There they wrote a document called the Fundamental Orders of Connecticut, which was the first formal constitution of any colonial government in North America. The Connecticut colonists soon established Yale College as a more liberal rival to Harvard.

Like Thomas Hooker, Roger Williams found himself in disagreement with Puritan authorities. Williams disapproved of any relationship between church and state; he felt that the two should be separated. People should be free to worship in whatever way they pleased; membership in a particular church should not affect people's civil rights. Williams was so outspoken on this issue that he was banished from Massachusetts. He established the colony of Providence, Rhode Island, in 1636. When Rhode Island was granted a royal charter in 1644, Williams insisted on a guarantee of religious freedom for all the colony's inhabitants.

Anne Hutchinson, another dissenter, soon sought sanctuary in Rhode Island. Although as a woman she could not be ordained a minister, she had become an unofficial religious leader soon after her arrival in Boston in 1634. In her home, she led discussions of the Bible and the sermons of the leading ministers of the city. Those meetings were widely popular, especially among women. However, many Bostonians disapproved of her meetings, believing that her growing influence threatened the authority of the ministers. As time passed, Hutchinson became more and more critical of the ministers who ran the city. She was arrested on a charge of weakening the authority of the church. Hutchinson put up a spirited and logical defense of her actions but lost her case. She was banished to Rhode Island.

The most shameful hour of the Massachusetts **theocracy** came in the 1690s with the Salem witch trials. Several young girls of the town of Salem accused various townspeople of witchcraft. Hundreds were arrested, and 19 of the accused were put to death, although no wrongdoing was proved. The courts believed that the accusation itself was enough evidence. Finally, protests from the surrounding community put a stop to the sensational trials and hangings. This disgraceful spectacle severely weakened the Puritan authority in New England from that time on. The colony would grow increasingly secular, although the Puritan beliefs would have a large effect on the mindset of the United States.

The Southern Colonies

Perhaps warned by the failure of theocracy in New England, other colonies espoused religious freedom and made it a part of their charters. Lord Baltimore established a Chesapeake colony; and when he died in 1632, it passed to his son, who named it Maryland. The colony had been intended as a refuge for Catholic immigrants who were persecuted by Anglicans in England, but soon it was opened to Protestants as well. Settlers of both Maryland and Virginia dedicated their efforts to growing tobacco, which the Jamestown colonists had proved was a highly profitable cash crop.

Tobacco meant huge farms, or **plantations.** This meant that a large labor force was required. At first indentured servants made up the labor pool, but once they had worked out their indentures and become free, they began to start small farms of their own. Small and large farmers did not get along well, since each encroached on the other's economic interests. In Bacon's Rebellion (1676), the small farmers attacked the Native Americans, whose lands they wanted for themselves. They also looted the large plantations and even took over the government in Jamestown for a short time. In the end, the rebellion was put down and the governing body of Virginia, called the House of Burgesses, declared that the Anglo-American colonists had the right to settle on Native American lands.

This outbreak of violence helped lead to an increase in the slave trade. The first record of any African slaves in North America was in the Chesapeake in 1640. After Bacon's Rebellion, tobacco and cotton planters in the South realized that they could not rely on the labor of indentured servants. They wanted a labor force over which they could exercise total and permanent control. African slaves fit their requirements perfectly. Because they looked different from Europeans, spoke languages Europeans could not understand, and were not Christians, it was easy for the Anglo-Americans to justify slavery to themselves on the grounds that Africans were racially inferior to Europeans. The isolation of the Africans in America provided a wall against escape that had stopped the enslavement of Native Americans in earlier attempts.

Carolina, named in honor of King Charles II, was originally one colony, founded in 1663. It eventually was divided into North Carolina and South Carolina. It was a colony of small farms and rice plantations. Growing rice and cotton demanded so much slave labor that by 1720 two-thirds of the population were slaves. Knowing they were outnumbered and fearing possible slave rebellions, the leaders of the Carolinas made their slave codes especially harsh.

Georgia had a beginning very different from that of the other colonies. It was a 1733 reclamation project for the poor of England. People who were heavily in debt could emigrate to Georgia and start over. With laws that forbade alcohol and slavery, Georgia failed to attract many immigrants. It did not begin to prosper until the 1750s.

The Mid-Atlantic Colonies

New Netherland was the one Atlantic coast colony founded by the Dutch. They famously purchased Manhattan from the Native Americans who lived there for a handful of cheap jewelry and founded the city of New Amsterdam there (although this story is not historically accurate). This island at the confluence of the Hudson and East rivers was a perfect location for trading. This was the beginning of a long history of European immigration to what was to become New York City. It was not exclusively a Dutch colony but attracted settlers from many nations.

In 1664 the English invaded New Amsterdam; its governor, Peter Stuyvesant, surrendered without a fight, and the colony was divided into two sections. One was renamed New York; the other, across the Hudson River, was called New Jersey.

Pennsylvania, given by King Charles II to William Penn in 1681, was an experiment in religious toleration. Penn was a Quaker who intended that all the inhabitants of his colony, including Native Americans, should have equal rights. Thousands of immigrants sailed to Pennsylvania, attracted by the promise of freedom and by its abundance of fertile farmland. Philadelphia, Penn's planned "City of Brotherly Love," soon became the largest city in the colonies.

The map below shows the original 13 British colonies, with the dates of their founding.

Tension between Colonists and Native Americans

When the English colonists first arrived on the shores of North America, they were powerless and weak. The Native Americans who first came across them extended friendship and help. They taught the newcomers how to grow crops, treat diseases and wounds, and survive freezing winters. The colonists accepted the help gratefully and signed peace treaties with the Native Americans, which both sides honored. At first, it appeared that it might be possible for both peoples to live side by side without conflict.

That state of affairs did not last. The expanding Anglo-American population made it impossible. As more and more people came to America and more and more children were born, the colonies chose to expand. That meant that they took over lands that belonged to the Native Americans. Often the

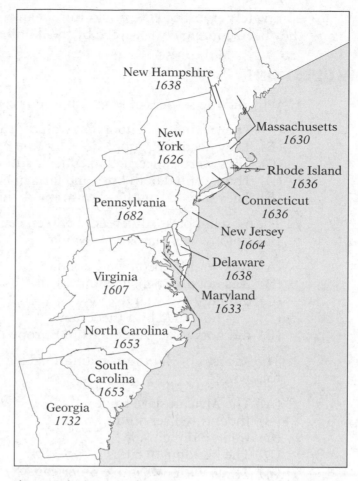

The 13 Colonies: Founding Dates

colonists passed laws that justified their theft to themselves and chose to ignore the treaties that they had signed previously. As had been the case when the Spaniards first reached American shores in the early 1500s, the Native Americans had no chance against European guns and organization. They were bound to lose.

However, the Native Americans did not give in easily. Over centuries of living in the forested Northeast, they had perfected guerrilla warfare tactics, taking their enemies by surprise in an ambush. Native Americans would choose a poorly defended target such as an isolated farmhouse. An attacking party would surround it, burn it to the ground, kill or steal all the animals, and kill or kidnap all the people in the place, although generally few casualties were inflicted by the natives. "Captive narratives" written by Anglo-Americans who survived the kidnappings and returned to their homes were among the most popular books in the colonies—the bestsellers of their day. These skirmishes often were used by the Europeans to justify the brutal extermination campaigns that followed, ignoring the role that their expansion played in the escalating conflict. The Puritans also would rationalize this through religion, claiming that the Native Americans were devils. This pattern of expansion would continue for the next 200 years.

Neither Native Americans nor Europeans considered any possibility of assimilation of the two groups. The Europeans would speak of assimilation and conversion, but there were very few actual efforts on those fronts. They believed that their cultures, languages, customs, religions, and ways of life had too little in common. To this day, many Native Americans have never completely embraced the Anglo-European culture and its customs, nor have they been completely accepted by the dominant Anglo-European culture.

REVIEW QUESTIONS

1. Why did the settlers of Massachusetts Bay found Harvard College?

    (A) They wanted a school that would rival Yale College in Connecticut.
    (B) They needed to supply jobs for unemployed professors.
    (C) They were concerned to educate future ministers of their church.
    (D) They wanted both boys and girls in New England to learn to read.
    (E) They insisted on the separation of church and state.

2. The most important difference between Pennsylvania and the Massachusetts Bay Colony was that Pennsylvania

    (A) was not founded by a Christian
    (B) was not an English colony
    (C) did not have a large city
    (D) was not ruled by a theocracy
    (E) did not attract settlers from Europe

3. The success of Southern plantations led to the increase of which of the following?

    (A) The African slave trade
    (B) Indentured servitude
    (C) Intercolonial trade
    (D) The building of cities
    (E) Trade with the Native Americans

4. Which of the following events was most responsible for the eventual disappearance of theocracy in Massachusetts?

    (A) The founding of Rhode Island
    (B) The establishment of Yale College
    (C) The banishment of Anne Hutchinson
    (D) The founding of Pennsylvania
    (E) The Salem witchcraft trials

Answers and Explanations

1. **C** The Puritans of Massachusetts Bay established Harvard as a training school for young men who wanted to enter the ministry because it was very important to them that their ministers be learned and educated.

2. **D** Pennsylvania was founded specifically to give its citizens religious freedom; unlike Massachusetts Bay, its government had no relationship to a particular church.

3. **A** The success of Southern plantations meant that a plentiful pool of cheap labor was needed. Indentured servants did not suffice because they eventually became free and bought farms of their own. Therefore, the plantation owners established a system of African slavery.

4. **E** The Salem witchcraft trials created a scandal throughout the colony. It was clear to the people that justice was not being served. The church officials who participated in the trials lost their standing in the community, and the reputation of the church was damaged permanently.

CHAPTER 3
COLONIAL LIFE

INTRODUCTION

After surviving the hard times of the first years in the New World, the European colonists settled down to the task of building a new society. Over the course of the next 200 years that society became distinctly American, not European.

Society centered on various institutions: the church, local politics, the business economy, and the family. Colonists lived in relatively small communities. The task of building the new towns and cities, creating institutions, cultivating land, and starting new businesses required the involvement of most of the community. Children began working alongside their parents as soon as they were old enough to look after themselves.

As the enslaved population continued to grow, Africans developed a society of their own. They held on to what they could of their African cultures while coping as well as they could with harsh conditions in a strange land.

Most colonists, of whatever home culture, could agree on one thing: they did not want interference from Europe. Religious freedom had been built into the constitutions of all the colonies except Plymouth and Massachusetts, and political freedom seemed to go hand in hand with religious freedom. The English government on the whole felt the same way and left the colonies alone to govern themselves as they saw fit. Spasmodic attempts at English control resulted in the strong assertion of colonial rights.

TIMELINE

1650   Parliament passes Navigation Acts requiring that all imports destined for colonies pass through Britain.

1686   King James II organizes northern colonies into the Dominion of New England; appoints Edmund Andros governor. Andros disbands General Courts.

1688–1689   Glorious Revolution in Britain; Catholic James II gives way to Protestant William and Mary. Bill of Rights establishes Parliament as true governing body; monarch rules in name only.

1689   The period of salutary neglect begins in the colonies.

1690   Slaves present in every one of the English colonies.

1730–1750   Great Awakening in colonies; widespread rise of Protestant religious fervor

KEY TERMS

abolitionist   one who believes that slavery is wrong and should be illegal

apprentice   boy or girl (usually boy) who exchanges full-time live-in labor for room, board, and being taught the trade of the master

Bill of Rights   passed by Parliament in 1689; established Parliament, the legislative body, as the supreme authority in the English government

censorship   government or military suppression of written or artistic works

Enlightenment   an intellectual and cultural movement of the eighteenth century that originated in France; emphasized the value of reason and the quality and freedom of the individual

Glorious Revolution   bloodless revolution in which the Protestants William and Mary replaced the Catholic James II as monarchs of Great Britain

Great Awakening   a series of Protestant religious revivals that took place from about the 1730s to the 1750s

indentured servitude   an arrangement by which, in exchange for passage to the New World, a person agreed to a term of servitude in the colonies; indentured servants often were treated brutally, but ultimately they received complete freedom

mercantilism   an economic theory that states that a nation should export more than it imports; colonies were to be a source of raw materials and subservient to the needs of the mother country

Middle Passage   the trip across the Atlantic from Africa to the Caribbean or the colonies

Navigation Acts   acts of Parliament passed beginning in 1650 that regulated colonial trade

slave codes   sets of laws that curtailed the activities of African slaves

Family and Community Life

The family was the most important unit of society in colonial America. Communities in the New World were quite small at first, and for a long time they remained relatively small compared with the same cities and towns today. A person often was related by blood or marriage to nearly every family in his or her village. Those close relationships connected colonial people to one another in a network of close bonds.

Every member of a family contributed to its welfare. Farming jobs were divided along gender lines, with men and boys doing the heavy outdoor work of farming and taking care of livestock while women and girls did the equally demanding indoor work of cooking, cleaning, washing, sewing, spinning, weaving, and raising children. In towns and cities, men worked at such jobs as printer, blacksmith, wheelwright, innkeeper, and lawyer. Many men owned their own businesses. As soon as he was old enough, a boy would become an **apprentice** to someone in a trade of his choice. Boys would provide full-time, live-in labor in exchange for free room and board and learning every aspect of the trade by working at it. The apprenticeship system was often harsh and arduous.

In the towns, women worked as hard as their sisters did on farms. They generally did not have the opportunities to take wage-earning jobs, but their hands were full with the work of running a house and bearing and raising children. Some women did earn money as servants, seamstresses, and midwives. If an innkeeper died, his wife often would carry on the business and take control of the profits. Widows were allowed to own property; many became quite wealthy. Women faced many obstacles in society, though, because they were completely legally controlled by the men in their lives. Widows, often with children, made up a large proportion of the colonial poor.

Life expectancy in colonial times was not high. Many children died when they were babies. Many women died of complications of childbirth. People of all ages died of illnesses that could be cured today with penicillin or antibiotics. Young people married in their middle to late teens, and young brides usually became pregnant very quickly; more children meant more pairs of hands to help with the work, and the more children a couple had, the more were likely to survive to adulthood.

Repeated pregnancies and the risks that went with them meant that women often died quite young. If a father of several children was widowed, he usually lost no time marrying again so that his children would have a mother. Men might have two or three wives in a lifetime. Widows often remarried as well; since they often inherited the husband's property and sometimes his business and since colonial laws made it hard for them to make it on their own, they were very desirable marriage partners.

Life expectancy was lower in the South than in the North. The marshy climate, the stifling heat and humidity, and the mosquitoes combined to foster germs and infection. The unsanitary conditions in which slaves were forced to live also contributed to the unhealthy climate. This meant that a Southern family was more likely than a Northern one to include relations such as stepparents and half sisters and half brothers.

In colonial times people did not recognize the modern concept of childhood as a carefree time of play. Children were valued because they would begin working as soon as they were old enough. Even young children could pull weeds in a garden, dust furniture, set the table, wash dishes, and plant seeds. Children began working very early on farms, right beside their parents. The harshness of colonial life made this a necessity. It was the same in cities; Benjamin Franklin's *Autobiography* documents his start in the printing trade when he was very young.

Work generally centered in and around the living space. In a city, a shopkeeper would have his business on the ground floor of the house, with the living area on the floor or floors above. A man might go out to work at a law office, but it would be only a short walk home for meals. Whereas the members of a modern-day family may have a number of different schedules and agendas, this was not the case in colonial times. Family members would have separate sets of chores, but all would eat together and would attend social occasions and church as a group.

Many people in the colonies also lived and worked under an arrangement called **indentured servitude.** Under this arrangement, in exchange for passage to the New World, a person agreed to work in the colonies as a servant for a period of years. Indentured servants often were treated brutally, but ultimately they received complete freedom.

Even among the dour Puritans and Pilgrims, colonial social life played an important role. Being so accustomed to death and hardship, people embraced chances to celebrate. Within a parish, a birth or wedding was always cause for celebration. People also gathered for harvest festivals, holiday feasts, and other large parties. In the colonies there was little spare time apart from work, but work often was combined with play. For example, when farmers harvested their corn, the whole village would gather for the "husking bee." Everyone would husk the cobs of fresh corn, which would be dried to make flour for the coming winter. The workers sang, joked, and laughed to make the time pass. The women of the village provided a hearty supper for the workers, and when anyone found a red ear of corn, it was used as bait in a "kissing game" among the younger people. Similarly, during the brief maple-sugaring season in the North, everyone in the community would come together to harvest the sap, cook it, and turn it into sugar and syrup. Festivities accompanied the hard work. Social events included everyone in a community; activities were not segregated by chronological age or generation.

The Growth of Slavery

Slavery grew rapidly as the colonies developed. The first Africans were brought to Jamestown in 1619 as bound servants. Even before legal restrictions were put in place, there were racial distinctions in the justice and social systems. In 1661, the colony of Virginia passed laws stating that slavery was legal; the next year the House of Burgesses made slave status hereditary. Massachusetts had passed laws against slavery in 1641; in 1670 those laws were amended to state that the children of slaves could be sold into slavery. By 1690 there were slaves in every colony, although there were far more in the South than in the North. This was a matter of economy and geography. Slaves were not in great demand north of Maryland because there were few large-scale farms or plantations, as the climate made them unprofitable. Those who lived in the North might be laborers or house servants, many of whom were able, over time, to save money and purchase their freedom.

There was resistance to slavery from the earliest days of the colonies. The Pennsylvania Quakers spoke out publicly against slavery as early as 1688. Benjamin Franklin founded the first antislavery society in the colonies. During the Revolutionary War, Abigail Adams noted the hypocrisy of Congress in demanding freedom for white Americans while denying it to African Americans. However, resistance from whites grew very slowly over the decades, and antislavery advocates were a very small minority. It was not until the nineteenth century that the **abolitionist** movement gained real power or influence.

Slavers would sail to Africa to capture Africans, usually in the regions along Africa's western coast. African tribes aided and abetted the slavers by helping to capture people from tribes hostile to their own. Once a slaver had enough captives to fill the hold of his ship, he would sail back across the Atlantic. Usually cargoes of slaves would be taken to the Caribbean, where planters purchased them to stay there and labor on the sugarcane plantations, or for transport north to the mainland plantations. At other times they were taken directly to the mainland colonies and sold at auction there.

The **Middle Passage,** as the trip across the Atlantic is known, was a nightmare for the African captives. They were crammed into the hold of the ship, far belowdecks, where there was no fresh air or light. They were kept in chains throughout the voyage. Because the traders insisted on maximum profit, they stuffed as many captives into a ship as it could hold. The slaves were placed side by side and end to end, each within a space no more than about two feet wide and six feet long. There were no sanitary facilities. Captives occasionally were taken on deck for fresh air; many threw themselves overboard to escape the terror. Between a third and a half died during the passage, and their bodies were thrown into the ocean. Still, 600,000 Africans survived the journey during the eighteenth century. In some colonies, such as South Carolina, Africans soon made up a majority of the population.

This 1789 slave-ship diagram drawn by the abolitionist Thomas Clarkson is the result of his detailed research and interviews he conducted with slavers.

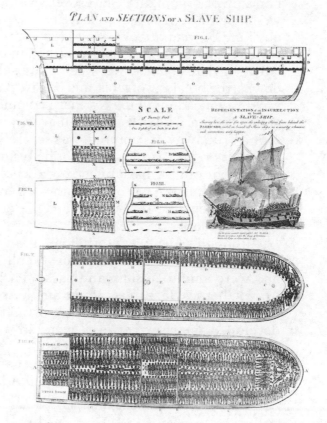

1789 diagram of hold of slave ship by Thomas Clarkson

Once they arrived in the Caribbean or North America, Africans were sold at auction. Captives were robbed of all dignity during this process: buyers forced their mouths open to look at their teeth, squeezed their arms and legs to test their muscle strength, and otherwise examined them as if they were livestock. There was no attempt to keep families together; buyers purchased only the types of workers they needed. Husbands and wives, children and parents often were parted for good on the auction block—an ironic situation considering the importance of religion and family in white colonial society.

Some slaves were put to work as house servants, but most Africans had been imported to do heavy outdoor labor on large farms or plantations. They sweated in the cotton, sugarcane, and tobacco fields of the Caribbean and the Southern colonies. They were given the minimum amount of food needed to remain alive and productive. They had no days off, received no pay, and worked constantly in all types of weather, often under the threat of whipping, beating, or even more severe punishments for any infraction of rules, as this was a system ruled by fear.

Female slaves had an even worse time than their male counterparts because they were sexually abused. No white man would incur any legal or social penalty for raping a black woman. It was very common for a slave to bear her master's children, who inherited her slave status. The irony of this was that slave masters often justified slavery as protecting white women from sexual assaults by freed blacks.

White colonists always were concerned about the possibility of slave rebellion. Therefore, the Southern colonies, where slaves were the most numerous, established legal **slave codes** that severely curtailed any possibilities of slaves bonding or organizing. Slaves were forbidden to meet in large groups. They were not allowed to marry, leave the plantation without permission, possess any kind of weapon, or learn to read or write. No well-organized, successful slave rebellion ever took place, although there were some large-scale revolts. Often slave resistance was much more subtle, taking the form of work slow-downs, the breaking of tools, and passive resistance. However, slaves frequently ran away, heading to the Northern colonies, where it was not too difficult to gain freedom. The risks in running away were great, and recapture was common. A runaway, if captured, was severely lashed. Some were punished even more severely; a runaway might be branded like livestock, have his or her tongue cut out, or have fingers or a whole hand chopped off and be left on the plantation as a warning to others. Slaves were considered valuable property, but they were replaceable, and therefore anyone deemed a troublemaker was expendable.

Although slaves were forbidden many things, they somehow managed to function and even to develop a lively culture of their own. They remembered and were able to sustain and pass on aspects of culture from their distant African homes. Jazz music, for example, is based on traditional African music. Slaves were also encouraged to absorb Christianity, at least up to a point, and developed their own style of worship with a call-and-response motif that comes straight from African culture.

African slavery remains the most shameful aspect of U.S. history. Many historians have noted, as did Abigail Adams, that slavery in a society that insisted on its own independence was rank hypocrisy.

Changes from Literacy, Education, and the Enlightenment

The United States of America since its beginnings was shaped by two forces that remain somewhat unreconciled to this day. The first was the influence of the **Enlightenment.**

The main ideas of the eighteenth-century Enlightenment that originated in France were that all men are born free and equal; people have the right to make their own laws and govern themselves; all forms of religion should be tolerated; and the press and the people must be free to write and speak their thoughts without **censorship.** Thinkers of the Enlightenment also argued that literacy and education are desirable goals. Through reading and education, people became aware of the world around them. They became able to think for themselves. Theoretically, education made a blacksmith the equal of an aristocrat and made it perfectly legitimate for a cobbler to criticize the king.

Colonial Americans believed that education was very important, although they felt this way originally for religious reasons. Protestants believed that everyone must read the Bible regularly, and so almost all colonial children were taught to read. Higher education was reserved for boys and the upper classes because only boys would become ministers or enter other professions, such as the law and medicine, in which education was clearly necessary. However, many girls throughout the colonies succeeded in getting a thorough education at home because they had enlightened parents or simply through their own persistence. Abigail Smith Adams, Mercy Otis Warren, and Phillis Wheatley are a few examples of women who received as good an education as any man of their times.

Widespread literacy also meant greater interest and participation in the political process. The colonies largely were left to govern themselves, with little interference from England. They all had representative assemblies of some sort, and men, mostly from the upper class, participated in them with enthusiasm, attending sessions regularly and arguing over which laws were best for the people. In colonial society, land ownership became the key to political power as it was thought that landowners had the greatest vested interest in society; thus, the defense of private property became entrenched in the American system. Politics and the Enlightenment often were restricted to a small elite who had the time, money, and leisure to engage in them.

The colonies had such an abundance of natural resources that colonists soon saw that an economy based on **mercantilism** was likely to bring them tremendous profits. They could make most of what they needed at home, and so their exports should stay well above their imports. The English realized that in the American colonies they had acquired a gold mine that would bring in wealth for many years to come. In response to the forces of the market, Parliament passed the **Navigation Acts** in 1650 and afterward and created a committee called the Lords of Trade to make sure the acts were enforced. Those acts required that all European goods exported to the colonies had to be routed through England, all colonial trade had to be carried out on ships owned by English subjects (the colonists, of course, were all English subjects), and colonial products such as tobacco, cotton, and sugar could be exported only to certain nations.

Those acts protected colonial trade but also hampered it to some extent. Traders in the colonies resented any law that cut into their profits. They reasoned that since they had not participated in making the laws that governed navigation, they did not have to follow them to the letter. Despite the efforts of the Lords of Trade to enforce the acts—including the revocation of the Massachusetts charter in 1684—smuggling was a thriving industry in the colonies. This flouting of faraway laws passed by Parliament presaged the revolution that was to come. The intermittent nature of colonial restrictions made it difficult to sustain control.

Changes from Religion and the Great Awakening

The second great force that has shaped American society and the American character was religious fervor. The Pilgrims and Puritans first came to America to establish moral Christian communities. They believed that their faith was the only true one and had little or no tolerance for those of other faiths. Instead, they tried to convert people to worship as they worshipped and to behave as they behaved.

The tyranny of those religions did not last long in the colonies. Outspoken people such as Anne Hutchinson and Roger Williams protested against it and founded or moved to more liberal colonies. Many people of many different religious faiths and sects were sailing to the New World. Tolerance became a necessity simply because the population was becoming so diverse. In addition, the forces of the Enlightenment encouraged people to think for themselves rather than blindly following the dictates of their particular church or minister.

However, religion was still a powerful force. It swept the colonies in a series of religious revivals known as the **Great Awakening** during the mid-1700s. Historians credit Jonathan Edwards of Connecticut and Massachusetts with launching the Great Awakening in New England around 1740. Edwards was an unforgettable preacher whose dramatic and impressive denunciations of sinners must have terrified his parishioners into leading blameless lives. Because Edwards suggested that God could be merciful to those who sincerely repented of their sins, many people were moved to confess their sins publicly and claim to be reborn in God's love. Since church doctrine preached predestination—God had chosen those who would be saved before they were born—Edwards was taking a risk by suggesting that a person could play an active role in his or her salvation. Church officials eventually dismissed him from the pulpit for his unorthodox teachings.

The Great Awakening continued nonetheless. George Whitefield, a revival preacher from England, drew crowds of thousands from 1738 onward. He was a celebrity before the concept of celebrity existed, receiving regular front-page coverage in colonial newspapers wherever he traveled. Whitefield was a powerful and charismatic speaker whose sermons inspired a surge in church membership and the building of new congregations. Many of the new churches were Baptist or Methodist.

Political Developments

The most important political event during this period of colonial development was put in motion by King James II of England. Unlike his relatively easygoing and tolerant older brother Charles II, from whom James had inherited the throne in 1685, the new king was a narrow-minded man who believed in absolute monarchy by divine right. James was convinced that his duty lay in strengthening royal authority over the distant colonies. He did that by authorizing the Lords of Trade to organize the Northern colonies into one political entity, the Dominion of New England. In 1686 James appointed Edmund Andros, a former colonial governor, to take charge of New England. Andros's first act was to disband the Massachusetts General Court and similar bodies in the other New England colonies. Naturally, he was cordially disliked on all sides. Thanks to the **Glorious Revolution** and the passage of the English **Bill of Rights,** the colonists soon were able to throw Andros out of office and restore their own legislative bodies.

The English on the other side of the Atlantic were equally displeased with their ruler. They had been a Protestant nation for too long to accept a Catholic king who apparently wished to covert the nation back to Catholicism. Charles II had been a Catholic, but he had not attempted to persecute Protestants, and he had been a charismatic man, enormously popular with his subjects. James, rigid and uncompromising, was easy to dislike. He fled the country when his daughter Mary and her husband, William of Orange, accepted an offer from Parliament to come and rule Britain jointly as Protestant monarchs. The Glorious Revolution began and ended without bloodshed, and Parliament soon passed a Bill of Rights that clarified its own authority, making the monarchy a constitutional rather than an absolute one. This example of the supremacy of the legislative body over the monarch was to make a great impression on the colonists in the years to come. The English model of government at that time is very similar to the model of government adopted by the colonists.

▄▄▄ REVIEW QUESTIONS

1. The Navigation Acts of the 1650s had all the following purposes EXCEPT:

   (A) to protect colonial trade
   (B) to increase profits for Great Britain
   (C) to maintain English control over colonial trade
   (D) to foster a mercantilist economy
   (E) to increase imports to the colonies while decreasing exports

2. A principal consequence of the Glorious Revolution in Britain was that

   (A) the New England colonists threw Edmund Andros out of office
   (B) England became a Catholic nation once again
   (C) a queen ruled England in her own right for the first time
   (D) the colonial assemblies began discussing the need for a militia
   (E) English Protestants began fleeing to the colonies for fear of religious persecution

3. The abolitionist movement had difficulty gaining supporters in the early 1800s because

   (A) African slaves were content with their status
   (B) there were no Africans in powerful positions in the government
   (C) Africans easily found ways to flout the system of slavery
   (D) Northern whites could ignore the wrongs of the slave system in the South and Southerners found it too profitable to end
   (E) Quakers were a majority in the colonies and spoke out against slavery at an early date

4. Which of the following people probably had the hardest and most thankless life in the colonies?

   (A) A farmer's wife
   (B) A female slave
   (C) A male slave
   (D) A cobbler
   (E) A blacksmith's apprentice

Answers and Explanations

1. **E** The Navigation Acts were intended in part to keep the level of colonial imports well below the level of colonial exports. Choice E states the opposite.

2. **A** Because the king who had appointed Andros was no longer on the throne, the colonists were able to put him out of power and restore the representative assemblies he had disbanded.

3. **D** Slaves were always in favor of abolition; abolitionism was a movement that succeeded in the end because of its white membership. Whites who did not see the effects of slavery on a daily basis either did not know or would not acknowledge its brutality, and Southerners had a strong economic incentive to maintain slavery as a system.

4. **B** Everyone in the colonies worked hard in one way or another. However, a slave had a much harder life than did any free person, and a female slave had the hardest time of all because she was subject to sexual abuse.

CHAPTER 4

CONFLICTS IN THE COLONIAL ERA

INTRODUCTION

Spain, France, and Great Britain were the three powerful European nations that became the first to explore North America and establish permanent footholds. All three nations claimed vast slices of the territory: the British along the Atlantic Coast, the Spanish on the West Coast and the Gulf of Mexico, and the French in all areas in the middle as well as much of Canada.

The British colonists were a great success story. They were prosperous and hearty, and their population grew considerably over the first decades. By the 1750s they began to flex their muscles and look for new lands to settle.

Royal charters had given the colonists permission to expand their territory westward as needed. However, expansion could happen only by denying the rights of rival claimants to the same land: the Native Americans and the French. The British did not have to organize an all-out war against the Native Americans. For the most part, they simply took whatever land they wanted; they were generally able to defeat the Native Americans, although the Native Americans never gave up and remained a constant threat.

The French were a different matter. The British and French shared a system of values, a cultural heritage, and an understanding of how to conduct a war. When both sides laid claim to land in the Ohio River Valley, war seemed inevitable. Neither the French colonists nor the British had a regular army in North America, and so Britain and France sent troops and officers. Although colonial volunteers played a large role in the war and Native Americans joined in first on one side and then on the other, the war was conducted along European lines and with European commanders.

The French and Indian War lasted from 1754 to around 1761. The final peace treaty signed in 1763 gave all French lands in Canada and east of the Mississippi River to Britain. Great Britain had won at a heavy financial cost, and Parliament immediately began discussing ways to force the colonies to help pay the war debt.

TIMELINE

1747 A group of Virginians forms the Ohio Company with the purpose of expanding settlement westward into the Ohio Valley.

1749 King George II grants the Ohio Company a charter and a large land grant, including the junction of the Allegheny, Monongahela, and Ohio rivers.

1751 The Ohio Company begins to settle the area.

1752 The French begin building a series of forts from which to attack the British colonists, including Fort Duquesne.

1754 Lieutenant-Colonel George Washington and 400 troops ride west to warn the French to leave British territory. The French refuse to leave. The British are defeated in the ensuing fight.

1755 England sends an army to the colonies; the British are defeated again at Fort Duquesne. Washington leads the retreat.

1756 The French and Indian War between Britain and France is formally declared.

1757 William Pitt becomes prime minister of Great Britain; directs all energy and resources into the war. French General Montcalm captures For Oswego and Fort William Henry.

1758 British army captures Forts Louisbourg and Frontenac. French burn Fort Duquesne rather than surrendering it. British rebuild it, naming it Fort Pitt.

1759 British forces take Fort Niagara and win the battle for Quebec on the Plains of Abraham.

1760 Canada surrenders to the British.

1762 To prevent the British from taking the Louisiana Territory as part of the terms of surrender, the French cede it to Spain in the Treaty of Fontainebleau.

1763 Treaty of Paris brings a formal end to the French and Indian War. England gains all territory formerly claimed by France east of the Mississippi River as well as all of Canada.

KEY TERMS

Albany Plan of Union   a plan of Benjamin Franklin's that stated that the colonies should unite for defense and protection

commander in chief   the most important military official in a nation; supreme officer in charge of the entire armed forces

Fort Duquesne   fort built by the French at the conjunction of the Allegheny, Monongahela, and Ohio rivers

French and Indian War   a war fought between 1754 and 1763 over colonial territory between the French and the British, with Native Americans fighting on both sides

Ohio Company   potential settlers of the Ohio Valley from Virginia

Plains of Abraham   a field directly on the outskirts of Quebec where the British won the French and Indian War

Treaty of Fontainebleau   1762 treaty that ceded the Louisiana Territory to Spain

Treaty of Paris   1763 treaty between the French and British, ending the French and Indian War; gave Britain all of Canada and New France

English against French

While the British colonists were settling the Atlantic Coast, the French had maintained a presence in North America. France claimed the entire central portion of the present-day United States, along with a large chunk of eastern Canada. Control of the Mississippi River was key to the French fur-trading industry. However, the French had settled very little of the area they claimed. They had built the cities of Quebec and Montreal in Canada, but for the most part they had been content to build trading posts along the Mississippi and other temporary settlements wherever they were needed.

The French got along reasonably well with the Native American population. Samuel de Champlain had set the tone for friendly relations between the French and the Native Americans when he first came to the shores of North America. For the fur traders to succeed in their work, they needed the Native Americans' help. The Native Americans were much better hunters than the French because they had been living on the land for centuries. They had built trails and knew where to find fur-bearing animals in large numbers. On their side, the Native Americans needed things from the French. They wanted to trade for weapons, horses, and metal tools more sophisticated and functional than those their people were able to make. Native Americans would hunt and trap and trade the furs for what they needed, providing a happy situation for both sides.

However, trouble lay ahead. Native Americans never before had spent so much time hunting or skinning the animals and preparing the fur pelts. This took time away from essential chores such as growing and hunting for food. Native Americans were suddenly in the position of having to trade for or purchase food, when for centuries they had been self-sufficient. The fur trade also meant that tribes became migratory. When they had decimated the fur-bearing animal population in one area, they had to move on, often into territory claimed by another tribe. This meant unprecedented contact and competition among the tribes and nations.

To some extent the fur trade and the complications it brought were controlled by the Iroquois Confederacy. The Iroquois chiefs often stepped between Western tribes and the Europeans to broker trades of the fur the Native Americans had gathered. The Iroquois were impartial between the French and English; they brokered trades in whatever way they believed was to their own advantage and that of their people. Neither the French nor the British had proved so trustworthy that the Native Americans felt great loyalty to either side.

Great Britain, France, and Spain fought over colonial territory just as they fought over their territorial boundaries in Europe. Spain had established itself in Mexico, Florida, California, and the Southwest; Britain, along the Atlantic coast; and France, over the rest of the continent. The map below shows North America in 1754.

All three nations recognized that the Native Americans would make valuable allies. The Native Americans were familiar with the land and were fierce, uncompromising fighters. They had learned to combine European weapons with guerrilla-style fighting, making themselves into a formidable enemy and a desirable ally. However, the Native Americans did not seem inclined to ally themselves with any particular group of colonists. They felt they should range their support on whichever side best furthered their own interests, although this usually tended to be the French.

Benjamin Franklin found the Iroquois Confederacy an impressive exercise in democratic rule. He proposed something similar for the colonies for their mutual defense. Franklin suggested as early as 1751 that the colonies

North America in 1754

should unite. He felt that some sort of union would strengthen and protect all the colonies. When representatives from seven colonies met in Albany, New York, to discuss questions of mutual defense, Franklin brought up his idea, which became known as the **Albany Plan of Union.** The colonial governments and faraway Parliament rejected Franklin's plan. The British were afraid it would weaken their authority over the colonies, and the representatives from one colony did not necessarily trust those from another.

Franklin drew this cartoon to illustrate why his plan of union was a good idea for the defense of the colonies. As a whole animal, the snake was well able to defend itself and to attack when necessary, but its individual pieces were helpless.

The French and Indian War

The conflict known in Europe as the Seven Years' War and in North America as the **French and Indian War** developed because France and Britain did not agree on the western boundaries of the British colonies. The British colonists believed—in many cases their royal charters explicitly stated—that they were entitled to spread out as far as they needed to. In practice, that effort to expand their borders to the west meant that the British were encroaching on territory claimed by France. This was also part of a larger struggle between the two countries that would lead some to call this the first world war. Britain and France were fighting in the Caribbean, India, and Europe to achieve the dominant empire.

The Ohio River Valley became the first arena of contention between the two European powers. In 1749, King George II had given a group of settlers known as the **Ohio Company** a large land grant in that area. However, the French laid claim to the same land. They built Fort Duquesne on the site of the present-day city of Pittsburgh, Pennsylvania, where the Allegheny and Monongahela rivers meet to form the Ohio. The British colonists swung immediately into action. The governor of Virginia appointed a 19-year-old named George Washington, who had always thirsted after a military career, to ride to **Fort Duquesne** and warn the French to leave British territory. He appointed Washington a lieutenant-colonel and authorized him and his troops to use force if the French ignored the warning. The date was 1754.

When Washington handed the French a letter warning them to leave the area, they laughed in his face, telling him that their claim to the land was as good as the British claim. Washington assigned some of his men to build a fort and left with others to bring back supplies. When he returned, he found that the French had taken the fort. Undaunted, the British troops built a new fort, which they named Necessity. In the ensuing fighting, the British side was defeated.

Both Britain and France sensed a perfect opportunity to stop the other nation from expanding its colonial holdings. Both European nations sent professional troops to the colonies. At that time the British colonies had no standing army and no trained military leaders. George Washington had lost the battle of Fort Duquesne because he had not learned the guerrilla-style warfare practiced by the Native Americans. Instead, he fought in the style he had read about in military histories in which two opposing armies faced one another across open fields. This convinced the Native Americans, who had allied themselves briefly with the British side at Fort Duquesne, that Washington was a fool and that the French were better fighters. Seeing no reason to ally themselves with the side that was bound to lose, the Native Americans ranged themselves in support of the French. This was also the result of years of better relations with the French and the fact that it was the British colonists who were expanding into Native American lands.

The British generals Edward Braddock and William Johnson conferred over their plan of attack. They decided to attack the French in three places: at Fort Duquesne, at Fort Niagara, and on the Atlantic coast of Nova Scotia. General Braddock was killed in the charge against Fort Duquesne; George Washington took over and led the retreat to safety. The British succeeded in forcing the French to evacuate Nova Scotia and claimed it for England. At Fort Niagara the French held the British back, but the British under General Johnson attacked again at Lake George and won a great victory in September 1755.

War was formally declared on May 8, 1756. The French Army under the command of the Marquis de Montcalm attacked a British garrison at Oswego on the Great Lakes. The Canadians and their Native American allies attacked the small American frontier towns and settlements in western New York and Pennsylvania. Meanwhile, the British and colonial forces blocked the mouth of the St. Lawrence River, which was a lifeline for the cities of Quebec and Montreal. British troops also launched attacks against Native American villages in the Ohio River Valley.

France gained the advantage with a successful siege of Fort William Henry on the shores of Lake George. In August 1757, Montcalm and his troops with their Native American allies destroyed the fort and killed the remaining British troops. The British lost control of the St. Lawrence River when a storm destroyed many of their ships.

Events took a turn for the better for the British side when reinforcements arrived. They took back the St. Lawrence and then captured Fort Frontenac in Quebec. In the Ohio Valley they mounted a determined assault on Fort Duquesne. The French eventually burned the fort rather than cede it to the enemy. The English built a new fort nearby, which they named Fort Pitt in honor of Prime Minister William Pitt. Pitt was something of a hero to the colonists, for as soon as he became prime minister he concentrated his efforts—and the British treasury—on winning the war in the colonies. His efforts as prime minister were instrumental in turning the tide in the war.

The next step was a direct attack on the city of Quebec. Under the command of General James Wolfe, the British laid siege to Quebec in 1759. After a battle on the **Plains of Abraham** outside the city on September 12, 1759, in which both Wolfe and Montcalm were killed, the British emerged victorious. The victory was due largely to the fact that the British Army had cannon and the French Army had none. The French surrendered formally on September 18, 1759.

In 1761 the fighting ended in America, although hostilities between the opponents continued elsewhere for two years. Representatives of the two nations signed the **Treaty of Paris** in 1763. By the terms of that treaty, the French gave Britain all of Canada and all French holdings east of the Mississippi River except New Orleans. To prevent Great Britain from gaining total control over the North American continent, France decided to cede the vast Louisiana Territory to Spain. That maneuver was accomplished in the **Treaty of Fontainebleau** in 1762. The map below shows North America in 1763.

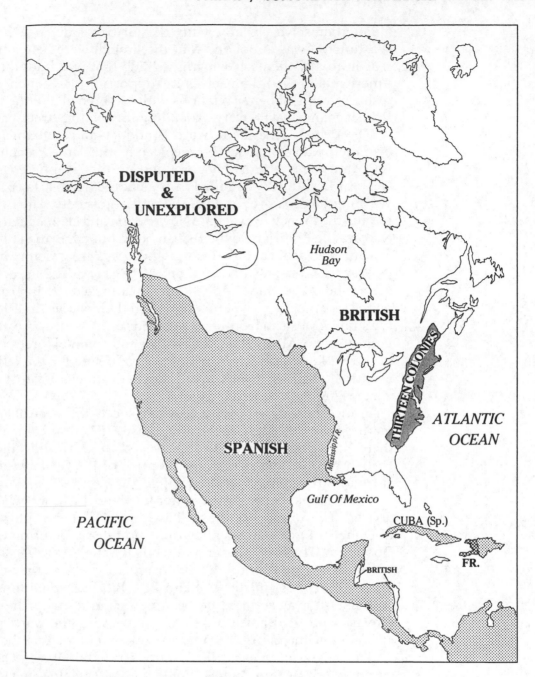

North America after the French and Indian War, 1763

George Washington

Throughout the war, the British general and commanders had treated George Washington with contempt in spite of the fact that he had held the title of **commander in chief** of the volunteer colonial army. Those experienced career military officers may have resented Washington because he was young; they may not have trusted him because he was American rather than English or because he did not have a particularly strong record in battle. They may have hesitated to treat him as an equal simply because he was a stranger to them. To Washington, it appeared that the British did not think of the colonists as fellow Englishmen. Deciding there was nothing he could accomplish against their distrust and contempt, Washington resigned from the army in 1759.

Washington's job had been thankless not only because the British command ignored him but because of the quality and character of the troops he commanded. None of the colonies had a standing army; all American troops in the French and Indian War were volunteers. To join the army, they had left their jobs, farms, and businesses behind. Since they served on a volunteer basis, they felt no compunction at deserting when they believed the time had come to go home to take care of their families, crops, or business affairs. They were liable to refuse to obey any orders with which they disagreed, feeling that their opinions were as good as those of their leaders. Under those circumstances, Washington had found command an exhausting task that challenged his ingenuity. Probably nothing but his great personal popularity and the respect his men felt for him held the volunteers together.

The Native American Role in the French and Indian War

Native Americans fought on the French side throughout most of the war. They had found French settlers and colonists cooperative and reasonably friendly compared with their British counterparts. Thus far, except in eastern Canada, the French had not tried to seize Native American lands or build permanent towns and cities. The French fur trade had brought financial prosperity and the means of acquiring weapons and modern tools to the Native Americans. Samuel de Champlain had set an example followed by others of learning Native American languages and customs.

When the British colonists arrived on the shores of the Atlantic, they too established cordial relations with the Native Americans. However, those relations did not last. As the colonial population grew, the British needed more land. The land that was there belonged to the Native Americans, but the British felt no hesitation about taking it. Because they were stronger and better organized, they were usually successful, engaging in a series of wars that amounted to extermination campaigns. The Native Americans retaliated by fighting back, ambushing, killing, and kidnapping settlers when they could, although usually on a small scale, as Native American wars tended to have fewer casualties then their European counterparts.

Because they had received better treatment from the French, the Native Americans allied with them during the war. However, they felt no genuine loyalty to the European colonists of either side. When the tide of war turned in favor of the British in the summer of 1758, the Iroquois went over to the British side.

Effects and Aftermath of the French and Indian War

The first and most obvious effect of the war was that British colonists no longer had to feel any concern about the French attacking their western borders. Second, George Washington and the rest of the American volunteer soldiers and officers had gained confidence and experience. France was a great military power, and they could take pride in the fact that their efforts had helped defeat it. Third, the war helped establish bonds among troops from different colonies. Up to that point colonists had tended to think of Virginia, New York, or Rhode Island as their "country," but now that men from the various colonies had fought a common enemy, they began to look at one another as friends and fellow countrymen. They were beginning to develop a common American identity, although at a very slow pace.

Britain had gained a prize of enormous value. The colony of Canada was rich in natural resources such as timber, fish, and furs. Canada also had a thriving and prosperous population. However, Britain had spent thousands of pounds to acquire that land. Britain had transported, equipped, supplied, and paid the troops throughout the war and now was faced with an enormous war debt. In the end, Parliament decided that since the war had been fought in part on behalf of the colonists, the colonists should bear some of the costs.

The French and Indian War marked the beginnings of mistrust between the colonies and Britain. Throughout the war, the British generals had questioned the loyalty of colonial officers such as George Washington, ignoring the fact that all the colonists were British subjects. On their side, the colonists resented the British assumption of authority in the conduct of the war. Those feelings of dislike and distrust would grow as Britain sought ways to force the colonists to help pay off the war debt.

REVIEW QUESTIONS

1. Britain defended the colonists against the French primarily because

    (A) William Pitt believed it was necessary to win the war quickly
    (B) Britain was protecting its own investment in the colonies
    (C) British military officers were personally loyal to colonial troops
    (D) the British and the Native Americans did not have friendly relations
    (E) Britain wanted to push Spain out of its American colonies

2. George Washington found the job of commander in chief of the colonial army thankless and exhausting for all the following reasons EXCEPT:

    (A) the regular desertion of his soldiers who wanted to return to look after their own affairs
    (B) the contempt and distrust with which the British army officers treated him
    (C) the fact that his soldiers often refused to obey orders of which they did not approve
    (D) his lack of enjoyment of or interest in the military life
    (E) the youth and inexperience that made it difficult for him to know the best course to pursue

3. The two maps in this chapter illustrate which result of the French and Indian War?

    (A) The colonists began to identify themselves as fellow Americans rather than as Virginians or New Yorkers.
    (B) Dislike and distrust began to grow between Britain and the colonies.
    (C) Individual colonies expanded their territory westward.
    (D) Britain more than doubled the size of its holdings in North America.
    (E) Spain more than doubled the size of its holdings in North America.

4. Before 1754 French activity in North America was directed primarily toward

(A) open warfare with Spanish colonists along the West Coast
(B) religious conversion of the Native Americans
(C) establishing the fur trade with the Native Americans
(D) border warfare with the British colonists
(E) building large cities along the Mississippi River

Answers and Explanations

1. **B** The British had made a commitment to the war before Pitt took office. The British military felt no personal loyalty to the colonial soldiers, who were strangers to them. The Native Americans were only a secondary factor in the war; it was largely about what the British saw as their rights to territory that the French also claimed.

2. **D** Washington had always desired a military career, and it is common knowledge that he was to continue to serve in the military throughout the American Revolution. The other four choices all contributed to his first experience of army command being mixed, at best.

3. **D** Choices A and B do not show on the map. Individual colonies did not grow in size; they were guaranteed the potential for expansion. Choice E is untrue: Spain gained territory, but not that much.

4. **C** The main purpose of the French in North America was to gain profits from the fur trade. French missionaries were involved in religious conversion, but that was a minor expense of energy and effort compared with the business affairs of the fur trade.

CHAPTER 5
THE ROAD TO REVOLUTION

INTRODUCTION

The French and Indian War led swiftly and inevitably to a second war: the American Revolution, or the War for Independence. This war did not break out overnight. Relations between Britain and the colonies deteriorated in several slow, painful stages.

Britain had allowed the colonies a great deal of freedom to handle their own affairs. In prosperous times that arrangement had worked very well for both sides. However, faced with a huge debt from the French and Indian War, Parliament wanted to exercise all its authority over the colonies. Much to the surprise of Great Britain, the colonies dug in their heels and argued that Parliament had no authority over them. Since they were not represented in Parliament, the colonists pointed out, they did not have to obey its laws. Britain retorted angrily that of course they had to obey; they were subjects of the British crown and had to obey all its laws.

Parliament passed a series of acts legalizing taxes on various imports to the colonies, such as molasses, tea, and paper. The colonists fought each act. As time went on, they began to feel that they had a common identity and were fighting a common enemy. After the Boston Massacre and the Boston Tea Party, the colonists called their first truly national assembly: the First Continental Congress of 1774. Although the delegates agreed not to break away from Great Britain and declare independence, they insisted on their rights. While they awaited a response to their latest petition to Parliament for redress of grievances, the first shots of the Revolutionary War were fired in Massachusetts.

TIMELINE

1763   Passage of Proclamation of 1763, setting aside lands between the 13 colonies and Mississippi River for Native Americans.

1764   Passage of Sugar Act.

March 1765   Passage of Stamp Act.

October 1765   Meeting of Stamp Act Congress in New York.

1766   Repeal of Stamp Act; passage of Declaratory Act asserting total parliamentary authority.

1767   Passage of Townshend Acts.

March 5, 1770   Boston Massacre.

December 16, 1773   Boston Tea Party.

1774   Passage of Coercive/Intolerable Acts and Quebec Act.

September 1774   First Continental Congress convenes in Philadelphia.

October 1774   Congress sends Declaration and Resolves to Britain.

KEY TERMS

Boston Massacre   a riot in Boston between soldiers and colonists on March 5, 1770

Boston Tea Party   December 16, 1773, raid on a cargo of tea on a merchant ship in Boston Harbor; Sons of Liberty disguised as Native Americans destroy entire cargo by dumping it overboard

Declaratory Act   a parliamentary Act passed in 1766, insisting on Parliament's total authority over the colonies

First Continental Congress   an official assembly of delegates from 12 of 13 colonies held in Philadelphia in September–October 1774 to discuss and enact a response to the Intolerable Acts

Galloway Plan of Union   suggestion by Joseph Galloway of Pennsylvania for an American national assembly to be led by a royally appointed president to serve as the American branch of Parliament; rejected by congressional vote

House of Commons   the more powerful legislative arm of the British Parliament; made up of popularly elected members from each district of Great Britain (membership in the House of Lords is hereditary, and the duties are largely ceremonial)

Intolerable Acts   four Acts of Parliament passed in early 1775 to punish Boston for the destruction of tea

Proclamation of 1763   a parliamentary edict that created new colonies of Quebec, East Florida, and West Florida and stated that only Native Americans could settle the land between the 13 colonies and the Mississippi River

redcoats   nickname colonists gave to British soldiers, derived from their scarlet-coated uniforms

Sons of Liberty   colonial groups formed to discuss and enact resistance to acts of Parliament and other British policies

Stamp Act   required the use of an official stamp on most paper goods and established a tax on stamped paper; passed in March 1765

Sugar Act   3-cents-a-gallon tax on imported molasses, to be paid by colonies; passed in April 1764

Townshend Acts   established taxes on imported paper, paint, tea, and glass; passed in 1767

The French and Indian War: Its Results and Aftermath

Great Britain had won the French and Indian War and driven France to the far side of the Mississippi River, gaining vast tracts of land in the process. However, that victory brought a number of complications and problems with it.

First, the war had been hugely expensive. Britain ended the war heavily in debt, with no ready means of payment. Second, the newly acquired territories would have to be populated and policed against any enemies who made rival claims to the same land. This meant that Britain would have to maintain a standing army in the colonies for the first time. Parliament also felt that the successful outcome of the war provided a perfect opportunity to overhaul the entire system of colonial government. The colonists had always ignored the Navigation Acts, and their local governments were too independent. Parliament intended to strengthen its authority over the colonies. It reasoned that since the colonies were protected by the British army and navy and the war was fought for the colonies' benefit, they should bear some of the cost.

British policy was in part responsible for the situation. The geographical distance between the colonies and the mother country was also a factor. It had been convenient to allow the colonies to govern themselves, with the mother country being much too far away to settle every problem that came up across the Atlantic. The **House of Commons** had no members who represented the colonies. No one living in Britain knew much about the circumstances and conditions in America, and thus nobody there could represent colonial interests. However, the burdens imposed by Parliament were not particularly heavy. The average colonist had a much lower tax rate than did the average citizen of Britain.

Each colony had its own constitution. No two were alike; the laws depended on when and how the colonies originally had been settled. Each colony had a governor. Royal governors in some colonies had been appointed by the British monarch; other colonies had locally elected American governors. Each colonial governor was the head of a legislative assembly of popularly elected men. Many of those assemblies from the beginning claimed that Parliament had no right to tax or legislate for them, although they rejected the idea of representation in Parliament as a viable solution. Any colonial representative would be outvoted consistently. What they wanted was a representative body of their own that reported to the king just as Parliament did.

Parliament passed the **Proclamation of 1763.** That edict made three new colonies out of the territory Britain had acquired in the Treaty of Paris. The colonies were Quebec, East Florida, and West Florida. All the lands between the 13 original colonies and the Mississippi River were left to the Native Americans to settle, and the proclamation made it illegal for settlers to buy any of that land from the Native Americans. Parliament's hope was that this segregation of the two peoples would end the strife between the British colonists and the Native Americans.

The Sugar Act

Parliament's next action was to crack down on abuses of the Navigation Acts. Those abuses were widespread and had gone on for many years. Colonial legislatures refused to pass laws putting a stop to smuggling, and even when governors disagreed with their legislatures, they were powerless to enforce the laws when every colonist appeared to be in league to continue the practice of smuggling and refusing to pay duty at the customs house. The man Parliament appointed to take charge of enforcing the Navigation Acts was George Grenville.

Grenville saw the Americans as disobedient subjects who had to be forced to obey Parliament. The quickest way to raise the money Britain needed for the war debt was to raise taxes on the colonists. Grenville initiated a shift in the taxation policy of the British. Previously taxes had been levied on goods when they were sold in Britain and thus were external taxes. Grenville imposed internal taxes on the colonies, a right the colonists claimed he did not have. His first move was to present the **Sugar Act** to Parliament in 1764.

The Sugar Act called for a 3-cents-a-gallon tax on all foreign molasses imported into the colonies. The colonies had always been required to pay a duty on foreign molasses, but Britain had never enforced that rule before. Now, however, it would do so. The Sugar Act stated that Parliament would appoint more cargo inspectors and give the Royal Navy the right to inspect any ship in American waters. If any ship failed to report its cargo or refused to pay the tax on it, the captain would be arrested and put on trial in the admiralty courts. Those courts had no juries.

Parliament passed the Sugar Act in April 1764. From New England to Georgia, many colonists reacted with dismay. It appeared to them that Parliament wanted to take away two of their most basic rights as British citizens: the right not to be taxed without their own consent and the right to a trial by jury. They believed that the 1689 Bill of Rights passed by Parliament gave them those rights because they were British citizens.

The colonists sent official letters to Britain, signed by their governors, to protest the Sugar Act. Colonial merchants knew that paying the molasses tax would cut into their profits. With the Royal Navy checking every ship, the colonists were unable to continue the profitable practice of smuggling. They pleaded with Britain to relax its inspections at least for small boats that traded locally.

Colonial newspaper editorials urged colonists to boycott British goods in protest. People should make their own clothing, brew their own beer, and raise their own livestock rather than depending on British imports. Men also expressed their displeasure with their fists. Rioting between working men and men of the Royal Navy became an everyday occurrence in port cities such as Boston. In an effort to smooth things over, Parliament lowered the tax on molasses to 1 cent per gallon in 1766. The colonists were not entirely satisfied, but they paid.

This would begin a downward cycle in the relations between the colonies and Britain. Parliament would enact a tax, and the colonies would resist through petition and violence. After a period of discontent, Parliament generally would remove the taxes, and this allowed for a period of calm until the financial situation demanded new taxes.

The Stamp Act

The Sugar Act had included one item that failed to pass. That item, passed in March 1765, became known as the **Stamp Act.** It required the use of an official stamp on most kinds of paper goods in the colonies and also charged a tax for the use of the paper. Newspapers, legal papers, property records, and legal and professional licenses were included under the Stamp Act. George Grenville appointed a stamp inspector for each colony. That official would pass out stamps and collect the taxes.

Passage of the Stamp Act touched off outraged reactions throughout the colonies. Although they might have accepted the Sugar Act as an attempt to regulate trade rather than a tax, the Stamp Act was clearly not related to trade. It was a tax pure and simple, and the colonists had been given no chance to vote on it.

In October 1765 a group of political leaders from nine colonies met in New York to discuss the colonial response to the Stamp Act. That gathering was called the Stamp Act Congress. The leaders agreed on active resistance to the stamp inspectors. **Sons of Liberty,** as colonial activist groups were called, encouraged the people to rob and tear down the homes of the stamp inspectors.

The colonists did that with enthusiasm, damaging the inspectors' property, hanging them in effigy, insulting them in newspaper articles, and making their lives miserable. Many stamp inspectors resigned in fear for their lives; all reported to Parliament that it was impossible to collect the stamp tax.

In Parliament in January 1766, William Pitt urged repeal of the Stamp Act. He pointed to the principle that Parliament had no legal right to tax the colonists without their consent. Benjamin Franklin, in London at the time of the debate, was called to Parliament to give the colonial view of the Stamp Act. He explained that Americans believed they had the same rights as all other British citizens—no taxation without representation—and that they would never consent to the stamp tax. Parliament repealed the act but published a **Declaratory Act** asserting its total authority over the colonies. The British position was that as subjects of the British Crown, the colonists were "virtually represented" in Parliament, as was the case with the other parts of the British Empire.

The Townshend Acts and Illegal Taxation

In 1767, Parliament tried again to raise money from the colonies. Chancellor of the Exchequer Charles Townshend recommended a series of acts taxing all imported paint, paper, glass, and tea. Since the colonists had grudgingly accepted the Sugar Act as a trade regulation rather than a tax, Townshend believed they would regard the new acts in the same light. He was mistaken. The colonists were furious. Led by Samuel Adams, a political activist from Boston, they complained in print that the **Townshend Acts** were simply more illegal attempts to tax them. Adams sent a circular letter to the governments of all the colonies, laying out the reasons for the colonial objections. Soon there were riots in the streets of the port cities again, most notably in Boston. Conditions grew so unsafe that British officials in Boston asked General Gage, the head of the standing army, to send troops to the city to maintain order. Adams's marshaling of public support into violence was even more remarkable in light of the fact that the taxes affected only an elite few in the colonies.

The Boston Massacre

The English soldiers quickly became the most despised people in Boston. On the night of March 5, 1770, tension between soldiers and citizens erupted into what became known as the **Boston Massacre.** A group of colonists, including the free African merchant seaman Crispus Attucks, jeered at a group of **redcoats.** Suddenly an American hurled a stone and then another. Attucks joined the attack, pushing one of the redcoats. A shot was fired, and moments later Attucks lay dead on the ground. In the ensuing melee, the soldiers shot and killed four more people. The next day, the Bostonians' bodies were carried to Faneuil Hall, where people paid their respects to the fallen as martyrs to a cause.

This engraving by the Bostonian silversmith Paul Revere shows a highly exaggerated account of the riot, depicting the British as brutal aggressors and the Bostonians as helpless victims. Although this was a distortion of the facts, the colonists eagerly embraced it. The engraving was reprinted and made available all over the colonies very shortly after the event. It is an excellent example of propaganda and helped unite the colonists against what they were beginning to perceive as a common enemy—Britain.

The Boston Massacre (engraving by Paul Revere)

The morning after the riot Samuel Adams rose to his feet in the Massachusetts Assembly and demanded the "total evacuation of the town by all regular troops." Royal Governor Hutchinson realized that Adams was right and that the situation in Boston had become untenable and unsafe. He ordered the redcoats to leave the city.

Months later the soldiers who had killed Attucks and the other rioters were tried for murder. John Adams, Samuel Adams's cousin, agreed to defend them. His decision was unpopular, but he stood fast on the principle that if the colonists demanded rights such as a fair trial for themselves, they had to be prepared to extend those rights to others. Because the colonists had been the aggressors, the jury agreed that the soldiers were not guilty of murder.

The Boston Tea Party

The colonists retaliated against the Townshend Acts by boycotting all tea that came from Britain. Instead they drank smuggled Dutch tea, which was cheaper because it was not taxed. As a result, Britain's East India Company had no buyers for the millions of pounds of tea in its warehouses. British merchants in India, who stood to lose a fortune, begged Parliament for help. Parliament agreed to allow the East India Company to sell its tea in the colonies at a special low price so that even with the tax it would be cheaper than Dutch tea. The colonists saw this agreement as an attempt to manipulate them into paying a tax they opposed on principle. They knew that if they bought the East India tea to save money, the British would have a hold over them in the longstanding quarrel over payment of taxes.

Various colonial merchants had agreed to sell the East India tea. The Sons of Liberty met in Philadelphia and New York in October and agreed not to accept the tea. This had the effect of making most merchants renege on their agreements to sell it. There was one crucial holdout, however; the sons of Massachusetts Royal Governor Thomas Hutchinson were merchants and held firm in their agreement to sell the East India tea.

On November 27, 1773, the *Dartmouth* sailed into Boston Harbor with a cargo of East India tea. No dockworker in Boston was willing to help unload it. On their side, the Hutchinsons refused to allow the *Dartmouth* to leave the port until the tea was unloaded and the duty was paid. The law was that the ship could be seized in 20 days for nonpayment of duty. If that happened, the tea would be unloaded and could be put on sale. The Sons of Liberty decided to unload the tea themselves—into Boston Harbor.

December 16 was the last day of grace before the customs house could seize the cargo. That night, a crowd of 200 "Indians" with feathers in their hair and hatchets in their hands stormed aboard the *Dartmouth*. They hacked the wooden crates of tea open and dumped them into the sea, cheered on by a great crowd of Bostonians on the docks.

The Sons of Liberty had planned well. They knew that no actual Native Americans would be blamed because the Native Americans had taken no part in the hostilities between Britain and the colonists. They also knew that they needed to keep their identities secret because they were committing a crime that constituted treason. The secret was well kept. To this day historians do not know exactly who boarded the *Dartmouth* that night.

The Results of the Boston Tea Party

News of the "**Boston Tea Party**" reached Britain in January 1774. Parliament agreed that Boston must be punished harshly, made an example to other colonies that might be tempted to defy Parliament's authority and steal and destroy valuable property in the process. Parliament promptly passed a series of acts that became known in the colonies as the "**Intolerable Acts.**"

Name of Act	What It Required	Effect
Boston Port Act	Closed the port of Boston until Boston agreed to pay East India company for *Dartmouth* cargo	Boston could not import any foreign goods or export to other nations
Massachusetts Government Act	Members of legislature to be appointed by king, no longer popularly elected	Revoked Massachusetts Charter of 1691; forbade town meetings for which governor had not given permission
Administration of Justice Act	Any royal official committing a capital offense to be tried in Britain or in any colony other than Massachusetts	Made it more likely that soldiers would get away with violence against citizens
Quartering Act	Colonists had to provide food and housing for British soldiers on demand	Robbed citizens of the right to privacy and security in their own homes

Parliament also passed the Quebec Act in 1774. That act gave the colony of Quebec a system of government that did not include a representative assembly or trial by jury. The colonists regarded this abrupt revocation of Canadians' rights as a portent for themselves.

The First Continental Congress and Its Accomplishments

Samuel Adams and the other Massachusetts Assembly members who were thrown out of office by the Intolerable Acts met privately to discuss their situation. They wrote to the assemblies of the other colonies, asking for their support in a total suspension of trade with Britain. Leaders from all the colonies except Georgia agreed to meet in Philadelphia at the beginning of September 1774 to take steps for the security of colonial rights, which everyone agreed were threatened seriously by a pattern of oppression from Britain.

Leaders from each colony decided who would best represent them in the **First Continental Congress.** Samuel and John Adams, the two radical leaders from Boston, would represent Massachusetts. Both men were well-read and well-educated graduates of Harvard College. Both rose to prominence around the time of the Stamp Act crisis. Samuel Adams was a political leader and a writer of great influence; John Adams was a lawyer whose interest in politics was equally passionate.

George Washington and Patrick Henry represented Virginia. Washington had acquired a distaste for the British during his days of being snubbed and shoved aside in the French and Indian War. Patrick Henry was a fiery liberal who rose to his feet the first day of Congress, exclaiming, "The distinctions between Virginians, Pennsylvanians, New Yorkers, and New Englanders are no more. I am no longer a Virginian, but an American!" John Dickinson, who had written a famous pamphlet opposing the Townshend Acts, represented Pennsylvania.

The delegates found that they agreed with one another on many of their major concerns. All were united in expressing outrage over the Intolerable Acts, which had been designed specifically to punish Boston and were harder on Massachusetts than on any other colony. "This day convinced me that America will support Massachusetts or perish with her," John Adams wrote in his diary one day after the debate. The unity of the colonies was especially significant in light of the lack of unity in the previous 30 years. The colonies had regarded each other with suspicion and distrust. Now they coalesced around the idea of colonial unity even though the only colony truly affected was Massachusetts.

By October the delegates had debated and approved a document called the Declaration and Resolves. It stated that since the colonists were not represented in Parliament, it had no authority over them; that they were entitled to elect their own local governments; and that the colonies would cut off all trade with Britain and boycott all British goods until the Intolerable Acts were repealed and the standing army was disbanded and sent back to Britain. Some trade would be cut off immediately; since Southern delegates argued forcefully for the right to trade their current cotton and tobacco crops, trade of those items would be suspended several months later, in 1775. The delegates also agreed that each colony should establish its own militia.

The Congress discussed the issue of breaking completely away from Great Britain or resolving their differences with the mother country and remaining part of the British Empire. Joseph Galloway, a Quaker delegate from Pennsylvania, believed that it would be best to steer a middle course. He suggested what came to be known as the **Galloway Plan of Union** to the Congress, giving each colony control of its own affairs but creating a national American assembly that would be a branch of the British Parliament. This national assembly would have representatives from all the colonies and be headed by a president-general who would be appointed by the monarch. The Plan of Union was rejected narrowly in a vote.

The delegates agreed to meet again in May if they had no positive response from London addressing their concerns. Just before that, on April 19, something happened that would give them a new topic for debate: open warfare would erupt in Massachusetts.

REVIEW QUESTIONS

1. The First Continental Congress was convened primarily to

   (A) discuss a unified colonial response to the Intolerable Acts
   (B) discuss a plan to unite the 13 colonies as an independent nation
   (C) raise a standing army that could protect the colonists against British oppression
   (D) arrive at a set of internal trade regulations that was fair to all colonies
   (E) plan a suspension of all trade with Great Britain

2. Why had Great Britain failed to enforce the Navigation Acts before 1763?

   (A) Smuggling had made the colonies, and therefore Britain, wealthier.
   (B) The royal governors in the colonies were disloyal to British interests.
   (C) Britain had no interest in what went on in the American colonies.
   (D) British representatives found it impossible to enforce laws that so many colonists were determined to ignore.
   (E) The colonists threatened the lives and property of the people paid to enforce the Navigation Acts.

3. The Sons of Liberty disguised themselves as Native Americans on the night of the Boston Tea Party for all these reasons EXCEPT:

   (A) They knew that Native Americans would never be accused or suffer any penalties for the destruction of the tea.
   (B) They did not want to be prosecuted for the crime of destroying property that was not theirs.
   (C) They wanted their friends and families to be able to say truthfully that they did not recognize them that night.
   (D) They knew that dressing up in costumes would add to the excitement and enthusiasm of the undertaking.
   (E) They hoped that Native Americans would be blamed for the storming of the *Dartmouth*.

4. Paul Revere chose to distort the facts in his engraving of the Boston Massacre primarily to

   (A) unite people from all the colonies against the aggressor, Britain
   (B) satisfy his creative instincts as an artist
   (C) ensure that the redcoats would not receive a fair trial
   (D) ensure that history would portray Britain as a villain
   (E) prove that Crispus Attucks and his friends had died the deaths of heroes

Answers and Explanations

1. **A** The immediate reason for convening the Congress was to agree on how the colonies, united in their mutual concerns, would respond to the Intolerable Acts.

2. **D** Choices B, C, and E are untrue statements. Choice A is misleading; the colonists profited from smuggling, but those profits did not accrue to Britain.

3. **E** The Sons of Liberty knew that there was no chance that Native Americans would be blamed for the crime. As an urban community, Boston had a very small Native American population.

4. **A** Revere knew perfectly well that his engraving would not have the power to accomplish choices C and D. He knew the engraving was inaccurate, and so he was not trying to achieve choice E. He probably did want to satisfy his artistic instincts, but his primary purpose was to create a piece of propaganda that would stir up sympathy and support for Massachusetts in the other colonies.

CHAPTER 6

THE AMERICAN REVOLUTION

INTRODUCTION

The Revolutionary War began on the morning of April 19, 1775, when someone fired a shot on Lexington Green just outside Boston. To this day no one knows who fired this first shot of the American War for Independence. It was only the first of many shots fired over the next six years.

At first sight no one would have thought that the Americans could defeat the British Army. American soldiers were volunteers who had little training and were not being paid. The British Army was famous throughout the world and had a glorious history. Its men were better equipped, better trained, and much more experienced.

The Americans had two major advantages: a knowledge of their own terrain and the ability to fight in the manner of Native Americans. They had learned the value of the Native American method of hiding behind cover and then leaping out to take an enemy by surprise. Most of the American victories in the war were brought off by stealth.

To the British, such a method of conducting a military campaign amounted to cheating. Armies should fight fairly, facing each other across an open field. That would not have been fair to the Americans, who were not trained or equipped to win such fights.

The passage of the Declaration of Independence in July 1776 put new heart into the army, which now had a true cause for which to fight. George Washington's leadership kept the army united under the worst conditions; the soldiers felt such personal loyalty to their commander that there was very little desertion from Valley Forge during the winter of 1777–1778 despite the dreadful conditions.

The alliance with France in 1778 was a second and welcome boost to American morale. With a powerful ally such as France, the United States knew that it could hang on long enough to defeat the redcoats. French and American forces finally cornered the British at Yorktown, Virginia, in 1781. Two years later, in the Treaty of Paris, Britain formally recognized the colonies as the independent United States of America.

TIMELINE

1775

April 19   Initial skirmishes at Lexington and Concord, Massachusetts.

May 10   Second Continental Congress begins its meeting.

June 15   George Washington assumes command of the Continental Army.

June 16   Battles of Breed's and Bunker Hill.

1776

January   *Common Sense* is published.

July 4   Declaration of Independence is approved and signed by the Second Continental Congress.

December 26   Battle of Trenton, New Jersey.

1777

January 3   Battle of Princeton, New Jersey.

September   Battle of Brandywine, Pennsylvania.

October 17   Battle of Saratoga, New York.

1778

February   France and America form a military alliance.

June   Battle of Monmouth, New Jersey.

1781

October   Hostilities cease with the British laying down of arms at Yorktown, Virginia.

1783   War ends; Treaty of Paris makes it official.

KEY TERMS

disperse   to break up, to scatter, to disband

Hessian   from the German province of Hesse

magazine   storehouse for weapons

mercenaries   troops who agree to fight on the side of a foreign power for payment

minuteman   volunteer soldier who agrees to be ready to fight at a minute's notice

siege   a military blockade that does not allow any people or goods to enter an area; thus, those inside will be starved into surrender

The "Shot Heard Round the World"

In 1775, Parliament replaced Royal Governor Hutchinson of Massachusetts with General Thomas Gage, charging him to use his troops to maintain order in Boston. Gage found himself unable to exert true authority. Although Parliament had revoked the colony's charter and disbanded its assembly, Gage knew what everyone knew: the assemblymen were continuing to gather and make plans. Gage was also well aware of the fury the Bostonians felt at having a standing army maintained in their city in peacetime.

The presence of the British troops made all the towns near Boston form their own militias. Those volunteer companies were known as **minutemen** because they agreed to be ready to take up arms against the enemy at a minute's notice. The colonies had no armies of their own, but there were many veterans of the French and Indian War who agreed to train the minutemen. Many of those volunteer soldiers were as young as 15 years old.

Concord, a sleepy village not far from Boston, was a favorite meeting place for the former assembly members. Samuel Adams, John Hancock, and the others agreed that Concord would be a good place to establish a **magazine.** It would be too dangerous to keep a stock of weapons in Boston, where the redcoats might discover it at any time.

In April 1775 General Gage decided to seize the weapons. He sent two patrols of men to Concord: one to storm the magazine and the other to arrest Adams and Hancock. The troops began their short journey after dark; Gage wanted to keep their mission quiet, hoping to catch the Americans by surprise. However, his plan was foiled by the Sons of Liberty, who had a number of spies watching the troops. On the night of April 18, when the British crossed the Charles River and began their march toward Concord, Paul Revere warned a friend to light two lanterns in the tower of Boston's Old North Church. The people north of Boston would see the signal and know that the British were coming. William Dawes mounted a fast horse and rode hard to Lexington to warn the people and summon the minutemen from their beds. Revere crossed the Charles and followed Dawes. The towns between Boston and Lexington, roused by the shouts of the riders, leaped into their clothes and grabbed their muskets.

On Lexington Green the redcoats and the minutemen faced each other for the first time. The British ordered the Americans to **disperse.** The Americans, outnumbered by more than 15 to 1 and unused to military discipline, were confused and disorderly. Some backed away. A shot rang out, then another and another. Seven minutemen and their commander were killed. Satisfied with having chased the rebels away, the British marched on to Concord, seized the weapons they found, and then turned back toward Lexington and Boston.

Each side claimed that the other fired first. No historian has been able to discover the truth, and even the eyewitness accounts differ.

As the British marched toward Concord, the minutemen began firing at them, using the underbrush and trees lining the sides of the road for cover. At Concord Bridge there was another skirmish between the minutemen and the redcoats. Many years later, Ralph Waldo Emerson commemorated the patriots' efforts in a poem in which he coined the famous phrase "the shot heard round the world." By the time the redcoats reached Boston, the Americans had killed more than 265 of them.

The Siege of Boston

The Second Continental Congress met in Philadelphia on May 10. The first topic of debate was the response to Lexington and Concord. The British use of arms against their fellow citizens had done more to unite the colonies than had any of the infuriating acts of Parliament. On June 14 Congress formally created the Continental Army, which was to raise six companies of soldiers in Pennsylvania, Maryland, and Virginia. John Adams rose to nominate George Washington—"a gentleman whose skill and experience as an officer, great talents, and universal character would unite the cordial exertions of the colonies better than any other person"—as commander in chief. He was elected unanimously. With his newly appointed staff officers, Washington rode north toward Boston. He and his men arrived just in time to hear of the battles of Breed's Hill and Bunker Hill.

The Lexington minutemen had followed the redcoats all the way back to Boston and had laid **siege** to it. Minutemen from all over New England had responded when they heard the news about Lexington. Thousands of them had come to Boston to support the siege and starve the British Army into surrender. With those reinforcements, the Americans outnumbered the British by about five to one; the British had no choice but to wait for help from outside. Meanwhile, many Bostonians left the city; those who stayed braved food shortages and stoppage of trade.

The Americans knew that if they had heavy artillery, they might fire on the redcoats and force a surrender. There were French and Indian War cannon at far-off Fort Ticonderoga, New York; both the Connecticut Assembly and the leaders of Massachusetts made plans to bring the artillery to Boston, each unaware of the other's action. New Hampshire's Ethan Allen and his Green Mountain Boys and the Massachusetts patriot Benedict Arnold joined forces, captured the cannon, and hauled them toward Boston.

In June, the British generals Burgoyne, Clinton, and Howe and 3,000 soldiers came to the aid of the besieged city of Boston. Burgoyne suggested an attack from the high ground overlooking Boston. The watchful Sons of Liberty discovered the plan. On the night of June 16, General Putnam and Colonel Prescott led a thousand soldiers to Breed's Hill, where they dug trenches and built a barricade. When the sun rose the next morning and the British saw what had happened, they fired on the Americans, who held their ground. With their scarlet and white uniforms glittering in the morning sun, the British made easy targets for the minutemen, one of whom later remembered General Putnam's warning: "Reserve your fire until the enemy approaches so near as to enable you to see the whites of their eyes!" Many British fell, but when the Americans began to run out of bullets, they were chased out of Charlestown, which the redcoats burned to the ground. The British had gained control of the heights but had lost more than twice as many men as the Americans had. This battle would have important symbolic effect as the valor of the colonials would convince many that they could face the British in battle.

From *Common Sense* to the Declaration of Independence

"We have it in our power to begin the world over again." With those simple words, a pamphlet called *Common Sense* boldly suggested that America should become an independent nation as soon as possible. After Bunker Hill, many Americans had begun discussing independence; *Common Sense* convinced many more.

The 39-year-old journalist Thomas Paine, a recent immigrant from England to the colonies, had failed at many jobs in his life: corset maker, customs clerk, teacher, and grocer. He began working on *Common Sense* in November 1775. Paine did not know much about the various acts of Parliament that had so angered the colonists. He argued for independence on general principles: all government was a necessary evil, but a hereditary monarchy such as the English had was the worst system of all. Paine urged that the American colonies adopt a new democratic system that would be based on talent, not on accidents of birth. Paine believed that if one nation set an example of democracy, others would follow. The events of 1775 had convinced him that this was the right time for the colonies to take that step. Many readers agreed; *Common Sense* sold 500,000 copies in 1776, one copy for every four or five people living in the colonies.

More and more colonial assemblies declared their support for independence from Britain. Others, however, believed that reconciliation was still possible.

John Dickinson of Pennsylvania was the leading conservative voice in Congress. He wrote a document called the Olive Branch Petition, a direct appeal to King George III to bring about peace between Parliament and the colonies. Congress voted to sign and send the Olive Branch Petition but also approved a Declaration for the Causes and Necessities of Taking Up Arms. That declaration was written by Thomas Jefferson and closed with the words "We most solemnly declare that we will preserve our liberties, being with one mind resolved to die free men rather than to live as slaves."

In June 1776, Richard Henry Lee of Virginia rose in Congress and read this resolution:

> that these united colonies are, and of right ought to be, a free and independent state; that they are absolved from all allegiance to the British Crown; and that all political connection between them and the state of Great Britain is, and ought to be, totally dissolved.

Three weeks later the delegates were debating the Declaration of Independence. That document had been written by Thomas Jefferson, a youthful, quiet, studious, and highly respected delegate from Virginia. The Declaration set forth the reasons for the separation from Britain. Jefferson sat almost silent through three days of fierce debate during which John Adams passionately defended every sentence of the Declaration while others raised objections to whole passages. The most crucial passage to be stricken referred to slavery as "cruel war against human nature itself." Southern delegates did not like the implication that slavery was wrong; for the sake of gaining independence, the Northern delegates consented to having the passage removed. The declaration finally was approved, and the Virginia resolution carried unanimously on July 2; it was made official on July 4. John Adams wrote to his wife, Abigail, that in the future, the anniversary of American independence would be celebrated "with pomp and parade, with shows, games, sports, guns, bells, bonfires, and illuminations, from one end of this continent to the other, from this time forward forevermore."

Washington Moves to Victory

The American forces were at a tremendous disadvantage. The British forces were better armed, better trained, and much greater in number. On top of that, the revolution never had the support of more than a third of the population; in fact, one third of the colonists supported the British. The British, however, were hamstrung by distance and inconsistent leadership.

Washington had arrived in Boston after the Battle of Bunker Hill. He immediately brought order and discipline to the troops camped around the city. His plan was to wait for the British to leave, as they would have to do sooner or later, or starve. However, the British were prepared to wait, and the Americans grew bored. They were volunteers and did not have the regular-army professional discipline of the British; also, they were not being paid a salary for their efforts. They had thought that war would be an exciting adventure, not just endless weeks of waiting for something to happen. Many of them returned to their homes. By January 1776 Washington had only about 10,000 men remaining.

In March, General Howe sent word to Washington, asking that the Continental Army allow his troops to leave the city peacefully. In exchange for safe passage out of the city, Howe promised that the British would not fire and would not burn Boston. Washington agreed. The British sailed out of Boston. They planned to take over New York City, cutting New England off from the rest of the colonies and crushing both sections in turn. Thousands of **Hessian mercenaries** were sailing across the Atlantic to reinforce the British troops.

Washington and the Continental Army moved south and set up headquarters in New York. In late June a British fleet arrived in New York Harbor. A month later British troops under General Howe landed in Brooklyn and proceeded to attack its American defenders. The Battle of Brooklyn was a great success for the British. Thousands of Americans were killed. Those who survived retreated to Manhattan. If Howe had attacked again right away, the safe retreat of the Continental Army would not have been possible, but Howe did nothing and the Americans were able to retreat in good order. They marched north through Manhattan and fought the British again at Harlem Heights. Meanwhile, the patriotic citizens of Manhattan set the city on fire, leaving the British with only smoking ruins. Washington's army eventually crossed the river to New Jersey. Washington would lose battles, but he would display an important strength. At this point he had not given up his belief in fighting the British in the open field, and this led to many grievous loses. However, he also displayed his ability to hold the army together in the worst circumstances. In many respects this would be his most formidable asset.

The Continental Army marched south to Trenton, which lies on the Delaware River, the border between New Jersey and Pennsylvania. They crossed to the Pennsylvania side in small boats and set up camp. The British remained in Trenton.

It was Christmastime. Washington suddenly wondered if he could turn the holiday into an American advantage. If he and his men slipped back into Trenton on Christmas night and attacked the next morning, they might take the Hessians by surprise. Between the late-afternoon dusk and the following dawn over 2,400 soldiers were ferried quietly back across the Delaware. The young officer Alexander Hamilton noticed the bloody tracks their feet left in the snow, but he also saw grim determination on every face.

Washington's daring plan succeeded. The Hessians had celebrated Christmas until late at night and were caught completely off guard by the Americans in the morning. Nearly 1,000 Hessians were taken prisoner, and their weapons were distributed among the American troops. Washington's great victory inspired many of his men to reenlist and inspired many others to join up for the first time.

Colonial Soldiers

Women, Native Americans, and African Americans all fought in the Revolutionary War. Washington originally had banned Africans from serving as soldiers. When Virginia's governor offered freedom to any slave who would fight on the British side and hundreds of slaves accepted, the U.S. Army began enlisting free Africans. Perhaps 5,000 of them fought in the war.

American soldiers faced tremendous hardships throughout the struggle. They were generally undersupplied, starving, and sick. Disease would kill more than battles did, and in the winter many would die from frostbite brought about through a lack of shelter, blankets, and shoes. They very rarely saw their promised wages and faced harsh discipline for infractions. Battlefield medicine was horrifyingly simple and ineffective. Although the officers managed to be well fed and protected, the average soldier struggled for survival.

Native Americans were considered valuable allies by both sides because of their knowledge of the terrain. On their part, the Native Americans were willing to fight for whichever side seemed most likely to respect their rights. The Cayuga, Mohawk, Onondaga, and Seneca fought for the British, and many Oneida and Tuscarora fought on the American side.

Many American women followed their husbands to war. They camped with the troops, working as nurses, cooks, and laundresses. Those women were in as much danger as the men, under constant threat of enemy fire. Mary Ludwig Hayes is famous for taking over a cannon at the Battle of Monmouth; Deborah Sampson disguised herself as a man and fought as Robert Shurtleff for many months before her masquerade was discovered.

Key Battles at Brandywine and Saratoga

In January 1777 Washington won the Battle of Princeton, pushing the British out of New Jersey for good. By September, however, General Howe had swung his troops around the American forces to attack them from the rear. His goal was to capture Philadelphia, the capital of the United States and the meeting place of Congress.

The battle was fought at Brandywine Creek, several miles from Philadelphia. The Americans were forced to retreat to Germantown, just north of the city. A week later the British attacked Paoli, a town about 25 miles west of the city. By the end of September the British were marching through the streets of Philadelphia.

In October, Washington attacked Howe's men in Germantown. The day was foggy, and the American troops panicked and ran in all directions. This was the fifth time Howe defeated Washington in battle. The ragtag colonial army gathered itself together and settled at Valley Forge for the winter. Although conditions were dreadful—deep snow, bitterly cold temperatures, little food, and no boots or clothing to replace the garments they had been wearing for months—few soldiers deserted. Washington somehow had gained the personal loyalty and respect of his troops. "They exhibited a degree of patience and fortitude which reflects on them the highest honor, and which ought ever to entitle them to the gratitude of their country," wrote one observer.

The army put the time to good use. Friedrich von Steuben, a career Prussian army officer who had befriended Benjamin Franklin in Paris, began working with the men, drilling them on a daily basis until they began to look as sharp and disciplined as the British regulars. In the spring Washington led his troops forth into battle at Monmouth, New Jersey. This was the first time the two armies had met in an open battle. When the American commander ordered his troops to retreat, George Washington lost his temper for the first time, swearing "until the leaves shook on the trees," according to one officer. Washington rallied his troops and continued the battle. There was no clear victory for either side, but the British had learned that the Americans were formidable opponents even in traditional European-style warfare.

In October 1777 the Americans pulled off a miracle by forcing the British to surrender at Saratoga, a small town in northern New York. That spring General Burgoyne had planned to march on Albany. He would lead troops from the north, taking back Fort Ticonderoga and Lake Champlain. Colonel St. Leger and his troops would approach Albany from the west.

General Benedict Arnold bribed a prisoner of war called Schuyler into giving false information to the Iroquois allies of the British. Schuyler, who could speak Iroquois, easily got them to persuade St. Leger's troops to retreat. Under Arnold's leadership and at the suggestion of Colonel Tadeusz Kosciuzko, who had come from Poland to help the American cause, the Americans grouped their cannon at the top of a cliff. Burgoyne's troops could not pass without marching directly into the line of fire. On October 17, Burgoyne surrendered. The Battle of Saratoga would bring the French into the war, providing an invaluable source of materials and a navy. This victory would convince them that the Americans had a chance at victory. The map below shows the battles in the north.

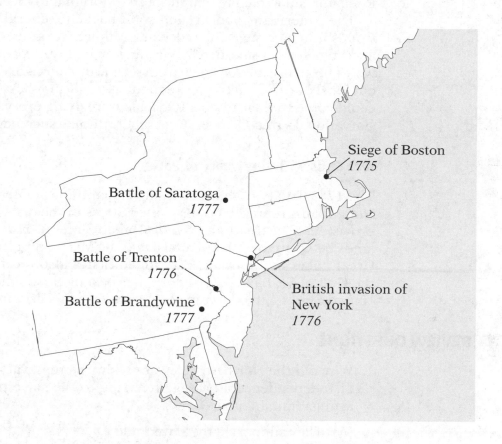

The War Turns in Favor of the Colonists

In December 1778 the British Army began a determined attack on the Southern colonies. Since the American Army had left the South largely undefended, the British commanders, General Cornwallis and General Clinton, thought they could easily conquer the South and then march north, taking control of each colony as they passed through it. They also believed that support for the revolution was weaker in that area. Washington's army was camping for the winter in New Jersey and was in no shape for a long march or a fight.

By the spring of 1781 the British had captured Georgia and were marching toward Charleston, South Carolina. General Clinton won a great victory at Charleston in May, capturing 5,400 American soldiers and a small fleet of ships.

General Gates was put in charge of the American Army in the South. His job was to stop the British advance and retake South Carolina. In a bloody battle at Camden, South Carolina, Gates lost his nerve. His soldiers retreated in a panic, giving the victory to the redcoats.

By October the British were threatening North Carolina. The British, under the command of General Ferguson, had taken a high hill, which gave them a strong position. The Americans charged the hill twice and were beaten back, but a third charge was successful. By the end of the battle all the British had been captured or killed. That loss made the British generals decide to march on to Virginia. By that time French troops, ships, and money had arrived in the United States. Washington and the French commander Rochambeau agreed to march south to Virginia to meet the enemy.

The Americans and French soon backed General Cornwallis and his troops into a corner. The redcoats occupied Yorktown, Virginia. American and French troops headed by Washington, Lafayette, and other commanders were able to fire on Yorktown from several directions at once. The British held out for six weeks, but they were running out of supplies and had no allies who could come to their rescue. Redcoats were dying every day from illness and starvation. In mid-October, General Cornwallis surrendered to Washington.

War Ends with the Treaty of Paris

The 1783 Treaty of Paris officially ended the war. Benjamin Franklin and John Adams represented the United States in the discussions of the treaty's provisions. The treaty granted the United States its independence and all the lands between the Atlantic Coast and the Mississippi River and between the Great Lakes and Florida. The United States also received fishing rights in the Gulf of St. Lawrence and off the coast of Newfoundland. In return, the United States agreed to repay any debt owed to Britain.

REVIEW QUESTIONS

1. Why did the Northern delegates allow the removal from the Declaration of Independence a passage referring to the slave trade as a "cruel war against human nature"?

   (A) They supported the slave trade.
   (B) They were slave owners from large plantations.
   (C) They did not like the implication that they were slaves of the king of Great Britain.
   (D) They thought the Southerners would not vote for independence if that passage was not removed.
   (E) They did not believe that this was the right time to free the slaves.

2. General Howe was determined to capture the city of Philadelphia primarily because

   (A) it was the capital city and such a capture would be prestigious
   (B) it was an important Atlantic seaport city
   (C) it had been the scene of most of the fierce resistance to the Acts of Parliament before the war began
   (D) it was the home of Benjamin Franklin
   (E) it was a Loyalist city and would welcome the arrival of the British

3. Which of the following lists the battles in the correct chronological order?

(A) Brandywine, Monmouth, Saratoga
(B) Saratoga, Brandywine, Monmouth
(C) Monmouth, Brandywine, Saratoga
(D) Saratoga, Monmouth, Brandywine
(E) Brandywine, Saratoga, Monmouth

4. What was the primary purpose of the Olive Branch Petition?

(A) To open trade between the United States and the Mediterranean nations of Greece and Italy
(B) To ask King George III to bring about a reconciliation between Parliament and the colonies
(C) To state the reasons for Americans to declare their independence from Great Britain
(D) To urge Americans to declare independence from a corrupt hereditary monarchy
(E) To justify America's decision to begin to take up arms against the redcoats

Answers and Explanations

1. **D** Some Northerners opposed slavery and the slave trade and did not live on large plantations. However, they thought that they had no choice but to give in to the Southerners' demands to remove this passage if they wanted the colonies to become independent.
2. **A** The British gained no strategic advantage by occupying the capital. Howe wanted to take the city because taking the enemy's capital city was traditional in warfare, and it looked like an important accomplishment.
3. **E** The Americans under Washington lost the Battle of Brandywine (September 1777) before the retreat to Valley Forge. The Battle of Saratoga took place in October 1777. The Battle of Monmouth took place in June 1778.
4. **B** Choice C describes the Declaration of Independence, choice D describes *Common Sense,* and choice E describes the "Causes and Necessities for Taking up Arms." Choice A is wrong because the Olive Branch Petition had nothing to do with olives.

CHAPTER 7

THE ARTICLES OF CONFEDERATION

INTRODUCTION

Shortly after the signing of the Declaration of Independence, Congress appointed a committee to begin work on a national constitution. The committee members produced the Articles of Confederation, which were debated and amended over the next year and a half before being passed in November 1777. It took until 1781 for the Articles of Confederation to be ratified by all 13 states.

The Articles of Confederation constituted a very poor attempt at making a working plan for a central government. They left far too much power with the states, although that was their goal. They did not create a national executive or judicial branch. They did not even give the legislature the power to collect the taxes that any national government needs to pay for things such as an army.

Unable to force the states to help pay for the costs of the revolution, Congress found itself with a huge war debt. When the states belatedly began raising taxes to help pay the debt, the people rebelled, believing that Congress was the British Parliament all over again. Political leaders such as James Madison and George Washington began speaking out against the Articles, urging that Congress try again and this time create a stronger central government with real authority to administrate the states. By 1787 it was clear that this was essential if the new nation was going to succeed.

TIMELINE

November 1777   Articles of Confederation approved by Congress.

March 1781   The last state, Maryland, ratifies the Articles of Confederation.

October 1781   Fighting ends at Yorktown.

September 1783   Treaty of Paris is signed, giving the United States all land east of the Mississippi River.

January 1786   Shays' Rebellion is put down in Massachusetts.

April 1787   Madison writes "Vices of the Political System of the United States."

May 1787   Philadelphia hosts the Constitutional Convention with delegates from all the states.

KEY TERMS

Articles of Confederation   the first attempt at a national constitution

constitution   a framework for the processes and principles that govern a state

depression   state of the economy in which unemployment rises and business activity falls

Northwest Ordinance   established rules for governing the Northwest Territory and listed a set of steps by which the territories in the Northwest Territory eventually could become states

Northwest Territory   parcel of land that includes present-day Wisconsin, Michigan, Indiana, Illinois, and Ohio

ratification   official approval

republic   a government in which the people elect representatives to govern them and make their laws

Shays' Rebellion   armed protest by Massachusetts farmers against taxes and seizure of land, led by Daniel Shays

veto   to refuse to sign legislation that another branch of government has approved

The Country's First Constitution

Between 1776 and 1780, 11 of the 13 United States had written new state constitutions; Connecticut and Rhode Island revised their royal charters. However, the Second Continental Congress had not yet written a national **constitution** for the United States. The exact form the government would take had not been decided.

The state governments relied on **republicanism,** a form of government in which the people elect representatives to govern them and make their laws. Although the United States often is described as a democracy, it is in fact a republic. In a democracy, the people rule themselves directly rather than electing anyone to do so for them.

The states had had bad experiences with the system of royal governors. Those men, naturally loyal to the British Crown, often **vetoed** legislation passed by the popularly elected assembly members. Therefore, in the state constitutions, the governors generally were popularly elected and were given strictly limited powers compared with those of the state legislatures. The leaders of the new state governments hoped that this system would make the governments more truly representative of the voters' needs.

Voting in the states was still a privilege rather than a right. Women, African Americans, and Native Americans could not vote. Only male property owners of European descent could vote. In effect, the government was in the hands of a wealthy elite.

State constitutions granted freedom of religion. Many of the leaders of the new state governments had been influenced strongly by thinkers of the European Enlightenment, and they feared the influence of religion on the state. Many also recognized that the United States was already a land of religious pluralism where Quakers, Anglicans, Protestants of all kinds, Jews, Catholics, and others all had to live and work side by side. It made sense to ensure that no American citizen could be penalized by the government for worshipping according to the dictates of conscience.

As the state governments began to take shape, Congress turned its attention to designing a national government. John Dickinson of Pennsylvania was put in charge of the committee to draft a plan for the new government.

On July 12, 1776, the **Articles of Confederation** were presented to Congress for debate. Congress adopted the plan on November 15, 1777. The Articles of Confederation did not truly create one nation from the 13 states. Instead, it created a loosely knit association of 13 sovereign powers that were guaranteed their independence and freedom. The Articles echoed the fear of a strong central government that had made each state draft a constitution that limited the powers of its governor.

The Power of the Legislative Branch

The national legislative body was to be called the Congress. Congress had the power to borrow and coin money, set a standard for a national currency, set and carry out foreign policy, control affairs between the United States and Native Americans, and settle any disputes between or among states. Congress could not require states to contribute money to the central government or provide recruits for the U.S. armed forces. The Articles of Confederation stated that expenses related to the army and to fighting wars would be paid from the national treasury but that it would be up to the states to decide how to raise the money.

Each state was to receive one vote in Congress regardless of the size of its population. Delegates to Congress were to be elected annually, and each state would have two to seven representatives. Congress agreed to allow Canada to join the Untied States if it wished to be admitted and stipulated that if any other colony wanted to join the United States, at least 9 of the 13 states would have to agree.

This chart shows the major provisions of the Articles of Confederation.

The Articles of Confederation	
Article I	Established "United Sates of America" as the name of the country.
Article II	Each state is to remain independent. All powers not expressly given to Congress remain with the states.
Article III	The states agree to assist one another if any one of them is attacked.
Article IV	Citizens may travel freely from one state to another. If a criminal flees from one state and is found in another, the second state will return him or her home for trial. Each state shall give full faith and credit to the laws of the rest.
Article V	Voters will elect two to seven representatives to Congress each year. Congress will meet each year on the first of November. Each state shall have one vote in Congress. Freedom of speech and debate in Congress is absolute.
Article VI	Only Congress has the power to set foreign policy, make treaties, conduct war, or maintain a standing army in times of peace. Each state shall maintain a militia and a proper quantity of weapons.
Article VII	State legislatures shall appoint military commanders.
Article VIII	Congress will fund war expenses from a national treasury; each state shall decide how to raise money to pay its share.

Article IX	Only Congress has the power to determine peace and war. Congress will settle all disputes between or among states. Congress has the sole power to fix weights and measures and coin money. A majority vote of the delegates is necessary for any congressional action.
Article X	Congress can take no legislative action without the agreement of at least nine delegates.
Article XI	Canada may join the Untied States if it approves the Articles of Confederation. No other territory can join the United States except by vote of nine states.
Article XII	The United States agrees to pay all debts it contracts.
Article XIII	Every state agrees to be bound by the authority of Congress. The union of the states is to be perpetual.

Executive and Judicial Powers

The Articles of Confederation did not provide for a president or any other chief executive of the new government or for a national court. No state wanted to give up its power to rule itself. Many delegates felt that the colonies' experience of the British government proved the case that each state should be left to govern itself rather than having to answer to a central authority.

Ratification

Congress agreed that **ratification** of the Articles of Confederation had to be unanimous. The major obstacle in the way of ratification was the disputed land between the settled coastal areas of the colonies and the Mississippi River. In fact, that land was claimed by the British and could not belong to any of the states unless they won the Revolutionary War, but the states proceeded on the assumption of a victory. Various colonies claimed the same parcels of land by their royal charters. States that claimed none of the land were concerned about the expansion of the rest. The Maryland legislature flatly refused to ratify the Articles of Confederation unless some of the other states gave up their rights to the disputed land.

Virginia and New York, the states that held the most land, set an example by ceding their claims to Congress. By 1781 other states had followed suit, and in March of that year Maryland, the final state to hold back, ratified the Articles of Confederation. This was the official birth of the United States of America.

Effects of the Articles of Confederation: The Northwest Ordinance

Congress immediately took steps to resolve the problem of disputed land in the West. The Land Ordinance of 1785 marked off all the land east of the Mississippi into townships and put up 640-acre lots in the townships for sale at the minimum price of $1 per acre. One section of each township was reserved for a public schoolhouse. The Land Ordinance of 1787, commonly called the **Northwest Ordinance,** established the rules for governing the **Northwest Territory.**

The following map shows the borders of the states as of 1781 and the Western lands each state claimed. The Northwest Territory, heavily outlined, includes the present-day states of Wisconsin, Michigan, Illinois, Indiana, and Ohio.

The United States in 1787

Congress believed that eventually the Northwest Territory would be settled and that the settlers would want to join the United States. Therefore, they established a process by which that would happen. First, the territory would be divided into three to five smaller parcels of land. Second, Congress would appoint a governor, a secretary, and three judges for each territory. Third, when the population of a territory reached 5,000 people, voters would elect a legislature that then could send a nonvoting delegate to Congress. Fourth, the territory would become eligible for statehood when the population reached 60,000. The territory would draft a state constitution; on congressional approval of the constitution, the territory would become a state. The organization of the Northwest Territory and the establishment of the process for the admission of new states were among the few accomplishments of the Articles government.

The Northwest Ordinance also guaranteed civil rights and banned slavery in the territories. Opposition to slavery had been growing among the

Northern delegates, who were uncomfortably aware of the irony of declaring their own independence while denying it to the African population, although they still generally considered this a Southern issue. However, the Southerners refused to give up the system of free labor that had brought them so much prosperity, and the Articles of Confederation gave Congress no power to do anything about slavery. The Northwest Ordinance stated that escaped slaves seeking sanctuary in the territories had to be returned to their owners.

Effects of the Articles of Confederation: The Economy

It quickly became apparent that the Articles of Confederation were not a sufficiently strong basis for a national government. Because Congress had no power over the states, it could accomplish very little. Any new legislation it wanted to pass required the support of nine states, and delegates within one state often could not agree on how to cast their vote let alone agree with delegates from other states.

Because Congress had given itself no power to tax the states or the people, it had great difficulty conducting the Revolutionary War. The troops often went without food, necessary supplies, boots, and uniforms because there was no way for Congress to purchase those items. States delayed paying their share into the treasury for those expenses, and Congress had no leverage to make them pay more or pay more promptly. George Washington and the other military commanders were probably more acutely aware than anyone of the weaknesses of the Articles of Confederation, since they saw the evidence of it every day in their struggles on the battlefield.

During the war the United States accumulated a substantial debt. After the war ended, Congress had no means to raise the taxes needed to pay the debt. Congress printed paper money and began to circulate it, but merchants refused to accept it, claiming that it had no value.

In 1784 an economic **depression** occurred. Unemployment rose, and business activity fell off. Britain had closed some of its markets to colonial commerce and then flooded the colonies with inexpensive goods. Colonial merchants could not compete with British prices and quickly began to lose money. The desperate economic situation led to **Shays' Rebellion** in 1786.

Daniel Shays was a farmer and a Revolutionary War captain. When the Massachusetts government, which was dominated by the coastal merchant elite, began raising taxes on land to help the economy recover and seized land for nonpayment of taxes, Shays and others rebelled. The tax hit them disproportionately, and they shut down debtor courts and marched on Springfield, intending to seize an arsenal of weapons stored there. The governor of Massachusetts called out the militia to stop them. When the fighting began in late January 1787, four of Shays' men were killed. By the end of February the rebellion had been put down.

Shays' Rebellion made it clear that the United States needed a stronger central government. Many political leaders agreed. James Madison of Virginia published his opinions in "Vices of the Political System of the United States" in April 1787. Madison argued that states had failed to comply with reasonable constitutional demands for money, that various states had trespassed on one another's rights, that states had entered into agreements with Native Americans in defiance of the Articles of Confederation, that the national economic depression made it clear that states would not work together voluntarily in defense of their common interests, and so on. Madison's clear, declarative statements and specific examples impressed many readers. George Washington, who had had every opportunity to observe the concrete results of Congress's impotence during the war, agreed with Madison, writing, "I predict the worst consequences from a half-starved, limping government, always moving upon crutches and tottering at every step."

Other factors would drive the delegates to reevaluate the Articles. Internationally the government had no foreign office and was thus unable to force the British to fulfill their obligations under the Treaty of Paris or stop the impressment of American sailors into service on British warships. The government was also unable to facilitate trade, and the multiple state currencies caused economic stagnation. In May 1787 delegates again gathered in Philadelphia to try to write a new federal constitution.

REVIEW QUESTIONS

1. The Articles of Confederation

   (A) were ratified by 9 of the 13 states and then became law
   (B) fixed the amount of the Revolutionary War debt Congress would have to repay
   (C) did not provide for an executive or judicial branch of the national government
   (D) established a strong central authority over the individual states
   (E) apportioned representation of each state according to its population

2. James Madison objected to the Articles of Confederation on all these grounds EXCEPT:

   (A) States were violating one another's rights.
   (B) Congress could not force states to pay their fair share of taxes.
   (C) States were making separate treaties with Native Americans.
   (D) Congress included delegates from each state.
   (E) States would never work together in their own best long-term interests.

3. All the following were direct or indirect consequences of the Articles of Confederation EXCEPT:

   (A) The United States acquired a large war debt.
   (B) The states gave up individual claims to lands outside their borders east of the Mississippi.
   (C) The Northwest Territory was divided into smaller territories, each with its own governor.
   (D) An economic depression hit the United States in 1784.
   (E) Daniel Shays led a farmers' rebellion in Massachusetts.

Answers and Explanations

1. **C** The Articles could not fix the debt because they were written during the war. They were ratified by all the states. They did not establish a strong central authority or provide for proportional representation.
2. **D** Madison did not object to each state having representation in Congress. He did object to the other four choices.
3. **A** The Articles of Confederation did not affect the amount of money the war cost.

CHAPTER 8

THE CONSTITUTION

INTRODUCTION

The Constitution of the United States was ratified in 1788 after months of closed debate among the framers of the document and months of argument in the public sphere once the document was written. When the first Congress convened in 1789, its members immediately began to write a series of amendments to the document. Those amendments, which were passed in 1791, are known as the Bill of Rights.

The framers of the Constitution had many interests to balance. They had to ensure that small and large states would be represented fairly in the national government. They had to make sure that the state and the national government would share the powers of government fairly. They needed to represent the interests of all the voters. They had to address the questions of slavery and the Native American population.

Compromise was the solution in every case. All the states had to agree to give up something they wanted in an attempt to be reasonably fair to all. In the end the Congress designed a government with checks and balances in its three branches. A president would be in charge of the executive branch for a four-year term. Congress would have two houses. In the lower house, the states would be represented according to population; in the upper house, each state would have an equal voice. A Supreme Court would constitute a judicial branch. Each branch would have certain checks on the powers of the other two.

Several states were dismayed by the fact that the Constitution ignored questions of individual rights. However, the required nine states did ratify the document. Congress's first action on meeting in May 1789, after the first national elections, was to draft a Bill of Rights that stipulated many important freedoms and privileges of ordinary citizens. Those 10 amendments were ratified by the states in 1791.

TIMELINE

1787

May 25   The Constitutional Convention is convened.

September 17   The Constitution is signed by the Constitutional Convention delegates.

October   First of the *Federalist Papers* is published in New York newspapers.

December 7   Delaware becomes the first state to ratify the Constitution.

1788

June 21   New Hampshire ratifies the Constitution, making it "the supreme law of the land."

1789

April 30   George Washington takes the oath of office as the first president.

1791   The Bill of Rights is ratified and becomes part of the amendments to the Constitution.

KEY TERMS

Antifederalists   opponents of the Constitution as originally written

bicameral   having two chambers or two houses

faction   special-interest group

Federalists   supporters of the Constitution

preamble   introduction

ratification   procedure for approval

separation of powers   division of authority into three branches of government, each with checks on the power of the others

suffrage   the right to vote

Three-Fifths Compromise   agreement that for purposes of taxation and representation, slaves would each count as three-fifths of a person

Proceedings of the Constitutional Convention

The Constitutional Convention began in Philadelphia on May 25. Like the Second Continental Congress, the Convention met in the State House in central Philadelphia. Because the Declaration of Independence was signed there, the building is known as Independence Hall. There were 55 delegates, many of whom had represented their colonies in the First and Second Continental Congresses. Benjamin Franklin, George Washington, Alexander Hamilton, and James Madison were among the delegates. Thomas Jefferson and John Adams, both on diplomatic missions in Europe, did not attend. Rhode Island sent no representatives. The delegates unanimously chose George Washington as president of the Convention. Those delegates did not represent a cross section of the American public. They were all white, male landowners, wealthy, and generally older.

The delegates' first decision was to keep the proceedings of the Convention secret. They would keep the doors and windows of Independence Hall closed during debates. All the delegates agreed not to discuss the proceedings with family members, friends, or journalists. The reason for the secrecy was to allow each man to speak without fear, sure that there would be no outside pressure or reprisals.

The delegates soon agreed that instead of revising the Articles of Confederation, they would discard them altogether and start anew. The new document they would prepare would be called the Constitution of the United States.

Most of the delegates were well-educated, well-off men. Many had studied law. Their background and education revealed major historical influences on the Constitution they would write. The first was the influence of the Roman republic, an ancient and long-lasting system of government that had a legislative branch (the Senate) and elected officials. Like Americans, Romans did not have universal **suffrage;** only male property owners could vote, and only males could hold office. A second influence was the British government. The Magna Carta, which had been signed by King John in 1215, established that all citizens, including the monarch, were equal under the laws of the land. It also set forth various individual rights, such as trial by jury. The English Bill of Rights of 1689 took the Magna Carta even further, setting forth more individual rights and establishing that the monarch could not take away those rights. A third influence was the writing of eighteenth-century philosophers such as Locke and Montesquieu. Montesquieu's *Spirit of the Laws* of 1748 had described and argued for the **separation of powers:** a three-branch government (executive, legislative, and judicial) in which each branch had certain checks on the authority of the others so that the government was balanced. Locke insisted on the rights of the governed to design the government that would rule them. The final important influence on the framers of the Constitution was their own experience of local government in the colonies, going back to the Mayflower Compact of 1620. Since the colonies had begun, they had run efficiently and well on a system of representative government. The framers were determined to design a national government that would be representative in the same way the state governments had been.

The Great Compromise

There were two primary causes of disagreement among the delegates. One was the issue of states' rights versus the powers of the central government. The other was the concern for equal representation for small and large states.

The first detailed plan for a new government was known as the Virginia Plan. It was proposed by Edmund Randolph of Virginia and supported by James Madison. The Virginia Plan called for a **bicameral** legislature in which each state would be represented in proportion to its population. Randolph's plan also included an executive branch and a judicial branch of the national government. Between May 30 and June 13, the delegates argued over Randolph's plan.

A second plan, proposed by William Patterson of New Jersey, was presented on June 16. The New Jersey Plan called for equal representation of all states in both houses of the legislature. The New Jersey Plan did not garner as much support as the Virginia Plan, although many of its ideas appeared in the final Constitution. The debate over the two plans would stall and almost cause an end to the Constitutional Convention.

On May 31, in an agreement known as the Great Compromise, the delegates voted in favor of a proposal that the people should directly elect the representatives in the lower house of the legislature. Although many of the delegates were wary of any form of direct democracy, they were prepared to go this far in their belief that the government should exist specifically to represent the concerns of the governed. However, they agreed that the legislature should be bicameral so that each house would provide a check on the power of the other. After lengthy debates during the month of June, they agreed that the members of the Senate would be chosen by the state legislatures rather than elected directly by the voters. To settle the question of equal representation of all the states, the delegates agreed that states would be represented proportionally in the House of Representatives, according to their populations, but represented equally in the Senate, with two votes for each state. That compromise was proposed by Roger Sherman of Connecticut, one of only four men who attended both the Second Continental Congress and the Constitutional Convention.

The debate over counting the population of each state was fierce. Southerners wanted their slaves counted toward the total population of their states, which meant they would have more representatives in the government, but not counted for the purpose of tax assessment, which meant they would pay less in taxes. Northern states protested that since Southerners considered their slaves property rather than people, the slaves should not be counted toward the total population or at least that the Southerners should not try to have it both ways. On July 11 the **Three-Fifths Compromise** was worked out: each slave would be counted as three-fifths of a person in determining the total population of a state.

In August the debate turned to national control of trade. Over Southern protests, the delegates agreed to give Congress the power to pass navigation acts. Over Northern protests, they agreed to prevent Congress from passing any laws restricting the slave trade until 1808. This compromise on the part of the Northern states sowed the seeds that would grow into the bitter racial divide that affected the country for generations to come.

By September 8 the debates had drawn the Convention to a close. The Convention appointed a committee to write the Constitution in its final form. Gouverneur Morris, a wealthy delegate from New York, completed most of that work by September 12. The Constitution was signed by the delegates on September 17. On that day Benjamin Franklin, at 81 the oldest of the delegates, made a speech praising the efforts of the Convention and urging the delegates to join in friendship and forget their differences.

> Mr. President, I confess that there are several parts of this convention which I do not at present approve, but I am not sure I shall never approve them; for having lived long, I have experienced many instances of being obliged by better information or fuller consideration, to change opinions even on important subjects, which I once thought right, but found to be otherwise. . . .
>
> In these sentiments, Sir, I agree to this Constitution with all its faults, if they are such, because I think a general government necessary for us, and there is no form of government what may be a blessing to the people if well administered, and believe farther that this is likely to be well administered, and can only end in despotism, as other forms have done before it, when the people shall become so corrupted as to need despotic government, being incapable of any other. . . .
>
> On the whole, Sir, I cannot help expressing a wish that every member of the Convention who may still have objections to it, would with me, on this occasion, doubt a little of his own infallibility—and to make manifest our unanimity, put his name to this instrument.

A Look at the Constitution

The Constitution begins with the following **preamble:**

> We the People of the United States, in order to form a more perfect Union, establish Justice, insure domestic Tranquility, provide for the common defense, promote the general Welfare, and secure the Blessings of Liberty to ourselves and our Posterity, do ordain and establish this Constitution for the United States of America.

The Preamble is remarkable for the first three words. "We the people" suggests that the government will be a democracy, not a republic, that rather than being written by representatives of the people, the Constitution was written and approved by the people themselves. This shows the framers' concern for the Lockian principle of government by the consent of the governed.

The Constitution is divided into seven articles, as follows:

Article I	Describes the legislative branch with two houses: a Senate and a House of Representatives. The senators are to be chosen by state legislatures, and there will be two for each state. The representatives are to be popularly elected, and there will be one for every 30,000 people in a state (excluding Native Americans and counting each slave as three-fifths of a person). Gives the rules by which the legislature will conduct business and pass laws.
Article II	Describes the executive branch, which will be headed by a president of the United States who will be chosen by a system known as the electoral college in which the voters choose electors who in turn cast votes for the president.
Article III	Describes the judicial branch, which will consist of a Supreme Court with nine justices who will serve for life, during good behavior.
Article IV	Describes the powers and rights of the states.
Article V	Describes the amendment process.
Article VI	States that the Constitution is the supreme law of the land and that no religious test will be administered as a qualification for office.
Article VII	States that the Constitution will become law when nine states have ratified it.

Checks and Balances in the Constitution

The Constitution was designed specifically so that no branch of the government could establish tyranny over either of the other two branches. Each branch has checks on the power of the others.

The president can veto congressional legislation. The president has the power to nominate Supreme Court justices. The president generally has the power to enforce the law and to nominate.

Congress can override a presidential veto with a two-thirds vote of both houses. Congress can refuse to appoint a Supreme Court justice nominated by the president. Congress can impeach a president for committing "high crimes or misdemeanors." It can remove a justice from the Supreme Court for the same reason. Congress generally makes the law and confirms nominations.

The Supreme Court can overturn congressional legislation it deems unconstitutional. The chief justice presides over the impeachment of a president. Justices serve for life, under good behavior, and are therefore not subject to outside pressure to keep their seats on the bench. The Supreme Court is the final judge of a law's constitutionality.

The people have the power of their votes. They can withhold their votes and refuse to reelect any president, senator, or representative they do not support.

The Ratification Process

Elbridge Gerry of Massachusetts and Edmund Randolph and Thomas Paine of Virginia refused to sign the Constitution, feeling that it gave too much power to the national government. Their refusal foreshadowed the struggle for **ratification** that would end in the addition of 10 amendments to the Constitution. Those amendments are known collectively as the Bill of Rights.

Those who supported the Constitution were called **Federalists** because they had designed a federal government, or one in which the national and state governments shared power and authority. Those who opposed the Constitution as originally written were known as **Antifederalists.** Both sides took their cases directly to the voters in pamphlets, speeches, and newspaper editorials.

The Antifederalists feared a repetition of what had happened between the colonies and Great Britain. They also worried that local interests would be ignored in favor of national ones, that a distant central government would ignore the people it had been designed to represent, and that the smaller and weaker states would come under the sway of the interest of the larger, more powerful states. Above all, the Antifederalists stressed the fact that the Constitution said nothing about the rights of individual citizens.

James Madison had been the best-prepared delegate at the Constitutional Convention. He had shut himself up in his Virginia home for months before the Convention, reading historical and political works as he considered what kind of government would best suit the United States. Madison kept detailed written notes of the debates in the Constitutional Convention that have been a priceless record for historians to study ever since.

Now Madison took pen in hand to defend the Constitution. Beginning in October 1787, a series of essays known collectively as the *Federalist Papers* began to appear in print. Signed with the name Publius, those essays presented a variety of reasoned arguments in favor of the Constitution. "Publius" was actually three men: Alexander Hamilton wrote 51 of the essays, Madison wrote 29, and John Jay wrote 5. The entire collection was published together in the spring of 1788.

By far the most famous of the Federalist Papers is Number 10, written by Madison. In this essay Publius discussed the danger of **faction.** He argued that the United States included so many factions that only a representative central government in which all the factions had an equal voice could possibly succeed, that smaller local governments were bound to discriminate in favor of the majority. With so many diverse interests in the national government, Publius argued, there would be no danger of any particular faction gaining a majority.

The Early Days of the Constitution

By May 1788 eight of the nine necessary states had ratified the Constitution: Delaware, Pennsylvania, New Jersey, Georgia, Connecticut, Massachusetts, Maryland, and South Carolina. The smaller states were the first to ratify as they needed the protection of the Constitution the most. In Virginia, one of the largest and most powerful states, whose ratification the framers deemed especially crucial to the success of the Constitution, debate was especially intense. Eventually Virginia ratified the Constitution with recommendations that it be amended. Led by the Antifederalist Patrick Henry, those who opposed the

Constitution offered the Congress a bill of rights and 20 suggested changes to the Constitution. New Hampshire became the ninth state to ratify, followed by Virginia and New York. On July 2, Congress announced that the Constitution had been ratified. On September 13, 1788, the first national elections were called. As everyone had expected, George Washington was elected the first president of the United States. John Adams came in second in the voting and in accordance with the Constitution was named vice president. The first Congress was made up of 59 representatives and 22 senators. At that time New York City was the national capital. George Washington took the oath of office on the steps of Federal Hall on Wall Street. A statue of him stands on that spot, commemorating the event. Congress convened in New York in March 1789.

The Bill of Rights Becomes Part of the Constitution

As the First Congress of the United States opened, James Madison immediately moved that Congress begin work on a Bill of Rights. On September 9, Congress submitted 12 amendments to the states. Ten of them were ratified and formally became part of the Constitution on December 15, 1791.

First Amendment	Guarantees freedom of religion, freedom of speech, freedom of the press, the right of peaceful assembly, and the right to petition the government for redress of grievances.
Second Amendment	States that the people have the right to bear arms as part of a well-regulated militia necessary to the state.
Third Amendment	Guarantees that private citizens cannot be forced to house soldiers in peacetime and can be forced to house them in wartime only by the passage of laws to that effect.
Fourth Amendment	Protects the people against unreasonable search and seizure of personal property. Requires probable cause for the issue of a search warrant.
Fifth Amendment	Protects persons accused of a criminal offense from self-incrimination; outlaws double jeopardy; requires a grand jury indictment for trial; requires due process of law.
Sixth Amendment	Guarantees a speedy and public trial by jury; requires that a person accused of a criminal offense be told the charges against him or her and be confronted with the evidence and guarantees the accused the right to present his or her own case and to legal representation.
Seventh Amendment	Requires a trial by jury in any case in which the disputed value of property exceeds $20.
Eighth Amendment	Bans excessive bail and cruel or unusual punishment.
Ninth Amendment	States that listing certain rights in the Constitution does not imply that the people do not have other rights as well.
Tenth Amendment	States that any powers not delegated to the national government are reserved to the states or to the people.

REVIEW QUESTIONS

1. The Antifederalists opposed the Constitution primarily because

   (A) they thought the United States should be ruled by a constitutional monarchy
   (B) they did not want the central government to have too much control over the states
   (C) they opposed slavery and wanted a constitution that would outlaw it
   (D) they demanded equal representation for all the states
   (E) they wanted the Constitution to include The Northwest Ordinances

2. Which of the following wrote the majority of the *Federalist Papers?*

   (A) Benjamin Franklin
   (B) Alexander Hamilton
   (C) John Jay
   (D) James Madison
   (E) George Washington

3. Why did the delegates agree to keep the proceedings of the Constitutional Convention secret?

   (A) They knew their work would be unpopular with their constituents.
   (B) They did not want to be subjected to any outside pressures or influences.
   (C) They had received a number of threats to their lives.
   (D) They knew there were many foreign spies hoping to betray them.
   (E) They did not want to provoke an uprising among the people.

4. All the following were important influences on the framers of the Constitution EXCEPT:

   (A) the Magna Carta
   (B) the English Bill of Rights
   (C) the Roman republic
   (D) *The Spirit of the Laws*
   (E) the *Federalist Papers*

Answers and Explanations

1. **B** The primary reason for opposition to the Constitution was a concern for states' rights. The desire for a Bill of Rights was a secondary consideration. The other choices are untrue statements.
2. **B** Hamilton wrote nearly two-thirds of the essays, Madison about one-third, and Jay only five. Washington and Franklin wrote none.
3. **B** The delegates wanted to have total freedom to say what they thought in debates. Therefore, they agreed not to discuss the proceedings outside the hall. The other four choices are untrue statements.
4. **E** The *Federalist Papers* were written later than the Constitution and in support of it, and so they could not have been an influence on the framers.

CHAPTER 9

ESTABLISHING A NEW NATION

INTRODUCTION

The first 25 years of the new nation were tumultuous. Many obstacles and challenges arose, some of which the framers of the Constitution had foreseen and others of which were unanticipated. During the first four presidential administrations the nation began to take shape.

George Washington set a precedent for the isolationism that was to characterize American foreign policy for many decades afterward. Washington refused to involve the United States in the French Revolution, and on leaving office in 1796 he warned his successors to avoid getting involved in foreign wars.

John Adams was the first president to represent a political party. He was the candidate of the Federalists, which had developed as the party that believed in a strong national government rather than one that was dominated by the states. Adams struggled successfully to maintain peace with France at the cost of signing the Alien and Sedition Acts. Many people believed that those acts were unconstitutional because they infringed on individual liberties guaranteed in the Bill of Rights. Kentucky and Virginia passed resolutions declaring that states did not have to obey unconstitutional laws.

Thomas Jefferson became president in 1800 and directed his envoy to seize the opportunity to purchase the Louisiana Territory from France, doubling the size of the United States. Under Jefferson, the Supreme Court established the principle of judicial review, which gave the Court the right to decide whether a law was unconstitutional and, if it was, to strike it down.

Under James Madison tension between the Native Americans and the United States finally broke out into war. U.S. troops defeated the Native American confederation at the Battle of Tippecanoe. Soon afterward the United States was plunged into war again, this time with Great Britain. In late 1814 the Treaty of Ghent ended the war, establishing an alliance with Britain that has continued uninterrupted to the present day.

TIMELINE

1789 George Washington inaugurated first president of the United States.

1791 Congress grants the charter for the Bank of the United States.

1794 Early challenges for the new government: Whiskey Rebellion; Jay's Treaty; Battle of Fallen Timbers.

1795 Pinckney's Treaty.

1796 John Adams elected president.

1798 Adams's trials as president: XYZ Affair, Alien and Sedition Acts, Virginia and Kentucky resolutions.

1800   Thomas Jefferson becomes third president.

1803   *Marbury v. Madison;* Louisiana Purchase.

1804–1806   Lewis and Clark expedition.

1807   Embargo Act established.

1808   James Madison becomes fourth president and third president from Virginia.

1812   United States declares war on Great Britain.

1815   Battle of New Orleans.

KEY TERMS

cabinet   group consisting of the vice president and heads of government departments who advise the president on policy

capitalism   an economic system in which business and industry are in private hands and the free market determines wages and prices

Democratic-Republicans   a political party that supported states' rights and individual rights over the rights of the central government

elastic clause   statement in the Constitution that Congress has the right to make "all necessary and proper" laws to enable it to enforce its own powers

Federalists   a political party that supported a strong central government that takes precedence over state governments

impressment   the practice of kidnapping men and forcing them to serve in the navy

judicial review   the right of the Supreme Court to decide whether a law is constitutional and to strike down any law it declares unconstitutional

mint   a factory where federal coins are manufactured and paper currency is printed

political parties   associations of people with a common domestic and foreign policy agenda for a nation

strict constructionist   a person who believes that the Constitution should be obeyed to the letter of what it says

unconstitutional   anything that contradicts the Constitution or that would be illegal under its laws

The Challenge of Organizing the New Government

George Washington was the obvious choice to lead the new nation he had helped create. He was not a profound political thinker like Adams, Jefferson, or Madison, and he knew it; he was a successful military commander. However, he had a characteristic unique among all the presidents who followed him: he was the universal choice of all the political leaders of the day. Washington commanded profound personal respect and affection from everyone who knew him and had worked with him. His popularity was an important ingredient in the success of the new nation for its first eight years simply because most people—leaders and ordinary citizens alike—trusted him and could agree to unite under his leadership.

Washington's first action was to decide on the title by which the president should be addressed. His choice, "president of the United States," reassured everyone that the United States would never turn into a monarchy. The title was a simple one and reinforced the notion that the president was no more exalted than any other U.S. citizen.

The first **cabinet** contained only five members, as follows:

Secretary of State Thomas Jefferson
Secretary of the Treasury Alexander Hamilton
Secretary of War Henry Knox
Attorney General Edmund Randolph
Postmaster General Samuel Osgood

The first Supreme Court had a chief justice, John Jay, and five associate justices.

Alexander Hamilton quickly achieved a prominent position in the administration. Hamilton was influenced by the Scottish economist Adam Smith, who believed in **capitalism,** the economic system in which private businesses run most industries and free-market competition determines wages and prices. Hamilton's agreement with Smith's philosophy and his comprehensive plan were largely responsible for the way the American economy took shape. He planned to encourage the nation's manufacturing, banking, and credit to strengthen its economic prospects.

Hamilton's first challenge was to pay off the national debt, which had soared to $77 million because of the war. He felt that it was important to pay the debt rather than allow it to mount so that the nation would have good credit with the rest of the world. Hamilton's plan involved selling new bonds to pay off old ones. He also declared that the federal government should be responsible for the debts the states currently owed. Since the Southern states already had paid their debts, they protested, arguing that the Northern states should be forced to pay just as they had paid. Hamilton compromised with Southern leaders by agreeing that the new national capital city would be in the South, on the border between Maryland and Virginia. This city, which stands outside state borders, would be called the District of Columbia; soon it was named Washington in honor of the first president.

Congress created the Bank of the United States in 1791. Its charter stated that it was to be owned jointly by the government and private investors and would operate for 20 years. Congress also created a **mint,** which began to produce the first national coins in 1792. The discussion over the bank would create the first conflict between loose and strict constructionists as they debated whether the bank was covered by the "just and proper clause."

Hamilton continued to cast about for ways to settle the government's debts. As many other political leaders had done throughout history to deal with debt, he created new taxes. A new tax on whiskey provoked an uprising among farmers in western Pennsylvania who had profited handsomely for years by turning their surplus grain crop into whiskey and trading it for supplies. The new tax on whiskey would take away their profits. When marshals tried to collect the tax from Pennsylvania farmers, the farmers resisted. They attacked the officials and planned a march of about 6,000 men on Philadelphia, the nation's temporary capital. Washington called out the militia to put down the Whiskey Rebellion, further establishing the supremacy of the federal government.

The conflicts created by Hamilton's economic plans would hasten the creation of political parties. Support for Hamilton would be strong among the Northern business communities and financial interests. Jefferson would appeal to "yeoman" farmers and gain the support of the Southern agricultural interests. This eventually would split Washington's cabinet, especially after Washington endorsed Hamilton's plans.

Washington and European Affairs

Meanwhile, Native Americans in the Northwest Territory were fighting to defend their lands from the encroaching settlers. Led by the Miami chief Michikinikwa ("Little Turtle"), over 1,000 Native Americans of various nations banded together and soundly defeated U.S. forces in a battle along the Wabash River in present-day Indiana. Washington responded by sending a larger militia west and putting General Anthony Wayne in charge. In 1794 the Americans defeated the Native Americans in the Battle of Fallen Timbers in present-day Ohio. The conflict was ended in 1795 by the Treaty of Greenville, under which Native Americans were paid $20,000 for lands in Ohio and Indiana.

In 1789 revolution broke out in France. Although the French were following the American example in fighting for the creation of a republic, the United States refused to help its Revolutionary War ally. George Washington, believing that the United States was unprepared to help fight a foreign war, issued a statement in 1793 that the nation would remain neutral. That decision was not popular in France, and not all Americans agreed with it.

The British also were causing the new nation a great deal of trouble. British ships frequently impressed Americans into service in the British Navy. Britain seized a fleet of U.S. ships in the West Indies, falsely claiming that those ships were trading with France. The British also were arming hostile Native Americans in the Northwest Territory. John Jay negotiated with the British, and in 1794 the two sides signed what became known as Jay's Treaty, under which the British agreed to abandon their North American forts. However, the British continued their practices of **impressment** and the arming of Native Americans. The treaty would prove extremely unpopular in the United States.

When Spain joined France in its struggle against Great Britain, the United States was able to sign Pinckney's Treaty with Spain. That treaty recognized the 31st parallel as the U.S. border with Spanish Florida and guaranteed U.S. navigation rights along the Mississippi River.

The Adams Administration

Washington was reelected president in 1792. In 1796 he announced that he would retire at the end of his second term. On leaving office, he urged his successors to "observe good faith and justice toward all nations" but to "steer clear of permanent alliances with any portion of the foreign world."

The nation's first **political parties** had developed during Washington's administration. Washington himself was above party politics and did not approve of them, but he remains the only president in American history to take that position. Factions developed quickly around the cabinet members Jefferson and Hamilton, who were at odds on most major issues. Hamilton believed in a powerful federal government, whereas Jefferson felt that most powers should be left to the states and the people. Hamilton believed in encouraging business and industry, whereas Jefferson felt that agriculture was the most important part of the economy. Jefferson was a **strict constructionist** who believed in the letter of the Constitution; Hamilton was a loose constructionist who argued that the Constitution had a built-in **elastic clause** so that laws could be made as new situations developed. Hamilton wanted an alliance with Britain; Jefferson wanted an alliance with France.

Jefferson's supporters called themselves **Democratic-Republicans,** Hamilton's supporters called themselves **Federalists.** Newspapers, which had a powerful influence on public opinion, took sides. Early newspapers were not unbiased sources of news but mouthpieces for political parties, engaging in mudslinging that would be shocking by today's standards.

John Adams, who supported Hamilton's Federalist views, won the greatest number of electoral votes in the 1796 election and became president. In a twist of fate, Jefferson, who was of the opposing party, won the second highest total of votes and under the Constitution became vice president. Adams and Jefferson had enjoyed a close friendship ever since their days in the Second Continental Congress. They had served together during diplomatic missions in Europe and despite their vastly different personalities had always gotten along well. However, their friendship could not stand up to their political differences.

Adams had never been popular among his political colleagues. He was too combative and forthright, an undiplomatic diplomat and a politician who did not know how to play political games. He was known as a warm and loyal friend, his integrity and honesty were agreed to be unimpeachable, and he was intellectually brilliant. However, he lacked the tact and reserve that characterized Washington and Jefferson.

The important events in Adams's administration involved foreign policy. In protest against Jay's Treaty, France had begun seizing American ships in the West Indies. Adams wanted to avoid war with France if possible. He sent diplomats to France to negotiate a settlement. Three French agents asked the Americans diplomats to pay France's foreign minister a heavy bribe and to lend France $10 million before any negotiations. When Adams informed Congress of that demand, he referred to the French agents as X, Y, and Z rather than revealing their names. The XYZ Affair turned public opinion even further against France.

Adams decided that the best chance to maintain peace lay in a show of strength. He poured money into building up the U.S. Navy. The ploy worked: the French minister Talleyrand agreed that France would stop seizing U.S. ships. Soon afterward U.S. diplomats signed a peace agreement with the French leader Napoleon Bonaparte, who did not want a war with the United States.

Hamilton and the rest of the Federalists were disappointed, They had wanted war with France and felt that Adams had made the United States look weak. Adams refused to give in, creating a split among the Federalists.

The low point of the Adams administration came with the passage of the Alien and Sedition Acts. Those acts, passed by Congress in 1798, allowed the president to deport any foreigner thought to be dangerous to the country and made it illegal to speak or act against the government. Many people thought that the acts infringed on the liberties guaranteed by the Bill of Rights. Jefferson and Madison, who found the acts outrageous, were instrumental in writing the

Kentucky and Virginia resolutions. Those state laws, passed in 1798 and 1799, claimed that a state could not be forced to obey a federal law if the law was **unconstitutional.**

Jefferson Is Elected President in 1800

Owing to the machinations of Alexander Hamilton, Thomas Jefferson was elected president in 1800. Jefferson and Aaron Burr were the Democratic-Republican candidates, Adams and Charles Pinckney the candidates of the Federalists. When the election resulted in a tie, it was thrown to the House of Representatives. In 35 attempts, the Representatives failed to break the tie. (Later in the session Congress passed the Twelfth Amendment, which would prevent further electoral crises of this kind.)

Hamilton disliked and distrusted Burr. He had never agreed with Jefferson, but he felt that compared with Burr, Jefferson would be the better president. He persuaded many of the electors to vote for Jefferson instead of Burr, thus swinging the election to him. Personal relations did not improve between Burr and Hamilton; four years after the election, Burr shot and killed Hamilton in a duel.

Before leaving office, Adams worked to secure the Federalist position in the government. He signed the Judiciary Act of 1801, which created a number of new circuit courts and federal judgeships, and then appointed many Federalists to the bench on the night before his term ended. Since Jefferson was opposed to the Federalist Party, that gesture struck him as a personal insult. The relationship between the two men had degenerated as Jefferson had worked to undermine Adams as vice president. Some time after both had retired from politics, Adams wrote a friendly letter to Jefferson, who eagerly responded; the two men maintained a lively correspondence for the rest of their lives. In an odd historical coincidence, both men died on July 4, 1826, the fiftieth anniversary of the signing of the Declaration of Independence whose adoption both had done so much to bring about.

The most significant of Adams's "midnight appointments" was that of Supreme Court Chief Justice John Marshall, who was to serve more than 30 years and establish many important legal precedents. The most important of those precedents was **judicial review,** established in a case called *Marbury v. Madison.* Marbury was one of the last-minute judges appointed by Adams; Jefferson had refused to allow Madison, his secretary of state, to permit Marbury to serve. Marbury sued Madison. The Supreme Court ruled against Marbury on the grounds that the Judiciary Act of 1801 was unconstitutional. This set the precedent for the Court to determine the legality of laws passed by Congress, an important judicial check on the power of the legislative branch.

The Louisiana Purchase

Jefferson's most important act as president was to double the size of the nation by purchasing the Louisiana Territory from France (see the following map). After the slave revolt in Haiti had destroyed France's power base in the West Indies, the French emperor Napoleon Bonaparte abandoned any hope of extending the French Empire in the western hemisphere. He decided to sell his North American territory and use the funds to finance his wars in Europe. James Monroe, acting as Jefferson's envoy, agreed to purchase the land for Napoleon's price: $15 million, or about 4 cents per acre.

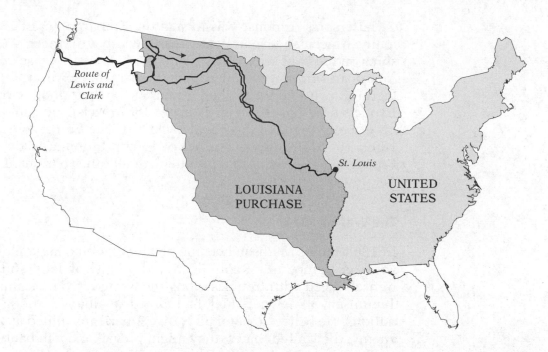

In May 1804 Meriwether Lewis and William Clark set out from St. Louis with a party of guides and explorers. Their written instructions from President Jefferson directed them to look for a water route across the continent to the Pacific Ocean, establish friendly relations with the Native Americans who lived in the territory, catalog examples of unfamiliar plants and animals, map the territory, and keep detailed written records of everything they observed and experienced. In the party was Sacagawea, the Shoshone wife of one of the French Canadians in the party. The legend that Sacagawea acted as guide and interpreter for the expedition is largely untrue; she knew only Shoshone languages and could not understand the speech of most of the other Native American tribes the expedition encountered. However, she played a crucial role in facilitating friendly contact between whites and Native Americans; her presence in the party appeared to the Native Americans to guarantee that the white men were trustworthy. On November 7, 1805, the party reached the Pacific Ocean. They learned that it was not possible to cross the continent by river.

At the same time, the explorer Zebulon Pike was investigating and mapping the regions to the west of the Mississippi Valley. He traveled west as far as the Rocky Mountains. The Colorado mountain Pike's Peak is named for him. When Pike ventured along the Rio Grande, he was arrested by the Spaniards who governed the area. They eventually released him, but they kept his written records. However, Pike recalled enough information to write a report detailing his discoveries in the Southwest.

The Embargo Act

In 1807 a British warship opened fire on the USS *Chesapeake*. The Americans had refused to allow the British, who claimed to be searching for deserters, to board. The British practice of impressing Americans into service had made all American captains wary of contact with British ships. The British crew killed three of the Americans and impressed four others.

Jefferson's response was to sign the Embargo Act of 1807, which halted many American exports. He reasoned that if there were no American ships on the high seas, British impressment would cease and that the lack of American shipping would cripple the British. However, farmers and manufacturers who no longer had a market for their goods protested furiously. Exports fell to one-fifth of their pre-1807 levels, and Jefferson realized that his attempt to make peace had backfired. The Embargo Act was repealed in 1809. The Non-Intercourse Act of 1809 prohibited trade with Britain and France but allowed it to continue with all other nations. Like the Embargo Act, it was ineffective.

The War of 1812

In 1808 James Madison became president with a large plurality of electoral votes. A Democratic-Republican and an ally of Jefferson, Madison found himself faced with troubles along the western frontier almost immediately. Tecumseh, a Shawnee chief, had forged an alliance among Native American nations. He believed that if all Native Americans united against the common enemy, the United States, they might prevail and win back their lands.

On November 7, 1811, General William Henry Harrison and his troops fought the Native Americans at a site on the Tippecanoe River in Indiana Territory. The Battle of Tippecanoe ended in defeat for the Native Americans and the failure of their attempt at a united confederation.

Senators Henry Clay of Kentucky and John C. Calhoun of South Carolina then led a public campaign for war with Great Britain, accusing the British of having provided the Native Americans with guns. Those "War Hawks" also saw this as a chance for the United States to gain territory in Canada. In 1812, Madison asked Congress to declare war.

War on land was not successful because Congress had been reluctant to spend money on equipping and paying the army. However, the Navy had had a buildup during the Adams administration and was well prepared for war. Sea battles and raids in the Great Lakes, in the Caribbean, and around the British isles brought many victories to the Americans, although they would not have a major effect on the rest of the war.

The British attacked Washington, D.C., in August 1814. First Lady Dolley Madison famously escaped from the White House only hours before the British troops burst through the front doors. The British then attacked Fort McHenry in Baltimore. Watching the battle, the prisoner of war Francis Scott Key wrote the words to what would later become the American national anthem. The British lost the battle, but in the peace negotiations that followed they retained the upper hand. Only their war weariness stopped them from imposing harsh terms. Meanwhile, in New Orleans, U.S. forces under General Andrew Jackson prepared to resist a British invasion. In a battle on January 8, 1815, the British were repulsed, but the U.S. victory had no real strategic importance. Shortly before the battle the Treaty of Ghent (Belgium) had been signed by U.S. and British representatives. Word of the successful treaty negotiations reached the White House at about the same time as news of the victory at New Orleans. That battle would allow the Americans to claim some measure of victory in an otherwise losing effort.

The War of 1812 had both positive and negative effects on the United States. On the one hand, it strengthened U.S. control over the Northwest Territory. Also, the Treaty of Ghent established friendly relations between

Great Britain and the United States that have lasted to the present day. On the other hand, the war divided the nation. New England Federalists, who opposed the war, met at the Hartford Convention to discuss seceding from the Union and negotiating a separate peace with Britain. The majority voted instead for a constitutional amendment limiting the powers of Congress and the Southern states. By the time the news of the Treaty of Ghent reached the United States, those who had backed the Hartford Convention were being accused of treason. The Federalist Party broke up a few years afterward.

REVIEW QUESTIONS

1. Around which two central figures were the Federalist and Democratic-Republican parties organized?

   (A) George Washington and John Adams
   (B) Alexander Hamilton and John Adams
   (C) Alexander Hamilton and Thomas Jefferson
   (D) Thomas Jefferson and James Madison
   (E) John Adams and Thomas Jefferson

2. What was the major aim of George Washington's foreign policy?

   (A) To remain friendly with but neutral toward all nations
   (B) To support the French monarchy during the French Revolution
   (C) To support the revolutionaries during the French Revolution
   (D) To stake a claim to the Louisiana territory
   (E) To settle the Northwest Territory as soon as possible

3. What was the Democratic-Republican response to the passage of the Alien and Sedition Acts?

   (A) The Treaty of Ghent
   (B) The Virginia and Kentucky resolutions
   (C) The Battle of Tippecanoe
   (D) The Judiciary Act
   (E) The Embargo Act

Answers and Explanations

1. **C** The two parties developed among the officers of the first cabinet. Hamilton headed one faction, and Jefferson the other.
2. **A** Washington believed that the United States should not become involved in foreign wars. He did not want the United States to take sides during the French Revolution. The expansion of U.S. claims to the West did not take place during his administration.
3. **B** The Virginia and Kentucky resolutions stated that if the federal government passed an unconstitutional law such as the Alien and Sedition Acts, the states did not have to obey it.

CHAPTER 10
THE EARLY NINETEENTH CENTURY

INTRODUCTION

The first quarter of the nineteenth century saw sweeping changes in the way Americans lived and worked. Migration, the Industrial Revolution, the rise to power of Andrew Jackson, and the change in Native American and foreign policy all affected American society.

The Industrial Revolution in the United States had truly begun in 1793 with the invention of the cotton gin, a machine that could process as much cotton in one day as 1,000 slaves could. Southern planters found that it multiplied their profits tenfold. The invention of the steamboat, which could sail upstream against the current, made it possible to move huge boatloads of cotton north, and this gave rise to the textile industry in New England. The steamboat and the building of the National Road to Illinois also made it easier for settlers hungry for new land to migrate west in record numbers. With the takeover of Florida from Spain and the admission of several new states, the nation was growing rapidly.

The Monroe Doctrine of 1823, which was conceived by Secretary of State John Quincy Adams, declared to the world that the United States would remain neutral in any conflict between a European nation and its colonies in the western hemisphere. However, the United States would regard any further attempt at European colonization in the western hemisphere or any European attempt to retake a colony that had declared itself independent as a threat against the United States. The United States alone did not have the power to enforce the doctrine; the support of Great Britain and its powerful navy also was required. However, the Monroe Doctrine set an important precedent for the way the United States viewed its role in the western hemisphere.

The election of Andrew Jackson in 1828 marked a new era in politics. Jackson was the first son of immigrants to be elected to office. He was the first "man of the people" elected to the presidency. He was the first to appoint people who were not drawn from the landowning or merchant elite to top posts in his administration. He was the first president to represent the new Democratic Party. As a military hero, Jackson was universally popular. His most notable action as president was the forced expulsion of Native Americans from the United States. He declared publicly that it was for the Native Americans' protection, although in fact it was intended to give U.S. settlers freedom to take Native American lands. The Southeastern tribes that were the target of the Indian Removal Act resisted, even fighting the Second Seminole War against U.S. troops, but to no avail. In 1838, the last of them were marched under federal guard to Oklahoma along the "Trail of Tears."

TIMELINE

1793   Invention of the cotton gin.

1807   First practical steamboat makes New York–Albany round trip.

1815–1819 Great Migration of settlers westward along National Road.

1816 Election of James Monroe; Era of Good Feelings.

1817 Rush-Bagot Agreement creates peace in Great Lakes region.

1819 United States takes over Florida in Adams-Onís Treaty.

1820 Missouri Compromise.

1823 Monroe Doctrine warns Europeans not to colonize in the Americas.

1824 Election of John Quincy Adams.

1828 Election of Andrew Jackson.

1830 Indian Removal Act expels Native Americans from United States.

1838 Remaining Native Americans forced by federal troops along "Trail of Tears" to Oklahoma Territory.

KEY TERMS

Adams-Onís Treaty Spain surrenders Florida to United States

cotton gin a machine that separated cotton fibers from cotton seeds

Democratic Party party formed around Andrew Jackson in 1820s; historically has represented the people rather than big business or the privileged class

Great Migration westward movement of settlers from 1815 to 1819

Indian Removal Act an act of Congress that forcibly expelled all Native Americans from the United States

Industrial Revolution the shift across the Western world from an agricultural society to a manufacturing one

Missouri Compromise a congressional agreement that Maine and Missouri would be admitted as states, one slave and the other free, and that slavery would be banned in all new states north of Missouri's southern border (excluding Missouri itself)

Monroe Doctrine statement that United States will remain neutral between the European powers and their Latin American colonies but will regard any further attempt to colonize in the western hemisphere as a direct threat to the United States

National Road paved road leading west from Baltimore to Vandalia, Illinois

Rush-Bagot Agreement limited the number of British and U.S. warships on the Great Lakes

steamboat a cargo or passenger boat powered by steam; the first boat not powered by human muscle

Trail of Tears the trail leading from the Southeast to Oklahoma Territory along which Native Americans were forced to march in 1838

Foreign Relations and the Monroe Doctrine

The collapse of the Federalist Party and the election of the Democratic-Republican James Monroe in 1816 marked the start of the so-called Era of

Good Feelings. For the first time in U.S. politics, partisan fighting was at a minimum. Candidates were chosen from within the Democratic Party, and national interest in politics began to decline.

President Monroe's first concern was to put relations with Great Britain on a sound footing after the War of 1812. Since peace in the Great Lakes region would benefit both Britain and the United States, Monroe's desire for disarmament in that region found a favorable reception in Britain. The **Rush-Bagot Agreement** of 1817 strictly limited the number of warships each nation could maintain on the Great Lakes. Britain and the United States also negotiated the border between the United States and Canada, establishing it at the 49th parallel, and agreed that they both would occupy the Oregon Territory until 1828, at which time they would set boundaries.

Meanwhile, Monroe was trying to come to terms with Spain over the Florida Territory. Spain had maintained its hold on Florida, which at that time stretched into the Gulf Coast areas of present-day Alabama, Mississippi, and Louisiana. The United States took over West Florida with little difficulty while Spain was distracted trying to quell revolts in many of its South American colonies. While Secretary of State John Quincy Adams negotiated with Spain to buy East Florida, General Andrew Jackson was fighting the First Seminole War. He and his troops had been ordered to West Florida to put down a revolt by the Seminole tribe, which was resisting land claims by U.S. settlers. However, Jackson did not stop at fighting the Native Americans; he ordered his men to seize Spanish forts in East Florida. After Jackson had exceeded his commission to the point of ordering the military execution of two British officials, European leaders condemned the United States. Monroe did not punish Jackson, but he did return the captured forts to Spain. Monroe argued that if the Spanish could not control the Seminole population, they must hand over Florida to the United States. Unable to match U.S. military force, Spain ceded Florida to the United States in the **Adams-Onís Treaty** of 1819.

People in the United States had been watching the series of rebellions in Spain's Latin American colonies with interest, as they watched every revolution of a colony against its mother country. The United States sided with the revolutionaries; European powers sided with the colonizers. Monroe knew that the European powers would help Spain retake the colonies if they could. In an 1823 speech to Congress he stated that the United States would remain neutral in any conflict between a Latin American colony and its European mother country. However, the United States would regard any attack on an independent Latin American republic or any further attempts to colonize the western hemisphere as an attack on the United States itself:

> With the existing colonies or dependencies of any European power we have not interfered and shall not interfere. . . . It is impossible that the allied powers [of Europe] should extend their political system to any portion of either continent [North or South America] without endangering our peace and happiness. . . . It is equally impossible, therefore, that we should behold such interposition in any form with indifference.

This statement, the terms of which largely had been worked out by John Quincy Adams, became known as the **Monroe Doctrine.**

Most Americans supported the Monroe Doctrine, although there were those who were apprehensive that it would force the United States to become involved in wars outside its borders. The effect of the Monroe Doctrine was what the administration had hoped: European nations made no further efforts to colonize in the western hemisphere. Although the United States was not powerful enough to enforce the doctrine, Great Britain also backed the idea; the British did not want to see the other European powers expand their empires. In future years, people in the United States would come to believe that under the Monroe Doctrine they had a special right to intervene in Latin America regardless of the wishes of people in those countries.

Economic Changes and the Industrial Revolution

Between 1805 and 1815 the United States experienced an economic depression. The fall in prices and rise in unemployment came about because the Napoleonic Wars in Europe meant fewer European buyers for U.S. goods; there also were a variety of U.S. trade restrictions in place. The South was at the point of economic collapse because there were no foreign buyers for its cotton.

With the return of peace in Europe and the shift in the Northeast to manufacturing rather than trade, markets opened again and profits soared. The government was able to provide frontier land grants to veterans. Between 1815 and 1819 the **Great Migration** saw record numbers of Americans moving westward from New York, Tennessee, Kentucky, and Ohio into Illinois and Indiana. Improved transportation, such as the building of the Cumberland or **National Road,** helped make this possible. This road, originally a trail blazed by General Edward Braddock in 1755, led from Baltimore to Cumberland, Maryland, through Wheeling, Virginia. It eventually was extended through Columbus, Ohio, to the town of Vandalia in central Illinois. This paved road provided a path for settlers migrating west and for trade in both directions. It even provided connections with flatboats that allowed settlers to travel down the Ohio River into the Mississippi Valley. Today the National Road is U.S. Route 40 (see the map below). The Great Migration ended with the Panic of 1819 (see Chapter 12). The cities along the National Road, once nothing but trading posts, became important manufacturing centers.

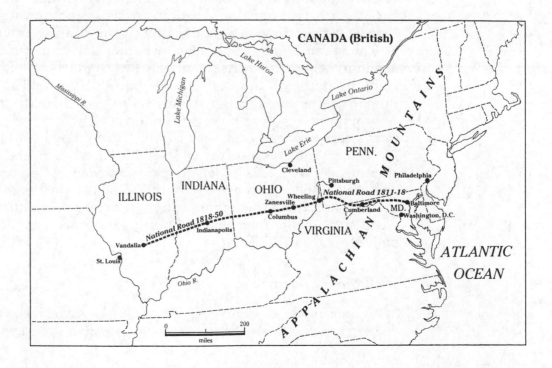

The **Industrial Revolution** was a vast, sweeping change in a world that in some respects had changed very little over all the preceding several centuries. People always had depended largely on the land for survival; both everyday and luxury goods were made one item at a time, by hand; and the key to the economy was the success or failure of the harvest.

With the beginning of manufacturing industries, everything changed. A variety of machines changed the way farmers sowed and harvested their crops. New methods of transportation changed the way crops were taken to market and expanded markets into new territory. Machines made it possible for people to assemble many products simultaneously. Though a slow process that would not be complete for over 50 years, this would divide the North and the South further.

The invention of the **cotton gin** in 1793 already had revolutionized the Southern economy. Cotton was a labor-intensive crop because the seeds and fibers had to be separated by hand after the cotton was picked. Eli Whitney of Massachusetts invented a machine ("gin" was short for "engine") that could comb seeds from cotton fibers automatically. In one day the cotton gin could process as much cotton as 1,000 slaves could process by hand. By 1800, cotton exports were 20 times what they had been nine years earlier, before the invention of the cotton gin. This made it possible for a Northern textile industry to develop. Southerners shipped their cotton north to be woven into cloth in the New England textile mills.

For slaves, the invention of the cotton gin spelled disaster. Slavery had begun slowly to decline because it had been outlawed in the North and was proving unprofitable in the long run in the South. It cost money to purchase, house, feed, and maintain a large slave population, but no matter how many slaves a plantation had, the work still took time. With the invention of the cotton gin, slavery suddenly became profitable again for both Southern plantation owners and Northern textile-mill owners. With the new profits, some Northerners began to drop their outspoken objections to slavery. The issue continued to be a political bone of contention between the North and the South; the North did not want the South to expand its power base, and a growing number of Northerners continued to object to slavery on ethical grounds, although they would continue to be in the minority for years to come.

The **steamboat** was another invention that changed business and the economy. America's many rivers provided an excellent "highway" system for trade by flatboat. The trouble was that flatboats had to be propelled by human power, and it was very difficult to pilot them upstream, against the flow of the water. In 1807, Robert Fulton of New York unveiled the first practical steam-powered boat, the *Clermont*. Beginning in 1811, there was regular steamboat service on the Ohio and Mississippi rivers. Southern plantation owners used steamboats to transport their cotton north to the textile mills in a fraction of the time it once had taken. The steamboat also sped up mail service, making communication from far-apart settlements and towns frequent and commonplace and uniting those who did not live geographically close.

John Quincy Adams

With the support of Henry Clay, John Quincy Adams won the presidency in 1824 in a contentious election. This son of former President John Adams had spent a lifetime in government circles. As a young man he had served his country as a diplomat, traveling as far away as Russia. As secretary of state under James Monroe he had negotiated the acquisition of Florida from Spain and conceived the Monroe Doctrine. Like his father, Adams was not personally popular, although for different reasons: The elder Adams had been too outspoken and argumentative, whereas the younger one was cold and haughty in manner. Despite his enormous intellectual achievements and the breadth of his vision for the nation, Adams served only one term as president, losing the 1828 election to the wildly popular war hero Andrew Jackson. The people of Massachusetts elected Adams to the U.S. Senate in 1830; he served there with distinction for 18 years, becoming well known throughout the nation as an abolitionist. Adams died in the chamber of the Senate in 1848.

The Spread of Slavery and the Missouri Compromise

As the United States expanded in size, the most important issue in congressional debates over the admission of new states was whether a new state would be a "slave state" or a "free state." Slaveholding states did not want to lose their power as a voting bloc in Congress; free states did not want slavery to spread any farther than it already had. Because slaves were counted, according to the Constitution, as three-fifths of a person but not allowed to vote, Southern whites were overrepresented in Congress in comparison to their actual numbers. Naturally, Northerners did not like that situation and wanted to contain it. Up to 1819 the balance had been maintained evenly, with 11 free states and 11 slaveholding states.

In 1819 Missouri applied for statehood. At that time its population included about 10,000 African slaves. Congressman James Tallmadge of New York pointed out that Missouri was in violation of the Northwest Ordinance of 1787, which had banned slavery in all U.S. territories. He proposed admitting Missouri to the Union on the condition that it adopt a plan for the gradual phasing out of slavery. Southern congressmen, seeing this as a threat to slavery everywhere, including their own states, reacted violently. Henry Clay eventually worked out the **Missouri Compromise,** which maintained the balance of power in Congress by admitting Missouri as a slave state and Maine as a free state. The Missouri Compromise also banned slavery in the territory north of Missouri's southern boundary (excluding Missouri itself) at latitude 36°30'. The Missouri Compromise silenced the division over the issue of slavery for the moment, but it solved nothing; it was only a palliative. The deep split over this issue would continue to haunt U.S. society for many decades.

Andrew Jackson and Native American Policy

Andrew Jackson won the presidential election of 1828, partly as the result of what is known today as negative campaigning. In 1824, when running for president against John Quincy Adams and Henry Clay, Jackson had started the rumor that Henry Clay and John Quincy Adams had made "a corrupt bargain" to win the presidency for Adams; he argued that Clay had thrown his support to Adams in exchange for being chosen secretary of state. The rumor tarnished both Adams's and Clay's reputations in spite of their denials, and Jackson was swept easily to victory in 1828.

Jackson was the first U.S. president who had not come from the American "aristocracy": he was neither a New England intellectual like the Adamses nor a Virginia planter like Jefferson, Madison, and Washington. The son of Scottish immigrants, Jackson was born in a log cabin in Tennessee, and he was the first "man of the people" to be elected to high office. By the time of his presidency he had established a large landholding fortune, but he nonetheless was able to appeal to the common man. He was the first president to appoint people from backgrounds like his own to administrative posts rather than believing that government should be run by the wealthy. Jackson believed that personal merit, not social rank, was the only requirement for holding political office. Popular among voters both for his "common touch" and for his military record, Jackson was the symbol around which the new **Democratic Party** organized itself.

During the Jacksonian era voting rights were expanded. Congress amended the Constitution to permit voters, rather than state legislatures, to elect their senators. States began dropping the requirement that voters own property. Voting was still a privilege of white adult males rather than a right of all adult citizens, but the number of voters nearly doubled between 1836 and 1840. Jackson wielded power that was based on the strength of his personality, in the process changing the nature of the presidency. He would utilize the veto as an instrument of policy, invoke a rotation system in office, and personalize many fights with political opponents.

During Jackson's presidency U.S. politicians began to come to a consensus on the question of Native American policy. U.S. citizens were so hungry for land that they consistently broke treaties and agreements made with Native Americans, encroaching on lands they formerly had agreed the Native Americans could keep. Many officials in the government began to agree that Native Americans should be moved to lands outside the borders of the United States. Jackson agreed with that point of view. He wrote that such a policy provided the Native Americans with necessary protection against the evils that white men would commit against them if they remained within the United States. In 1830 Jackson signed the **Indian Removal Act,** which forced Native Americans living east of the Mississippi to move to Indian Territory in present-day Oklahoma. The act promised that that land would belong to the Native Americans perpetually.

The Native Americans did not leave their ancestral lands willingly. In Florida the Seminole, led by Osceola, fought the Second Seminole War from 1835 to 1842. The United States declared the war over in 1842, having forcibly ejected thousands of Seminoles from their land and having killed hundreds more. In Georgia the Cherokee people took the state to court after fulfilling all the requirements set forth by the state for them to keep their land. Chief Justice John Marshall ruled that Georgia had no right to take away Native American lands, but despite that victory, the Cherokee received no federal protection from settlers who stole their property. In 1835 the Cherokee signed a treaty accepting money and land in Indian Territory in exchange for their Southeastern lands. They agreed to vacate Georgia by 1838. When that date arrived, federal troops were sent to the Southeast to eject all Native Americans who had not yet moved west. That forced 800-mile march is known as the **Trail of Tears** because so many Native Americans died along the way.

REVIEW QUESTIONS

1. All the following major changes first occurred in U.S. society between 1790 and 1825 EXCEPT:

    (A) More than 100,000 Americans migrated westward.
    (B) The Industrial Revolution changed the economy and the way people worked.
    (C) The Erie Canal was completed.
    (D) Voting rights were expanded to include white men who did not own property.
    (E) Political leaders began disagreeing over the question of slavery.

2. The Missouri Compromise stated all the following EXCEPT:

    (A) Missouri would be admitted to the Union as a slaveholding state.
    (B) Maine would be admitted to the Union as a free state.
    (C) Slavery would be outlawed north of Missouri's southern border, except in Missouri itself.
    (D) No future state would be admitted to the Union as a slaveholding state.
    (E) The balance of power in Congress would remain even, with 12 free states and 12 slaveholding states.

3. How did the invention of the cotton gin affect the South?

    (A) Planters divided their large plantations into smaller farms.
    (B) The economy boomed because one gin could do the work of 1,000 slaves.
    (C) Slavery began to be less profitable and started to die out.
    (D) Southerners began to build textile mills and make their own cloth for export and trade.
    (E) Southerners began building factories to manufacture more cotton gins.

4. What was the purpose of the Monroe Doctrine?

    (A) To support democracy all over the world
    (B) To ally the United States with European interests
    (C) To encourage Latin American revolutionaries to rise up against the European colonial powers
    (D) To warn European nations not to invade or colonize the western hemisphere
    (E) To declare American neutrality in relations between Latin America and Europe

Answers and Explanations

1. **E** Political leaders had been disagreeing on the question of slavery ever since the debate over including Jefferson's reference to "cruel war against human nature" in the Declaration of Independence. This was not new to the nineteenth century. The other four choices all describe phenomena that had not happened before 1790.

2. **D** The Southern states never would have agreed to the idea that no future states would be slave states; the essence of the compromise was to try to maintain a balance of power that would satisfy those on both sides on the issue.

3. **B** One cotton gin could process as much cotton in a day as 1,000 slaves could. This made slavery more profitable. The textile industry developed in the North, not the South; the South planted and harvested the cotton and then shipped it north, where the mills were. The gin did not make the South an industrial or manufacturing society; it remained an agricultural society.

4. **D** The Monroe Doctrine stated that the United States would not interfere in conflicts between the European powers and their Latin American colonies but that the United States would regard any European attempt to colonize more territory in the western hemisphere or to retake a colony that had declared its independence as a threat to the United States. Therefore, choice D is correct.

CHAPTER 11
RELIGION AND REFORM

INTRODUCTION

The early nineteenth century was a time of great change in U.S. society. With independence firmly established and the new government proving workable, people turned their attention to two major issues that had been swept aside in the need for unanimity on the question of independence: the rights and freedom of women and slaves.

Throughout the nineteenth century and well into the twentieth, both groups would have to continue the fight for equal rights and equal treatment. The women's rights movement and the abolitionist movement shared many goals and many leaders. Both movements had strong arguments on their side, principally the irony and hypocrisy of a nation founded on a document stating that "all men are created equal" denying equality to its entire female population for no better reason than outworn tradition and to perhaps 10 percent of its male population solely on the basis of skin color.

A wave of religious fervor swept the nation from the 1790s to about the 1830s. The Second Great Awakening helped fuel the struggle for full civil rights for all; many preachers pointed out that it was a sin to hold human beings in slavery and that women were equal to men in the eyes of God. The evangelical revival also gave rise to the temperance movement, in which women literally stormed saloons and destroyed their stores of spirituous liquors.

In Washington a new political party had risen to combat Jacksonian democracy. The Whigs elected their first president, William Henry Harrison, in 1840. They would continue to be a force in politics for the next 20 years.

TIMELINE

1790s–1830s   Second Great Awakening.

1820s   Beginning of temperance movement; founding of American Temperance Society.

1822   Establishment of Monrovia (now Liberia) on the west coast of Africa.

1831   Nat Turner rebellion in Virginia; first issue of *The Liberator*.

1834   Birth of the Whig Party.

1836   Election of Martin Van Buren.

1839   Publication of *American Slavery as It Is*.

1840   Election of William Henry Harrison.

1848   Seneca Falls Women's Rights Convention; New York passes Married Women's Property Act.

KEY TERMS

abolitionist   one who advocated a gradual or immediate end to slavery

Declaration of Sentiments   a document published by the Seneca Falls Convention, listing its grievances and advocating reform

literate   able to read and write

Second Great Awakening   an evangelical Protestant religious revival that began about 1790

Seneca Falls Convention   1848 meeting at Seneca Falls, New York, to discuss reform in the area of women's rights

temperance   moderation in or abstention from the consumption of alcohol

temperance advocate   one who supports temperance

utopian   ideal; a utopian society is one without flaws

Whig   a member of a political party created in 1834 in opposition to the Democratic Party

Political Developments

Although Andrew Jackson was very well liked among the general population, there were many in office who disliked and distrusted his policies. A new political party, the **Whigs,** came into existence in 1834, born of opposition to the Democratic Party that had grown up around Jackson's candidacy for president.

The Whigs were a mixture of people who opposed Jackson on personal grounds and those who felt that he was abusing his power and shifting the presidency toward something close to a monarchy. The leaders of the Whigs were Senators Daniel Webster and Henry Clay. They took their party name from Revolutionary days, when the British Whigs had advocated a relaxation of Parliament's authority over the colonies.

The Whigs ran their first candidates for president in 1836: William Henry Harrison, the hero of the War of 1812; Hugh White; and Daniel Webster. None of the three garnered nearly as many votes as Martin Van Buren, who had been Andrew Jackson's vice president. Van Buren was a New York City politician who had proved a valuable political ally for Jackson but lacked Jackson's personal popularity.

In 1840 the Whigs tried again. This time they succeeded in capturing the White House. During a spirited and hard-fought campaign they painted Van Buren as a remote aristocrat and called themselves "the party of the people." Although William Henry Harrison had an aristocratic background—he was from a wealthy family, and his father had signed the Declaration of Independence—the Whigs successfully portrayed him as a common man with a log-cabin past, just like Andrew Jackson. Harrison also capitalized on his military career, reminding the voters of his victory at the Battle of Tippecanoe. "Tippecanoe and Tyler, too!" became the rallying cry of the campaign, and Harrison and his vice president, John Tyler of Virginia, were elected. The popular vote was close, but Harrison won almost four times as many electoral votes as Van Buren. Harrison ended up serving the shortest term of any U.S. president; after delivering his lengthy inaugural address in the rain, he fell ill and did not recover. He died only one month into his term. Vice President John Tyler became the first person to step into office when a president died before his term was over.

Literature

Ever since the early colonial days, the United States had been a **literate** society. Because Puritans had wanted everyone to be able to read the Bible, all children were taught to read. This did not mean that all Americans could read and write, but the majority had had some schooling, and more and more people were continuing their education beyond the grammar school level. Although higher education was not standard for girls, it was beginning to be available. Southern states passed laws making it illegal to teach slaves to read or write, but many slaves managed to learn in spite of the ban. In 1833 Oberlin College in northeast Ohio opened its doors, providing the first opportunity in the United States for women to earn a four-year college degree. Two years later it became the first U.S. college to admit African-American students.

In the early 1800s Americans were beginning to produce more imaginative literature that was intended for entertainment rather than political information or religious edification. Most American literature of note in this period came from the Northeast. An entire literary community developed around Concord, Massachusetts, where Herman Melville, Nathaniel Hawthorne, Henry David Thoreau, Ralph Waldo Emerson, and Louisa May Alcott were all near neighbors of one another. Some of those writers also participated in a famous experimental community called Brook Farm. They produced the first great works of American literature, setting forth many themes and ideas that would become a permanent part of the American mindset. Henry Wadsworth Longfellow became the first American to earn a living by writing poetry; Edgar Allan Poe of Baltimore was a pioneer in the field of detective and horror fiction; and Walt Whitman of New York and Emily Dickinson of Massachusetts broke literary ground with their poems.

Literary Figures	Major Works	Genre
Louisa May Alcott	*Little Women* *An Old-Fashioned Girl* *Work*	Children's fiction Adult fiction Gothic short stories
Ralph Waldo Emerson	*On Friendship* *Self-Reliance*	Essays Philosophy
Henry David Thoreau	*Walden* *Civil Disobedience*	Memoirs Philosophy Essays
Nathaniel Hawthorne	*The Scarlet Letter* *Tanglewood Tales*	Novels, short stories, children's fiction Short stories
Edgar Allan Poe	"The Fall of the House of Usher" "The Tell-Tale Heart" "The Cask of Amontillado" "The Purloined Letter" "The Raven"	Horror fiction Detective fiction Poetry
Walt Whitman	*Leaves of Grass*	Poetry (free-verse)
Emily Dickinson	Poems	Poetry
Herman Melville	*Moby-Dick* *White-Jacket* "Bartleby the Scrivener"	Novels, short stories

The Second Great Awakening

The Great Awakening of the 1740s and 1750s had created a rise in the number of Protestant congregations in America. The new philosophy of salvation by being converted (in modern terminology, "born again") to sincere repentance for sins and faith in God had flown in the face of the Puritan concept of salvation by predestination alone. Large numbers of people in the United States embraced the idea that they could play a role in their own salvation.

The **Second Great Awakening** began as early as the 1790s in upstate New York and continued through the 1830s. Religious revival meetings conducted by fiery evangelical preachers sometimes drew up to 20,000 people. Like the first Great Awakening, the Second Great Awakening caused a surge in church membership among Protestants, especially Methodists and Baptists. The movement appealed strongly to women and to African Americans, even giving rise to a black Methodist denomination known as the African Methodist Episcopal (AME) Church. Those religious movements often led to reform movements that focused on improving human conditions. Penitentiary reform, aid to the poor, and some of the first insane asylums were all major aspects of this era.

Utopian communities based on religion and philosophy sprang up throughout the United States between 1800 and 1850. People came together with a vision of an ideal society in which everyone would contribute to the good of the whole group. Work, ownership of property, and family life all would be shared. Although most of those communities would be short-lived, a few, such as the Oneida Experiment, would succeed for a considerable time.

The religious revival of the early nineteenth century also gave rise to the **temperance** movement. That movement, which discouraged the consumption of alcohol, was organized and led largely by Protestant women, who established the American Temperance society in the 1820s. In the early 1800s no respectable woman would have been seen in a saloon or a bar; the targets of the movement were men. **Temperance advocates** believed that alcohol was a dangerous temptation to men to spend their wages on drink instead of on groceries and to spend their time in brothels or saloons instead of with their wives and children.

The women who led the temperance movement were no more subtle than the patriots who had dumped chests of tea into Boston Harbor in 1774. They became famous for their aggressive approach to their work—striding into saloons, smashing the glass windows, and taking hatchets to kegs of whiskey, rum, and other spirits till the liquor ran in streams along the floorboards. The movement was effective; by the mid-1800s the national consumption of alcohol had dropped. Temperance advocates continued their fight throughout the nineteenth century. In 1917 they would reach the pinnacle of success with the passage of the Eighteenth Amendment, known as "Prohibition" because it prohibited the sale of alcoholic beverages. (Prohibition would be repealed in 1933, having proved a resounding failure.)

The Abolitionist Movement

The Second Great Awakening also helped reinforce the **abolitionist** movement that had been in existence since the earliest days of the colonies. The Pennsylvania Quakers had always spoken out against slavery. The first antislavery society in America was founded by Benjamin Franklin. Ministers of the Great Awakening preached that each individual must live without sin and urge others to do likewise; holding another human being in slavery, of course, was regarded as a sin. Even a slave owner such as Thomas Jefferson had recognized the hypocrisy of founding a slaveholding nation with a document stating that all men were created equal.

By the early 1800s most Northern states had outlawed slavery. The next step was to try to end it in the South. One idea that took root was to send African Americans back to Africa to establish a democratic nation of their own. That nation, established in 1822 on the west coast of Africa, was called Monrovia after President James Monroe (today it is called Liberia). Some 1,400 African Americans had settled in the new nation by 1830.

Most African Americans, however, had a different goal. They did not want to go to Africa, which to most of them was a foreign land. Most African Americans had been born in the United States and regarded it as their home. Their goal was freedom from and equality with white people; they wanted to be treated as free citizens of the United States, with the same rights and privileges as white people. By 1826 there were more than 143 antislavery societies throughout the country, many of them organized and run by free blacks; though initially few in number, black and white activists would continue the fight for abolition and equality.

Many did not want to wait for gradual changes in the law. They wanted immediate action. Nat Turner, a slave born in 1800, led an armed uprising in August 1831. The area around Southampton, Virginia, quickly became a scene of terror as Turner and his followers killed any white people they came across; eventually, 50 or 60 people fell victim to the enraged slave and his army. The rebellion did not last long because Turner's army was far too small to sustain a war; in the end, he and his followers (along with many innocent African Americans) were captured and hanged. Southern states were quick to pass harsh new laws that curtailed the few rights and freedoms slaves enjoyed. William Lloyd Garrison, a white journalist, started his famous abolitionist newspaper *The Liberator* in response to the Turner rebellion. Like Turner, Garrison did not believe in waiting for freedom:

> Urge me not to use moderation in a cause like the present. I am in earnest—I will not equivocate—I will not excuse—I will not retreat a single inch—AND I WILL BE HEARD. . . .

Women's Rights

As the nineteenth century began, women in the United States still were not permitted to vote or hold office. By law, women had few rights to property or earnings. They could not obtain custody of their children in case of divorce. There were few colleges or professions open to women. At best, women were second-class citizens in a republic founded on the notion that "all men are created equal." (Interestingly, the Constitution of the United States does not specify that only men can hold office; it uses the word "person" to refer to the president, senators, representatives, and Supreme Court justices.)

During the Revolutionary War, Abigail Adams had urged her husband to "remember the ladies" in the new government that was being designed. John Adams returned a laughing answer by letter and did not bring up Abigail's idea in congressional debates. However, many women agreed with Abigail Adams. They argued that they were educated and literate, as capable of forming opinions as their husbands; since they had to obey the laws of the land, it was only right that they be allowed to vote. Otherwise they were in the same position as the colonists before the Revolution: they were unrepresented in their own government. In effect, they were slaves.

During the 1830s Sarah and Angelina Grimké, Quakers from South Carolina, began speaking and writing against slavery and for women's rights. In 1839 Angelina Grimké and her husband, Theodore Weld, published *American Slavery as It Is,* a document that was to sway the opinions of many in favor of the cause of abolition. When ministers sneered publicly at the Grimkés for daring to speak to mixed audiences of men and women, claiming that such work was appropriate only for men, the Grimkés fought back:

> Men and women were created equal. They are both moral and account-able beings, and whatever is right for man to do, is right for woman.
>
> It is a woman's right to have a voice in all the laws and regulations by which she is to be governed, whether in Church or State.

In 1840 the American reformers Elizabeth Cady Stanton and Lucretia Mott attended a World Anti-Slavery Convention in London. They were out-raged to learn that women were not welcome; the convention leaders finally agreed to allow them into the hall, but only if they would sit behind a curtain that screened them from the male participants in the convention. The two women vowed to fight such prejudices. In 1848 they organized the **Seneca Falls Convention,** the first national meeting ever held in the United States on the subject of women's rights. More than 300 people came to the small town of Seneca Falls in New York to hear the speeches. The convention resulted in the **Declaration of Sentiments,** which called for legal and social reform. Its language echoed that of the Declaration of Independence, with the ironic twist of showing how the men who wrote and approved that document had ignored half the population of the United States:

> We hold these truths to be self-evident, that all men and women are created equal, that they are endowed by their creator with certain inalienable rights, that among these are life, liberty, and the pursuit of happiness.
>
> The history of mankind is a history of repeated injuries and usurpa-tions on the part of man toward woman, having as a direct object the establishment of an absolute tyranny over her. To prove this, let facts be submitted to a candid world.
>
> He has never permitted her to exercise her inalienable right to the elective franchise.
>
> He has taken from her all right in property, even to the wages she earns.
>
> He has denied her the facilities for obtaining a thorough education, all colleges being closed against her.
>
> He has endeavored, in every way that he could, to destroy her confidence in her own powers, to lessen her self-respect, and to make her willing to lead a dependent and abject life.
>
> Resolved, That woman is man's equal—was intended to be so by the creator, and the highest good of the race demands that she should be recognized as such.

Lucy Stone, one of the first women to graduate from Oberlin College, became a famous advocate of abolition and women's rights. Stone kept her maiden name when she married; for some years afterward any woman who did the same thing was called a "Lucy Stoner." Susan B. Anthony, who became close friends with Elizabeth Cady Stanton, focused her efforts on fighting for political rights for women. She argued that until women had political rights, they would have no other rights. When Anthony boldly went to the polls and cast a vote, she was arrested. However, she was successful in her fight for reform in property rights. In 1848 New York passed the Married Women's Property Act, which entitled married women to own property. In 1860 the act was amended to include a woman's right to control her own earnings. Other states passed similar laws.

Limits of Antebellum Reform

Apart from abolition, the social movements of the antebellum (pre–Civil War) period primarily addressed the concerns of the developing middle class. Only middle- and upper-class women had time to be concerned about issues such as higher education, voting rights, and the right to be heard in public. Working-class women had very different concerns. If they had had time, they would have fought for higher wages, better working conditions, and better living conditions in poor neighborhoods. However, they were too busy with the struggle for survival. The condition of the working class, especially in the city, was harsh in terms of work, living conditions, and economic status. Working-class people would have to wait until the next century for society as a whole to address their concerns.

REVIEW QUESTIONS

1. Who among the following did not belong to the literary community in Concord, Massachusetts?

   (A) Louisa May Alcott
   (B) Nathaniel Hawthorne
   (C) Bronson Alcott
   (D) Edgar Allan Poe
   (E) Henry David Thoreau

2. What happened at the Seneca Falls Convention?

   (A) A constitutional amendment was passed granting women the right to vote.
   (B) A Declaration of Sentiments listing women's grievances was signed and published.
   (C) A riot broke out between those who supported and those who opposed women's rights.
   (D) The president of the United States pledged to make women's rights a major campaign issue.
   (E) Newspaper articles supporting the abolition of slavery were read and discussed.

3. The rebellion of Nat Turner had all the following effects EXCEPT:

   (A) Fifty or sixty white people were killed.
   (B) The Southern states passed harsh new laws limiting the rights of slaves.
   (C) Southerners blamed William Lloyd Garrison and *The Liberator* for the uprising.
   (D) Nat Turner and several of his followers were hanged as criminals.
   (E) The rebellion inspired other successful uprisings throughout the South.

4. The Second Great Awakening gave rise to or supported all the following movements EXCEPT:

   (A) women's education
   (B) temperance
   (C) abolition
   (D) women's suffrage
   (E) the Whig Party

Answers and Explanations

1. **D** Both Alcotts, Hawthorne, and Thoreau were all near neighbors of one another in Concord. Poe was from Maryland; he lived in several cities along the eastern seaboard, but never in Concord.
2. **B** The Seneca Falls Convention is important because it was the first national meeting in the United States on the issue of women's rights. No riot broke out, the president did not attend, and the convention did not have the power to pass a constitutional amendment.
3. **E** Turner's rebellion was put down harshly. His army was too small to fight effectively against the United States. Because his rebellion resulted in harsher laws against slaves' rights, it would have been difficult for another rebellion to take place.
4. **E** The Second Great Awakening was a religious movement. Because its leaders regarded all Christians as equal in the eyes of God, it supported equal rights for all. It opposed the free consumption of alcohol because alcohol led people into sinful pleasures. Almost all evangelical Protestants supported the Whig Party.

CHAPTER 12

THE MARKET REVOLUTION, 1812–1845

INTRODUCTION

As the nineteenth century began, the United States started to develop two distinct cultures: one in the South and one in the North. Advances in technology and transportation allowed the South to expand its agriculture at the same time that the North began developing industry and business. As the years went on, the two societies had less and less in common.

Both Southern and Northern cultures were divided into social and economic classes. In the North there were the very wealthy, the middle class, and the urban poor. Many of the urban poor were newly arrived immigrants; in the 1830s and 1840s most of those immigrants came from Ireland. Lacking the money to buy land and farm it, they became a laboring class. They worked in mines and factories, built national roads and canals, and turned their hand to any other job or work that paid wages.

The beginning of the nineteenth century also marked the continuation of the struggle between the power of the federal government and the rights of the states to govern themselves. Southern states insisted that they were under no compulsion to obey any laws they found unconstitutional, such as tariff acts that drove up the prices of foreign goods. Financial panics in 1819 and 1837 suggested that a strong national bank was a necessity, but many remained unconvinced of this.

TIMELINE

1811 Congress does not renew the charter of the Bank of the United States.

1815 Construction of the National Road begins.

1816 Congress creates the Second Bank of the United States.

1816 Tariff Act of 1816 imposes a 25 percent tax on imported manufactured goods.

1817 Construction of Erie Canal begins.

1818 Second Bank calls in all state loans, causing Panic of 1819.

1828 New tariff act doubles tax on imports; Calhoun writes an essay stating the doctrine of nullification.

1830 Locomotives come into use as a means of transportation.

1836 Andrew Jackson closes the Second Bank, touching off the Panic of 1837.

KEY TERMS

American System Henry Clay's proposal for a national bank, protective tariffs, and a national transportation system

canal   a human-made waterway cut through an area of land to link two bodies of water

doctrine of nullification   an argument stating that since the states had formed the Union, the states had the final authority over laws and could ignore any law they deemed unconstitutional

Know-Nothing Party   a political party founded by those with nativist beliefs

market revolution   a vast expansion of markets in which manufacturers and producers could sell goods and products

nativism   the belief that immigrants do not deserve the same rights and privileges as native-born Americans

panic   a financial crisis in which banks fail and close and those who have accounts there lose their savings

slave narrative   the autobiography of a former slave, emphasizing the horrifying conditions from which he or she had escaped

tariff   a tax imposed on foreign goods sold in the domestic market; intended to support the purchase of domestically made goods

The Market Economy

The U.S. economy really began to take shape in the first quarter of the nineteenth century. Congress had refused to renew the charter of the Bank of the United States in 1811; as a result, the government had to look to state banks for funds to repay the debt from the War of 1812. Since state banks did not always have the gold or silver to back up their paper currency, other banks often would refuse to honor it. Speaker of the House of Representatives Henry Clay of Kentucky offered a solution to the emerging economic crisis. His proposal, called the **American System,** consisted of three parts:

- Creation of a national bank to establish a standard national currency and fund the federal government
- Enactment of protective **tariffs** on imports, which would encourage people to buy articles made in the United States and thus provide a spur to U.S. industry
- Creation of a national transportation system of roads and canals on which natural resources and manufactured goods could be hauled, uniting the industrial and agricultural sectors of the nation and allowing each to benefit from the other

Many of Clay's colleagues in Congress believed that his plan was a sensible one. In 1816 they sent a bill to President Madison, asking for a charter for the Second Bank of the United States. Madison promptly signed the bill into law.

The next step was protective tariffs. Congress soon passed the Tariff Act of 1816, which established a 25 percent tax on imported manufactured goods. This drove up the price of imports to such a degree that Southern planters, afraid that European nations would retaliate by taxing American cotton, protested. However, Northerners were happy to avoid the tariff and purchase locally made goods; they benefited from the act because almost all U.S. factories were in the North.

The Tariff Act funded the solution of the last issue: the national transportation system. Congress decided to use the money brought in by the tariff to pay for the building of roads and **canals.** The National Road from Baltimore to Vandalia, Illinois, was begun in 1815, and the Erie Canal in 1817. Within 10 years, this 363-mile canal provided a direct and efficient trade route from the Hudson River to Lake Erie.

The third element of the national transportation system was the railroad. The first locomotives came into use in the United States around 1830. At that time the steam-powered "iron horse" lost a race to a horse of flesh and blood; however, mechanical knowledge advanced quickly, and the train soon could outperform any live animal. By 1850 trains were running over thousands of miles of track. Well before the end of the century Americans would have a transcontinental railroad.

The transportation boom created new markets for goods. Before the existence of steamboats that could take goods upstream and canals that could carry goods inland from the ocean, Americans had sold most of what they manufactured and grew in local markets. Now they could expand to new territories with thousands of new customers. This created a **market revolution.** As profits grew, so did the sizes of towns and the movement of settlers. Skilled artisans, who always had manufactured items one at a time, began to give way to mass production and factories.

Some of the inventions that made the Industrial Revolution are listed below.

Spinning jenny	Mechanical loom invented by James Hargreaves of Great Britain; brought to the United States by Samuel Slater in 1789
Interchangeable parts	Mass-produced, identical parts for machines, tools, and weapons, allowing for mass production by the assembly of standardized parts
Cotton gin	Machine that separates cotton seeds from cotton fibers in a fraction of the time it takes a person to do the task by hand
Steamboat	Boat whose steam power allows it to travel upstream against the current, something that formerly had been very difficult; enabled Southern planters to send cotton north in bulk, giving rise the to Northern textile industry

Economic Panic

In 1818 the Second Bank called in all outstanding loans from state banks. Those banks had borrowed more money than they could pay back, and the result was the Panic of 1819. In a frantic attempt to get enough money to pay their debt to the government, banks foreclosed on mortgages and called in loans to customers; this is typical of the early stages of a **panic.** In turn, individual borrowers could not pay back the banks on such short notice, and many had to sell their homes or businesses. With no one to buy the businesses, they closed down, and their workers were suddenly unemployed. The resulting economic depression lasted for several years.

In 1828 a new tariff act doubled the rates set in the tariff act of 1816. Southerners, who had not supported the first act, were furious over the new one. They complained bitterly about the infringement of the federal government on states' rights. John C. Calhoun, who originally had supported the use of the import taxes to pay for roads and canals, was so alienated by the new act that he wrote an essay arguing that no state should be forced to obey any act of Congress it believed to be unconstitutional. Because the states had created the federal government, the states should have greater power. The position Calhoun took in his essay became known as the **doctrine of nullification.**

Many voters agreed with Calhoun. Henry Clay, ever the compromiser, successfully urged Congress to pass a reduction in the new tariff. For Southerners that was not enough. South Carolina took the lead, passing resolutions declaring the tariff acts null and void and refusing to pay any tariffs to the federal government. If the government tried to collect tariffs, South Carolina threatened, it would secede from the United States. President Jackson responded by calling up federal troops and threatening an invasion of South Carolina. Clay stepped in and urged a further compromise that lowered the tariff rates gradually over the course of 10 years. Placated for the moment, South Carolinians dropped their threats. The tension during this period is known as the Nullification Crisis.

President Andrew Jackson looked with disfavor on the Second Bank, believing that it catered to the interests of the wealthy at the expense of the common working people. The voters apparently agreed with Jackson; when the fate of the bank became a major campaign issue in 1836, Jackson easily defeated his opponent, Henry Clay, who supported renewing the bank's charter. Once reelected, Jackson took steps to close down the Second Bank. He transferred funds to various state banks rather than into the federal bank. Bank president Nicholas Biddle attempted to save the bank by triggering a financial crisis, hoping to show Jackson and the public that they should support an institution that stabilized the national economy. Neither Jackson nor the public was converted to this view; instead, they felt that Biddle was demonstrating conclusively that the bank was a tool to be used against the public.

The Second Bank closed down in 1836. State banks meanwhile lent money readily, allowing speculators to buy land. The speculators resold the land at inflated prices, clearing a fast profit. As land prices soared, so did all other prices. President Jackson tried to stem the tide of inflation by stating that the federal government would accept only gold and silver as payment for public land—no paper currency would be accepted. Land sales dropped precipitously because few people had gold or silver. People tried to trade paper money for gold and silver at the banks, and the banks quickly ran out of gold and silver and then failed. This so-called Panic of 1837 resulted in an economic depression from which the nation did not begin to recover until 1843. The lack of a national banking structure would haunt the United States for decades.

The Northern Economy

During the early nineteenth century the urban economy in the North quickly developed three distinct social classes: the poor, the middle class, and the wealthy. Though greater than in Europe, social mobility remained limited throughout this period.

The nineteenth century was a lean time for the urban poor. There were no regulations to protect them either in the workplace or at home. Employers set wages as low as they could and demanded as many working hours as they dared so that their profits would be greater. The modern concept of the weekend did not exist; Sunday was the only day of rest, and a normal workday lasted from 10 to 14 hours. There were no labor unions or minimum-wage laws to protect workers' interests. If one worker found the wages too low, another would gladly take his place. America's high rate of immigration meant that workers were easy to replace; therefore, employers did not see the need to spend money or time making the workplace safe. At textile mills, for instance, workers constantly inhaled the lint and fluff that were by-products of their work. This eventually led to serious health complications. Fires and other serious accidents were common. It became clear that management would make no attempt to alter this situation unless forced to do so by laws or by pressure from workers' organizations.

Life at home was no better for the poor. They were crowded into apartment buildings without heat or running water. Cities had no sewer systems. There were no public laws to protect urban dwellers. In this situation, disease spread rapidly. Landlords could allow buildings to fall into serious states of disrepair, and the poor had no recourse to the law. There were few public facilities such as baths, swimming pools, or even green parks where children could play.

Everyone in a poor family worked except for the very youngest children. There were no child-labor laws in the early nineteenth century, and children as young as age five were expected to put in a full day of work. Factories and mines readily hired children; their small size made them the best workers for jobs that involved squeezing into tight spaces. No poor family would send a child to school when he or she was able to help earn the money so desperately needed for survival.

The urban middle class lived very differently. This class was made up primarily of people who owned their own small businesses or had good positions in larger businesses. Lawyers, teachers, professors, clergymen, artisans, and shopkeepers were all members of the middle class. These people generally lived comfortable though not luxurious lives.

Because the middle class wanted to appear as distinct as possible from the poorer class, middle-class women did not work. Although in colonial times it had been a matter of pride that everyone in a family worked, the middle class made it a matter of pride that its women could afford not to work. Respectable middle-class women were supposed to stay at home, managing the house and raising the children, while the men went out to work at a profession. Middle-class families usually could afford a cook and a maid; that meant that prosperous housewives lived lives of enforced idleness. They also lacked any legal rights and protections, being utterly dependent on their husbands for protection.

Being confined to such a narrow sphere of activity created deep discontent among many women who had enough intelligence and education to imagine and desire wider horizons than those provided by home and hearth. "The Yellow Wallpaper," an 1892 short story by Charlotte Perkins Gilman, sums up the plight of nineteenth-century middle-class women in its chilling portrait of a young married woman literally driven mad by a husband who refuses to let her write or take part in any other intellectual or physical activity because it might be too much for her nerves. The boredom of respectability helped give rise to the women's rights movement, in which women began to demand a college education, fight for the right to study for professions, and be allowed to have honorable goals other than marriage and motherhood. The women who led the national fight for social, education, and political reform were almost all middle-class women (see Chapter 11).

Wealthy society lived in an atmosphere far removed from the circle of the poor or the middle class. This small group of people who owned a disproportionate amount of the community's wealth spent their time together.

Wealthy men were involved in politics and had inherited incomes to manage. Wealthy women organized entertainment events for themselves and their friends. The children of the upper class were educated to follow in the footsteps of their parents. Sometimes the wealthy patronized the performing arts or did charitable work.

Growth of Immigration and Labor Unions

Northern cities grew like weeds for one simple reason: immigration. Thousands of Europeans crossed the Atlantic every year, searching for financial opportunities, an escape from wretched conditions at home, and ownership of property.

During the mid-1800s most immigrants came from Ireland. The potato famine of the 1840s had destroyed that nation's staple crop, causing widespread starvation. Hundreds of thousands of Irish, having nowhere else to go, sailed west, lured by the promise of opportunity in the United States. Once they arrived in the United States, they were too poor to buy land and live as they had lived in Ireland, as subsistence farmers. They remained in the cities, snatching at the opportunities for factory work. Those who moved westward from the Atlantic Coast provided most of the labor that built the roads, laid the railroad tracks, and dug the Erie Canal. Irishmen also turned their hand to mining coal in Pennsylvania and unloading freight in Ohio. Irishwomen worked as laundresses, seamstresses, servants, and factory hands.

With their distinctive brogue and their different religious faith (nearly all Irish immigrants were Roman Catholics), the Irish encountered more than their share of prejudice in the United States. Protestant Anglo-Saxons had continued to be the dominant group in the United States, controlling most of the money and power, and they despised the Irish. Like the generations that followed them, Americans of the 1830s and 1840s refused to acknowledge the fact that they too, or their parents or grandparents, had immigrated to the United States just as the Irish had, and for the same reasons.

In concrete terms, prejudice meant that landlords might refuse to rent to Irish families or might ask unreasonably high rents. Factory owners might refuse to hire Irish workers or offer them lower wages. They sometimes would reserve the most difficult and dangerous jobs for the Irish. This anti-immigrant prejudice gave rise to **nativism,** the belief that certain rights and privileges should be reserved for native-born Americans. Nativists showed their displeasure with immigrants by vandalizing Irish Catholic churches, attacking immigrants in the streets, and trying to change laws to restrict immigrants' rights. The nativists eventually formed their own political party, called the **Know-Nothing Party** in honor of a typical party member's response when asked about nativist activities: "I know nothing of that."

However, the Irish proved tough enough to survive and even to triumph. By the 1880s many of them had gained enormous political power in major cities such as Boston and New York.

German immigrants also flooded the United States during this era. Most of them settled in the major cities or the rural areas surrounding the Great Lakes. Germans tended to become small farmers or skilled artisans. German immigrants had a high rate of success because they generally came to the United States with enough money to be self-sufficient once they arrived. Most German immigrants knew that they could rely for help on relatives or friends who already had settled in the United States.

The Southern Economy

Southern society was so different from society in the North that the United States was in many ways two separate countries. The agricultural South and the industrial North had little in common. Their climates and topography were different, their sources of income were different, the businesses in which they worked were different, and their ideas on the subject of slave labor and their notions of how the federal government should be run were poles apart.

In the South there were four social and economic classes: wealthy planters, small farmers, poor whites, and slaves. Rich planters who owned 50 or more slaves were relatively few in number. They might own hundreds or thousands of acres of land on which they grew cotton and also sometimes rice or sugarcane. With a vast number of slaves and also with paid employees, a plantation owner was like a medieval lord. He and his wife, and often their grown sons and daughters, worked together to oversee the day-to-day operations of their land. The planter ran a business like any other business; he had accounts to keep, correspondence to write, trades to make, and so on. The planter's lady was responsible for the general welfare of everyone who lived on the plantation; she ran the household, looked after and treated the sick, and managed the staff of house slaves. Though few in number, rich planters controlled a disproportionate amount of wealth and almost all the political and social power. Owning slaves was the only way into elite Southern society.

Small farmers might or might not own a few slaves. They were largely self-sufficient, growing what they needed for themselves and trading their surplus crops for cash and manufactured goods or for things they could not grow, such as spices, tea, and tools.

The "poor white" class was poor because its members lived on barren soil. The majority of good land was dominated by the planter elite. When a farmer could not coax a good crop from his land, his family was bound to suffer. The poorest Southerners owned no slaves. They subsisted on what they could grow and lived in log cabins. They had no leisure for education and nowhere to go to get it. Many of them were illiterate. They had very little hope of improving their lot in life.

Slaves were paid nothing for their work, although they were on call every hour of every day. Because they were valuable "property," the plantation owner gave them food and housing and a certain amount of care when they fell ill. But since the owner's purpose was to make the greatest possible profit, the slaves were given no luxuries and very few comforts. They were housed in shacks, given the poorest-quality food and not much of it, and clothed in castoffs from the owner's family or clothing they made themselves from the poorest and roughest fabrics. They knew better than to appeal for medical care unless they were seriously ill; no slave wanted to be branded a troublemaker or a complainer. Plantation owners knew that they had to maintain a healthy and strong workforce to turn a profit, but they convinced themselves that African slaves could subsist and even thrive on starvation diets and a seven-day workweek. This was a system that was predicated on fear. Violence was a constant threat and reality, slave families were split up, and rape of female slaves was common. A system of slave catchers was in place to capture runaway slaves or kidnap free blacks. Whites who were not slaveholders often were forced to be a part of those patrols. Returned runaway slaves often were maimed and left on the plantation as an example to others.

But somehow, despite the nightmare conditions under which they were forced to live, slaves maintained a rich culture of their own. It was a patchwork quilt of memories of a variety of cultures from their home continent of Africa, blended with European-derived elements they had acquired in the New World. Spirituals, for instance, combine African musical elements with Christian lyrics. Slaves told stories, sang, and danced to entertain themselves and each other. Many slave women became skilled in the art of using herbs to heal the sick. Although it was a crime to teach a slave to read or write, many slaves managed to learn anyway; during the mid-1800s the **slave narrative** became a popular and widely read type of autobiography. Escaped slaves, most famously Frederick Douglass, wrote of experiences such as starvation, brutal physical punishments, and the constant restraint of their liberty in the hope that readers would be converted to the cause of abolition.

REVIEW QUESTIONS

1. All these inventions helped revolutionize the U.S. economy in the early nineteenth century EXCEPT:

   (A) the cotton gin
   (B) the locomotive
   (C) the incandescent lightbulb
   (D) the steamboat
   (E) the spinning jenny

2. Which of the following social classes did NOT make up a significant part of Southern society?

   (A) Wealthy planters
   (B) Immigrants
   (C) Slaves
   (D) Small farmers
   (E) "Poor whites"

3. Which of the following was the primary reason for the wave of Irish immigration in the 1840s?

   (A) Desire to buy land
   (B) Desire for economic opportunity
   (C) Widespread starvation in the wake of the potato famine
   (D) Religious oppression
   (E) Political oppression from Great Britain

Answers and Explanations

1. **C** Thomas Edison did not invent the incandescent lightbulb in 1879 but he created the first practical lightbulb and the electrical system to support it. All the other inventions date from this period and had a profound effect on the U.S. economy.
2. **B** Immigrants did not travel to the South because there was no industry and because all the jobs they might have taken in agriculture were filled by slaves.
3. **C** There is some truth in all five choices, but for thousands of Irish peasants, the most urgent reason to go to the United States was that they did not have enough food.

CHAPTER 13

NATIONAL EXPANSION AND SECTIONAL DIVISION, 1830–1850

INTRODUCTION

During the 20 years from 1830 to 1850, the United States continued to expand its territory. It fought a successful war of conquest against Mexico, gaining vast amounts of western and southwestern land in exchange for a cash payment. It admitted two of its largest states, Texas and California, into the Union. It reached a settlement with Great Britain that gave it control of the Oregon Country south of the present Canadian border.

People flowed westward in a steady stream to settle the new territory. Late in 1848 news reached the East that gold had been discovered in California in January. The number of westward migrants multiplied overnight as people dropped everything to grab a share of the gold.

The trail westward led through the Great Plains, which had been set aside as Native American territory. Native Americans had prospered on that land, hunting wild buffalo and migrating with the herds. The thousands of pioneers traveling west disrupted their lifestyle and decimated the buffalo population; travelers on the Oregon Trail killed the buffalo for food to sustain them on their journey west. At an 1851 conference the United States and the Native Americans reached an agreement highly favorable to the United States. The Native Americans of the Plains would confine themselves to certain areas rather than ranging freely, and the United States would pay them in food and trade goods in exchange.

As new states applied to enter the Union, Congress continued to be unable to resolve the issue of slavery. Southern states threatened to leave the Union if any measures favorable to abolition were passed. In the end, they allowed California to enter the Union as a free state only at the price of the Fugitive Slave Act of 1850, a law that established such harsh measures against escaped slaves that it turned many people in the North into antislavery activists.

TIMELINE

1830 Mexico bans further U.S. immigration to Texas, bans slavery in Texas.

1836 Siege of the Alamo; Texas wins independence from Mexico as "Lone Star Republic."

1844 James K. Polk elected president.

1845 John O'Sullivan coins the phrase "Manifest Destiny."

Texas admitted to United States; Mexico breaks off diplomatic relations with United States.

1846   Mexican War begins.

Wilmot Proviso defeated in Congress.

United States and Great Britain agree to divide Oregon at present-day Canadian border.

1847   Treaty of Guadalupe-Hidalgo ends Mexican War; United States gains territory in exchange for money.

1848   Zachary Taylor elected president; Free-Soil Party founded.

1849   California Gold Rush begins.

1850   Compromise of 1850; passage of Fugitive Slave Act of 1850.

Zachary Taylor dies in office; Millard Fillmore becomes president.

1851   Conference with Native American tribes of the Great Plains; settled on terms highly favorable to United States.

1853   Gadsden Purchase.

KEY TERMS

Compromise of 1850   a proposal by Henry Clay that California be admitted as a free state in exchange for the passage of a tougher Fugitive Slave Act

duress   force

entrepreneur   a person who goes into business for himself or herself

Free-Soil Party   a political party founded in 1848 to support and promote abolitionism

Fugitive Slave Act   a law passed in 1850 that drastically toughened the regulations dealing with slaves who had escaped to free states or territories

Gadsden Purchase   purchase of parts of present-day New Mexico and Arizona

Gold Rush of 1849   a massive movement westward in search of gold in California

Manifest Destiny   literally meaning "obvious fate"; a phrase used to justify U.S. expansion westward to the Pacific coast; basically, the belief that God meant the United States to have that land

Mexican Cession   lands ceded to the United States in the Treaty of Guadalupe-Hidalgo

secede   withdraw from membership in a group or confederation, in this case the United States

Underground Railroad   organization of people who conducted escaping slaves north to freedom

wagon trains   large groups of covered wagons drawn by oxen or very strong horses

Wilmot Proviso   a defeated amendment to a congressional bill proposing that no slavery be allowed in territory acquired in the Mexican War

"Manifest Destiny"

Ever since the founding of the British colonies in North America, people had looked westward for new opportunities. By 1840 the original 13 colonies had expanded halfway across the continent. In 1845 the magazine editor John O'Sullivan put into words what many people in the United States had been thinking: it was obvious that the United States should expand to fill the borders of North America between Canada and Mexico, all the way to the Pacific Ocean.

> The American claim is by the right of our manifest destiny to overspread and to possess the whole of the continent which Providence has given us for the development of the great experiment of liberty.

People who agreed with O'Sullivan's view of **Manifest Destiny** ignored the fact that others already claimed some of the Western lands. A vast tract of land called the Oregon Country, for example, was claimed in part by Native Americans, Russia, Great Britain, Spain, and the United States. In the Rush-Bagot Agreement of 1817 the United States and Britain had agreed to occupy the territory jointly. At that point Russia and Spain gave up their claims. The rights of the Native Americans, as always, were irrelevant as far as the United States and the European powers were concerned.

In 1846 President James K. Polk, despite his earlier campaign promises, signed an agreement with Britain, dividing the Oregon Country along the present U.S.–Canadian border. The British moved north of the line, and the United States took control of the southern portion, renaming it the Oregon Territory. The territory eventually became the present-day states of Oregon, Washington, and Idaho.

The fur trade thrived in the Northwest until about 1830, by which time the beaver population had been decimated and beaver fur was going out of fashion. When settlers began moving west to Oregon, they were able to take advantage of trails blazed by the Native Americans and the fur traders. An African American, James Beckworth, attempting to find his way across the Sierra Nevadas, discovered a route to California that later was traveled by thousands of pioneers heading west. Marcus and Narcissa Whitman, missionaries who planned to build a school for the Cayuse Native Americans who lived in the territory, became the first white family to settle permanently in Oregon in 1836.

Seven years later the first **wagon trains** undertook the trek along the Oregon Trail. Families traveling west would wait in Independence, Missouri, until a large group of families had gathered. The wagons then would set off together. This ensured that no pioneer family would be without help if people fell ill or a pregnant woman went into labor. A large group of wagons was also less vulnerable to attack by thieves or Native American raiders.

This map shows the route the pioneers traveled. There were so many of them that the ruts their wagon wheels dug in the Great Plains are still visible today.

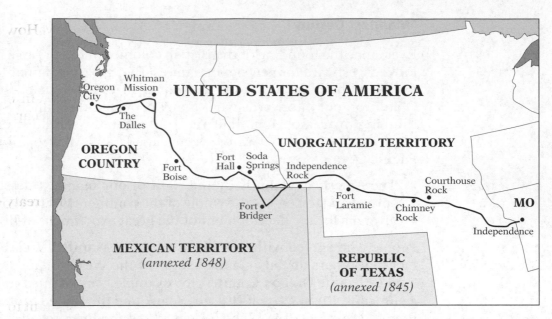

The Oregon Trail

Travelers left Independence in May so that they would be sure to get across the mountains by October, before the heavy snows made travel impossible. This meant traveling 12 hours a day. The pioneers faced many obstacles. The weather was capricious, sometimes stiflingly hot and sometimes pouring with rain for days on end. Covered wagons provided little shelter. Illness, which came frequently, spread quickly from one family to another in the close conditions of the camps. Many women were pregnant when the journey began and had to give birth out in the open along the trail, since there were no hospitals or doctors; many of them died of complications from the births. The Whitmans were only one of many families who adopted children who had been orphaned on the Oregon Trail. Apart from replenishing the stock of fresh water and shooting game to cook and eat, it was not possible to restock any supplies during the journey. If people had not brought along what they needed, they had to find ways to manage without it.

However, the pioneers were on the whole a tough and enduring group of people. Thousands of them reached Oregon safely between 1840 and 1860.

The Republic of Texas

At that time most of present-day Texas belonged to Mexico. However, this had not stopped U.S. citizens from settling in Texas, particularly after 1821, when Mexico won its independence from Spain. The Mexican government held out inducements to U.S. settlers, offering them low prices on land and reminding them that as residents of Mexico they would not have to pay U.S. taxes. From Mexico's point of view, a large U.S. population in northeast Texas was desirable for more than one reason. The settlers from the United States would draw the fire of the Apache and Comanche raiders to whom northeastern Texas was home, and once the settlers were living in Texas, they presumably would side with Mexico against any attempted U.S. invasion.

By 1830 so many U.S. settlers had come to Texas that they outnumbered the Mexican Texans two to one. Worried that those Anglo-American settlers would be loyal to U.S. interests, Mexico banned further immigration from the United States and prohibited slavery in the territory. However, both bans proved unenforceable.

In 1833 General Antonio Lopez de Santa Anna was elected president of Mexico. He soon changed his presidency into a military dictatorship. Residents of Texas rebelled against Santa Anna's government. In 1835 Texans captured the town of San Antonio. In early 1836 Santa Anna arrived at the head of an army to subdue the revolt. The Mexicans laid siege to the Alamo, a fort near San Antonio where the Texans were holding their position. On March 6, Santa Anna's army battled for and won control of the fort. In April, led by Sam Houston, the Texans fought the Mexicans again near the San Jacinto River. They took Santa Anna prisoner and forced him to sign a treaty granting Texas its independence. Sam Houston was elected the first president of the Republic of Texas in 1836. Mexico, pointing out that Santa Anna had signed the treaty under **duress,** refused to recognize Texan independence.

In 1837, Texas applied to the U.S. Congress for statehood. Since Northerners in Congress did not want to admit another slaveholding state to the Union and even some Southern congressmen were hesitant to take a step that would infuriate the Mexican government, Texas remained an independent republic from 1836 until 1845.

The Mexican War

In 1844 the Democrat James K. Polk, a former governor of Tennessee, became president. He was elected on a campaign promise to annex Texas and on his outspoken support of western expansion in general. Henry Clay and James Birney, Polk's opponents, ignored the issue of Texas in their campaigns. Polk won by a narrow margin of the popular vote.

The admission of Texas as a state in 1845 proved that Congress had been right to hesitate; Mexico immediately broke off diplomatic relations with the United States, claiming that Texas was a Mexican state and that its annexation amounted to a declaration of war against Mexico. In addition, Texas claimed that its southern border was the Rio Grande, whereas Mexico insisted that the border of the Mexican state of Texas was the Rio Nueces, which lay substantially east of the Rio Grande and was supported by most documentation. The U.S. government inherited this border dispute when it granted Texas statehood.

President Polk hoped to avoid war with Mexico. His first step was to offer Mexico a total of $30 million for both Texas and California if Mexico would accept the Rio Grande as the border. John Slidell, Polk's envoy, met a frosty reception in Mexico City. Mexico underwent a change of regime in December 1845, and Slidell soon discovered that negotiation with the new president, Mariano Paredes, would not be possible.

President Polk stationed troops in the disputed territory, and on April 24, 1846, Mexican forces crossed the Rio Grande and attacked General Zachary Taylor's troops. By May 9 the U.S. forces had driven the Mexicans back across the river. When the news arrived in Washington, Congress officially declared war on Mexico.

Fighting continued until 1847. General Winfield Scott and his troops eventually ended the war by laying siege to Mexico City. The Mexicans were forced to surrender on September 14. The following February, the two sides signed the Treaty of Guadalupe-Hidalgo. The terms of the treaty gave the United States a vast tract of land known as the **Mexican Cession** that included the present-day states of California, Nevada, and Utah and parts of Arizona, New Mexico, Colorado, and Wyoming. Mexico also gave up its claims to Texas. In return, the United States paid Mexico $15 million and agreed to pay all damages claimed by U.S. citizens against the Mexican government. The United States also assured all Mexicans living in the Mexican Cession that they would be granted full U.S. citizenship.

Treaty of Guadalupe-Hidalgo, 1848	
U.S. Grants to Mexico	**Mexico Grants to United States**
• $15 million	• Mexican Cession, including present-day states of California, Nevada, and Utah and parts of Arizona, New Mexico, Colorado, and Wyoming
• Payment of all claims made by U.S. citizens against Mexican government	• All claims to Texas
• Full U.S. citizenship to all Mexicans living within borders of Mexican Cession	• Recognition of Rio Grande as border between Mexico and United States

The Election of 1848

When Texas applied for admission to the United States as a slaveholding state, Congress once again faced a disturbance of the balance of power between Northern and Southern states. Congress agreed to admit Texas as a slave state, adding that the Texas state legislature could divide the territory into as many as five states (all slaveholding). Congress also extended westward the line of the Missouri Compromise, north of which no slavery was permitted. In 1846, as Congress considered the possibility of purchasing territory from Mexico, Representative David Wilmot of Pennsylvania suggested the **Wilmot Proviso,** which stipulated that slavery would not be allowed in any of this new territory. Southerners threatened to **secede** from the Union over the Wilmot proviso, and after heated debate it was defeated.

This dispute over the slave or free status of the formerly Mexican territory became the key issue in the 1848 presidential election. Opponents of slavery formed the **Free-Soil Party,** represented by Martin Van Buren and Charles Francis Adams. The Whigs chose Zachary Taylor and Millard Fillmore as their candidates. The Mexican War hero Taylor was a slaveholder, but he did not comment on the issue of slavery during the campaign. Free-Soil candidates probably swung the election to Taylor, and in addition they won several seats in the House of Representatives. The Free-Soil victories ensured that abolitionist forces would continue to have a voice in the government.

California Gold

At first the Western territories acquired from Mexico had no organized governments. Congress was too busy debating the issue of slavery in the territories to turn its attention to other issues of government. That situation changed abruptly when the following statement appeared in a newspaper:

> GOLD MINE FOUND.—In the newly made raceway of the Saw Mill recently erected by Captain Sutter, on the American Fork, gold has been found in considerable quantities.

The discovery of gold at Sutter's Mill in January 1848 touched off a nation-wide craze. Men gathered their possessions and headed west in what became known as the **Gold Rush of 1849.** People traveled to California not only from the East but from other continents. Prospectors were American, African American, Chinese, and Mexican. Many were young men who had no ties at home and thus found it easy to drop everything in the search for quick riches. Western society during the gold rush was wild and lawless. Crime was rife. Miners and prospectors forced Native Americans off land that held the promise of rich gold strikes. Racial discrimination against miners who were not U.S. citizens abounded.

In the wake of the "forty-niners," many **entrepreneurs** traveled west. They could see that there were fortunes to be made in providing services such as saloons, restaurants, boardinghouses, laundry, and stores for the miners. In this way the Gold Rush gave rise to one of the classic elements of U.S. culture—blue jeans. Levi Strauss, an immigrant tailor from Germany, made a fortune on his sturdy denim work trousers, which featured a diagonal twill weave, in essence an extra layer of threads in the fabric. This made them hold up better than any other clothing under the tough working conditions in the gold mines. Levis, as they are called, are probably the most commonly worn garment in the United States today.

The Compromise of 1850

California's application for statehood in 1850 threw Congress into turmoil. Southern leaders refused to consider allowing another free state into the Union. They did not want the balance of power disturbed unless it was going to be in their favor, and California's leaders had made it clear that they did not want to permit slavery in their state.

Once again, it was up to Henry Clay to find a way to get both sides to meet halfway. Clay offered the **Compromise of 1850** to Congress. It proposed an exchange by which California would enter the Union as a free state but Congress would agree to sign a new **Fugitive Slave Act** into law.

That act would force all U.S. citizens in free and slaveholding states alike to help slave owners recover escaped slaves. At that time any slave who set foot over the border of a free state automatically gained his or her freedom. The new act would change that. A slave's status would travel with him or her. The act also stated that even if the slave had escaped long before 1850, the former owner could reclaim the slave. This meant that all free African Americans were in danger of losing their freedom. The act called for special commissions to hear cases of disputed ownership, denied African Americans the right to testify in their own defense, and set a higher fee for the commissioners for cases in which the slave owner won.

The passage of the Fugitive Slave Act had several effects. Hundreds of thousands of free African Americans afraid of being returned to slavery crossed the northern border into Canada to escape the reach of U.S. laws. The **Underground Railroad** became more active than ever before. And thousands of whites living in free states, who had always been inclined to oppose slavery, became active abolitionists when the government tried to force them to collaborate in the Fugitive Slave Act.

The Gadsden Purchase

In 1853 Secretary of War Jefferson Davis suggested to the ambassador to Mexico, James Gadsden, that Gadsden offer Mexico $10 million for a long, narrow piece of land between Texas and California, south of the Gila River. In need of cash after losing the war, Mexico agreed to the offer. On December 30, 1853, the deal was signed. The **Gadsden Purchase** added one more piece to the giant jigsaw puzzle of the United States. Today this land is part of the states of New Mexico and Arizona.

The Fate of the Plains Tribes

U.S. expansion meant that the "permanent Indian frontier" guaranteed by the Jackson administration became a fiction. First, the pioneers migrating from east to west along the Oregon and California trails had to travel through Native American territory. Native Americans were willing to accept this as long as the settlers were only passing through rather than claiming any of the land for themselves. Native Americans and settlers even traded with one another along the journey, and few migrating pioneers were killed in Native American raids or killed any Native Americans.

The Native Americans of the Plains of central North America had managed to remain independent and prosperous largely because of horses. Spanish explorers had brought the first horses to North America. Once the Native Americans learned to breed and ride horses, they had a much easier time chasing and killing buffalo and following the buffalo herds when they moved. This migratory lifestyle suited the people of the Plains very well.

Once the United States acquired clear title to the Oregon Country and to California and Texas, the Permanent Indian Frontier was no longer the western limit of the United States. Native American territory lay in the middle, between two sections of settled country. Migrating pioneers replenished their food supplies by killing buffalo they encountered on the journey west. Seeking safety, the buffalo herds changed their patterns of migration and grazing, leaving the Native Americans no choice but to follow the herds. This led tribes to violate one another's hunting grounds in the interest of survival, and intertribal warfare resulted.

The stream of westward migration only grew with time. Between 1849 and 1850, more than 50,000 people traveled across the plains to California, many in search of gold. That amount of traffic decimated the buffalo herds and put the continued existence of the Sioux tribes in peril. Conflicts between Native Americans and settlers grew as the whites infringed on Native American land. At the urging of concerned Indian agents of the federal government, the White House agreed to hold a conference with the Plains tribes, in which both sides would come to an agreement about compensation to the Native Americans for their damages and access across the plains for the pioneers.

The conference was held in 1851 near Fort Laramie in present-day Wyoming. More than 10,000 Native Americans from various Plains tribes attended. Colonel David Mitchell, speaking for the United States, outlined the terms of the proposal. The Native Americans would agree to cease intertribal warfare; each tribe would promise to remain within its own mutually agreed borders. The Native Americans also would agree that all westbound immigrants could travel through the Plains in safety. They would agree to allow the U.S. government to build forts and roads in the Plains. In return, the United States would pay each tribe $50,000 in food and trade goods for the next 50 years. The U.S. government was proceeding on the theory that the Native American tribes of the Plains by that time would have become successful farmers.

The treaty had the following effects: It deprived the Native Americans of their customary ability to range freely over the Plains, making it more difficult for them to hunt and making them more dependent on charity from the U.S. government. It moved most tribes out of what would become Kansas and Nebraska into the Dakotas, Montana, Wyoming, the foothills of the Rocky Mountains, and Oklahoma. It deprived Native Americans of their sovereignty over the Great Plains, which had been promised to them and their heirs in perpetuity. It also hastened the end of the hunting culture of the Plains; with continued migration from east to west and the prospect of the construction of roads and forts, it was clear that the great buffalo herds were doomed.

REVIEW QUESTIONS

1. Between 1830 and 1850, the United States gained land that would become all the following present-day states EXCEPT:

   (A) California
   (B) North Dakota
   (C) Washington
   (D) Oregon
   (E) Texas

2. The Gold Rush of 1849 had all the following immediate effects on California society EXCEPT:

   (A) The population became more ethnically diverse.
   (B) Many entrepreneurs made their fortunes from the miners.
   (C) The population grew by many thousands.
   (D) More and more people turned to farming to make a living.
   (E) Society became violent and lawless.

3. The Fugitive Slave Act of 1850 made it legal to do which of the following?

   (A) Prevent an African American from testifying in his or her own defense
   (B) Help a slave escape to a free state
   (C) Become a free person simply by crossing the border into a free state
   (D) Join the Free-Soil Party and speak out in favor of abolition
   (E) Execute any slave who was proved to have escaped from his or her owner

Answers and Explanations

1. **B** The United States gained Oregon and Washington in an 1846 agreement with Britain, Texas became a state in 1846, and California was part of the Mexican Cession of 1848. The Dakota Territory continued to belong, at least in name, to the Native Americans of the Plains.

2. **D** People traveled to California during the Gold Rush because they wanted to get rich from gold, not by farming. Because so many people traveled west, the California population grew rapidly. Because most of those people were single men competing fiercely with one another for riches, crime rates were high.

3. **A** The act specifically stated that African Americans accused of being escaped slaves could not testify before the commission hearing the case. People had every right to join the Free-Soil Party without reference to the Fugitive Slave Act. The U.S. government never passed a law that permitted the execution of escaped slaves. Choices B and C are the opposite of what the act required.

CHAPTER 14

A HOUSE DIVIDED, 1820–1860

INTRODUCTION

The issue of slavery continued to divide the nation. None of Henry Clay's famous compromises had altered the basic situation: in the South there was a system of enforced labor, based on racial discrimination, in which the workers were paid no wages and had no rights. Just as Northerners were determined to end slavery throughout the nation, Southerners refused to consider changing the economic and social system that had made them wealthy. Instead, they wanted to spread their system westward.

The Western states showed no desire to allow slavery. California insisted on entering the Union as a free state, as did Oregon. When Senator Stephen Douglas of Illinois proposed that the Kansas and Nebraska territories be allowed to decide for themselves whether they wanted to be slaveholding or free, he provoked outraged reactions on all sides. Northerners were furious because the Kansas-Nebraska Act overturned the Missouri Compromise, which had outlawed slavery in the territories. Southerners were angry because they thought Douglas should have fought to make Kansas a slave territory.

In the Dred Scott Case of 1857, the Supreme Court declared that a slave was a slave no matter where he or she traveled, even into free territory. The Court also stated that since slaves were property and the Fifth Amendment protected property rights, any law prohibiting slavery anywhere was unconstitutional.

Many people took action on both sides of the issue. Missouri "Border Ruffians" stormed into Kansas Territory before an election and illegally voted a proslavery legislature into office. John Brown and his supporters tried unsuccessfully to start an armed slave uprising in Harpers Ferry. Harriet Beecher Stowe published *Uncle Tom's Cabin,* a dramatic story that opened the eyes of Northerners to the corrupting influence of slavery on everyone it touched. And in Illinois a self-educated lawyer named Abraham Lincoln decided to run for national office.

To Southerners, Lincoln's election to the White House in 1860 was the final straw. Seven Southern states rapidly seceded from the Union, declaring themselves the Confederate States of America.

TIMELINE

1845   *Narrative of the Life of Frederick Douglass* published.

1850   Fugitive Slave Act passed.

1852   *Uncle Tom's Cabin* published.

   Franklin Pierce elected president.

1854   Kansas-Nebraska Act.

   Republican Party formed.

1855   Kansas elections.

1856   Pottawatomie Massacre.

James Buchanan elected president.

Dred Scott v. Sanford.

1858   Lincoln-Douglas debates.

1859   Raid on Harpers Ferry.

1860   Abraham Lincoln elected president.

KEY TERMS

arsenal   place for the manufacture and storage of weapons and military equipment

Border Ruffians   nickname given to proslavery Missouri men who crossed the border into Kansas to commit crimes against Free-Staters

bounty hunter   one who was paid to track down and capture escaped slaves and force them to return to the South

Confederate States of America   also CSA or "the Confederacy": a group of 11 slaveholding states that seceded from the United States in 1860 and 1861

popular sovereignty   the right of the people of a state or territory to organize their own government, specifically to choose for themselves whether their territory will allow slavery

Pottawatomie Massacre   brutal murder of five proslavery men at Pottawatomie Creek settlement in Kansas; led by John Brown

Republican Party   a political party founded in 1854 to support candidates who opposed the expansion of slavery

sectionalism   patriotic identification with one's state or region rather than one's nation

Sectional Division

As time went on, it became more and more clear that people in the United States felt more loyalty to their state and region than they did to the nation as a whole. They thought of themselves as Virginians or New Yorkers, Northerners or Southerners, not simply as Americans.

Sectionalism continued to thrive because of the split in attitudes toward slavery. The Northern states had outlawed it in Revolutionary War days or soon afterward, and the Southern states were determined to maintain it. Each of the two sections of the country was determined to force the other to give in. More than once the South threatened to secede from the United States if certain antislavery measures were passed. The issue of slavery began to crowd out all other concerns as the nation moved toward a crisis.

The nation was nearly broken apart when California asked to be admitted to the Union as a free state. Debate raged in Congress. Senator Henry Foote of Mississippi even leveled a gun across the chamber at Senator Thomas Hart Benton of Missouri, who would not back down even in the face of that threat. "Stand out of the way and let the assassin fire!" he thundered as other senators hurried to intervene.

By that time Henry Clay, veteran of so many congressional debates and author of so many compromises, was a tired old man of 73. Clay urged his colleagues to try to come to an agreement for the sake of the nation as a whole. South Carolina Senator John C. Calhoun, who had been Andrew Jackson's vice president and who was even more frail and ill than Clay, scorned Clay's suggestion. "Let the states agree to part in peace," he wrote. "If you are unwilling that we should part in peace, tell us so, and we shall know what to do."

Daniel Webster of Massachusetts was the next to speak. He supported Clay, urging the senators to preserve the Union. "There can be no such thing as peaceable secession," Webster warned the Senate. "Peaceable secession is an utter impossibility."

Both John Calhoun and President Zachary Taylor died in 1850. The new president, Millard Fillmore, agreed with Webster and Clay that it was more important to preserve the Union than to abolish or even check the spread of slavery. Under the Compromise of 1850, California entered the Union as a free state and a new, harsh Fugitive Slave Act was passed (see Chapter 13).

The Abolitionist Movement

To the chagrin of Southerners, the passage of the Fugitive Slave Act had the effect of energizing the abolitionist movement in the North. Most Northerners opposed the institution of slavery, but many had taken no active steps against it.

In 1845 an autobiography called *Narrative of the Life of Frederick Douglass* appeared in print. This book belonged to the genre known as slave narratives: stories of the brutal repression from which slaves such as Douglass had been skillful and lucky enough to escape. In the years after the publication of the *Narrative*, Douglass became well known as a public speaker, most frequently on the issue of abolition. Reading his book convinced many people that slavery was evil.

In 1852 Harriet Beecher Stowe shocked the reading public with the epic novel *Uncle Tom's Cabin*. Stowe's novel included a wide variety of characters and viewpoints: male and female, free and enslaved, enlightened and bigoted, young and old, educated and ignorant, Northern and Southern. The novel reveals the evil effects of the slave system on everyone it touches: it corrupts people who are good and noble in other respects into believing that Africans are not fully human.

In the novel's most memorable sequence, the slave Eliza escapes with her baby, determined to cross the Ohio River into freedom. When she reaches the river, it is choked by great drifting chunks of ice. With courage born of desperation, Eliza leaps into the river. The **bounty hunters** who have been chasing her stop on the riverbank, watching incredulously as she jumps from one ice block to the next until she is safely across.

In the United States, Stowe's novel outsold every book except the Bible in the years leading up to the Civil War. It was translated into several languages and made her an international celebrity. It opened the eyes of many Northerners to the realities of slavery as portrayed in its pages and reinforced the abolitionist beliefs of many more. The novel was banned in the South; Southerners who read it dismissed it as the ravings of a crazy woman.

New Political Parties

As the battle between the proslavery and antislavery factions continued and the South seemed to be gaining more and more ground, Northerners formed new political parties to combat the spread of slavery and maintain their power base in Washington. The Free-Soil Party, formed in 1848, did not win any electoral votes in the presidential election. However, the party supported a number of candidates for congressional seats, several of whom were elected.

In 1852, the Free-Soilers tried for the White House once again. Their candidate was John Hale of New Hampshire, running against the Democrat Franklin Pierce and the Whig General Winfield Scott, who had been in command of the U.S. troops that had laid siege to Mexico City in 1847. Pierce won in a landslide of electoral votes, and the Free-Soilers gave up the struggle. The Whigs also accepted this defeat as final; they were never again to play a significant role in U.S. politics.

In 1854, the remnants of the Whig Party and the Free-Soil Party joined antislavery members of the Know-Nothing and Democratic parties. This group formed a strong coalition of men determined to end the expansion of slavery in the United States. They called their new party the **Republican Party**. In 1856 they supported John C Frémont for president. Frémont, a career army officer and a topographical engineer in peacetime, made a strong showing, but the Democratic candidate James Buchanan carried the South and thus won the presidency.

Kansas-Nebraska Act

In 1854 Senator Stephen Douglas of Illinois, soon to go down in history as Abraham Lincoln's most famous political opponent, introduced the Kansas-Nebraska Act into Congress. The act proposed the following:

- That the unorganized territory north of the 37th parallel and west of the Missouri River be divided into two sections, one called Nebraska and the other called Kansas
- That the territories set up their own governments on the basis of **popular sovereignty**
- That once the territories were organized, Congress would proceed with plans for a transcontinental railroad

Popular sovereignty meant that the people who settled Kansas and Nebraska could decide for themselves how their governments would work. As everyone in Congress knew, the real meaning of this proposal was that the territories would decide for themselves whether they would be slaveholding or free states. This provision of the act violated the Missouri Compromise of 1820, which had banned slavery in the territory north of Missouri's southern border (see Chapter 10 and the map below).

Nicknamed the "Little Giant" for the combination of his short stature and forceful personality, Douglas was a native of Vermont who had settled in Illinois and first been elected to Congress in 1842. He championed the issues of westward expansion and states' rights. In Douglas's view, the federal government had no right to interfere in the issue of whether a territory or state should be slaveholding or free; the people of that state or territory should decide for themselves. He also was a strong supporter of a transcontinental railroad, which had been stalled because of the slavery issue.

The Kansas-Nebraska Act became law in 1854. Douglas had hoped it would be received as a compromise, since he knew that Kansas probably would be settled by slavers from the neighboring Southern states and Nebraska by abolitionists from the North. He was dismayed to discover that it only divided Congress and the nation further. People argued against the repeal of the

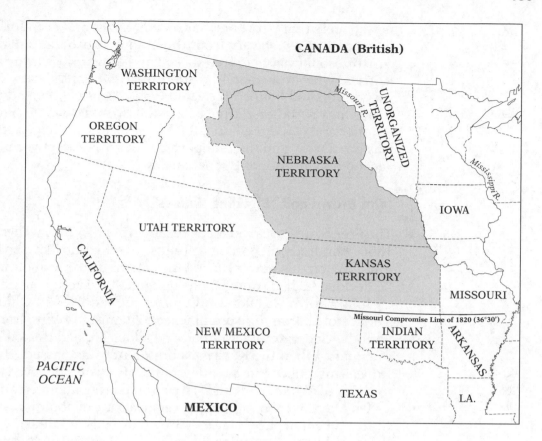

Missouri Compromise on various grounds. Some were abolitionists on principle and wanted to stop the spread of slavery. Some argued that if slavery were allowed in the territories, white people no longer would migrate west in search of jobs; businesses would never pay wages when they could force slaves to work for nothing. For the same reason, white workers already settled in the West would be forced out.

Both abolitionist and proslavery groups urged people to move into the territories. Both sides knew that if they could gain a majority among the population of Kansas and Nebraska, the votes on the slavery issue would be decided in their favor. The issue was moot in Nebraska Territory; it was far enough north that it was settled, as Douglas had foreseen, by Northerners who had no desire to own slaves. Southerners did not travel far enough north to create a powerful voice in Nebraska politics, and an antislavery legislature was elected easily.

In Kansas the situation was very different. Although Kansas did not have the right climate for growing cotton, and therefore few Southerners seriously intended to extend slavery into that territory, Southern politicians were determined to enlarge their political base and acquire more senators and representatives who would vote their way in Congress.

The election that would choose the Kansas legislature was to be held in March 1855. Just before the election, 5,000 proslavery Missouri voters marched into Kansas. Those "**Border Ruffians**" had no right to vote there since they were not residents of the territory, but they were armed and violent. They were ready to kill anyone at the polling places who tried to prevent them from voting. The result was that a proslavery legislature was elected. That legislature immediately passed laws making it a crime to criticize slavery, banning newspapers that wrote antislavery editorials, and even forbidding preachers to speak against slavery from the pulpit. Those flagrant violations of their constitutional rights to free speech and a free press infuriated the people of Kansas, who immediately elected their own antislavery legislature, which was dominated by the Free State Party. Kansas now had two governments. It was only a matter of time before the two sides would have to confront one another and settle the issue of which was to run the territory. The governor was proslavery and thus supported the proslavery government, and this was accepted by President Buchanan.

John Brown and "Bleeding Kansas"

The Free State Party had made the town of Lawrence its headquarters. In May 1856, hundreds of Border Ruffians marched on Lawrence and sacked the town. When this news reached the ears of the fiery abolitionist John Brown, he decided he had waited long enough to take action against the slavers.

John Brown was born in Connecticut and lived in Ohio and upstate New York before becoming a prominent abolitionist in Pennsylvania. He had worked with the Underground Railroad and all his life had treated African Americans as equals. When the Kansas-Nebraska Act was passed, Brown foresaw that Kansas might become a battleground. He always believed that only an armed uprising of abolitionists and slaves would bring about emancipation.

On May 23, 1856, Brown led a small group of abolitionists to Pottawatomie Creek, a center of proslavers. Brown and his small army kidnapped five of them and hacked their bodies to pieces. The **Pottawatomie Massacre** outraged Southerners and gave the territory the nickname "Bleeding Kansas." In the Senate, Charles Sumner of Massachusetts delivered a scathing speech blaming the violence on the slavers who had not been content to accept the Missouri Compromise. Two days later Congressman Preston Brooks of South Carolina retaliated by accosting Sumner in the Senate chamber and attempting to beat him to death. That murderous attack polarized people further; many who had been neutral were converted to fervent abolitionists, whereas voters in Brooks's home district sent him gifts to show their approval.

In Kansas, the Free State Legislature broke up in July 1856, convinced that since the majority of the people were antislavery, the principle of popular sovereignty eventually would make Kansas a free territory and then a free state. This indeed happened. The voters elected abolitionists to the legislature, and Kansas drafted a free-state constitution in 1859.

Dred Scott Decision

In 1857, the Supreme Court took a stand on the issue of slave status. A Missouri slave named Dred Scott had traveled with his owner to Illinois and Minnesota, which were free territories. Scott sued for his freedom on the grounds that he had lived on free soil for four years. The Court ruled against him, stating that slave status traveled with the person and that Scott had not carried free status back to Missouri with him when he returned there. Chief Justice Roger Taney added that he believed the framers of the Constitution had perceived Africans as "an inferior order, and unfit associates for the white race" and had never intended the Constitution to apply to them. Taney went on to argue that since slaves were property and the Fifth Amendment prevented anyone from being deprived of property without due process of law, any law against slavery was unconstitutional. The Missouri Compromise had been unconstitutional because it prevented a person from taking his or her property (i.e., slaves) into free territory. In practice, this decision meant that Congress had no right to ban slavery anywhere; it had no power to contain the spread of slavery westward or even into the North.

Dred Scott v. Sanford had several immediate effects. First, newly elected President James Buchanan refused to recognize the free-state government in Kansas. Second, Westerners and Northerners alike reacted with dismay to the idea that slavery could expand throughout the country. The West became increasingly closely connected with the North both economically and politically; thus, the South grew more isolated from the rest of the nation.

Frederick Douglass summed up the antislavery reaction to the Dred Scott decision:

> I ask, then, any man to read the Constitution, and tell me where, if he can, in what particular that instrument affords the slightest sanction of slavery? . . .
>
> This very attempt to blot out forever the hopes of an enslaved people may be one necessary link in the chain of events preparatory to the downfall and complete overthrow of the whole slave system.

The Lincoln-Douglas Debates

In 1858, one of the most important figures in U.S. history appeared on the national political scene. Abraham Lincoln, a self-educated Illinois lawyer, had served one term in the House of Representatives, but until now he had not been a nationally known figure. He returned to politics over the question of slavery, which he opposed, stating plainly that "no man is good enough to govern another without that other's consent." At the Republican convention of 1858, Lincoln gave one of the most famous speeches of his career.

> "A house divided against itself cannot stand." I believe this government cannot endure permanently half slave and half free. I do not expect the Union to be dissolved—I do not expect the house to fall—but I do expect it will cease to be divided. It will become all one thing, or all the other.

The Republican candidate Lincoln ran against the Democratic candidate Stephen Douglas. The two held a series of seven debates between August and October 1858. They argued the important issue of the day—slavery—at length in each appearance. Both men defended their positions on the Dred Scott decision, the theory of popular sovereignty, the Compromise of 1850, and the expansion of slavery. Huge crowds turned out to hear the two men speak. In the end, Douglas defeated Lincoln by a slim margin of votes. However, he soon would lose to Lincoln in a much more important race.

Harpers Ferry

On October 16, 1859, John Brown struck what many people referred to afterward as the first blow of the Civil War. Brown left Kansas and came east with the intention of raising an African-American army. His belief in the power of arms to end slavery speedily was unaltered. He captured the interest and excitement of many men, but during the months before he was ready to take action, many of his supporters grew uneasy or lost faith in Brown.

During the night of October 16, Brown and his small remaining band of followers seized the federal **arsenal** at Harpers Ferry, Virginia (today it is within the borders of West Virginia), and took 60 hostages. Brown was devastated when no slaves came to the aid of his army. Within 36 hours the Virginia militia, led by Colonel Robert E. Lee, surrounded the arsenal, killed many of Brown's men, and compelled the rest to surrender. On December 2, 1859, John Brown was hanged as a traitor. Henry David Thoreau spoke for all enslaved Africans and abolitionists when he wrote that Brown had been "a brave and humane man." Southerners, of course, had the opposite reaction. To them, Brown was a terrorist whose act amounted to a declaration of war on them and their way of life. In response to this the South rebuilt its militia system, and many began to see the divisions as irreconcilable.

The Election of 1860

In 1860 the Republicans nominated Abraham Lincoln for president. The Democrats, for the first time in many years, were not agreed on a favorite candidate. The Democratic convention nominated Stephen Douglas, but Southerners found him too moderate. They nominated John Breckinridge to run against Douglas and Lincoln.

People cast their ballots along strictly geographical lines. The deep South voted for Breckinridge, and the Pacific coastal states, Midwest, and Northeast voted for Lincoln. Constitutional Party candidate John Bell of Tennessee won in Virginia, Tennessee, and Kentucky, but this accounted for fewer than 6,000 votes. Stephen Douglas carried only the state of Missouri, although his total popular vote was only 500,000 fewer than what Lincoln received (see the electoral map below).

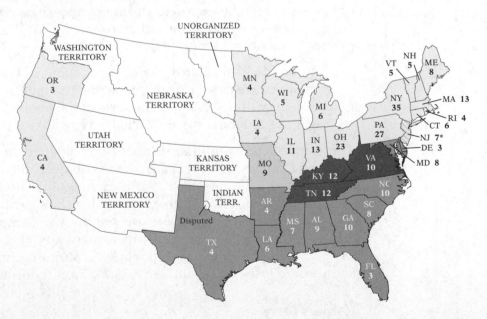

Candidate	Party	Electoral Vote	Popular Vote	Percentage of Popular Vote
☐ Lincoln	Republican	180	1,865,593	39.8
◻ Douglas	Northern Democrat	12	1,382,713	29.5
◼ Breckinridge	Southern Democrat	72	848,356	18.1
■ Bell	Constitutional Union	39	592,906	12.6

*New Jersey cast four electoral votes for Lincoln and three for Douglas.

Lincoln became president because the proslavery faction had not agreed to support a single candidate, instead splintering its vote between two candidates. Although Lincoln had stated publicly and repeatedly that he had neither the constitutional authority nor the desire to abolish slavery in the states where it already existed, Southerners hated him. Days after his election, South Carolina seceded from the Union. Alabama, Florida, Georgia, Louisiana, Mississippi, and Texas followed in rapid succession. Those states soon drew up a constitution for the **Confederate States of America** and elected Jefferson Davis of Mississippi as their president. President James Buchanan did not know what to do and decided to leave the problem to the incoming President Lincoln.

REVIEW QUESTIONS

1. The immediate cause of Southern secession from the Union was

   (A) the raid on Harpers Ferry
   (B) the Pottawatomie Massacre
   (C) the election of Abraham Lincoln
   (D) the passage of the Kansas-Nebraska Act
   (E) the determination of Kansas to be a free state

2. In his opinion in the case of *Dred Scott v. Sanford,* Chief Justice Taney stated all the following EXCEPT:

   (A) The Fifth Amendment protected slaveowners' rights to their property.
   (B) The Missouri Compromise had been unconstitutional because it violated slaveowners' property rights.
   (C) The framers of the Constitution clearly had not intended the Constitution to apply to anyone of African descent.
   (D) Slave status did not depend on geography but traveled everywhere with a person who was a slave.
   (E) As long as society provided separate but equal opportunities to African slaves, it did not have to do anything more for them.

3. Why did Thoreau and other abolitionists praise John Brown?

   (A) They approved of using violence to change laws.
   (B) They looked forward eagerly to a war between North and South.
   (C) They wanted to see as many slavers killed as possible.
   (D) They admired his long history of helping African Americans and dealing fairly with them.
   (E) They felt that Brown had taken an appropriate revenge for Congressman Brooks's attack on Senator Sumner.

Answers and Explanations

1. **C** South Carolina seceded right after Lincoln's election. Choices A and B contributed to Southern dislike and distrust of the North, but the election of a Republican president was the immediate cause of secession.
2. **E** Choice E describes a doctrine that would become famous in a later Supreme Court case, *Plessy v. Ferguson.* In 1857, Africans were still slaves, and no Southerner was suggesting that they deserved equality.

3. **D** Before the Pottawatomie Massacre and the raid on Harpers Ferry, Brown had been a distinguished abolitionist. He had been a part of the Underground Railroad and had helped free African Americans and escaped slaves with food, money, and whatever else they needed. He had spoken out forcefully in favor of abolition. Northerners honored him for his career. Even those who deplored his violent acts agreed with his principles.

CHAPTER 15
THE CIVIL WAR, 1861–1865

INTRODUCTION

Few were surprised when the bitter sectional violence that had divided the nation escalated into an all-out war. The election of the Republican Abraham Lincoln had convinced many in the South that they would never succeed in their ambition to spread slavery throughout the nation. Eventually, 11 states would secede from the Union, forming the rival Confederate State of America.

The Confederacy faced many disadvantages at the start of the war. It was much smaller than the Union and had a much lower population of boys and young men who could serve in the military. The South had few factories, little heavy industry, and much less money than the North. However, it did have greatly superior generals. This fact alone made the Civil War last three years longer than it probably would have otherwise.

At first the South won a string of important victories. However, in 1863, when Confederate troops invaded the North and were defeated at Gettysburg, they lost all hope of winning the war. They would never penetrate into the Northern states again. The Battle of Gettysburg was lost on the same day that Vicksburg, Mississippi, fell to Union troops. The war dragged on for another year and a half, but in April 1865 the Confederacy surrendered to the Union.

The cost to both sides was heavy. An entire generation died on the battlefield or from wounds, disease, or starvation—more than 600,000 boys and young men. (This was roughly 20 times the number of soldiers who had died in all previous American wars combined.) There had been little fighting in the North, but many Southern towns and major cities had been battle sites and were largely or entirely in ruins. Railroad lines had to be rebuilt and mail service reestablished. Slaves freed by the Emancipation Proclamation found themselves homeless, with no jobs to go to. The defeated South felt a bitter hatred toward the Northerners, a destructive emotion that would flourish in the South for many decades to come and that found immediate expression in the assassination of President Lincoln by an emotionally unstable Southern sympathizer. Perhaps most daunting of all, the South would have to adjust to building a society that could function and prosper without slave labor.

TIMELINE

1861

April   Fall of Fort Sumter, South Carolina.

   Four more states secede from Union; West Virginia secedes from Virginia.

July   First Battle of Bull Run, Virginia (Battle of Manassas).

1862

February   Fall of Forts Lee and Donaldson, Tennessee.

April   Battle of Shiloh, Tennessee.

   Fall of New Orleans and Memphis.

September   Battle of Antietam, Maryland.

Lincoln issues preliminary Emancipation Proclamation.

November   Burnside replaces McClellan as commander of U.S. Army.

December   Battle of Fredericksburg, Maryland.

1863

January 1   Emancipation Proclamation frees all slaves in the Confederacy.

May   Battle of Chancellorsville, Virginia.

June   Siege of Vicksburg, Mississippi, begins.

July   Attack on Fort Wagner, South Carolina.

Battle of Gettysburg, Pennsylvania.

Battle of Vicksburg.

November   Lincoln gives Gettysburg Address.

1864

Battles of Wilderness, Spotsylvania, Cold Harbor.

August   Siege of Richmond, Virginia, begins.

September   Fall of Atlanta, Georgia.

October   Union victories in Shenandoah Valley.

November   Lincoln reelected.

Burning of Atlanta.

1865

April   Battle of Petersburg, Virginia.

Fall of Richmond.

Confederates surrender at Appomattox, Virginia.

Assassination of President Lincoln.

KEY TERMS

anachronism   something that properly belongs to a time long past

assassination   murder of a national leader

attrition   act of wearing down, exhausting, using up

casualties   those who die in battle

emancipation   freedom from slavery

enlist   sign up for military service voluntarily

reinforcements   fresh troops to replace those who have died or been discharged

serfdom   a system of enforced labor

shelled   fired on with heavy artillery

President Abraham Lincoln

Abraham Lincoln took office in circumstances no president before him had faced. Pressures bore in on Lincoln from all sides, urging him to compromise, give in, or let the South go its own way. The fact that Lincoln was married to Mary Todd, a Southern woman whose brothers were in the Confederate Army, made many people sneer that the president was clearly unfit to lead a war against the South. Despite all this, Lincoln never wavered in his conviction that slavery must not spread beyond the current slaveholding states or his determination to bring the Southern states back into the Union.

Like Andrew Jackson, Lincoln was born in poverty in a log cabin. He worked hard on his father's farm by day and read every book he could borrow by lamplight at night. At six feet four inches, he towered over most of the men of his day. Lincoln practiced law for some time before serving one term in Congress, then running for the Senate, and finally winning the presidency. In his series of debates with Stephen Douglas he proved that he was a powerful and eloquent public speaker; like future presidents Roosevelt, Kennedy, and Clinton, Lincoln also had a shrewd sense of humor that created a warm bond between him and the voters. Lincoln remains one of the greatest political thinkers and writers in U.S. history.

Strengths and Weaknesses of the North and the South

The strengths of the Union were obvious from the beginning. In terms of population, the Union was more than twice the size of the Confederacy—and one-third of the Confederate population were slaves. With a larger population, the North would have a larger fighting force, a greater pool from which to draw **reinforcements** and replace **casualties,** and more people who could take over essential noncombat jobs in industry. In resources, the North also had the advantage. It controlled well over 80 percent of the nation's material resources and its factories and industries. This meant that it could produce necessary uniforms, supplies, and weapons, without relying on foreign allies or going into debt. The North had about four times as much cash on deposit in banks as the South did. It commanded the loyalty of the federal navy, which was to prove a key weapon in the war; the South would have to build its own navy.

Perhaps most important, the South was fighting for a cause that was bound to lose. By outlawing slavery during the late 1700s and early 1800s, the North had moved with the times while the South refused to recognize that slavery had become an **anachronism**. For example, **serfdom** in Russia was dying out more or less peacefully just as the South was preparing to go to war in defense of slavery. Nevertheless, the strength of their belief was a motivating factor for many Southerners.

The South had few advantages. Southern leaders hoped for an alliance with Great Britain and France, which were two important buyers of Southern cotton. The South also had the most skilled military leaders. Robert E. Lee was so highly regarded that Lincoln asked him to take command of the Union Army. Torn between his loyalty to the United States and his opposition to secession on one side and his love for his native Virginia on the other, Lee refused. He resigned from the U.S. Army and soon found himself in command of the Confederate Army.

The Start of the War

In April 1861 the Confederates fired on Fort Sumter in Charleston Harbor in South Carolina. The Confederates had taken over federal arsenals and forts throughout the South. Fort Sumter refused to surrender, appealing to the White House for help when supplies began to run low. Lincoln notified the Confederacy that he was sending supplies for the fort but no troops or weapons. The Confederates called on the fort's commander to surrender. When he refused, the Confederates **shelled** the fort.

On April 15 the Union formally declared war. Lincoln called for 75,000 volunteer troops to put down the rebellion, although for only three-month enlistments, since Lincoln, like many others, thought it would be a short war. Virginia, North Carolina, Arkansas, and Tennessee immediately seceded from the Union rather than take up arms against the Confederacy. The mountainous region of western Virginia, where there was little support for slavery, soon seceded from Virginia and was granted statehood as West Virginia in 1863 (see the map below).

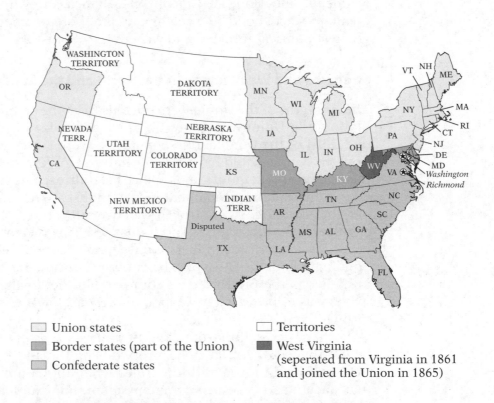

☐ Union states

▨ Border states (part of the Union)

▨ Confederate states

☐ Territories

■ West Virginia
(seperated from Virginia in 1861
and joined the Union in 1865)

On July 21, 1861, the first full-scale battle of the war began. The Confederate and Union troops faced each other at Bull Run Creek near Manassas, Virginia. The Union Army was winning the battle when Southern reinforcements arrived; seeing the fresh troops advancing on them, the Union soldiers began a disorganized, chaotic retreat toward Washington.

The First Battle of Bull Run had contradictory effects on the two sides. It made the South complacent; many Confederate soldiers went home after the battle, convinced the South would win the war easily. The South failed to take advantage of the victory by marching immediately on Washington, the Union capital; some historians believe that if that had happened, the war might have ended quickly in a Southern victory.

For the North, the loss was sobering. The Union had learned that in spite of its tremendous advantages, it would not be easy to defeat the Confederate army. Military training began in earnest in the North.

Goals and Strategies

	Union	**Confederacy**
GOALS	Restore the Union	Defend the Confederacy
STRATEGIES	• Capture Richmond, Virginia • Gain control of the Mississippi River • Use the federal navy to blockade the South • Divide the South geographically along the Mississippi, fighting a two-front war	• Outlast the North • If to their advantage, invade the North through the Shenandoah Valley

War over the Mississippi

Early in the war, General Winfield Scott advocated what came to be called the Anaconda Plan (see the chart above) to divide and conquer the Confederacy. At first this was rejected as too conservative, but over time it was vindicated and slowly adopted as the North's plan for the war. Almost immediately Lincoln adopted the blockade aspects.

In February 1862, Union troops captured Forts Henry and Donelson and the city of Nashville in Tennessee. Those successes accomplished three things. First, the North gained control of Kentucky and western Tennessee, a power base from which it could invade the western half of the South. Second, the Union troops gained confidence that ultimately the North would win the war. Third, a fierce, determined, and courageous Union officer named Ulysses S. Grant rose to prominence.

In the spring of 1862 General Grant marched his troops toward the Mississippi. They broke camp near a little church called Shiloh to wait for reinforcements. The Confederates took them by surprise with a fierce attack. Grant's troops were pushed back to the Tennessee River, but he refused to surrender. When Union reinforcements arrived during the night, the battle began again. After two days of terrible fighting, the Union won. This series of battles gave the North the advantage in the fight for control over the Mississippi River and the river valley. Both sides had lost thousands of men. The capture of New Orleans by the U.S. Navy, which steadily shelled the two forts that guarded the approach to the city until the Confederates surrendered, combined with later victories at Vicksburg, ultimately allowed the Union to cut the Confederacy in two.

The Army of the Potomac

While Grant led successful campaigns in the West and the South, General George McClellan led the Army of the Potomac against Confederate forces led by Johnston and Lee near the capital cities of Washington and Richmond. Although McClellan excelled at military discipline and trained his recruits well, he was not a capable or skilled commander. The Army of the Potomac won no decisive victories under his leadership. In September 1862 the Confederates won a second battle at Bull Run, and their forces moved north into Maryland.

The Battle of Antietam, fought near Antietam Creek in Maryland, stalled the Confederate attempt to invade the North. Two Union soldiers found a discarded piece of paper that turned out to be a copy of the Confederate battle plan. They immediately passed the information on to General McClellan. By the end of the daylong battle, more than 25,000 men lay dead on the battlefield. The Confederates had failed to win a victory on Union soil. They retreated to Virginia. That loss persuaded Great Britain not to enter the war on the side of the Confederacy.

The Emancipation Proclamation

At the start of 1863, in a move that would deprive the Confederacy of slave labor and bring additional men into the Union Army, Lincoln issued the Emancipation Proclamation. This document stated that as of January 1, 1863, all slaves in any territory in rebellion against the United States would be "then, thenceforward, and forever free." This gave Confederate states a chance to rejoin the Union and keep their slaves; the Proclamation did not extend freedom to any slaves held within the Union (four slaveholding states had not seceded with the rest). However, the Confederacy spurned the offer. On the first day of 1863, according to Union law, **emancipation** meant that slavery was formally and officially over in the old South.

Many slaves already had escaped from their Confederate owners and made their way to the Union lines. When the Emancipation Proclamation went into effect, Lincoln signed an order allowing African Americans to **enlist** in the Union army. In the end, nearly 180,000 of them would serve, many with distinction. African Americans provided an important source of reinforcements for the exhausted Union Army.

The Confederates won a great victory at Fredericksburg, Virginia, just before the Emancipation Proclamation was due to take effect. Lee was able to establish his troops on high ground overlooking an open plain. The Confederates were in a perfect position to fire on the Union troops when they crossed the plain. Four months later the South scored another victory at Chancellorsville, where Generals Lee and Jackson organized an ingenious double-pronged attack against the Union Army. During the battle, however, the South suffered a severe blow. Confederate troops shot "Stonewall" Jackson, mistaking him for an enemy soldier. Jackson, who had been one of the ablest generals in the Confederate Army, died of his wounds a week later.

Gettysburg: The Turning Point

In 1863 Lee decided to take his troops north, following his original plan to win the war on Union territory. He gathered 75,000 troops at the sleepy town of Gettysburg in eastern Pennsylvania. This location would become the major battle and the turning point of the war. Union and Confederate troops fought from July 1 through July 3, 1863, in the hills and farmland around the town. The Union troops were able to maintain the high ground and thus won the battle. The Confederate Army never again would penetrate into Union territory.

The cost was high on both sides; in three days of fighting, more than 50,000 men and boys died.

At a dedication ceremony for a cemetery for the war dead, Abraham Lincoln gave the most famous speech in American history: the Gettysburg Address. He alluded to the Declaration of Independence, quoting Jefferson's phrase "all men are created equal." He spoke of the contributions of the thousands of dead soldiers to the cause of liberty. He finished with these words:

"... we here highly resolve that these dead shall not have died in vain; that this nation, under God, shall have a new birth of freedom; and that government of the people, by the people, for the people, shall not perish from the earth."

Lincoln had realized by this time that of all his generals, only Ulysses S. Grant seemed determined on victory and only Grant would stick to the task until it was completed. Grant laid siege to Vicksburg, Mississippi, knowing that the Union Army could command an important strategic position from the bluffs overlooking the river. The siege was successful. On July 3, 1863, the last day of the Battle of Gettysburg, the Union troops gained control of the Mississippi River and effectively made it impossible for the western Confederacy to come to Lee's aid. In 1864, Lincoln named Grant supreme commander of the Union Army.

The War of Attrition

Grant's strategy was to fight a war of **attrition.** He would lead the Union troops in a march on Richmond. Grant knew that the Union had the advantage of numbers. No matter how many men the Union lost, they could be replaced; the South had no pool from which it could draw reinforcements. Therefore, every casualty was for more costly to the South than to the North. People described Grant as a butcher because so many of his men were lost—60,000 in one month in 1864—but they agreed he would never back down. The Union was winning the war of attrition.

Meanwhile, Union forces under General William Tecumseh Sherman marched toward Atlanta, destroying important Southern railroads and factories that lay in their path. Sherman's men burned the city of Atlanta after they captured it. This Union victory helped ensure President Lincoln's reelection. Sherman's men then continued east, taking the port city of Savannah in December. Because Sherman attacked important economic assets and resources—warehouses, stores of food, railroads—civilians throughout the South suffered. Sherman's strategy was effective, but it strengthened the deep hatred Southerners felt toward "Yankees."

In April 1865, Richmond fell to the Union Army. Unable to get his army through Union lines to regroup, General Lee surrendered to General Grant. The terms of surrender were signed at the courthouse in the little village of Appomattox, Virginia. To look at the two generals, no one would have imagined that Grant was the victor: He wore a creased, stained common soldier's uniform that had seen much hard wear in battle, whereas Lee was resplendent in full-dress Confederate grays, with a ceremonial sword at his side.

Grant was generous in victory. He ordered his troops to share their rations with the Confederate soldiers, many of whom were starving. He insisted that Southern soldiers be allowed to keep their guns, horses, and mules so that they would be able to hunt for food and rebuild their farms.

The Assassination of Lincoln

Across the South people received news of the defeat with bitterness that would take many decades to heal. One excitable young man, the dashing stage actor John Wilkes Booth, was crushed by the news of the Union victory. Booth blamed Lincoln, whom he viewed as the colonists had viewed King George III: as a tyrant.

On the night of April 14 Lincoln and his wife were attending a performance at Ford's Theater in Washington. The ushers all knew Booth and did not question his presence in the theater. He crept up the stairs to the presidential box, overpowered the one guard at the door, and pushed the curtain aside. He pulled out a pistol, shot the president in the head at close range, and then vaulted over the railing of the box and leaped to the stage below, possibly shouting *Sic semper tyrannis!* (meaning "Thus always to tyrants!"). Booth then pushed past the horrified actors and escaped through the theater's back door. Lincoln immediately was carried across the street to the nearest house, and a doctor was summoned. The doctor could do nothing, and Lincoln died early the next day. This marked the first time a U.S. president had died from **assassination.**

Booth had expected to be hailed as a hero striking a blow for individual liberty; instead he was vilified as a murderer, hunted by federal troops, and soon cornered. Having broken his ankle in his leap to the stage of the theater, Booth did not get very far. He took refuge in a barn. When troops found him a few days after the assassination, they ordered him to surrender to them. When he refused to come out, they set fire to the barn. Booth died of a gunshot wound; although one of the federal police claimed to have fired the shot, many believe Booth shot himself rather than be hanged as a traitor.

Lincoln had been greatly loved throughout the North. His funeral procession, which took his body by railroad to Illinois, was watched in silence by millions of mourners along the route. Future president Theodore Roosevelt, then a six-year-old child, always recalled watching the procession from the upstairs windows of his family home in New York City. Vice President Andrew Johnson immediately became president and was faced with the heavy task of helping the South rebuild.

REVIEW QUESTIONS

1. The Union strategy for winning the war included all the following EXCEPT:

   (A) dividing the Confederacy along the Mississippi River and conquering both halves in turn
   (B) taking control of the Mississippi so that the South could not use it for trade or communication
   (C) blockading Confederate ports so that no supplies or reinforcements could come in
   (D) capturing and killing Confederate President Jefferson Davis
   (E) capturing the capital city of Richmond, Virginia

2. The Union was more likely to win a war of attrition because

   (A) it had a larger pool of available reinforcements and could resupply its troops
   (B) the Confederates had not been able to march farther north than Maryland
   (C) the Confederate officers did not know how to fight a war of attrition
   (D) African Americans fought only on the Union side
   (E) its military leaders had no command of strategy and tactics

3. The Emancipation Proclamation, by implication, extended which of the following offers to Confederate states?

   (A) They could keep their slaves if they abandoned the Confederacy and rejoined the Union.
   (B) The war would continue until they freed their slaves.
   (C) The Union would pay them for their slaves if they would agree to free them.
   (D) The Union would surrender if they agreed to free their slaves.
   (E) The Confederacy could exist as an independent nation if it would build an impregnable border between its territory and that of the United States.

Answers and Explanations

1. **D** The Union Army never intended to kill or capture Jefferson Davis. The other four choices were clearly important points in winning a war.
2. **A** A war of attrition is a war fought without quarter to exhaust the troops, supplies, and resources of the enemy. The South had far fewer of those things to begin with, and so was more likely to lose a war of attrition.
3. **A** The Emancipation Proclamation freed only the slaves who lived in states "in rebellion against the Union." It did not free the slaves in Maryland, Delaware, Kentucky, and Missouri, slaveholding states that had remained in the Union. The implication was clear: If any Confederate state rejoined the Union, it could continue to be a slaveholding state.

CHAPTER 16
RECONSTRUCTION, 1865–1877

INTRODUCTION

The Civil War ended in 1865, but the war for African-American civil and political rights was by no means over. The first battle in that long war was called Reconstruction. A Republican Congress was eager to reform the old Confederacy along the lines of the North, where all citizens had the right to vote and no one owned another person as property. However, two obstacles stood in the way. One was President Andrew Johnson, who took office after Lincoln was assassinated. Johnson had sided with the Union, but he despised African Americans and did not lend his support to any laws giving them rights. The other was the old guard of the Confederacy, who were determined to restore Southern society to exactly what it had been before the war. Southerners were forced to accept the Thirteenth Amendment, which made slavery illegal, but they passed many laws curtailing the rights and privileges of African citizens.

Republicans were able to do something about the first obstacle. Congress passed a series of laws over President Johnson's veto that made it possible for African Americans to vote, hold political office, and enjoy other important civil rights. However, no Congress ever convened would be able to remove deep-seated prejudice, bitterness in defeat, and racism simply by passing laws. Using terrorist tactics of violence and intimidation, the South managed to defeat Reconstruction reforms and push African Americans back down to the lowest rung on the social and economic ladder. It would take a century to enforce the three civil rights amendments that were passed between 1865 and 1870.

TIMELINE

1863 Proclamation of Amnesty and Reconstruction.

1864 Freedmen's Bureau established.

1865 President Lincoln assassinated.

Vice President Andrew Johnson becomes president.

Black Codes passed in former Confederate states.

1866 Passage of Civil Rights Act of 1866.

1867 Reconstruction Acts of 1867.

Andrew Johnson impeached; acquitted on all charges.

1868 Fourteenth Amendment ratified.

Ulysses S. Grant elected president.

1870 Fifteenth Amendment ratified.

▨ KEY TERMS

Black Codes   unconstitutional laws passed in former Confederate states to deprive freedmen of their civil rights

company stores/houses   housing and stores owned by the company, where workers were forced to live and buy their food and supplies; rents and prices were often higher than market rates

crop-lien system   the ability to charge purchases against the profit that would be made from the harvest and sale of the year's crops

Freedmen's Bureau   a government office set up to give emergency aid to African Americans in the devastated South

Jim Crow   a popular minstrel-show song and character; nickname for segregationist law codes passed in the former Confederate states after Reconstruction

Ku Klux Klan   a white terrorist organization formed after the Civil War to drive Republicans out of office and defeat Reconstruction

lynching   the kidnapping and murder of a person, usually an African American, by a vigilante mob

minstrel   a white song-and-dance actor appearing in blackface makeup as a caricature of an African

Reconstruction   era of rebuilding society and the economy in the old Confederacy after the Civil War

sharecropping   the exchange of labor for farmland, tools, a cabin, and a share of the crop; usually resulted in grinding poverty

Reconstruction Plans under Lincoln

President Abraham Lincoln had begun planning for the post–Civil War era long before the war ended. Lincoln had never envisioned any ending other than the preservation of the United States. On that assumption, he knew that sweeping changes would come to the South. The old Confederacy would have to adjust to a new society in which races were equal and a new economy not supported by slave labor. In 1863 he issued the Proclamation of Amnesty and Reconstruction. It offered a full pardon to all Southerners who swore that they would henceforth obey the U.S. Constitution and accept new federal laws that would end slavery. It stated that any Confederate state would be entitled to rejoin the Union and form a new state government as soon as 10 percent of its population took this oath.

Many members of Congress, especially Republicans, did not like this "Ten Percent Plan"; they thought it took too much on trust. In 1864 they passed a rival **Reconstruction** plan called the Wade-Davis bill after its two sponsors, Benjamin Franklin Wade and Henry Winter Davis. This bill required 50 percent of each state's population to take a loyalty oath and forbade any reconstruction of the government until slavery was abolished. Lincoln would not sign the bill, claiming it was too inflexible.

However, Congress and Lincoln did agree on the creation of the **Freedmen's Bureau.** This office had been created to distribute food and clothing to Southerners who had lost everything in the devastation of war. The Freedmen's Bureau also set up schools and hospitals and helped people find jobs.

President Lincoln was assassinated in April 1865, just days after the Confederacy surrendered at Appomattox. John Wilkes Booth killed Lincoln in a misguided attempt to avenge the South; Lincoln was widely known for compassion and had shown every indication that he would treat Southerners with mercy and justice.

Reconstruction under Andrew Johnson

Vice President Andrew Johnson was as different from Lincoln as could be. Although a self-made man, like Lincoln, who had never identified himself with the slave-owning class, Johnson was a Southerner and a profound racist. He supported the Union but had no sympathy with or liking for African Americans. Johnson believed that any Reconstruction government in the South should be run only by whites.

A few weeks after taking office President Johnson pardoned all former Confederate rebels. He also issued a plan for readmission to the union that had only three requirements:

- Abolition of slavery
- Nullification of the 1861 Acts of Secession
- Ending of payment of any debts the Confederate government owed to individuals

Former Confederate government and military leaders retained a great deal of power under Johnson's plan. They took over the new state legislatures, where they could pass any laws they liked. Not surprisingly, they passed a variety of laws, called **Black Codes,** that tried to return Southern society to the way it had been before the war. For example, they did not grant voting rights to freedmen. Mississippi even refused to ratify the Thirteenth Amendment, which abolished slavery throughout the nation.

Black Codes were different in every state, but they had the same goal: to suppress freedmen and deprive them of their full civil rights. They banned African Americans from serving on juries, owning guns, and traveling without a permit. They segregated the school systems. They passed local laws limiting freedmen's job opportunities other than field labor. In short, they were a blatant attempt to reestablish slavery in fact if not in name.

Congress Takes Action

Congress was sharply divided over the issues involved in Reconstruction. Radical Republicans declared that if the South were allowed to rebuild itself along the lines of the Black Codes, the Civil War had been fought for nothing.

Congress took a first step by extending the authority of the Freedmen's Bureau. That agency had been intended to operate only for one year, but Congress decided to keep it open. President Johnson vetoed the bill, claiming that the freedmen were not entitled to perpetual charity from the U.S. government. Congress angrily retaliated by passing the Civil Rights Act of 1866, which stated that everyone born in the United States was a citizen and as such was entitled to full civil rights. President Johnson vetoed the Civil Rights Act on the grounds that the federal government had no right to make such a law. Congress contemptuously overrode the president's veto and took the same action to keep the Freedmen's Bureau in operation.

In 1868 the Fourteenth Amendment became part of the Constitution. This amendment declared that anyone born or naturalized in the United States was a citizen and could not be deprived of life, liberty, or property without due process of law. It also promised all citizens the equal protection of the law. It did not give African-American men voting rights, but it did tie the number of congressional representatives per state to a state's total population of voters. This meant that if the Southern states allowed freedmen to vote, those states would have greater representation in Washington.

Radical Reconstruction

The year 1868 was a congressional election year, with one-third of the Senate and the full House of Representatives at stake. White violence against freedmen in the South had become common, and a number of people had been killed. Northerners overwhelmingly supported Republican candidates in the election, since it appeared to them that Johnson's policies were likely to overturn everything they had fought for in the Civil War.

Congress immediately passed a law, over Johnson's veto, that gave freedmen living in Washington, D.C., the right to vote. Next, they passed the Reconstruction Acts of 1867. Congress believed that the race riots, including an especially violent confrontation in New Orleans in 1866, proved that the South would never conform to the laws of the United States unless it was forced to do so. Therefore, the Reconstruction Acts divided the old Confederacy (except Tennessee, which already was reconstructed) into five military districts, to be occupied by U.S. troops until each district was in full compliance with the Fourteenth Amendment and each state had written a new state constitution giving freedmen the vote and the right to hold office.

The Impeachment of Andrew Johnson

Certain that President Johnson would not support the Reconstruction Acts, which had been passed over his veto, Congress passed a law called the Tenure of Office Act. It required Senate approval for the president to fire any government official who had been confirmed by the Senate.

Johnson believed the law was unconstitutional and promptly fired Secretary of War Edwin Stanton, who supported Radical Reconstruction. Congress immediately impeached Johnson on the grounds that he had violated the Tenure of Office Act, made "scandalous speeches," and "brought Congress into disgrace."

The truth of the matter was that Congress deliberately had passed the Tenure of Office Act with the purpose of provoking Johnson. Republicans believed that he was incompetent to lead the nation; they did not like his leniency toward the leaders of the old Confederacy or his refusal to sign any laws that granted rights to freedmen. Unfortunately for the Republicans, political disagreement with Congress was not grounds for removal from office. After an eight-week trial in which it became clear that Johnson had not committed high crimes or misdemeanors—the only legal grounds for impeachment—the president was acquitted by a margin of one vote.

The Election of 1868

The Radical Republicans had overreached themselves in their attempt to impeach the president on trumped-up grounds. The Republican Party was now afraid of losing power in Washington. Republican leaders decided that the best thing to do would be to support the candidate who seemed most assured of an easy victory at the polls. This man was Ulysses S. Grant, who had no experience in politics. Like George Washington and Andrew Jackson before him, Grant was popular with the public purely on the grounds of his success in the military. In the end, because of the support of African-American voters in the South, Grant won a narrow victory over New York's governor, Horatio Seymour.

Acknowledging the importance to their party of the new group of voters, Republican congressional representatives proposed the Fifteenth Amendment, which read:

> The right of citizens of the United States to vote shall not be denied or abridged by the United States or by any state on account of race, color, or previous condition of servitude.

The Fifteenth Amendment was ratified in 1870. It caused an unintended schism in the women's suffrage movement; because it ignored the question of women's rights, many suffragist leaders refused to support it. This caused anger and resentment among African-American women, who felt that the women's movement should support the Fifteenth Amendment and then use it as a lever to fight for their own rights.

Civil Rights Amendments	
Amendment	**Provisions**
Thirteenth	Abolished slavery throughout the United States
Fourteenth	Granted U.S. citizenship to all persons born or naturalized in the United States; granted due process of law and equal protection to all citizens
Fifteenth	Gave African-American men age 21 or older the right to vote

African Americans took full advantage of their first chance to participate in the political process. All former Confederate states were required to write new state constitutions; there were African-American delegates present at all those constitutional conventions. African Americans were elected to state legislatures, to the U.S. Congress, and to a variety of state and local offices.

Thwarted in their attempts to restore the prewar status quo, the former Confederate loyalists reacted by forming a terrorist organization called the **Ku Klux Klan.** Wearing hoods and robes to hide their identities, white men formed mobs throughout the old Confederacy. They attacked and murdered Republican legislators, both white and black. They attacked and killed any African American who crossed their paths, especially those who had achieved economic or political success. They burned homes, businesses, churches, and schools belonging to African Americans. This was worsened by the fact that these men acted without fear of prosecution from the local white authorities, who often sympathized with them.

African Americans responded in a variety of ways. They destroyed property that belonged to Klan members. They protected anyone they knew was likely to be attacked. They appealed to the federal government for help.

Congress passed the Enforcement Acts of 1870 and 1871, allowing the federal government to use military force against terrorist groups and to prosecute the terrorists. Klan membership declined after those acts were passed.

1876: Election and Compromise

Active Republican support for Reconstruction faded as time passed. Republican efforts had been so successful that the politicians felt that their work was completed and began turning their attention to the economy. The Panic of 1873 threw many people out of work. Democrats found new support among thousands of small businessmen and small farmers, many of whom blamed Reconstruction projects for the economic depression. In the 1874 elections Democrats regained the majority of seats in the House of Representatives. Congress did pass the Civil Rights Act of 1875, prohibiting segregation and discrimination in public places such as restaurants, but this was to be the last gasp of an active federal effort toward Reconstruction.

Seizing their moment of strength and support among the voting public, the Democrats used terrorist tactics—including murder—to prevent African Americans from voting for Republican candidates in state elections. In 1876 the Democrats used similar tactics in support of the presidential candidate Samuel Tilden. Tilden won the popular vote, but the electoral votes in four states were disputed, and in the Compromise of 1877 Congress agreed to name the Republican Rutherford B. Hayes president in exchange for the withdrawal of federal troops from the South. Without the support of those troops, the last of the Reconstruction governments quickly collapsed. It would take nearly 100 years for African Americans to have their full civil rights recognized again in the South.

The Rise of Jim Crow Laws

The Southern economy still depended on cotton, rice, and tobacco. The large plantations still existed. The crops still had to be harvested. A large labor force was still necessary. However, Southerners would have to find a way to make their economy function with a paid labor force.

A system known as **sharecropping** developed. A poor farmer would work a piece of land in exchange for a house or cabin on the farm, tools, a mule, and a share of the crop he or she cultivated. This meant that the owner did not have to pay wages until harvest time. Farmers had to buy edibles, tools, and supplies on credit, charging them against the money they would earn when they sold their share of the crop. This meant, of course, that when farmers were paid, they immediately had to turn over most of the money to pay their debts. The **crop-lien** system ensured that sharecroppers would remain poor. Although the South had begun to rebuild its railroads and industrialize to some extent, factory workers were forced to buy high-priced goods on credit at **company stores** and to live at high rents in **company housing.** They were no better off than sharecroppers.

Along with this economic subjugation, those in power in the South installed a system of political and social discrimination. The Civil War had not changed the racist attitudes of the old guard of the Confederacy; instead, it had reinforced the defeated planter class in its determination to restore its supremacy. When African Americans resisted unconstitutional segregationist laws, whites reacted with violence. As the century wore on, **lynching** became common. A white mob would kidnap a black person who had offended it in some way—perhaps only by failing to stand back to allow a white woman to pass him on the street, perhaps by operating a successful small business. The mob would kill the victim, usually by hanging him or her from a tree. They usually would leave the body where it was as a symbol they hoped would terrorize and further subjugate the local African-American population. There were thousands of lynchings throughout the South in the last decades of the nineteenth century.

Local and state legislatures passed unconstitutional laws requiring payment of poll taxes and passage of literacy tests before a person could vote. Although there were many poor and illiterate whites in the South, only African Americans who were likely Republican voters were required to take the tests and pay the taxes. When they failed to do so, they were barred from voting. Many of the discriminatory laws that had been enacted in the Black Codes were reinstated. They were known popularly as "**Jim Crow**" laws, after a song lyric. During the 1830s the white actor Thomas Rice performed a vaudeville act in which he blacked his face, danced a jig, and sang a song containing the phrase "jump Jim Crow." The character became popular, and many other actors performed similar **minstrel** acts. Many of the racist stereotypes of African Americans in popular culture, which would persist until the time of World War II, were based on the comic exaggerations that white minstrel-show actors had invented to get laughs from the audience.

African Americans protested that the Jim Crow laws were unconstitutional. In 1883, the Supreme Court declared that the federal government could not apply the Fourteenth Amendment to privately owned businesses. Later, when an African-American man named Homer Plessy insisted that he had bought a full-fare railroad ticket and had the right to ride in any car of the train he wanted, the case went all the way to the Supreme Court. In an 1896 decision known as *Plessy v. Ferguson,* the Court ruled that as long as a business provided "separate but equal" facilities for customers, it was not in violation of the Fourteenth Amendment. Justice John Harlan famously dissented, standing up strongly for the full civil rights of African Americans under the Constitution. Ironically, he based part of his argument on racist grounds, pointing out that although the Chinese were a different and in his eyes clearly inferior race, Chinese people had the right to ride in first-class railroad cars. How, then could the Court deny the same right to an African American? Harlan went on to write, "Our Constitution is color-blind and neither knows nor tolerates classes among citizens."

Many African Americans resisted Jim Crow laws, and many achieved a success that was truly remarkable in the face of the obstacles put in their path. One example was Ida B. Wells, who began as a reporter and eventually owned her own newspaper. She became nationally known as a fighter for African-American and women's rights and a leader of an antilynching campaign.

REVIEW QUESTIONS

1. Andrew Johnson was impeached primarily because he

    (A) dismissed Edwin M. Stanton from a cabinet post
    (B) disagreed with the congressional majority on domestic policy
    (C) committed high crimes and misdemeanors
    (D) prevented Congress from enacting any legislation that would propel Reconstruction forward
    (E) failed to carry out any projects that President Lincoln had planned to enact

2. Southern Democrats did all the following to bar likely Republican voters from the polls EXCEPT:

   (A) threatened them with violence
   (B) charged a poll tax they could not afford
   (C) made them take a literacy test they were likely to fail
   (D) shot them to death
   (E) passed laws that denied them the right to vote

3. Many active supporters of the women's suffrage movement opposed the Fifteenth Amendment because

   (A) the women's movement did not care about the rights of African Americans
   (B) white suffragists thought that their concerns were more important than those of African Americans
   (C) women were angry that the Fifteenth Amendment did not give them the right to vote
   (D) suffragists did not want African Americans to have voting rights
   (E) women were afraid that the Fifteenth Amendment would jeopardize their fight for women's suffrage

Answers and Explanations

1. **B** Congress deliberately provoked Johnson to break the law known as the Tenure of Office Act so that it would have grounds on which to impeach him. The Republican majority wanted to remove Johnson from office because they believed he was far too lenient toward the old Confederacy. He committed no high crimes; he had no power to prevent Congress from enacting legislation over his veto; and Lincoln was killed so suddenly that he left no plans in place for Reconstruction.

2. **E** The Fifteenth Amendment guarantees African Americans the constitutional right to vote. No state or local legislature could pass a law denying that right; no such law would have stood the test of a lawsuit.

3. **C** Suffragists wanted all adults to have equal rights to vote. They were in no way opposed to African Americans having that right. They refused to support the Fifteenth Amendment only because they thought it did not go far enough; they wanted an amendment that would give all adults the right to vote.

CHAPTER 17
WESTWARD MOVEMENT, 1860–1898

INTRODUCTION

The years after the Civil War were a time of great change and development west of the Mississippi River. For the Native Americans, those years brought disaster. For most other Americans, the West offered opportunity and freedom.

The United States had no intention of making Native Americans welcome in the country that had been stolen from them. They continued to push Native Americans farther and farther from their ancestral lands and take more and more land and freedom from them. Indians always had been willing to negotiate, but the U.S. government did not honor treaties with them. When negotiation failed, the Native Americans resisted with force of arms, but they could not match the strength and numbers of the federal troops. By the end of the nineteenth century they were forced onto reservations and were facing the end of their former dominance over the North American continent.

The U.S. government and big business between them worked hard to settle the West. The government offered land free to any homesteader who would claim it and farm it for five years. It also offered tremendous land grants to any companies willing to build railroads. Companies jumped at the offer, and the railroads became the largest employers of the day, hiring millions of people to work on every aspect of developing and building the national transportation system. Big companies also purchased Western lands where gold and silver had been discovered and hired miners to get the precious metals from the ground. The government made prairie land free for ranchers' cattle to range on, making ranching an attractive and profitable venture for many entrepreneurs, large and small.

TIMELINE

1849	California Gold Rush.
1851	Fort Laramie Treaty.
1859	Comstock Lode discovered.
1862	Santee Sioux uprising.
	Government Land Acts.
	United States Department of Agriculture established.
1864	Sand Creek Massacre.
1867	Treaty of Medicine Lodge.
	Purchase of Alaska from Russia.
1868	Second Fort Laramie Treaty.
1869	Transcontinental railroad is completed.
1870–1890	Cattle boom in the Southwest.

1876 Battle of Little Bighorn.

1890 Ghost Dance movement.

Wounded Knee Massacre.

KEY TERMS

brand   a mark seared into the flesh of cattle with a hot iron; used to identify each animal as the property of a particular rancher

cowboy   a hired man who looked after a rancher's cattle, rounded them up, and drove them to the railroad to be shipped east

homestead   land given to a settler by the government on condition that the settler farmed the land and lived on it for five years

reservation   land set aside, or reserved, for Native Americans, on which no outsiders had the right to settle; generally the worst land in the area

roundup   gathering of cattle from the open range

Conflicts with Native Americans in the Great Plains

As people continued to migrate westward in search of California gold, farmland, and other economic opportunities, they continued to grab space that the government had set aside for Native Americans. Again and again the U.S. government broke its word to the Native Americans. Since Europeans first arrived in North America, they steadily had pushed the Native Americans farther and farther west, driving them from their ancestral lands. Since Native American culture was very specifically tied to land, topography, and climate, Native Americans took some time to adjust to living in new lands. That situation was worsened when the United States began intentionally slaughtering the buffalo to remove the Indians' food supply.

In 1851 the U.S. government had guaranteed the Plains tribes that they would be left alone in their defined territories, or **reservations.** In exchange for ceasing to hunt buffalo all over the Great Plains, many Native Americans accepted money and a guarantee of a yearly delivery of supplies worth thousands of dollars (see Chapter 13).

Reality did not accord with the terms of the treaty. The United States continued to take land, shrinking the size of the reservations. Supplies were not delivered as had been promised. Since the treaties had limited the Native Americans' opportunity to provide for themselves by hunting, they depended on those supplies for survival. Without them, some tribes were in grave danger of starvation.

A deep cultural divide existed between people of Western European descent and Native Americans. Native Americans' experience of dealing with other tribes had been limited and had not taught them that treaties were easily broken. Europeans, in contrast, had warred among themselves for hundreds of years (France against England, Spain against France, Germany against Austria) and never took anything on trust. To people of European descent, making a treaty on the best terms possible and then breaking it as soon as necessary was often the way to pursue foreign policy. To Native Americans broken promises were bewildering and ended by causing deep resentment and fury toward the U.S. government and its people.

Armed conflict was unavoidable in light of the U.S. failure to deal honestly and honorably with the Native Americans. In 1862, when the Santee Sioux were starving because the government had failed to deliver the promised supplies, they banded together, attacked local Bureau of Indian Affairs offices, and raided local farms for food. The U.S. troops, which were better organized and had more and better weapons, quickly quelled the raid. They executed several of the Sioux and forced the tribe to move to Dakota Territory and later to Nebraska.

Over time the Native Americans came to realize that there was no reason to honor any treaty the U.S. government and military had violated repeatedly. The Plains tribal culture was migratory, and the Plains tribes were not content living on reservations. They frequently strayed away to hunt buffalo or simply to feel that they were free to go where they pleased. U.S. troops were ordered to try to contain them on their reservations. Sometimes the two groups clashed, and men on both sides were wounded or killed.

Sand Creek in the Colorado Territory was the site of an especially shameful episode. Colonel John Chivington of the U.S. Army deliberately ordered his troops to fire on a large group of Cheyenne, almost all women and children, none of whom had attacked the U.S. troops or done anything to provoke an attack. Chivington's troops massacred 200 Cheyenne that day. When national newspapers printed the story of the Sand Creek Massacre, people were horrified. A congressional committee investigated and condemned the massacre, calling for reform in Native American affairs. Unfortunately, slaughters like this were not uncommon.

Meanwhile, Native American tribes took direct violent action against farmers and troops on the Great Plains. The U.S. government called for peace in the Treaty of Medicine Lodge. Native Americans of the Southern Plains moved to reservations in Oklahoma Territory. In the Second Fort Laramie Treaty of 1868, the Sioux agreed to move to South Dakota, to an area they named the Black Hills. For once the United States had moved a tribe of Native Americans to rich, fertile lands.

However, the U.S. government could not leave well enough alone. In 1874, U.S. troops invaded the reservation, examining the land for any signs of gold in the ground. When they discovered that there was gold in the Black Hills, the government ordered the Native Americans to move again. The Sioux refused to move and took up arms.

Much to the surprise of the U.S. authorities, the Sioux and their Cheyenne allies won two major battles with the U.S. Army: the battles of the Rosebud and the Little Bighorn. At Little Bighorn, General George Armstrong Custer and all his troops were killed. The U.S. army redoubled its efforts to police the Sioux, and in the end they were forced to surrender and move to new reservations.

In these times of great trouble Native Americans turned to religion for solace and hope. A Paiute named Wovoka assured the Plains tribes that a ritual dance called the Ghost Dance would bring their ancestors back and ward off further U.S. attempts to destroy Native American culture. The U.S. military, afraid that the Ghost Dance movement would spread and give rise to further armed conflict, decided to arrest Sitting Bull. A fight broke out when U.S. troops approached Sitting Bull's cabin, and the troops killed several Native Americans, including Sitting Bull.

The unnecessary death of their great leader made some Sioux furious and discouraged others. Many of them traveled west toward the Pine Ridge reservation with their leader, Big Foot. One night in December 1890, the Sioux camped along Wounded Knee Creek on the South Dakota–Nebraska border. Five hundred U.S. troops surrounded them in the morning and demanded their guns. The Sioux surrendered, but the troops began shooting anyway. At the end of the Wounded Knee Massacre, 150 Sioux and about 30 U.S. soldiers lay dead. The Sioux gave up all further attempts at resistance after this incident. In the West, the U.S. Army succeeded in relocating the Nez Percé and the Apache.

Settling the Plains and the West

The federal government was eager to settle the Western lands as quickly as possible. The acquisition of territory in the Treaty of Guadalupe-Hidalgo and the discovery of gold in California provided great incentives to Easterners to move to the West. Even during the dark days of the Civil War, the federal government continued its efforts to move people westward. The table below shows three of the most important laws the government passed in this regard.

Government Land Acts of 1862	
Homestead Act	Anyone who staked a claim to up to 160 acres of land could keep it if he or she farmed and lived on the land for five years
Pacific Railway Act	Railroad companies could apply for land grants on which to develop and build a transcontinental railroad system
Morrill Act	Granted 17 million acres of federal land to the states, requiring that they sell that land and use the money to found agricultural and engineering colleges

The Pacific Railway Act had many effects beyond facilitating the development of a transportation system. The railroads became the biggest employers of the day, hiring thousands of people to survey the land, level the grade over which the trains would pass, lay the ties and the track, manufacture the cars and seats, build and staff the depots and stations, and drive the trains. The railroads also sold off surplus land to create **homesteads,** further encouraging settlement. Chinese immigrants proved to be experts at this kind of work, particularly because of their knowledge of explosives, and the Central Pacific Railroad brought thousands of Chinese to the United States during the 1860s.

The first transcontinental railroad was completed in May 1869. The Central Pacific railway company began laying track at San Francisco and built toward the east, across the Sierra Nevada mountains. The Union Pacific began at Omaha and built westward. They met at Promontory Point, Utah, near the north shore of the Great Salt Lake (see the map below). The railroad was built largely with immigrant labor: Chinese laid the track for the Central Pacific, and the Union Pacific workers were overwhelmingly Irish, supplemented by young Civil War veterans and freedmen. The conditions they labored under were tremendously difficult.

Families in search of farmland had gone westward with the first wagon trains. Then, in the years before the Civil War, a flood of young single men had traveled westward in search of gold, opportunity, freedom, and adventure. Beginning in 1865, with the war over, the pattern of westward migration changed. Three main groups traveled westward: immigrants, freedmen, and middle-class whites.

So many immigrants had flooded into Northeastern port cities that conditions had become overcrowded, unsanitary, and in many cases desperate. Many immigrants had been farmers in their native countries and knew that they would have to travel westward beyond the cities to find land. The Homestead Act made it possible for millions of poor immigrants to start afresh in the American West. Immigrants from Scandinavian countries and Central and Eastern European nations such as Poland, Austria, and Sweden settled on the Great Plains in large numbers.

The Emancipation Proclamation had freed African Americans in the South, but it had left them to fend for themselves. As slaves, they had been sure of receiving shelter and regular meals, however inadequate; now that they were homeless and in a location devastated by war, they would be lucky to find work and survive. Reconstruction programs gave African Americans high hopes for the future, but all too soon the Southern Democrats prevailed over the Reconstructionists and reinstated much of the old system of segregation and oppression. African Americans traveled west to find good jobs on the railroad, mine gold and silver, claim homesteads, work on cattle ranches, and escape the subjugation in which the old guard were determined to make them live. In 1879 alone more than 20,000 African Americans left the South.

Farming

So many farmers moving in such a short time to the same geographical area created new problems. The Great Plains had abundant grassy land that was perfect for cattle to graze on or for the cultivation of grain but lacked water and timber. Without a reliable water supply, farmers could not irrigate their crops; without timber, they could not build houses or barns. In 1862 the government created the U.S. Department of Agriculture to help settlers address those problems. They needed to develop techniques that came to be called dry farming and incorporated mulch, windmills, and irrigation.

The two writers who captured westward migration and farming on the Great Plains in the greatest detail were Willa Cather and Laura Ingalls Wilder. Cather traveled from Virginia to Nebraska with her family in 1873. She wrote several classic novels of immigrant pioneers on the Great Plains. *My Ántonia* (1927) tells the story of a Bohemian (south German) family adjusting to life on the Great Plains. Wilder was born in Wisconsin. As a child, she traveled in a covered wagon to Indian Territory in Oklahoma, to Minnesota, and finally to the Dakota Territory, where her family settled for good. She recounted the story of her childhood and girlhood in a famous series of books called the "Little House" stories. *By the Shores of Silver Lake, Little House on the Prairie,* and the rest of the series constitute a valuable history of the migrant pioneer experience in the 1870s and 1880s.

Ranching

The **cowboy** is a popular figure of American myth who really existed, although differently than portrayed in the popular literature. The first Spaniards who came to the New World saw immediately that the Southwest was an ideal place to raise the cattle they had brought with them. Three hundred years later Texans were still raising cattle. The industry spread across the Great Plains as the buffalo population dwindled and died out. Ranchers also raised sheep, but this brought on fierce clashes between sheep ranchers and cattle ranchers. Each believed that the other's livestock was eating too much of the grass. As ranching spread west and north, the government determined that ranchers could allow their cattle to graze freely on the open range. Water was scarce in the Southwest, and every successful rancher owned property near a water source.

Cowboys led a harsh outdoor life and earned little money. During the years of the great cattle boom after the Civil War, they were a mixed group of freedmen, Mexicans, Mexican Americans, and white Civil War veterans. The most important job of the cowboys was to herd the cattle from the ranches to the railroads. First, there was the **roundup;** the cattle had to be gathered from the open range and identified as a particular rancher's property by means of a **brand.** The cowboys then drove thousands of cattle over hundreds of miles, usually to railroad depots in Kansas. Besides being outdoors in all types of weather throughout the long drive, cowboys had to watch for stampedes and prevent cattle from straying from the herd. They had to worry about unexpected problems with the weather and with getting the cattle across flooded rivers. Once they got the cattle to the depot, the cowboys would be paid for their hard work—and usually would spend their pay immediately, drinking and gambling in the towns.

All cowboys were male, but women worked as hard on the ranch as men did. They had to take care of not just the family but all the hands on the ranch. Women made and mended the clothing, raised the children, and doctored the sick. They also knew how to fire guns, fix anything that got broken, use a branding iron, and herd cattle or sheep to pasture.

A combination of factors ended the cattle boom around 1890. First, ranchers had been so successful that the supply of cattle was starting to exceed the demand; that meant that prices for beef were falling. Second, the invention of barbed wire allowed ranchers to fence off their lands so that others could not have access to water or grass on their property. That drove many small ranchers and farmers out of business. Third, seven straight months of severe blizzards in 1886–1887 (described by Laura Ingalls Wilder in *The Long Winter*) killed up to 90 percent of the herds. Many ranchers survived by expanding their sheep herds. The era of the cowboy was effectively over.

Mining

The California Gold Rush of 1849 ushered in an era of mining in the West. After the discovery of gold at Sutter's Mill, the next strike was at Pike's Peak in Colorado in 1858. In 1859, a rich silver vein was tapped in the Carson River valley in present-day Nevada. The Comstock Lode turned out to be worth more than $500 million. Miners also found gold in the Klondike district on the border of Alaska Territory, which was acquired by President Johnson's Secretary of State William Seward in 1867. Seward had been criticized roundly for the purchase; people called Alaska "Seward's Folly" or "Johnson's Polar Bear Garden." They were silenced when the miners struck gold. The United States paid Russia $7.2 million for Alaska; by 1900, people from the United States had mined hundreds of millions of dollars' worth of gold from the new territory.

Mining communities were largely male, and only the strongest could survive in them. Immigrant miners from all nations found themselves forced out by those who had been born in the United States or the territories. Violence abounded, partly because there was no law enforcement authority. Miners had to settle their differences by themselves, and vigilante "justice" was swift and merciless. The vast majority of money was made by the corporations, not by the individuals looking for ore on their own.

REVIEW QUESTIONS

1. The U.S. government insisted on moving Native Americans to reservations primarily because

   (A) settlers from the East were greedy for the Native Americans' ancestral lands
   (B) Native American hunting practices threatened the survival of the buffalo
   (C) Native Americans were better at farming and technology than were Americans of European descent
   (D) settlers from the East did not understand Native American languages
   (E) government authorities were afraid of a planned Native American rebellion

2. The Pacific Railway Act had all the following effects EXCEPT:

   (A) the arrival in California of thousands of Chinese immigrants
   (B) a rise in the national rate of employment
   (C) an increase in westward migration by people in search of jobs with the railroad
   (D) the sale of surplus railroad land to homesteaders
   (E) a decline in production in the steel industry

3. African Americans traveled west after the Civil War for all the following reasons EXCEPT:

   (A) to work on the railroad
   (B) to escape racial segregation
   (C) to work in the fur-trading industry
   (D) to mine gold and silver
   (E) to claim homesteads for themselves and their families

Answers and Explanations

1. **A** Native Americans were never numerous enough or aggressive enough to threaten the United States in any way. Americans of European descent forced Native Americans off their land for only one reason: they wanted the land for themselves.

2. **E** The railroad became one of the largest employers in the nation. It actively recruited Chinese to come to the United States to work. People moved west to buy railroad land for farms and to work on the railroad. The steel industry expanded production because it made railroad tracks and parts of railroad cars.

3. **C** The fur-trading industry had died out before the Civil War. People were still hunting and trapping animals for their fur, but there was no longer a major industry to attract people to the West en masse.

CHAPTER 18

THE RISE OF BIG BUSINESS AND THE GILDED AGE, 1870–1896

INTRODUCTION

While the issue of Reconstruction was dividing the nation, a tremendous economic boom was going on. The Second Industrial Revolution was a period of enormous change in U.S. society. Inventions that would have seemed miraculous to a previous generation—instant long-distance written communication (telegraph), the ability to speak to someone in another city (telephone), a machine that could produce a perfectly printed letter (typewriter)—became everyday and commonplace in the new world of the postwar nineteenth century.

The technological breakthroughs caused a boom in heavy industry. Since it was much easier and cheaper to convert iron ore to steel, there was a surplus of steel, which could be put to a variety of uses, such as building and bridge construction. Men who were the heads of large corporations made fortunes. The workers to whose labor they owed those fortunes, in contrast, eked out a miserable existence. Toward the end of the century, workers finally began to organize into unions and strike for a reasonable living wage and an eight-hour workday.

Hundreds of thousands of immigrants came to the United States in the second half of the century, principally from Europe and China. They formed a lively and colorful presence in cities, where they gathered in small replicas of their old neighborhoods at home. The new industry also gave rise to a thriving middle class of professionals, highly trained workers, managers, and of course buyers of all the mass-produced consumer goods that were becoming so common. The upper classes acquired three-quarters of all the wealth in the nation. They were the class that gave rise to the term "Gilded Age" by which the era is known.

TIMELINE

1837 Morse invents telegraph and Morse Code.

1848 Karl Marx and Friedrich Engels publish *The Communist Manifesto*.

circa 1850–1900 Second Industrial Revolution.

1850s Bessemer process of converting iron ore to steel is perfected.

1853 Otis invents the elevator.

1876 Alexander Graham Bell invents the telephone.

1879 Thomas Edison and Lewis Latimer invent and perfect the lightbulb.

1882 Congress passes the Chinese Exclusion Act.

1886 Great Upheaval.

Haymarket Riot.

Samuel Gompers founds the American Federation of Labor.

1890   Congress passes the Sherman Antitrust Act.

1899   Thorstein Veblen publishes *Theory of the Leisure Class.*

KEY TERMS

blacklist   to ban from employment

capitalism   an economic system in which businesses are privately owned and a free market determines prices

communism   an economic system without private property and classes in which the people own businesses and industries and all people are entitled to take what they need from the common store

labor union   an organization of workers for their mutual protection and to fight for their common interests

laissez-faire   a system of capitalism in which the government is not involved; inherently probusiness.

monopoly   control of an entire industry by one board of trustees

Second Industrial Revolution   shift of U.S. society and economy from small businesses to giant corporations and industries

shares of stock   certificates of ownership of a small part of a corporation; available for individual purchase

Social Darwinism   a sociological and philosophical theory that claims that Charles Darwin's ideas about the natural evolution of species also govern human society, and that the "fittest" (those most able to compete) deserve to gain wealth and power.

stock market   place where shareholders can buy, sell, and trade shares

stockbroker   a person who handles stock transactions

strike   a protest in which workers walk off the job until management negotiates a satisfactory agreement

trust   a group of businesses run by the same board of trustees as one corporation

Technological Revolutions

The Western world had undergone one Industrial Revolution in the early 1800s with the development of the cotton gin and the power loom. That Industrial Revolution had changed U.S. society drastically and had caused the economy to expand dramatically. At midcentury, the **Second Industrial Revolution** came along, shaking up U.S. society and the economy once again. Innovations, new technological processes, and new machines appeared throughout the second half of the nineteenth century.

The factor that played the most important role in the Second Industrial Revolution was the development of the Bessemer process. Henry Bessemer from Great Britain and William Kelley from the United States both discovered a new, efficient way to convert iron ore into steel. That method, called the Bessemer process, led to a rise in steel production, which in turn made many things possible. Steel was needed for railroad ties, train parts, machines and engines of all types, and girders in buildings. Steel gave the United States a completely different appearance. A continent that had been pastoral and relatively undisturbed by large-scale development was now heavily populated, featuring cities full of skyscrapers, with railroads crossing from one ocean to the other and with heavy machinery everywhere.

The table below shows some of the key inventions and technological breakthroughs of the Second Industrial Revolution.

Date	Inventor	Process or Machine
1837	Samuel F. B. Morse	Telegraph Morse code
1850s	Henry Bessemer William Kelly	Bessemer process
1853	Elisha Otis	Mechanized elevator
1867	Christopher Sholes	Typewriter
1876	Alexander Graham Bell	Telephone
1877	Thomas Alva Edison	Phonograph
1879	Edison/Lewis Latimer	Lightbulb
circa 1880	Elijah McCoy	Oil-lubricating cup for machinery
1880s	George Westinghouse Westinghouse/Nicola Tesla	Compressed-air brake High-voltage alternating electric current (AC)
1893	Charles and Frank Duryea	First practical motorcar in the United States
1903	Wilbur and Orville Wright	First piloted airplane flight

The Growth of Big Business

Technological innovations that led to the possibility of mass production on a grand scale naturally gave rise to an era of big business. The system of **capitalism** that developed in the United States was founded on the constitutional right to own private property and a disinclination to allow a central government to control everything. In a capitalist system, businesses and industries are privately owned by people who have invested money in them. A free market determines the value of goods and services. If goods are abundant, the price goes down; if goods become scarce, the price goes up. The system of limited government involvement came to be called **laissez-faire,** a French expression that translates as "let it be." This system inherently favored the wealthy as it was the working and poorer classes that needed the protection of the government.

Businesses exist to make profits; every action a business owner takes is geared toward greater financial returns. In the case of the post–Civil War U.S.

business boom, this meant that the workers suffered. Because government did not regulate business practices, owners were allowed to pay whatever wages they saw fit and to install safety devices only if they chose to. Because of the continual influx of immigrant labor, owners saw no need to pay high wages or to follow safety regulations that would cost money. Workers were cheap and easily replaced, and their wages and working conditions were one of the easiest places for a business owner to save money.

Two competing political philosophies were formed in reaction to the rise of big business. One was **communism,** formulated by the German philosopher Karl Marx. Marx argued that because the workers were the ones who actually did all the work, they deserved the greatest share of the profits. He argued that all property should be owned by the whole community, not by private individuals. Each person should work as hard as he or she could and take from the common pool all the goods and services he or she needed. The other new philosophy was called **Social Darwinism.** It applied the biological notion of "survival of the fittest" to human society. According to this theory, the strongest survive and the weak die out. Political thinkers and sociologists argued that if a society helped its weaker classes, it would be a weaker society. Therefore, the laboring class and the poor should be left to struggle. Those who deserved to succeed would succeed; it was better for society as a whole if the rest fell by the wayside. This theory was linked to the idea of a meritocracy, a society in which those who work hard get ahead. Those in charge of the economy argued that they had achieved their status through their own effort, often ignoring the fact that most rich people were born wealthy.

The traditional form of business in the United States until the Civil War had been the small business. It usually was owned and operated by one or two people and a small staff. Small businessmen could not afford to run a giant industry on the new model. Therefore, those who wanted to set up a big business started corporations. Instead of bearing the whole cost themselves, owners sold **shares of stock** in the company. Stocks were purchased by ordinary men and women, none of whom owned enough shares to have any control over the way the business was run. However, they did get a return on their investment at regular intervals if the corporation was successful.

The establishment of the big corporation gave rise to the **stock market.** In the stock market people could buy, sell, and trade their shares. The people who advised them and handled their transaction were called **stockbrokers.** Many stockbrokers became fabulously wealthy.

Some corporations joined to form **trusts.** A board of trustees ran all the corporations in a trust as a single enterprise. When a trust gains control of all the corporations in one industry, it becomes a **monopoly.** Monopolies take two forms: vertical, in which one company controls all levels of production and distribution, and horizontal, in which one company controls all the enterprises at a single level. Monopolies benefit business owners because they eliminate competition. Consumers of course prefer to have several corporations offering goods or services so that they can choose the ones they prefer; this competition forces businesses to make products attractive and affordable. Public criticism of trusts grew throughout the last years of the nineteenth century as many of the trusts engaged in destructive business practices. With the power of monopoly they were able to crush competition through bribery, kickbacks, rebates, corruption, and other unethical and illegal practices.

The table below shows some of the key figures in U.S. big business during the Second Industrial Revolution.

Industrialists	Industries
Andrew Carnegie	Carnegie Steel Company
John D. Rockefeller	Standard Oil
Cornelius Vanderbilt	New York Central Railroad; many other railroads
George Westinghouse	Westinghouse Air Brake Company
George Pullman	Pullman passenger-railroad-car manufacturing company
John Wanamaker R. H. Macy Marshall Field	Department stores
Frank Woolworth	Five-and-ten-cent stores

The new industries gave rise to still newer industries in their turn. For example, the large corporations gave rise to unprecedented activity in the stock market, and a whole new industry was built up around that activity. Another new industry was advertising. Corporations wanted people to buy their products or come to them for services. Advertising was one way to bring their products to the attention of the public. Corporations spent a great deal of money on posters, newspaper advertisements, and other kinds of marketing to appeal to shoppers. Corporations hired artists to design logos that the public would recognize and remember. Department stores provided fancy paper bags and packages and wrappings in which people could take their purchases home. Many companies made their products available by mail order to those who lived in rural areas; the appearance in a rural mailbox of the latest Sears, Roebuck or Montgomery Ward catalogue was an event. For the first time mass marketing began to have an effect on the mindset of consumers as local production began to decline.

Industrialization and Workers

As big businesses grew, urban middle-class and wealthy people enjoyed an era of unprecedented consumer choices on which to spend their money. New stores were opening everywhere. Clothing and other items that once had been expensive were being mass-produced in great quantities. Fancy toys, books, furniture, and other goods of all kinds, both useful and frivolous, were for sale on every block of every major city.

When small businesses protested the existence of trusts, Congress reluctantly acted by passing the Sherman Antitrust Act. That act banned trusts and monopolies but failed to state exactly what a monopoly or a trust was. Without strong leadership in Washington that was determined to fight the abuses of big business, it was impossible to enforce. Many loopholes were formed as corporations reorganized to avoid accountability, forming interlocking directories and holding companies through mergers.

For the laboring class the era was one of great hardship. The government did not regulate business, preferring to leave it to regulate itself. When the government did step in, it normally ruled in favor of the business owners, not the workers. Corruption was the rule of the day as people unabashedly used their offices for personal gain. For example, Congress might establish protective tariffs on U.S.-produced goods so that people would buy them in preference to more expensive imports. However, Congress ignored the concerns of those whose work made the economy prosperous: the welders, miners, dyers, tailors, porters, teamsters, and other working people.

Wages were as low as owners could set them. If one person refused to work for a low wage, a hungrier and poorer person would agree to do so. Laborers worked six days a week, often for 12 to 14 hours per day. Children went to work as soon as they were old enough; management valued juvenile workers because their wages were lower and they were too young to protest or fight the dreadful working conditions that prevailed.

Factories were generally extremely hot, dark, and unhealthy places. In many industries, such as coal and cotton, the air was filled with deadly contaminants. There were no guaranteed lunch or dinner breaks and no place except outside the building to sit down for a few moments of respite. If a worker fell ill, he or she usually would try to conceal it; staying home because of illness generally meant the permanent loss of the job. If a worker was hurt on the job and unable to continue, he was fired and no compensation was offered. Life in the factories generally left a person broken, penniless, and injured.

By 1890, 10 percent of the U.S. population owned 75 percent of the wealth, and workers were lucky to earn $500 in an entire year. The government continued to ignore the situation and in fact sided openly with business owners. The workers would have to take care of themselves.

Slowly, workers realized that they had power. First, they were far more numerous than owners. Strength lay in their numbers. Second, they were essential to the economy. Without their efforts, owners could not become wealthy. Third, they had the power to band together. If all workers protested, perhaps management could be forced to listen to their concerns.

The first attempts to organize **labor unions** began soon after the Civil War. One of the first unions to form was the Knights of Labor. This was a national union begun by Philadelphia garment workers under the leadership of Uriah Stephens. It began as a union for white male workers, but in the 1880s it expanded to include women and African Americans (although it excluded Chinese workers). Membership was open to both skilled and unskilled workers of all types. Important leaders of the Knights of Labor included Terence V. Powderly and Mary Harris "Mother" Jones.

By 1886 the union had over 700,000 members and was growing. The union fought for an eight-hour workday, equal pay for equal work (at that time women were paid less than men, and black workers less than white), and the passage of laws against child labor. The creation of unions is all the more impressive when one considers the forces arrayed against it.

The Great Strikes

The **strike** was, and continues to be, the most effective weapon union workers have ever had against management. The strike is the protest of last resort. Workers walk off the job in protest when management ignores their demands or when labor and management fail to negotiate an agreement. A strike is effective because a business cannot operate without workers. For every day that a factory is closed or a railroad does not operate, owners lose enormous amounts of money—and consumers will transfer their patronage to rival businesses. Therefore, it is in management's interest to settle a strike quickly.

In the early days of unions, strikes were quite risky for workers. First, there were so many immigrants coming to the United States that an owner could replace a business's entire labor force very quickly. Second, workers went without pay during a strike, and it was a much greater hardship to them to lose a day's pay than it was to an owner to lose a day's profits. However, workers struck in spite of the risks. One of the reasons labor unions traditionally ask their members for dues is to support those who go out on strike so that they and their families do not have to suffer.

Successful labor strikes helped union membership rise. In 1877 railroad workers in 14 states went on strike despite the threatening appearance on the scene of federal troops attempting to force them to return to work.

The early 1880s brought economic depression to the nation. During a depression, businesses cut back by firing workers and lowering the wages of those who remain on the job, sometimes not telling them in advance and withholding the money when it comes time for payment after the work has been done. Nationwide wage cuts led to a successful railroad strike in 1884 and a violent year of labor-management clashes known as the Great Upheaval of 1886.

In May 1886 a labor strike in Chicago led to a clash between strikers and the police. When four strikers were killed by the police, a rally was called for the next day at Haymarket Square. The protest was peaceful, and the mayor ordered the police to let it disperse peacefully. Suddenly 200 policemen arrived and began to assault the peaceful protestors violently. Eventually a bomb exploded. Seven police officers were killed, and many were wounded. The police arrested hundreds and eventually put several prominent anarchists (only one of whom had actually been present) on trial. They were tried for incitement to murder, and the courts convicted all eight and executed four in spite of the fact that extremely little evidence was presented at the trial.

Worker activism slowed after the Haymarket Riot, and union membership dwindled. Employers began fighting labor unions by **blacklisting** any worker who tried to organize his or her colleagues. They forced newly hired workers to sign agreements never to join a union. They brought in strikebreakers (often paid thugs) to force laborers to return to work. And of course they hired replacement workers. The owners were very effective in stopping union formation, largely because they were supported by the government. City, state, and federal authorities often would send in troops, suspend constitutional rights, and convict strikers while ignoring the violence and illegality of the strikebreakers.

Skilled workers decided to form their own union. In 1886 Samuel Gompers formed the American Federation of Labor (AF of L or AFL) for skilled workers. The AFL was founded, like all labor unions, to fight for the rights of workers, but all too often it colluded with management to the detriment of its members. The American Railway Union, which struck against the Pullman company in 1894, was defeated permanently when the strike failed.

Social Classes

Edith Wharton and Henry James were the most important novelists who recorded the lives of the upper classes of this era, those whose lifestyle the socialist Thorstein Veblen described as "conspicuous consumption" in 1899.

Both were from New York City. Wharton belonged to the upper classes, where her love of books was considered a bizarre peculiarity, especially in a girl; James's family was solidly and comfortably middle-class and intellectual. Two of James's brothers were officers in the 54th Massachusetts regiment in the Civil War; another brother was the famous psychiatrist William James.

In novels such as *The House of Mirth* and *The Age of Innocence* and *The Wings of the Dove* and *The Golden Bowl*, Wharton and James wrote about idle, wealthy society people and about the middle-class or newly rich people who schemed and plotted to marry into that class or enter it by some other means. People in the upper strata of society married within their own social set, spent months every year traveling in Europe, and paid servants to do all the manual labor in their houses. These people lived largely on inherited incomes; men might "go to an office" for a few hours a day or sit on a board of trustees of an organization, but the upper class was an idle class for the most part. It was this class that gave rise to the phrase "Gilded Age" that people used to refer to the 1890s.

There was an enormously wealthy class that was not considered "high society." This class, formed from the giant industrialists and financiers who had made their money in big business, took pride in the source of its wealth. They often had far more money to spend than did the members of the old guard of society, and their lives were even more conspicuous for consumption. They lived in enormous mansions and might spend thousands of dollars to give a party. Their wealth was borne on the backs of the workers they employed for miserable wages in wretched conditions. Some of them became philanthropists in their later years, endowing libraries, schools, and museums.

The middle class expanded greatly during this era. The rise of industry had created millions of jobs for educated trained workers such as engineers, architects, lawyers, stockbrokers, and doctors. Young middle-class women had more limited prospects than their brothers, but many urban businesses welcomed them into the workforce. Female sales clerks and secretaries earned less than their male counterparts but worked just as efficiently; therefore, they were sought after to some extent by business owners. Young women who could do so often left the workforce when they got married; after that they remained home to raise children and run a household. Many of them also found time for volunteer work, such as involvement in the ongoing struggle for women's suffrage or settlement-house work in the cities. Women in this era were still limited in their rights, being unable to vote, own property, or sue for divorce in most places.

The lowest class was composed largely of recent immigrants and made up the majority of the urban population. At this time in U.S. history most immigrants to New York's Ellis Island—hundreds of thousands each year—came from Italy and from Central and Eastern Europe. At the same time, a flood of Chinese crossed the Pacific, landing at Angel Island off the California coast.

Because the new immigrants did not speak English, they were temporarily isolated from mainstream U.S. life and from other immigrants of different nationalities. They generally formed their own small communities in New York and other cities, and that provided some continuity with home. They had neighbors who spoke their language and could help them find work. They also contributed some of the little money they had toward building churches in their new neighborhoods. The church would serve as an important community center. Conditions in those cities were often horrendous, and new immigrants often were taken advantage of by the very people who were supposed to help them (see Chapter 19).

Immigrants took the lowest-paying jobs in business and industry. Many had been skilled workers at home but had no money to establish a business in the United States. They had to take any work that came in order not to starve. Because they were newcomers, they often did not know their own rights, and owners found it easy to bully and intimidate them.

Much of the vitality of U.S. cities from that day to the present has been due to the immigrant presence. Immigrant populations continued to cook familiar dishes, publish newspapers in their own languages, and observe religious and cultural festivals as they had done at home.

Immigrants faced discrimination both socially and professionally. The previous generation of immigrants were often the least ready to welcome the newcomers now that they had been in the country for some time and could feel that they were "real Americans." As immigration continued to rise, a nativist movement grew up in protest against it. Nativists feared that the immigrants from so many different cultures would alter U.S. society drastically. They did not want immigrants bringing in new ideas or ways of thinking. They did not want immigrants lowering the working wage or taking jobs from those who had been born in the United States. It was easy for nativists to forget that their own families had been immigrants.

The group that suffered most from the nativist attitude was the Chinese, probably because they seemed more "foreign" than did European immigrants. Whereas people in the United States could recognize and understand words in many European languages and perhaps even speak one or two of them fluently, they found the Chinese language incomprehensible. Whereas Europeans dressed more or less like people in the United States, Chinese did not. Whereas Europeans looked just like Americans whose forebears had come from Europe, the Chinese had distinctive and different physical characteristics. All these factors combined to make the Chinese an easy target for prejudice. In 1882, Congress passed a law called the Chinese Exclusion Act. It denied U.S. citizenship to anyone born in China; this meant that no Chinese immigrants could ever acquire it (although their children born in the United States were automatically citizens). The Chinese Exclusion Act also banned further Chinese immigration to the United States.

REVIEW QUESTIONS

1. All the following inventions were developed during the Second Industrial Revolution EXCEPT:

   (A) the lightbulb
   (B) the telephone
   (C) the air brake
   (D) the cotton gin
   (E) the typewriter

2. In a dispute with owners or management, workers had all the following advantages EXCEPT:

   (A) There were far more of them.
   (B) No business could function without them.
   (C) They could form unions to help them survive financially during strikes.
   (D) Owners stood to lose substantial profits if workers refused to work.
   (E) They could not be replaced easily.

3. In the early 1900's, nativists supported restrictions on immigration for all the following reasons EXCEPT:

(A) They did not want U.S. culture changed.
(B) They did not want to learn to speak foreign languages.
(C) They feared that immigrants would lower the working wage.
(D) They thought immigrants might bring in ideas, values, and ways of thinking that would not fit in.
(E) They feared that immigrants would take jobs away from workers born in the United States.

Answers and Explanations

1. **D** The cotton gin was developed in 1793, during the first Industrial Revolution.
2. **E** Unskilled workers could be replaced readily and easily because of the constant influx of immigrants, who needed to find work right away. Workers were able to survive financially during strikes because their unions helped them.
3. **B** Until the major wave of Latin American immigration in the late twentieth century, there was no fear that any person in the United States would have to learn a language other than English.

CHAPTER 19

POLITICS AND THE CALL FOR REFORM, 1865–1900

INTRODUCTION

The second half of the nineteenth century brought prosperity to many and poverty to many more. Immigrants continued to flood the United States in the millions, usually taking the lowest-paying jobs and living in the poorest housing because they had no other options. This situation meant that business owners, managers, and landlords had little incentive to improve wages or living and working conditions. However, many people tried to do something on an individual basis. The settlement-house movement brought help into the neighborhoods where it was most needed. Political machines also provided essential improvements to cities, such as sewer systems, although at a price.

As manufacturing and service workers began to unionize and demand better working conditions, farmers began to try to do the same thing. National and regional Alliance movements formed, bringing farmers together to address their most important financial and political concerns. By the end of the century the Alliance movements had won major concessions.

People who were well off financially saw no need for reform, and those who profited from the widespread corruption in politics and business did not seek reform either. On the other side, millions of people clamored for a more democratic society, feeling that the United States had become a nation ruled by the wealthy for the wealthy. Most presidential elections of the era turned on the question of reform. Some progress was made, but major reforms would have to wait until the turn of the century and the rise to the presidency of the pugnacious, determined, fearless Theodore Roosevelt.

TIMELINE

1860s   2.3 million immigrants enter the United States.

William Marcy Tweed becomes political boss of New York City.

1867   National Grange movement founded.

1870s   2.8 million immigrants enter the United States.

Farmers' Alliance Movement begins.

1872   Ulysses S. Grant reelected president.

1876   Rutherford B. Hayes elected president.

1880s   5.2 million immigrants enter the United States.

1880   James A. Garfield elected president.

1881   Garfield shot; Chester A. Arthur becomes president.

1883   Congress passes the Pendleton Civil Service Act.

1884   Grover Cleveland elected president.

1888   First mass-transit system in the United States (Richmond, Virginia).

Benjamin Harrison elected president.

1889   Jane Addams opens Hull House in Chicago.

1890s   3.7 million immigrants enter the United States.

1892   Grover Cleveland elected president for the second time.

1896   William McKinley elected president.

KEY TERMS

cooperative   an organization in which a group of people with similar interests pool their resources to help one another financially

gold standard   agreement that a bill of paper money was worth its face value in gold

graft   money a political boss expected from constituents and companies in return for addressing their concerns or securing them a business contract

mudslinging   making vicious personal accusations about a candidate for high office

political boss   the man unofficially in charge of a political machine

political machine   a well-run local political organization, usually in a major city, that controls the elected and appointed offices, generally through corruption.

Populist Party   a political party founded in the 1890s to address the concerns of the poor and working classes

precinct captain   the man who dealt directly with voters in his district within the city by working with the political machine

settlement house   a neighborhood community, cultural, and social-service center

tenement   technically, any building containing residential units for rent; historically, a cheaply constructed, poorly maintained rental building for the poorer classes

The Rise of the Big Cities

The enormous influx of immigration made cities such as New York grow. Hundreds of thousands of immigrants came to the United States each year, and a great many of them settled in the port of entry. This skyrocketing population created many changes in the cities. New buildings were constructed to house the growing population. New schools and hospitals opened. A mass transit system was put into operation. **Settlement houses** came into existence in the poorest neighborhoods.

Many immigrants could afford nothing better than a room in a **tenement.** By 1900, well over 1.5 million New Yorkers lived in tenements. An entire family would live in one room. Tenements had no elevators or running water. Many rooms had windows that opened only onto dark air shafts or alleys, with the wall of the neighboring building almost close enough to touch; some had no windows at all. With no public garbage collection or proper sanitation, the neighborhood streets were appalling. There were no rent regulations, and so a landlord could demand whatever rent he or she wanted; tenants had only two choices: pay it or go somewhere else. A landlord was under no obligation to maintain the property in good condition. Cities became dark and crime-infested places. Jacob Riis documented tenement life in an important work of photojournalism called *How the Other Half Lives* (1890). Many prosperous people were horrified when Riis's work opened their eyes to the miserable conditions in which their neighbors were living. People began calling for reform.

In most immigrant families everyone who was old enough went out to work or brought work home. Italian women in New York, for instance, made decorative paper flowers at home, being paid woefully little; however, they were able to enlist their young children to help, and the mother and children could work together without supervision, taking breaks when they liked. In general, to make enough money to subsist, everyone in the family had to work.

The settlement-house movement began in the 1880s with the goal of helping urban working families and immigrants. Jane Addams and Ellen Gates Starr established one of the first settlement houses, Hull House, in Chicago in 1889. Addams's goals were to

- Offer classes to laborers and immigrants
- Bring culture and the arts to poor neighborhoods
- Establish a safe day-care center for the young children of working parents
- Give young middle-class women training for a career in education or social work
- Provide the neighborhood with a community center

Hull House accomplished all this and more. People from the neighborhood could go to a concert at Hull House, view an art show, take English lessons, learn to read, and send their children to classes. Hull House provided a place to hold dances, parties, and political meetings. Settlement-house workers could help a woman find a doctor for her sick child. They did their best to help people find jobs when they were thrown out of work.

Settlement houses such as Hull House and New York City's Greenwich House succeeded because they were part of the neighborhood. Settlement-house volunteers usually lived in the house and were part of the neighborhood and its activities. To the working poor this made the house a community center rather than a source of charitable handouts. Unfortunately, those institutions were limited in their ability to help and were not supported by the government.

After 1860 more and more states began passing laws that required all children to go to school. Nativists wanted the schools to teach immigrants to become "good Americans" and lose their native customs. By 1900 over 70 percent of all children in the United States were attending school. More and more colleges also opened as the population continued to grow. However, reform was needed. Many schools, especially those in poor urban neighborhoods, did not have adequate space or facilities for the students. In addition, colleges were usually too expensive for any but comfortably off middle-class parents or wealthy ones to send their children there. The wages paid to immigrants and laborers were so low that they continued to send their children out to work.

As the cities grew larger, they needed mass-transit systems so that people living far from the center could come downtown. Richmond, Virginia, became the first city to have a trolley system (1888). In the early 1900s New York City began operating its first subway lines. The subway tunnels were dug largely by Italian immigrant laborers; Italians also were hired to pave the walls of each subway station with decorative tile mosaics because they were skilled at that kind of tile work.

Big-City Politics

When immigrants came to the city, they often were greeted by representatives of the local **political machines.** These were large-scale corrupt organizations that virtually ran the cities. The machines would help immigrants find work and housing and obtain citizenship in exchange for their loyalty in the upcoming elections. If a voter did not vote the way the machine politician wanted (this was an era before the secret ballot), he or she might incur violence from the machine's local thugs. The **precinct captain** would control his ethnic area, often living in the community and reporting up a hierarchy to the **political (or party) boss.**

Historical study and opinion about the political machines have changed over time. Machines used to be seen as extraordinarily corrupt and lacking any redeeming characteristics. A more balanced view has developed. The political machines did engage in **graft,** fraud, and kickbacks as well as widespread voter fraud and violence. They fleeced their cities for millions and oversaw a system of patronage that rewarded loyalty. However, bosses also provided services to the public that other elected officials could not. The cities had grown very quickly and haphazardly, and the confusing laws and jurisdictions were unable to keep up. Into the gap came the political bosses. Political bosses saw to it that streets were paved, water and sewer systems were installed and maintained, sidewalks were constructed, and fences were put up around dangerous construction sites. They backed major urban improvement projects that employed thousands of immigrants. Many were of recent immigrant stock themselves, in many cases Irish; they understood the problems of their constituents and helped them. They might have done this only to ensure voter loyalty so that they could continue their corrupt practices, but they undoubtedly accomplished a lot.

A political boss was an important man. William Marcy Tweed, the boss of New York City throughout the 1860s, is synonymous with Tammany Hall, the downtown building where political meetings were held. He became the symbol of political bosses and one of the most corrupt. It is estimated that he stole between $45 million and $200 million. Tweed eventually was discredited in part by the political cartoons of Thomas Nast. Another political boss, John "Honey Fitz" Fitzgerald, became mayor of Boston; his grandson John Fitzgerald Kennedy would become president.

Politics in Washington

During the heyday of the political bosses' authority over the cities, Ulysses S. Grant was president of the United States. Republicans, fearing for the future of Reconstruction, felt that Grant's popularity as a war hero would ensure his election. He won a narrow victory thanks to the vote of African Americans in the South (see Chapter 16).

The Grant years in Washington proved to be an era of political scandals. Jay Gould and James Fisk, who had made fortunes in finance, wanted to acquire a monopoly over the gold market. To drive up the price of gold, they wanted to keep as little of it in circulation as possible. That meant persuading President Grant not to sell gold from the U.S. Treasury. When Grant refused to be a party to any such scheme, Gould defied him, spreading rumors that the government would sell no more gold. Speculators took fright and began buying and selling gold. Determined to defeat Gould and his cronies, Grant immediately ordered the sale of $4 million worth of the government's gold. That ruined Gould's scheme, but it also drove the price of gold down so suddenly that many investors and speculators lost everything they had risked in the market.

In 1872 the public became aware of a scheme hatched a few years previously by Schuyler Colfax, Grant's vice president. That plot had involved a group of congressmen who had pocketed money that came from Colfax's construction company. That company, Crédit Mobilier, had overcharged the Union Pacific Railroad by millions, and those undeclared profits had gone straight into the pockets of Colfax and his cronies. Many other scandals would come to light, marking this as one of the most corrupt eras in U.S. history. Grant's only involvement seemed to be trusting his corrupt advisors and no personal corruption was found, but the scandal surfaced during his presidency and his reputation was tarnished by association.

In this climate of scandal, the reformer and newspaper editor Horace Greeley ran for president. He was backed by a liberal faction of the Republican Party and also by many Democrats who wanted Grant out of office. However, Grant's popularity was high with the voters, and he easily won the election. Greeley died less than a month later.

An 1874 scandal over the taxation of whiskey spurred the growth of the reforming spirit throughout the country. Voters had begun, with good reason, to distrust their political leaders, many of whom were growing fabulously wealthy by taking bribes. The 1876 election pitted two reformers against each other: Rutherford B. Hayes and Samuel Tilden. The election was thrown to the House of Representatives, and in a compromise over issues connected with Reconstruction (see Chapter 16), Hayes was chosen.

When Hayes banned employees of the federal government from taking part in political campaigns, he caused a split in his own party. The Stalwarts opposed civil service reform; the Half-Breeds supported it. The Stalwarts wanted the system of patronage to continue, whereas the Half-Breeds supported Hayes's idea of a civil service staffed by employees who had passed an examination and thus were hired on merit rather than because of family or political connections.

The fierce conflict between Republican factions made Hayes decide not to run for reelection. The Republicans were still divided, but they agreed to compromise. Half-Breed James A. Garfield was their nominee for president, and Stalwart Chester A. Arthur was his running mate. With Reconstruction over, there seemed little difference to many voters between Republicans and Democrats, and the election of 1880 was very close. Garfield won a narrow victory over Winfield Scott, who had served with distinction in the Mexican and Civil wars. However, his presidency was brief. In early July 1881 Charles Guiteau, a Stalwart supporter, shot Garfield in a train station. The shoulder wound Garfield received was relatively minor, and he almost certainly would have survived with better medical care, although with a bullet in his shoulder for the rest of his life. However, medical science at that time was primitive, and doctors continued to dig for the bullet. Unable to heal and recover under those conditions, Garfield continued to weaken, and he died a few days after the shooting.

In reaction to the assassination, Chester A. Arthur vowed to push through the reforms Garfield had planned. He signed the Pendleton Civil Service Act into law in 1883, requiring competitive examinations for about 10 percent of all civil service jobs. Naturally, Arthur lost the support of the Stalwarts, and they nominated the Half-Breed James Blaine for president in 1884. Mugwumps—a nickname given to reform-minded Republicans—deserted their party and supported the Democrat Grover Cleveland, who had fought Tammany Hall when he was governor of New York. Cleveland won a narrow victory in a campaign in which he held himself above the vicious **mudslinging** engaged in by supporters on both sides.

As president, Cleveland immediately began advancing government reforms. He extended the Pendleton Act to cover many more government positions. His reforming zeal made him unpopular among many career politicians, but he nevertheless succeeded in winning the nomination in 1888. He won the popular vote but lost the electoral vote to the Republican Benjamin Harrison. Harrison and the Republicans abandoned Cleveland's reform program, spending so much money to reward their supporters that they were nicknamed "the Billion Dollar Congress."

Attempts at reform during this period were very limited and ineffective. The general mindset of many, if not most, in Congress and in other public offices was that profiting from their offices was natural and acceptable and that they could do this and still work for the greater good. It would take pressure from outside the government to enact real change.

Populism

Although major reforms in big business and labor would have to wait until after the turn of the century, reform did take place in agriculture. The first step toward assistance had been the creation of the U.S. Department of Agriculture (see Chapter 17). The next step occurred when farmers realized that, like laborers in the manufacturing and service sectors of the economy, they could organize. Together they were strong, whereas individually they were powerless.

During the late 1800s farmers faced many challenges. Some of them were in desperate economic straits. Their profits had gone down while their expenses had gone up. Ironically, success had led to failure; after years of bountiful harvests, the supply of fresh produce and grain was exceeding the demand. This meant that prices fell. Meanwhile, the railroads continued to raise prices for shipping, and manufacturers who sold equipment such as plows also were charging more. Farmers had little choice but to go into debt. They were also the victims of forces beyond their control. The agricultural markets had become global, and a bumper crop in the Ukraine could destroy their harvests. They often blamed their troubles on the banks and businessmen they dealt with, at times unjustifiably.

Oliver Kelley founded the National Grange in 1867 as a social organization for farmers, but as their troubles grew, it became a voice for farmers' mutual concerns. The Grange began to address political and economic issues. Grange members formed **cooperatives** to buy equipment and supplies in bulk, thereby saving money. They put their crops together and pooled the costs of shipping and hauling. They also pressured state legislatures to regulate railroad freight and grain storage costs. During the 1870s their insistence began paying off as many farming states passed laws to standardize such rates. In 1887 the Grange farmers had their first taste of national success when

Congress passed the Interstate Commerce Act. That act stated that railroads had to charge reasonable rates, could not make refunds to large shippers secretly, and could not charge more for a short haul than for a long-distance haul. It also created an Interstate Commerce Commission to regulate the railroads but gave the commission so little means to enforce its authority that it was useless.

The Farmers' Alliance began in Texas during the 1870s. It organized cooperatives, offered farmers low-cost insurance, and constituted a powerful political lobby for tougher bank regulations and government ownership of the transportation system. The Alliance also called for tax relief for farmers.

In the South there were two Farmers' Alliance groups: the Southern Alliance and the Colored Farmers' Alliance. Like every other aspect of Southern life, the Alliance movement was racially segregated despite the fact that the farmers had common concerns. By 1900, the Colored Farmers' Alliance had largely disappeared; it did not have the power to fight both the Southern Alliance and the interests of big business.

Farmers wanted more money in circulation because that would help them pay their debts. They urged the printing of more paper money and a return to the coining of silver, which Congress had ended in 1873 in a return to the **gold standard.** That standard limited the amount of money in circulation to the amount of gold owned by the U.S. government. In 1878 and 1890 Congress passed acts legalizing the coining of silver in the hope that it would help a poor economy. This did not happen fast enough for the farmers, who successfully backed numerous candidates for office in the 1890 congressional elections. Prosilver candidates won over 40 seats in Congress as well as several governorships. The silver issue came to dominate the farmers' lobby. More silver meant more money in circulation, and that made debt easier to pay back and raw materials more profitable. The gold standard meant less money in circulation, which made loans retain their value and made raw materials less expensive, a situation that favored banks and business.

The Alliance movement gave rise to a new political party: the **Populist Party.** The key planks in the Populist platform were

- A graduated income tax
- Regulation of banks
- Government ownership of the railroads and the telegraph lines
- Unlimited coinage of silver
- Restrictions on immigration
- A shorter workday
- Voting reforms

The Populist candidate for president in 1892 was James Weaver, running against the incumbent president Benjamin Harrison and the Democrat Grover Cleveland. With the support of labor behind him, Cleveland became the only president in U.S. history to serve nonconsecutive terms in office. However, Weaver won a million popular votes and 22 electoral votes.

In response to a severe financial panic in 1893 that was triggered by the failure of one of the major railroad companies, President Cleveland decided to return the nation to the gold standard. Many disagreed with his decision, and once again silver became the major issue in a presidential campaign. In 1896 William Jennings Bryan ran for the Democrats against the Republican

William McKinley. The Populists decided to support Bryan rather than running a candidate of their own because Bryan was an outspoken proponent of abandoning the gold standard and coining more silver.

Bryan was a colorful character: a lawyer and a charismatic public speaker. Some time later he and Clarence Darrow would oppose each other in the controversial Scopes trial, which would decide the fate of a Kansas schoolteacher who had taught evolution in the classroom. At the 1890 Democratic convention Bryan gave the famous "Cross of Gold" speech, arguing passionately for the coinage of silver:

> We have petitioned, and our petitions have been scorned; we have entreated, and our entreaties have been disregarded; we have begged, and they have mocked when our calamity came. We beg no longer; we entreat no more; we petition no more. We defy them! . . . We will answer their demand for a gold standard by saying to them: You shall not press down upon the brow of labor this crown of thorns, you shall not crucify mankind upon a cross of gold!

The election came to be seen as a referendum on the Populists and the establishment, centering mostly on the issue of money coinage. The quiet Republican candidate William McKinley won a narrow victory over Bryan. Voting split along economic lines; most who were prosperous or comfortably off voted for McKinley because they had nothing to gain from an increase of money in circulation. The Populist Party would never succeed in shedding its image as a farmers' party and appeal to the masses of people in the cities. That would come later with the Progressive Party. However, the demands for reform were clear and would be addressed in the near future by a man as charismatic as Bryan: William McKinley's vice president, Theodore Roosevelt.

REVIEW QUESTIONS

1. The settlement-house movement had all the following goals EXCEPT:

   (A) to train young women for careers in education or social work
   (B) to integrate city school systems
   (C) to provide a day-care center for the young children of working parents
   (D) to provide a social gathering place in a neighborhood
   (E) to offer classes in English and other subjects for children and adults

2. The Populist Party was founded with all the following goals EXCEPT:

   (A) to support the coinage of silver
   (B) to return to the gold standard
   (C) to push for government ownership of the railroads
   (D) to regulate the banks
   (E) to restrict immigration

3. In the late 1870s, the Republican Party was divided primarily over the issue of

   (A) the gold standard
   (B) civil-service reform
   (C) racial segregation
   (D) women's rights
   (E) raising taxes

Answers and Explanations

1. **B** The settlement-house movement did not concern itself with fighting for integration in the school system.
2. **B** The Populists were opposed to the gold standard.
3. **B** Republicans either supported civil-service reform or opposed it. Since this issue directly affected who would hold government jobs, it was important to the political party and caused a split when the two sides could not agree.

CHAPTER 20

THEODORE ROOSEVELT AND THE PROGRESSIVE MOVEMENT, 1900–1920

INTRODUCTION

The turn of the new century brought relief to the laboring classes that had had such a severe struggle during the second half of the 1800s. Finally, a president came to the White House who would fight on behalf of the people.

Theodore Roosevelt believed that as president it was his responsibility to look after the welfare of all the people, not only the wealthy. Roosevelt shared the concerns of the Progressive movement that had developed in the middle class. He believed that all people in the United States should prosper and that business had to be regulated, since it clearly could not be trusted to treat either its workers or its customers fairly when left to its own devices.

Under Roosevelt and his successor, William Howard Taft, the federal government sued trusts and monopolies on about 150 occasions. Congress passed important legislation that would regulate the way business was done. Roosevelt was concerned with reform on all levels: social, political, and economic.

The Progressives who were Roosevelt's staunch supporters were also active. They pushed for local and state political reforms. They succeeded in making many changes in the election process, all of which gave the people a greater direct voice in their own government.

Investigative journalists and novelists also concerned themselves with present-day social ills. Magazine articles exposed the shady and dishonest business dealings of men such as John D. Rockefeller of Standard Oil. Full-length books informed readers about immigrants' living and working conditions in city slums and big factories. When comfortable middle-class people realized that those issues affected them directly, they were alarmed and pushed for change.

When Woodrow Wilson became president in 1912, he continued to fight for reform. Wilson signed much important legislation that protected workers and regulated business practices. He reformed the national financial system, creating the powerful Federal Reserve.

The ratification of the Nineteenth Amendment marked the greatest triumph of the era of reform. After fighting for well over a century, women in the United States finally gained the right to vote.

TIMELINE

1890   National American Woman Suffrage Association founded.

1901   William McKinley assassinated; Theodore Roosevelt becomes president.

1902   Newlands Reclamation Act.

   United Mine Workers strike.

1903   Elkins Act.

1904   Roosevelt reelected.

1906   Upton Sinclair publishes *The Jungle*.

Hepburn Act.

Pure Food and Drug Act.

1908   William Howard Taft elected president.

1909   Payne-Aldrich Tariff.

1912   Creation of Progressive "Bull Moose" Party.

Woodrow Wilson elected president.

1913   Sixteenth Amendment and Seventeenth Amendment ratified.

1914   Congressional Union for Woman Suffrage founded.

Clayton Antitrust Act.

1916   Federal Farm Loan Act.

Adamson Act.

1920   Nineteenth Amendment ratified.

KEY TERMS

Bull Moose Party   an offshoot of the Republican Party that was created to support Theodore Roosevelt's candidacy for the presidency in 1912

conservation   preservation and protection of the natural resources of the land, such as forests

direct primary   a primary election in which voters vote directly for candidates, not for electors

initiative   any issue placed on the ballot at the behest of voters

muckraker   nickname given to investigative journalists of the Progressive Era

New Nationalism   name for the domestic agenda called for by Theodore Roosevelt during the 1910 election

Progressive   a person who supported reforms in urban living and working conditions, politics, and government

Progressive Party   a collection of reform groups that wanted to change the structure of government and society; grew out of the labor movement and farmers' movement

recall   a special election in which voters can remove a public official from office before his or her term is up

referendum   any law placed on the ballot for voters to confirm or veto

secret ballot   a piece of paper listing candidates for office; all look exactly alike so that no one can see whom an individual has voted for

Square Deal   name for the domestic agenda of President Theodore Roosevelt's second term

trustbuster   a nickname applied to Theodore Roosevelt, who fought the trusts

The Progressive Era

Whereas the Populists had been motivated largely by concern for the plight of farmers, the **Progressives** were filled with reforming zeal by the ills of urban life. Their mission was to wipe out political corruption; improve living conditions, especially in poor neighborhoods; and support workplace legislation. Progressives did not believe that an upper class should enjoy luxuries while oppressing and starving the lower classes. They believed that all social classes should be able to live decently and in reasonable comfort, earn a fair living wage that would support their families, and get an education. U.S. society was prosperous; it was only fair that all levels of society should reap the benefits of the prosperity they all played a role in creating.

Progressivism attracted a variety of groups. The prosperous middle class, which had grown by several million people since 1870, would join with labor and farmers. Both men and women played active roles in the movement. Although it was becoming much more common for middle-class women to earn a college degree, it was still difficult for them to find acceptance in many professions. The Progressive movement gave them a chance to put their knowledge and skills to use.

One of the most important concerns of Progressives was abuse in big business. Progressives were well aware that the laborers, not the owners, did all the hard work and were therefore responsible for the profits of which they received so meager a share.

Most workers in the United States worked 10, 12, or even 14 hours a day, six days a week. The modern concept of the weekend did not exist, and workers were not paid extra for working overtime. There was no guaranteed minimum wage. Businesses were unregulated, and so they did not have to put safety regulations in place. Long working hours led to exhaustion, and exhaustion led to clumsiness; workers often were maimed severely or killed in industrial accidents either because unsafe practices were in place or because they were half asleep on the job. Progressives called for an eight-hour workday, a minimum wage across all industries, safer working conditions, and an end to child labor. They believed that working parents should be paid enough to allow their children to go to school.

The Muckrakers

Naturally, business owners opposed the Progressives. The Progressives retaliated by exposing the worst practices of the big businesses in the daily press. Theodore Roosevelt was the first to apply the term "**muckrakers**" to the investigative journalists of the day. He initially meant this negatively, but in time would come to support them. One issue of *McClure's Magazine* advertised the following articles on its front cover:

> PITTSBURGH: A CITY ASHAMED
> LINCOLN STEFFENS'S exposure of another type of municipal grafting; how Pittsburgh differs from St. Louis and Minneapolis.
> IDA M. TARBELL on the Standard [Oil] tactics which brought on the famous oil crisis of 1878.

Trusts and monopolies were unpopular with most people in the United States because they drove up prices by eliminating free-market competition for customers. Readers snapped up copies of *McClure's* and other magazines and newspapers, glad to see the truth about the hated business tycoons exposed. Many muckrakers even wrote full-length books such as *Following the Color Line* by Ray Stannard Baker and *The Shame of the Cities* by Lincoln Steffens. Novelists picked up on many of the same themes. In 1906 Upton Sinclair's *The Jungle* exposed the shocking practices of the meatpacking industry. Horrified meat-eating readers of *The Jungle*, knowing that they could count on support from the White House, pushed for reform in the industry. A government inspector's report read in part as follows:

> We saw meat shoveled from filthy wooden floors, piled on tables rarely washed, pushed from room to room in rotten box carts. In all of which processes it was in the way of gathering dirt, splinters, floor filth, and the expectoration of tuberculosis and other diseased workers.

Reform under Roosevelt

Vice President Theodore Roosevelt, Spanish-American War hero (see Chapter 21) and former governor of New York, became the nation's youngest president when William McKinley was assassinated in 1901. Roosevelt was fearless, outspoken, charismatic, and determined to govern as he saw fit rather than answering to special interests. Although fervently opposed to anything like communism or radicalism, he believed that reform was necessary. He referred to his domestic goals as "a square deal, no less and no more" for all citizens. Roosevelt believed that big business had a role to play in society, but he also knew that business owners put their profits above all other considerations. Therefore, Roosevelt was determined to force them, by law, to obey regulations that would ensure fair hours, wages, and working conditions for laborers. He did not believe that all trusts were bad and sought to regulate only those he saw as detrimental to social welfare.

Economic Reforms

When the United Mine Workers struck in 1902, Roosevelt immediately had a chance to put his **Square Deal** program into action. The miners were striking for recognition of their union and for higher wages. Roosevelt approached the workers and the owners and offered to appoint a commission of arbitrators who would hear both sides and settle the dispute. Neither the workers nor the owners liked the sound of that proposal. Owners were afraid of Roosevelt because he had stated clearly that he believed in regulating big business. Workers distrusted him because no previous president had ever supported them in a dispute. Roosevelt was offended by the imperious attitude of the owners and threatened to use the army to run the mines. After that threat the owners came to the table, and both sides agreed to the president's proposal. The commission ruled that the owners had to raise wages and shorten hours but that they did not have to recognize or bargain with the union. This was the first time any president had achieved a result that protected workers and the public, at least to some extent. Both sides were at least somewhat satisfied for the moment with the commission's ruling.

The U.S. government sued the Northern Securities Company, a railroad monopoly that controlled shipping from Chicago to the Northwest. The courts sided with the government, claiming that the Northern Securities Company violated the Sherman Antitrust Act. So many lawsuits followed that Roosevelt was nicknamed a **"trustbuster."** Roosevelt also attempted to strengthen the government's power to regulate the railroads. The 1903 Elkins Act and the 1906 Hepburn Act gave the Interstate Commerce Commission (ICC) its first real authority to enforce rules. Those new ICC powers later were extended by Roosevelt's successor, William Howard Taft.

Roosevelt acknowledged growing public concern with the food and drug industry. That industry was, like all others, unregulated at the time Roosevelt took office. There were no ingredient labels on packaged foods or medicines. Quack doctors could package anything they wanted and sell it as a cure-all for headaches, pains, and other physical ills. Dangerous drugs such as opium were available over the counter. Also, no one but the workers knew what went on in the plants where foods were processed and packaged. *The Jungle* opened readers' eyes to the unsanitary conditions that prevailed in such plants and proved beyond doubt that regulation of the industry was necessary for the sake of public health and welfare.

In 1906 Roosevelt signed the Pure Food and Drug Act into law. It required that all containers of anything edible be clearly labeled with the ingredients. It banned the manufacture, sale, or transportation across state lines of harmful or poisonous substances.

The following table shows the key elements in Roosevelt's program of reform.

1902	Newlands Reclamation Act	Stated that money from the sale of federal land was to be used to irrigate and reclaim land
1903	Elkins Act	Outlawed rebates to shipping companies
1906	Hepburn Act	Authorized the ICC to set railroad rates and regulate all companies engaged in interstate commerce
1906	Meat Inspection Act	Required federal inspection of meat shipped across state lines
1906	Pure Food and Drug Act	Outlawed the manufacture or sale of harmful substances Required ingredient labels on food and drug containers

Conservation and the Environment

Roosevelt was the first president to involve the federal government in protecting and preserving the environment. As a child Roosevelt had been fascinated by birds and animals and had declared that he would grow up to be a naturalist. As an adult he had owned and operated a ranch and had been a big-game hunter in Africa. Roosevelt loved the outdoors and the natural wilderness and was determined to use his authority as president to protect it.

Roosevelt's friend Gifford Pinchot first coined the word **"conservation"** to describe the protection of the natural environment. Roosevelt set aside millions of acres of federally owned land, including the Grand Canyon and the Petrified Forest, as forest reserves and national parks. Conservatives of that era supported Roosevelt's actions, noting that Pinchot was right: The natural resources that fed big business had to be protected so that they continued to be productive.

Political Reform

The Progressives also involved themselves in political reform. They were determined to give the voters a greater voice in their own government and to wipe out the big-city political machines. Voters also complained about national politics, viewing their senators and congressmen as far too submissive to the big business owners who had paid so much money to get them elected.

The first step the Progressives took was to fight for reform in local elections. In those elections the people voted for delegates who then nominated candidates for office. Progressives supported the **direct primary,** in which voters cast their votes directly for the candidate. Between 1902 and 1916 most states switched to a direct-primary system.

The Constitution states that members of the House of Representatives will be elected directly by the people but senators are to be appointed by the state legislatures. The Progressives saw no reason for this system to continue. They believed that the political machines had too much influence over the state legislatures and that the people should choose their own representatives. In 1913 the Seventeenth Amendment was ratified, giving the people the right to vote directly for senators.

The Progressives also fought for a secret, uniform ballot. At that time political parties printed their own ballots in different colors, and so anyone could see how anyone else was voting. That made it easy for the political machines and other powerful vested interests to identify, confront, and threaten a person who was not voting the way they wanted him to vote. With a uniform ballot, voting would be private and secret. By 1910 most states had bowed to Progressive pressure and converted to a **secret ballot.**

Progressives also believed that the people needed a mechanism by which they could propose legislation. The table below shows three measures for which they fought that would make this possible. All were adopted by most states by 1916.

Initiative	If 5 to 15 percent of all voters sign a petition proposing legislation, it must appear on the ballot.
Recall	Voters have the power to remove an elected official from office by vote before his or her term ends.
Referendum	If 5 to 15 percent of all voters sign a petition, a recently passed law must be placed on the ballot so that voters can approve or veto it.

Many Progressives ran for local political office. Some became mayors and were able to play a key role in reforming big-city politics. Samuel M. "Golden Rule" Jones of Toledo and Tom Johnson of Cleveland were Progressive mayors in big Ohio cities. They accomplished goals such as reforming the police force, establishing fair local tax systems, opening schools for young children, and improving urban living conditions. Some Progressives, such as Theodore Roosevelt and Robert La Follette of Wisconsin, became state governors. Their influence on reform at the state level was profound and effective. Many of their fellow governors followed their example.

The Progressive movement never succeeded in becoming a national party. Some Progressives would win local or even state elections, but nationally they could not crack the two-party system. The established parties had greater resources and were able to siphon away voters by appealing to them on limited issues. Republicans such as Roosevelt and Democrats such as Wilson would run as the candidate of the Progressive wing of their party.

Reform under Taft

William Howard Taft, who had served in Roosevelt's cabinet, was elected president in 1908 with Roosevelt's support. Taft continued many of the programs Roosevelt had initiated. His administration filed nearly a hundred lawsuits against trusts. He extended the amount of land the government set aside as reserves. He supported the elimination of child labor. He signed the Department of Labor into law. Under Taft, Congress passed laws mandating safer working conditions in mines and an eight-hour working day for the laborers in any company that did business with the federal government. Under Taft, the Sixteenth Amendment was proposed. That amendment established that the government could tax individual income and that the tax would be proportional to the amount of money earned. The Sixteenth Amendment was ratified in 1913, shortly after Taft left office.

Taft was not the same type of man as Roosevelt, and this would cause him to lose a lot of support. He did not believe the president's job was to lobby Congress and in fact often claimed that he did not want to be president. Taft lost the support of Roosevelt and the Progressive wing of the Republican Party when he signed the Payne-Aldrich Tariff into law. That tariff raised the prices of consumer goods and made people accuse Taft of breaking faith with the voters. Taft also had a falling-out with Gifford Pinchot over the sale of a vast tract of land in Alaska to the timber industry. In fact, Taft had an extremely positive record on environmental and reform legislation, but the perception of Roosevelt and the public was that he had failed. During the congressional elections of 1910 Roosevelt actively supported candidates who opposed Taft. His program, which he called **New Nationalism,** called for laws that would protect the people. The goals of New Nationalism were better and safer working conditions, support for public health, and the regulation of big business. "The citizens of the United States must effectively control the mighty commercial forces which they have themselves called into being," stated Roosevelt.

Roosevelt decided to run for president again in 1912. When Taft managed to win the Republican Party nomination at the convention in spite of the popularity of his opponent, Roosevelt's supporters created the National **Progressive Party,** also called the **Bull Moose Party.** Roosevelt ran as a third-party candidate. With the Republicans divided between Roosevelt and Taft, the Democratic candidate—the quiet, scholarly Woodrow Wilson, governor of New Jersey—won a landslide of electoral votes to become president in 1912. Like both Taft and Roosevelt, Wilson was a Progressive by inclination. He described his domestic agenda as "the New Freedom."

Reform under Wilson

Wilson was determined to lower tariffs. In 1913 he signed into law the Underwood Tariff Act. That act pushed tariffs down to their lowest levels in 50 years. Next, he addressed banking reform. Democrats and Progressives favored a banking system run by the government. Conservatives argued that private banks should have more control. Wilson compromised by signing the Federal Reserve Act of 1913. That act created a national board to oversee the banking system and 12 Federal Reserve banks that were under combined federal and private control. Private banks could borrow money from the Federal Reserve banks. This bill helped farmers by making it possible for them to borrow money at lower interest rates.

Like Roosevelt and Taft, Wilson believed in regulating big business. In 1914 he signed the Clayton Antitrust Act into law. That act clarified the nebulous Sherman Antitrust Act by stating specifically what corporations could and could not do. It protected small businesses from being swallowed up by larger ones.

Under Wilson, Congress passed the Federal Farm Loan Act of 1916. That law, which was hailed with jubilation by farmers across the country, set up a special banking system for farmers only. Any farmer could borrow from one of the federal farm-loan banks at a low interest rate.

Like Roosevelt, Wilson believed in arbitration of labor strikes. A national railroad strike in 1916 led to the passage of the Adamson Act, which reduced the working day for railroaders from 10 to 8 hours but maintained their wages at preset levels. The strike was averted, with the workers gaining an important victory. Wilson also supported congressional legislation that for the first time offered financial compensation to workers injured on the job.

The Nineteenth Amendment

The most important reform of all—because it involved over 50 percent of the U.S. population—gained enough ground during Wilson's presidency to become law in 1920. The passage of the Nineteenth Amendment finally granted adult women the right to vote.

In 1890 Elizabeth Cady Stanton and Susan B. Anthony had helped found the National American Woman Suffrage Association. The association pushed for voting rights for women on the state level and by 1901 had succeeded in four western states. In 1914 Alice Paul formed the Congressional Union for Woman Suffrage; two years later it became the National Woman's Party. The party's goal was simple: to pass an amendment giving women the vote.

Paul and her followers picketed the White House daily, pointing out the inconsistency of Wilson's position: he supported workers but denied women their rights. The protesters used speeches of Wilson that stated that all people who consent to a government deserve a say in that government. The Washington, D.C., commissioner had the protesters arrested for "obstructing traffic," and many were sentenced to months in jail (the charges were dropped later). In jail those women faced brutality and violence for exercising their constitutionally protected right to protest. Many went on hunger strikes as a form of protest. All those tactics kept the struggle for suffrage in the newspapers and before the public.

In 1916 Carrie Chapman Catt devised what later was called "Catt's Winning Plan." That plan called for campaigning simultaneously for suffrage on both the federal and state levels and compromising for partial suffrage in states that resisted the movement. Adopting her ideas, the association won victories in several states, getting legislation passed that gave women the vote. When the United States entered World War I, women proved their importance to the nation by playing a major role in the war effort. President Wilson, after the story of the women in jail broke in the papers, spoke out in favor of universal suffrage in 1918. The Nineteenth Amendment was ratified in 1920.

REVIEW QUESTIONS

1. Theodore Roosevelt believed that big business should be regulated federally primarily because

   (A) it was wrong for so few people to control so much money and property
   (B) owners would not take proper care of the welfare of their workers or customers unless forced to by law
   (C) businesses were not efficiently run or profitable
   (D) too many people bought imported goods rather than goods made in the United States
   (E) businesses were destroying too great a proportion of the nation's natural resources

2. The Seventeenth Amendment, ratified in 1913, established which of the following?

   (A) Secret ballots in local elections
   (B) A direct primary
   (C) Direct popular election of senators
   (D) An eight-hour workday
   (E) A federal minimum wage

3. Conservatives supported environmental legislation under Roosevelt and Taft because

   (A) they did not want the natural resources of the United States to die out or be used up
   (B) they wanted a place in which to go hunting
   (C) they always sided with the owners in labor disputes
   (D) they opposed regulation of big business
   (E) they did not want certain rare species of birds or animals to become extinct

Answers and Explanations

1. **B** Roosevelt wanted to establish laws that businesses would have to obey because he had ample evidence that businesses were concerned only with profits, not with the health and safety of their workers or customers.

2. **C** Choices A, B, D, and E have never been the subject of constitutional amendments, although all have been passed into law or established by custom. The Seventeenth Amendment overturned a provision of the Constitution that gave state legislatures the power to choose senators.

3. **A** Conservatives supported the interests of big business. They understood that protecting the environment meant that it would continue to renew itself, providing big business with timber, fuel, coal, and other resources for all time.

CHAPTER 21
THE UNITED STATES BECOMES A WORLD POWER

INTRODUCTION

Although the United States had acquired an empire, it was one continuous tract of land on one continent (apart from the Alaska territory). Unlike the great European powers, the United States had not traveled the world, acquiring faraway colonies. That changed as the nineteenth century gave way to the twentieth.

The United States had grown dependent on certain raw materials and goods it could not produce for itself, such as rubber, sugar, and coffee. It produced a huge surplus of grain and a vast array of manufactured goods for which it had insufficient markets abroad. To many people in the United States, it was clearly time to expand—to acquire new trade markets and colonize nations to increase the country's power. A colony could provide the United States with what it needed at favorable prices, and it would purchase what the United States wanted to export, again at a rate favorable to the country. Colonies in strategic parts of the world also could provide bases for the growing U.S. Navy.

The United States acquired a valuable colony in the Hawaiian Islands in the central Pacific Ocean. Hawaii became a U.S. territory and served as a valuable trading partner and naval base. As a result of the Spanish-American War, the United States acquired the territories of Guam, Puerto Rico, and the Philippines. It also made Cuba a protectorate.

The United States made perhaps its most important acquisition in 1903, when it signed a treaty with Panama that gave it complete control over the zone where a canal that connected the Pacific and Atlantic oceans was under construction. The United States hired Caribbean workers to complete the job, and the Panama Canal opened with great fanfare in 1914. This period also saw the beginning of the U.S. tendency to be "the policeman of the world" with its continual uninvited incursions into the affairs of Latin American nations.

TIMELINE

1875 Hawaii and the United States sign a treaty exempting Hawaiian sugar from U.S. tariffs.

1880s French begin to dig the Panama Canal.

1890 McKinley Tariff repeals 1875 treaty with Hawaii.

1893 Americans take over the Hawaiian government; Queen Liliuokalani resigns.

1898 United States annexes Hawaii.

Battleship *Maine* explodes off Cuba.

Congress recognizes Cuban independence from Spain and declares war on Spain.

Spain cedes Guam, Puerto Rico, and Philippines to the United States.

1899 Open Door Policy.

United States acquires control over Samoa.

1900 Boxer Rebellion.

Foraker Act.

1902 Philippine Government Act.

Platt Amendment.

1903 Hay–Bunau-Varilla Treaty.

1905 Roosevelt brokers peace treaty between Russia and Japan.

1914 Panama Canal completed.

1916 Jones Act of 1916.

1917 Jones Act of 1917.

KEY TERMS

dollar diplomacy the use of economic means to control foreign relations with Latin American nations

imperialism desire to annex foreign nations as one's own colonies

jingoism the beliefs and practices of those who support an aggressive foreign policy

missionary diplomacy Wilson's foreign policy, which was a mix of moralism and self-interest

protectorate a nation that accepts a measure of control by a stronger nation in exchange for protection from other nations

Roosevelt Corollary 1904 statement of U.S. foreign policy toward Latin America

yellow fever a fatal disease carried by biting insects in hot, humid climates

yellow journalism sensational newspaper stories printed without regard for the facts

Pressure to Expand

While domestic reforms were under way at home, the United States developed a new agenda outside its borders. The United States had a history of conquering land and subjugating the people who already lived there to expand its influence, but until the late 1800s that tendency had been confined to North America. From the late 1800s until World War I, the United States began flexing its muscles and testing its powers overseas. In doing this it took on an **imperialist** persona somewhat like that of the European powers. It became a great power ready to acquire and rule colonies of its own.

The country's desire for expansion was motivated by the same factors that drove European colonization during the Age of Exploration. The United States wanted to establish new markets for its exports, acquire lands with abundant natural resources that the United States lacked, and gain a reputation as a major military and political force in world affairs. Some people in the United States also argued that the country had a moral duty to spread democracy through the world, although others felt that invading and taking control of a foreign nation was not moral or justifiable. Others would rationalize this with an argument of racial superiority, stating that the people in South America and the Pacific were inferior and needed the United States to "civilize" them.

The United States already had long-established trade relationships with European nations. To expand markets for its abundance of grain, crops, and manufactured goods, it looked to Africa, Asia, and the Caribbean and Pacific islands. By this time European nations already had colonized the better part of Africa, gaining control over its vast riches of diamonds and silver and other precious metals. Therefore, the United States turned its attention to the islands of the Pacific. Because of their climate, those islands were or could be made major producers of sugar, rubber, coffee, and other crops and goods that the United States could not supply for itself.

China and Japan

The United States had begun trading with China in the late 1700s. In 1843 China extended trade options with the West by opening five ports for trade. After losing an 1895 war with Japan, China was weakened, and four European nations were quick to take advantage and seize exclusive trade rights over various parts of that nation. Afraid of being left out in the cold, the United States proposed the so-called Open Door Policy, which contained three principles:

- Any nation with trade rights in China would share those rights with all other nations.
- Chinese officials would be put in charge of collecting tariffs and duties on imports and exports.
- Harbor, trade, and tariff rates would be equal for all nations trading with China.

It is important to note that the opinion of people in China never was considered and that this policy was forced on them against their wishes. The European nations that received official notice of the Open Door Policy ignored it; the United States took their silence for consent. After the Boxer Rebellion of 1900, Secretary of State John Hay reiterated the Open Door Policy.

Trade between the United States and the island nation of Japan had begun in 1854, when the United States forced Japan to end its centuries of isolation. Japan had had no contact at all with the outside world in hundreds of years, but it soon launched a program of rapid modernization. It quickly became a world power. In 1904 Japan attacked Russia. The United States brokered a peace treaty between the two nations in 1905, for which President Roosevelt was awarded the Nobel Peace Prize.

Hawaii

In 1875 the United States signed a treaty with King Kalakaua of the Hawaiian Islands, 2,000 miles off the coast of California. The Hawaiian Islands consist of eight large islands, the largest of which is called Hawaii. U.S. officials decided that Hawaii would make an excellent naval base and fueling station for merchant ships. The treaty granted Hawaii an exemption from tariffs on the sugar it exported to the United States. This was an enormous economic benefit to Hawaii. In exchange, Kalakaua agreed not to cede any territory to any foreign power. When the United States tried to improve the terms of the treaty in 1886 by demanding full control over Pearl Harbor, which it wanted for a naval base, Kalakaua refused. In the meantime, a group of U.S. interests secretly formed the Hawaiian League. Those traders, planters, and merchants wanted the exemption from the sugar tariff to continue. They decided that they had to overthrow the Hawaiian government and influence the U.S. government to annex Hawaii. Their first step was to force Kalakaua to sign the "Bayonet Constitution" (so called because the king was forced to sign it at gunpoint). That constitution limited the monarch's power and the right of Hawaiians to hold political office. In 1890 the McKinley Tariff granted all nations the right to ship sugar to the United States duty-free. The price of sugar fell, and the Hawaiian economy felt the impact.

In 1891 Liliuokalani succeeded Kalakaua as monarch of Hawaii. She made it clear that she intended to maintain the independence of her people. Supporters of the Hawaiian League staged a major protest when she announced that she intended to overturn the illegal Bayonet Constitution. With support from armed U.S. Marines, the Hawaiian League installed Sanford Dole as the president of a new government. Rather than see Hawaiian lives lost in battle, Liliuokalani stepped down from the throne.

When the Dole government petitioned the United States for annexation, President Grover Cleveland ordered an investigation. Disgusted by the flagrant illegality of the "revolution," which had been led by U.S. expatriates who had been given no authority by their government, Cleveland ordered the Dole government disbanded. However, Sanford Dole defied the president, refusing to step down. Cleveland was not willing to go to war to restore Liliuokalani to her throne, but he stood his ground in refusing to annex Hawaii. President William McKinley annexed Hawaii in 1898, ignoring the protests of the vast majority of Hawaiians. Hawaii became a U.S. territory in 1900, and U.S. companies continued to control vast plantations in Hawaii on which workers labored under harsh conditions.

The Spanish-American War

> You take the Spanish-American war. . . . That was Mr. Kane's war. We didn't really have anything to fight about. But do you think if it hadn't been for that war of Mr. Kane's we'd have the Panama Canal?

In 1941 a muckraking film biography of the newspaper publisher William Randolph Hearst called *Citizen Kane* opened in theaters across the United States. The film makes newspaper editor and owner Charles Foster Kane (a thinly disguised stand-in for Hearst) responsible for deliberately provoking the Spanish-American War by running inflammatory headlines in his newspapers. This was no exaggeration on the part of the filmmakers.

Hearst believed that his most important responsibility as the owner of the *New York Journal* was to sell more papers. He soon acquired the reputation of one who would print any story, no matter how outrageous, to attract the reading public. The sensational stories that became the *Journal*'s trademark were nicknamed "**yellow journalism**" after a character in a newspaper comic strip. Hearst was not terribly concerned with facts. He was interested in printing anything that would make someone buy a copy of his paper rather than that of a rival.

The large Caribbean islands of Puerto Rico and Cuba were the only remaining colonies of the once large Spanish Empire in the West. Cubans had been fighting sporadically for their independence since 1860. Spanish authorities had kept the upper hand and tried to break the spirit of the revolutionaries by exiling many of their leaders from the island. In 1896 the Spanish Army herded tens of thousands of Cubans into concentration camps, where many of them died of hunger and sickness. Hearst knew that the dramatic events in Cuba would interest his readers. He encouraged his reporters to exaggerate the facts and stir up U.S. resentment against Spain. Many people in the United States sympathized with the Cuban revolutionaries, who were fighting a tyrant on the other side of the Atlantic just as the American colonists had resisted Great Britain. *Journal* stories deliberately played on that sympathy, actively pressuring the U.S. government to declare war on Spain. President McKinley resisted the pressure.

In 1898 the U.S. battleship *Maine*, anchored off the Cuban coast in case its crew should be needed to protect U.S. property or lives, exploded without warning. What caused the explosion is still unknown; independent investigations at the time suggested that it might have been an accident or an underwater mine. Few people seriously believed the Spanish were to blame, as Spanish diplomats had been working hard to avoid a confrontation with the United States. Ignoring the facts, Hearst put the story of the *Maine* on the front page for several days, with headlines such as the following:

- THE WARSHIP *MAINE* WAS SPLIT IN TWO BY AN ENEMY'S SECRET INFERNAL MACHINE.
- THE WHOLE COUNTRY THRILLS WITH THE WAR FEVER
- HOW THE *MAINE* ACTUALLY LOOKS AS IT LIES, WRECKED BY SPANISH TREACHERY, IN HAVANA BAY

Hearst had deliberately stirred the public to a fever pitch of indignation against Spain with what one historian later referred to as the "acme of ruthless, truthless newspaper **jingoism.**" With the people clamoring for action, McKinley felt that he had no choice but to demand concessions from the Spanish. Even after the concessions were accepted, Congress voted to take up arms against Spain. Congress officially recognized Cuba's independence from Spain and then formally declared that the United States would use military force to help Cuba secure independence. On April 25, 1898, Congress declared war. It would be fought on three fronts: in Cuba, Puerto Rico, and the Philippines (where Admiral Dewey had already been sent), which served at the time as a Spanish naval base.

Commodore George Dewey led a fleet of U.S. warships from the coast of Hong Kong to the Philippines a few days after Congress declared war. The U.S. ships opened fire on the Spanish fleet guarding Manila's harbor, easily overpowering them. Filipinos had been rebelling against Spanish rule for two years and were easily enlisted to help the United States conquer Manila. The war ended in the Philippines in August 1898.

Although the navy had been successful in the Philippines, the army was not adequately prepared for the land battles it would have to fight in Cuba. The United States did not maintain a large standing army in peacetime, and the only uniforms the soldiers were supplied with were made of heavy wool, which was unsuitable for the tropical climate of Cuba.

Theodore Roosevelt had joined the army and been placed in command of a cavalry unit nicknamed the Rough Riders whose goal was to capture the high ground above the city of Santiago. The Rough Riders charged up the hill under a hail of Spanish bullets and had control of the high ground by nightfall.

Through his contacts with the media and reporters, Roosevelt would use this battle to solidify his reputation. The U.S. Navy sank the entire Spanish fleet off the coast of Cuba, and the war ended two weeks later when Spain surrendered. Fighting in Puerto Rico already had ended. The United States agreed to pay Spain $20 million for the Philippines. Cuba gained its independence from Spain. Spain ceded Guam to the United States.

After the War: The Philippines

After the defeat of the Spanish fleet, the Filipino patriot Emiliano Aguinaldo took the lead in setting up a provisional government. Aguinaldo became the island nation's first president. The Filipinos had been given no say in the matter of their annexation by the United States and were furious because the United States had promised them independence in exchange for rebelling against Spain. However, the United States had other plans for the Philippines. It would serve as a naval base. It would function as a handy central location for trade of Asian and U.S. goods, saving thousands of miles of transport. It would provide a new market for U.S. goods. It could produce goods that the United States needed to import at forced favorable rates.

From their point of view, the Filipinos felt that U.S. annexation amounted to a betrayal. Armed conflict raged between a U.S. army of occupation and Filipino patriots for three years. The Filipinos utilized guerrilla warfare, and the United States resorted to brutal tactics. Finally, in 1902 the United States brought the rebellion under control, although sporadic fighting would continue for years. The U.S. Congress then passed the Philippine Government Act, which established a bicameral legislature and a governor. Filipinos would elect their own representatives to the lower house; the United States would appoint the governor and the members of the upper house. In 1916 the United States relented further and passed the Jones Act of 1916, giving Filipinos the right to elect members of the upper house, although the United States continued to control the country.

After the War: Cuba and Puerto Rico

Having been pushed into a war he did not support, President McKinley acted decisively once the war was over. He installed temporary governments in Cuba and Puerto Rico, claiming that the United States had to be in charge until order was restored. McKinley appointed Leonard Wood governor of Cuba. Wood immediately took two practical steps to improve everyday life in Cuba: he provided money for the construction of schools and established a sanitation system that deprived mosquitoes of their breeding grounds by draining pools of standing water and thus removing the constant threat of **yellow fever.** He also allowed U.S. companies to take over the important industries.

Despite those points in his favor, Wood was an autocrat. He joined the U.S. Congress in insisting that Cuba adopt the so-called Platt Amendment to the Cuban constitution, making the island a **protectorate** of the United States and requiring Cuba to sell or rent land to the United States for a naval base. If Cuba accepted the Platt Amendment, U.S. troops of occupation would leave the island. The Cuban legislature reluctantly voted for the amendment in 1902. Theodore Roosevelt commented that "there was little independence left in Cuba under the Platt Amendment." The next year Cuba and the United States signed a trade agreement that profited both countries.

Puerto Rico was at first ruled just as the Philippines had been, with a U.S.-appointed governor and senate and a Puerto Rican–elected House of Representatives. The Jones Act of 1917 restored to Puerto Ricans the right to elect their own senate.

The Panama Canal

The French were the first to try to construct a canal across the isthmus of Panama to link the Atlantic and Pacific oceans. Ferdinand de Lesseps, a French engineer, had designed and overseen the construction of the Suez Canal in Egypt and was confident of success in Panama. However, the effort was a failure. Thousands of workers died of yellow fever and dysentery, and the French abandoned the project.

The United States watched the progress of the canal project with interest and stepped in as soon as the French gave up the attempt. In 1903 Secretary of State John Hay proposed a bargain to the government of Colombia, of which Panama was then a part. Colombia would give the United States a 99-year lease on the Canal Zone, a strip of land 6 miles wide and 50 miles long, across Panama. In exchange, the United States would pay Colombia $10 million outright and $250,000 a year afterward. The Colombians did not accept the bargain.

However, Colombia had not reckoned with the actions of Panamanian rebels who believed that a deal for the canal with the United States would help achieve Panamanian independence. In 1903 Philippe Bunau-Varilla, the chief engineer of the canal project, brokered a deal between the rebels and the U.S. government. The United States agreed to support the rebels against Colombia in exchange for permanent sovereignty over a 10-mile-wide canal zone. Colombia quickly capitulated, Panama became independent, and the U.S.-controlled Canal Zone was established. Construction of the Panama Canal was completed in 1914 (see the map below). Most of the workers had been recruited from the Caribbean islands. They faced many dangers, including sudden avalanches of earth and disease. Six thousand workers would die before the project was completed.

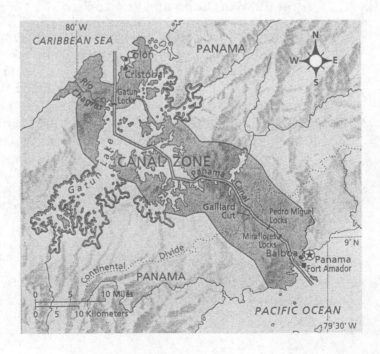

Promoting Economic Growth

To gain economic control over various Latin American nations, the United States frequently intervened in their affairs. In 1904 President Theodore Roosevelt proclaimed the so-called **Roosevelt Corollary** to the Monroe Doctrine, outlining U.S. policy toward Latin America:

> . . . under no circumstances will the United States use the Monroe Doctrine as a cloak for territorial aggression. We desire peace with all the world, but. . . . [t]here are, of course, limits to the wrongs which any self-respecting nation can endure. It is always possible that wrong actions toward this Nation, or toward citizens of this Nation . . . may result in our having to take action to protect our rights; but such action will not be taken with a view to territorial aggression, and it will be taken at all only with extreme reluctance and when it has become evident that every other resource has been exhausted.

By using the phrase "to protect American interests," the corollary was vague enough to justify almost any action. When Latin American nations could not repay bank loans to Europe and European nations threatened to use force to collect on their loans, the United States intervened, generally without consulting the Latin American nations concerned. U.S. intervention generally came in the form of an army of occupation, which usually stayed in place for some years. This marked a change in U.S. foreign policy from reactive to proactive and damaged relations with Latin American countries for years to come.

When William Howard Taft succeeded Roosevelt as president, U.S. policy shifted. Taft believed in **dollar diplomacy:** investing U.S. money in Latin American nations. That way those nations would owe money to the United States, not to Europe. They would have trade relations with the United States. The United States would build businesses in those nations and hire workers there.

Woodrow Wilson, who took office after Taft, felt that politics, not economics, was the way to gain influence over Latin America. He used military force to help rebels establish constitutional governments throughout Latin America. This **missionary diplomacy** was often a confusing mix of self-interest and moralism. A good example was the situation in Mexico, where Wilson sent troops to arrest Pancho Villa, a rebel who had led raids across the U.S. border. At the same time, Wilson demanded that Mexico remedy inequality in wealth between the upper and lower classes (something that no government would do in the United States).

REVIEW QUESTIONS

1. The United States became an imperialist nation in the late 1800s for all the following reasons EXCEPT:

   (A) desire to establish new markets for U.S. goods
   (B) interest in acquiring naval bases in strategic locations
   (C) need to obtain inexpensive access to certain goods that the United States could not produce for itself, such as sugar and rubber
   (D) desire to put an end to tyranny in foreign nations
   (E) wish to be considered a powerful force in world affairs

2. By 1920 the United States had acquired partial or total control over all the following EXCEPT:

   (A) the Canal Zone
   (B) Puerto Rico
   (C) China
   (D) the Philippines
   (E) Guam

3. Which of the following did the Roosevelt Corollary modify?

   (A) The Monroe Doctrine
   (B) The Platt Amendment
   (C) The Hawaiian constitution
   (D) The Hay–Bunau-Varilla Treaty
   (E) The Open Door Policy

Answers and Explanations

1. **D** The United States did not depose any foreign tyrants for another hundred years. This was never a goal of late nineteenth-century imperialism.
2. **C** The United States had a trade relationship with China but controlled no part of that country or its government.
3. **A** The Monroe Doctrine established U.S. foreign policy toward Latin America and any nation that had colonies there. The Roosevelt Corollary restated and modified U.S. policy toward Latin America.

CHAPTER 22

WORLD WAR I AND ITS AFTERMATH, 1914–1920

INTRODUCTION

The United States had entered the twentieth century an isolated nation both geographically and politically. It played no role in conflicts between other nations but simply pursued its own territorial conquests and fought wars involving its own direct concerns.

The Spanish-American War marked the beginning of the end of that period of isolation. For the first time the nation fought a war that took place outside the contiguous United States. This marked the country's involvement in the affairs of Europe and colonialism but limited that involvement to places far from the centers of world power.

World War I marked the first major role in world affairs for the United States. The war began in 1914, but the United States did not become directly involved in it until three years of fighting had gone by. The United States supplied money and arms to the Allied Powers as early as 1916 but did not declare war on the Central Powers until 1917. The first U.S. troops did not enter the trenches until 1918.

The United States came out of the war in a strong position. The traditional European powers—Britain, France, and Germany—were severely weakened. Millions of their young men had been slaughtered, their armies and navies were destroyed, their economies were devastated, and much French land and many villages lay in ruins. By contrast, the United States had lost relatively few soldiers and ships, and its home front had been far away from the fighting. The war effort had had a positive effect on the U.S. economy.

The fact that the war might have been avoided led President Woodrow Wilson to insist on the creation of a League of Nations, an international organization in which representatives of member nations would discuss conflicts at a roundtable, attempting to resolve them peacefully. In Wilson's vision, armed conflict would be a last resort. If one nation behaved aggressively, all other nations would unite against it, effectively putting a stop to its attacks or encroachments. That vision became a reality in 1920, but without U.S. participation. A full-scale United Nations, which all the great powers of the world would join, would have to wait until after World War II—a war that might have been prevented if Wilson's dream of a modern roundtable had come true.

TIMELINE

1908   Austria-Hungary annexes Bosnia-Herzegovina.

1914

June 28   Gavrilo Princip assassinates Archduke Franz Ferdinand of Austria-Hungary.

July 28   Austria-Hungary declares war on Serbia.

July 30   Russian troops mobilize against Austria-Hungary.

August 1   Germany declares war on Russia.

August 3   Germany declares war on France; German troops invade Belgium.

September 6–7   Battle of the Marne.

October 29   Turkey enters the war on the side of the Central Powers.

November 10–18   First Battle of Ypres.

1915

Trench warfare begins.

United States begins giving financial support to the Allies.

Great Migration of African Americans to Northern states begins (1915–1930).

April 22   Germans pioneer the use of poison gas in war at Second Battle of Ypres.

April 26   Italy signs Treaty of London.

May 7   German U-boats sink the *Lusitania*.

May 24   Italy enters the war on the Allied side.

November 15   British forced to withdraw from Dardanelles in defeat.

1916

National Defense Act.

"Lafayette Escadrilles" (U.S. volunteer airmen) begin fighting in France.

February 21   Battle of Verdun begins (ends July 1916).

May 31   Battle of Jutland.

July 1   Battle of the Somme begins (ends November 1916).

September   Allied Powers pioneer the use of the tank in battle.

1917

Selective Service Act.

February 3   United States severs diplomatic relations with Germany.

March 1   Publication of the Zimmerman Telegram.

March 16   Czar Nicholas II of Russia abdicates.

April 4   United States declares war on Germany.

June 9   Espionage Act.

July 21–November 10   Battle of Passchendaele.

October 21   U.S. troops arrive on Western Front.

November 2   Balfour Declaration.

November 7   Bolshevik Revolution.

1918

January 8   Woodrow Wilson gives "Fourteen Points" speech.

February 23   Treaty of Brest-Litovsk.

September–October   Massive flu epidemic kills tens of millions.

November 11   Germany surrenders; armistice signed.

1919

June 28   Peace conference and signing of the Treaty of Versailles.

September   Wilson has a severe stroke.

KEY TERMS

Allied Powers   Britain and France; later included Italy and United States

armistice   cease-fire agreement

Bolshevik Party   a Russian political party of radical socialists

Central Powers   Germany, Austria-Hungary, Bulgaria, and the Ottoman Empire

Fourteen Points   Woodrow Wilson's program for world peace

mutiny   defiance of military or naval authority

no-man's-land   the zone between two lines of trenches

reparations   financial compensation for damage done

Schlieffen Plan   German war plan involving a two-front war against France in the west and Russia in the east

Selective Service Act   established a military draft in which young men registered and then waited to be called for duty

superpower   a nation that is clearly wealthier, mightier, and less vulnerable than all other nations

trench warfare   armed combat between two sides that have dug trench fortifications in the ground

U-boat   nickname for *unterseeboot* (pronounced oohn • tehr • SAY • boat); in English, submarine or, more specifically, a German submarine.

Causes of World War I

The spark that touched off World War I—called "the Great War" at the time—was territorial conflict. Both Serbia and Austria-Hungary claimed the right to control the tiny kingdom of Bosnia-Herzegovina. Austria annexed the territory in 1908, provoking Serbian anger and vows of revenge.

In June 1914 Archduke Franz Ferdinand and Archduchess Sophie of Austria-Hungary were visiting Sarajevo, the capital city of Bosnia. As they rode through the streets in an open car, a Serbian nationalist named Gavrilo Princip shot and killed them. Austria soon declared war on Serbia. Serbia's ally Russia then threatened to attack Austria. Austria was allied with Germany, and the Germans responded to the Russian threat by declaring war on Russia and also on its ally France. A few days later, when German troops invaded Belgium on their way to France, Great Britain declared war on Germany.

World War I had its roots in nineteenth-century imperialism. An arms race and conflict over territory had been brewing for many years. Many countries believed that a quick war would be necessary to determine once and for all who was going to be in charge of Europe. Many interlocking treaties and alliances would draw the countries and their colonial empires into the war. The German war plan, called the **Schlieffen Plan,** was to conquer Belgium and France so that Britain would be unable to bring troops to continental Europe and then to conquer Russia in the east. That plan bogged down after the German offensive was stopped in France at the First Battle of the Marne.

The war pitted the **Allied Powers**—Britain, France, and Russia—against the **Central Powers**—Germany, Austria-Hungary, the Ottoman Empire, and Bulgaria. The United States and Italy later entered the war on the Allied side.

Much of World War I was fought in the trenches that both sides had dug—hundreds of miles of them, stretching roughly along the north-south axis of Europe, from Nieuport on the North Sea coast of Belgium to the border of Switzerland. This trench zone was called the Western Front. The trenches served the soldiers on both sides as both home and fort throughout four years of fighting. German and Allied trenches were sometimes only a few dozen yards apart. The zone that separated them was called **no-man's-land.** On orders, soldiers would leap out of the trenches and cross no-man's-land to attack the enemy, usually facing a hail of machine-gun bullets that slaughtered millions on both sides (see the map below). The great tragedy of **trench warfare** was that only a mile or so of land was ever gained on either side—millions of young men died in no-man's-land and in the trenches for nothing.

Allied trenches were terrible places. They had been dug hastily on the assumption that the war would be over quickly; therefore, they lacked any comforts or amenities. They were muddy, often ankle- or knee-deep in rainwater, damp all the time, frigid in winter and broiling in summer. Soldiers found it impossible to keep the rats away from their stores of food or to keep their personal property—books, cigarettes, letters from home—clean and dry. The Allied generals proved unimaginative, continually sending their soldiers over the top to run at the German lines, no matter how unsuccessfully. German trenches were somewhat more comfortable; the German Army had used planks to pave its trenches with flooring and walls and had even installed electricity.

World War I was the first modern war. No soldier had ever experienced anything like it. The officers were mainly older men, veterans of nineteenth-century wars who had fought in cavalry regiments and still thought of war as an honorable duty and a gallant adventure. This war was fought with machine guns, tanks, and poison gas. It was fought by submarines under the water and pilots in the air. The casualties were tremendous as tactics slowly caught up with the new technology.

The United States Enters the War

Although the United States maintained an official policy of strict neutrality, few Americans felt neutral about the war. Millions of them were recent immigrants or the children or grandchildren of immigrants from the nations at war in Europe. They still had emotional ties to those nations, and most still had family in Europe. The heritage argument split the U.S. public, but most were united in the idea that they did not want to be involved militarily.

It clearly would not be possible for the United States to remain detached for long. International alliances demanded that the United States commit itself to one side or the other. Both Britain and Germany violated U.S. neutrality on the seas.

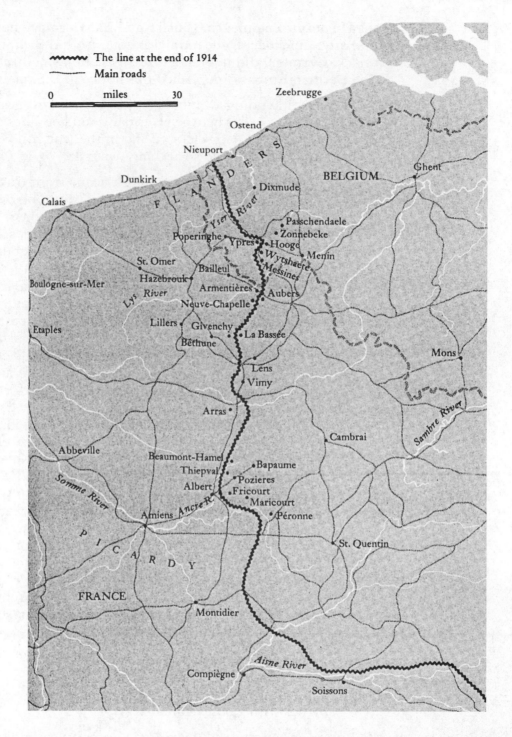

The British Navy blockaded Germany and set mines in the North Sea. The British insisted on searching all ships entering the North Sea and intercepting any goods that appeared to be bound for Germany. This included U.S. ships. Wilson registered official protests with the British government, but the practice continued.

Germany had built an impressive fleet of *unterseeboots*—submarines. Those **U-boats,** as they were called, were a highly effective weapon in the war because they could not be detected. They could sail quietly underwater and then suddenly blow up a ship on the surface that had had no warning of their approach. Part of the Germans' war plan from the beginning had been to use the U-boats to cripple the British Navy. The Germans had openly announced that any ship entering the naval war zone around Britain might be subject to attack; Germany did not recognize any nation's neutrality in the war zone. The German Embassy published this notice in U.S. newspapers:

> Travelers intending to embark on the Atlantic voyage are reminded that a state of war exists between Germany and her allies and Great Britain and her allies . . . travelers sailing in the war zone on ships of Great Britain or her allies do so at their own risk.

Warnings like this did not stop Americans from traveling; Wilson stated that any injury to U.S. citizens or property would be considered a violation of neutrality and the United States would not let it pass. Wilson asserted that the United States had a right to trade with both sides, essentially profiting from the conflict. It is important to note that the president also sold weapons to the British in spite of a promise not to.

On May 7, 1915, German U-boats sank the *Lusitania,* a British passenger liner. More than a hundred U.S. citizens were lost, as well as a shipment of U.S. arms destined for Britain. People in the United States were furious. Wilson demanded that Germany halt submarine warfare on civilian merchant ships. By 1916 the United States no longer could claim even a pretence of neutrality. It had sold millions of dollars' worth of arms to the Allies and had provided billions of dollars in financial support for their war effort.

Wilson took several steps in 1916 to prepare the United States for war, although he still hoped to avoid it. He signed the National Defense Act, which doubled the size of the armed forces. He built up the size of the National Guard. He signed a bill that gave millions of dollars to the Navy. Most people in the United States shared Wilson's earnest hope that those preparations would prove unnecessary. In the presidential election of 1916 Wilson campaigned as the candidate who would keep the United States out of war. Theodore Roosevelt publicly stated that he considered it the nation's duty to send troops to Europe without delay; he failed to win his party's nomination for president. Wilson won the election over Charles Evans Hughes, whom Roosevelt reluctantly supported. Voters associated Hughes with Roosevelt's eagerness for war and backed away from supporting him. A political advertisement that appeared in the papers on Election Day accurately captured voters' sentiments:

> You Are Working—*Not Fighting!*
> Alive and Happy;—*Not cannon Fodder!*
> Wilson and Peace with Honor?
> or
> Hughes with Roosevelt and War?

Europeans interpreted Wilson's victory as a clear indication that the United States would stay out of the war. However, Germany provoked the United States again and again by resuming U-boat attacks on all ships, including merchant ships. In March, U.S. newspapers published the Zimmerman Telegram, sent by the German foreign secretary Arthur Zimmerman to the German minister in Mexico, suggesting an alliance between Germany and Mexico against the United States. In case of a German victory, stated the telegram, Mexico would be given back a large portion of the southwestern parts of the United States. Americans regarded the telegram as a clear threat, and Wilson decided that he had no choice but to ask Congress to declare war. It did so on April 4, 1917.

The U.S. Army

Much as in the Civil War, the United States could not rely on an all-volunteer army. So few men volunteered for service that Congress passed the **Selective Service Act,** requiring all men and boys between the ages of 21 and 30 (later the age range was extended to 18 to 45) to register with local draft boards. Troops were racially segregated, with many of the worst duties being assigned to Latinos, Native Americans, foreign-born soldiers, and African Americans. All those diverse groups served bravely, many with distinction. The military service of 10,000 Native Americans persuaded Congress to pass a 1924 law granting all Native Americans U.S. citizenship. Thousands of women eagerly grasped the opportunity to go overseas as well. They were not allowed to join the Army in combat positions, but the Medical Corps welcomed them as nurses, doctors, and ambulance drivers. Many more women sailed to Europe as volunteers with the Red Cross and other charitable agencies.

The first U.S. troops reached France in June 1917. On July 4 they were in Paris. One officer saluted the tomb of Lafayette and said aloud: "Lafayette, we are here!" acknowledging that the United States was repaying the debt it owed to the French for coming to its aid during the Revolutionary War.

U.S. warships escorted merchant ships that carried urgently needed supplies for the relief of the Allies as well as U.S. troops and volunteers. This effectively checkmated the U-boat offensive. The United States also laid mines in the North Sea, which was the route the U-boats traveled on their way home to Germany.

The Home Front

The United States needed money to pay for the war. The federal government took several steps to raise money and conserve resources. First, Congress raised taxes. That brought the government added revenue of about $10 billion. Second, the government sold war bonds and persuaded Americans through advertising that it was their patriotic duty to buy them. The newly created Food and Fuel Administrations regulated the production and supply of crops and coal. People in the United States began growing their own vegetables in what were called "victory gardens." People went without meat on certain days of the week and without bread on others. The Fuel Administration promoted "heatless Mondays" so that people would conserve fuel at least one day a week.

The War Industries Board began regulating steel and other big industries, setting their prices and production levels. Many people loudly objected to that interference with free enterprise. However, they went quiet when profits soared.

The National War Labor Board heard and decided disputes between workers and management. In keeping with the reforming spirit of the Progressive Era, the board often decided in favor of the workers. Union membership rose to unprecedented levels. Many unions agreed not to agitate for better pay and working conditions because it was a time of war (even though business leaders were making billions in profit). Since so many men had left their jobs to join the Army or Navy, thousands of women took their place in a variety of jobs, from bricklayer to teamster.

African Americans also took advantage of the improved opportunities created by the war effort. Between about 1915 and 1930 hundreds of thousands of African Americans moved from the segregated South to the North, where they hoped to find jobs that paid well and a respite from racial discrimination. That movement came to be known as the Great Migration. The migrants soon found that there was no lack of racial prejudice in the North; still, they were able to earn more money.

Many people felt that the U.S. government was manipulating the poor and the workers to fight a war that would benefit only the wealthy and powerful. The Socialist Party, led by Eugene Debs, was especially active against the war. So were the Industrial Workers of the World, the Quakers, and other organizations. Labor strikes organized specifically to protest the war drove Congress to pass the Espionage and Sedition Acts, which made it illegal to "utter, print, write, or publish any disloyal or abusive language" about the government, the flag, or the military. Stating "I am against the war" became a crime punishable with prison time. Although those acts clearly violated the First Amendment, hundreds of people were convicted and sent to prison for speaking out. Eugene Debs, after his trial for violating the acts, looked the judge in the eye and stated firmly:

> Your Honor, years ago I recognized my kinship with all living beings, and I made up my mind that I was not one bit better than the meanest of earth. I said then, and I say now, that while there is a lower class, I am in it, while there is a criminal element I am of it, and while there is a soul in prison, I am not free.

So many union leaders were jailed that many unions were left leaderless. Even though the jail sentences often were overturned by appeals courts, much of the union movement was weakened for years to come.

The Turning of the Tide: Victory and Armistice

In the fall of 1917 many French troops began to **mutiny.** They had been fighting in the trenches for over three years, making no advances, seeing their comrades blown to pieces beside them, and knowing that all the while the generals were safe, well behind the lines of fire. They refused to go on fighting. New heart was brought to the French and the other Allied troops by the arrival of the first U.S. soldiers.

Events took an unexpected turn when Russia decided to abandon the war. Anger against the war and the czar's government had been stirring in Russia for some time, and it finally boiled over in the streets in 1917. The czar abdicated. After a power struggle of several more months with the socialists, the more radical **Bolshevik Party** seized power. Its leader, Vladimir Ilyich Lenin, signed the Treaty of Brest-Litovsk with Germany in early 1918.

The Germans now launched a final, massive attack on the Western Front. Because of the fresh U.S. troops, the Allies were able to beat them back. Then the Allies launched their own attack. Fighting raged through the spring and summer and into the autumn of 1918. Finally, in the Battle of the Argonne Forest, it became clear that Germany would have to surrender. One African-American regiment fought so bravely at the Argonne Forest that France later awarded it the Croix de Guerre, that nation's highest military honor.

On November 9 Kaiser Wilhelm II of Germany abdicated, and early in the morning of November 11 the leaders on both sides signed the **armistice.** At 11 a.m., the guns stopped firing.

Woodrow Wilson's Fourteen Points, the Treaty of Versailles, and the League of Nations

Before the war had ended, Woodrow Wilson and his advisors had laid out an impressive plan for maintaining world peace. Wilson's plan, called the **Fourteen Points,** was disclosed to Congress in a speech in January:

> What we demand in this war, therefore, is . . . that the world be made fit and safe to live in; and particularly that it be made safe for every peace-loving nation which, like our own, wishes to live its own life, determine its own institutions, be assured of justice and fair dealing by the other peoples of the world as against force and selfish aggression.

Wilson then laid out the "Fourteen Points" of his program for peace. The first five points were general, describing how international relations should be conducted in the future. Those points included an argument for free trade and free access to the seas among all nations. The next eight points dealt specifically with how the map of Europe should appear at the end of the war: that all armies of occupation return home, that national frontiers be drawn along appropriate ethnic borders, and that no European nation should maintain dominion over another that wished to be independent. He did not apply those programs to the non-Europeans who were a part of the various European colonial empires.

The final point stated that an international organization must be formed that would protect the interests of large and small nations on an equal basis. Representatives of member nations would work together to maintain world peace and settle any international disputes across a table before resorting to the battlefield.

People in the United States responded positively to Wilson's idea for a League of Nations, and Wilson insisted that a clause establishing the league be included in the Treaty of Versailles. To obtain this he was forced by the French and British governments to abandon the rest of the Fourteen Points and agree to very harsh terms for Germany.

The peace conference convened in January 1919 at Versailles, the old French royal palace in the countryside near Paris. Versailles was a symbol of the power of France, and its selection as the place to sign the treaty was a deliberate attempt to intimidate the Germans. The conference itself had been arranged carefully to humiliate the German representatives. They were forced to travel to Versailles by a local train through many of the major battlefields and to view the destruction for which the treaty would demand that they take sole blame.

Provisions of the Treaty of Versailles

The treaty contained the following provisions, among others:

- Created new nations, such as Czechoslovakia and Yugoslavia, by taking territory from Austria
- Recognized the independence of Poland, Finland, Latvia, Lithuania, and Estonia, which formerly had been ruled by Russia
- Returned the Alsace-Lorraine region to France from Germany
- Gave France control of Germany's Saarland region until 1934
- Disarmed Germany and ordered it not to rearm

- Forced Germany to admit full responsibility for the war
- Charged Germany billions of dollars in **reparations** to other nations

Wilson opposed the final two clauses. He saw no point in heaping so much blame on Germany, which had suffered as much as any other European nation had. He also knew, as did all the other leaders, that Germany could not possibly pay reparations on such a massive scale. However, the French and British representatives insisted on putting all the blame on Germany. They felt that to do otherwise would be to dishonor the memories of the millions of Allied soldiers who had fallen during the war.

Wilson returned to the United States in July 1919 and laid the Treaty of Versailles before Congress. As a result of the objections of a faction led by Senator Henry Cabot Lodge, Congress refused to approve the treaty. Lodge and his followers were immovably opposed to the League of Nations. Another group of senators agreed to accept the League of Nations but did not like a provision in it that committed the United States to defend any member nation that was attacked by an outsider. Wilson refused to bend on this issue and, hoping to sway public opinion to his side, embarked on a speaking tour of the country. During the tour he experienced a severe stroke; he survived and served out his term, but historians agree that he exercised little control over events from then on. The League of Nations became a reality, but without U.S. participation.

The Costs of War

Twenty million people—an entire generation of Europeans—died during the war of battle wounds or disease. Thirty million more were missing or living with severe wounds or amputations. The rich farmlands of Belgium and France, which had been the major battlefields of the war, were laid waste. European industry was in ruins.

Moreover, "an age was dead and gone," as Wilson stated in a 1918 speech. The tank had replaced the cavalry regiment. The machine gun had replaced the bayonet. For a generation, innocence had been murdered brutally. The writer Ernest Hemingway flatly stated that "words such as glory, honor, courage, or hallow were obscene" compared to cold facts such as the name of a dead soldier or the number of a regiment. "In the summer of 1914," wrote the historian Paul Fussell, "no one would have understood what [Hemingway] was talking about." After the war, people understood only too well.

The United States came out of the war relatively unscathed. Over 100,000 U.S. soldiers had lost their lives, but no fighting had taken place on U.S. soil. The economy at home was prosperous from the war effort, and industrial production had increased. Since the European nations were devastated and exhausted, their towns destroyed, their resources spent, and millions of their young men dead, the United States emerged from the war as a major power, stronger by far than the European powers. Although U.S. participation in the war had been relatively minor compared with that of France or Britain, the United States participated in the peace process on equal terms with the Allies. This showed conclusively that the balance of international power had shifted from the Old World to the New. The United States had entered a century in which it would be considered a **superpower,** although its first act would be to return to isolationism.

REVIEW QUESTIONS

1. All of the following nations were allied with the Central Powers EXCEPT:

   (A) France
   (B) Germany
   (C) Turkey
   (D) Bulgaria
   (E) Austria-Hungary

2. The United States came out of World War I in a strong international position primarily because

   (A) it had founded the League of Nations
   (B) it had lost relatively few of its fighting forces and its economy was prosperous
   (C) it had had a successful socialist revolution
   (D) it was geographically isolated from Europe
   (E) it had dictated the terms of the Treaty of Versailles

3. The Treaty of Versailles stated all the following EXCEPT:

   (A) Germany would have to pay reparations to Allied nations.
   (B) Alsace-Lorraine would be returned to France.
   (C) New nations called Czechoslovakia and Yugoslavia would be established.
   (D) Russia would be known as the Soviet Union.
   (E) Germany would accept total blame for the war.

Answers and Explanations

1. **A** France fought with the Allied Powers. The German war plan was to invade and conquer Belgium and France; therefore, France and Germany could not have been allies.

2. **B** The United States came out of the war in a strong position because fighting had not taken place in the United States; therefore, its industries were intact and in fact were operating at peak production. It had entered the war so late that relatively few of its soldiers had been killed, whereas the European nations had seen their armies decimated.

3. **D** The name change from Russia to the Soviet Union occurred as a result of the Bolshevik Revolution, not the Treaty of Versailles.

CHAPTER 23
THE JAZZ AGE

INTRODUCTION

The Jazz Age, the Roaring Twenties, the era of the flapper—the decade between the Treaty of Versailles and the stock market crash has many names. Many people view it as the true beginning of the twentieth century: the beginning of the modern era. For the first time it seemed that almost everyone owned a car. The piano that had once adorned most people's living rooms was being sold to make room for a radio and a phonograph. People watched moving pictures on theater screens and bought hard black disks with the latest jazz tunes recorded on them.

After World War I ended, people in the United States enjoyed a decade of prosperity. Although conditions for the working class were not good during the 1920s—they lost many of the gains they had made during the Progressive Era—times were good for almost everyone else. The rich grew richer, and there were more expensive toys for them to spend their money on. Women made the most of the freedoms they had won during the war, changing everything about their appearance, clothing, and behavior.

An explosion of artistic creations acknowledged the darker side of life. Artists who had come of age as members of the "Lost Generation" wrote about the death of innocence in the trenches of World War I and about the impossibility of romance in the modern world. On the surface, jazz music was cheerful and catchy, but it was built on slave songs and the blues. Segregation existed in nightclubs that African Americans could enter only if they were performing on stage.

Politically, the 1920s marked a return to conservatism. Three Republican presidents gave tax cuts to the wealthy but refused to pass any legislation that would protect the workers who were responsible for the profits. The party of the Jazz Age ended as suddenly as it had begun—on October 24, 1929, the stock market crashed.

TIMELINE

1919   Chicago White Sox take bribes to throw the World Series to the Cincinnati Reds.

Eighteenth Amendment ratified.

Volstead Act.

1920   First radio broadcasts.

1923   Equal Rights Amendment proposed to Congress.

1925   Scopes trial.

F. Scott Fitzgerald publishes *The Great Gatsby*.

1927   Charles Lindbergh completes the first solo flight across the Atlantic.

Babe Ruth hits 60 home runs for the New York Yankees.

Ford Motor Company introduces the "Model A."

Warner Brothers releases *The Jazz Singer*, the first full-length motion picture with sound.

1929   St. Valentine's Day Massacre.

1931   Empire State Building completed.

1933   Twenty-First Amendment ratified, repealing Eighteenth Amendment.

KEY TERMS

assembly line   a method of factory construction in which each item passes workers on a conveyor belt, with each worker adding the next part to it

bathtub gin   an alcoholic drink distilled in private homes, usually in the bathtub

Black Sox   nickname for the members of the Chicago White Sox who threw the 1919 World Series

bootleg   adjective meaning "illegal"

evolution   a scientific theory stating that human beings evolved from other primates

flapper   a modern young woman who played sports, bobbed her hair, and wore short skirts

Harlem Renaissance   an artistic movement led by African Americans that centered on Harlem in New York City

Lost Generation   a name coined by Gertrude Stein to describe American writers and artists who had lost their illusions of glory and honor during World War I

normalcy   a word coined by Warren G. Harding meaning "normality"

organized crime   illegal activity on a large scale, run like a business with an organizational structure

Prohibition   the era during which the Eighteenth Amendment was in effect

speakeasy   any club that sold liquor illegally

St. Valentine's Day Massacre   February 14, 1929, violent gang confrontation in Chicago that resulted in seven deaths

"Untouchables"   a squad of FBI agents who worked only on cases dealing with violations of Prohibition

The "Return to Normalcy"

After the war President Herbert Hoover would embark on the "return to normalcy." Basically, this meant that he wanted an end to the Progressive Era. The government would use the Espionage Act to destroy union leadership, and the courts would rule against the right to strike. Progressive legislation would come to an end, and business would be freed from regulations on safety, pay, and consumer protection. Women would be forced out of their jobs, and African-American soldiers returning from the war would endure a series of race riots throughout the country.

One of the first indications of this shift was the so-called Red Scare. After the Bolshevik Revolution in Russia, paranoia about communism ran rampant in the United States. After a series of bombings in New York City, the government was given increased power to arrest people. Attorney General A. Mitchell Palmer was allowed to arrest, detain, and search thousands of suspected anarchists. This process resulted in relatively few arrests but was followed by large-scale deportations. The Red Scare reached its peak with the trial of two Italian-born anarchists, Nicola Sacco and Bartolomeo Vanzetti, for murder. The evidence against the defendants was in dispute, but they were convicted and sentenced to death. The case received international attention and dispute.

The Arts

The nickname "the Jazz Age" perfectly sums up the tone of life during the 1920s. For those who could afford it, the decade was one long party. The economy was booming; wealthy and middle-class Americans had plenty of money to spend. A greater variety of consumer goods was available, and a flood of advertisements tempted the money out of people's pockets.

The name "Jazz Age" comes, of course, from jazz—the popular music of the era. Jazz is a combination of spirituals, work songs, the blues, and ragtime. It is made up of a variety of African musical elements such as syncopation, call and response, and the famous "blue note"—literally, a note that does not belong in the major scale. These elements, blended with the European musical elements of harmony and melody, all combined to create a truly American musical form.

Jazz bands usually featured trumpets, trombones, saxophones, clarinets, a piano, and drums. All the members of a jazz band were talented improvisers and soloists. They worked on a basic tune, changing it around in almost every conceivable way. Jazz was upbeat while recognizing the sorrows that lay beneath the African-American experience. The new sound was more than just popular—it was a craze. The new technologies of recorded music and concerts broadcast over the radio helped spread the popularity of jazz; anyone with a radio could enjoy it, not just those who lived in a big city with jazz clubs. Artists such as Jelly Roll Morton and Duke Ellington would rise to prominence in this new age of celebrity.

After they recovered from the shock of the Black Sox scandal (see below), people returned to cheering baseball players with the arrival of George Herman "Babe" Ruth. Born in Baltimore, Ruth was a star pitcher, but he had such power and skill as a hitter that he was soon made an outfielder so that he could play every day. In 1927, Ruth hit 60 home runs—his nearest competitor that year hit only 19. Besides his talent, Ruth had an expansive personality perfectly suited to the Jazz Age. He smoked big cigars, wore an ankle-length fur coat in the winter, dressed snappily, ate heartily, and spent money lavishly. His celebrity made him bigger than the game, and his exploits were followed by millions.

Architecture began changing the look of cities in the United States during the 1920s. New York City's Chrysler Building, completed in 1930, soared to a height of 77 stories; across town, the Empire State Building topped it a few months later at 102 stories. With their steel-girder construction, their escalators and fast elevators, their sparkling rows of glass windows and chrome trim, and the breathtaking views from their rooftop observatories, buildings like these epitomized modern times.

Two major artistic movements peaked during the 1920s: the **Harlem Renaissance** and the **Lost Generation.** The Harlem Renaissance was a direct result of the Great Migration of African Americans to the North. Many African Americans settled in Harlem, a neighborhood in New York City. They formed a community of creative artists: musicians, writers, photographers, painters, and poets. Poet Langston Hughes, novelist Nella Larsen, poet and prose writer James Weldon Johnson, and jazz musicians Duke Ellington and Louis Armstrong were key figures in the Harlem Renaissance. African-American activists hoped that by promoting the arts they could change the images of blacks in the United States from the Jim Crow stereotype to a more positive image. This era, while achieving few tangible goals, would prepare the way in terms of organization and activism for the later civil rights movement.

Ironically, Harlem was a segregated neighborhood. The Cotton Club, perhaps the most famous nightclub of the era, featured the best-known black musicians of the day. However, African Americans could enter the Cotton Club only through the stage door; they were not permitted to be part of the all-white audience. Some African Americans fought such discrimination by example. The dance team of Harold and Fayard Nicholas, young boys during the 1920s, often were called to join the Cotton Club audience after their act by patrons who wanted to fuss over the two engaging children. Fayard Nicholas recalled years later that he and his brother had struck their own quiet blow for integration: polite, well-dressed, and tidy, they proved that African Americans were in no way unfit to sit with whites in any audience.

In 1924 Paul Robeson attracted enormous attention when he became the first African-American actor to play the Shakespearean role of Othello opposite a white actress playing Desdemona. Robeson was universally acknowledged as a splendid talent, but that did not prevent people from directing racial slurs at him in hotel elevators and other public places.

The expatriate writer Gertrude Stein named her artistic friends of the 1920s "the Lost Generation." Ernest Hemingway, F. Scott and Zelda Fitzgerald, John Dos Passos, Dorothy Parker, John Steinbeck, Dashiell Hammett, and many others had been disillusioned by the failure of world leaders to resolve their differences peacefully or speedily and by the horrors of trench warfare. Their writing took on a cynical edge that was new to American literature. F. Scott Fitzgerald's *The Great Gatsby* perfectly captured the Jazz Age—its gaiety, its cynicism, and its essential hollowness. The story of Gatsby shows that there was no place for romanticism anymore. Similarly, Ernest Hemingway's *The Sun Also Rises* (1926) depicted the generation that had survived the war but had suffered permanent psychological and physical damage.

Politics in the 1920s

In 1920 the Republican Party hack Warren G. Harding ran for president against the Democrat James Cox. Harding coined the word "**normalcy**" to describe what he thought the United States needed after the dramatic and chaotic years of World War I. Cox, in contrast, seemed to promise continued involvement in foreign affairs as his campaign focused on the League of Nations. Historians generally agree that Harding was neither intelligent nor talented, but the voters liked the sound of a focus on domestic problems rather than foreign affairs, and Harding was elected in a landslide. As president he was more interested in partying at the White House than in the duties of the office.

Harding did not share the goals of the Progressives. His administration reduced taxes on wealthy Americans and also reduced government spending. By 1922 the government debt had turned into a surplus. In 1922 Congress raised tariffs to their highest levels ever, and that encouraged people to buy goods made in the United States. Lowering taxes on the wealthy would encourage them to spend the money they had saved on their taxes; this supposedly would stimulate the economy, and the benefits would "trickle down" to the poorer classes. The economy prospered under this trickle-down policy (at least in the short term), but poor and working-class families—which far outnumbered wealthy families—grew poorer, not richer. The actions of the administration would weaken the working class further by attacking and destroying the power of unions. Harding's aim of reestablishing normalcy meant tough times for many people in the United States.

Businesses took advantage of their increased prosperity by merging, in effect recreating the monopolies and trusts that had been outlawed under the Progressives. The federal government had ceased to enforce antitrust laws. However, workers did not get their fair share of the profits. Whereas owners' profits increased by 60 percent over the decade, workers' incomes rose only 10 percent, and that increase was offset by inflation. Although the nation was prosperous on the surface, there was a growing inequity in the distribution of wealth and poverty.

The last days of the Harding administration and the beginning of the Coolidge administration were disturbed when corruption in the White House came to light. Several of Harding's close associates had been given cabinet positions and were discovered to have abused their power by stealing millions of dollars. Harding died before it could be ascertained whether he had played a role in the scandals. Calvin Coolidge, his vice president, took action as soon as he took office; he fired the officials implicated in the scandals.

Because the economy was prospering, Coolidge was reelected easily in 1924. He cut taxes on the wealthy even more than Harding had and kept government spending at an all-time low. Coolidge opposed laws designed to help workers, claiming that such programs would not be good for the national economy. He was unabashedly probusiness, stating that "the business of America is business."

Herbert Hoover, Coolidge's secretary of commerce, was elected president in 1928. His opponent was Alfred Smith, the popular governor of New York and a Catholic. Smith was the first non-Protestant to run for president. Protestants conveniently forgot their own Puritan history of refusing to separate church and state, claiming that Smith would bow to the authority of the Pope in Rome. Ironically, Protestant ministers who feared the Pope's influence on a Catholic president used their influence and authority to urge their congregations to vote against Smith. Smith dismissed those scare tactics as ridiculous, pointing out that 19 times in his political career he had taken an oath of office in which he had sworn to uphold the Constitution. Despite the fact that not he but his opponents were proving themselves religiously intolerant, Smith lost the election; the continued economic prosperity under Republican administrations and Smith's opposition to Prohibition combined with Protestant paranoia to defeat him. However, he made a strong enough showing that Democrats hoped to regain the White House eventually.

Social Changes in the 1920s

One of the most notable changes that took place during 1920s was in the way women behaved, spoke, and dressed. During World War I, women had worked at traditionally male jobs such as house painting, stone masonry, plastering, and driving trucks. In 1920 women finally won the right to vote. Having come this far, women would not turn back. They felt that it was time for society to recognize their equality and their freedom to do what they wanted, as men had always done.

Women threw off the restrictions that had dictated fashion for many years. Until the 1920s skirts were worn long, with the hems coming down to the tops of the shoes. Women's dress consisted of corsets, stays, and other confining undergarments. Bodices of dresses were boned to make the body conform to the shape of the gown. Women never cut their hair; they grew it long and thick, pinning it up in braids, knots, twists, or whatever the fashion of the decade called for. Suffragists had begun to set an example against the most extreme of those fashions—for example, they shortened skirts to ankle length for ease in walking—but it was left to the **flapper** to bury them for good.

In the flapper era women cut their hair as short as a boy's. They shortened their skirts to just below the knee, showing legs in sheer silk stockings and feet in pretty shoes. Their loose-fitting party dresses were made of sheer fabrics, sleeveless, backless, and cut low in the front. Day dresses were more modest but still had short skirts and a comfortable, loose-fitting shape. Undergarments were skimpy and comfortable. Corsets were a thing of the past. The flapper was determined to flaunt her freedom.

Flappers also behaved very differently than did the women of past decades. They smoked, drove their own automobiles, and played sports, and many of them held jobs or took part in daring adventures such as flying planes. They laughed at the notion of chaperones. In the past, when a young man called on a girl, the two were not left alone together; in the 1920s that changed.

The phenomenon of mass entertainment was new to the 1920s. Radio broadcasts and movies meant that the same entertainment was available all over the country rather than being different in every location.

One thing that drastically changed the American landscape was the rise in popularity of the automobile. Henry Ford installed an **assembly line** that drove down the price of his sturdy, efficient little cars even further. The car would travel slowly through the factory along a conveyor belt. As it passed each worker, that worker would add the next part. When it reached the end of the line, the automobile would be finished.

This method had several advantages. It doubled production and reduced costs. It made each worker an expert at installing a particular car part. However, it also eliminated the sense of satisfaction workers once had been able to take in making something with their own hands. Workers who had been artisans were reduced to the level of machines, lessening their ability to ask for higher wages.

Automobiles were a huge success with customers. By the end of the decade there was one car on the road for every five people. That meant a huge change in the way cities looked; now there were cars parked along every street, with more cars trying to edge their way through the busy traffic. Established cities such as Boston and Philadelphia had not been designed to accommodate cars; houses had no driveways or garages. People simply parked their cars where they could, and that impeded the flow of traffic along the narrow streets. Newer cities such as Los Angeles and Chicago, which were still very much under construction in the 1920s, took cars into account in the architecture and city planning: Their streets were wider, for one thing. Cars also added to what was rapidly becoming a severe air-pollution problem.

Automobiles made it possible to travel as quickly as the railroad, but on one's own schedule. People in business no longer had to live within easy walking distance of their jobs; they could drive. This eventually became a major factor in the development of suburbs and urban sprawl.

Another technological change of the 1920s was the spread of the use of electricity. By 1930, more than two-thirds of all homes in the United States had electricity. This changed the rhythms of family life, which once had been dictated largely by sunrise and sunset. Now people could keep lights on as long as they chose. They also had new entertainment options: radios and phonographs. Recorded music was truly revolutionary; until this technology was developed, people had to be in the room with the performer to hear music. Now it was available at the turn of a crank. Whereas in one generation a piano had been present in almost every middle-class living room, now it was replaced by the radio and phonograph.

Organized Crime: The Black Sox Scandal and Prohibition

For **organized crime** the 1920s was an era of publicity and huge profits. Organized crime functioned in much the same way as the political machines of the 1860s and 1870s (see Chapter 19). An organized-crime boss was at the top of the pyramid. Several trusted associates worked directly with him. Under them were a much larger number of criminals who dealt directly with saloon owners, wholesalers, jockeys and ballplayers, and anyone else the boss wanted to use to make a profit. Instead of pressuring those people to vote a certain way, gamblers would pressure athletes to lose a race or throw a game. Once a person had given in to the pressure and committed a crime, the boss had a hold over him and could use that hold to blackmail the person into continuing to do what the crooks and gamblers wanted him to do.

In 1919 gamblers worked on members of baseball's Chicago White Sox, persuading them to throw the World Series, which they were heavily favored to win, to the Cincinnati Reds. An upset victory by the Reds would make the gamblers a fortune because they would be betting against the odds—putting up less money and winning more.

Players were persuadable because major league baseball was still a harsh system. Although baseball was a big business like any other—the biggest entertainment business in the United States in the Jazz Age—the government regarded it as a sport and did not regulate it as it did other businesses. Major league baseball was a monopoly, but one that enjoyed an exemption from antitrust laws. Every player, when hired, signed a contract stating that the ball club had the right to renew his services at the end of each season for the following season and to trade him to another club without consulting him. The player could not negotiate with any other club; no owner would hire him if he tried. This meant that players were literally indentured servants. Owners controlled salaries, keeping them as low as possible so that their profits would be greater. Frequently they offered bonuses and then refused to pay them. The players had no agents and no union to protect them. They had no reason to feel any loyalty to the owners. Gamblers, knowing there was money to be made, often offered players attractive sums of money to throw games.

However, before the World Series of 1919, this had been done on a relatively small scale. The players' motivation was very simple: they were severely underpaid and undervalued, with no leverage to fight for higher wages or better working conditions, and the gamblers offered them good money. In the end, eight White Sox players agreed to throw the World Series.

It was not long before the fix was discovered. Word had spread among gamblers, and the odds, which had heavily favored the White Sox, shortened so much that it became clear that something was going on. Cincinnati won the series. When the players eventually confessed in court, the nation was shocked. At that time baseball was the only professional team sport and was enormously popular. Eliot Asinof summed up the national reaction in his book about the "**Black Sox**" scandal:

> There is no way to gauge the extent of the damage on the American psyche. It is impossible to add up bitterness like a batting average. How great was the layer of cynicism that settled over the nation? How many kids developed tolerance for a lie, for a betrayal, for corruption itself?

The era of **Prohibition** began in 1919, when the temperance advocates saw their dream of a constitutional amendment against alcohol consumption become a reality. The Eighteenth Amendment made it illegal to consume or sell alcoholic beverages or transport them across state lines. The Eighteenth Amendment proved to be a resounding failure. Although alcoholism and related deaths declined, Prohibition had a number of unfortunate side effects that the temperance advocates had failed to anticipate.

The one thing Prohibition did not do was stop anybody from drinking. Most people in the United States, if questioned, would have agreed that many saloons should be closed and that people should not drink to excess, but they had never envisioned being unable to drink a beer in the evening or order wine in a restaurant. The vast majority of people in the United States decided that the law was not reasonable, and they broke it on an everyday basis. A new word—**speakeasy**—came into being to describe a nightclub where illegal or **bootleg** whiskey and other drinks were sold. **Bathtub gin** was distilled in homes across the country.

Because consumers continued to provide a market for alcohol and its production had been made illegitimate, gangsters were handed a perfect opportunity to make fortunes. Al Capone and his mobsters soon controlled most of the sales of liquor in the Chicago area. Wars between gangs over control of alcohol production and sales developed. The climax came on February 14, 1929, when Capone's gang mowed down seven members of a rival gang with machine guns. That incident became known as the **St. Valentine's Day Massacre.**

The mobsters also were able to corrupt local law enforcement. Bribery and threats were used to keep the police away from the speakeasies and bootlegging operations. There was so much violent crime associated with Prohibition that the FBI established a special branch of agents to deal solely with Prohibition cases. This agency, headed by Detective Elliot Ness, was called "**the Untouchables.**"

Prohibition was repealed in 1933.

The Scopes Trial

Two major influences on life and thought in the United States—Enlightenment reason and fundamentalist religion—clashed in a Tennessee courtroom in 1925. The state of Tennessee had passed a law that outlawed the teaching of the theory of **evolution** in its public schools. Fundamentalist Christians rejected the theory that human beings had evolved from more primitive life-forms. They claimed that since the Bible stated that God had created human beings in His image, evolution could not possibly be true. Fundamentalists saw this as an attack on the basis of their belief system and sought to ban the theory from being taught in schools.

The science teacher John Scopes taught evolution anyway, having read that the American Civil Liberties Union was willing to pay the costs of defending any teacher who defied the Tennessee law. The ACLU believed the law was unconstitutional. The Scopes trial would put that belief to the test.

Clarence Darrow, one of the nation's most famous criminal lawyers, agreed to defend Scopes. Former congressman William Jennings Bryan appeared for the prosecution. The judge refused to allow any scientific experts to testify about evolution, clearly exposing his profundamentalist bias. Darrow's response was to put Bryan on the witness stand and ask him questions about the Bible. Since many statements in the Bible contradict one another and many others are ambiguous, Bryan was made to look foolish in trying to protest that every word of the Bible is literally true. Nevertheless, the court found Scopes guilty and fined him $100. In the end the Scopes trial failed to resolve disputes over the teaching of evolution.

REVIEW QUESTIONS

1. All the following characterized the 1920s EXCEPT:

   (A) a rise in organized crime
   (B) a wave of prolabor legislation
   (C) the development of mass entertainment
   (D) technological advances such as the radio
   (E) the rise in popularity of the automobile

2. Who were "the Untouchables"?

   (A) Chicago White Sox baseball players who threw the World Series in 1919
   (B) Organized criminals who worked for Al Capone
   (C) The murderers involved in the St. Valentine's Day Massacre
   (D) Characters in a novel by Ernest Hemingway
   (E) FBI detectives who worked on cases involving violations of Prohibition

3. All the following characterized the flapper EXCEPT:

   (A) bobbed hair
   (B) short skirts
   (C) participation in sports
   (D) political activism
   (E) cigarette smoking

Answers and Explanations

1. **B** Presidents Harding, Coolidge, and Hoover did not support Progressive programs that helped labor. They were much more inclined to favor laws that helped business owners.

2. **E** "The Untouchables" worked for Detective Elliot Ness. Their squad was created because Prohibition had given rise to numerous violent crimes.

3. **D** Although flappers sometimes participated in serious events such as the fight for the Equal Rights Amendment, the term "flapper" generally was used to describe idle, rich society girls who spent most of their time shopping, flirting, and going to parties.

CHAPTER 24

THE GREAT DEPRESSION

INTRODUCTION

In later October 1929 the United States entered the worst economic crisis in its history. The stock market crashed, and the Great Depression began.

The Great Depression was worse than the many other financial panics the United States had weathered since the 1790s. It was much more widespread, and it lasted much longer. Across the nation, banks failed, businesses closed down, and workers were laid off. Landlords evicted tenants who could not pay the rent. Lenders foreclosed on borrowers who could not meet their payment obligations. To the average person living in the United States, it appeared that suddenly, no matter where one looked, no one had any money.

Most people blamed the crisis on President Herbert Hoover for two reasons: He had failed to predict it, and once it happened, he seemed both unwilling and unable to do anything about it. In 1932 Hoover lost his bid for reelection to an individual who struck most voters as being both willing and able to help them: Franklin Delano Roosevelt.

Roosevelt immediately set in motion a group of programs called the New Deal. Those programs were intended to offer immediate relief in the form of jobs to those who needed it most, create conditions under which the economy would recover, and install safeguards so that no such major financial crisis could ever occur again. The New Deal did not end the Depression, but it did many positive things: It created millions of jobs. It paid workers to build bridges, highways, and public buildings. It kept hundreds of artists employed entertaining those who badly needed occasional escape from their daily worries. It restored the nation's banks to a sound financial footing. During Roosevelt's first term the total percentage of unemployed workers dropped by about 8 percent. Unsurprisingly, he was reelected in the greatest landslide in 100 years.

TIMELINE

1928   Herbert Hoover elected president.

1929   Stock market crashes.

1930   Smoot-Hawley Tariff.

1930–1932   Bank failures across the nation.

1932   Franklin D. Roosevelt elected president.

1933   Fifteen million Americans unemployed.

New Deal programs put into action.

1934   Second New Deal programs created.

1936   Roosevelt reelected president.

Margaret Mitchell publishes *Gone With the Wind*.

1939   Marian Anderson sings at Lincoln Memorial.

John Steinbeck publishes *The Grapes of Wrath*.

KEY TERMS

Dust Bowl   Great Plains region devastated by severe droughts during the mid-1930s

Great Depression   a severe economic crisis that lasted from the stock market crash of 1929 until the United States entered World War II in 1941

Hooverville   a community of homeless people living in oversized cardboard boxes or makeshift shanties

margin buying   purchasing stocks with borrowed money with the intent of making a profit and repaying the loan when the stock prices rise

New Deal   the name President Franklin D. Roosevelt gave to his plan for the nation's economic relief and recovery

Okies   a derogatory name for Oklahoma farmers who drove west on Route 66 to California to find work

rugged individualism   President Hoover's term for gaining what one had by hard work rather than depending on charity or the government

The Stock Market Crash

The party of the Jazz Age, which no one had believed would end, ended abruptly—with a crash. On October 24, 1929, investors suddenly began selling their shares of stock. So much selling without anyone buying caused prices to plummet. On October 29 the frantic selling began again. By the end of that day 16 million shares of stock had been offered for sale. By the end of December 1929 investors in the stock market had lost over $30 billion—more than it had cost the U.S. government to contribute money, weapons, and troops to World War I.

The simple cause of the stock market crash was that people all over the country had gotten into the habit of buying things they could not afford. The practice of buying on credit had become common during the 1920s. People did not buy stocks on credit, but they did borrow money to buy stocks in a practice called **margin buying.** Speculators would borrow money to buy stock, then keep an eye on its value and sell it as soon as its price went up. The large number of speculators meant that share prices were constantly fluctuating, usually in an upward direction.

This speculation was exacerbated by the fact that businesses often misreported and sometimes lied outright about their profits. To drive up prices, businesses would hide losses and build up inventory. Widespread insider trading and abuse allowed many to manipulate the system to their benefit, to the detriment of the majority of investors. The market was booming, but only on the insubstantial foundation of unpaid debt. The only industries that truly were making money were the automobile and steel industries. When they announced that they would make less of a profit, the house of cards collapsed.

Buyers suddenly lost confidence in the market and began selling their shares. Share prices dropped, and the debts fell due. Banks failed because people could not repay their loans, and banks' deposits were lost in the market collapse. When a bank failed, all its depositors lost whatever money they had saved, including many thousands of people who had never invested in the stock market or gone into debt from buying on credit. There was no mechanism in place to protect them. Many people panicked at the news of the bank failures and tried to withdraw their money from their own banks, only to be told that the money was no longer there.

Like individuals, businesses lost money when the banks closed. Many businesses failed because they could not pay their debts. When businesses failed, all their workers were left without jobs. By 1933 the U.S. gross national product was only about half of what it had been in 1929. More than 50,000 businesses had failed, and 13.5 million people—more than 20 percent of the wage-earning population—had lost their jobs. That widespread unemployment would lead to an avalanche of other problems, including evictions, hunger, and sickness.

The era ushered in by the stock market crash was known as the **Great Depression.** An economic depression occurs when prices and wages fall and unemployment rises. The Great Depression got its name because it lasted for more than a decade, which is highly unusual for an economic crisis.

Hoover's Response to the Depression

President Herbert Hoover stated publicly that "the Government should not support the people." Himself a self-made man, Hoover believed in **rugged individualism:** people rescuing themselves by their own efforts. For quite some time he refused to accept that the economic crisis was so widespread and so grave that people could not help themselves no matter how much they wanted to. Nor could he accept the instability of the U.S. system, preferring to blame it on international causes. Eventually, between the public, the newspaper reports, and his advisors, Hoover was persuaded to take steps to help the needy. His administration spent hundreds of millions of dollars on public-works projects such as the construction of Boulder (later Hoover) Dam on the Colorado River. The Federal Farm Board, established in 1929, lent farmers money and bought up tons of their surplus crops that no one else could afford. However, those policies did not go far enough to help the people who needed it most, and economic conditions did not improve.

Millions of people in the United States who had always worked hard and supported themselves and their families were suddenly destitute. Some of those who lost fortunes in the stock market committed suicide. Others found themselves begging for food or money, standing in long lines outside missions and charities for free bowls of soup or sandwiches. Many young people, especially boys, went out on their own, sneaking aboard railway boxcars and riding freight trains for free, going long distances across the country in search of work.

Landlords regularly evicted those who could not pay rent. Often they would wait until a tenant who owed money had left his or her apartment and then change the locks and either throw the person's belongings out into the street or keep them as part payment for the rent. Homeowners also were evicted; many could not make their mortgage payments, and their houses were taken away from them. Newly homeless people formed communities called **Hoovervilles** in ironic tribute to the president who had made it all possible. Shelters in those makeshift communities were made of oversize cardboard boxes, packing crates for large items such as grand pianos, scraps of tin, boards, and any other building material that was available. Hoovervilles usually were formed in vacant lots, under bridges, or on the outskirts of towns.

The fact that they named their shantytowns Hoovervilles showed that the people in the United States who were suffering the greatest misery during the

Depression blamed the president. Hoover ran for reelection in 1932 although he knew he had almost no chance of winning. His opponent was the dynamic governor of New York, Franklin Delano Roosevelt. At the Democratic convention Roosevelt placed the blame for the economic situation squarely on the White House, stating firmly that Republican leaders had "failed in national vision, because in disaster they have held out no hope." Roosevelt won the election in a popular and electoral landslide, carrying 42 states and winning 7 million more votes than Hoover. Voters extended their blame for current conditions to the entire Republican Party; the Democrats won substantial majorities in both houses of Congress.

President and Mrs. Roosevelt

FDR, as Roosevelt often was called, was a distant cousin of the former president Theodore Roosevelt. FDR grew up in a wealthy New York family and married his cousin Eleanor Roosevelt (the former president's niece), who always joked that she accepted him only because it would save her having to have the monograms on her luggage changed.

Both Roosevelts were unique personalities. FDR quickly became a symbol of hope for the people. He was a natty dresser, with his hat tilted back and his cigarette holder clamped between his teeth at a jaunty angle. He exuded confidence, decisiveness, and good cheer. To see him riding in a car or even standing behind a podium, no one would imagine that this strong, vigorous-looking man could not walk unaided—and then could take only a few steps. A severe bout of polio in 1921 had confined FDR permanently to a wheelchair. He never allowed his physical disability to prevent him from taking on any challenge or let it defeat his optimism or his courage. In an amazing feat he was able to keep his disability from the American public throughout most of his presidency. The start of his first inaugural address summed up his outlook on life brilliantly:

> First of all, let me assert my firm belief that the only thing we have to fear is fear itself—nameless, unreasoning, unjustified terror which paralyzes needed efforts to convert retreat into advance.

Partly because her husband's disability made frequent long-distance travel very difficult for him and partly because of her own convictions about her duty as first lady, Eleanor Roosevelt made more of her position in the White House than had any of her predecessors. She wrote a daily newspaper column and traveled all over the country making speeches, inspecting the living conditions of those left destitute by the Depression, and speaking to them personally, listening to their individual concerns and taking careful notes of her impressions back to the president. Most of the people who met Mrs. Roosevelt were impressed by her unfailing courtesy and kindness. FDR considered Eleanor one of his most observant and valued advisers.

FDR and the Early Phases of the New Deal

"I pledge you, I pledge myself, to a new deal for the American people," FDR told the cheering crowds at the Democratic nominating convention in 1932. The **New Deal** marked a complete break with the Republican policies of the 1920s. It consisted of 15 programs designed to bring relief to the economy and the people. Roosevelt considered his New Deal to be a "war against the emergency," and as soon as he took office, he asked Congress to grant him special powers to take action. The New Deal marked a shift in the balance of national power from the legislative branch to the executive that Washington had not seen since the Civil War. In its way, the Great Depression was every bit as much a national crisis, and strong leadership was essential. Congress agreed with the president that emergency measures were called for and promptly passed all 15 of the New Deal programs. Much of the New Deal was grounded in Keynesian economics, a theory that gives the government responsibility for jump-starting the economy and spending its way out of a depression. Direct relief and government deficits were essential to improving the nation's economic state.

The following table lists the programs of the New Deal and what they accomplished.

1933	
Emergency Banking Act	Temporarily closed down all banks, examined their books, and reopened those which were solvent
Farm Credit Administration	Made low-interest, long-term loans to farmers for mortgages, equipment, and taxes
Economy Act	Proposed to balance the federal budget
Civilian Conservation Corps	Paid $30 a month to young men age 18 to 25 to work in national parks and plant trees throughout the West
Federal Emergency Relief Administration	Distributed $500 million to states for direct aid to families Matched every $3 cities and towns spent on relief projects with $1 in federal aid
Agricultural Adjustment Administration	Paid farmers to grow less, thus raising prices (later declared unconstitutional)
Tennessee Valley Authority	Built dams, provided electricity, and otherwise greatly improved conditions in the Tennessee Valley, one of the nation's poorest regions
Home Owners Loan Corporation	Made low-interest, long-term mortgage loans; protected people from losing their houses
Banking Act of 1933	Created FDIC (see next row) and authorized branch banking
Federal Deposit Insurance Corporation	Insured individual bank deposits up to $5,000
National Recovery Administration	Regulated businesses by establishing minimum wages and other standards to protect workers
Public Works Administration	Contracted private firms to hire millions of people to build bridges, post offices, highways, etc.
Civil Works Administration	Created millions of low-skill jobs such as cleaning city streets

1934	
Securities and Exchange Commission	Regulated companies that sold stocks and bonds
Federal Housing Administration	Insured all bank loans made for construction and repair of houses

FDR had designed the programs of the New Deal with three main goals: to bring immediate relief to those who were suffering, to bring the economy back to prosperity, and to put safeguards in place so that the same situation would not occur again. Programs such as the Civil Works Administration and the Public Works Administration accomplished the first goal. The Agricultural Adjustment Administration and the Tennessee Valley Authority helped accomplish the second goal. New organizations such as the Securities and Exchange Commission and the Federal Deposit Insurance Corporation were put into place with an eye toward the third goal.

Despite the relief it provided to millions across the country, not everyone supported the New Deal. African Americans regarded it with a wary eye because it did not always give them the same benefits whites received. The National Recovery Administration set lower wages for black workers, and other programs segregated them from white workers. Roosevelt also refused to support a federal antilynching law. Throughout his long tenure in the White House, FDR was a pragmatist, not an idealist. He always believed that the larger picture of a situation was more important than any individual details. In his view, pressing for civil rights legislation was less important than doing the best possible job to lead the nation out of the Depression. In many respects though, Roosevelt was able to gain the support of African Americans not because the New Deal specifically included minorities but because it did not specifically exclude them as did many government actions before it.

However, FDR showed his support for civil rights in other ways. He signed the Indian Reorganization Act of 1934 into law. That legislation attempted to help Native Americans both financially and socially. FDR appointed more than 100 African Americans to a wide variety of government jobs. He also appointed the first female cabinet secretary, Frances Perkins.

Many of the actions FDR took to help African Americans were taken at Eleanor Roosevelt's urging. Mrs. Roosevelt was a champion of civil rights. She made national headlines in 1939 when the Daughters of the American Revolution (DAR) withdrew a concert booking for Marian Anderson, one of the greatest classical singers of the era, because of racial prejudice. Mrs. Roosevelt was a DAR member. When she learned that the DAR had denied Anderson the chance to perform at Constitution Hall, she immediately and publicly resigned from the organization. She then arranged for Anderson to sing the planned concert from the steps of the Lincoln Memorial. Nearly 75,000 people stood quietly on the grounds outside the memorial, shoulder to shoulder, to hear Anderson sing.

Despite FDR's enormous popularity across the nation, his New Deal programs had many critics. The Republicans hated him and his programs, claiming that he was turning the United States into a socialist society and destroying big business and free enterprise. Not all Democrats supported the New Deal either; some thought it did not go far enough, and others thought it should include different programs. Newly prominent demagogues such as Huey Long, Francis Townsend, and Father Coughlin proposed radical solutions that were embraced by many people.

The New Deal did not pull the nation out of the Great Depression. However, it did substantially improve the lives of millions of people for both the short term and the long term. The programs of the New Deal would help stabilize the country and bring hope to millions. Some of the programs it created, such as the Federal Deposit Insurance Corporation, have continued to provide safeguards against another depression. The New Deal brought electricity and indoor plumbing to many regions where such improvements had been found in very few homes. This improved public health and sanitation as well as people's standard of living. During the New Deal, the South's economy finally began to rely more on modern industry and less on cash crops such as cotton.

The Second New Deal

The 1934 congressional elections showed that no matter what the critics thought, the public was solidly in favor of the New Deal. Democrats gained even more seats in Congress. That put FDR in a position to initiate more programs that he hoped would help the economy recover over the long term rather than simply bring immediate relief to those who needed it.

The "Second New Deal" included three especially important programs. One was the Works Progress Administration (WPA). Created in 1935, it replaced the Civil Works Administration. The WPA employed more than 8 million people over eight years in construction work, research projects, and teaching jobs. It set aside $300 million for Federal Project Number One, which employed thousands of writers, actors, painters, designers, and musicians. The purpose of Federal One was twofold: to provide jobs for unemployed artists and to encourage pride in American arts and culture by supporting artists financially.

The Social Security Act of 1935 provided unemployment insurance to those who lost their jobs, guaranteed all U.S. workers a government pension once they turned 65, and made payments to disabled workers and the widows and children of workers. All workers paid a small percentage of each paycheck into a government-administered fund. Once they reached age 65, they would receive monthly checks based on the average yearly amount of their earnings. In this way, Social Security paid for itself.

In 1936 FDR ran for reelection against the Republican Alfred M. Landon, the governor of Kansas. Union and Socialist Party candidates also appeared on the ballot. FDR found it an easy campaign since all he had to do was remind farmers, workers, and businessmen that they were better off now than they had been when he took office. FDR won the election in the greatest landslide in a century, carrying every state except Vermont and Maine and winning 11 million more votes than Landon.

The Dust Bowl

Severe droughts during the mid-1930s turned the Great Plains into the "**Dust Bowl.**" The soil of the central plains of the United States did not retain moisture well to begin with. This was why it was such good soil for growing wheat and corn; those two crops thrive in that type of soil. However, this also meant that trouble would occur if there was a significant drop in rainfall. The Great

Plains had so few major natural sources of water that it was not easy to irrigate crops. Farmers normally depended on regular rainfall.

It did not rain for months on end. The loose topsoil blew about in the frequent high winds, creating dust storms. Across 50 million acres of land, crops failed or yielded poorly. To counteract the effects of the drought, the Civilian Conservation Corps planted millions of trees throughout the Dust Bowl. Those trees created windbreaks that helped reduce the erosion of the soil substantially by 1939.

By that time many small farmers had lost everything. Tenant farmers had been forced off their land; owners, deciding there was no sense in keeping barren land, mailed eviction notices to tenants and then sent in heavy tractors to tear up the soil. The tractors did not go around the farmhouses but steamrolled over them. Farmers—some of whom had farmed that land for generations—protested, but in vain. Before the tractors came, they loaded their few belongings into shabby old trucks and drove west along Route 66, hoping to find work in the California fruit orchards. The novelist John Steinbeck made the journey with one family of Oklahoma farmers, or "**Okies,**" as they came to be called, and recorded the experience in his classic novel *The Grapes of Wrath*. Steinbeck described in detail the fierce competition for jobs picking fruit and harvesting cotton. Since so many people were desperate for work, the growers offered lower and lower wages, knowing that no one could afford to turn down their offers. The migrant workers had no unions, and whenever anyone tried to argue for decent housing or attempted to organize the other workers, the growers would bring in the police to arrest the "troublemakers" on trumped-up charges.

Opponents of the New Deal might dismiss *The Grapes of Wrath* as fiction, but they could not do the same with the photojournalism of Dorothea Lange, Walker Evans, Gordon Parks, and Margaret Bourke-White. Their cameras captured the toil and endurance of migrant workers, sharecroppers, and the homeless under appalling living conditions. *Migrant Mother,* a photograph taken by Lange in 1936, is something of a poster image summarizing the misery of the Great Depression. After seeing photographs like *Migrant Mother,* Californians began insisting on decent housing and sanitary conditions for the millions of seasonal migrant workers.

Escape

Whenever they could, people in the United States escaped the difficulties of everyday life by seeking entertainment. It cost nothing to listen to the radio, which broadcast the latest jazz, dance music of the big bands, classical concerts, and comedy programs such as *The Jack Benny Show.* One October night in 1938, as people changed radio stations to see what was playing, they were startled to hear what purported to be a news flash that aliens from Mars had invaded the United States. Something of a nationwide panic was halted only when the radio network was able to explain that it was a fictional news flash, part of a science-fiction dramatization of H. G. Wells's *The War of the Worlds.* Those who had been listening to director Orson Welles's Mercury Theater broadcast from the beginning had known that it was a dramatization all along and were amused by the panic.

For a few cents per person a whole family could spend an entire day at the movie house. They would see a newsreel, cartoons, a first feature, live entertainment, and then a second feature. The Hollywood movie studio system was one of the few industries that paid good salaries throughout the 1930s. Hollywood produced hundreds of films a year throughout the decade. By the late 1930s some films were being shot in Technicolor, attracting even more moviegoers than before.

The most popular novel of the decade was *Gone With the Wind*, written by the Atlanta housewife Margaret Mitchell to entertain herself while she recovered from an ankle injury. This sweeping, romantic story of Civil War heroine Scarlett O'Hara captivated the entire nation; readers cheered for Scarlett as she endured starvation and poverty like their own and came out on top. In 1939 *Gone With the Wind* was made into an equally popular and acclaimed Technicolor film.

REVIEW QUESTIONS

1. All the following were contributing causes of the Great Depression EXCEPT:

   (A) margin buying
   (B) frequent fluctuations in share prices
   (C) widespread bank failures
   (D) the existence of Hoovervilles
   (E) widespread business failures

2. Which of the following New Deal programs was intended to ensure that no Great Depression could occur again in the future?

   (A) Federal Deposit Insurance Corporation
   (B) Farm Credit Administration
   (C) Tennessee Valley Authority
   (D) Public Works Administration
   (E) Civilian Conservation Corps

3. After they drove west from the Dust Bowl seeking work in California, most farmers

   (A) found good jobs and soon returned to prosperity
   (B) competed with thousands like themselves for poorly paid work
   (C) got arrested protesting unfair working conditions
   (D) crossed the border into Mexico to find work
   (E) petitioned the White House for help in fighting the growers' association

Answers and Explanations

1. **D** The Great Depression gave rise to Hoovervilles, not the other way around.
2. **A** The FDIC insures deposits so that if a bank fails, individuals cannot lose the money they have deposited there. This would protect people from losing everything if a financial panic occurred.
3. **B** The California fruit and vegetable growers could offer whatever wages they cared to because they knew the Okies and other migrants were desperate for work. Naturally, they set wages very low. Farmers had no choice but to accept the offers or starve.

CHAPTER 25

WORLD WAR II (PART I)

INTRODUCTION

Historians agree that the peace treaty signed at the end of World War I made World War II probable. Many people see the two as one war with a long intermission during which nations rearmed and prepared for the second act.

Germany had been forced to surrender on such humiliating terms that it was not surprising that Germans resented the situation and wanted revenge. After all, Germany, like other nations, had suffered terrible losses during the war, and Germans saw no reason why they should bear the entire burden of guilt.

The reparations demanded by the Allies were impossible to pay. The worldwide economic depression had hit Germany harder than almost any other nation. Paper money in Germany was all but worthless. People were starving and discontented. They looked everywhere for determined leadership and found it in the figure of a seemingly insignificant Austrian named Adolf Hitler. Hitler had a remarkable ability to stir up the enthusiasm of a crowd, along with an obsessive hatred of the Allies for their treatment of Germany after the war. He was able to use those qualities to take control of the German government as an unquestioned dictator. It soon became apparent that he planned to rearm Germany and expand his rule over the rest of Europe. In 1939 he launched World War II.

At the same time, Japan was abandoning treaties signed with the Allied Powers and expanding its control over the Chinese province of Manchuria and over the Pacific. When Japan perceived the United States as a threat to its expansion, it launched an attack on the U.S. naval base at Pearl Harbor. That attack brought the United States into the war against both Japan and Germany.

The change to a war economy pulled the United States out of the Depression. People who believed the war was coming decided to reelect Franklin Roosevelt to an unprecedented third term as president. As he had guided the nation through the worst of the Depression, Roosevelt would continue to guide it through war.

TIMELINE

1921	Washington Conference.
	Four-Power Treaty and Nine-Power Treaty.
	Mussolini founds Fascist Party in Italy.
1922	Mussolini becomes prime minister.
1924	Dawes Plan.
	Vladimir Lenin dies; Joseph Stalin takes control of Soviet Union.
1933	Adolf Hitler becomes chancellor of Germany.
	Good Neighbor Policy.

1935	Nuremberg Laws deprive German Jews of citizenship.
1936	Germany annexes Rhineland.
	Germany and Italy unite as Axis Powers.
1937	Japan invades China.
1938	Munich Conference.
	Germany annexes Austria.
1939	Germany and Soviet Union sign nonaggression pact.
	Germany and Soviet Union take over Poland from opposite sides.
	Britain and France declare war on Germany.
1940	Germany invades Belgium; marches on to France; Allies retreat at Dunkirk.
	Winston Churchill becomes prime minister of Great Britain.
	Italy declares war on France and Great Britain.
1941	Lend-Lease Act.
	United States and Great Britain sign Atlantic Charter.
	Germany invades Soviet Union.
	Japan bombs U.S. naval base at Pearl Harbor.
	United States declares war on Japan.

KEY TERMS

Allied Powers   France, Great Britain, and later the United States and the Soviet Union

appeasement   policy of agreeing to demands made by others

Axis Powers   Germany and Italy

blitz   term used to describe German bombing of London and other British cities

blitzkrieg   literally, "lightning war"; a violent, sudden, overpowering attack made without warning

disarmament   voluntary reduction in stocks of weapons, ships, tanks, war planes, and bombs

Fascist Party   an Italian political party founded by Benito Mussolini

Nazi Party   abbreviation for the National Socialist German Workers' Party, led by Hitler from 1921 onward

German Expansionism and the Outbreak of World War II

Woodrow Wilson had been right to try to dissuade the victorious nations in World War I from demanding an admission of war guilt and impossible reparations from Germany. The result was that monetary inflation in Germany reached epic proportions; a wheelbarrow full of money was barely enough to buy a loaf of bread, and people sometimes papered over cracks in the walls of their apartments with German marks because they were literally not worth the paper they were printed on. The German reaction was resentment and a determination to regain the nation's status as a world power. As soon as Adolf Hitler took power in 1933, he began the process of rearmament that had been outlawed by the Treaty of Versailles.

Hitler had been a failure all his life, often living on charity and unable to settle down to any particular job until World War I broke out. He then served in the German Army and bitterly resented Germany's defeat. After the war, as head of the National Socialist Party (**Nazi Party**), he used his extraordinary ability to stir the emotions of crowds to gain power and then his equally uncanny ability to intimidate others to reach the top position in the German government. It was not long before Hitler discarded the democratic title "Chancellor of Germany" in exchange for the imperial "Fuehrer of the Third Reich." With the eager collaboration of the majority of Germans, this foreign nobody had made himself an absolute dictator. Among Hitler's first acts were repressive laws aimed at Germany's Jews, whom the Nazis blamed for the nation's economic and social ills.

Totalitarian governments also had risen to power in the Soviet Union and Italy. After the death in 1924 of Vladimir Lenin, who had led the 1917 Bolshevik Revolution against the tsar, Joseph Stalin took over the Soviet government. With the power of the Communist Party and the Red Army behind him, Stalin reorganized large and small farms estates into vast cooperatives on which people were forced to work. Anyone who disagreed with official Soviet policy was sent to a labor camp. Historians estimate that Stalin had more than 30 million people murdered in his attempt to eliminate any influence opposed to his own.

In Italy, Benito Mussolini founded the **Fascist Party** in 1921. The next year, Mussolini forced the king to make him a dictator. From then on the Fascists and the Italian Army ruled the country. Italy pushed into North Africa, where it soon controlled Libya and Ethiopia. Fascism is a type of regime that corrupts the mechanics of government through violence and appeals to nationalism and militarism. Both Italy and Germany were fascist states, and later they formed an alliance and became the **Axis Powers.**

With Germany rearmed, Hitler in 1936 ordered his troops into the Rhineland, which had been a demilitarized zone. In 1938 Germany annexed Austria, and in 1939 it took control of Czechoslovakia after Britain and France gave in to Hitler's demands at a conference at Munich, Germany. In September 1939, Hitler and Stalin secretly signed a pact agreeing that neither would attack the other and that they would invade Poland from opposite sides and divide it between them. When the invasion of Poland began, both France and Britain declared war on Germany.

1940–1941: Events in Europe

In 1940, German armies pushed westward in a fast-moving campaign called the **blitzkrieg.** Britain and France (now called the **Allied Powers**) were unable to stop them, and Belgium, the Netherlands, and France soon were conquered. It became clear at this dangerous point, with the Germans only a few miles away across the English Channel, that a change in British leadership was overdue. Winston Churchill, who had warned Parliament for years about German rearmament and its probable consequences and had vigorously opposed earlier leaders' **appeasement** policies (policies based on offering concessions to Hitler), became the new prime minister on May 10. No wartime leader in history ever played a more important role than Churchill in maintaining his nation's morale. Churchill's complete lack of fear of Hitler and refusal even to consider the possibility of a British defeat inspired and encouraged the British people.

Churchill and the royal family also set an example of courage by remaining in London throughout the German bombing campaign called the **blitz.** The German air force, the Luftwaffe, bombed London and other British cities on a nightly basis in a deliberate attempt to frighten the British people and make them lose heart for the fight. One of Churchill's most important contributions to the war was his refusal to be intimidated by those tactics.

Unable to conquer Britain, Hitler in 1941 launched a surprise attack on the Soviet Union. The Soviets were taken completely unaware but soon rallied a fierce opposition against the invaders. The Soviet Union joined the Allied side in the war, and its enormous army would play a crucial part in the outcome.

U.S. Neutrality

Since the end of World War I most people in the United States had supported a foreign policy of neutrality, hoping to remain on friendly terms with all nations and not be dragged into conflicts with any. Owing to its huge size and geographical isolation from Europe and Asia, the United States felt invulnerable to attack and thus felt no need to have any foreign alliances for its own protection. Congress felt that it spoke for the people when it refused to join either the League of Nations or the World Court.

However, the United States was included in various diplomatic meetings during the 1920s and 1930s. Those meetings discussed world **disarmament.** The Washington Conference of 1921 resulted in three major treaties, as outlined in the table below.

Five-Power Naval Treaty	United States, Britain, Italy, France, Japan	British and U.S. navies to be same size Japanese Navy to be 60 percent of that size French and Italian navies to be 50 percent of size of Japanese Navy
Four-Power Treaty	Britain, United States, France, Japan	All four nations to respect one another's territories in the Pacific
Nine-Power Treaty	Britain, United States, France, Italy, Japan, Belgium, China, Netherlands, Portugal	Guaranteed China's territorial integrity and upheld Open Door Policy

The United States also pulled back on its imperialist tactics toward Latin America. President Roosevelt announced what was dubbed the "Good Neighbor Policy," in which he pledged that the United States would respect the rights of its neighbors and hope to be treated by them with the same respect.

Roosevelt withdrew troops from Latin American nations, agreed to Cuba's request to repeal the Platt Amendment, and put relations with Mexico on a better footing.

The United States reduced the World War I debt owed by Allied nations. Because it was clearly impossible for Germany to make reparations as had been agreed after the war, the Dawes Plan of 1924 drew up a new schedule for the payment of German reparations.

In 1940 Roosevelt ran for reelection again. This marked the first time any president had run for a third consecutive term in office. Historians agree that if the world had been at peace in 1940, Roosevelt probably would have thrown his support to another prominent Democratic leader rather than seeking reelection. However, because it was likely that the United States would soon be at war again, Roosevelt decided to run. He had the overwhelming support of his party. The Republican Wendell Wilkie, a former Democrat and New Deal supporter who had no political experience, opposed him.

The economy was beginning to recover from the worst of the Great Depression, and the issue of greatest concern to voters was whether the United States would take part in the war. Both Wilkie and Roosevelt pledged to keep the United States neutral—Wilkie at all costs, Roosevelt if possible. Roosevelt made it clear that the United States would not seek a battle with any nation but would defend itself immediately if it were attacked directly.

Roosevelt won the election decisively, winning 449 electoral votes of a possible 531 and nearly 55 percent of the popular vote. "What counted," wrote one historian, "was the feeling that in a dangerous world the United States had better not change horses in midstream."

After the election, Roosevelt made several moves to aid the beleaguered British. Under the "Lend-Lease" Act of 1941, U.S. military aid was sent to Britain and other nations whose defense was deemed "vital to the defense of the United States." Also in 1941, Roosevelt and Churchill met to issue the so-called Atlantic Charter, a document spelling out the aims of the democratic nations' war against the Axis Powers.

Pearl Harbor: The United States Enters the War

Japan had not observed the provisions of the treaties it had signed at the Washington Conference. Instead, it had invaded and taken over Manchuria in eastern China. It had also attacked U.S. ships near Nanking (now Nanjing), China, in 1937. Increasingly sharp demands had been exchanged between Japanese and U.S. diplomats, and series of sanctions had been implemented. Japan finally decided that it had to challenge the United States as a world power. As part of that plan, Japanese leaders formed an alliance with the Axis Powers, Germany and Italy.

The United States maintained a substantial naval base at Pearl Harbor, Hawaii (still a U.S. territory rather than a state). A large part of the U.S. Pacific Fleet rode at anchor in Pearl Harbor, and hundreds of planes sat on the base's airfields. U.S. officials had intercepted coded messages and knew that a Japanese attack was being planned, but they were unable to find out where or when. The public knew nothing of this.

With no warning, Japan began bombing the base at 8 a.m. on December 7. The U.S. Navy was completely unprepared for the attack. The Japanese destroyed 20 warships and 200 airplanes. About 2,400 Americans were killed in the attack.

After the attack President Roosevelt went on the radio and said, "Yesterday, December 7, 1941—a date which will live in infamy—the United States was suddenly and deliberately attacked by naval and air forces of the empire of Japan." The attack on Pearl Harbor left the United States no choice but to declare war on Japan. A few days later Japan's ally Germany declared war on the United States.

Mobilization in the United States

World War II was the catalyst that brought the U.S. economy out of the Depression. After the attack on Pearl Harbor, all thought of neutrality was forgotten. The United States was committed to defeating Japan and also to helping the Allied Powers defeat the Germans. People in the United States readily accepted war rationing of goods such as sugar, coffee, cigarettes, silk (needed for parachutes), tires, and canned goods. Clothing styles changed to save fabric: Skirts were shorter; dress styles were plainer, without flounces or ruffles; trouser cuffs were eliminated or narrowed; and hems were tiny.

Between 1940 and 1943 the number of people employed in U.S. factories that made weapons and ammunition increased by more than 450,000. Unemployment dropped to below 1929 levels, and wages rose. The military employed hundreds of thousands, including women. Many of them ended up going overseas to support the war effort in Europe or in the Pacific.

Military Campaigns in the Pacific, 1942–1943

Japan followed the attack on Pearl Harbor with similar attacks on U.S. and British bases in the Philippines, Burma, Hong Kong, and other places. After the onslaught on the Philippines, General Douglas MacArthur led a U.S. retreat to Australia. The Japanese took thousands of U.S. prisoners at Bataan near Manila and forced them on a death march through the jungle on the way to the prison camps. More than 10,000 of the prisoners died.

By 1942 Japan was attempting to establish an "island fortress," two defensive lines of islands in the Pacific. The United States developed the policy of "island hopping" to combat that defense. In the Battle of the Coral Sea, British and U.S. forces fought back the Japanese advance. In the Battle of Midway, the United States again defeated the Japanese Air Force and Navy. By conquering the island of Guadalcanal and defeating Japanese naval forces off the nearby Solomon Islands, U.S. forces blocked a possible Japanese invasion of Australia.

The United States had one major advantage over the Japanese: Whereas U.S. interceptors were able to decode Japanese radio messages, the Japanese had no luck with U.S. codes. The United States had established a special corps of Navajo Indians who broadcast messages in their own language. Since the Japanese had no knowledge of Navajo, they were never able to crack the code, which would have given them advance warning of U.S. troop movements and other plans.

Military Campaigns in Europe and North Africa

The Axis Powers had the upper hand in European fighting until late 1942. Their armies were the aggressors; they had been preparing for war for years and were well organized to fight. They also controlled the vast majority of

Europe and a sizable chunk of North Africa. However, the fact that they were trying to fight a war on several fronts at once weakened and divided their forces. Allied forces hoped to exploit that weakness.

Allied advantages included numerical strength and geography. The Soviet Union and the United States between them had huge populations to draw from for troops. The German and Italian forces were much smaller because the populations of those countries were much smaller. U.S. industries were also a major asset for the Allies: the United States could produce huge quantities of weapons, ammunition, ships, tankers, and planes.

A campaign was fought in North Africa throughout 1942. British forces led by General Bernard Montgomery pursued German forces led by Field Marshal Erwin Rommel, who was one of the most skilled commanders on either side. However, Rommel was outnumbered and had to retreat after the Battle of El Alamein.

Meanwhile, German armies invading the Soviet Union marched east to Leningrad and laid siege to it. The people of the city underwent slow starvation for many months before the siege was lifted. Other German armies pushed eastward across the Ukraine toward the Volga River. Finally, in early 1943 the Soviets succeeded in penning up the invading Germans in the city of Stalingrad, starving them into surrender. The combination of the victories in the Soviet Union and North Africa turned the tide of the war in the Allies' favor.

REVIEW QUESTIONS

1. All the following nations were under Axis control by the end of 1940 EXCEPT:

   (A) Poland
   (B) the Soviet Union
   (C) France
   (D) Italy
   (E) the Netherlands

2. All the following were U.S. victories in the Pacific EXCEPT:

   (A) Bataan
   (B) Guadalcanal
   (C) Coral Sea
   (D) Midway
   (E) Solomon Islands

3. Which of the following was the purpose of the Lend-Lease Act?

   (A) To guarantee the territorial integrity of China
   (B) To permit Roosevelt to run for a third presidential term
   (C) To set limits on the size of the British and Japanese navies
   (D) To spell out the war aims of the Allied Powers
   (E) To provide military aid to defend Britain and other Allied countries

Answers and Explanations

1. **B** The Soviet Union was not invaded by the Germans until 1941 and was never controlled entirely by the Axis Powers.
2. **A** The Japanese defeated U.S. forces at Bataan in 1942.
3. **E** The purpose of the Lend-Lease Act of 1941 was to provide military aid to Britain and other countries whose defense was considered vital to the defense of the United States.

CHAPTER 26
WORLD WAR II (PART II)

INTRODUCTION

World War II raged on until 1945. The Allies won battles steadily from 1942 onward, but the Germans and Japanese proved to be stubborn and tough enemies, very difficult to defeat. All the ingenuity of the Allied Powers was necessary to win the war.

Racial prejudice played an important role in the war. In Europe, the Nazi regime was based largely on racial prejudice. Hitler had a fixed, obsessive hatred for anyone who was not of purebred Aryan descent, especially Jews. His government methodically tracked down Jews throughout the German-controlled territories, revoked their constitutional privileges, and forced them into concentration camps where they were starved, tortured, and executed in gas chambers. Millions of other non-Aryans, such as Gypsies and Slavs, also were dragged to the death camps.

On the Allied side too there was racial prejudice. In the United States the federal government rounded up tens of thousands of Japanese Americans and imprisoned them in hastily constructed camps in the West. Since no similar measures were taken against German Americans or Italian Americans, it was clear that this action was due to racial prejudice. The excuse was fear that the prisoners might feel enough loyalty to their country of origin to betray the United States to the Japanese. There was never any specific evidence against any individual.

In the spring of 1945, with the Soviets invading Berlin, Hitler committed suicide. The Germans surrendered unconditionally within the week. Japan held out somewhat longer, refusing to surrender until the United States dropped nuclear bombs on the cities of Hiroshima and Nagasaki.

In terms of lives lost and damage done, World War II was by far the costliest war in history. As it ended, the Allies began to realize that they would have to take extraordinary steps to prevent a similar conflict from occurring again.

TIMELINE

1942   Allies invade North Africa.

Germans begin transporting Jews to concentration camps, where they and many others are slaughtered.

1943   Soviets defeat Germany at Stalingrad.

Axis forces surrender in North Africa.

Mussolini deposed; assassinated in 1944 by Italian freedom fighters.

Italy signs armistice with Allies.

1944

June 4   Rome falls to Allies.

June 6   D-Day; landing of Allied forces on Normandy beaches.

August 25 Allies liberate Paris from German occupation.

October Battle of Leyte Gulf.

December Battle of the Bulge.

1945

February Yalta Conference.

Battle of Iwo Jima.

March Allies invade Germany.

April Battle of Okinawa.

Death of Roosevelt; Harry S. Truman becomes president.

Soviet forces enter Berlin.

April 30 Hitler commits suicide.

May 7 Germans surrender; VE Day.

July Potsdam Conference.

August 6 United States drops atomic bomb on Hiroshima, Japan.

August 8 Soviet Union declares war on Japan; invades Manchuria.

August 9 United States drops atomic bomb on Nagasaki, Japan.

September 2 Japan signs surrender.

KEY TERMS

Aryans people of pure German or Anglo-Saxon descent

concentration camps camps set up mainly in Eastern Europe for Jews and others to be confined in before being killed

D-Day June 6, 1944, the date of the Allied invasion of occupied France

Holocaust deliberate genocide by Germans of 6 million European Jews

internment imprisonment

Manhattan Project a secret research project by Allied scientists to develop the atomic bomb

VE Day "Victory in Europe" Day, May 8, 1945

Roosevelt's Fourth Term

As 1944 wore on, it was clear that the war might last another year. Believing that it was his clear duty to remain in charge until the war ended, Roosevelt ran for reelection once again, this time against the Republican Thomas E. Dewey. The popular vote was relatively close—26 million votes for Roosevelt, 22 million for Dewey—but the incumbent once again carried a huge electoral majority. On the whole, people in the United States shared Roosevelt's belief that a transition to a new president during a time of war would not be a good idea.

Roosevelt compiled a remarkable record as one of the country's great war leaders, yet the record of his administration included one distinct black mark. In 1941, at the urging of West Coast politicians and business and labor leaders after Japan's attack on Pearl Harbor, Roosevelt signed legislation ordering the forced evacuation of all West Coast residents who were Japanese immigrants or the children of Japanese immigrants. There was no reason to believe that any of those people were disloyal to the United States, and those who had been born in the United States were full citizens. Yet there was enough fear of those people and prejudice against them that the federal government relocated about 120,000 of them to **internment** camps in the Western states. Despite this violation of their rights, many Japanese Americans enlisted in the army and served with distinction. Those who did not enlist were not released from the camps until 1945.

War in North Africa and Europe: 1942–1944

When the U.S. forces arrived in Europe, they planned with Allied leaders to begin their attack in the Mediterranean region. Under the command of General Dwight D. Eisenhower, the Allies invaded North Africa in November 1942. Allied troops landed in Morocco and Algeria, two French colonial territories then under the control of the puppet "Vichy" regime set up in France under German rule. The Vichy soldiers put up little resistance, but the Allies soon were forced to combat battle-hardened German troops. Fighting continued until May 1943, when the Allies forced the surrender of German forces in Tunisia, the last Axis stronghold in Africa.

With North Africa under their control, the Allies turned their attention to Italy. They invaded Sicily in July 1943 and soon controlled it. From there they intended to launch an attack on the Italian mainland. Italy gave way promptly; many Italians were weary of the fascist regime and felt little loyalty to Mussolini. The king of Italy had Mussolini arrested, and a new government sought an armistice with the Allies. However, the Germans soon rescued Mussolini and set up a new power base for him in northern Italy. German troops entered the Italian peninsula and blocked further Allied progress. Fierce battles raged for months, and the Allies reached Rome in central Italy only in June 1944.

Throughout 1943 the Allied air forces bombed Germany. The goals of the bombing campaign were to destroy railroad lines, munitions factories, weapons arsenals, and other strategic locations. The Allies also hoped to break the spirit of the German people by destroying their cities, just as the German air attacks on Great Britain had been intended to break the British spirit. Allied bombs killed tens of thousands of German civilians and destroyed about 70 percent of all the buildings in virtually every large city in Germany, including some of its oldest and most beautiful cities, such as Dresden.

At sea, Allied warships fought the Battle of the Atlantic against German submarines, which managed to sink many ships carrying supplies to Great Britain. The tide of battle turned only when the Allies began using sonar to locate and destroy the German submarines. By 1944 the Allies had taken control of the seas.

After much debate, U.S. and British leaders agreed that to win the war against Germany (and to relieve the German pressure on the Soviet Union in the east), they would need to send an army across the English Channel into France and from there into Germany itself. However, in order to build up a force that was large enough and well enough trained and supplied to take on the Germans, it was necessary to wait until the spring of 1944. The secret plan was to invade France along the beaches of Normandy. It was called Operation Overlord and placed under the command of General Eisenhower.

The Germans had fortified the beaches with mines and tank traps, but they were unsure about where and when the invasion would take place. On June 6, 1944 (**D-Day**), 150,000 Allied troops crossed the English Channel from Britain either in planes or aboard transports. Though many were killed, the troops were able to overrun the beaches and begin marching south and east. Meanwhile, another Allied force invaded southern France and started marching north. On August 25, 1944, the Allies marched into Paris and liberated that city from German occupation.

Allied troops continued marching east toward the Low Countries and Germany, but in December the Germans launched a fierce counterattack assault in the Ardennes region of Belgium and northern France. They pushed the Allied forces back so far in one place that they bulged into the line of defense, nearly breaking through; this gave the Battle of the Bulge its name. The Allies were outnumbered by more than two to one but flatly refused to give in to the Germans' demand to surrender. When reinforcements came, the Allies pushed the Germans back. By January the Germans knew that they had lost the Battle of the Bulge. It was clear to everyone but Hitler that Germany would have to surrender.

In February 1945 Winston Churchill, Franklin Roosevelt, and Joseph Stalin met at Yalta in the Soviet Union to plan for peace. Stalin promised that the Soviet Union would join the fight against Japan within three months of Germany's surrender. The three leaders then agreed that along with France, they would occupy Germany after the war. They also discussed plans for a new League of Nations.

Surrender in Europe: VE Day

After tremendous battles against German armies all across Eastern Europe, Soviet troops marched westward toward Berlin in early 1945. Meanwhile, Allied troops entered Germany from the west. In late April 1945 the Soviets became the first to enter Hitler's capital city. Hitler, rather than be robbed of his power and face punishment for his crimes, committed suicide on April 30. A few days earlier in Italy, Mussolini had been captured and executed by Italian antifascists. On May 7 Germany surrendered, ending the war in Europe. People in the Allied countries called the date **VE** (Victory in Europe) **Day.**

As Allied troops entered the territories under German control, they discovered the **concentration camps** where so many Jews and other non-Aryans from all over Europe had been sent to be killed. Hitler, who had a maniacal hatred of Jews, had established a methodical system of registering them in their home towns and cities, rounding them up, herding them into concentration camps, and then exterminating them. This notorious Nazi practice soon was extended to Gypsies, Poles, Slavs, Catholics, the mentally and physically disabled, and any others who did not meet the Nazi definition of "**Aryan.**" In all, nearly 12 million people, about half of them Jews, were slaughtered by the Nazis. The deliberate massacre of European Jews is known to history as the **Holocaust.**

Roosevelt and other Allied leaders had been at least peripherally aware of Hitler's intentions toward non-Aryans for some time. However, because their attention was focused totally on the larger war effort, Allied officials had made no special plans to capture the camps or disrupt their operations. Roosevelt and others chose instead to focus on ending the war as quickly as possible, which in turn would eliminate the camps. News of the camps' existence had never been made public in the United States. As a result, when Allied soldiers reached the camps, they were completely unprepared for the horrors they found: people with registration numbers branded on their arms, many starved to two-thirds or even one-half their normal body weight, exhausted and ill. There was large-scale cremation equipment at some camps and massive common graves at all of them. There were huge, neatly sorted piles of human hair, gold and silver dental fillings, eyeglasses, clothing, and shoes. Almost all the camp guards had either committed suicide or fled in terror of the approaching Allied armies.

War in the Pacific

Numerous islands and island chains lie scattered across the Pacific Ocean between Japan and Australia. Early in the war most of them were controlled by Japan. The Allied plan was to use the U.S. Marines, who had the reputation of being the toughest branch of the armed forces, to take over certain key islands and use them as power bases as they made their way north toward Japan. That plan for attack was put into action in November 1943 in the Gilbert Islands. U.S. troops quickly took over Makin Island, but neighboring Tarawa was heavily fortified and also protected by a surrounding coral reef. Nearly 3,000 U.S. Marines were killed or wounded in the assault on Tarawa, but in the end the United States claimed the island. The Marines moved on to secure the Marshall Islands and then moved north toward the Marianas. Thousands on both sides died in the battles for Saipan and Guam (see the map below).

By August 1944 the United States had taken control of the Marianas and their valuable airstrips. By October, U.S. forces were poised to take back the Philippine Islands. The Battle of Leyte Gulf became the decisive battle in the war between Japan and the United States. In February 1945, U.S. troops finally entered the capital city of Manila, and the battle was over.

The United States used the Pacific islands as air bases from which to send out bombing raids on Japan. The planes bombed most of Japan's major cities, doing heavy damage. Still, the Japanese refused to surrender. In February 1945 the marines met the Japanese again on the island of Iwo Jima, only 75 miles from Japan's main island. In one of the most brutal battles of the war, in which thousands on both sides were killed, the United States finally gained a victory after six weeks of fighting. Loud cheers broke out among the U.S. troops when they saw their flag go up atop Mount Suribachi.

One more battle remained in the Pacific, since Iwo Jima had not brought about a Japanese surrender. U.S. forces invaded Okinawa unchallenged. Five days later Japanese troops opened fire on them. About 150,000 soldiers, two-thirds of them Japanese, were killed in the fighting.

Hiroshima and the Surrender of Japan

Roosevelt did not live to see VE Day. He died on April 12 in Warm Springs, Georgia, where he had a favorite retreat. Roosevelt had been president for so many years and had courageously held the nation together through such hard times that people were shaken by his passing as they had not been at the death of any president since Abraham Lincoln. With Roosevelt's death, Vice President Harry S. Truman took office.

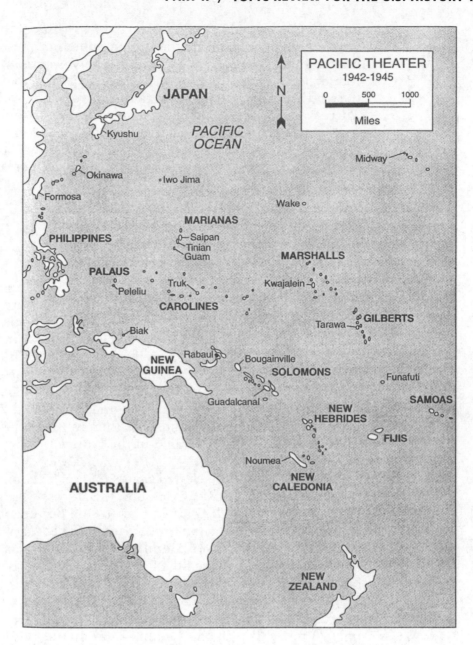

The news from Europe made it clear that the German surrender was imminent. This meant that Truman could turn all his attention to the war against Japan. Faced with the Japanese refusal to surrender, Truman decided to use the deadliest weapon in history: the atomic bomb, the world's first nuclear weapon.

European and U.S. scientists had developed the bomb between 1942 and 1945 in a research project called the **Manhattan Project.** The first bomb was tested successfully in New Mexico in July 1945. It was clear that the bomb would wreak unimaginable destruction; nevertheless, Truman believed that it would save the lives of U.S. troops by ending the fighting immediately. On August 6 the United States dropped the first atomic bomb on the Japanese city of Hiroshima. The blast killed over 75,000 people and laid every building in the city completely flat. A second bomb was dropped on Nagasaki three days later. Truman was proved correct in his belief that the bomb would bring about immediate surrender; the Japanese, stunned at the damage and the number of deaths, surrendered on September 2. (Few, including Truman, had any idea at the time of the serious long-term damage the explosions caused to the environment and to the people exposed to the radiation; that did not become apparent until some time later.)

Results of the War

The Allied forces had beaten back the German attempt to conquer Europe. The Nazi Party was disbanded and discredited; those of its key figures who had not committed suicide or fled to South America soon were put on trial as war criminals. Japan's military warlords were overthrown. Both nations lost all the territory they had annexed during the war.

Estimates of the number of lives lost vary. The number was certainly in the millions, with the Soviet Union being by far the hardest hit. Between 7 million and 10 million Soviet soldiers died during World War II, more than the soldiers of all the other fighting nations combined. The U.S. armed forces, by contrast, lost approximately 400,000 soldiers. Millions of civilians died as a result of disease, starvation, massacre, deliberate execution, and bombing.

Much of Central Europe lay in ruins. Germany was heavily damaged by bombing. Cities and villages across the Soviet Union and Poland had been reduced to piles of stones. Transportation systems were wrecked. Everyday necessities such as fresh water, fuel, electricity, and food were unavailable. Sanitation was impossible in bombed-out cities. Governments were in disarray or had been removed from power. Japan was in as bad a state as any nation in Europe. As they gathered for a peace conference at Potsdam in Germany, Allied leaders had the enormous task of rebuilding before them.

The Potsdam Conference

The Allied leaders met at Potsdam in July 1945. President Truman represented the United States, Stalin the Soviet Union, and Churchill and his successor, Clement Attlee, Great Britain.

Provisions of the Potsdam Conference

- Austria and Germany each would be divided into four zones of occupation: Soviet, British, U.S., and French.
- Vienna and Berlin (inside the Soviet zone) also would be divided into four zones, as above (see the map below).
- The Allies would help rebuild German industry and reestablish local governments.
- German refugees would be returned to their homes.
- Poland would retain the German territory it had claimed after the war.
- Germany would make reparations to all the Allied nations, with the Soviet Union receiving the largest share as the greatest sufferer.

The Allied leaders were somewhat suspicious of one another. Stalin did not want the United States imposing a capitalist economy on Germany; on his side, Truman did not want the Soviets to gain too much control over Poland and Eastern Europe. These suspicions continued to grow as time went on. Before long they would lead the world into the Cold War.

GERMANY 1945   **BERLIN 1945**

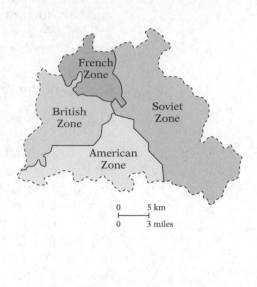

REVIEW QUESTIONS

1. The Battle of the Bulge took place when Allied troops

   (A) invaded North Africa
   (B) approached Germany's western border
   (C) fought German troops in Italy
   (D) landed on the beaches of Normandy
   (E) fought the Japanese at Iwo Jima

2. Which of the following was among the reasons why President Truman decided to drop atomic bombs on Japan?

   (A) He wanted to free the Philippines from Japanese occupation.
   (B) He feared a Japanese invasion of the United States.
   (C) He believed the bombing would shorten the war and save U.S. lives.
   (D) He wanted to impress the British with U.S. strength.
   (E) He wanted to destroy every city in Japan.

3. The Potsdam Conference provided for all the following EXCEPT:

   (A) the division of Germany into four occupied zones
   (B) the payment of reparations to the Allies
   (C) the reorganization of the Soviet government
   (D) the acknowledgment that Poland could keep the German territory it had claimed
   (E) the conversion of the German economy to agriculture and light industry.

Answers and Explanations

1. **B** The Battle of the Bulge took place in late 1944 as Allied troops in Belgium approached Germany's western border. The Germans sought to stop the Allied advance but in the end were defeated, allowing the Allies to enter Germany in early 1945.

2. **C** Truman believed that when the Japanese saw the destruction that an atomic bomb could create, they would surrender, making it unnecessary to invade Japan and put U.S. solders' lives at further risk. After two atomic bombs were dropped on Japanese cities, the Japanese government surrendered.

3. **C** The Soviets were on the winning side in the war; therefore, there was no reason for them to undertake any reorganization of their government, and nobody proposed this.

CHAPTER 27

POSTWAR AMERICA, 1945–1960

INTRODUCTION

World War II was over, but it did not bring peace to the world. Instead, it ushered in a new era of conflict known as the Cold War that was to last for 40 years. The Soviet Union and the United States were the only superpowers to emerge from the destruction of the war. They had antithetical systems of government, and their economic policies were opposed to each other. The Soviets already had spread a mantle of control over most of Eastern Europe. For the next 40 years the United States would try to keep Soviet power from spreading any farther. However, this had to be done carefully and delicately to avoid provoking a nuclear war that both sides knew could destroy the world. By 1949 both the Soviet Union and the United States had begun to stockpile nuclear weapons.

Fear of the Soviet Union made many people afraid that communists and other leftists in the United States were Soviet agents. Congressional investigations pandered to that public fear, ruining many lives with accusations and allegations.

People in the United States enjoyed an era of prosperity and plenty after the hard times of the Great Depression. The GI Bill of Rights gave veterans a chance to get a college education, buy a farm, attend training school for a particular profession, or start a business. This enabled many to marry, start families, and move to the newly built suburbs. People were buying cars, television sets, and other consumer goods in large quantities.

In U.S. society the first steps were taken toward racial integration. African Americans' service in the war had convinced many whites that they deserved to be treated equally. Federal legislation and important Supreme Court decisions desegregated public schools and public transportation by the mid-1950s. The Brooklyn Dodgers baseball team set an example of integration in private business by signing Jackie Robinson in 1947.

TIMELINE

1945   Potsdam Conference.

Nuremberg Trials.

Founding of United Nations.

Winston Churchill gives "Iron Curtain" speech.

Allies divide Korea into two zones.

1945–1952   U.S. occupation of Japan.

1947   Brooklyn Dodgers sign Jackie Robinson.

1948   Marshall Plan goes into effect.

Truman reelected president.

1949   North Atlantic Treaty Organization founded.

1950   North Korea invades South Korea.

U.S. and UN forces defend South Korea.

1952   *Brown v. Board of Education.*

Dwight D. Eisenhower elected president.

1953   Korean armistice signed.

1955–56   Montgomery bus boycott.

1956   Eisenhower reelected.

KEY TERMS

blacklisted   denied work, especially for political reasons

containment   measures to prevent a country from extending its power over other countries or regions

Cold War   standoff between the Soviet Union and United States that lasted from about 1945 to 1989; "cold" because no battles were fought

Iron Curtain   a phrase coined by Winston Churchill to identify the invisible border between democratic Western Europe and communist Eastern Europe

Marshall Plan   name for the European Recovery Program designed by General George C. Marshall that provided European nations with $17 billion in U.S. aid

McCarthyism   a term used to describe the anticommunist hysteria that was promulgated by the false accusations of U.S. Senator Joseph McCarthy

satellite   a country that is under the political and military control of another country

Truman Doctrine   stated that the Unites States would offer economic and military assistance to any free country that attempted to resist subjugation by an outside power

The Founding of the United Nations

The League of Nations had failed to prevent World War II. World leaders agreed that they needed to design a new international peacekeeping organization that had more power. The United States agreed to host the planning meetings. Delegates from the United States, China, the Soviet Union, and Great Britain proposed an organization that would be called the United Nations. Delegates from the Soviet Union and the United States argued over several points but eventually compromised on key issues. Delegates from 50 nations then met to discuss the proposal and write a charter for the UN. It established a General Assembly in which all member nations would have an equal voice and a Security Council made up of five permanent members (the United States, Great Britain, the Soviet Union, China, and France) with veto power and 10 rotating members.

A large majority in the Senate voted in favor of U.S. participation in the UN. The UN headquarters was established in New York City. One of its first tasks was to write and pass a universal Declaration of Human Rights. President Truman appointed Eleanor Roosevelt to serve as one of the delegates. Roosevelt played a crucial role in getting the declaration passed.

The Beginnings of the Cold War

One of the results of World War II was that the great European powers were severely weakened. Germany was divided and powerless; other nations had lost millions of their people and had had their industries, infrastructure, and cities badly damaged by bombs and battles. Only two nations emerged from the struggle as great powers: the United States and the Soviet Union. Tension had strained their alliance even during the war.

During World War II the Soviets had marched westward against Germany and had taken over every country through which their army passed. Poland, Estonia, Latvia, Lithuania, Romania, and eastern Germany were now **satellite** nations under Soviet control. The Soviets also had taken control of Manchuria, a formerly Japanese-controlled province in eastern China. Stalin claimed that for its own security, the Soviet Union needed to ensure this zone of friendly nations between itself and Western Europe. Stalin wanted to ensure that the Soviets would not be invaded from the west again (see the map below).

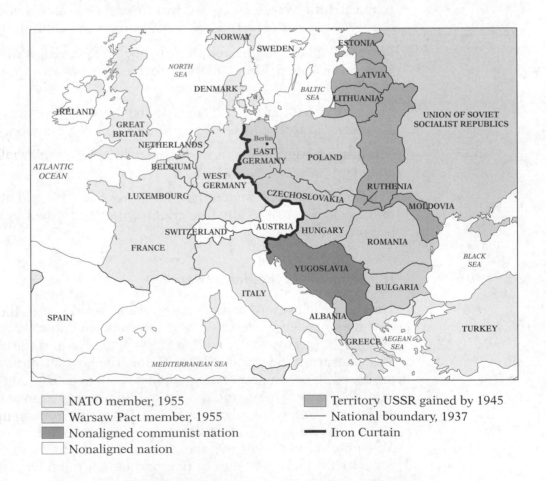

In 1946, former British prime minister Winston Churchill accepted an invitation to speak at Fulton College in Missouri. Missouri was President Truman's home state, and Truman personally escorted Churchill to his speaking engagement. In a lengthy address on the current state of world affairs, Churchill spoke the following memorable sentences:

> From Stettin in the Baltic to Trieste in the Adriatic, an iron curtain has descended across the Continent. Behind that line lie all the capitals of the ancient states of Central and Eastern Europe. Warsaw, Berlin, Prague, Vienna, Budapest, Belgrade, Bucharest, and Sofia, all these famous cities and the populations around them lie in what I must call the Soviet sphere, and all are subject in one form or another not only to Soviet influence but to a very high and, in many cases, increasing measure of control from Moscow.

Many Americans did not want to acknowledge the truth of Churchill's perceptions; they wanted to believe that the victory over the Nazis had made the world safe. However, most people recognized that Churchill was correct. The immediate U.S. response was to adopt a policy called **containment.** The United States believed that it might be possible to prevent Soviet influence from spreading any farther and that this was a necessary first step in pushing the Soviets back within the borders of their own territory. In what became known as the **Truman Doctrine,** President Truman stated that the United States would support any nation or region that the Soviets threatened to take over or subjugate.

The first Soviet threat of expansion was in the Dardanelles, the strait linking the Black Sea with the Aegean and Mediterranean seas. Since control of the strait would give the Soviets an important strategic advantage in the Mediterranean, the United States immediately agreed to give Greece and Turkey, the nations on either side of the straits, $400 million worth of aid to hold off the Soviets.

The United States also provided billions of dollars in aid to European nations to help them rebuild and recover from the devastation of World War II. That foreign aid plan was created by General George C. Marshall, the secretary of state and former army chief of staff. Under what soon became known as the **Marshall Plan,** aid would be provided to any European nation that requested it. Congress balked at first at the amount of money involved but gave in when communist forces took over the government of Czechoslovakia in 1948. The Marshall Plan ultimately helped rebuild the economies of almost all the nations in Western Europe. Stalin regarded the Marshall Plan as a blatant attempt by the United States to buy influence in Europe and prevented any nation behind the **Iron Curtain** from participating in it. For its part, the United States refused to give aid to any country that did not meet its standards for a capitalist democratic government.

A contrast was soon visible between the two groups of nations on opposite sides of the Iron Curtain. Western nations were able to rebuild their economies and their infrastructure. They held elections and reestablished their governments, all of which were republican or democratic to a greater or lesser degree. They began to trade internationally once again, building up their treasuries and their relations with other nations.

Behind the Iron Curtain conditions were different. Employment was nearly 100 percent because in communist nations people were guaranteed jobs. However, wages were low and there was little for people to spend money on. People had to wait in line for hours every day to buy necessities; luxuries were completely out of reach. The state owned and ran all businesses and industries, and so people took little personal pride in their jobs.

The contrast was strongest in the city of Berlin. Berlin was many miles behind the Iron Curtain, but since it had been divided into zones of occupation at the end of the war (see the map in Chapter 26), only East Berlin was controlled by the Soviets. Britain, France, and the United States had combined their zones to create West Berlin, a small island of thriving capitalism that was made prosperous by Marshall Plan aid from the West.

In 1948, when the three Western sections were united despite promises to the contrary made earlier at Yalta, the Soviets blockaded all ground access to West Berlin, claiming that since it was in East Germany, they had the right to do this. The United States immediately organized the Berlin Airlift. Supply planes brought food, medicines, and other essentials into West Berlin on a daily basis until the Soviets recognized defeat and ended the blockade in 1949. Soon afterward West Germany officially broke from East Germany as the Federal Republic of Germany. Soviet-backed East Germany reorganized itself as the German Democratic Republic.

The Korean War

As part of the peace settlement in 1945, the Allies had divided the Korean peninsula into two zones. North Korea was occupied by Soviet troops, and South Korea by U.S. troops. Like the divisions of Berlin and Vienna, this began as a temporary measure. However, the Soviets insisted on maintaining control of North Korea, which soon was governed by communists and declared itself the People's Republic of Korea. South Korea, which had a democratically elected president, was known as the Republic of Korea.

The United States and the Soviets pulled their troops out of Korea in 1949 without resolving the tension between the two Koreas, which were bound to clash because of their different systems of government. North Korea invaded South Korea on June 25, 1950. The UN called for an immediate cease-fire, and UN forces, primarily U.S. troops, immediately went on duty to defend South Korea. When U.S. troops under General Douglas MacArthur neared the Chinese border, Chinese forces entered the conflict on the North Korean side.

When Dwight D. Eisenhower was elected president in 1952 (see below), he pledged to end the Korean War. By July 1953, with Eisenhower threatening the use of nuclear weapons against North Korea, both sides agreed to an armistice. The terms restored the status quo before the war. Korea was divided along the 38th parallel, with the northern half under communist rule and the southern half under democratic rule.

Anticommunist Hysteria and McCarthyism

The desire to contain the spread of communism overseas affected life at home. A small number of people in the United States belonged to the Communist Party. They believed in many of its ideals, especially its claim that workers should have control over economic decisions. Communism had been especially appealing during the 1930s and the war years because it was the opposite of fascism.

Any U.S. citizen is free to belong to any political party; it has never been a crime to be a communist. During the **Cold War,** many people in the United States ignored this fact. Their irrational fears created a "Red Scare" (red being the symbolic color of communism) in which it became unsafe to be a communist, have communist sympathies, or be suspected of being a communist.

In 1938 the House of Representatives had created the House Un-American Activities Committee to investigate fascist groups. In 1947 that committee began investigating suspected communists. Its investigation of many prominent people in the Hollywood film industry made national headlines. (During the war many Hollywood figures had been hired to make pro-Soviet films because the Soviet Union and the United States were allies. Afterward their participation in those projects often would be used against them.) A group of writers and directors who became known as the Hollywood Ten invoked their constitutional right not to answer the committee's questions. They were jailed briefly, and then they were **blacklisted** in Hollywood. Hollywood studios existed to make profits and did not want their films boycotted by audiences that had been influenced by anticommunist hysteria. Fearing the blacklist, many Hollywood figures gave the committee the names of anyone they thought might be a communist or a communist sympathizer. Others, such as Humphrey Bogart, Katharine Hepburn, and Lauren Bacall, courageously opposed the committee.

The Hollywood Ten were not the only people whose lives and careers were ruined. The FBI investigated any group or individual who was accused of being a communist. Many prominent writers and university professors were investigated. So was Paul Robeson, an internationally acclaimed concert singer and actor. Robeson, like many other African Americans, had spoken publicly about the unequal treatment of blacks in the United States. He had been to the Soviet Union and had spoken favorably about race relations in that country. When Robeson refused to answer the committee's questions about his politics, pointing out that such questions were illegal, his passport was taken away. Since no one in the United States would hire a suspected communist, he was effectively deprived of the means to earn a living.

The hysteria worsened after a series of high-profile spy cases. Julius and Ethel Rosenberg were accused and convicted of giving the Soviets the secret to the atomic bomb. Alger Hiss, a State Department official who had been present at the Yalta Conference, was convicted of perjury after the statute of limitations has passed on spy charges. Although later evidence would prove that Hiss and possibly Julius Rosenberg were spies, at the time they were convicted, the evidence against them was outweighed by the hysteria.

In 1950 a little-known Wisconsin senator named Joseph McCarthy falsely claimed to have a list of more than 200 communists currently employed in the U.S. State Department. That claim, made at a press conference, touched off an era of hysteria unparalleled since the Puritan "witch hunts" of the 1600s. McCarthy used his sudden rise to national prominence to ruin the lives of hundreds of people by making unsubstantiated accusations against them. By 1954 McCarthy had been discredited. It had become clear to the entire country, after committee hearings were broadcast on television, that there was no evidence behind any of his charges (although this provided little solace to those whose lives were ruined). Ever since this disgraceful era in U.S. history, the term "**McCarthyism**" has been used to identify dirty political tactics like his: hurling unfounded accusations, slandering opponents, and trying to gain the support of the public by playing on its fears and prejudices.

The Truman and Eisenhower Administrations

Truman's administration was faced with numerous challenges, including the threat of nuclear war abroad and anticommunist hysteria at home.

Truman, a plainspoken, solidly middle-class Midwesterner, was not a man to back down when faced by a challenge: he was stubborn, determined, and steadfast in his convictions.

Truman. supported the GI Bill of Rights, which provided money for veterans to go to college, start businesses, and buy farms or houses. Millions of U.S. citizens from the lower classes became the first in their families to get a college education; in the past, most college graduates had been wealthy or upper-middle-class persons. In effect, this made U.S. society far more democratic than it had ever been.

Truman also felt that more progress needed to be made in the area of civil rights. He ended racial segregation in the armed forces and the federal bureaucracy, and in 1952 he supported congressional repeal of the 1882 Chinese Exclusion Act, which had barred Chinese immigrants from entering the country and denied naturalization to those already there. White Southern Democrats were outraged by Truman's support for African Americans and vowed not to vote for him in 1948. Truman campaigned vigorously and scored an upset victory against his Republican opponent, Thomas A. Dewey.

During his second term in office Truman proposed a series of programs modeled on the New Deal and called the "Fair Deal." His programs had limited success in a Congress that was no longer as heavily controlled by Democrats as it had been under Roosevelt. However, under Truman's administration, the minimum wage went up and Social Security was expanded to cover millions more people.

The popular World War II hero Dwight D. Eisenhower, whom everyone called "Ike," was elected president in 1952. Eisenhower described himself as fiscally Republican but socially Democratic. He reduced the size of the federal bureaucracy and cut farm subsidies, but he also expanded Social Security and unemployment benefits, increased the minimum wage, and increased spending on education.

Eisenhower found himself participating in a nuclear arms race with the Soviet Union. Until 1949 the United States had been the only nation that had the technology to make nuclear weapons. However, Soviet scientists, following the same research path as the participants in the Manhattan Project, had built their own bomb by 1949. From then on both nations stockpiled nuclear weapons. Each side wanted to have so many weapons that the other side would be reluctant to launch an attack. Neither side wanted to provoke a nuclear war. The bombs dropped on Japan had made it clear that such a war could destroy the world. The United States spent a staggering amount of money on defense; by 1960 it had about 19,000 nuclear weapons, about five times as many as the Soviet Union.

Social Changes 1945–1960

The two biggest changes in everyday life in the United States after World War II were migration to the suburbs and the invention of television. Many suburbs were planned communities that were built outside major cities on large tracts of land. One of the most famous was Levittown, New York, on Long Island near New York City. Levittown was a community of more or less identical houses with garages, driveways, wide streets, and spreading lawns. Newly married veterans and those who already had families thought the suburbs were an ideal place to raise children. Because houses and cars were affordable in the postwar era, it was possible to live in the suburbs and work in the city. By 1960 almost one-third of the U.S. population had moved to the suburbs. The move to the suburbs and the subsequent reallocation of tax dollars would lead to a decline in the quality of life in the cities.

The other major change was the new recreational pastime of watching television. This "radio with pictures" was universally popular. People could watch a variety of programs on television: news broadcasts, comedies such as *I Love Lucy*, sporting events such as baseball games, game shows such as *The $64,000 Question*, and dramas such as *Playhouse 90*. Since anyone who owned a television could turn it on at any time, television networks could not charge audiences money. Instead, they paid their expenses by selling airtime to advertisers that knew that their commercials would be viewed by thousands, perhaps millions, of people in their homes.

Civil Rights

Several important steps toward racial integration were made during the 1940s and 1950s. One was President Truman's integration of the armed forces and the federal bureaucracy. Another was Jackie Robinson's appearance in a Brooklyn Dodgers uniform in 1947. Until that spring major league baseball had had an unofficial "whites only" policy. African Americans had their own Negro Leagues featuring stars such as Satchel Paige, Oscar Charleston, and Cool Papa Bell. Dodgers general manager Branch Rickey, determined to bring quality players to his team regardless of race, sought out Robinson and offered him a contract. When players on other teams threatened to go on strike rather than play against an African American, National League president Ford Frick stated firmly:

> I do not care if half the league strikes . . . I don't care if it wrecks the National League for five years. This is the United States of America, and one citizen has as much right to play as any other. The National League will go down the line with Robinson whatever the consequences.

Robinson endured a difficult season of taunts, jeers, and death threats from the public and a measure of hostility from many players. However, his superb skills eventually won his teammates and the fans over to his side. Other teams began hiring black players, and soon the Negro Leagues folded. Since baseball was played almost every day over the course of a six-month season, fans saw integration at work on a daily basis. This had a mitigating effect on many people's prejudices.

In Montgomery, Alabama, an African-American woman named Rosa Parks refused to give up her bus seat to a white passenger. The rule on buses was that white passengers sat in the front and black passengers sat in the back; if the front seats were filled, blacks had to give up their seats to whites. Because Parks refused to give up her seat, she was arrested. In response, African Americans launched a citywide bus boycott, and the National Association for the Advancement of Colored People (NAACP) appealed Parks's case. In November 1956 the Supreme Court declared that segregated seating on city buses was unconstitutional. This case brought an African-American minister and activist named Martin Luther King, Jr., into prominence for the first time. It also showed the power of mass action as a tool for change.

Another blow to segregation came in 1952, when the Supreme Court heard a case called *Brown v. Board of Education*. The African-American lawyer Thurgood Marshall argued that segregation by race in public schools was unconstitutional. The court ruled in his favor, noting that segregated school systems were by nature unequal. That decision made segregation illegal in public school systems.

Many white Southerners reacted to the ruling with fury. Throughout the South school integration happened slowly and painfully. The first black students to attend white schools had to be escorted by armed guards, but that did not stop white people from throwing rotten vegetables at them, jeering at them, and calling them foul names. However, the students continued to attend school in spite of constant harassment and threats. They were among the bravest Americans to play a role in the civil rights movement that would shape the following decade.

REVIEW QUESTIONS

1. Which of the following prompted the first use of UN military forces?

   (A) Tension between the Soviet Union and the United States
   (B) The nuclear arms race between the Soviet Union and the United States
   (C) The North Korean invasion of South Korea
   (D) The international agreement to put Nazi officials on trial for their crimes
   (E) Anticommunist hysteria in the United States

2. The primary purpose of the Marshall Plan was to

   (A) reestablish democratic governments in Western Europe
   (B) provide military assistance to Britain and its empire
   (C) offer financial aid for reconstruction to European nations
   (D) help Japan rebuild its cities and its economy
   (E) increase U.S. power in the world

3. All the following advances were made in race relations in the United States between 1940 and 1960 EXCEPT:

   (A) In Brown Vs. Board of Education, the U.S. Supreme Court declared that segregated public schools were unconstitutional.
   (B) Public transportation was desegregated.
   (C) Major league baseball was desegregated.
   (D) The Chinese Exclusion Act was repealed.
   (E) A voting rights act was passed.

Answers and Explanations

1. **C** When North Korea invaded South Korea in 1950, the UN called for a cease-fire and then sent UN troops (mostly U.S. military forces) to defend South Korea.
2. **C** The Marshall Plan offered financial aid to rebuild bombed-out locations and reestablish economies on a sound footing to any European nation that had participated in World War II. No nation behind the Iron Curtain accepted the aid.
3. **E** The Voting Rights Act was not passed until 1965, under President Lyndon B. Johnson.

CHAPTER 28

THE NEW FRONTIER AND THE CIVIL RIGHTS MOVEMENT

INTRODUCTION

The presidential election of 1960 brought the Democratic Party back to the White House. John F. Kennedy took over the helm of U.S. politics at a challenging and dangerous time, when the threat of nuclear war was at its height and Cold War tensions were growing.

At home, the civil rights movement that had begun in the 1950s continued to make advances. Under the leadership of Martin Luther King, Jr., African Americans organized nonviolent protests throughout the segregated South. The quiet, well-organized protesters, exercising their First Amendment rights to "peaceably assemble," provided a strong contrast to the brutal armed policemen and the jeering crowds of segregationists. The protesters won public opinion over to their side, and by 1964 the Civil Rights Act had been signed into law, ending segregation in fact nearly 100 years after the civil rights amendments to the Constitution had ended it in law.

In foreign affairs the United States was brought to the brink of nuclear war at least twice. East German officials under Soviet control, deciding to stop once and for all the exodus of East Germans to West Berlin, built the Berlin Wall. The United States did not want to go to war over this issue, but Kennedy did fly to Berlin and give a strongly worded speech claiming that communist rule clearly had failed when the East German government had to build a wall to keep people from leaving. Closer to home, a crisis developed when the Soviets installed nuclear missiles in Cuba, 90 miles from the United States. During a tense two weeks, Kennedy responded with a naval blockade of Cuba. Although both nations were poised for nuclear war, the Soviet premier, Nikita Khrushchev, agreed at the last moment to withdraw the missiles, ushering in a new era of attempts to find common ground between the two superpowers.

The nation and the world went into shock when Kennedy was assassinated on a campaign trip to Dallas, Texas. Lyndon B. Johnson took over the presidency and was soon to reshape the nation's domestic policies.

TIMELINE

1960   John F. Kennedy elected president.

Civil rights protestors conduct sit-ins in the South.

Student Nonviolent Coordinating Committee formed.

1961   Summit meeting between the United States and the Soviet Union.

Berlin Wall is constructed.

1962   Cuban missile crisis.

279

1963 Limited Nuclear Test Ban Treaty.

Civil rights protests in Birmingham, Alabama.

Martin Luther King gives "I Have a Dream" speech in Washington.

Kennedy assassinated; Lyndon B. Johnson becomes president.

1964 Twenty-Fourth Amendment ratified.

Civil Rights Act of 1964.

KEY TERMS

Berlin Wall a barbed-wire fence, later a concrete wall, erected around the perimeter of West Berlin to prevent East Germans from leaving the Soviet-controlled region

civil rights movement an organized push for desegregation, especially in the South

Cuban missile crisis a situation that developed when the Soviets installed nuclear missiles in Cuba

New Frontier name for President John F. Kennedy's domestic programs

Peace Corps a federal volunteer program in which Americans served for two years in a foreign country as teachers, doctors, farmers, or engineers

sit-in a form of peaceful protest in which people sit in an area and refuse to move

The Election of 1960

During President Truman's first term in office Congress passed the Twenty-Second Amendment, which limited a president to two terms in office. The Republican majority in Congress wanted to ensure that no Democratic president would ever again, like Franklin Roosevelt, be elected to four terms. If this amendment had not been ratified, the popular Dwight D. Eisenhower might well have served a third term; however, he had to step down in 1960.

The election of 1960 pitted the Democrat John F. Kennedy of Massachusetts against the Republican Richard Nixon of California. Both men had been elected to the U.S. Senate in 1946; Kennedy had served there ever since, and Nixon had been Eisenhower's vice president since 1952 and hoped to benefit from Eisenhower's enormous popularity. As a Catholic, Kennedy faced the same prejudice and bigotry that had helped defeat Al Smith in 1928, but Protestants as a whole had grown somewhat more tolerant in the intervening years, and Kennedy assured voters that he believed in the strict separation of church and state. As a result, religion was not a decisive factor in the election.

Kennedy was a charming and witty man whom audiences found irresistibly attractive. His appearance and personality combined to convey a youthful energy and optimism that people found appealing. Kennedy was also a highly skilled campaigner, good at dealing with people and with the press. Nixon's style was quite different. Nixon had considerable political experience and was highly intelligent, but his stiff manner, distrust and suspicion of reporters, and determination to ignore advisors and make all his own campaign decisions helped defeat him. He also was handicapped in many people's minds by his association with the House Un-American Activities Committee and the McCarthy-style campaigning tactics he had used throughout his political career.

The contrast between the two candidates was never more apparent than during the first televised presidential debates in history. Kennedy, utilizing makeup and consultants, looked pleasant, open, and relaxed on camera; he also had a considerable command of the facts on the issues that came up in questions. The cameras were not nearly so kind to Nixon, and Kennedy's unexpected skills as a debater put Nixon on the defensive. In November the popular vote was so close that the outcome took a few days to call, but in the end Kennedy was elected.

The Kennedy White House was characterized by style and flair. Much of this was due to the first lady, Jacqueline Bouvier Kennedy. Mrs. Kennedy came from an upper-class family, had been educated in Paris, spoke French and Spanish fluently, dressed stylishly, and charmed everyone with her beautiful manners. The Kennedys were the youngest couple ever to live in the White House, and their two toddlers were popular subjects for photographers.

Domestic Policy: The New Frontier

In domestic policy, Kennedy moved energetically to propose a set of initiatives he called the "New Frontier." These included programs to extend federal benefits for education, health, and welfare—ideas long promoted by Democrats. But even though the Democratic Party controlled both houses of Congress, conservative Southerners refused to support Kennedy's proposals, and as a result, many of his domestic policy initiatives produced little in the way of tangible results.

Foreign Policy: Cuba and Berlin

As soon as he took office, Kennedy was forced to deal with pressing foreign policy concerns. Eisenhower's years in office had done nothing to resolve the Cold War hostility with the Soviet Union. In 1959 the rebel leader Fidel Castro had seized power in Cuba, turning it into a communist state that he ruled as military dictator. The presence of a communist nation only 90 miles from the U.S. coast was a grave concern. Before Eisenhower left office, the Central Intelligence Agency (CIA) had developed a plan to remove Castro from power. Kennedy approved the plan, which called for a force of Cuban exiles to invade the island at a coral reef known as the Bay of Pigs. The invasion was a disastrous failure that strengthened the alliance between the Soviet Union and Cuba and increased the hostility that both nations felt toward the United States.

Another crisis developed in Europe, where West Berlin remained a small island of Western-style capitalism and freedom in a sea of communism. The Soviets were well aware that every year hundreds of thousands of East Germans decided to escape political oppression and seek better economic opportunities by walking across the border into West Berlin and then relocating to West Germany or another Western nation. In August 1961, without warning, the Soviet-controlled East German government began constructing a heavy barbed-wire fence around the perimeter of West Berlin. Since the fence was entirely on East German land, people in West Berlin could not stop the construction. The fence ended all legal westward travel; from that time on East Germans had to have special permits to cross the barrier for limited periods. Many still found ways to cross the wire hidden in trunks of cars or clinging to the undercarriage of trains or openly, by making a run for it. Some were successful; hundreds were shot by border guards. In time, the fence was replaced with a high concrete wall guarded by soldiers and dogs. The **Berlin Wall** soon became the most recognizable symbol of the Cold War.

Kennedy did not want to go to war over the Berlin Wall, but he also did not want to appear weak to the Soviets or to U.S. voters. In June 1961 he traveled to Berlin and made a speech on the western side of the wall, denouncing communist rule as a failure and noting that in the West "we have never had to build a wall to keep our people in, to prevent them from leaving us."

The Soviet premier, Nikita Khrushchev, who had met Kennedy face to face at a European summit, felt that the U.S. president was inexperienced and weak. Khrushchev therefore decided to test the United States by sending nuclear arms to the Soviet Union's ally Cuba. The missiles in Cuba posed the threat of a nuclear attack on the United States.

In response to the **Cuban missile crisis,** Kennedy established a naval blockade of Cuba. He ordered the U.S. Navy to turn back all armed Soviet ships headed for the island. Both sides prepared for battle. Soviet ships approached the blockade, but at the last minute Khrushchev offered to withdraw the missiles from Cuba if the United States would withdraw its missiles from sites in Turkey where they were aimed at the Soviet Union. The offer was accepted, and the threat of war was averted.

This was the closest the two nations were to come to launching a nuclear war. Both Kennedy and Khrushchev acknowledged that they could not allow such a war to happen. From then on the two nations began to try to find common ground and to achieve what later became known as détente, or "peaceful coexistence." In 1963, with Great Britain, the two nations signed the Limited Nuclear Test Ban Treaty, which ended the testing of nuclear bombs in the atmosphere and underwater.

Kennedy had continued Eisenhower's policy of stockpiling nuclear weapons but also had created programs of his own to contain communism in a more peaceful and constructive way. The **Peace Corps** recruited people in the United States to serve in a variety of foreign countries for two-year terms as teachers, farmers, engineers, doctors, and so on. When it began, the Peace Corps served 44 nations. This program helped foreign economies recover, brought new technology to developing nations, and created good relations between them and the United States. It continues to this day.

The Civil Rights Movement

The **civil rights movement** is the name for the post–World War II campaign for the rights that African Americans had been granted on paper during and after the Civil War but often had been denied in reality. During the late 1940s and the 1950s, African Americans (and many sympathetic whites) began an organized campaign to do away with discrimination and segregation, especially in the states of the former Confederacy (see Chapter 27). President Kennedy supported the goals of the civil rights movement; his successor, Lyndon Johnson, passed substantial federal civil rights legislation. Both sometimes were obliged to send federal troops to the South to deal with outbreaks of brutality between the police and protestors.

In 1957, Martin Luther King, Jr., became the leader of the Southern Christian Leadership Conference (SCLC). This association of black church organizations adopted the philosophy of nonviolent resistance King had learned from studying the writings of Mohandas Gandhi of India. Young followers of King and the SCLC formed their own organization, the Student Nonviolent Coordinating Committee (SNCC). Jesse Jackson, who later would run for president of the United States, played a major role in SNCC activities.

The SNCC launched a campaign of **sit-ins** in Southern cities in 1958. Small groups of black students would go to "whites-only" lunch counters and sit down. When service was refused, they would refuse to leave. They remained until closing, studying their books, and returned the next day. Onlookers taunted them, poured ketchup and sugar over their heads, and threw food at them. The sit-ins continued into 1960 and made national headlines. In the end the students' determination and perseverance paid off when restaurants all across the South began serving black customers.

Participation in the civil rights movement was dangerous. Southern police and segregationists were frequently guilty of brutally beating protestors and committing other acts of violence. In the first years of school desegregation, armed guards had to protect black students from possible harm. In 1963, the secretary of the National Association for the Advancement of Colored People (NAACP), Medgar Evers, was shot and killed.

The nonviolent protests advocated by King worked because they provoked violence among the segregationists, putting them in an unfavorable light in the eyes of the general public. It was clear to most of the country by this time that the era of segregation had come to an end and that Jim Crow laws were unconstitutional.

In 1963 the SCLC began concentrating its nonviolent protests in the city of Birmingham, Alabama. Many school-age children took part in the nonviolent protests, which drew a great deal of newspaper and television coverage. People across the country were horrified at the photographs and films of armed policemen setting dogs on crowds of peaceful protestors or turning fire hoses on large groups that included small children. Public opinion quickly was won over to the side of the protestors.

In the summer of 1963 the protesters gained one of their most important objectives. President Kennedy asked Congress to make segregation illegal in public places. To celebrate that success and keep the movement in the public eye, civil rights leaders organized a rally at the Lincoln Memorial in Washington, D.C. At the rally, in the most famous speech of his career, King described his dream of what the United States might become when it finally lived up to its promise that all men were created equal:

> When we let [freedom] ring from every village and every hamlet, from every state and every city, we will be able to speed up that day when all of God's children, black men and white men, Jews and Gentiles, Protestants and Catholics, will be able to join hands and sing in the words of the old Negro spiritual, "Free at last! Free at last! Thank God Almighty, we are free at last!"

A year later, as King looked on, Lyndon Johnson signed the Civil Rights Act of 1964 into law on July 2. The act had the following provisions:

- Banned racial, gender, religious, and ethnic discrimination in employment
- Made segregation illegal in all public places

- Allowed the federal government to sue public school systems that did not obey desegregation laws
- Removed certain voter-registration restrictions

Space Race

When he became president, Kennedy challenged the scientific community to put a man on the moon by the end of the decade. Both the United States and the Soviets already had begun experimenting with space flight. In 1961, the Soviet astronaut Yuri Gagarin became the first human being to orbit the earth. The United States matched that achievement in 1962 when John Glenn duplicated Gagarin's feat. Throughout the 1960s U.S. and Soviet space programs raced to be the first one to have an astronaut walk on the surface of the moon. The Apollo program finally accomplished that goal in 1969.

Assassination

On the morning of November 22, 1963, the president and the first lady were riding in an open car through the streets of Dallas, Texas. As the motorcade passed, a young malcontent named Lee Harvey Oswald opened fire on the president from the window of a schoolbook warehouse. Kennedy was killed, and within hours Vice President Lyndon B. Johnson took the oath of office. Oswald was apprehended promptly but was shot by a gunman named Jack Ruby, who died in prison before he could be tried. (An investigation headed by Supreme Court Chief Justice Earl Warren later determined that both gunmen had acted alone, but this did not prevent a lively industry of conspiracy theorists from springing up.)

REVIEW QUESTIONS

1. The Civil Rights Act of 1964 had all the following provisions EXCEPT:

   (A) It banned racial, gender, religious, and ethnic discrimination in employment.
   (B) It removed certain voter-registration restrictions.
   (C) It made segregation illegal in all public places.
   (D) It allowed the federal government to sue public schools that did not desegregate.
   (E) It integrated the federal government and the armed forces.

2. The Cuban missile crisis ended when

   (A) the Soviets agreed to withdraw their missiles from Cuba if U.S. missiles were withdrawn from sites in Turkey
   (B) President Kennedy ordered the U.S. Navy to turn back Soviet ships headed for Cuba
   (C) a CIA-sponsored invasion of Cuba by Cuban exiles was defeated at the Bay of Pigs
   (D) President Kennedy was assassinated
   (E) the East German government built a wall around the perimeter of West Berlin

3. All the following characterized the civil rights movement EXCEPT:

(A) advocating legislation that would outlaw segregation
(B) nonviolent demonstrations
(C) sit-ins at segregated lunch counters and restaurants
(D) police brutality against civil rights marchers
(E) violent attacks on segregated restaurants and other public facilities

Answers and Explanations

1. **E** The federal bureaucracy and the armed forces were integrated during the 1940s under President Truman.
2. **A** War was averted and the crisis ended when the Soviets agreed to withdraw their missiles from Cuba if U.S. missiles aimed at the Soviet Union were withdrawn from sites in Turkey.
3. **E** Most civil rights protesters believed in nonviolence. Those who took part in sit-ins at lunch counters, restaurants, and other public facilities were generally peaceful, even when attacked by prosegregation whites.

CHAPTER 29

THE GREAT SOCIETY

INTRODUCTION

A career politician from Texas, Lyndon Johnson seemed at first glance an unlikely champion of civil rights and antipoverty legislation. Nonetheless, he became the president most responsible for ending racial segregation and pushed important social legislation through Congress that continues to protect the needy.

Johnson became president when Kennedy was assassinated. After winning reelection in 1964, Johnson launched a major social legislation program known as the Great Society. As a result of his programs, millions of people in the United States were able to leave poverty behind.

The civil rights movement had not ended with the signing of the Civil Rights Act of 1964. African Americans continued to fight for their rights, especially at the polls. By 1968 millions of previously unregistered African Americans had registered to vote, participating in the political process for the first time.

In the same era, many women participated in efforts to obtain rights equal to those of men. Women formed lobbying and political organizations and campaigned for greater social and economic equality.

TIMELINE

1962   Rachel Carson publishes *Silent Spring*.

1963   Lyndon B. Johnson becomes president when Kennedy is assassinated.

1964   War on Poverty.

Civil Rights Act.

Johnson reelected president.

Twenty-Fourth Amendment ratified.

1965   Great Society.

Medicare and Medicaid founded.

Malcolm X assassinated.

Selma, Alabama, voting registration drive.

Department of Housing and Urban Development established.

Corporation for Public Broadcasting created.

Voting Rights Act.

1966   Black Panther Party founded.

1968   Poor People's Campaign.

Martin Luther King, Jr., assassinated.

Robert F. Kennedy assassinated.

KEY TERMS

black power   the idea that African Americans can mobilize their own political and economic power to compel others to respect their rights

Great Society   a set of social programs promoted by President Lyndon B. Johnson and enacted into law by his administration

Lyndon B. Johnson

Lyndon B. Johnson had run for the presidential nomination in 1960 against John F. Kennedy. At the Democratic Party convention, Kennedy had startled his closest advisors by asking Johnson to be his running mate.

Born and raised in Texas, Johnson had been a schoolteacher before running for Congress. He had served as Senate majority leader and compiled an impressive record of getting legislation passed. His presence on the Democratic ticket helped win many votes in the South; this was Johnson's own region, and he was well liked there.

Although Johnson's years of experience would have been of great value to the Kennedy administration, Kennedy's advisors disliked and distrusted him and largely ignored him. However, when Johnson suddenly was elevated to the presidency in 1963, he asked all of Kennedy's cabinet members to stay on. Johnson intended to see Kennedy's policies through, especially in the area of civil rights.

Johnson, who described himself as "an old Roosevelt New Dealer," was fully committed to social programs that would give opportunities to the poorest classes in society. In January 1964 he announced the launching of a "War on Poverty." He proposed the creation of the Office of Economic Opportunity, which would administer a number of antipoverty programs such as Head Start, a preschool education program, and the Job Corps, a work training program for young people. Johnson also created the first program of aid for Native Americans that allowed the tribes themselves to administer the money and decide how it would be used to reduce poverty on reservations.

In 1964 Johnson ran for reelection. His Republican opponent was Senator Barry Goldwater, a conservative whose extreme positions on many issues were not popular among most voters. Johnson won in November in a popular and electoral landslide.

The Great Society

Johnson introduced his vision for the United States, which he called the **Great Society,** in speeches in the spring of 1965. He described a country that provided equal social and economic opportunity for all. Johnson wasted no time trying to make his vision a reality. He used his tremendous skills as a negotiator to get legislation for important social programs passed. All but about 20 of some 200 bills he presented to Congress became law between 1964 and 1968.

The table below shows the key programs of the Great Society.

Another area in which the Great Society strove for improvement was environmental legislation. In 1962 a marine biologist named Rachel Carson had published a book called *Silent Spring* in which she described the damage done to wildlife by the pesticides used in farming. Carson's book aroused public support for laws protecting the environment. Thanks to her book,

Job Corps	Work training program for people age 16 to 21
Head Start	Preschool education program for children from low-income families
Elementary and Secondary Education Act	Provided federal funding for schools in poor regions
Medicare	Federally funded health insurance for people age 65 and over
Medicaid	Federally funded health insurance for the needy
Corporation for Public Broadcasting	Federally and privately funded television network whose mission was to show educational programming
Omnibus Housing Act	Funded urban renewal and housing assistance for low-income families

DDT, the most harmful of the pesticides, was banned. Johnson urged Congress to pass laws that would control and improve air and water quality, along with other environmental bills.

Supreme Court rulings during the 1960s strengthened the principle of equality before the law. Led by Chief Justice Earl Warren, the Court set several important precedents. *Gideon v. Wainwright* stated that courts must provide attorneys for accused criminals who could not afford their own. *Escobedo v. Illinois* stated that an accused person had the right to have an attorney present during questioning by the police. *Miranda v. Arizona* stated that anyone being arrested must be informed of the right to remain silent and have an attorney. Under these decisions, people from even the most disadvantaged segments of society were assured of their constitutional legal rights to due process and equality before the law.

The Great Society helped many people escape poverty and improve their lives, but before long it was overshadowed by the Vietnam War (see Chapter 30), and funding was diverted from domestic social programs to the military. By the time Johnson left office, the Great Society had lost its momentum. However, some of its most important programs are still in place, providing important services to those who need them.

Civil Rights

A major focus of the civil rights movement during the mid-1960s was a drive to increase the number of African-American voters, particularly in the South. In many Southern states Jim Crow laws restricting registration had long discouraged African Americans from voting. Civil rights activists organized voter registration drives in many parts of the South. In the summer of 1964, known as "Freedom Summer," white volunteers joined African-American civil rights activists in a drive to register black voters in Mississippi. Public sympathy for the movement rose after three young voting-rights activists were found dead, murdered by segregationists.

In early 1965 in Alabama, Martin Luther King, Jr., and others organized a march from Selma to Montgomery to protest legal obstacles that prevented African Americans from voting. When police attacked the marchers, public opinion was outraged. President Johnson immediately called for a voting rights bill, which Congress passed in the summer of 1965. The Voting Rights Act put the voter registration process under federal, not state, control. Federal officials traveled south and began registering voters. African-American voter registration rose in the segregated South by more than 225 percent in some areas by 1968.

As the 1960s wore on—and as social and economic equality proved more difficult to achieve than mere legal equality—King's belief in nonviolence as an effective weapon began to lose its influence. Other black leaders emerged, including many who wanted African Americans to take more active measures.

The Nation of Islam, or Black Muslims, urged African Americans to create their own republic within the United States. A leading spokesman for the group was the fiery orator Malcolm X, who, like many other Black Muslims, had rejected his family name because it had originated in slavery. He criticized King and the other nonviolent leaders and urged a policy of black separatism and empowerment. Malcolm X later broke with the Nation of Islam and began promoting more moderate views, but in 1965 he was assassinated.

Activists who questioned the values of nonviolence and racial integration began calling for **"black power."** The term was coined by Stokely Carmichael of the Student Nonviolent Coordinating Committee. The idea it expressed was that African Americans could mobilize their own political and economic power to compel others to respect their rights. One group promoting black power was the Black Panther Party, many of whose members openly carried guns and vowed to defend themselves by force if necessary.

Throughout the mid-1960s racial tensions increased, particularly in many inner-city African-American neighborhoods. During several summers, violent disturbances broke out, often after confrontations between African Americans and white police officers. The worst disturbances took place in Detroit, Los Angeles, and Newark, New Jersey, leaving many dead. Those events caused many middle-class whites to lose sympathy for the civil rights movement and to call instead for "law and order."

In April 1968 the movement suffered another blow when Martin Luther King was assassinated by a sniper. The cause of civil rights had lost its most eloquent spokesman.

The Women's Movement

Throughout U.S. history women as a group had experienced unequal treatment under the law and in society at large. Women were subject to many legal restrictions, barred from many educational institutions, and discouraged from entering many professions. Society expected married women to stay at home and raise children rather than participate in the workforce. Women workers earned lower salaries than men in comparable jobs.

By the 1960s some aspects of that situation had changed. During the war years many women had worked in traditionally male jobs. More middle- and upper-class women were getting a college education. Some were obtaining highly paid skilled jobs. However, there were still inequities in the system. Few women were hired for government posts or elected to office. Women generally continued to be paid less than men to do the same jobs.

The Equal Pay Act of 1963 required certain employers to pay male and female workers the same wage for the same job, but it covered only about one-third of all working women. The Civil Rights Act of 1964 offered some improvement: It included a provision called Title VII that outlawed sexual discrimination in employment.

In June 1966, Betty Friedan (the author of a bestselling profeminist book called *The Feminine Mystique*), Gloria Steinem, and other women activists formed the National Organization for Women (NOW). Since its inception NOW has lobbied Washington politicians to ensure social and economic equality for women. In later years feminist activists would help achieve increased equity for women in the workplace and in fields such as sports and education.

REVIEW QUESTIONS

1. All the following are programs of the Great Society EXCEPT:

    (A) the National Organization for Women
    (B) Head Start
    (C) the Corporation for Public Broadcasting
    (D) Medicare
    (E) Medicaid

2. A major achievement of the civil rights movement in the 1960s was

    (A) equality in pay for white and African-American workers doing the same jobs
    (B) a huge increase in the number of African-American voters in the South
    (C) equal access to higher education for African Americans
    (D) appointment of African Americans to leading posts in major corporations
    (E) election of African-American majorities in state legislatures

3. President Johnson called for a voting rights bill in 1965 after

    (A) Martin Luther King., Jr., was assassinated
    (B) he defeated the Republican Barry Goldwater in a landslide election
    (C) Betty Friedan and others formed the National Organization for Women
    (D) racial disturbances broke out in Detroit and Los Angeles
    (E) a protest march let by Martin Luther King, Jr., was met with violence

Answers and Explanations

1. **A** The National Organization for Women is not a federal program.
2. **B** One of the great achievements of the 1960s civil rights movement was the registration of huge numbers of African-American voters in the Southern states.
3. **E** Johnson called for passage of a voting rights act after a protest march led by Martin Luther King, Jr., was met with violence near Selma, Alabama.

CHAPTER 30

THE VIETNAM WAR

INTRODUCTION

The Vietnam War was unlike any other war in which the United States had participated. It lasted more than 10 years, over time it lost support at home, it was never formally declared by Congress, and it ended in an inglorious defeat. It was also the occasion for millions of people in the United States to lose faith in their government, a malaise with effects that continue to this day.

The United States became involved in Vietnam because U.S. leaders did not want to see communism spread any farther in Asia than it already had. When Vietnam, formerly a French possession, declared its independence under the communist leader Ho Chi Minh, the United States did not support it. Instead, the United States helped broker an international agreement that Vietnam would be divided into two nations—North Vietnam and South Vietnam— that would reunite and hold elections in 1946. However, that agreement was never carried out. Ho and his followers consolidated their power in North Vietnam and began sending aid to communist guerrillas, called the Vietcong, in the south. Meanwhile, in South Vietnam, the United States backed an anti-communist government led by Ngo Dinh Diem and began sending troops to train the South Vietnamese Army. Deservedly unpopular, Diem was assassinated in 1963.

Starting in 1965, President Lyndon Johnson sent hundreds of thousands more U.S. troops to Vietnam and launched a sustained bombing campaign. However, the North Vietnamese and the Vietcong proved impossible to pin down in conventional battle. They fought the war on their terms, by jungle ambush. U.S. bombs proved ineffective at anything except pointless destruction.

Richard Nixon became president in 1968 on a promise to end the war. Instead, however, he increased the bombing and expanded the war into nearby Cambodia. Nevertheless, unable to defeat the Vietnamese and under pressure from an increasingly disillusioned American public, the U.S. government began withdrawing its troops. Eventually, in 1975, the North Vietnamese succeeded in taking over all of Vietnam, and the United States was forced to accept a humiliating defeat.

The war and the U.S. government's handling of it severely damaged the American psyche. The healing process began only in 1982 with the unveiling of the Vietnam War Memorial on the mall in Washington, D.C.

TIMELINE

1940 Japanese occupy French Indochina (Vietnam).

1941 Ho Chi Minh organizes the Vietminh.

1945 Japan withdraws from Indochina.

Vietminh declare Vietnamese Independence.

1946 United States allies with French against Vietnamese.

1954 Vietminh defeat French at Dien Bien Phu.

Geneva Conference on Indochina: Vietnam divided along 17th parallel.

1955   Ngo Dinh Diem becomes president of Republic of Vietnam (South Vietnam).

1960   National Liberation Front and Vietcong begin attacking South Vietnam.

1961–1963   U.S. troops go to South Vietnam as military advisors, then combatants.

1963   Diem assassinated.

Congress passes Tonkin Gulf Resolution.

1965   Johnson institutes military draft.

Operation Rolling Thunder.

First national antiwar demonstration in Washington, D.C.

1966   Congressional hearings on Vietnam.

1968   Tet Offensive.

Robert F. Kennedy assassinated.

Richard Nixon elected president.

1969   U.S. troop withdrawals begin.

U.S. bombing of Cambodia.

1970   Kent State massacre.

Congress repeals Tonkin Gulf Resolution.

1971   Twenty-Sixth Amendment is ratified.

New York Times begins publishing "Pentagon Papers."

1972   Major North Vietnamese invasion of South Vietnam.

Nixon reelected.

1973   Cease-fire agreement between United States and North Vietnam.

Congress passes War Powers Act.

1975   Saigon evacuated; South Vietnam surrenders to North Vietnam.

1982   Vietnam War Memorial dedicated.

KEY TERMS

Agent Orange   a toxic chemical U.S. soldiers used to strip forested land and poison plants

conscientious objector   one who refuses to serve in the military on the grounds of conscience, religion, or morals

domino theory   the belief that if one Southeast Asian nation converted to communist rule, they all would do so

French Indochina   term for a Southeast Asian region, including Laos, Vietnam, and Cambodia, under French control from 1883 to 1940

Ho Chi Minh Trail   a network of jungle paths leading from North Vietnam to South Vietnam

Pentagon Papers   documents published beginning in 1971 that showed that the U.S. government had lied about involvement in Vietnam

Tet Offensive   a major North Vietnamese assault on January 30, 1968, New Year's Day or "Tet" in Vietnam; showed that U.S. forces were not in control in Vietnam

Tonkin Gulf Resolution   gave the U.S. president authority to commit troops to a war without seeking congressional approval

Vietcong   U.S. name for Southern Vietminh, who wanted to overthrow the government of South Vietnam after the national division; name stands for "Vietnamese Communists"

Vietminh   Vietnamese freedom fighters, also known as League for the Independence of Vietnam; founded 1941 by Ho Chi Minh

War Powers Act   set a 60-day limit on a president's power to commit troops to a foreign war without congressional approval

Background: Vietnam

Vietnam occupies a part of the Indochinese peninsula in Southeast Asia. It is a long, narrow country that is bordered on one side by the South China Sea and on the other by Cambodia and Laos. China borders Vietnam on the north. In 1883, during the period of European colonization in Asia and the Pacific, the French invaded Vietnam, Cambodia, and Laos. France took control of all three nations, combining them into one colony called **French Indochina.** Nevertheless, many Vietnamese resisted French control, and over time, groups emerged seeking independence.

During World War II Japan occupied French Indochina. In 1941 Vietnamese, led by Ho Chi Minh, organized a resistance movement known as the **Vietminh,** or the League for the Independence of Vietnam. The Vietminh were ready when World War II ended and Japan withdrew. Ho declared Vietnamese independence from France in August 1945. The French did not accept that, and the United States supported France both because it was a longtime ally and because Ho and many of his followers were communists.

At that time in the Cold War communists were active in independence movements in many European colonies, and people in the United States feared that those movements would lead to communist takeovers and the expansion of Soviet influence. Those fears were heightened when communists took power in China in 1949. Many people believed in the so-called **domino theory:** the idea that if one country was taken over by communists, those nearby would be taken over as well. As a result, the United States poured money into the French effort to regain control over Indochina, while the Vietminh received aid from China. The guerrilla tactics of the Vietminh were very effective against the French. At Dien Bien Phu in northern Vietnam, Vietminh forces trapped French troops, whom they outnumbered by more than three to one. The French expected U.S. reinforcements that never came; President Eisenhower did not want to commit U.S. troops to another ground war in Asia so soon after their return from Korea. The French surrendered on May 7, 1954.

After the French defeat there was a peace conference in Geneva involving several nations: France, Vietnam, Cambodia, Laos, China, the Soviet Union, Great Britain, and the United States. Each nation pursued its own agenda. China wanted to limit U.S. influence in Asia and did not want a strong, united independent Vietnam. The United States wanted to limit communist influence in the region. In the end Vietnam was divided along the 17th parallel, with the Vietminh taking control in North Vietnam and the French taking control in the south. With the United States abstaining, the other nations agreed that in 1956 Vietnam would hold general elections and reunify the nation under one government.

In South Vietnam the Eisenhower administration threw its support behind Ngo Dinh Diem, who had been a government official under French rule. After a disputed election, Diem became president of the Republic of South Vietnam in 1955. Diem was ruthless and corrupt. As time went on, he also became increasingly unpopular, in part because as a Catholic he alienated the Buddhist majority. He also implemented policies that favored the wealthy.

Backed by the United States, Diem refused to hold national reunification elections in 1956 as agreed in Geneva. He did not believe he could win an election against Ho Chi Minh, and he did not want to step down from the presidency. Communists and others in South Vietnam organized underground resistance to the Diem government. In 1960 they formed an organization called the National Liberation Front (NLF) with the goal of overthrowing Diem and reuniting the nation. The Vietminh in North Vietnam began sending weapons to the NLF, which became known popularly as the **Vietcong.**

The United States Sends Troops

Eisenhower was the first U.S. president to send troops to Vietnam, although the number was limited to several hundred "military advisors" whose job was to train the official army of South Vietnam. After 1960 President Kennedy, who shared Eisenhower's apprehension about the spread of communism in Asia, sent more troops. By 1963 there were more than 16,000 U.S. troops in Vietnam, and they were no longer serving only in a training capacity. Because of the fierce assaults of the Vietcong, Kennedy authorized U.S. troops to fight. Nearly 500 Americans had been killed or wounded in combat, although no war had been declared.

In 1963 Diem launched a brutal campaign of repression against Buddhist groups in South Vietnam. Anxious to maintain stability, the U.S. government threw its support to a group of South Vietnamese who intended to unseat Diem. Soon afterward, Diem and his brother were murdered brutally. Three weeks later, President Kennedy was assassinated. It was then up to Lyndon Johnson to deal with U.S. involvement in Vietnam.

The Vietnam War Expands

On July 30, 1964, after a series of events that are still in dispute, U.S. Navy ships in the Gulf of Tonkin off North Vietnam reported that they had been attacked by North Vietnamese torpedo boats. At that time President Johnson was campaigning for president against the Republican challenger Barry Goldwater. Goldwater had tried to portray the president as "soft" on Vietnam. Knowing he needed to appear aggressive in the eyes of the voters, Johnson decided to step up the Navy's presence in the gulf. On August 4, after another reported North Vietnamese attack, Johnson ordered an air attack on North Vietnamese bases and patrol boats. At midnight Johnson spoke to the U.S. public

on television, informing it of the "unprovoked attacks" by the North Vietnamese and stating that he had asked Congress to authorize the use of military
force against North Vietnam. With the **Tonkin Gulf Resolution,** Congress
effectively signed away its constitutional power to declare war.

In November, Johnson was reelected president. Early in 1965 he ordered
the Selective Service to begin sending out draft notices. College students, who
were mainly from upper- or middle-income families, received deferments;
consequently, those drafted were largely from lower-income families. In 1965
almost 25 percent of all U.S. casualties were African Americans although they
made up only about 10 percent of the total U.S. population. Hispanics also
served in disproportionate numbers. More than 10,000 women served in
Vietnam as field nurses and in other positions where they were in the thick
of fighting, although they did not carry guns in combat. More than 40,000
more women served as volunteers with organizations such as the Red Cross.

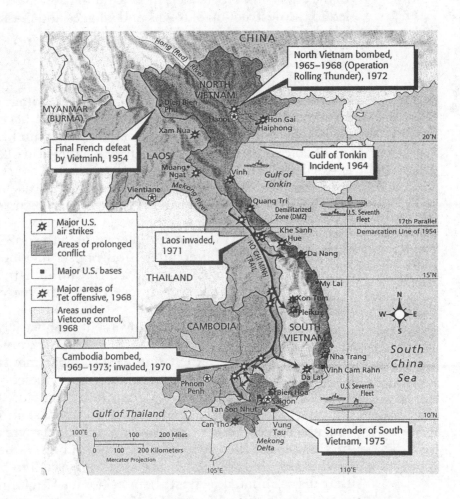

Combat in Vietnam 1965–1968

Hoping to bring the war to a speedy end, in 1965 Johnson ordered an air war
and bombing campaign called Operation Rolling Thunder against the North
Vietnamese and the Vietcong. However, the operation did not succeed. The
Vietnamese were adept at guerrilla warfare, hiding in the jungles and fre-
quently ambushing U.S. troops. Supplies from North Vietnam reached the
Vietcong in the south along the **Ho Chi Minh Trail,** a complicated pathway

through the jungles. Bombing was of no avail against the jungle route. If a U.S. bomb destroyed a bridge, the Vietcong rebuilt it or swam the river it crossed. The Vietcong also built a series of underground bomb shelters where they could hide themselves, their weapons, and their supplies in safety.

Conventional bombs were not the only U.S. weapons. Firebombs filled with napalm and cluster bombs that showered sharp slivers of metal were commonly used weapons. Troops sprayed forests with a deadly chemical known as **Agent Orange.** It killed most vegetation, thus robbing the Vietcong of their jungle cover.

When aerial bombing proved ineffective, the United States tried ground war. Between 1965 and 1967 another 300,000 U.S. troops were sent to Vietnam. However, hampered by their unfamiliarity with jungle terrain and guerrilla-style warfare, the U.S. forces made little progress. As the fighting increased, hundreds of thousands of Vietnamese civilians were killed, caught in the cross fire. U.S. tactics, though failing to weaken the Vietcong, sometimes led to the destruction of towns and villages and massacres of the population.

Protest at Home

The Vietnam War was the first war that people in the United States watched on television. Americans had seen newsreel footage of World War II and the Korean War, but by the 1960s television had become big business. News networks sent reporters and cameras to Vietnam to cover the action.

People soon discovered that there was a world of difference between reading articles in newspapers and seeing video coverage on television. A reporter might give a vivid description of horrors in words, but it was still an account that kept the reader safely detached. Moving pictures, seen on a daily basis, were something else. The public soon became aware that the optimistic statements from the White House did not match the unrelenting combat they saw on television night after night. Journalists in Vietnam who saw firsthand what was happening also criticized the administration for having lost control of the war. As the war dragged on, many people in the United States began turning against it.

People joined the antiwar movement for a variety of reasons. Some were pacifists who did not believe in any war. Some wanted their tax dollars to go to social programs rather than to the Department of Defense. Some were afraid that the war would escalate into a nuclear conflict. Some did not believe in the "domino theory" that was used to justify the war. Some argued that the war was a civil war among Vietnamese in which the United States had no business interfering. Many who had relatives and friends in the armed forces wanted their loved ones to return home safely. Civil rights activists were angry that so many black men were asked to fight and die for a nation that discriminated against them at home. Muhammad Ali was only one of many who requested **conscientious objector** status on religious grounds.

On April 17, 1965, a group called Students for a Democratic Society held the first national antiwar protest. Twenty thousand people came to Washington, D.C., to demonstrate against the war. Antiwar demonstrations continued for the next 10 years. Many young men refused to be drafted or fled to Canada.

The antiwar movement divided the generations. The protesters included many young people, but most older people felt that it was unpatriotic to protest against the government.

The Tet Offensive

On Tet (January 30, 1968), the Vietnamese New Year, the North Vietnamese and the Vietcong launched a major offensive against U.S. troops and their allies, fighting them even in the streets of downtown Saigon, the capital of South Vietnam, in what came to be known as the **Tet Offensive.** The attackers were repelled, but the offensive was a tactical success for the North because it proved that the United States had nowhere near the control it claimed in Vietnam. Public opinion in the United States shifted dramatically against the war.

In March 1968 President Johnson announced that he would not run for reelection (he was eligible to do so under the Twenty-Second Amendment because he had served less than two years of Kennedy's term). The leading Democratic contender for the office was the enormously popular Senator Robert F. Kennedy, who had served in his brother's cabinet as attorney general. Kennedy had called for a negotiated settlement in Vietnam. When he was shot down by an assassin after the California primary election, the Democrats lost their best hope of keeping the White House. The Republican Richard Nixon, claiming that he had a secret plan to end the war and promising "law and order" at home, was elected in a close contest over Johnson's vice president, Hubert Humphrey.

Nixon and Secretary of State Henry Kissinger planned to withdraw U.S. troops gradually and turn the war over to the South Vietnamese. Nixon hoped that that strategy would result in a stable, noncommunist South Vietnam. The North Vietnamese agreed to peace talks, but only on condition that the United States set a date for the withdrawal of all troops. As it turned out, withdrawal was a slow process; there were still 240,000 U.S. soldiers in Vietnam at the end of Nixon's first term.

Early in 1969 Nixon ordered the bombing of Cambodia, a neutral nation that bordered Vietnam, believing that Vietcong forces were taking refuge on Cambodian territory. In a flagrant abuse of his powers, Nixon informed no one—not Congress, not the voters, not even key military leaders—about the bombing. In 1970, after the Cambodian government was overthrown in a U.S.-backed coup, Nixon finally revealed his strategy. He then sent tens of thousands of U.S. ground troops into Cambodia.

The invasion of Cambodia outraged many in Congress and the public. Congress repealed the Tonkin Gulf Resolution, and when Nixon refused to acknowledge the repeal, Congress cut off funding for the war. Later, in 1973, Congress passed the **War Powers Act,** which allowed a president to commit troops to a foreign war for only 60 days without congressional approval.

The invasion of Cambodia also touched off a new wave of antiwar demonstrations across the United States. At Kent State University in Ohio, National Guard troops were sent in to restore order. The troops fired at random into a large group of students, killing four and wounding nine more. The Kent State Massacre and a similar incident a few days later at Jackson State College in Mississippi shocked the nation.

In 1971 a former Department of Defense official named Daniel Ellsberg gave copies of secret government documents to the *New York Times*. Those documents, which became known as the **Pentagon Papers,** revealed that successive U.S. administrations had lied to the public about their policies and actions in Vietnam. Public support for the war, which had been waning, was eroded further by this concrete evidence of bad faith.

In the spring of 1972 Nixon ordered a new bombing campaign against North Vietnam. The North Vietnamese responded with a major invasion of

South Vietnam. Secretary of State Kissinger and the Vietnamese leader Le Duc Tho had been meeting secretly since 1969, trying to reach a peace settlement agreeable to both sides. In January 1973, after a final fierce bombing assault by the United States failed to force a surrender, Le Duc Tho and Kissinger agreed to the following terms:

- A cease-fire was declared.
- The United States would help rebuild South Vietnam.
- Prisoners of war would be exchanged.

In 1975 the military government that had been established in South Vietnam collapsed. North Vietnamese troops invaded Saigon. The last U.S. troops, as well as over 100,000 Vietnamese, were evacuated. On April 30, 1975, South Vietnam surrendered.

REVIEW QUESTIONS

1. Which of the following presidents sent troops to Vietnam?

   (A) Truman, Eisenhower, and Kennedy
   (B) Eisenhower, Kennedy, Johnson, and Nixon
   (C) Johnson and Nixon
   (D) Kennedy and Johnson
   (E) Johnson

2. Which of the following was NOT settled in the U.S.–North Vietnamese peace agreement of 1973?

   (A) An exchange of prisoners of war
   (B) The political future of South Vietnam
   (C) The withdrawal of U.S. troops
   (D) The end of U.S. military aid to South Vietnam
   (E) A cease-fire

3. All the following turned people in the United States against the Vietnam War EXCEPT:

   (A) the Kent State and Jackson State massacres
   (B) publication of the Pentagon Papers
   (C) disclosure of the bombing of Cambodia
   (D) repeal of the Tonkin Gulf Resolution
   (E) revulsion against the horrors of war as shown on television news broadcasts

Answers and Explanations

1. **B** Eisenhower was the first president who sent troops to Vietnam. Kennedy sent more troops, and Johnson sent many more. Nixon also sent troops to both Vietnam and Cambodia but eventually was obliged to begin the U.S. withdrawal.
2. **B** The peace agreement did not settle the future of South Vietnam.
3. **D** The repeal of the Tonkin Gulf Resolution was a result, not a cause, of antiwar sentiment.

CHAPTER 31
WATERGATE AND ITS AFTERMATH

INTRODUCTION

June 17, 1972, Nine o'clock Saturday morning. Early for the telephone. Woodward fumbled for the receiver and snapped awake. The city editor of the *Washington Post* was on the line. Five men had been arrested earlier that morning in a burglary at Democratic headquarters, carrying photographic equipment and electronic gear. Could he come in?

Elected president by a narrow margin of 500,000 votes in 1968, Richard Nixon intended to stay president for a second term. More than that, he ordered his closest aides to see to it that he would be reelected by the largest landslide in history, telling them he did not care how they did it as long as it was done. The actions those aides took, with Nixon's full knowledge and approval, eventually led to the break-in at the Watergate buildings in Washington, D.C., and to the newspaper investigations later described in the book *All the President's Men* (1974).

Nixon achieved notable success in foreign affairs, easing relations with the Soviet Union and paving the way for better relations with China. His domestic policies were neither coherent nor successful; both inflation and unemployment rose while he was in office. However, his major legacy to the nation was the high crimes and misdemeanors he committed while in office.

It became clear that the Committee to Re-elect the President had paid the Watergate burglars. Because that committee was run entirely from the White House and everyone in Washington knew that nothing happened in the White House without Nixon's approval, people began to realize that Nixon must have known about the burglary and about other crimes that were uncovered in the following months by reporters from the *Washington Post*. The reporters eventually traced a conspiracy, run directly from the Oval Office, to subvert the electoral process and ensure Nixon's reelection.

Nixon might not have been forced to resign the presidency if there had not been clear evidence against him in the form of tape recordings of confidential Oval Office conversations. Nixon had authorized the recordings because he wanted to preserve his legacy for history. That plan backfired on him when the existence of the tapes was revealed to the grand jury investigating the Watergate crimes. Never before in history had a president resigned; Nixon became the first to do so rather than face up to what he had done.

TIMELINE

1968 Richard Nixon elected president.

1969 Warren Burger appointed to Supreme Court.

1970 Congress creates Environmental Protection Agency.

1971 Nixon aides begin to compile "enemies list."

1972   Nixon visits China.

Nixon visits Soviet Union; signs SALT Treaty.

Break-in at Democratic headquarters in Watergate buildings.

Nixon reelected.

1973–1974   Energy crisis.

1973   Senate begins investigating Watergate scandals.

Vice President Agnew resigns; replaced by Gerald Ford.

Saturday Night Massacre.

1974   Taped Oval Office conversations made public.

Nixon resigns; Ford becomes president.

Ford pardons Nixon.

KEY TERMS

CREEP   the **C**ommittee to **Re-e**lect the **P**resident; established to back Nixon in the 1972 election

Deep Throat   code name for source of information for *Washington Post* reporters working on Watergate story

détente   lessening of tension; peaceful coexistence

inflation   a constant trend toward rising prices

OPEC   the **O**rganization of **P**etroleum-**E**xporting **C**ountries; founded in 1960

realpolitik   "politics of realism"; a philosophy of politics based on material interests rather than ethics

SALT   the **S**trategic **A**rms **L**imitation **T**alks; held between the Soviet Union and the United States with the goal of limiting intercontinental nuclear missiles

Saturday Night Massacre   resignation of the attorney general and his assistant over their refusal to fire Watergate Special Prosecutor Archibald Cox

Watergate   catchall name given to the corruption and high crimes that eventually forced Nixon to resign from office

Richard Nixon began his political career in his native state of California, running for Congress in the 1950s. He won his campaigns by taking advantage of the current "Red Scare" and accusing his opponents of sympathizing with communism. Once elected to the House of Representatives, Nixon became a prominent member of the House Un-American Activities Committee (HUAC). Later he became vice president under Dwight D. Eisenhower.

When Nixon ran for president in 1960, the political reporter Theodore H. White wrote of him:

The brotherhood of the press was considered by Mr. Nixon and his staff, not a brotherhood, but a conspiracy, and a hostile conspiracy at that. . . . What he thought, what he planned, what he wished to express, Nixon kept to himself, believing (until too late in the campaign) that he could reach the American people over the heads of the press.

After he lost the election to Kennedy, Nixon returned to California, where he ran for governor in 1962. During that campaign he deliberately leveled false charges at his Democratic opponent, Governor Pat Brown, for example, sending out mailings purporting to come from the Democratic Party and releasing doctored photographs showing Brown with people he had never met. Those unethical tactics failed to win Nixon the election. However, he would use them again in the future.

The 1968 Election

Nixon ran for president in 1968, a year in which people in the United States desperately wanted some stability in society. John F. Kennedy, Martin Luther King, Jr., the civil rights activist Medgar Evers, the African-American radical Malcolm X, and Senator Robert F. Kennedy had been assassinated. The Alabama governor and conservative presidential candidate George Wallace had been paralyzed by an assassin's bullet. War in Vietnam raged on with no end in sight. War protesters continued to demonstrate. Nixon capitalized on that unrest by depicting himself as a law-and-order candidate who would restore peace both at home and abroad.

The Democratic Party was deeply divided over Vietnam. Antiwar demonstrators clashed violently with the police in Chicago during the Democratic Party convention. Many conservatives, including many people in the older generation, were shocked at the way the protestors defied the authorities. Feeling uncertain and afraid as the protests mounted and resenting what they viewed as the protestors' disrespect for traditional American values, many of those people turned away from the Democratic Party to vote for Nixon, who won the presidency over Hubert Humphrey by about 500,000 votes.

Domestic Policy under Nixon

Nixon did not support many of Johnson's Great Society programs. In his view, those programs were charitable handouts, not attempts to provide opportunities to poor people. Under the Great Society, the number of people on public assistance had doubled. In response, Nixon proposed a Family Assistance Plan under which adults receiving welfare payments would work in exchange for a guaranteed minimum salary. The Senate did not pass that plan.

Nixon did not believe in civil rights legislation. He also opposed it on political grounds because it was unpopular among white Southern voters, whom the Republicans were trying to attract. As a result, many white Southerners switched allegiance from the Democrats to Nixon's Republican Party. In 1971 Nixon opposed a Supreme Court ruling that schools could be integrated by busing students to achieve racial balance. Nixon had four opportunities to appoint a new justice to the Supreme Court. All of his choices were conservative, two of them so conservative that the Senate refused to confirm them. In the end, the new Chief Justice was Warren Burger, and the three new associate justices were Harry Blackmun, Lewis Powell, and William Rehnquist. Over the years Burger and Blackmun proved to be much more moderate in their decisions than Nixon had anticipated.

In 1973 a crisis arose over the high price of petroleum. The United States had become heavily dependent on imported oil, much of it from Arab countries in the Middle East that resented U.S. support for Israel. After a war in 1973 between Israel and its Arab neighbors, the oil-producing Arab countries, which accounted for a majority of the members of the Organization of Petroleum-Exporting Countries (**OPEC**), decided to retaliate against the United States and other supporters of Israel first by refusing to ship any oil at all and later by drastically raising its price. By December 1973 the price of oil had risen by nearly 400 percent. That "energy crisis" caused severe economic problems in the United States as the prices of oil-dependent goods and services rose dramatically. **Inflation** (a constant trend toward rising prices) remained a problem for years afterward.

Under Nixon the first serious efforts were made to protect the environment from degradation and pollution. One major step was the creation in 1970 of the Environmental Protection Agency.

Foreign Policy

In the area of foreign policy Nixon worked closely with his secretary of state, the German-born Henry Kissinger. Kissinger was one of very few associates whom the president trusted. The two agreed on an approach called **realpolitik,** a political philosophy based on material interests rather than idealism. Nixon believed in supporting any allies of the United States even if some of them engaged in policies that might offend the U.S. public. For a description of Nixon and Kissinger's Vietnam policy, see Chapter 30.

By the 1970s China and the Soviet Union, the world's two great communist powers, had become hostile to each other. Nixon felt that the United States could gain an advantage by establishing friendly relations with China. (Relations with China had been severed after the communists took power there in 1949.) In 1972 Nixon traveled to China for a summit meting with the Chinese premier, Chou En-lai. Nixon and Chou agreed to work together to maintain peace in the Pacific and develop trade relations between China and the United States. Nixon also agreed to withdraw U.S. troops from Taiwan (which China regarded as a province in rebellion) if the Chinese would agree to do the same thing in North Vietnam. This development astounded people in the United States because it reversed the longstanding U.S. policy of supporting the Taiwanese in their bid for independence from China.

After China, Nixon traveled to the Soviet Union, where he met Soviet leader Leonid Brezhnev. The two leaders signed the **SALT** (Strategic Arms Limitation Talks) Treaty limiting the number of intercontinental nuclear missiles each could have. They also agreed to relax trade restrictions and bring their nations closer to a friendly understanding. That policy of promoting better relations between the two hostile countries was called **détente.**

Watergate

Early in the morning of June 17, 1972, police arrested five burglars in the Democratic Party offices in the Watergate buildings in Washington, D.C. The men had wiretapping equipment and cameras. Because this was a local crime story, the *Washington Post* city editor sent two reporters, Carl Bernstein and Bob Woodward, to cover the break-in. The two men pursued the story for months, uncovering new leads and evidence of crimes that led straight to the Oval Office. In August 1974 Nixon resigned the presidency to avoid impeachment for his crimes, which came to be known under the catchall title **Watergate.**

When planning his reelection campaign in 1971, Nixon had developed the ambition, according to Kissinger, of winning "by the biggest electoral land-slide in history." Nixon was determined to take any action, even if illegal, to bring about that result. When the Pentagon Papers were released, he ordered his aides to stop further "leaks" from the White House. A group called the Plumbers (so called because their purpose was to stop leaks) was formed; its members were authorized to take any action at all to ensure Nixon's reelec-tion. The Watergate burglars were Plumbers. Their aim was to obtain useful or embarrassing information from Democratic Party files.

To prepare for the 1972 election, Nixon and his staff had formed the Com-mittee to Re-elect the President, known as CRP or **CREEP.** Woodward and Bernstein soon learned that it was from CREEP that the Watergate burglars had received payment. This was a clear link to the president. Everyone knew that no one took any important action in the Nixon White House without presidential approval.

Meanwhile, in the 1972 presidential race, Nixon was opposed by the Dem-ocratic Senator George McGovern, a committed opponent of the Vietnam War. With strong support from conservatives, especially white Southern voters (plus all manner of campaign "dirty tricks" by paid Nixon staffers), Nixon won in a landslide, carrying every state but Massachusetts.

During the campaign the Democratic Party was unable to capitalize on the flow of Watergate stories. Nixon denied all knowledge of the Watergate bur-glary, and White House spokesmen denied all allegations published in the *Post* and other newspapers.

After the election, however, the stories kept coming. Many men and women who worked or had worked in the Nixon White House, including the unnamed **Deep Throat,** were willing to talk to Woodward and Bernstein about what they had witnessed. Congress began calling for investigations. Finally, during a Senate investigation led by Senator Sam Ervin of North Carolina, the pres-ident's attorney, John Dean, testified about the administration's complicity in the burglary and the attempted cover-up that had followed. The hearings were televised nationally; for weeks on end, millions of people watched in amaze-ment as the structure of secrecy around Nixon slowly crumbled.

Nixon continued to deny his own involvement until one witness mentioned that there was a secret tape-recording system in the Oval Office. Senate inves-tigators subpoenaed the tapes immediately. Nixon refused to surrender them, claiming that as chief executive, he enjoyed the privilege of keeping his private conversations private.

At that point a new scandal arose: Nixon's vice president, Spiro Agnew, was accused of evading income taxes when he was governor of Maryland. Agnew resigned his office in a plea-bargain agreement. Nixon appointed the House minority leader, the Republican Gerald Ford of Michigan, to take his place.

The courts rejected Nixon's argument of executive privilege and ordered him to turn over the tapes. Special Prosecutor Archibald Cox ordered Nixon to surrender the tapes to the federal grand jury investigating Watergate. Nixon responded by ordering his attorney general, Elliot Richardson, to fire Cox. Rather than carry out the order, Richardson resigned. Deputy Attorney General William Ruckelshaus also resigned on receiving the same order. Solicitor General Robert Bork fired Cox. That series of events became known as the **Saturday Night Massacre.**

Nixon appealed his case to the Supreme Court. Ironically, his own appointees ruled against him. Chief Justice Burger stated that the tapes were important evidence in a criminal case and that Nixon had no right to withhold them. The president's privilege, he wrote, "cannot prevail over the fundamental demands of due process of law in the fair administration of criminal justice."

Woodward and Bernstein were warned that some of the tapes contained deliberate erasures. Less than two weeks later, the grand jury confirmed that there was an 18 1/2-minute gap on one of the tapes. The fact that the tapes had been partially erased tended to confirm suspicions of Nixon's guilt.

The House Judiciary Committee then began to discuss bringing impeachment proceedings against the president. Rather than face impeachment, Nixon resigned on August 9, 1974. Gerald Ford then became president.

The Pardon

Ford was a good-humored, affable man who was well liked by congressional colleagues from both parties. However, in a gesture that shocked the entire country, Ford pardoned Nixon one month after taking office, stating that he intended the pardon to be a healing gesture. Resigning from the presidency had put Nixon beyond the reach of impeachment; the pardon meant that he could not be tried for the crimes he had committed.

After Watergate many people believed that "the system had worked" and proved the strength of U.S. democracy, but many others became deeply cynical about politics and politicians. Many people no longer believed what government officials told them. Some were angry that Nixon had "gotten away with it." Others believed that the whole affair was a partisan conspiracy. Still others turned away from politics completely, convinced that the whole process was corrupt.

REVIEW QUESTIONS

1. Nixon's foreign policy of détente was meant to improve relations between the United States and

    (A) North Vietnam
    (B) Cambodia
    (C) Taiwan
    (D) China
    (E) the Soviet Union

2. The "energy crisis" of 1973 started when

    (A) Arab countries refused to ship petroleum to countries friendly to Israel
    (B) Congress refused to authorize oil drilling in Alaska
    (C) oil reserves in Texas and Oklahoma began to run dry
    (D) the public refused to support the building of nuclear power plants
    (E) the United States decided to end all imports of foreign petroleum

3. The Watergate burglars were

    (A) newspaper reporters investigating a crime story
    (B) FBI agents looking for evidence of wrongdoing by Nixon
    (C) thieves looking for money in the Democratic Party offices
    (D) operatives in the pay of Nixon's reelection committee
    (E) Democratic Party members looking for evidence to discredit Republicans

Answers and Explanations

1. **E** Détente was the name given to efforts by the Nixon administration to improve relations with the Soviet Union. One result of détente was the Strategic Arms Limitation Talks.

2. **A** The energy crisis of 1973 started after a war between Israel and its Arab neighbors. The Arab oil-producing countries decided to punish countries friendly to Israel by stopping all oil exports to them and later by raising the price of oil drastically.

3. **D** The Watergate burglars were operatives in the pay of the White House–based Committee to Re-elect the President.

CHAPTER 32

THE REAGAN ERA AND THE END OF THE COLD WAR

INTRODUCTION

As the 1976 elections drew near, many people in the United States were eager for a change in leadership. Primarily, they wanted a leader who could restore their faith in government. In a close election, the Democrat Jimmy Carter defeated Gerald Ford. Carter was a former state governor with no experience of Washington politics; that seemed a point in his favor to voters who were sick of Washington. The Carter presidency, however, was ineffective on many levels.

In 1980 Ronald Reagan became president. Reagan was a Republican but attracted many Democratic voters. He promised to balance the federal budget, but instead he ran up the highest deficits in history. His successor George Bush, elected in 1988, continued Reagan's policies, but by then the economic boom of the 1980s was over. Rising prices, rising unemployment, widespread buying on credit, and stock market fluctuations all contributed to growing unease in the electorate.

In foreign affairs, Reagan administration officials secretly financed an anticommunist rebel army in Nicaragua despite a congressional amendment forbidding such aid. When the aid was revealed, Reagan's opponents were outraged, but his supporters defended the Nicaragua policy. In the end, two Reagan officials were convicted of crimes related to the Nicaragua policy, but the convictions were overturned.

The Cold War ended during the Reagan-Bush years, and with it ended the long-standing hostility between the United States and the now-defunct Soviet Union. In 1991, Iraq invaded Kuwait, and a U.S.-led force under United Nations auspices was dispatched to the Persian Gulf to repel the invaders.

TIMELINE

1973   *Roe v. Wade.*

1976   Jimmy Carter elected president.

1979   Three Mile Island accident.

Camp David Accords.

Sandinistas overthrow the government in Nicaragua.

1980   Ronald Reagan elected president.

Polish workers strike for the right to form unions.

1984   Reagan reelected.

1985   Mikhail Gorbachev becomes premier of the Soviet Union.

1986   Disclosure of illegal support of Nicaraguan Contras by Reagan White House.

1988   George Bush elected president.

1989 Berlin Wall comes down.

1991 Soviet Union breaks up.

East Germany and West Germany form Federal Republic of Germany under one government.

Persian Gulf War.

KEY TERMS

apartheid Afrikaans word meaning "separateness"; official racial segregation policy in force in South Africa until the 1990s

Camp David Accords a peace agreement made between President Anwar al-Sadat of Egypt and Prime Minister Menachem Begin of Israel, brokered by President Jimmy Carter

Contras Nicaraguan fighters recruited, trained, and financed by the CIA; opposed to the Sandinista government

glasnost Russian for "openness"; the name of Premier Mikhail Gorbachev's proclaimed new government policy for the Soviet Union

Iran-Contra a shorthand term used to describe Reagan officials' illegal attempts to finance the Nicaraguan Contras by selling arms to Iran

Moral Majority a conservative political organization of fundamentalist Christians

New Right conservative organizations that backed Ronald Reagan in the 1980s

Operation Desert Storm U.S.-led military attack on Iraq to drive Iraqi invaders out of Kuwait

perestroika name for the restructuring of the Soviet economy under Premier Mikhail Gorbachev

pro-choice position in support of *Roe v. Wade;* belief that a woman has the right to have an abortion during the first three months of pregnancy

pro-life position in opposition to *Roe v. Wade* on the grounds that a fetus is a human being from the moment of conception

Reagan Democrats Democrats who were disenchanted enough with the Carter presidency to cross party lines and vote for Ronald Reagan

Reaganomics the policy of "trickle-down" or "supply-side" economics followed by the Reagan Administration

Sandinistas Nicaraguan rebels who ousted the dictator Somoza; aided by the Soviets

Solidarity trade union of Polish shipyard and dock workers

Star Wars nickname for a proposed space-based missile defense system

Three Mile Island location of a nuclear power plant in Pennsylvania that was the site of a serious accident in 1979

The Presidency of Jimmy Carter

Gerald Ford served out the remainder of Nixon's term and ran for reelection in 1976. In a fairly close election, he lost to the Democratic candidate, Jimmy Carter, the former governor of Georgia. The crimes committed by Nixon and many of his aides, Ford's subsequent pardon of Nixon, and the generally shaky economy made many people turn away from the Republican Party in the hopes that a Democrat might prove a better steward of the nation.

Carter was quiet, scholarly, and soft-spoken. He had no experience in national politics, and that appealed to voters who had had enough of Washington insiders after Watergate. Carter also was unimpeachably honest. However, he exhibited little understanding of the mood of the nation, and he did not know how to respond to many people's everyday concerns. At a time when the nation badly needed a strong leader, Carter did not give an impression of strength and confidence.

Domestically, Carter's presidency was largely unsuccessful. The nation was in the grip of a social and economic malaise that the White House could not shake. Prices, which had been rising since the time of the Vietnam War and the "energy crisis" of 1973, continued to increase. In 1979 OPEC again drastically raised the price of oil, leading to a new energy crisis and long lines of cars at gas stations. Carter argued that the United States needed to depend more on nuclear energy and less on foreign oil, but just at that time a nuclear reactor at **Three Mile Island** in Pennsylvania failed, forcing the evacuation of tens of thousands of people from the area.

Carter was more successful in foreign affairs. He urged the Senate to ratify a series of treaties giving full control of the Panama Canal to the Panamanians. That move was popular in Latin American countries, most of which continued to regard the United States with suspicion. Carter also condemned South Africa's policy of **apartheid,** or enforced racial segregation. Carter's opposition to apartheid increased international respect for the United States. Carter's greatest achievement was his brokering of a peace treaty between Egypt and Israel, which had been at war for 30 years. In September 1978 Egyptian President Anwar al-Sadat and Israeli Prime Minister Menachem Begin met with Carter at Camp David, the presidential retreat in Maryland, to negotiate. The result of the **Camp David Accords** was a formal peace treaty between Egypt and Israel.

In spite of these accomplishments, Carter lost much support as a result of events in Iran. After the fall of the U.S.-backed shah, religious leaders in Iran set up a theocratic government. When the shah was allowed to enter the United States for cancer treatment, Iranian students took hostages at the U.S. embassy in Tehran. After a failed rescue attempt, the hostages eventually were released, but not before Carter had lost the 1980 election.

The Election of 1980

Carter ran for reelection in 1980 but lost by over 8 million votes to the California Republican Ronald Reagan. Even die-hard Democratic voters felt that Carter had been a remarkably ineffective president. Many people found Reagan, a former movie actor who once had been a Democrat, an attractive alternative; those people crossed party lines to vote Republican and became known as **Reagan Democrats.** Reagan campaigned on promises to balance the federal budget, cut taxes, and "get government off the backs of the American people."

A political movement called the **New Right,** spearheaded by a fundamentalist religious group called the **Moral Majority,** united behind Reagan, providing his strongest base of support. Reagan and the Moral Majority shared many views, notably opposition to abortion, equal rights for women, and gun control.

During the Reagan era the issue of abortion rights came increasingly to divide U.S. society. In 1973 the Supreme Court had decided a famous case called *Roe v. Wade* that concerned abortion rights. In *Roe,* the Court ruled that the government had no right to prevent a woman from having an abortion during the first three months of pregnancy. During the last six months the state could block an abortion, but not if a doctor determined that it was necessary to the mother's life and health.

Democratic Party candidates generally have supported *Roe,* claiming that the mother should have the right to choose whether to have an abortion. This position has become known as **pro-choice.** The Moral Majority and the rest of the New Right, along with the Republican Party, generally have opposed *Roe* and have urged that it be overturned. They believe that from the moment of conception, a fetus is a human life and the mother has no right to terminate that life. This view is called **pro-life.**

Reaganomics

"**Reaganomics**" was the name people gave to Reagan's theory of "trickle-down" or "supply-side" economics. Like many conservatives before him, Reagan believed in removing regulations on big business and cutting taxes. According to this theory, when wealthy business owners are taxed less, they invest the savings in their businesses (the "supply side"), thus increasing output, creating jobs, and eventually benefiting society as a whole. When the theory had been put into practice under past presidents, it had worked only partially; the profits never quite "trickled down" to the lower middle class or to workers, who watched prices go up while their incomes stayed the same. However, by 1983 Reagan's policies resulted in a substantial drop in the rate of inflation and a stock-market boom. For those who were well off to begin with, the Reagan years meant great prosperity.

Under Reagan, Congress cut spending on social programs. This meant that poor and working-class people suffered by being deprived of benefits they needed for survival. Unemployment was high across the nation, especially in old manufacturing centers in the Midwest and in major cities. People bought more on credit, and their debts increased.

The End of the Cold War

The Cold War had dragged on for 40 years with no real move on either side toward a settlement or a significant lessening of tension. Reagan's solution to the Cold War was to build up U.S. armed forces. He believed that a mighty U.S. military, heavily armed with the latest weaponry, would frighten the communist nations into abandoning the Cold War. He even proposed a space-based missile defense system called the Strategic Defense Initiative that was nicknamed **Star Wars** after a popular science-fiction/fantasy movie. This system was never tested successfully.

Reagan's military buildup forced the Soviets to follow his example, and the cost brought their already shaky economy to the brink of ruin. However, the end of the Cold War was brought about mainly by events in the Soviet Union and Eastern Europe.

By the 1980s many Eastern European nations had had enough of being forced to live under communist governments that were controlled by the Soviets. The first successful act of rebellion took place in 1980 in Poland, where workers struck for the right to form a noncommunist union called **Solidarity.**

In 1985 Mikhail Gorbachev became the premier of the Soviet Union. To remedy the economic and social ills that plagued the country, Gorbachev called for policies of **glasnost,** or openness, and **perestroika,** or restructuring of the economy and society. Gorbachev called for increases in foreign trade and reductions in military spending. During a 1987 meeting, Gorbachev and Reagan signed the Intermediate-Range Nuclear Forces Treaty, eliminating all medium-range nuclear missiles from Europe.

In July 1988 Gorbachev announced to Eastern European leaders that the Soviet Union no longer was prepared to intervene militarily to defend communist regimes in Eastern Europe; those regimes would have to defend themselves. The results were immediate free elections in Poland and Hungary and, soon afterward, the fall of the communist governments of Romania and Czechoslovakia.

In 1989 the East German government announced that it no longer would prevent East Germans from traveling to the West. Television viewers all over the world watched astounded as young Germans attacked the Berlin Wall on both sides with sledgehammers and pickaxes. After nearly 50 years, the Iron Curtain had finally been removed. In 1990, East Germany and West Germany were reunited under one government.

The map below shows the changes in Central and Eastern Europe after the removal of the Iron Curtain. Compare it with the map in Chapter 28.

The Breakup of the Soviet Union

In 1991 the Soviet Union itself broke up. The Soviet republics, of which Russia was one, became separate countries. The breakup brought an end to the long-standing enmity between Russia and the United States. President Reagan's successor, George Bush, hailed that moment in history as the beginning of a new world order "in which freedom and respect for human rights find a home among all nations."

Iran-Contra

In 1979 a revolution had occurred in Nicaragua. Rebels called **Sandinistas** had ousted the dictator Anastasio Somoza and won subsequent elections. When Reagan took office in 1980, he claimed that the Sandinistas were receiving Soviet aid. Reagan therefore cut off all U.S. aid to Nicaragua. As a result, the Sandinistas sought closer ties with the Soviet Union. Reagan then decided to provide U.S. support to the **Contras,** a rebel army trained and paid by the CIA. He hoped that the Contras would defeat the Sandinistas. The Contras engaged in many acts of violence and brutality.

Even though Reagan was a popular president and argued that a Contra victory would bring democracy to Nicaragua, many people in the United States, remembering the experience of Vietnam, were wary of intervening in a civil conflict in another nation. In 1984 Congress passed the Boland Amendment, which barred the White House, the CIA, and all other government agencies from aiding the Contras.

In 1986 the U.S. public learned that Reagan officials had secretly sent financial aid to the Contras, using money earned by selling weapons to Iran. That arrangement, dubbed **Iran-Contra** in the press, was illegal under the Boland Amendment. Responding to public outrage, Reagan ordered an investigation. He was cleared of any role in the affair, but the investigation led to criminal charges against Lieutenant Colonel Oliver North and Admiral John Poindexter. Both were convicted, but the convictions later were over-turned on a technicality. The affair further divided Reagan's supporters and opponents. Supporters believed that the Contras' cause was just and that for the officials involved, the end justified the means. Opponents believed that the officials involved deserved punishment for their role in the affair and also that Reagan had been directly involved but his aides had covered up for him.

The Gulf War

In 1990 Iraq invaded Kuwait. In the United Nations member countries approved an ultimatum demanding that Iraq withdraw. When Iraq refused, Congress approved U.S. participation in a UN-sponsored attack. Beginning on January 16, 1991, U.S.-led forces, including troops from Great Britain, France, Egypt, and Saudi Arabia, engaged in a bombing attack on Iraq and an invasion of Kuwait called **Operation Desert Storm.** An estimated 100,000 Iraqis were killed, and the bombs extensively damaged Iraqi cities in about two months of fighting. The war was quick and efficient and was considered a great success by people in the United States because there were only about 600 U.S. casualties.

Reagan, Bush, and the Supreme Court

Presidents Reagan and Bush both had the opportunity to appoint Supreme Court justices. In 1981 Reagan proposed Sandra Day O'Connor of Texas. O'Connor was nominally a conservative but in time gained a reputation as a moderate. Reagan also nominated Robert Bork, who had served in the Nixon Administration, but the Senate refused to confirm Bork.

When Thurgood Marshall, a Johnson appointee and the first African American to sit on the Court, retired in 1991, President Bush nominated Clarence Thomas, an extremely conservative African American, to replace him. Controversy erupted at the confirmation hearing when a law professor named Anita Hill accused Thomas of sexual harassment. Thomas responded by likening the hearing to a "lynching," a racially charged comparison that was called unfair by Thomas's opponents. Eventually the Senate confirmed the nomination.

Bush and Economic Affairs

Ronald Reagan had promised to balance the federal budget, but his business-friendly policies had the opposite effect. The federal deficit soared under Reagan and also under his successor Bush. By the time President Bush left office in 1992, the deficit stood at $291 billion. Bush was forced to take the politically unpopular step of raising taxes to try to boost government revenue and offset the deficit, but the deficit was so immense that the higher taxes accomplished little. Unemployment rose as Bush cut social programs to try to balance the budget. As the election year of 1992 began, it was clear that if the Democrats could find a strong candidate to challenge Bush, they would have a very good chance to take back the White House.

REVIEW QUESTIONS

1. President Jimmy Carter helped work out a peace agreement between

   (A) Palestine and Israel
   (B) Israel and Egypt
   (C) Egypt and Jordan
   (D) Iraq and Kuwait
   (E) East Germany and West Germany

2. The Cold War ended primarily because

   (A) Germans destroyed the Berlin Wall
   (B) Soviet leader Mikhail Gorbachev introduced new policies
   (C) the United States defeated communism in Vietnam
   (D) the United States created a rebel army in Nicaragua
   (E) the workers of Poland staged a series of strikes

3. The Gulf War of 1991 was fought to liberate

   (A) Iran
   (B) Israel
   (C) Kuwait
   (D) Saudi Arabia
   (E) Nicaragua

Answers and Explanations

1. **B** Carter invited the leaders of Israel and Egypt to Camp David to give them the chance to make a peace agreement in 1979.
2. **B** As premier of the Soviet Union, Gorbachev exercised power over the entire Iron Curtain region. His policies led to the collapse of communist rule and the end of the Cold War.
3. **C** The Gulf War of 1991 took place after Iraq invaded and conquered Kuwait. The U.S.-led forces defeated the Iraqis and liberated Kuwait.

CHAPTER 33

THE 1990s AND THE EARLY 21ST CENTURY

INTRODUCTION

In 1992 Bill Clinton became the first Democratic president in 12 years. He gained a reputation as a "centrist" by following not only many traditional Democratic policies but also many policies usually associated with Republicans, such as fiscal responsibility and balancing the budget. He also pleased Democrats by supporting the "pro-choice" position on abortion, protection for the environment, health-care and education reform, and antipoverty legislation.

Under Clinton, what had been an enormous federal deficit became a surplus. Unemployment fell to low levels, and wages rose. A series of important environmental laws were passed. Clinton also signed the Family and Medical Leave Act, providing unpaid leave to workers who needed it for reasons of childbirth, infant care, or a family medical emergency.

Clinton made many opponents among Republicans and other conservatives, and when personal scandals arose during his second term, some hoped he would be forced to resign in disgrace. However, Clinton remained popular with the public, and even when a White House scandal led the House of Representatives to vote for his impeachment, the Senate declined to convict him.

In the 2000 presidential election George W. Bush lost the popular vote to Clinton's vice president, Al Gore. However, Bush won the electoral vote and became president after the Supreme Court stopped a recount of disputed election results in Florida.

In 2001 a group of mostly Saudi terrorists carried out a devastating attack on New York City and Washington, D.C. In retaliation, the Bush administration launched an attack on Afghanistan, where the Saudi mastermind of the terrorist plot, Osama bin Laden, was known to be hiding. Bin Laden never was found, but in early 2003 the Bush administration launched another war in the Middle East. Claiming that Iraq, then ruled by a despot named Saddam Hussein, possessed "weapons of mass destruction" that posed an imminent threat, Bush sought United Nations approval for an invasion. Although that approval was not given, the United States and its ally Great Britain, with token participation from a few smaller countries, invaded Iraq in March 2003. No weapons were found, but Hussein eventually was captured. Iraqi insurgents then launched a protracted conflict with U.S. and British troops.

George W. Bush was reelected in 2004 and his government was criticized for its handling of Hurricane Katrina. Several economic crises marked Bush's second term, leading to Democrats taking over both houses of Congress in 2006 and the rapid rise to power of Illinois Senator Barack Obama, who won the presidency in 2008. Obama was the first African-American president in United States' history. His administration focused on dealing with continuing global and domestic terrorism, the struggle for economic recovery, and expanding healthcare coverage and civil rights to all Americans.

TIMELINE

1992	Bill Clinton elected president.
	Family and Medical Leave Act passed.
	Failure of health-care reform.
1996	Clinton reelected.
2000	George W. Bush becomes president by Supreme Court decision.
2001	Terrorist attacks on World Trade Center and Pentagon.
	U.S.-led forces invade Afghanistan.
2003	U.S.-led forces invade Iraq.
	U.S. forces capture Saddam Hussein.
	George Bush gives "Mission Accomplished" speech
	Secretary of State Colin Powell departs; replaced by Condoleezza Rice
	Massachusetts legalizes marriage between homosexual couples
	New Yorker breaks Abu Ghraib story
2004	George W. Bush reelected.
2005	Hurricane Katrina destroys much of New Orleans, displacing thousands
	Justice O'Connor retires from Supreme Court; Chief Justice Rehnquist dies
2006	Midterm elections move control of both houses of Congress to Democrats
	Secretary of Defense Donald Rumsfeld resigns
2007	Attorney General Alberto Gonzalez resigns
	Housing market collapses; millions in default of mortgage payments
2008	Gasoline prices rise to $4 per gallon
	Democrats nominate Barack Obama for President
	Republicans nominate John McCain for President
	The stock market loses nearly 1800 points in one week
	Barack Obama is elected President of the United States
2009	Obama signs $787 billion stimulus package
	Justice Sonia Sotomayor sworn in
	Fort Hood Shooting
2010	Affordable Care Act passed
	Deepwater Horizon oil spill in the Gulf of Mexico
	Mid-term elections give Republicans a majority in the House
	WikiLeaks releases classified documents
	"Don't Ask, Don't Tell" repealed

2011   Tucson shooting

Death of Osama bin Laden

U.S. debt ceiling crisis and credit-rating downgrade

Occupy Wall Street movement begins

2012   Hurricane Sandy devastates the East Coast

Barack Obama is elected to a second term

Sandy Hook Elementary School shooting

2013   Boston Marathon bombings

Global surveillance disclosures

2014   U.S. sends troops back to Iraq to fight Islamic State

Michael Brown shot by Ferguson, MO police officer, igniting protests and riots

Republicans take control of the Senate and retain control of the House

President Obama announces restoration of diplomatic relations with Cuba

Marijuana is legalized in several states

2015   Justice Department reports widespread racial bias in Ferguson police department

Freddie Gray's death in police custody leads to riots in Baltimore

Same-sex marriage legalized in all states

KEY TERMS

al Qaeda   literally "the Base"; an international network of terrorists financed and run by the Saudi Osama bin Laden

detainees   Bush Administration term for Iraq War prisoners

foreclosure   repossession of a mortgaged house by the lender when the borrower cannot make the mortgage payments

Geneva Conventions   a series of international agreements governing the treatment of prisoners of war

hybrid   an automobile that runs on a combination of electricity and gasoline

Islamic State, ISIL, ISIS a terrorist organization devoted to establishing an Islamic caliphate

New Democrat   one who supports conservative fiscal policies along with social programs traditionally popular with Democrats

Reform Party   an alternative political party founded in 1992 by the Texas businessman Ross Perot

Taliban   an Islamic fundamentalist regime that ruled Afghanistan

Tea Party an alternative political party, made up primarily of ultra-conservative Republicans

The Election of 1992

As the 1992 presidential election approached, Governor Bill Clinton of Arkansas stood out among Democratic candidates for his self-confidence and eagerness to tackle difficult problems. He was backed by many so-called **New Democrats,** who embraced not only traditional Democratic concerns for social programs and the environment but also Republican ideas such as fiscal responsibility and cutbacks in the government bureaucracy. Clinton won the Democratic nomination and chose Senator Al Gore of Tennessee as his running mate. With two Southerners on the ticket, Democrats hoped to improve their showing among the growing number of Republican white voters in the South.

The Republicans renominated President George Bush as their candidate, but Bush's popularity suffered because economic conditions had worsened and also because Bush had raised some taxes after promising not to do so. The campaign was enlivened by the emergence of a third candidate, the Texas businessman Ross Perot. Backed by the newly formed **Reform Party,** Perot argued that government should be run on strict business principles. His views attracted many Republican voters but also some Democrats.

In November Clinton gained a decisive victory over Bush, winning 370 electoral votes. Perot received 19 percent of the popular vote, an extraordinarily high total for a third-party candidate.

Clinton's Domestic Policy

Clinton began his term by instituting measures that were popular among Democrats. A government rule banning abortion counseling at federally funded clinics was revoked. At Clinton's urging, Congress passed the Family and Medical Leave Act, which required large companies to provide employees with unpaid leave to deal with childbirth, infant care, or a family medical emergency. Clinton's main focus, however, was a proposal for government reform of the largely private health-care insurance system. The proposal, which would have extended health insurance to many who otherwise could not afford it, was opposed vigorously by the health-care industry. In the end, it failed to win congressional approval.

On the economic front Clinton's policies were more successful. Clinton cut government spending and increased taxes, mainly for people at the upper-income level. By the end of Clinton's first term the federal government deficit had been reduced by about half. New laws were passed to protect the environment, and strict new requirements were imposed on recipients of public assistance (known popularly as "welfare"). As a result, the number of people receiving assistance was reduced dramatically.

Clinton enjoyed wide popularity, but many conservatives disliked him and undertook efforts to discredit him and his policies. In his second term Clinton inadvertently provided ammunition to his critics by engaging in an affair with a young White House intern and then lying about it to investigators who were looking into other alleged improprieties. When the affair was made public, there were calls for Clinton's resignation, and some in Congress backed a move to impeach him. However, Clinton remained popular with the voters, many of whom did not regard lying about a private matter as an impeachable offense. In the end, even thought the House voted for impeachment, the Senate declined to convict Clinton or remove him from office.

The Election of 2000

In 2000 Clinton's vice president, Al Gore, ran for president against Governor George W. Bush of Texas, a son of the former president. The election was very close. Gore won the popular vote, but Bush appeared to have a slim lead in electoral votes. However, his lead depended on the outcome in Florida, where the vote count was disputed. The election remained in doubt while both sides argued. Bush finally took Gore to court to try to stop a recount. In the end the case went to the Supreme Court, which voted 5–4, conservative judges against liberals, to bar a recount. As a result, Florida's electoral votes went to Bush, who was declared president.

The Presidency of George W. Bush

The presidency of George W. Bush began under the cloud of the disputed 2000 election. Bush promoted policies that were popular with business and with the most conservative wing of the Republican Party. At his urging, Congress passed a large tax cut that soon turned the federal government's Clinton-era financial surplus into a deficit. In foreign affairs Bush officials reversed longstanding policies of international cooperation, reneging on international arms-control agreements and rejecting participation in international efforts to protect the environment.

September 11, 2001

On a sunny September morning in 2001 a group of mostly Saudi terrorists hijacked four U.S. passenger jets and embarked on suicide missions. Two of the planes were crashed deliberately into the World Trade Center towers in New York City. The third was crashed into the Pentagon in Washington. The fourth, probably targeting either the Capitol or the White House, crashed in Pennsylvania after the passengers fought with the hijackers. In the attacks, more than 3,000 people were killed.

The mastermind behind the attacks was Osama bin Laden, a wealthy Saudi exile and Islamic extremist who had organized and financed guerrillas fighting Soviet invaders in Afghanistan in the 1970s. A sworn enemy of the Saudi monarchy and other Middle Eastern rulers as well as their Western allies, including the United States, bin Laden had used his enormous fortune to finance an international network of Islamic fundamentalist terrorists known as **al Qaeda.**

The Bush administration decided to respond to the attacks by launching an all-out war on terrorism. The first target was Afghanistan, where bin Laden and his al Qaeda supporters were living under the protection of an Islamic fundamentalist regime called the **Taliban.** The attack on Afghanistan began on October 7, 2001. By early 2002 the Taliban had been ousted, but bin Laden remained at large.

War in Iraq

The Bush Administration next decided to attack Iraq. The Persian Gulf War of 1990 had left the military dictator Saddam Hussein in power on condition that Iraq abandon its attempts to build nuclear weapons. UN inspectors had been appointed to oversee Iraqi disarmament, but they encountered stubborn obstruction from Hussein's government. Denied access to crucial sites, the inspectors eventually gave up and left.

Bush administration officials argued that Iraq had violated UN resolutions requiring weapons inspections and that the country now possessed dangerous "weapons of mass destruction." They also claimed to have evidence of links between the Iraqi government and the terrorists of al Qaeda. The Bush administration pressed the United Nations to authorize an immediate invasion. The UN sent weapons inspectors back to Iraq, but when no weapons were found, the UN Security Council declined to back an invasion. However, claiming imminent danger, the U.S. government prepared to send in troops. Great Britain supported the invasion and several other countries offered token participation, but many major U.S. allies stood aloof. At home opinion on the invasion was divided; many opposed the war, but many others accepted the administration's claims or believed that the war would bring democracy to the Middle East.

The invasion began in March 2003 and quickly ousted Saddam Hussein and his government. Many Iraqis were killed, but U.S. losses were comparatively low. No Iraqi "weapons of mass destruction" were found. In December 2003 the U.S. military captured Hussein and installed a governing council. Free elections were held in the following year; but important groups refused to participate, and armed insurgents attacked U.S. forces and the Iraqis allied with them.

In 2004 Bush was reelected president, beating back an ineffective challenge by Democratic Senator John Kerry of Massachusetts.

Detainees

The Bush Administration's policies toward prisoners taken during the Iraq War were controversial. The White House maintained a variety of arguments to support its interpretation of both law and custom in its treatment of the prisoners.

First, the Administration argued that terrorists were not prisoners of war because they did not belong to an official national army. Therefore, such prisoners, called **detainees** by the Administration, had none of the rights set forth in a longstanding series of international agreements called the **Geneva Conventions**. Second, the Administration held the vast majority of the detainees outside the United States, arguing that constitutional rights such as the writ of habeas corpus applied only inside American borders. In *Boumedienne* v. *Bush*, the Supreme Court sided against the White House and in favor of the prisoners' rights.

Some of the current detainees were in prison for several years. They were not permitted certain rights, including the right to speak with an attorney and the right to summon witnesses on their own behalf. They were frequently subjected to harsh interrogation techniques, which some critics of these practices believed constituted torture. The Administration maintained that such techniques were necessary in order to obtain valuable information.

In 2004, the television show *60 Minutes II* broke a story about the Abu Ghraib prison in Baghdad, Iraq. The television broadcast and a subsequent Seymour Hersh article in the *New Yorker* magazine showed photographs and described in great detail American soldiers torturing Arab suspects. Some of the suspects died under the torture and abuse. Responding to public outrage, the military court-martialed a few low-ranking soldiers and one or two officers. Secretary of Defense Donald Rumsfeld responded to public protests by resigning at the end of 2006. No charges were brought against the commander of U.S. forces in Iraq, and the Administration continued to insist that its treatment of detainees did not constitute torture.

Changes on the Supreme Court

In 2005, Justice Sandra Day O'Connor announced her retirement; shortly after, Chief Justice William Rehnquist died. George Bush nominated conservative judges John Roberts and Samuel Alito to replace them. Congress confirmed both justices, with Roberts named Chief Justice.

Hurricane Katrina

New Orleans, on the Gulf of Mexico at the mouth of the Mississippi River, is vulnerable to hurricanes because of its position below seal level. In late August 2005, when Hurricane Katrina approached the city, most of the population fled. Some people refused to leave their homes. Several thousand others, unable to find any way out of the city, were given emergency shelter in the New Orleans Superdome, on safe high ground.

When the hurricane struck, much of New Orleans and several surrounding parishes were submerged under 15 feet of water. The storm completely destroyed the local power systems. At the Superdome, refugees were trapped without light, food, or functioning sanitary facilities. It was days before they were rescued.

Flood survivors who remained in the city were driven to looting for basic supplies and food. The National Guard helped to restore order. Over the following months, the Federal Emergency Management Agency (FEMA) provided temporary housing for those who had lost everything. The results of Hurricane Katrina were catastrophic: large numbers of people were left homeless and whole neighborhoods were destroyed. Many victims who fled elsewhere were unable to return because of financial limitations or because they had no home to return to. Many of the city's poorer residents were forced to leave New Orleans permanently.

Economic Crises

Three major economic crises occurred during Bush's second term: a housing crisis, a sharp rise in the price of gasoline, and a severe slump in the stock market that affected financial markets all over the world.

The Housing Crisis

During the early 2000s, millions of Americans bought homes using so-called "sub-prime" mortgages. These were loans either at much higher rates than normal or with low introductory rates that later skyrocketed to extremely high rates. Many people were unable to keep up with interest payments and when home values began declining in 2007, they began defaulting on their loans. Unable to collect payments, banks and mortgage companies began **foreclosing** or taking possession of, huge numbers of homes. Burdened with bad debts, banks soon found themselves in serious financial difficulties.

By the summer of 2008, many were in such poor financial shape that they hoped to be purchased by larger, healthier banks.

Rising Gasoline Prices

The price of gasoline began to rise during the Iraq War. In 2008, it went above $4 a gallon for the first time in history. Americans reacted by buying more fuel-efficient cars and **hybrid** vehicles, or by abandoning their cars and taking mass transit whenever possible. Rural farm workers were the hardest hit; dependent on cars and trucks because there was no mass transit where they lived, some could no longer afford to go to work because of the gas prices.

The Financial Crash

In the fall of 2008, major financial corporations that had invested heavily in sub-prime mortgages began experiencing severe economic problems. Several of the largest ones, including Bear Stearns and Lehman Brothers, collapsed, touching off a global stock-market fall. Stocks listed in the New York Stock Exchange lost trillions of dollars in value. The government was forced to bail out the quasi-governmental mortgage-holding corporations called Fannie Mae and Freddie Mac. Bailouts were also offered to other banks and financial institutions. In the mean time, however, the financial system and the economy that depended on it continued to deteriorate.

The 2008 Election

Senators Barack Obama of Illinois and Hillary Clinton of New York became the main contenders for the Democratic presidential nomination. After a lengthy primary election, Senator Barack Obama emerged as the Democratic nominee and chose Senator Joe Biden of Delaware, an early contender in the primary, as his running mate. On the Republican side, Senator John McCain, a renowned Vietnam War veteran, quickly clinched his party's nomination. McCain named Governor Sarah Palin of Alaska as his running mate. Palin, a fundamentalist Christian and foe of abortion rights, was embraced by religious conservatives.

McCain and Obama entered the final two-month run for the White House nearly even in the polls, but in the wake of the growing housing crisis and financial crash, Obama's popularity increased and he carried the election on November 4 with a decisive majority of 365 electoral votes, defeating McCain's 173 electoral votes. Obama won several states that had voted Republican in the previous election: Ohio, Indiana, Florida, North Carolina, Virginia, Colorado, Nevada, and New Mexico. Obama's election was a historic event in that he was the first African-American to win the Presidency. Obama was inaugurated and took office as President in January 2009.

Obama's Presidency

In early 2009, President Obama signed executive orders closing all secret detention camps and prisons and banning coercive interrogation methods. He also signed a $787 billion stimulus package intended to stimulate the economy. In March of 2010, President Obama signed the Patient Protection and Affordable Care Act, also known as the ACA, or "Obamacare," into law. This law exacerbated the growing division between Republicans and Democrats. A new movement, called the Tea Party, began having protests against big government and promoting individual freedom, fiscal responsibility, and conservative moral and constitutional views.

The Continuing War on Terror

After years of searching, U.S. military forces finally located and killed Osama bin Laden in Pakistan in 2011. Also in 2011, the last U.S. troops were withdrawn from Iraq, but in 2014 a small number of troops were ordered back to help Iraqi and Kurdish forces battle the Islamic State of Iraq and the Levant (ISIL). The group originally was tied to al Qaeda, but al Qaeda broke ties with ISIL in 2014. A dramatic incident of "homegrown terrorism" occurred with the bombing of the Boston Marathon in 2013 by two brothers who claimed to have been influenced by Islamic extremism, but were not directly connected with any group. Mass shootings by individuals dominated the news, including the 2009 Ft. Hood shooting, the 2011 Tucson shooting of Representative Gabrielle Giffords that killed six others, and the Sandy Hook Elementary School shooting that left 20 children and six staff members dead.

Big Brother

During George W. Bush's administration, the Patriot Act gave the government unprecedented power as it struggled to deal with terrorism. Americans began to get increasingly concerned about compromising their rights, especially their right to privacy. In 2010, WikiLeaks began releasing classified documents to the international press. In 2013, Edward Snowden leaked classified information to investigative journalists who exposed several domestic surveillance programs run by the NSA, including the PRISM data mining program.

Landmark Rulings

In 2009, the first Hispanic Supreme Court justice, Sonia Sotomayor, was confirmed to replace Justice David Souter, who retired. She was the third woman ever appointed to the court, and one of the youngest justices to serve. In 2010, Justice Elena Kagan joined the court, becoming the fourth female Supreme Court Justice.

Several landmark cases were heard during President Obama's two terms. In *Citizens United v. Federal Election Commission* (2010), the court ruled that the government cannot restrict corporate spending for political campaigns. This ruling was controversial, with a vote of 5-4, and President Obama expressed disapproval of the verdict, calling it a victory for Wall Street and big business.

Republicans in Congress made many, many attempts to dismantle Obama's healthcare law, but in 2012 the court upheld the ACA and the expansion of Medicaid. A further decision in 2015 upheld another key provision of the ACA.

The Supreme Court under President Obama promoted civil rights in the area of marriage equality with several rulings on the issue of same-sex marriage, finally ruling in 2015 with *Obergefell v. Hodges* that same-sex couples have a fundamental right to marry and that all states must recognize same-sex marriages as legal.

In what was seen by many as a move backwards for civil rights, in 2013 the court struck down Section 4b of the Voting Rights Act because the majority felt that the need for congressional approval of voting law changes was based on old data and was no longer needed. Judge Ginsburg wrote a strong dissent, fearing that voter discrimination would resurge. President Obama and Attorney General Eric Holder both expressed disappointment with the decision. As feared by opponents of the decision, within hours Texas and Mississippi officials pledged to enforce voter ID laws that had been previously overruled. Texas and six other states have indeed done so since the decision.

REVIEW QUESTIONS

1. President Bill Clinton suffered defeat in Congress when he

   (A) sought to reform the nation's largely private system of health-care insurance
   (B) attempted to reduce the federal government's financial deficit
   (C) tried to impose strict requirements on recipients of public assistance
   (D) sought passage of an act requiring corporations to provide workers with unpaid leave to cope with family medical emergencies
   (E) chose Senator Al Gore to be his vice president

2. The presidential election of 2000 was decided when

   (A) a recount of votes in Florida showed that Bush had won the popular vote
   (B) a recount of electoral votes was ordered by the Supreme Court
   (C) a vote recount in Florida was barred by the Supreme Court, effectively making Bush president
   (D) a recount of the popular vote nationwide showed that Gore was the loser
   (E) Republicans agreed to permit a recount of the popular vote in Florida

3. The Bush administration launched the war in Iraq in 2003 in alliance with

   (A) the United Nations Security Council
   (B) Saudi Arabia and other Middle Eastern countries
   (C) Germany, France, and other major U.S. allies
   (D) Great Britain, along with token forces from several smaller countries
   (E) no other countries or international organizations

4. At the start of his term, President Barack Obama faced all the following challenges in office EXCEPT:
   (A) a housing and mortgage crisis
   (B) flood relief for the city of New Orleans
   (C) a war in Iraq
   (D) a crashing stock market
   (E) soaring unemployment

5. Increased reliance on computers has led to national concern over

    (A) the minimum wage paid to workers
    (B) outsourcing of jobs
    (C) environmental pollution
    (D) using alternative sources of energy
    (E) the right to privacy

Answers and Explanations

1. **A** Clinton suffered the greatest defeat of his administration when his ambitious health-care insurance reform plan was defeated in Congress.
2. **C** The presidential election of 2000 remained undecided until the Supreme Court voted to bar a recount of disputed popular votes in Florida. As a result, that state's electoral votes went to Bush, who thus became president.
3. **D** The Bush administration launched the war in Iraq in 2003 in alliance with Great Britain. A number of smaller countries sent token forces to support the war effort. The United Nations declined to approve the war, and major U.S. allies such as Germany and France stood aloof.
4. **B** The flooding caused by Hurricane Katrina took place in August 2005, well before Obama's inauguration in January 2009.
5. **E** Revelations about the number and scope of domestic surveillance programs have caused many Americans to be concerned about their right to privacy and the security of their data.

PART III
SIX FULL LENGTH PRACTICE TESTS

PRACTICE TEST 1
U.S. HISTORY

The following Practice Test is designed to be just like the real SAT U.S. History test. It matches the actual test in content coverage and level of difficulty.

When you are finished with the test, determine your score and carefully read the answer explanations for the questions you answered incorrectly. Identify any weak areas by determining the areas in which you made the most errors. Review those chapters of the book first. Then, as time permits, go back and review your stronger areas.

Allow 1 hour to take the test. Time yourself and work uninterrupted. If you run out of time, take note of where you ended when time ran out. Remember that you lose $\frac{1}{4}$ of a point for each incorrect answer. Because of this penalty, do not guess on a question unless you can eliminate one or more of the answers. Your score is calculated by using the following formula:

Number of correct answers $- \frac{1}{4}$ (Number of incorrect answers)

This Practice Test will be an accurate reflection of how you'll do on test day if you treat it as the real examination. Here are some hints on how to take the test under conditions similar to those of the actual exam.

- Complete the test in one sitting.
- Time yourself.
- Tear out your Answer Sheet and fill in the ovals just as you would on the actual test day.
- Become familiar with the directions to the test and the reference information provided. You'll save time on the actual test day by already being familiar with this information.

PRACTICE TEST 1

U.S. HISTORY

ANSWER SHEET

Tear out this answer sheet and use it to mark your answers.

There are 100 lines of numbered ovals on this answer sheet. If there are more lines than you need, leave the remainder blank.

1. Ⓐ Ⓑ Ⓒ Ⓓ Ⓔ	26. Ⓐ Ⓑ Ⓒ Ⓓ Ⓔ	51. Ⓐ Ⓑ Ⓒ Ⓓ Ⓔ	76. Ⓐ Ⓑ Ⓒ Ⓓ Ⓔ
2. Ⓐ Ⓑ Ⓒ Ⓓ Ⓔ	27. Ⓐ Ⓑ Ⓒ Ⓓ Ⓔ	52. Ⓐ Ⓑ Ⓒ Ⓓ Ⓔ	77. Ⓐ Ⓑ Ⓒ Ⓓ Ⓔ
3. Ⓐ Ⓑ Ⓒ Ⓓ Ⓔ	28. Ⓐ Ⓑ Ⓒ Ⓓ Ⓔ	53. Ⓐ Ⓑ Ⓒ Ⓓ Ⓔ	78. Ⓐ Ⓑ Ⓒ Ⓓ Ⓔ
4. Ⓐ Ⓑ Ⓒ Ⓓ Ⓔ	29. Ⓐ Ⓑ Ⓒ Ⓓ Ⓔ	54. Ⓐ Ⓑ Ⓒ Ⓓ Ⓔ	79. Ⓐ Ⓑ Ⓒ Ⓓ Ⓔ
5. Ⓐ Ⓑ Ⓒ Ⓓ Ⓔ	30. Ⓐ Ⓑ Ⓒ Ⓓ Ⓔ	55. Ⓐ Ⓑ Ⓒ Ⓓ Ⓔ	80. Ⓐ Ⓑ Ⓒ Ⓓ Ⓔ
6. Ⓐ Ⓑ Ⓒ Ⓓ Ⓔ	31. Ⓐ Ⓑ Ⓒ Ⓓ Ⓔ	56. Ⓐ Ⓑ Ⓒ Ⓓ Ⓔ	81. Ⓐ Ⓑ Ⓒ Ⓓ Ⓔ
7. Ⓐ Ⓑ Ⓒ Ⓓ Ⓔ	32. Ⓐ Ⓑ Ⓒ Ⓓ Ⓔ	57. Ⓐ Ⓑ Ⓒ Ⓓ Ⓔ	82. Ⓐ Ⓑ Ⓒ Ⓓ Ⓔ
8. Ⓐ Ⓑ Ⓒ Ⓓ Ⓔ	33. Ⓐ Ⓑ Ⓒ Ⓓ Ⓔ	58. Ⓐ Ⓑ Ⓒ Ⓓ Ⓔ	83. Ⓐ Ⓑ Ⓒ Ⓓ Ⓔ
9. Ⓐ Ⓑ Ⓒ Ⓓ Ⓔ	34. Ⓐ Ⓑ Ⓒ Ⓓ Ⓔ	59. Ⓐ Ⓑ Ⓒ Ⓓ Ⓔ	84. Ⓐ Ⓑ Ⓒ Ⓓ Ⓔ
10. Ⓐ Ⓑ Ⓒ Ⓓ Ⓔ	35. Ⓐ Ⓑ Ⓒ Ⓓ Ⓔ	60. Ⓐ Ⓑ Ⓒ Ⓓ Ⓔ	85. Ⓐ Ⓑ Ⓒ Ⓓ Ⓔ
11. Ⓐ Ⓑ Ⓒ Ⓓ Ⓔ	36. Ⓐ Ⓑ Ⓒ Ⓓ Ⓔ	61. Ⓐ Ⓑ Ⓒ Ⓓ Ⓔ	86. Ⓐ Ⓑ Ⓒ Ⓓ Ⓔ
12. Ⓐ Ⓑ Ⓒ Ⓓ Ⓔ	37. Ⓐ Ⓑ Ⓒ Ⓓ Ⓔ	62. Ⓐ Ⓑ Ⓒ Ⓓ Ⓔ	87. Ⓐ Ⓑ Ⓒ Ⓓ Ⓔ
13. Ⓐ Ⓑ Ⓒ Ⓓ Ⓔ	38. Ⓐ Ⓑ Ⓒ Ⓓ Ⓔ	63. Ⓐ Ⓑ Ⓒ Ⓓ Ⓔ	88. Ⓐ Ⓑ Ⓒ Ⓓ Ⓔ
14. Ⓐ Ⓑ Ⓒ Ⓓ Ⓔ	39. Ⓐ Ⓑ Ⓒ Ⓓ Ⓔ	64. Ⓐ Ⓑ Ⓒ Ⓓ Ⓔ	89. Ⓐ Ⓑ Ⓒ Ⓓ Ⓔ
15. Ⓐ Ⓑ Ⓒ Ⓓ Ⓔ	40. Ⓐ Ⓑ Ⓒ Ⓓ Ⓔ	65. Ⓐ Ⓑ Ⓒ Ⓓ Ⓔ	90. Ⓐ Ⓑ Ⓒ Ⓓ Ⓔ
16. Ⓐ Ⓑ Ⓒ Ⓓ Ⓔ	41. Ⓐ Ⓑ Ⓒ Ⓓ Ⓔ	66. Ⓐ Ⓑ Ⓒ Ⓓ Ⓔ	91. Ⓐ Ⓑ Ⓒ Ⓓ Ⓔ
17. Ⓐ Ⓑ Ⓒ Ⓓ Ⓔ	42. Ⓐ Ⓑ Ⓒ Ⓓ Ⓔ	67. Ⓐ Ⓑ Ⓒ Ⓓ Ⓔ	92. Ⓐ Ⓑ Ⓒ Ⓓ Ⓔ
18. Ⓐ Ⓑ Ⓒ Ⓓ Ⓔ	43. Ⓐ Ⓑ Ⓒ Ⓓ Ⓔ	68. Ⓐ Ⓑ Ⓒ Ⓓ Ⓔ	93. Ⓐ Ⓑ Ⓒ Ⓓ Ⓔ
19. Ⓐ Ⓑ Ⓒ Ⓓ Ⓔ	44. Ⓐ Ⓑ Ⓒ Ⓓ Ⓔ	69. Ⓐ Ⓑ Ⓒ Ⓓ Ⓔ	94. Ⓐ Ⓑ Ⓒ Ⓓ Ⓔ
20. Ⓐ Ⓑ Ⓒ Ⓓ Ⓔ	45. Ⓐ Ⓑ Ⓒ Ⓓ Ⓔ	70. Ⓐ Ⓑ Ⓒ Ⓓ Ⓔ	95. Ⓐ Ⓑ Ⓒ Ⓓ Ⓔ
21. Ⓐ Ⓑ Ⓒ Ⓓ Ⓔ	46. Ⓐ Ⓑ Ⓒ Ⓓ Ⓔ	71. Ⓐ Ⓑ Ⓒ Ⓓ Ⓔ	96. Ⓐ Ⓑ Ⓒ Ⓓ Ⓔ
22. Ⓐ Ⓑ Ⓒ Ⓓ Ⓔ	47. Ⓐ Ⓑ Ⓒ Ⓓ Ⓔ	72. Ⓐ Ⓑ Ⓒ Ⓓ Ⓔ	97. Ⓐ Ⓑ Ⓒ Ⓓ Ⓔ
23. Ⓐ Ⓑ Ⓒ Ⓓ Ⓔ	48. Ⓐ Ⓑ Ⓒ Ⓓ Ⓔ	73. Ⓐ Ⓑ Ⓒ Ⓓ Ⓔ	98. Ⓐ Ⓑ Ⓒ Ⓓ Ⓔ
24. Ⓐ Ⓑ Ⓒ Ⓓ Ⓔ	49. Ⓐ Ⓑ Ⓒ Ⓓ Ⓔ	74. Ⓐ Ⓑ Ⓒ Ⓓ Ⓔ	99. Ⓐ Ⓑ Ⓒ Ⓓ Ⓔ
25. Ⓐ Ⓑ Ⓒ Ⓓ Ⓔ	50. Ⓐ Ⓑ Ⓒ Ⓓ Ⓔ	75. Ⓐ Ⓑ Ⓒ Ⓓ Ⓔ	100. Ⓐ Ⓑ Ⓒ Ⓓ Ⓔ

PRACTICE TEST 1
Time: 60 Minutes

<u>Directions</u>: Each of the questions or incomplete statements below is followed by five suggested answers or completions. Select the one that is best in each case and then fill in the corresponding oval on the answer sheet.

1. "Slavery now stands erect, clanking its chains on the territory of Kansas, surrounded by a code of death, and trampling upon all cherished liberties."

   This statement was most likely made by a(n)

   (A) Whig
   (B) "muckraker"
   (C) plantation owner
   (D) Democrat
   (E) abolitionist

2. The president's power to veto a bill is checked by Congress's power to

   (A) override the veto with a two-thirds majority vote
   (B) filibuster
   (C) call for a referendum
   (D) petition the states
   (E) impeach

3. The Olmec, the Maya, the Toltec, the Aztec, and the Inca are the earliest major civilizations of the Americas and are termed the

   (A) Paleolithic migrations
   (B) cultures of "blue men"
   (C) Mesoamerican cultures
   (D) Tewa nations
   (E) sun worshippers

4. Even though the Tea Act of 1773 lowered the price of East India tea, the colonists opposed it primarily because

   (A) the British were selling the colonies inferior tea
   (B) the price of the tea included a tax the colonists did not want to pay
   (C) the Dutch threatened to stop trading with the colonies
   (D) the act gave trading privileges to Dutch merchants over colonial merchants
   (E) the British colonial governors took the tea for themselves

5. Most European immigrants at the turn of the nineteenth century passed through:

   (A) Castle Garden, New York
   (B) Roosevelt Island, New York
   (C) The Port of Boston, Massachusetts
   (D) Ellis Island, New York
   (E) Plymouth, Massachusetts

6. Henry Clay's proposal that Maine enter the Union as a free state and Missouri enter as a slave state was called

   (A) the Maine Compromise
   (B) the Missouri Compromise
   (C) the Clay Compromise
   (D) Clay's Folly
   (E) the Know-Nothing Agreement

7. In a 1906 speech, Theodore Roosevelt described a man with a muckrake who "fixes his eyes . . . only on that which is vile and debasing." His speech gave rise to the new word *muckrakers,* referring to

   (A) farmers in lowland areas
   (B) trial lawyers
   (C) religious leaders
   (D) judges in criminal courts
   (E) investigative journalists

8. The only United States president who was not a member of a Protestant sect was

   (A) Franklin D. Roosevelt
   (B) Harry S Truman
   (C) Dwight D. Eisenhower
   (D) John F. Kennedy
   (E) Lyndon B. Johnson

GO ON TO THE NEXT PAGE

PRACTICE TEST—*Continued*

Europe in 1922

9. Several countries on this map were conquered by Germany in 1940, causing the United States to sign the Atlantic Charter with Great Britain. Two of the conquered countries were

   (A) Switzerland and France
   (B) France and Spain
   (C) Belgium and France
   (D) Belgium and Portugal
   (E) Switzerland and Luxembourg

10. In the aftermath of President Kennedy's assassination, a commission was formed to review the evidence and publish a report. The commission was headed by

    (A) Vice President Lyndon B. Johnson
    (B) Pierre Salinger
    (C) Senator J. William Fulbright
    (D) Attorney General Robert F. Kennedy
    (E) Chief Justice Earl Warren

11. The Fourteen Points, presented in January 1918, were

    (A) Winston Churchill's plans for dealing with Hitler
    (B) American suffragists' demands for women's rights
    (C) Woodrow Wilson's plan for building peace in the post–World War I world
    (D) sections of the income tax amendment to the Constitution
    (E) the Socialist Party's proposal for economic fairness

12. White Southerners were opposed to Northerners who traveled south after the Civil War to work for racial justice and/or make money. They called these people:

    (A) mugwumps
    (B) Whigs
    (C) dog robbers
    (D) Southern sympathizers
    (E) carpetbaggers

13. President James Monroe issued the Monroe Doctrine in 1823, warning European powers not to establish new colonies in the western hemisphere. This policy was supported by

    (A) Spain
    (B) Russia
    (C) England
    (D) France
    (E) Cuba

GO ON TO THE NEXT PAGE

PRACTICE TEST—*Continued*

14. The voyage that brought African captives across the Atlantic to the Americas and the West Indies is referred to as the

    (A) Middle Passage
    (B) Northwest Passage
    (C) China Passage
    (D) Passage to India
    (E) Bermuda Passage

15. Gifford Pinchot is associated with a movement that began in the nineteenth century and focused on protecting the country's natural environment. This movement is called the

    (A) Greenpeace movement
    (B) emancipation movement
    (C) enfranchisement movement
    (D) conservationist movement
    (E) emigration movement

16. "Tippecanoe and Tyler, too" was a campaign slogan in the presidential election of 1840. "Tippecanoe" refers to

    (A) John Tyler
    (B) Andrew Jackson
    (C) Benjamin Harrison
    (D) William Henry Harrison
    (E) George Rogers Clark

17. Beginning in 1663 with Carolina, a second wave of colonization in British North America was facilitated by

    (A) the restoration of Oliver Cromwell and the Puritans to power in Great Britain
    (B) King George II of Great Britain
    (C) the restoration of the monarchy in Britain and land grants in the New World from Charles II to his supporters
    (D) the voyages of exploration by John Cabot
    (E) peace pacts between French missionaries and Native American tribes

18. Jazz, flappers, bathtub gin, red-hot flannels, speakeasies, and radio stations were all elements of the era known as

    (A) the Gay Nineties
    (B) the Roaring Twenties
    (C) the Fabulous Sixties
    (D) Reconstruction
    (E) the turn of the century

19. The first U.S. military response to a suspected terrorist act came in 1986 when President Ronald Reagan ordered a bombing attack on which country?

    (A) Syria
    (B) Pakistan
    (C) Turkey
    (D) Uganda
    (E) Libya

20. Automation in the 1950s and 1960s brought about what two significant economic changes in the United States?

    (A) Increased hiring and tax cuts
    (B) An increase in manufacturing jobs and lower unemployment
    (C) Reductions in farm employment and elimination of factory jobs
    (D) Higher taxes and inflation
    (E) No changes

21. The U.S. pressured Cuba to accept the Platt Amendment in 1901. It made Cuba a protectorate of the United States. A protectorate is a

    (A) U.S. possession
    (B) country that promises to help protect the United States
    (C) country that contributes soldiers to the U.S. Army
    (D) country that accepts U.S. protection in exchange for the right of the United States to intervene in its affairs
    (E) country that is protected from U.S. aggression

22. The Fifteenth Amendment tried to ensure the right of black men to vote. The first presidential election after the ratification of the Fifteenth Amendment was in

    (A) 1864
    (B) 1920
    (C) 1860
    (D) 1960
    (E) 1872

GO ON TO THE NEXT PAGE

PRACTICE TEST—*Continued*

23. Which number on the map marks the Northwest Territory?

    (A) I
    (B) II
    (C) III
    (D) IV
    (E) V

24. The Spanish explorer Vasco Nunez de Balboa, the first European to cross the isthmus of Panama, saw a body of water he thought was the South Sea. It was actually the

    (A) Atlantic Ocean
    (B) Pacific Ocean
    (C) Gulf of Mexico
    (D) Indian Ocean
    (E) Caribbean Sea

25. The route known as the Oregon Trail followed the Platte River

    (A) across the Appalachians and into Ohio
    (B) across the Rio Grande and up the California coast to Oregon
    (C) across the Great Plains to the Rocky Mountains and then into Oregon along the Snake River
    (D) across the Mississippi and along the Missouri River to the Badlands and into Canada
    (E) across the desert and up the Sierra Nevadas to Oregon

26. Ralph Nader became prominent during the 1960s as an advocate for

    (A) transportation improvements
    (B) education reform
    (C) consumer interests
    (D) congressional term limits
    (E) vegetarianism

27. On March 12, 1933, President Franklin D. Roosevelt made a radio broadcast from the White House to explain his reasons for closing U.S. banks for a few days. This grew into a regular series of broadcasts that became known as

    (A) "fireside chats"
    (B) "The FDR Hour"
    (C) "The State of the Union"
    (D) "America Today"
    (E) "This Week in the News"

GO ON TO THE NEXT PAGE

PRACTICE TEST—*Continued*

28. The "British Invasion" of 1964 refers to

    (A) an attack by Great Britain on the U.S. Virgin Islands
    (B) an increase in British immigration to Canada
    (C) the sale of British-made automobiles in the United States
    (D) the introduction of popular British rock bands to U.S. audiences
    (E) the broadcast of British television shows in the United States

29. The first union of skilled workers, founded by Samuel L. Gompers in 1886, was called the

    (A) Congress of Industrial Organizations (CIO)
    (B) U.S. Department of Labor
    (C) International Ladies' Garment Workers' Union (ILGWU)
    (D) American Federation of Labor (AFL)
    (E) Industrial Workers of the World (IWW)

30. The first shots of the Revolutionary War were fired in which colony?

    (A) Massachusetts
    (B) Virginia
    (C) New Hampshire
    (D) Pennsylvania
    (E) New York

31. In *The American Crisis, no. 1,* Thomas Paine referred to "the summer soldier and the sunshine patriot." Whom did he mean?

    (A) Traitors to the U.S. Army
    (B) People who had supported independence before the war but changed their minds once it began
    (C) Colonists who had remained loyal to Great Britain all along
    (D) Soldiers who fired on the mobs during the Boston Massacre
    (E) Redcoats who fired on the minutemen, who were British subjects like themselves

32. Which of the following was NOT a primary aim of the Progressive movement of the early 1900s?

    (A) Passing laws that would improve slum conditions in large cities
    (B) Teaching immigrants to read, write, and speak English
    (C) Supporting the passage of legislation that would make the workplace safer
    (D) Creating public baths, parks, and playgrounds in urban areas
    (E) Making English the official language of the United States

33. The 1938 panic in which people thought that the earth was being attacked by hostile aliens from Mars was caused by a

    (A) radio broadcast of H. G. Wells's *The War of the Worlds* by Orson Welles and the Mercury Theater
    (B) series of swaths cut into mysterious symbolic shapes in Midwestern cornfields
    (C) power blackout that darkened the Northeast from Boston to Washington, D.C.
    (D) series of tornadoes in the Southeast in which many people disappeared
    (E) mysterious cloud formation hovering over the face of the moon

34. Why did the writer Gertrude Stein describe Ernest Hemingway, F. Scott Fitzgerald, and other artistic and literary Americans as a "lost generation" during the 1920s?

    (A) They preferred to live in Europe, not the United States.
    (B) They had fought recently on the losing side in World War I.
    (C) They were disillusioned by the experience of World War I.
    (D) They had lost all feeling of American patriotism.
    (E) They despised society and lived isolated lives.

35. The Emancipation Proclamation of January 1, 1863,

    (A) freed all slaves in the United States
    (B) freed all slaves in the Confederate States
    (C) required all slaves to register with the government
    (D) gave all adult male slaves the right to vote
    (E) gave all adult male slaves the right to enlist in the Union Army

36. "From Stettin in the Baltic to Trieste on the Adriatic, an iron curtain has descended across the continent."

    The phrase "iron curtain," coined in 1947, refers to the

    (A) Marshall Plan, which provided millions of dollars in U.S. aid to any nation in Europe that requested it
    (B) Allied invasion of Normandy during World War II
    (C) borderline between nations under Soviet communist influence and the rest of the world
    (D) borderline between Northern and Southern Europe
    (E) concrete wall that divided East Berlin from West Berlin

GO ON TO THE NEXT PAGE

PRACTICE TEST—*Continued*

37. Jane Addams opened Hull House in Chicago in 1889 for all the following reasons EXCEPT:

    (A) providing meaningful career opportunities for young women
    (B) improving living conditions in the immediate neighborhood
    (C) providing a day-care center for the young children of working parents
    (D) teaching English and other subjects to newly arrived immigrants
    (E) eliminating racial segregation throughout the city of Chicago

38. "Labor is prior to, and independent of, capital. Capital is only the fruit of labor, and could never have existed if labor had not first existed. Labor is the superior of capital and deserves much the higher consideration."

    Which of the following would the speaker of this quotation most likely support?

    (A) Prohibition
    (B) Socialism
    (C) Segregation
    (D) Progressivism
    (E) Capitalism

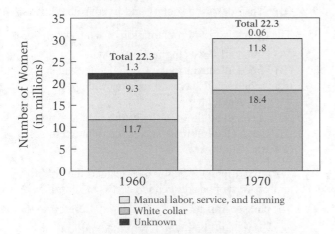

39. Which of the following statements do the data shown on this graph support?

    (A) The greatest rise in the number of working women over the decade was among farmers.
    (B) In 1960, a working woman was most likely to have a job in the field of manual labor.
    (C) Over the course of the decade, about 7 million women joined the white-collar workforce.
    (D) About 3 million women moved from the manual-labor category into the white-collar category.
    (E) Between 1960 and 1970, the number of working women doubled.

40. People in the United States lost confidence in President Herbert Hoover primarily because

    (A) his policies did not bring about an economic recovery
    (B) the Hoover Dam was an environmental disaster
    (C) the judges he appointed to the Supreme Court were incompetent
    (D) he outlawed membership in the Socialist and Communist parties
    (E) he established the Federal Farm Board in 1929

41. The primary purpose of the Lewis and Clark expedition of 1804–1806 was to

    (A) make accurate maps of the Louisiana Territory
    (B) search for a water route across North America from the Atlantic to the Pacific
    (C) register all the Native American tribes living in the Louisiana Territory
    (D) study the various types of plant and animals in the Louisiana Territory
    (E) establish friendly relations with the Native American tribes of the Pacific Coast

42. Which of the following would give a historian the clearest insight into the reasons for the way the Constitution was written?

    (A) Minutes and transcripts of debates to the Constitutional Convention
    (B) The diary of a Convention delegate such as James Madison or Benjamin Franklin
    (C) A copy of the *Federalist Papers*
    (D) Newspaper editorials published during the Constitutional Convention
    (E) A copy of the Constitution

43. Which of the following facts supports the theory that the War of 1812 brought about economic prosperity in the United States?

    (A) The USS *Constitution* destroyed several British warships.
    (B) Andrew Jackson led his troops to victory in the Battle of New Orleans.
    (C) Great Britain and the United States became allies after the war ended.
    (D) Trade embargoes forced U.S. manufacturers to expand operations.
    (E) The Treaty of Ghent strengthened U.S. control over the Northwest Territory.

GO ON TO THE NEXT PAGE

PRACTICE TEST—*Continued*

44. What took place during the Saturday Night Massacre?

   (A) A mob of Bostonians threw stones at British troops, who retaliated by firing on them.
   (B) General George Armstrong Custer and all his troops were killed at the Battle of Little Bighorn.
   (C) Attorney General Eliot Richardson and Deputy Attorney General William Ruckelshaus resigned rather than obey President Nixon's order to fire Special Prosecutor Archibald Cox.
   (D) George Washington and his troops captured and imprisoned the entire Hessian force at Trenton, New Jersey.
   (E) The stock market crashed on October 24, 1929, and some prominent people who had lost their fortunes committed suicide.

45. Which nation was NOT involved in the 1921 Four-Power Treaty, an agreement to respect territorial claims in the Pacific?

   (A) France
   (B) Great Britain
   (C) Japan
   (D) The Netherlands
   (E) The United States

46. Which novel was a catalyst for reform in the meat-packing industry under President Theodore Roosevelt?

   (A) *Manhattan Transfer* by John Dos Passos
   (B) *The Jungle* by Upton Sinclair
   (C) *Babbitt* by Sinclair Lewis
   (D) *The Octopus* by Frank Norris
   (E) *The Grapes of Wrath* by John Steinbeck

47. African Americans moved west in large numbers after the Civil War for all the following reasons EXCEPT:

   (A) to look for greater racial tolerance and economic opportunity
   (B) to take advantage of the opportunities offered by the Harlem Renaissance
   (C) to escape violent persecution by angry white Southerners
   (D) to acquire farmland that the Homestead Act made available for free to the first people to claim it
   (E) to work on building the railroad that soon would connect the East Coast and the West Coast

48. Which of the following was NOT proposed in 1850 to the U.S. Senate as a compromise between proslavery and antislavery factions?

   (A) Admission to the United States of California as a free state
   (B) Continuation of slavery in the District of Columbia
   (C) Passage of tougher fugitive slave legislation
   (D) Purchase of its claim to New Mexico Territory from Texas
   (E) Division of Texas into two new territories: New Mexico and Utah

49. Which of the following most aptly supports the assertion that Native Americans have suffered the worst discrimination of all groups in U.S. history?

   (A) Native Americans taught the colonists to grow corn and gather plants that were safe and nutritious to eat.
   (B) European explorers and colonists introduced Native Americans to the horse as a working animal and to pigs and chickens as sources of food.
   (C) Native Americans and Europeans had different cultural values.
   (D) Congress did not grant universal U.S. citizenship for Native Americans until 1924.
   (E) The European invaders and colonists of North America refused to learn Native American languages.

50. Which war did young Americans protest by burning their draft cards and draft notices, fleeing to Canada, and demonstrating against the administration?

   (A) Korean War
   (B) Vietnam War
   (C) Persian Gulf War
   (D) War in Afghanistan
   (E) Iraq War

GO ON TO THE NEXT PAGE →

PRACTICE TEST—*Continued*

51. Which statement most aptly supports the theory that the Black Sox scandal of 1919 was a result of the exploitation of labor by management?

(A) F. Scott Fitzgerald referred to the scandal as "playing with the faith of fifty million people."

(B) The baseball players were in effect indentured servants with no right to strike or to accept offers from other teams.

(C) The eight White Sox players accused of conspiring to cheat were acquitted in a jury trial.

(D) Baseball commissioner Kenesaw Mountain Landis permanently banned the eight "Black Sox" from professional baseball.

(E) Millions of Americans were cheated in their expectation of seeing a fairly contested World Series.

52. Which of the following is the correct chronological order of the three Civil War battles?

(A) Antietam, Gettysburg, Shiloh

(B) Gettysburg, Shiloh, Antietam

(C) Shiloh, Gettysburg, Antietam

(D) Gettysburg, Antietam, Shiloh

(E) Shiloh, Antietam, Gettysburg

53. "And the dispossessed, the migrants, flowed into California, two hundred and fifty thousand, and three hundred thousand. Behind them new tractors were going on to the land and the tenants were being forced off. And new waves were on the way, new waves of the dispossessed and the homeless, hardened, intent, and dangerous."

The author of this quotation is describing

(A) pioneers riding westward along the Oregon Trail

(B) prospectors hurrying to California during the Gold Rush of 1849

(C) farmers leaving the Dust Bowl during the Great Depression

(D) Mexicans crossing the Rio Grande into the United States

(E) African Americans migrating west during Reconstruction

54. What was the most significant result of the Battle of Little Bighorn?

(A) The U.S. Army redoubled its efforts to move Native Americans to reservations.

(B) The U.S. 7th Cavalry troops were all killed in the battle.

(C) The 7th Cavalry attacked the Lakota at dawn after riding all night.

(D) The Lakota felt more confident about their ability to fight the U.S. Army.

(E) The Native American tribes of the southern plains agreed to move to Indian Territory.

55. Everyday life in the United States changed after the Second Industrial Revolution in all the following ways EXCEPT:

(A) More people worked in factories.

(B) Electricity changed the way people worked and played.

(C) People could travel longer distances in a fraction of the time.

(D) Instant long-distance communication became commonplace.

(E) The percentage of women working in offices declined as factory work opened up opportunities for women.

56. The Mexican-American War was caused primarily by

(A) a border dispute between Mexico and Texas

(B) an unpaid debt that Mexico owed the United States

(C) the involvement of the United States in the 1836 Texas revolution

(D) the overthrow of the Mexican administration and its replacement by a military regime

(E) the Texan siege of the Spanish mission/fort known as the Alamo

57. The primary reason the Confederate Army lost the Battle of Gettysburg was that

(A) the Union troops did not have sufficient reinforcements to win the battle

(B) Confederate General Robert E. Lee was a strategically gifted commander

(C) the Union forces were able to hold the high ground northwest of Gettysburg

(D) the Confederate troops retreated south after Pickett's Charge

(E) Union troops vastly outnumbered the Confederates

58. The earliest example of republican government in North America is the

(A) Mayflower Compact

(B) Articles of Confederation

(C) Iroquois Confederacy

(D) Gettysburg Address

(E) U.S. Constitution

GO ON TO THE NEXT PAGE

PRACTICE TEST—*Continued*

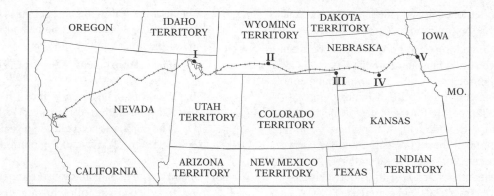

59. Which dot on the map represents the site where the Union Pacific and Central Pacific railroads met to form the transcontinental railroad in 1869?

    (A) I
    (B) II
    (C) III
    (D) IV
    (E) V

60. As the Constitutional Convention ended, Benjamin Franklin commented about a half-sun with its rays painted on George Washington's chair that "now at length I have the happiness to know that it is a rising and not a setting sun." Franklin meant these words as

    (A) a criticism of the delegates to the Convention who did not share his faith in the Constitution
    (B) an indication that he knew that the fight for the ratification of the Constitution would be difficult
    (C) a joke about the poor quality of the furniture in Independence Hall
    (D) an expression of hope and optimism for the new government he had helped design
    (E) a criticism of the painter of the chair

61. The heavy line drawn across the map below shows the

    (A) route of the De Soto party of Spanish explorers
    (B) route of the Lewis and Clark expedition
    (C) Oregon Trail
    (D) Northwest Passage
    (E) Wilderness Road

62. The Farmers' Alliance of the 1870s was founded with all the following goals EXCEPT:

    (A) organizing cooperatives to buy equipment and market farm products
    (B) offering farmers low-cost insurance
    (C) lobbying for tougher bank regulations
    (D) helping members in times of hardship such as drought
    (E) supporting private ownership of national railroads

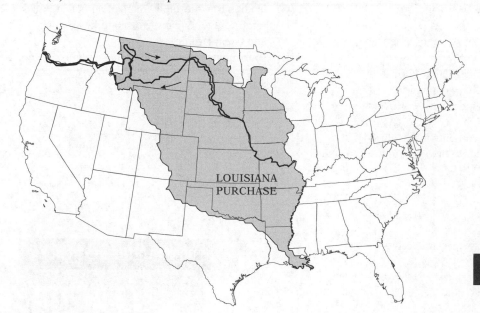

GO ON TO THE NEXT PAGE ▶

PRACTICE TEST—*Continued*

63. Pocahontas's friendship with the Jamestown colonists was historically important because she

    (A) encouraged trust and good relations between Native Americans and colonists
    (B) set other Native American women an example by marrying John Rolfe of Jamestown
    (C) made it possible for the Native Americans and colonists to trade with one another
    (D) ensured that the colonists granted the Native Americans full equal legal rights
    (E) permanently ended hostilities between the Native Americans and colonists

64. Which factor contributed most to the rise of membership in labor unions between 1915 and 1920?

    (A) The efforts of progressive reformers
    (B) The expansion of the open shop
    (C) The fire at the Triangle Shirtwaist Company
    (D) The passage of the Fourteenth Amendment
    (E) The exclusion of unskilled workers

65. Which event did NOT lead directly to the annexation of Hawaii as a U.S. territory in 1898?

    (A) Passage of the McKinley Tariff of 1890
    (B) Formation of the Secret Hawaiian League in 1886
    (C) Election of William McKinley to the presidency in 1898
    (D) Rebellion of Hawaiian supporters of annexation in 1893
    (E) Coronation of Queen Liliuokalani of Hawaii in 1891

66. What is the significance of the 54th Massachusetts Infantry regiment of the Union Army?

    (A) It began the Civil War by firing on Fort Sumter.
    (B) It was composed entirely of African-American soldiers and officers.
    (C) It was the first African-American regiment to play a major role in a military campaign.
    (D) It was an aristocratic regiment whose officers refused any pay.
    (E) It included a number of women who disguised themselves as men in order to take part in combat.

67. Which of the following best supports the theory that the United States had imperialist ambitions as of the end of the nineteenth century?

    (A) The establishment of the Open Door Policy in 1899
    (B) The Russo-Japanese War of 1904
    (C) The annexation of Hawaii in 1898
    (D) The popularity of yellow journalism in 1890s
    (E) The start of Mexican Revolution in 1910

68. Spanish and Spanish-sponsored parties explored and/or settled all the following areas of North America EXCEPT:

    (A) the northern Atlantic coast
    (B) the Gulf of Mexico
    (C) the Pacific coast
    (D) the Southwest
    (E) the Mississippi valley

69. Soon after World War I broke out in Europe, people in the United States became outraged against Germany because of the 1915 sinking of the

    (A) *Titanic*
    (B) *Maine*
    (C) *Lusitania*
    (D) *Constitution*
    (E) *Hindenburg*

70. The development of atomic technology affected daily life in the United States in all the following ways EXCEPT:

    (A) encouraging schools to teach more math and science classes
    (B) contributing to the popularity of science-fiction literature and movies
    (C) leading to widespread fears of a nuclear attack
    (D) reinforcing the fear of former allies France and Great Britain
    (E) spurring people to build or make bomb shelters

GO ON TO THE NEXT PAGE

PRACTICE TEST—*Continued*

71. Which of the following is NOT guaranteed in the Bill of Rights?

    (A) Freedom from cruel and unusual punishment for crimes

    (B) Possession of rights other than those listed in the Constitution

    (C) Protection against search and seizure of property without a warrant

    (D) The right to remain silent if arrested and tried for a crime

    (E) The right to vote for all free males age 21 or over

Percentage of Support for the Vietnam War by Race and Gender, 1966 and 1970

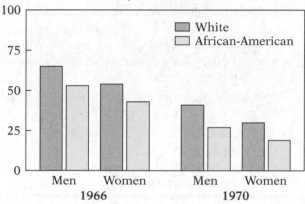

72. Which of the following statements is supported by the data in the bar graph above?

    (A) In 1966, African Americans did not support the Vietnam War.

    (B) In 1970, more women than men supported the Vietnam War.

    (C) Support for the Vietnam War dropped among all Americans between 1966 and 1970.

    (D) Between 1966 and 1970, support for the war dropped by a greater percentage among white women than in any other category.

    (E) A higher percentage of African-American men than white women supported the war.

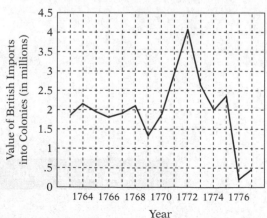

73. According to the graph, which of the following had the greatest negative impact on the value of British imports to the colonies?

    (A) Passage of the Sugar Act, 1764

    (B) Passage of Stamp Act, 1765

    (C) British troops arriving in Boston, 1768

    (D) Townshend Acts repealed, 1770

    (E) Passage of Intolerable Acts, 1774

74. "Fourscore and seven years ago, our fathers brought forth on this continent a new nation, conceived in liberty, and dedicated to the proposition that all men are created equal."

    To which of the following events is the speaker of this quotation alluding?

    (A) Signing of the Declaration of Independence

    (B) Ratification of the Constitution

    (C) Passage of the Bill of Rights

    (D) Repeal of Prohibition

    (E) Passage of the Civil Rights Act

75. "We believe that America had something better to offer mankind than those aims she is now pursuing. . . . She has lost her unique position as a potential leader in the progress of civilization and has taken up her place simply as one of the grasping and selfish nations of the present day."

    The speaker of this quotation most likely opposed the

    (A) Lewis and Clark expedition

    (B) California gold rush

    (C) annexation of the Philippines

    (D) Philadelphia Centennial Exhibition

    (E) passage of the Nineteenth Amendment

76. Congress passed the War Powers Act in response to the

    (A) Korean War

    (B) Vietnam War

    (C) Persian Gulf War

    (D) Six-Day War

    (E) Iraq War

GO ON TO THE NEXT PAGE

PRACTICE TEST—*Continued*

77. The 1783 Treaty of Paris granted the United States all the following EXCEPT:

    (A) British recognition of the United States as an independent nation
    (B) all territory between the 13 states and the Mississippi River
    (C) the right to maintain a standing army in the former colonies
    (D) British acceptance of U.S. payment of all debts owed by the colonies
    (E) fishing rights in the Gulf of St. Lawrence

78. Which of the following made it possible for the United States to govern and control the Canal Zone in Panama?

    (A) The Hay–Bunau-Varilla Treaty
    (B) The Platt Amendment
    (C) The Jones Act
    (D) The Foraker Act
    (E) The Roosevelt Corollary

79. "I think we came, without really knowing it, to make the memorial our wailing wall. We came to find the names of those we lost in the war, as if by tracing the letters cut into the granite we could find what was left of ourselves. . . ."

    The speaker most likely is referring to the

    (A) Ellis Island memorial
    (B) Lincoln Memorial
    (C) Vietnam War Memorial
    (D) Washington Monument
    (E) Tomb of the Unknown Soldier

80. All the following people were key figures in the Watergate scandal EXCEPT:

    (A) Richard M. Nixon
    (B) John Dean III
    (C) James McCord
    (D) Robert Bork
    (E) Robert S. McNamara

81. "Every nation, in every region, now has a decision to make. Either you are with us, or you are with the terrorists. From this day forward, any nation that continues to harbor or support terrorism will be regarded by the United Sates as a hostile regime."

    These words most likely were spoken by which president?

    (A) Abraham Lincoln
    (B) Ulysses S. Grant
    (C) Woodrow Wilson
    (D) Franklin D. Roosevelt
    (E) George W. Bush

82. What was the connection between political machines of the late 1800s and the need for city services?

    (A) Political bosses often supported public projects.
    (B) Voters who wanted city services boycotted the polls on election day.
    (C) The federal government took over public-works projects during the New Deal era.
    (D) The New York City subway system was built by the Tweed political machine.
    (E) The political machines refused all interest in public-works projects.

83. "Reformation *must* be effected; the foundation of southern institutions, both political, municipal, and social must be broken up and *relaid,* or all our blood and treasure have been spent in vain. . . . Without this, this government can never be, as it has never been, a true republic."

    The author of the above statement most likely opposed the

    (A) Black Codes
    (B) Civil Rights Act
    (C) Platt Amendment
    (D) Seneca Falls Convention
    (E) Tenure of Office Act

84. Which of the following women is NOT famous for her activities in wartime?

    (A) Clara Barton
    (B) Mary Ludwig Hayes
    (C) Deborah Sampson
    (D) Susan B. Anthony
    (E) Tokyo Rose

85. The maintenance of the peace and safety of the United States was the stated aim of the

    (A) XYZ Affair
    (B) Alien and Sedition Acts
    (C) Bill of Rights
    (D) *Federalist Papers*
    (E) Louisiana Purchase

GO ON TO THE NEXT PAGE →

PRACTICE TEST—*Continued*

86. To which author did Abraham Lincoln jokingly say, on meeting her, "So you're the little lady who started this great war"?

    (A) Edith Wharton
    (B) Harriet Beecher Stowe
    (C) Zorah Neale Hurston
    (D) Louisa May Alcott
    (E) Mary Mapes Dodge

87. Which of the following happened for the fist time during the presidential election of 1828?

    (A) A Federalist won the election.
    (B) Free African Americans voted.
    (C) The voters, not the state legislatures, chose the electors.
    (D) Native Americans voted.
    (E) A war hero won the election.

88. Which president's domestic programs were collectively known as the Great Society?

    (A) Franklin D. Roosevelt
    (B) Harry S. Truman
    (C) Dwight D. Eisenhower
    (D) John F. Kennedy
    (E) Lyndon B. Johnson

89. Over which issue did Congress agree to permit or withhold statehood from territories that applied for it between 1828 and 1860?

    (A) Free public education
    (B) Land grants to farmers
    (C) Slavery
    (D) Temperance
    (E) Woman suffrage

90. At the time of the Louisiana Purchase, which country did NOT claim any land in North America?

    (A) France
    (B) Great Britain
    (C) Holland
    (D) Spain
    (E) United States

STOP

IF YOU FINISH BEFORE TIME RUNS OUT, GO BACK AND CHECK YOUR WORK.

ANSWER KEY

1. E	21. D	41. B	61. B	81. E
2. A	22. E	42. A	62. E	82. A
3. C	23. C	43. D	63. A	83. A
4. B	24. B	44. C	64. A	84. D
5. D	25. C	45. D	65. E	85. B
6. B	26. C	46. B	66. C	86. B
7. E	27. A	47. B	67. C	87. C
8. D	28. D	48. E	68. A	88. E
9. C	29. D	49. D	69. C	89. C
10. E	30. A	50. B	70. D	90. C
11. C	31. B	51. B	71. E	
12. E	32. E	52. E	72. C	
13. C	33. A	53. C	73. E	
14. A	34. C	54. A	74. A	
15. D	35. B	55. E	75. C	
16. D	36. C	56. A	76. B	
17. C	37. E	57. C	77. C	
18. B	38. B	58. C	78. A	
19. E	39. C	59. A	79. C	
20. C	40. A	60. D	80. E	

ANSWERS AND EXPLANATIONS

1. **E** Abolitionists opposed the spread of slavery into new states and territories.

2. **A** This information is taken directly from the Constitution.

3. **C** "Mesoamerican" refers to people from this geographical area and time period.

4. **B** The colonists knew that if they gave in and paid the tax for the sake of saving money, Britain would have a hold over them the next time it ordered them to pay a tax.

5. **D** Most European immigrants at the turn of the century and afterward passed through Ellis Island in New York Harbor.

6. **B** Missouri's status as a slave/free state was the issue over which a compromise needed to be reached. Maine would never have been a slave state.

7. **E** Roosevelt was coining a metaphor comparing the literal muck in the stables with the figurative muck that journalists uncovered when they investigated scandals.

8. **D** Kennedy was a Catholic; all other U.S. Presidents were Protestants of one sect or another, even those who were only nominally religious.

9. **C** The Germans marched through and conquered Belgium on their way to doing the same thing in France.

10. **E** The Chief Justice of the Supreme Court was presumed to be above any political feeling about the assassination and thus could weigh evidence objectively.

11. **C** President Wilson presented the Fourteen Points to assure the people of the United States that the country fought the World War for a moral cause and for peace. However, Wilson had to compromise or eliminate almost all his points. The final Treaty of Versailles accepted only about four of Wilson's points.

12. **E** A "carpetbag" was an upholstered traveling bag carried by many Northerners and the source of their nickname.

13. **C** The Monroe Doctrine was aimed at conservative governments in Spain, Russia, and France. Cuba was a colony of Spain. England supported the policy and wanted to cosign the document. However, Secretary of State John Quincy Adams convinced President Monroe to issue it independently.

14. **A** The Northwest Passage was a mythical water route from the Atlantic to the Pacific, and *A Passage to India* is a novel by E. M. Forster.

15. **D** Greenpeace is a name that dates from much later in time, and the other choices are not relevant.

16. **D** Harrison was nicknamed for the Battle of Tippecanoe, which took place in west-central Indiana.

17. **C** The second wave of colonization began with the restoration. The other choices are too late or early in time or are false.

18. **B** All the items listed are specifically associated with the 1920s, when they were shocking and new.

19. **E** The U.S. government suspected that the Libyan leader Muammar Gadhafi had ordered an attack on a West Berlin nightclub that killed a U.S. soldier in 1986.

20. **C** Automation meant a gradual change from an agricultural and manufacturing economy to a service economy.

21. **D** This is the correct definition of a protectorate.

22. **E** The Fifteenth Amendment was passed by Congress in 1869 and ratified in 1870. The first presidential election it affected would have been in 1872.

23. **C** The Northwest Territory consisted of Michigan, Wisconsin, Indiana, Illinois, and Ohio.

24. **B** The Pacific Ocean is what lies on the western side of the isthmus of Panama.

25. **C** European fur traders drove the first wagons across the Great Plains to the eastern slopes of the Rockies to mark the beginning of the Oregon Trail in the 1830s.

26. **C** Nader has continued to be known for his concern for consumer interests as a presidential candidate.

27. **A** The "fireside chats" received their name as a way to invoke a cozy, friendly, and nostalgic atmosphere for people listening to the radio broadcasts.

28. **D** The enormously popular Beatles, a British rock group, first came to the United States in 1964. Americans had been able to see British films since the 1930s; the other choices are irrelevant.

29. **D** The first union of skilled workers in the United States was the American Federation of Labor (AFL).

30. **A** The minutemen and the redcoats faced each other as enemies in war for the first time at the village green at Lexington, Massachusetts.

31. **B** Paine was referring to those who gave up the idea of independence when they saw that it would mean hard times and sacrifice in the short term.

32. **E** The notion of needing to make English an official language had not occurred to anyone at the time.

33. **A** The play script included a written "we interrupt this broadcast" section that fooled many people who had not tuned in to the start of the show into thinking it was a real, spontaneous interruption of the broadcast to announce an invasion.

34. **C** Stein meant that the writers and artists and the generation they represented had lost their illusions of honor and glory in the trenches of World War I.

35. **B** The Emancipation Proclamation specifically refers to slaves in states that are "currently in rebellion against the Union." It did not free any slaves held in other areas.

36. **C** The phrase "iron curtain" referred primarily to the border between Soviet-controlled countries in Eastern Europe and the nations of Western Europe.

37. **E** Addams did not attempt to end segregation, except on the most local, concrete level by treating people equally.

38. **B** The philosophy of socialism is the one that most closely echoes the speaker's idea that the fruits of labor should belong to the laborer.

39. **C** The other four choices misstate the data shown in the graph.

40. **A** People judged Hoover mainly by their own bank balances. The other four choices are either untrue or irrelevant.

41. **B** This was the stated purpose of the expedition in President Jefferson's written instructions to Lewis and Clark. The other purposes, such as befriending the Native Americans and cataloging flora and fauna, were secondary.

42. **A** The diary would give only one person's opinions; the *Federalist Papers* discuss only one side of the issue; there were no newspaper editorials published because the debates were secret; and the finished Constitution does not reveal the debate that went into its making.

43. **D** The question asks about the economy, and choice D is the only one that refers to an economic factor.

44. **C** Choice A refers to the Boston Massacre, B to the Battle of Little Bighorn, D to the Battle of Trenton, and E to Black Tuesday.

45. **D** The Netherlands was not involved in the Four-Power Treaty even though it owned the Asian colony known as the Dutch East Indies (now Indonesia).

46. **B** *The Jungle* exposed the horrors of the lack of regulations in the meat-packing industry, and it shocked many meat-eating readers into demanding reforms.

47. **B** The Harlem Renaissance took place in the 1920s in New York City. The question asks why African Americans moved west.

48. **E** The division of Texas would not have helped the two factions to agree.

49. **D** Although Native Americans were here first, they had to wait the longest time for full citizenship, voting rights, and so on.

50. **B** The enormously unpopular Vietnam War is famous for the student and youth protests it engendered.

51. **B** Only management, not the players, had the right to terminate a perpetual contract. Therefore, management could keep salaries and benefits low and a player had no possibility of finding work elsewhere because no other team would hire him. Players agreed to throw the World Series for money because they naturally felt no loyalty to management.

52. **E** Shiloh was in the spring of 1862, Antietam in the fall of 1862, and Gettysburg in the spring of 1863.

53. **C** The quotation makes it clear that the migrants have been forced from their homes in areas east of California and that they were tenants there; this accurately describes the farmers of the Dust Bowl.

54. **A** This was the most important result in the long run. This battle was the last stand of the Native Americans against moving to the reservations.

55. **E** Women represented about 3 percent of office workers in 1870 and about 53 percent in 1930.

56. **A** All the choices are true, but only A was the spark that actually set off the war in a direct sense.

57. **C** The Confederates lost thousands of men when they tried to storm the hill; high ground is always an advantage in battle.

58. **C** The Iroquois Confederacy long predates any of the Anglo-American efforts at republican government.

59. **A** The Union Pacific and the Central Pacific met at Promontory Point, Utah.

60. **D** Sunrise is a perennial metaphor for hope and optimism.

61. **B** The Lewis and Clark expedition set out from St. Louis, traveling west along the Missouri River and ending the journey on the Pacific Coast on the border of present-day Washington and Oregon.

62. **E** The Alliance opposed private ownership of the railroads, which Alliance members felt should be owned and operated by the government.

63. **A** Pocahontas brought about good relations between the two groups because both sides liked and trusted her; therefore, they were more willing to like and trust each other.

64. **A** Choices B and E would discourage union membership, the Fourteenth Amendment is not relevant, and the Triangle fire contributed only indirectly; it was the efforts of the reformers after the fire to pass legislation that made union membership go up.

65. **E** All the other choices led directly or indirectly to the goal of annexation.

66. **C** The 54th Massachusetts was not all-black; the officers of the regiment were white. This regiment did not fire on Fort Sumter, and the officers did not volunteer to fight without pay. The attack on Fort Wagner was the first time a black regiment had been given an important role to play in U.S. military history.

67. **C** The annexation of territory is the best direct indication of imperialist ambitions.

68. **A** The Spaniards explored the West and the Southwest north of Mexico, the entire Gulf coast area, and the Mississippi valley; Hernando de Soto and his party were the first Europeans to see the Mississippi River. The Spaniards did not explore the Atlantic Coast north of Florida.

69. **C** The *Titanic* sank in 1912 when it hit an iceberg; the *Hindenburg* was an airship that exploded; the *Maine* was blown up during the Spanish-American War; and the *Constitution* is still intact.

70. **D** France and England were not "former" allies; they were still allied with the United States after World War II.

71. **E** The Bill of Rights includes nothing about the right to vote. Voting rights are specified elsewhere in the Constitution.

72. **C** The other statements are not supported by the data shown in the graph.

73. **E** The graph does not show as steep a drop in imports after any of the other four choices as after the passage of the Intolerable Acts.

74. **A** The phrase "all men are created equal" is a quotation from the Declaration of Independence.

75. **C** The speaker of the quotation clearly opposes imperialism. The annexation of the Philippines is the only choice that the general public would have regarded as imperialist.

76. **B** The War Powers Act was passed in 1973, long after the Korean War and long before the wars in choices C and E. The United States did not participate in the Six-Day War.

77. **C** The United States did not need the permission of a foreign power to maintain a standing army in its own territory.

78. **A** Bunau-Varilla was the ruler of Panama and the person with the authority to make a treaty involving the Canal Zone with the United States.

79. **C** The speaker clearly is referring to a war memorial, and there are no names carved on the Tomb of the Unknown Soldier because it is a memorial to unidentified soldiers.

80. **E** McNamara was secretary of defense in the administration of Lyndon B. Johnson. The other four choices were members of the Nixon White House that was responsible for the scandal.

81. **E** The word "terrorists" indicates that the quotation dates from no earlier than the 1990s.

82. **A** The political bosses were in favor of city services and pushed for them as long as they could make a considerable amount of money.

83. **A** The references to "southern institutions" and "all our blood and Treasure" indicate that this quotation came from the Civil War era. The speaker worries that the effort will all be in vain. Black Codes were laws passed in the South that attempted to return African Americans to a legal status very close to slavery. The speaker would have supported the Civil Rights Act. The other choices are not as relevant.

84. **D** Clara Barton was a Civil War nurse, Mary Hayes and Deborah Sampson took part in the Revolutionary War fighting, and Tokyo Rose was a radio broadcaster during World War II.

85. **B** This was the stated aim of the Alien and Sedition Acts, although they were an infringement on American civil liberties.

86. **B** Stowe was the author of *Uncle Tom's Cabin*, which converted many people to abolitionism and aroused outrage against the system of slavery.

87. **C** The Constitution had been amended to allow direct popular election of the electors. Federalists already had served as president; African Americans and Native Americans did not have the franchise until many years later; and the first war hero to win an election was George Washington.

88. **E** Johnson's domestic program was called the Great Society because it had enormous ambitions for changing "society," that is, everyday American life, by promoting civil rights and other important programs to help the poor, the working class, and minorities.

89. **C** Whether the nation as a whole would be primarily slaveholding, primarily free, or a balance of the two was a thorny issue in Congress throughout the era specified in the question.

90. **C** France owned the Louisiana Territory, Britain owned Canada, Spain owned Mexico and Texas, and the United States owned itself.

PRACTICE TEST 1

▋ SCORE SHEET

Number of questions correct: _____

Less: 0.25 × number of questions wrong: _____

(Remember that omitted questions ares not counted as wrong.)

Raw score: _____

Raw Score	Scaled Score	Raw Score	Scaled Score	Raw Score	Scaled Score	Raw Score	Scaled Score	Raw Score	Scaled Score
90	800	65	710	40	550	15	420	−10	300
89	800	64	700	39	550	14	420	−11	290
88	800	63	700	38	540	13	410	−12	290
87	800	62	690	37	540	12	410	−13	280
86	800	61	680	36	530	11	400	−14	280
85	800	60	680	35	530	10	400	−15	270
84	800	59	670	34	520	9	390	−16	260
83	800	58	660	33	520	8	390	−17	260
82	800	57	660	32	510	7	380	−18	250
81	800	56	650	31	510	6	380	−19	240
80	790	55	640	30	500	5	370	−20	230
79	780	54	630	29	500	4	370	−21	230
78	780	53	630	28	490	3	360	−22	230
77	770	52	620	27	480	2	360		
76	760	51	620	26	480	1	350		
75	760	50	610	25	470	0	350		
74	750	49	610	24	470	−1	340		
73	750	48	600	23	460	−2	340		
72	740	47	600	22	460	−3	330		
71	740	46	590	21	450	−4	330		
70	730	45	590	20	450	−5	320		
69	730	44	580	19	440	−6	320		
68	720	43	570	18	440	−7	320		
67	720	42	560	17	430	−8	310		
66	710	41	560	16	430	−9	310		

Note: This is only a sample scoring scale. Scoring scales differ from exam to exam.

U.S. HISTORY

The following Practice Test is designed to be just like the real SAT U.S. History test. It matches the actual test in content coverage and level of difficulty.

When you are finished with the test, determine your score and carefully read the answer explanations for the questions you answered incorrectly. Identify any weak areas by determining the areas in which you made the most errors. Review those chapters of the book first. Then, as time permits, go back and review your stronger areas.

Allow 1 hour to take the test. Time yourself and work uninterrupted. If you run out of time, take note of where you ended when time ran out. Remember that you lose $\frac{1}{4}$ of a point for each incorrect answer. Because of this penalty, do not guess on a question unless you can eliminate one or more of the answers. Your score is calculated by using the following formula:

Number of correct answers $- \frac{1}{4}$ (Number of incorrect answers)

This Practice Test will be an accurate reflection of how you'll do on test day if you treat it as the real examination. Here are some hints on how to take the test under conditions similar to those of the actual examination:

- Complete the test in one sitting.
- Time yourself.
- Tear out your Answer Sheet and fill in the ovals just as you would on the actual test day.
- Become familiar with the directions to the test and the reference information provided. You'll save time on the actual test day by already being familiar with this information.

PRACTICE TEST 2
U.S. HISTORY

ANSWER SHEET

Tear out this answer sheet and use it to mark your answers.

There are 100 lines of numbered ovals on this answer sheet. If there are more lines than you need, leave the remainder blank.

1. Ⓐ Ⓑ Ⓒ Ⓓ Ⓔ	26. Ⓐ Ⓑ Ⓒ Ⓓ Ⓔ	51. Ⓐ Ⓑ Ⓒ Ⓓ Ⓔ	76. Ⓐ Ⓑ Ⓒ Ⓓ Ⓔ
2. Ⓐ Ⓑ Ⓒ Ⓓ Ⓔ	27. Ⓐ Ⓑ Ⓒ Ⓓ Ⓔ	52. Ⓐ Ⓑ Ⓒ Ⓓ Ⓔ	77. Ⓐ Ⓑ Ⓒ Ⓓ Ⓔ
3. Ⓐ Ⓑ Ⓒ Ⓓ Ⓔ	28. Ⓐ Ⓑ Ⓒ Ⓓ Ⓔ	53. Ⓐ Ⓑ Ⓒ Ⓓ Ⓔ	78. Ⓐ Ⓑ Ⓒ Ⓓ Ⓔ
4. Ⓐ Ⓑ Ⓒ Ⓓ Ⓔ	29. Ⓐ Ⓑ Ⓒ Ⓓ Ⓔ	54. Ⓐ Ⓑ Ⓒ Ⓓ Ⓔ	79. Ⓐ Ⓑ Ⓒ Ⓓ Ⓔ
5. Ⓐ Ⓑ Ⓒ Ⓓ Ⓔ	30. Ⓐ Ⓑ Ⓒ Ⓓ Ⓔ	55. Ⓐ Ⓑ Ⓒ Ⓓ Ⓔ	80. Ⓐ Ⓑ Ⓒ Ⓓ Ⓔ
6. Ⓐ Ⓑ Ⓒ Ⓓ Ⓔ	31. Ⓐ Ⓑ Ⓒ Ⓓ Ⓔ	56. Ⓐ Ⓑ Ⓒ Ⓓ Ⓔ	81. Ⓐ Ⓑ Ⓒ Ⓓ Ⓔ
7. Ⓐ Ⓑ Ⓒ Ⓓ Ⓔ	32. Ⓐ Ⓑ Ⓒ Ⓓ Ⓔ	57. Ⓐ Ⓑ Ⓒ Ⓓ Ⓔ	82. Ⓐ Ⓑ Ⓒ Ⓓ Ⓔ
8. Ⓐ Ⓑ Ⓒ Ⓓ Ⓔ	33. Ⓐ Ⓑ Ⓒ Ⓓ Ⓔ	58. Ⓐ Ⓑ Ⓒ Ⓓ Ⓔ	83. Ⓐ Ⓑ Ⓒ Ⓓ Ⓔ
9. Ⓐ Ⓑ Ⓒ Ⓓ Ⓔ	34. Ⓐ Ⓑ Ⓒ Ⓓ Ⓔ	59. Ⓐ Ⓑ Ⓒ Ⓓ Ⓔ	84. Ⓐ Ⓑ Ⓒ Ⓓ Ⓔ
10. Ⓐ Ⓑ Ⓒ Ⓓ Ⓔ	35. Ⓐ Ⓑ Ⓒ Ⓓ Ⓔ	60. Ⓐ Ⓑ Ⓒ Ⓓ Ⓔ	85. Ⓐ Ⓑ Ⓒ Ⓓ Ⓔ
11. Ⓐ Ⓑ Ⓒ Ⓓ Ⓔ	36. Ⓐ Ⓑ Ⓒ Ⓓ Ⓔ	61. Ⓐ Ⓑ Ⓒ Ⓓ Ⓔ	86. Ⓐ Ⓑ Ⓒ Ⓓ Ⓔ
12. Ⓐ Ⓑ Ⓒ Ⓓ Ⓔ	37. Ⓐ Ⓑ Ⓒ Ⓓ Ⓔ	62. Ⓐ Ⓑ Ⓒ Ⓓ Ⓔ	87. Ⓐ Ⓑ Ⓒ Ⓓ Ⓔ
13. Ⓐ Ⓑ Ⓒ Ⓓ Ⓔ	38. Ⓐ Ⓑ Ⓒ Ⓓ Ⓔ	63. Ⓐ Ⓑ Ⓒ Ⓓ Ⓔ	88. Ⓐ Ⓑ Ⓒ Ⓓ Ⓔ
14. Ⓐ Ⓑ Ⓒ Ⓓ Ⓔ	39. Ⓐ Ⓑ Ⓒ Ⓓ Ⓔ	64. Ⓐ Ⓑ Ⓒ Ⓓ Ⓔ	89. Ⓐ Ⓑ Ⓒ Ⓓ Ⓔ
15. Ⓐ Ⓑ Ⓒ Ⓓ Ⓔ	40. Ⓐ Ⓑ Ⓒ Ⓓ Ⓔ	65. Ⓐ Ⓑ Ⓒ Ⓓ Ⓔ	90. Ⓐ Ⓑ Ⓒ Ⓓ Ⓔ
16. Ⓐ Ⓑ Ⓒ Ⓓ Ⓔ	41. Ⓐ Ⓑ Ⓒ Ⓓ Ⓔ	66. Ⓐ Ⓑ Ⓒ Ⓓ Ⓔ	91. Ⓐ Ⓑ Ⓒ Ⓓ Ⓔ
17. Ⓐ Ⓑ Ⓒ Ⓓ Ⓔ	42. Ⓐ Ⓑ Ⓒ Ⓓ Ⓔ	67. Ⓐ Ⓑ Ⓒ Ⓓ Ⓔ	92. Ⓐ Ⓑ Ⓒ Ⓓ Ⓔ
18. Ⓐ Ⓑ Ⓒ Ⓓ Ⓔ	43. Ⓐ Ⓑ Ⓒ Ⓓ Ⓔ	68. Ⓐ Ⓑ Ⓒ Ⓓ Ⓔ	93. Ⓐ Ⓑ Ⓒ Ⓓ Ⓔ
19. Ⓐ Ⓑ Ⓒ Ⓓ Ⓔ	44. Ⓐ Ⓑ Ⓒ Ⓓ Ⓔ	69. Ⓐ Ⓑ Ⓒ Ⓓ Ⓔ	94. Ⓐ Ⓑ Ⓒ Ⓓ Ⓔ
20. Ⓐ Ⓑ Ⓒ Ⓓ Ⓔ	45. Ⓐ Ⓑ Ⓒ Ⓓ Ⓔ	70. Ⓐ Ⓑ Ⓒ Ⓓ Ⓔ	95. Ⓐ Ⓑ Ⓒ Ⓓ Ⓔ
21. Ⓐ Ⓑ Ⓒ Ⓓ Ⓔ	46. Ⓐ Ⓑ Ⓒ Ⓓ Ⓔ	71. Ⓐ Ⓑ Ⓒ Ⓓ Ⓔ	96. Ⓐ Ⓑ Ⓒ Ⓓ Ⓔ
22. Ⓐ Ⓑ Ⓒ Ⓓ Ⓔ	47. Ⓐ Ⓑ Ⓒ Ⓓ Ⓔ	72. Ⓐ Ⓑ Ⓒ Ⓓ Ⓔ	97. Ⓐ Ⓑ Ⓒ Ⓓ Ⓔ
23. Ⓐ Ⓑ Ⓒ Ⓓ Ⓔ	48. Ⓐ Ⓑ Ⓒ Ⓓ Ⓔ	73. Ⓐ Ⓑ Ⓒ Ⓓ Ⓔ	98. Ⓐ Ⓑ Ⓒ Ⓓ Ⓔ
24. Ⓐ Ⓑ Ⓒ Ⓓ Ⓔ	49. Ⓐ Ⓑ Ⓒ Ⓓ Ⓔ	74. Ⓐ Ⓑ Ⓒ Ⓓ Ⓔ	99. Ⓐ Ⓑ Ⓒ Ⓓ Ⓔ
25. Ⓐ Ⓑ Ⓒ Ⓓ Ⓔ	50. Ⓐ Ⓑ Ⓒ Ⓓ Ⓔ	75. Ⓐ Ⓑ Ⓒ Ⓓ Ⓔ	100. Ⓐ Ⓑ Ⓒ Ⓓ Ⓔ

PRACTICE TEST 2
Time: 60 Minutes

<u>Directions</u>: Each of the questions or incomplete statements below is followed by five suggested answers or completions. Select the one that is best in each case and then fill in the corresponding oval on the answer sheet.

1. The Reconstruction amendments affected the right to suffrage of

   (A) African-American voters
   (B) female voters
   (C) voters between the ages of 18 and 21
   (D) Native American voters
   (E) Ku Klux Klan members

2. Which of the following authors was NOT a member of the "Lost Generation"?

   (A) John Dos Passos
   (B) F. Scott Fitzgerald
   (C) Ernest Hemingway
   (D) John Steinbeck
   (E) Jack Kerouac

3. Which of the following supports the thesis that George Washington was unique among U.S. presidents?

   (A) He was from Virginia.
   (B) He was the universal choice for president among politicians of all parties.
   (C) He had served with distinction in the military.
   (D) He warned the nation against involvement in foreign wars.
   (E) He easily might easily have been elected to a third term if he had run for reelection.

4. This political cartoon alludes to an experiment with electricity performed by

   (A) Ulysses S. Grant
   (B) Benjamin Franklin
   (C) Thomas Edison
   (D) Henry Ford
   (E) Leonardo da Vinci

5. What did the Platt Amendment of 1902 establish?

   (A) U.S. sovereignty over the Panama Canal Zone
   (B) Panama's status as an independent nation
   (C) General Leonard Wood as governor of Cuba
   (D) Cuba's status as a protectorate of the United States
   (E) Puerto Ricans' status as U.S. citizens

6. What was one major purpose of the settlement-house movement of the 1880s and 1890s?

   (A) To provide day care for the young children of working parents
   (B) To lead the fight for woman suffrage
   (C) To organize a fight for racial integration in major cities
   (D) To lead rent strikes against slum landlords
   (E) To publish newspapers that revealed political graft and corruption

GO ON TO THE NEXT PAGE

PRACTICE TEST—*Continued*

7. Jackie Robinson's first appearance in a Brooklyn Dodgers uniform in 1947 struck an important blow for civil rights because he

   (A) won the first rookie of the year award after the 1947 season
   (B) brought the Negro League style of play to the major leagues for the first time
   (C) proved to thousands of fans every day that there was no legitimate reason to exclude African-American players from major league baseball
   (D) received death threats from people who believed that baseball and society should remain segregated
   (E) was honored by having his number retired by major league baseball in 1997

8. Which two painters are considered the originators of a typically American style of painting?

   (A) Diego Rivera and Grant Wood
   (B) Andy Warhol and Thomas Nast
   (C) Marcel Duchamp and Jackson Pollock
   (D) Matthew Brady and Robert Henri
   (E) Thomas Eakins and Winslow Homer

9. Which of the following journalists played a key role in the disclosure of criminal activity in the Nixon administration?

   (A) Theodore H. White
   (B) Bob Woodward
   (C) Ida Tarbell
   (D) Walter Winchell
   (E) Hunter S. Thompson

10. The Lewis and Clark expedition set out with all the following purposes EXCEPT:

    (A) finding a water route across North America to the Pacific Ocean
    (B) making accurate maps of the Louisiana Territory
    (C) establishing friendly relations with Native American tribes living in the Louisiana Territory
    (D) identifying appropriate sites for major cities to be founded and built
    (E) cataloging species of plants and animals as yet unknown in the United States

11. "Freedom has many difficulties and democracy is not perfect, but we have never had to put up a wall to keep our people in, to keep them from leaving us."

    The speaker most likely made this speech during which of the following conflicts?

    (A) World War I
    (B) World War II
    (C) Cold War
    (D) Korean War
    (E) Vietnam War

12. Martin Luther King, Jr.'s, belief in a nonviolent approach to achieving civil rights for African Americans was influenced primarily by

    (A) Buddha
    (B) John Locke
    (C) Mohandas Gandhi
    (D) Plato
    (E) Confucius

13. The huge influx of European immigrants throughout the nineteenth century helped give rise to which of the following forms of entertainment in the United States?

    (A) Opera
    (B) Baseball
    (C) Television
    (D) Tennis
    (E) Horse racing

14. All the following are included in the "Four Freedoms" President Franklin D. Roosevelt described to Congress in 1941 EXCEPT:

    (A) freedom to worship in one's own way
    (B) freedom from fear
    (C) freedom of speech and expression
    (D) freedom to overthrow a tyrannical government
    (E) freedom from want

15. Which important legal principle did Chief Justice John Marshall establish in *Marbury v. Madison*?

    (A) Presumption of innocence
    (B) Right to remain silent
    (C) Majority rule
    (D) Judicial review
    (E) Constitutional law

GO ON TO THE NEXT PAGE

PRACTICE TEST—*Continued*

16. Which nineteenth-century author created the prototype of the strong, silent American hero of fiction
and drama, who keeps his own counsel and relies
only on his own judgment?

    (A) Edgar Allan Poe
    (B) James Fenimore Cooper
    (C) Herman Melville
    (D) Walt Whitman
    (E) Nathaniel Hawthorne

17. The phrase "conspicuous consumption" was first
used to describe the upper classes during the

    (A) 1890s
    (B) 1920s
    (C) 1940s
    (D) 1960s
    (E) 1980s

18. In what way was the purchase of the Louisiana
Territory inconsistent with Thomas Jefferson's political beliefs?

    (A) He did not think it was right to take any more
        land from the Native Americans.
    (B) He did not think the United States should
        continue expanding to the west.
    (C) He believed the Constitution should be
        interpreted according to the letter.
    (D) He believed that the French would attack the
        United States after the sale of the land.
    (E) He felt it was his duty as president to take
        advantage of the opportunity to buy the land.

19. What was the immediate U.S. response to the
September 11, 2001, attacks on the World Trade
Center and the Pentagon?

    (A) An invasion of Afghanistan
    (B) An invasion of Iraq
    (C) The disbanding of the United Nations
    (D) The introduction of a military draft
    (E) The suspension of the current session of
        Congress

20. Which treaty granted the United States full
sovereignty over the Panama Canal Zone?

    (A) Treaty of Guadalupe Hidalgo
    (B) Brest-Litovsk Treaty
    (C) Treaty of Versailles
    (D) Hay–Bunau-Varilla Treaty
    (E) Treaty of Tordesillas

21. Promontory Point, Utah, is historically significant as
the site of the

    (A) realization by Lewis and Clark that there was
        no water route to the Pacific Ocean
    (B) tests for the first atomic weapons created by
        the United States
    (C) meeting of the Union Pacific and Central
        Pacific railroads
    (D) first permanent settlement built by the
        Anasazi
    (E) colony of Mormons established by Brigham
        Young and his followers

22. Which of the following was the primary cause of the
Boston Massacre?

    (A) Passage of the Stamp Act
    (B) Passage of the Sugar Act
    (C) Boston Tea Party
    (D) Revocation of the royal charter of
        Massachusetts
    (E) Installation of British troops in Boston during
        peacetime

23. To which of the following does this cartoon refer?

    (A) The purchase of Alaska by William H. Seward
    (B) The concern people in the United States felt
        over the building of the Berlin Wall
    (C) The Russian Revolution of 1917 and the
        assassination of the Russian royal family
    (D) The World War II alliance between the United
        States and the Soviet Union
    (E) The fear of Soviet communism felt by people
        in the United States during the McCarthy era

GO ON TO THE NEXT PAGE ▶

PRACTICE TEST—*Continued*

24. The Progressive movement of the early 1900s had all the following goals EXCEPT:

    (A) creating public parks and playground in cities
    (B) providing recent immigrants with an opportunity to learn English
    (C) supporting legislation against urban slum landlords
    (D) fighting for laws that would make the urban workplace safer
    (E) preventing racial segregation in American cities

25. "Our policy is directed not against any country or doctrine but against hunger, poverty, desperation and chaos. Its purpose should be the revival of a working economy in the world so as to permit the emergence of political and social conditions in which free institutions can exist."

    The speaker of this quotation most likely is referring to which of the following?

    (A) The Lend-Lease Act
    (B) The Marshall Plan
    (C) The Schlieffen Plan
    (D) The Embargo Act
    (E) The War Powers Act

26. To check the executive's power to veto a bill passed by Congress, the legislative branch of the government can

    (A) impeach the president
    (B) filibuster the veto
    (C) petition the states
    (D) amend the Constitution
    (E) override the veto

27. Which of the following did Woodrow Wilson's "Fourteen Points" speech to Congress NOT call for?

    (A) Reduction of national armaments
    (B) Return of Alsace-Lorraine to France
    (C) Formation of an association of nations
    (D) Restoration of the Russian monarchy
    (E) Freedom of navigation in international waters

28. "The survival of the fittest is simply the survival of the strong, which implies and would better be called the destruction of the weak. If nature progresses through the destruction of the weak, man progresses through the protection of the weak."

    The speaker of the above quotation most likely opposed

    (A) progressivism
    (B) Social Darwinism
    (C) Prohibition
    (D) labor unions
    (E) woman suffrage

29. Which of the following inventions was necessary to the success of the multistory skyscraper?

    (A) Giuseppe Marconi's radio telegraph
    (B) Thomas Edison's lightbulb
    (C) Elisha Otis's elevator
    (D) Henry Ford's Model-T automobile
    (E) Alexander Graham Bell's telephone

30. "Follow the money," "Deep Throat," and "expletive deleted" are all phrases associated with the

    (A) Watergate scandal that brought about the resignation of President Nixon
    (B) impeachment of President William Clinton
    (C) XYZ Affair of the Adams administration
    (D) impeachment of President Andrew Johnson
    (E) Teapot Dome scandal of the Harding administration

31. The 1921 Four-Power Treaty stated that France, Great Britain, Japan, and the United States would

    (A) respect one another's claims to territory in the Pacific
    (B) maintain navies of equal size
    (C) provide aid if any of the other three nations were attacked by a foreign power
    (D) work together to establish free trade with China
    (E) eliminate tariffs on imports from the other three nations signing the treaty

32. All the following suggest that President Theodore Roosevelt did not support the interests of large corporations EXCEPT:

    (A) He signed laws that broke up monopolies into smaller business.
    (B) He ordered an investigation into the practices of the food-processing and food-manufacturing industry.
    (C) He allowed U.S. Steel to absorb the Tennessee Coal and Iron Company during the panic of 1907.
    (D) He signed laws that gave the government the authority to regulate the railroads.
    (E) He encouraged arbitration of labor disputes.

GO ON TO THE NEXT PAGE ➡

PRACTICE TEST—*Continued*

33. Which of the following was NOT a cause of the Mexican-American War?

    (A) U.S. support of Texas in the 1836 Texas Revolution
    (B) Nonpayment of the debt owed by Mexico to the United States
    (C) Border disputes between Mexico and Texas
    (D) U.S. desire for California
    (E) The Mexican siege of the Alamo

34. Which advantage did the Union NOT have over the Confederacy at the beginning of the Civil War?

    (A) Control over the majority of the nation's industry and material resources
    (B) Location of major national railroads in Union states
    (C) Loyalty and support of the U.S. Navy
    (D) A larger population and thus a larger pool of available soldiers
    (E) Superior, more experienced military leaders

35. The late nineteenth-century revolution in industry and technology affected the nature of work in U.S. society in all the following ways EXCEPT:

    (A) Workers migrated to cities to find jobs, shifting the population.
    (B) The growth of industry meant increasing numbers of women left the workforce and returned to domestic work.
    (C) The long-distance communications industry was created.
    (D) There was an increasing division between work life and home life.
    (E) More jobs became available in the railroad industry.

36. The United States declared war on Germany directly after

    (A) sinking of the *Lusitania* by German U-boats
    (B) signing of the *Sussex* Pledge by Germany
    (C) passage of the National Defense Act of 1916
    (D) establishment of the International Red Cross Organization
    (E) publication of the Zimmerman Telegram in U.S. newspapers

37. Northerners who opposed the Civil War showed their opposition by

    (A) joining the Confederate Army
    (B) leaving the country for Canada and Great Britain
    (C) flying the Confederate flag
    (D) protesting the draft and starting antiwar riots with speeches and articles
    (E) trying to nullify the election of Abraham Lincoln to the presidency

38. Patrick Henry showed his support for the cause of independence primarily by

    (A) writing pamphlets
    (B) making speeches against the British Crown
    (C) writing the Declaration of Independence
    (D) printing seditious newspaper articles in defiance of the colonial authorities
    (E) organizing the Boston Tea Party

39. By the early 1930s, the U.S. film industry had made which of the following major changes?

    (A) From silent films to talking pictures
    (B) From black-and-white to color film
    (C) From a studio system to an independent film industry
    (D) From filming primarily in Hollywood to filming on location all over the country
    (E) From Cinemascope to Kinescope

40. "[There is] a contest between the producing classes and the money power of the country. . . . Working-men are entitled to a just proportion of the proceeds of their labor." Which of these men made this statement in 1894?

    (A) Banker J. P. Morgan
    (B) Auto manufacturer Henry Ford
    (C) Railroad owner George Pullman
    (D) Labor leader Eugene V. Debs
    (E) President Grover Cleveland

41. The economy of the antebellum South was primarily dependent on

    (A) shipping and trade
    (B) manufacturing and skilled labor
    (C) government employment
    (D) land and slaves
    (E) foreign investment

42. The Anasazi are the ancestors of which Native American nation?

    (A) Iroquois
    (B) Pueblo
    (C) Cherokee
    (D) Seminole
    (E) Choctaw

GO ON TO THE NEXT PAGE

PRACTICE TEST—*Continued*

43. The United States adopted neutrality laws in the 1930s as a response to the rise of which form of government in Europe?

    (A) Anarchy
    (B) Autocracy
    (C) Communism
    (D) Monarchy
    (E) Fascism

44. "This atrocious decision furnishes final confirmation of the already well-known fact that, under the Constitution and government of the United States, the colored people are nothing and can be nothing but an alien, disenfranchised, and degraded class."

    The speaker of the above quotation probably was reacting to which of the following Supreme Court decisions?

    (A) *Dred Scott v. Sanford*
    (B) *Powell v. Alabama*
    (C) *Korematsu v. United States*
    (D) *Sweatt v. Painter*
    (E) *Gideon v. Wainwright*

45. Which one of the following men did NOT succeed to the presidency when the president under whom he served was assassinated?

    (A) Theodore Roosevelt
    (B) Franklin D. Roosevelt
    (C) Lyndon B. Johnson
    (D) Andrew Johnson
    (E) Chester A. Arthur

46. Which of the following American regional novelists is known for his or her stories of the Great Plains states?

    (A) Willa Cather
    (B) Mark Twain
    (C) Bret Harte
    (D) Jack London
    (E) Edith Wharton

47. Brigham Young is significant in U.S. history because he

    (A) led a migration of Mormons to settle in the territory of Utah in the late 1840s
    (B) denounced the U.S. treaty with Mexico after the Alamo
    (C) led settlers to California in the 1830s
    (D) denounced the Mormon practice of polygamy
    (E) led an attack on the Ute nation in aid of non-Mormon settlers in 1857

48. Which of the following was a 1912 Olympic competitor called at the time "the greatest athlete in the world"?

    (A) Jim Brown
    (B) Jesse Owens
    (C) Bob Mathias
    (D) Jim Thorpe
    (E) Rafer Johnson

49. The emphasis of the Great Awakening of the mid-1700s was on individual salvation by

    (A) separation of church and state
    (B) predestination
    (C) faith in the absolute power of God
    (D) the nonexistence of heaven or hell
    (E) the divinity of the English monarch

50. All the following have been traditional targets of Ku Klux Klan violence EXCEPT:

    (A) African Americans
    (B) Catholics
    (C) Jews
    (D) immigrants
    (E) Lutherans

51. Which new technology had the most profound effect on U.S. society in the 1980s?

    (A) The fuel-injection engine
    (B) The SST
    (C) The *Challenger* space shuttle
    (D) The DVD player
    (E) The personal computer

52. Which quote below is from Thomas Jefferson's first inaugural address?

    (A) "We have called by different names, brethren of the same principle. We are all Republicans, we are all Federalists."
    (B) "Let me assert my firm belief that we have nothing to fear but fear itself"
    (C) "Ask not what America will do for you, but what together we can do for the freedom of man."
    (D) "Now we are engaged in a great civil war, testing whether that nation, or any nation so conceived and so dedicated can long endure."
    (E) "It is time to reawaken this industrial giant, to get government back within its means, and to lighten our punitive tax burden."

GO ON TO THE NEXT PAGE ➤

PRACTICE TEST—*Continued*

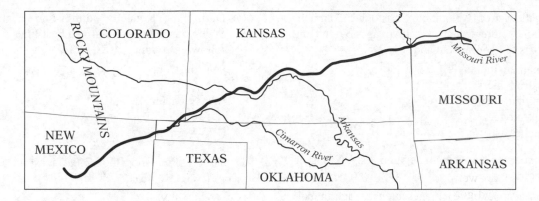

53. In 1821 William Becknell loaded a wagon with tools, clothing, and other goods and blazed the trade route shown on the map above. It is known as the

    (A) Chisholm Trail
    (B) Oregon Trail
    (C) Wilderness Road
    (D) California Road
    (E) Santa Fe Trail

54. "See to it that every man has a square deal, no less and no more" was Theodore Roosevelt's 1904 campaign promise to

    (A) map out square lots of free land in the Oklahoma Territory
    (B) limit trusts, promote public health, and improve working conditions
    (C) balance the federal budget
    (D) grant oil companies the right to buy smaller companies
    (E) institute a flat-rate income tax

55. The Supreme Court's decision in *Brown v. Board of Education* made it illegal to

    (A) have an abortion
    (B) teach evolution in public schools
    (C) segregate public schools by race
    (D) pray in a public school
    (E) recite the Pledge of Allegiance in a public school

56. The usual reaction of the stock market to a political crisis is

    (A) for the Stock Exchange to close for a week
    (B) a rise in stock prices and an increase in buying
    (C) the stoppage of payment on government bonds
    (D) a fall in stock prices and an increase in selling
    (E) an increase in foreign investment

57. "Beware, commies, spies, traitors, and foreign agents! Captain America, all loyal free men behind him, is looking for you."

    This quotation refers to a

    (A) vaudeville star
    (B) presidential radio announcement
    (C) newspaper column
    (D) radio drama
    (E) comic book superhero

58. The success of which of these nineteenth-century inventions was a direct result of the growth of the railroads?

    (A) Telephone
    (B) Automobile
    (C) Threshing machine
    (D) Telegraph
    (E) Colt revolver

59. A two-thirds majority in each house of Congress and a national convention called by Congress at the request of two-thirds of the state legislatures are the two ways of initially

    (A) proposing an amendment to the Constitution
    (B) recalling the president
    (C) ratifying an amendment to the Constitution
    (D) repealing an amendment to the Constitution
    (E) declaring war on a foreign power

GO ON TO THE NEXT PAGE ➜

PRACTICE TEST—*Continued*

60. During the Age of Exploration, Christopher Columbus and other explorers planned their voyages by studying the charts of geographers and

    (A) mathematicians
    (B) astronomers
    (C) military generals
    (D) astrologers
    (E) alchemists

61. The temperance movement began in the 1820s as an attempt to

    (A) bring about more lenient sentences for criminals
    (B) lessen the restrictions on immigration from Ireland
    (C) persuade Congress to be tolerant of Native American religious practices
    (D) bring reform to insane asylums and prisons
    (E) persuade people to limit their consumption of alcohol

62. Which of the following was NOT created or passed under the New Deal?

    (A) Works Progress Administration
    (B) Social Security Act
    (C) Civil Rights Act
    (D) Securities and Exchange Commission
    (E) Civilian Conservation Corps

63. In which state did no Civil War battles take place?

    (A) New York
    (B) Pennsylvania
    (C) Maryland
    (D) Virginia
    (E) South Carolina

64. All the following statements about the mill workers of Lowell, Massachusetts, in the 1840s are true EXCEPT:

    (A) They were strictly supervised at all times.
    (B) They worked more than 70 hours in a normal week.
    (C) Most of them came from wealthy families.
    (D) They wrote and published their own magazine.
    (E) Nearly all of them were female.

65. All the following foreign travelers to the United States wrote famous books on their observations of American society EXCEPT:

    (A) Alexis de Tocqueville
    (B) Frances Trollope
    (C) Fanny Kemble
    (D) Charles Dickens
    (E) Oscar Wilde

66. During the Kennedy administration, the United States was involved in armed hostilities with all the following countries EXCEPT:

    (A) the Congo
    (B) Laos
    (C) Vietnam
    (D) Cuba
    (E) North Korea

67. The cry "Remember the *Maine*!" is associated with the

    (A) Mexican War
    (B) Civil War
    (C) Spanish-American War
    (D) First World War
    (E) Cuban Missile Crisis

68. How did the colonists react to the passage of the Tea Act of 1773?

    (A) They tarred and feathered the stamp inspectors.
    (B) They drank only tea that had been smuggled in from Holland.
    (C) They called for the revocation of the royal charter of Massachusetts.
    (D) They began cultivating coffee since they could no longer drink tea.
    (E) They called for delegates from all the colonies to meet in Philadelphia.

69. Why did the Pony Express last for only 18 months?

    (A) Too many of the riders and horses died from exhaustion and abuse.
    (B) The mail the riders carried was too valuable to be put at constant risk of attack from robbers.
    (C) The completion of the transcontinental telegraph system made the Pony Express obsolete.
    (D) The mail service became too expensive for the owners to continue with it.
    (E) The Civil War put an end to all mail service in the United States.

GO ON TO THE NEXT PAGE →

PRACTICE TEST—*Continued*

70. What was the purpose of the colonial committees of correspondence?

   (A) To keep the public informed of British violations of colonial rights
   (B) To maintain a mail-delivery service among the 13 colonies
   (C) To write letters to Parliament protesting the unpopular measures it passed
   (D) To circulate anonymous letters accusing specific British officials of crimes
   (E) To convene a national convention of delegates to discuss colonial independence from Britain

71. The impact of the Smoot-Hawley Tariff of 1930 was

   (A) a reduction of the tariff on imports from Germany that caused public outrage
   (B) a lower duty on Canadian goods that caused hard times in the Great Lakes states
   (C) high tariffs that contributed to a global economic downturn in the 1930s
   (D) an export tax on tobacco
   (E) higher salaries for senators

72. "The Star-Spangled Banner" was composed during the War of 1812 and celebrates the survival of

   (A) Fort Ticonderoga in New York
   (B) Fort Duquesne in western Pennsylvania
   (C) Fort McHenry in Maryland
   (D) Fort Sumter in South Carolina
   (E) Fort Vincennes in Ohio

73. The term "dogfights" refers to what kind of fighting in what war?

   (A) Hand-to-hand combat in Korea
   (B) Naval skirmishes in the War of 1812
   (C) Canine corps actions by Germany and the United States in World War II
   (D) Jungle battles in the Spanish-American War
   (E) Aerial combat in World War I

74. Dwight D. Eisenhower was elected President in 1952 on his promises to

   (A) boost the economy, reform government, and end the Korean War
   (B) bring peace to Europe and end the Great Depression
   (C) establish a United Nations and abolish the income tax
   (D) stop the growth of labor unions and attack communist Cuba
   (E) implement the Great Society and sign an alliance with the Soviet Union

75. President Jimmy Carter created the Department of Energy in 1977 primarily in response to the

   (A) depletion of U.S. coal resources
   (B) growth of kerosene as a heat source
   (C) surplus of electrical power
   (D) popularity of nuclear power plants
   (E) skyrocketing price of foreign oil

76. All the following were activists for the ratification of the Nineteenth Amendment EXCEPT:

   (A) Harriet Stanton Blatch
   (B) Harriet Beecher Stowe
   (C) Susan B. Anthony
   (D) Carrie Chapman Catt
   (E) Alice Paul

77. The American colonists dubbed all the following measures of Parliament the "Intolerable Acts" EXCEPT:

   (A) the Administration of Justice Act
   (B) the Boston Port Act
   (C) the Massachusetts Government Act
   (D) the Quartering Act
   (E) the Stamp Act

78. All the following are Mesoamerican cultures EXCEPT:

   (A) the Aztec
   (B) the Olmec
   (C) the Maya
   (D) the Toltec
   (E) the Sioux

79. The Monroe Doctrine states that the United States will

   (A) not allow any European power to colonize U.S. territory
   (B) view any attempt to colonize Latin America as hostile toward the United States
   (C) encourage Latin American colonies to rebel against their European mother countries
   (D) actively support Latin American revolutions and wars for independence
   (E) support European powers that want to colonize Latin America

GO ON TO THE NEXT PAGE

PRACTICE TEST—*Continued*

80. What caused the United States to agree to sign the Atlantic Charter with Great Britain in 1940?

    (A) Germany's conquest of Belgium and France
    (B) Germany's invasion of Austria
    (C) Hitler's rise to power in Germany
    (D) Mussolini's rise to power in Italy
    (E) Switzerland's declaration of neutrality

81. Which source would give a historian the most accurate information about race relations in the Mississippi Valley in the years after the Civil War?

    (A) A copy of *The Adventures of Huckleberry Finn* by Mark Twain
    (B) The song lyrics of Stephen Foster
    (C) The diary of the governor of Arkansas during that period
    (D) Tax rolls of the region
    (E) Records of local and state laws of the region

82. Which of the following was an important cultural symbol of the 1920s?

    (A) Bathtub gin
    (B) Bread lines
    (C) Rosie the Riveter
    (D) Bomb shelters
    (E) Poodle skirts

83. This political cartoon most likely dates from

    (A) 1776
    (B) 1788
    (C) 1861
    (D) 1865
    (E) 1918

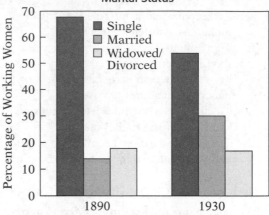

Percentage of Working Women, 1890 and 1930, by Marital Status

84. Which of the following statements is supported by the graph?

    (A) The number of divorced women in the United States fell between 1890 and 1930.
    (B) There were more married women in the United States in 1890 than in 1930.
    (C) The percentage of working women who were single fell over time, whereas the percentage of working women who were married rose.
    (D) In 1930 most working women were or had once been married.
    (E) In 1890 the majority of the female population of the United States was unmarried.

85. What does the rise in U.S. manufacturing during the War of 1812 suggest about that war's effect on the U.S. economy?

    (A) The economy prospered as people in the United States became less dependent on imports.
    (B) The economy plummeted as trade levels fell to record lows.
    (C) The economy began shifting from agriculture to manufacturing.
    (D) The economy became dependent on the health of the national bank and the stock market.
    (E) The economy suffered from a rise in imports and a lack of markets for exports.

GO ON TO THE NEXT PAGE →

PRACTICE TEST—*Continued*

86. Which colony wrote the 1776 resolution stating that "these united colonies, are, and of right ought to be, free and independent states"?

    (A) Massachusetts
    (B) Pennsylvania
    (C) Rhode Island
    (D) New York
    (E) Virginia

87. The Proclamation of 1763 required which of the following?

    (A) That fur traders obtain permission before settling in the territory west of the Appalachian Mountains
    (B) That no Native Americans be permitted to settle along the colonial frontier
    (C) That Britain give up control of all the land between the Atlantic coast and the Mississippi River
    (D) That France give up Haiti to Britain
    (E) That Spain give up its North American colonies to Britain

88. Why did the Iroquois decide to throw their support behind Britain near the end of the French and Indian War?

    (A) The British had treated the Iroquois better than the French had treated them.
    (B) The Iroquois felt some personal loyalty to the British.
    (C) The Iroquois accurately predicted that the British would win the war, and they did not want to side with the losers.
    (D) The Iroquois had planned all along to betray the French at a strategic moment.
    (E) The Iroquois were determined to drive the French out of Canada.

89. Which region of the country did NOT vote heavily for Abraham Lincoln in the election of 1860?

    (A) Southeast
    (B) Great Lakes
    (C) Northeast
    (D) Pacific Coast
    (E) Mid-Atlantic

90. At the time of the Louisiana Purchase, all the following countries claimed territory in North America EXCEPT:

    (A) France
    (B) Great Britain
    (C) Holland
    (D) Spain
    (E) United States

S T O P

IF YOU FINISH BEFORE TIME RUNS OUT, GO BACK AND CHECK YOUR WORK.

ANSWER KEY

1. A	21. C	41. D	61. E	81. E
2. E	22. E	42. B	62. C	82. A
3. B	23. A	43. E	63. A	83. B
4. B	24. E	44. A	64. C	84. C
5. D	25. B	45. B	65. E	85. A
6. A	26. E	46. A	66. E	86. E
7. C	27. D	47. A	67. C	87. A
8. E	28. B	48. D	68. B	88. C
9. B	29. C	49. C	69. C	89. A
10. D	30. A	50. E	70. A	90. C
11. C	31. A	51. E	71. C	
12. C	32. C	52. A	72. C	
13. A	33. E	53. E	73. E	
14. D	34. E	54. B	74. A	
15. D	35. B	55. C	75. E	
16. B	36. E	56. D	76. B	
17. A	37. D	57. E	77. E	
18. C	38. B	58. D	78. E	
19. A	39. A	59. C	79. B	
20. D	40. D	60. B	80. A	

ANSWERS AND EXPLANATIONS

1. **A** The Thirteenth, Fourteenth, and Fifteenth Amendments, known as the Reconstruction Amendments, attempted to ensure that newly freed slavers in the South had certain constitutionally protected rights. The Fifteenth Amendment states that, "The rights of citizens of the United States to vote shall not be denied or abridged by the United States or by any State on account of race, color, or previous condition of servitude."

2. **E** Kerouac was a member of the Beat Generation of the late 1950s–early 1960s.

3. **B** The other four choices describe other presidents besides Washington, but only Washington was the universal choice as the leader of all politicians of his day.

4. **B** Benjamin Franklin was nearly electrocuted when lightning struck a key he tied to a kite he flew during a thunderstorm in his famous experiment.

5. **D** The Platt Amendment is an amendment to Cuba's constitution, not to the U.S., Puerto Rican, or Panamanian constitution.

6. **A** Settlement houses were not hotbeds of political activity, but they tried to accomplish practical good on a neighborhood level.

7. **C** All five statements are true, but only choice C describes Robinson's important contribution to civil rights. Baseball was watched and listened to on radio by millions every day, and Robinson's example made it clear to them that an African American was the equal of a white man on the playing field and by implication everywhere else.

8. **E** Some of the other choices are either not American (Rivera and Duchamp) or not painters (Brady and Nast). Homer and Eakins are known for proving by example that American painting did not have to echo the European past.

9. **B** Bob Woodward and Carl Bernstein were the *Washington Post* reporters who followed the story of the Watergate break-in all the way to the end. The other journalists had no association with Watergate.

10. **D** Lewis and Clark and their party were not concerned with establishing cities on the plains of the Midwest.

11. **C** The reference to the Berlin Wall indicates that the speech was made during the Cold War.

12. **C** Gandhi famously led the citizens of India to independence from Britain by using nonviolent resistance. King adopted Gandhi's ideas and methods.

13. **A** To Europeans, opera was popular entertainment in their own languages. Many had been professional musicians in Europe and helped establish symphonic music and opera as professional entertainments in the United States.

14. **D** The Four Freedoms do not include the freedom to rise up against tyranny.

15. **D** Marshall set the precedent for judicial review by declaring the Judiciary Act of 1801 unconstitutional. That became an important judicial check on the legislative branch.

16. **B** Cooper's hero Hawkeye/Deerslayer/Natty Bumppo was the prototype of the strong, silent, self-reliant American hero familiar to movie audiences throughout the twentieth century and to readers of Hemingway and many other fiction writers.

17. **A** The social historian Thorstein Veblen coined this phrase in 1899 in *Theory of the Leisure Classes*.

18. **C** Jefferson believed in strict construction of the Constitution, and that document did not explicitly give the president the authority to enlarge the nation. Therefore, his purchase of the Louisiana Territory was inconsistent with his beliefs.

19. **A** The United States invaded Afghanistan in the belief that Osama bin Ladin, head of a terrorist cell, had been responsible for the attacks and would be found and captured there. The U.S. also wanted to remove Afghanistan's Taliban government, which had provided support to al-Qaeda.

20. **D** Guadalupe-Hidalgo ended the Mexican-American War (1848). Brest-Litovsk ended Russia's participation in World War I (1918), and the Treaty of Versailles (1919) officially ended World War I. The Treaty of Tordesillas (1494) divided South America between the Spanish and Portuguese.

21. **C** The Union Pacific and Central Pacific railroads, whose builders were working from opposite directions, met at Promontory Point in 1869 to create the first transcontinental railroad.

22. **E** The Boston Massacre took place because Bostonians resented the presence in their city of a standing army during peacetime.

23. **A** The two men in the cartoon are William Seward and President Andrew Johnson. They are taking a huge chunk of ice with them to "cool down" congressional opposition to the purchase of Alaska.

24. **E** The Progressives as a group had no intention of trying to prevent racial segregation in American cities.

25. **B** The quotation clearly refers to a worldwide aid program, which matches the description of the Marshall Plan.

26. **E** A two-thirds vote is required to override a presidential veto.

27. **D** The Fourteen Points do not call for reversing the Russian Revolution.

28. **B** Social Darwinism applies the biological survival of the fittest to civilized society. The speaker of the quotation opposes this theory, suggesting rather that human beings have the responsibility to help those who are weak.

29. **C** Without elevators, people had to walk upstairs; people would not walk up more than about five or six flights. To make taller buildings practical for use, the elevator was essential.

30. **A** Choice A is correct; "follow the money" was the advice of "Deep Throat," the anonymous source of information that led to the disclosure of criminal activity in the Nixon White House. "Expletive deleted" refers to obscene language deleted from Nixon's tape-recorded conversations.

31. **A** The Four-Power Treaty was an agreement to respect territorial claims in the Pacific.

32. **C** In 1907, E. H. Gary and H. C. Frick met privately with Theodore Roosevelt and convinced him to allow U.S. Steel to absorb the Tennessee Coal and Iron Company in violation of the Sherman Anti-Trust Act. Four years later, President William Taft's administration filed antitrust action against U.S. Steel when it became apparent that Roosevelt had been too accommodating to corporate interests.

33. **E** The siege of the Alamo long predated the Mexican War and was not a cause of it.

34. **E** Confederate military leaders were initially more gifted in tactics, strategy, and leadership than were their Union counterparts.

35. **B** Between 1870 and 1900, the number of American women grew by half, but the number in wage-earning jobs jumped by almost two-thirds.

36. **E** The Zimmerman Telegram was the last straw that swung U.S. public opinion against Germany enough for a declaration of war.

37. **D** Northerners who disagreed with the war protested the war.

38. **B** Patrick Henry is best known for his "Give me liberty or give me death" speech in the Virginia House of Burgesses.

39. **A** The other major changes in motion pictures happened at a later time. The conversion from silents to talkies occurred around the end of the 1920s.

40. **D** It is clear that the speaker supported labor, not management, and of the five choices, only Debs would have taken that position.

41. **D** The South depended on forced labor to cultivate and harvest its cotton and rice crops.

42. **B** The Anasazi settled originally at the Four Corners and then moved south and eventually became known as the Pueblo, a nation made up of the Zuñi and other Southwestern tribes.

43. **E** The neutrality laws were a response to the threat of war in Europe caused by the rise of fascist governments in Germany and Italy.

44. **A** The quotation clearly refers to a case decided against an African American. The other four choices either did not involve the issue of race or were decided in favor of African Americans.

45. **B** Franklin D. Roosevelt succeeded Herbert Hoover, who was not assassinated.

46. **A** Twain wrote about the Mississippi Valley, Wharton about New York City, Harte about the West, and London about the Northwest. Cather's stories are set in the heart of the "bread basket" section of the country, such as her native Nebraska.

47. **A** Brigham Young is famous as the leader of the Mormons.

48. **D** The Native American track star Jim Thorpe was widely considered one of the greatest athletes in history.

49. **C** The Great Awakening was radical because it contradicted the Puritan belief that salvation was predestined. It suggested instead that people could be "born again" and choose to save themselves through their faith.

50. **E** The Ku Klux Klan is a white-supremacist group that does not consider mainstream Protestants a target population.

51. **E** The other technologies listed either predate or postdate the 1980s.

52. **A** The reference to Republicans and Federalists shows that this must have been spoken by Jefferson.

53. **E** The Santa Fe Trail led to the Southwest, as shown on the map.

54. **B** Roosevelt was promising to be fair to all the voters, especially the working people of the United States.

55. **C** *Brown* is famous as the decision that did away with the concept of "separate but equal" status for African Americans and everyone else.

56. **D** During any national crisis, people panic and want to sell their stocks. Since the supply of available stocks rises rapidly, the price falls.

57. **E** Captain America was a comic book character who first appeared in 1941.

58. **D** The railroad made the telegraph possible. The railroad carried people to distant locations, thus creating a need for long-distance communication and also sending people out to string the telegraph wires and build and staff the telegraph offices.

59. **C** There are two ways to ratify an amendment to the Constitution, both of which are described accurately in this choice.

60. **B** Sailors used the position of the stars at night to navigate.

61. **E** The word "temperance" in the context of politics and social history specifically refers to alcohol consumption.

62. **C** Civil rights acts were passed during the administrations of Andrew Johnson, Ulysses Grant, Dwight Eisenhower and Lyndon B. Johnson, not Franklin D. Roosevelt.

63. **A** The Confederate Army did not penetrate the Union any farther north than Pennsylvania.

64. **C** The mill workers in Lowell in the 1840s did publish a magazine, they were strictly supervised, they were almost all female, and they did work more than 70 hours a week. However, most of them were from poor families.

65. **E** Tocqueville's *Democracy in America*, Trollope's *Domestic Manners of the Americans*, Dickens's *American Notes for General Circulation*, and Fanny Kemble's *Journal* all famously document the travelers' experiences of the United States. Wilde traveled to the United States but did not write about his journey.

66. **E** The Korean War ended several years before Kennedy became president.

67. **C** When the *Maine* was mysteriously blown up, Hearst newspapers used "Remember the *Maine*!" as a rallying cry in favor of the war.

68. **B** The immediate colonial response was to boycott East India tea and drink only smuggled Dutch tea.

69. **C** The Pony Express service had been advertised as the fastest available, but the telegraph transmitted messages instantaneously.

70. **A** The task of the committees was to correspond with similar committees in other colonies so that the general public would be aware of British abuses of colonial rights.

71. **C** The Smoot-Hawley Tariff of 1930 reduced trade and contributed to a global economic downturn in the following decade.

72. **C** Francis Scott Key watched the Battle of Ft. McHenry, which inspired him to write the words to the national anthem.

73. **E** The term "dogfights" refers to aerial combat between fighter planes used by both sides in World War I.

74. **A** Dwight D. Eisenhower was elected president in 1952 on his promises to boost the economy, reform government, and end the Korean War.

75. **E** Gasoline rationing in response to higher oil prices is a famous event of the Carter presidency.

76. **B** Harriet Beecher Stowe is famous for being the author of *Uncle Tom's Cabin,* not for her activity in support of woman suffrage.

77. **E** The Stamp Act had been passed and repealed well before the passage of the Intolerable Acts. Those were passed in response to the Boston Tea Party.

78. **E** The Mesoamerican cultures were the first civilizations established in the Americas. The Sioux were not among those civilizations.

79. **B** The Monroe Doctrine states that the United States will remain neutral between the European powers and any of their present Latin American colonies but will regard any further attempt at colonization in the western hemisphere as an attack on itself.

80. **A** The Atlantic Charter was signed after the German Army invaded and conquered Belgium and then France.

81. **E** The other choices would all give some insight into the question, but the laws of the time and place would provide the most accurate data on the status of the races.

82. **A** Breadlines symbolize the 1930s, Rosie the Riveter the 1940s, and bomb shelters and poodle skirts the 1950s. "Bathtub gin" came into existence because of Prohibition, which was in force throughout the 1920s.

83. **B** The cartoon shows the colonies ratifying the Constitution and thus achieving statehood in chronological order, beginning with Delaware. Therefore, the correct date is clearly the one after the Revolutionary War and before the Civil War and World War I.

84. **C** Choice C is the only one supported by the bar graph. The graph does not deal with all U.S. women but specifically with working women.

85. **A** It is logical to assume that if domestic manufacturing rises, imports will fall, and therefore the economy will be less dependent on them. Money spent will be spent on domestic products; therefore, it will remain in the country, and the domestic economy will profit.

86. **E** Richard Henry Lee of Virginia proposed this House of Burgesses resolution to Congress in June 1776.

87. **A** The Proclamation of 1763 ended the French and Indian War, stripped France of its claims to lands east of the Mississippi, and stated that only Native Americans could settle that land.

88. **C** The Native Americans felt no personal loyalty to either side. They acted in what they believed to be their own best interests, choosing to side with the winner.

89. **A** John Breckenridge won all the states of the deep South, including the Southeast. In most of the South, Abraham Lincoln was not even on the ballot.

90. **C** France owned the Louisiana Territory, Britain owned Canada, Spain owned Mexico and Texas, and the United States owned itself.

■ SCORE SHEET

Number of questions correct: _____

Less: 0.25 × number of questions wrong: _____

(Remember that omitted questions ares not counted as wrong.)

Raw score: _____

Raw Score	Scaled Score	Raw Score	Scaled Score	Raw Score	Scaled Score	Raw Score	Scaled Score	Raw Score	Scaled Score
90	800	65	710	40	550	15	420	−10	300
89	800	64	700	39	550	14	420	−11	290
88	800	63	700	38	540	13	410	−12	290
87	800	62	690	37	540	12	410	−13	280
86	800	61	680	36	530	11	400	−14	280
85	800	60	680	35	530	10	400	−15	270
84	800	59	670	34	520	9	390	−16	260
83	800	58	660	33	520	8	390	−17	260
82	800	57	660	32	510	7	380	−18	250
81	800	56	650	31	510	6	380	−19	240
80	790	55	640	30	500	5	370	−20	230
79	780	54	630	29	500	4	370	−21	230
78	780	53	630	28	490	3	360	−22	230
77	770	52	620	27	480	2	360		
76	760	51	620	26	480	1	350		
75	760	50	610	25	470	0	350		
74	750	49	610	24	470	−1	340		
73	750	48	600	23	460	−2	340		
72	740	47	600	22	460	−3	330		
71	740	46	590	21	450	−4	330		
70	730	45	590	20	450	−5	320		
69	730	44	580	19	440	−6	320		
68	720	43	570	18	440	−7	320		
67	720	42	560	17	430	−8	310		
66	710	41	560	16	430	−9	310		

Note: This is only a sample scoring scale. Scoring scales differ from exam to exam.

PRACTICE TEST 3
U.S. HISTORY

The following Practice Test is designed to be just like the real SAT U.S. History test. It matches the actual test in content coverage and level of difficulty.

When you are finished with the test, determine your score and carefully read the answer explanations for the questions you answered incorrectly. Identify any weak areas by determining the areas in which you made the most errors. Review those chapters of the book first. Then, as time permits, go back and review your stronger areas.

Allow 1 hour to take the test. Time yourself and work uninterrupted. If you run out of time, take note of where you ended when time ran out. Remember that you lose $\frac{1}{4}$ of a point for each incorrect answer. Because of this penalty, do not guess on a question unless you can eliminate one or more of the answers. Your score is calculated by using the following formula:

$$\text{Number of correct answers} - \frac{1}{4}(\text{Number of incorrect answers})$$

This Practice Test will be an accurate reflection of how you'll do on test day if you treat it as the real examination. Here are some hints on how to take the test under conditions similar to those of the actual examination:

- Complete the test in one sitting.
- Time yourself.
- Tear out your Answer Sheet and fill in the ovals just as you would on the actual test day.
- Become familiar with the directions to the test and the reference information provided. You'll save time on the actual test day by already being familiar with this information.

PRACTICE TEST 3
U.S. HISTORY

ANSWER SHEET

Tear out this answer sheet and use it to mark your answers.

There are 100 lines of numbered ovals on this answer sheet. If there are more lines than you need, leave the remainder blank.

1. Ⓐ Ⓑ Ⓒ Ⓓ Ⓔ	26. Ⓐ Ⓑ Ⓒ Ⓓ Ⓔ	51. Ⓐ Ⓑ Ⓒ Ⓓ Ⓔ	76. Ⓐ Ⓑ Ⓒ Ⓓ Ⓔ
2. Ⓐ Ⓑ Ⓒ Ⓓ Ⓔ	27. Ⓐ Ⓑ Ⓒ Ⓓ Ⓔ	52. Ⓐ Ⓑ Ⓒ Ⓓ Ⓔ	77. Ⓐ Ⓑ Ⓒ Ⓓ Ⓔ
3. Ⓐ Ⓑ Ⓒ Ⓓ Ⓔ	28. Ⓐ Ⓑ Ⓒ Ⓓ Ⓔ	53. Ⓐ Ⓑ Ⓒ Ⓓ Ⓔ	78. Ⓐ Ⓑ Ⓒ Ⓓ Ⓔ
4. Ⓐ Ⓑ Ⓒ Ⓓ Ⓔ	29. Ⓐ Ⓑ Ⓒ Ⓓ Ⓔ	54. Ⓐ Ⓑ Ⓒ Ⓓ Ⓔ	79. Ⓐ Ⓑ Ⓒ Ⓓ Ⓔ
5. Ⓐ Ⓑ Ⓒ Ⓓ Ⓔ	30. Ⓐ Ⓑ Ⓒ Ⓓ Ⓔ	55. Ⓐ Ⓑ Ⓒ Ⓓ Ⓔ	80. Ⓐ Ⓑ Ⓒ Ⓓ Ⓔ
6. Ⓐ Ⓑ Ⓒ Ⓓ Ⓔ	31. Ⓐ Ⓑ Ⓒ Ⓓ Ⓔ	56. Ⓐ Ⓑ Ⓒ Ⓓ Ⓔ	81. Ⓐ Ⓑ Ⓒ Ⓓ Ⓔ
7. Ⓐ Ⓑ Ⓒ Ⓓ Ⓔ	32. Ⓐ Ⓑ Ⓒ Ⓓ Ⓔ	57. Ⓐ Ⓑ Ⓒ Ⓓ Ⓔ	82. Ⓐ Ⓑ Ⓒ Ⓓ Ⓔ
8. Ⓐ Ⓑ Ⓒ Ⓓ Ⓔ	33. Ⓐ Ⓑ Ⓒ Ⓓ Ⓔ	58. Ⓐ Ⓑ Ⓒ Ⓓ Ⓔ	83. Ⓐ Ⓑ Ⓒ Ⓓ Ⓔ
9. Ⓐ Ⓑ Ⓒ Ⓓ Ⓔ	34. Ⓐ Ⓑ Ⓒ Ⓓ Ⓔ	59. Ⓐ Ⓑ Ⓒ Ⓓ Ⓔ	84. Ⓐ Ⓑ Ⓒ Ⓓ Ⓔ
10. Ⓐ Ⓑ Ⓒ Ⓓ Ⓔ	35. Ⓐ Ⓑ Ⓒ Ⓓ Ⓔ	60. Ⓐ Ⓑ Ⓒ Ⓓ Ⓔ	85. Ⓐ Ⓑ Ⓒ Ⓓ Ⓔ
11. Ⓐ Ⓑ Ⓒ Ⓓ Ⓔ	36. Ⓐ Ⓑ Ⓒ Ⓓ Ⓔ	61. Ⓐ Ⓑ Ⓒ Ⓓ Ⓔ	86. Ⓐ Ⓑ Ⓒ Ⓓ Ⓔ
12. Ⓐ Ⓑ Ⓒ Ⓓ Ⓔ	37. Ⓐ Ⓑ Ⓒ Ⓓ Ⓔ	62. Ⓐ Ⓑ Ⓒ Ⓓ Ⓔ	87. Ⓐ Ⓑ Ⓒ Ⓓ Ⓔ
13. Ⓐ Ⓑ Ⓒ Ⓓ Ⓔ	38. Ⓐ Ⓑ Ⓒ Ⓓ Ⓔ	63. Ⓐ Ⓑ Ⓒ Ⓓ Ⓔ	88. Ⓐ Ⓑ Ⓒ Ⓓ Ⓔ
14. Ⓐ Ⓑ Ⓒ Ⓓ Ⓔ	39. Ⓐ Ⓑ Ⓒ Ⓓ Ⓔ	64. Ⓐ Ⓑ Ⓒ Ⓓ Ⓔ	89. Ⓐ Ⓑ Ⓒ Ⓓ Ⓔ
15. Ⓐ Ⓑ Ⓒ Ⓓ Ⓔ	40. Ⓐ Ⓑ Ⓒ Ⓓ Ⓔ	65. Ⓐ Ⓑ Ⓒ Ⓓ Ⓔ	90. Ⓐ Ⓑ Ⓒ Ⓓ Ⓔ
16. Ⓐ Ⓑ Ⓒ Ⓓ Ⓔ	41. Ⓐ Ⓑ Ⓒ Ⓓ Ⓔ	66. Ⓐ Ⓑ Ⓒ Ⓓ Ⓔ	91. Ⓐ Ⓑ Ⓒ Ⓓ Ⓔ
17. Ⓐ Ⓑ Ⓒ Ⓓ Ⓔ	42. Ⓐ Ⓑ Ⓒ Ⓓ Ⓔ	67. Ⓐ Ⓑ Ⓒ Ⓓ Ⓔ	92. Ⓐ Ⓑ Ⓒ Ⓓ Ⓔ
18. Ⓐ Ⓑ Ⓒ Ⓓ Ⓔ	43. Ⓐ Ⓑ Ⓒ Ⓓ Ⓔ	68. Ⓐ Ⓑ Ⓒ Ⓓ Ⓔ	93. Ⓐ Ⓑ Ⓒ Ⓓ Ⓔ
19. Ⓐ Ⓑ Ⓒ Ⓓ Ⓔ	44. Ⓐ Ⓑ Ⓒ Ⓓ Ⓔ	69. Ⓐ Ⓑ Ⓒ Ⓓ Ⓔ	94. Ⓐ Ⓑ Ⓒ Ⓓ Ⓔ
20. Ⓐ Ⓑ Ⓒ Ⓓ Ⓔ	45. Ⓐ Ⓑ Ⓒ Ⓓ Ⓔ	70. Ⓐ Ⓑ Ⓒ Ⓓ Ⓔ	95. Ⓐ Ⓑ Ⓒ Ⓓ Ⓔ
21. Ⓐ Ⓑ Ⓒ Ⓓ Ⓔ	46. Ⓐ Ⓑ Ⓒ Ⓓ Ⓔ	71. Ⓐ Ⓑ Ⓒ Ⓓ Ⓔ	96. Ⓐ Ⓑ Ⓒ Ⓓ Ⓔ
22. Ⓐ Ⓑ Ⓒ Ⓓ Ⓔ	47. Ⓐ Ⓑ Ⓒ Ⓓ Ⓔ	72. Ⓐ Ⓑ Ⓒ Ⓓ Ⓔ	97. Ⓐ Ⓑ Ⓒ Ⓓ Ⓔ
23. Ⓐ Ⓑ Ⓒ Ⓓ Ⓔ	48. Ⓐ Ⓑ Ⓒ Ⓓ Ⓔ	73. Ⓐ Ⓑ Ⓒ Ⓓ Ⓔ	98. Ⓐ Ⓑ Ⓒ Ⓓ Ⓔ
24. Ⓐ Ⓑ Ⓒ Ⓓ Ⓔ	49. Ⓐ Ⓑ Ⓒ Ⓓ Ⓔ	74. Ⓐ Ⓑ Ⓒ Ⓓ Ⓔ	99. Ⓐ Ⓑ Ⓒ Ⓓ Ⓔ
25. Ⓐ Ⓑ Ⓒ Ⓓ Ⓔ	50. Ⓐ Ⓑ Ⓒ Ⓓ Ⓔ	75. Ⓐ Ⓑ Ⓒ Ⓓ Ⓔ	100. Ⓐ Ⓑ Ⓒ Ⓓ Ⓔ

PRACTICE TEST 3
Time: 60 Minutes

Directions: Each of the questions or incomplete statements below is followed by five suggested answers or completions. Select the one that is best in each case and then fill in the corresponding oval on the answer sheet.

1. The civil rights leader Martin Luther King, Jr., advocated and practiced nonviolent protests in the manner of

   (A) David Duke
   (B) Mahatma Gandhi
   (C) Golda Meir
   (D) Toussaint L'Ouverture
   (E) David Ben-Gurion

2. American colonists opposed the Tea Act for all the following reasons EXCEPT:

   (A) the high price of tea from the East India Company compared to other tea available in America
   (B) the tax added to the price of the East India tea
   (C) the advantage the Tea Act gave to British merchants over colonial ones
   (D) the fact that they had never voted on the Tea Act
   (E) the belief that if they accepted the East India tea, Parliament would begin taxing other products

3. The map below shows the route of the

   (A) Oregon Trail
   (B) Wilderness Road
   (C) Pony Express
   (D) Trail of Tears
   (E) Union Pacific railroad

4. The Missouri Compromise proposed that

   (A) the United States remain evenly balanced between slaveholding states and free states
   (B) slavery would be allowed only in territories and states south of the northern border of Missouri
   (C) the slave trade would end permanently, but slaveholding states would not have to change their status
   (D) all slaves would be emancipated, but would continue working on plantations for wages
   (E) plantation owners could keep their slaves but would sign legal agreements to treat them humanely

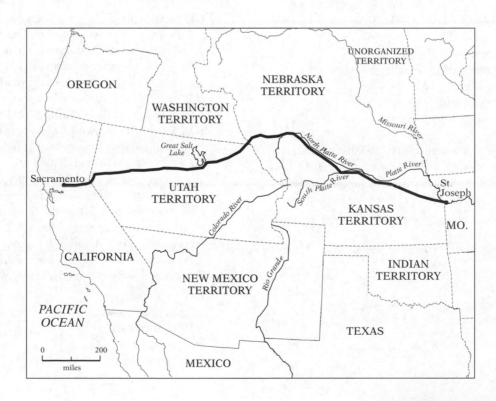

GO ON TO THE NEXT PAGE

PRACTICE TEST—*Continued*

5. "... if I had thought of it at all I would have thought of it as a thing that merely *happened*, the end of some inevitable chain. It never occurred to me that one man could start to play with the faith of fifty million people—with the single-mindedness of a burglar blowing a safe."

   Author F. Scott Fitzgerald was referring to the

   (A) outbreak of the Civil War
   (B) bombing of Pearl Harbor
   (C) break-in at the Democratic national headquarters in the Watergate buildings
   (D) assassination of President John F. Kennedy
   (E) fixing of the 1919 World Series

6. The Northwest Territory included which present-day states?

   (A) Oregon and Washington
   (B) Colorado, Wyoming, Arizona, and New Mexico
   (C) Wisconsin, Michigan, Illinois, Indiana, and Ohio
   (D) Idaho, Montana, South Dakota, and North Dakota
   (E) Maine, New Hampshire, and Vermont

7. The *Federalist Papers* were written to persuade people to support the ratification of the

   (A) Constitution
   (B) Declaration of Independence
   (C) Bill of Rights
   (D) Treaty of Paris
   (E) Northwest Ordinance

8. "I have here in my hand a list of 205 that were known to the Secretary of State as being members of the Communist Party and who nevertheless are still working and shaping the policy of the State Department."

   This statement began a brief period in U.S. history that became known for

   (A) reform
   (B) Reconstruction
   (C) McCarthyism
   (D) Watergate
   (E) Reaganomics

9. Which major legal precedent was established in the Supreme Court case *Marbury v. Madison?*

   (A) An accused person would be presumed innocent until proved guilty.
   (B) The United Sates would fight in the defense of any Latin American nation being attacked or invaded by an outside power.
   (C) A president would not be allowed to declare war on a foreign nation without the consent of Congress.
   (D) The Supreme Court would have the right to decide whether a law was constitutional and to strike it down if it was not.
   (E) Any person accused of a crime would have the right to refuse to testify in court.

10. Elizabeth Cady Stanton, Carrie Chapman Catt, and Alice Paul are all famous for leading the fight for

    (A) temperance
    (B) Prohibition
    (C) woman suffrage
    (D) civil rights
    (E) education reform

11. The "Hollywood Ten" were

    (A) scriptwriters who were blacklisted in Hollywood for refusing to answer questions posed by the House Un-American Activities Committee
    (B) California beatniks who refused to obey laws against selling and smoking marijuana
    (C) actors and actresses who appeared in propaganda films during World War II
    (D) movie-studio owners who conspired to run their industry on a system of indentured servitude of the performers
    (E) movie-studio technicians who led a famous labor strike that resulted in better wages and working hours across the film industry

12. Because they investigated the seamy underside of U.S. business and society, some journalists of the first decade of the twentieth century were known as

    (A) muckrakers
    (B) mugwumps
    (C) communists
    (D) socialists
    (E) carpetbaggers

GO ON TO THE NEXT PAGE

PRACTICE TEST—*Continued*

13. Which U.S. president ordered two atomic bombs dropped on Japan in 1945?

    (A) Franklin D. Roosevelt
    (B) Harry S. Truman
    (C) Dwight D. Eisenhower
    (D) John F. Kennedy
    (E) Lyndon B. Johnson

14. What did President Richard Nixon do to bring about the Saturday Night Massacre?

    (A) Ordered a break-in at the Democratic Party headquarters in the Watergate buildings
    (B) Ordered the attorney general to fire the special prosecutor who was investigating the administration
    (C) Demanded that *Washington Post* editor Ben Bradlee fire reporters Carl Bernstein and Bob Woodward
    (D) Refused to surrender taped Oval Office conversations to the Senate committee holding hearings on Watergate
    (E) Appointed Gerald R. Ford vice president of the United States

15. The stock market crash of October 29, 1929, had all the following effects EXCEPT:

    (A) Shareholders were forced to sell their stocks at huge losses.
    (B) Businesses failed when banks called in loans they could not repay immediately.
    (C) Brokers demanded immediate payment of money owed to them for stocks purchased on margin.
    (D) Borrowers began defaulting on their loan payments to banks, triggering widespread bank failures.
    (E) More and more people began buying on credit because there was a shortage of cash.

16. When President Andrew Jackson stated that he wanted to expel all Native Americans from the United States because he was concerned for their safety, all the following facts suggest that he was not sincere EXCEPT:

    (A) The Southeastern tribes owned some of the best cotton-growing land in the region.
    (B) As a general, Jackson had led an illegal war against the Seminole tribes in Florida and profited financially and politically from the resulting peace treaty.
    (C) Jackson had a long reputation as an Indian fighter dating back to his defeat of the Creek in the Battle of Horseshoe Bend in 1814.
    (D) In 1814 General Jackson had forced Creek tribes to sell lands to him and his friends for much less than it was worth.
    (E) The Five Civilized Tribes of the Southeast had developed societies similar to the European ones that had invaded and conquered their lands.

17. All the following factors combined to cause the high death rate in the Triangle Shirtwaist Company fire EXCEPT:

    (A) The business occupied the upper three floors of the building, well above ground level.
    (B) The fire doors were locked from the outside.
    (C) The only fire escape gave way beneath the weight of the escaping workers.
    (D) The only owners did not enact any of the safety regulations the workers' union had requested repeatedly.
    (E) A large strike by women's shirtwaist makers in 1909 began at the Triangle Company.

18. Which president's domestic and foreign policy programs were collectively known as the New Frontier?

    (A) John F. Kennedy
    (B) Lyndon B. Johnson
    (C) Gerald R. Ford
    (D) Jimmy Carter
    (E) Bill Clinton

GO ON TO THE NEXT PAGE

PRACTICE TEST—*Continued*

19. All the following were important figures in the civil rights movement of the 1960s EXCEPT:

    (A) Jesse Jackson
    (B) Martin Luther King, Jr.
    (C) Fannie Lou Hamer
    (D) Medgar Evers
    (E) Jim Crow

20. In which present-day state did the Union Pacific meet the Central Pacific to complete the first transcontinental railroad?

    (A) Kansas
    (B) Nebraska
    (C) Missouri
    (D) Colorado
    (E) Utah

21. Industrialization developed slowly in the South for all the following reasons EXCEPT:

    (A) Most Southerners preferred to invest in land and slaves, not factories.
    (B) There was no way to transport cotton upstream to the Northern textile mills.
    (C) Planters did not want to pay taxes that might have promoted manufacturing.
    (D) Immigrants who might have staffed factories did not travel to the South because the region relied on slave labor.
    (E) The majority of the Southern population had little or no money to spend on manufactured goods.

22. Which of the following was NOT a factor in ending the cattle boom of the late 1800s?

    (A) The supply of cattle became too great for the demand, bringing prices down.
    (B) The use of barbed wire to fence off land led to range wars among ranchers.
    (C) Severe weather conditions in the period 1885–1887 killed hundreds of cattle.
    (D) The U.S. government set aside some of the best grazing land for displaced Native American tribes.
    (E) Once the open range was fenced off, ranchers had to buy land, and that ate up their profits.

23. All the following facts support the thesis that the Puritan society in New England was a theocracy EXCEPT:

    (A) Only men were allowed to be ministers.
    (B) Only church members were eligible for political office.
    (C) Only church members could vote on political issues.
    (D) Religious dissenters were banished from the colony.
    (E) Moral offenses were considered civil crimes and punished as such.

24. "Upwards of 100 gallons of spirits were poured not down people's throats but on the sand and I believe there is now none in the place."

    This statement most likely describes the actions of a

    (A) political boss
    (B) temperance advocate
    (C) yellow journalist
    (D) suffragist
    (E) war protester

25. The "gag rule" of 1837 prevented which issue from being discussed or debated in the House of Representatives?

    (A) Abolition
    (B) Secession
    (C) Reform
    (D) Censorship
    (E) Taxation

GO ON TO THE NEXT PAGE

PRACTICE TEST—*Continued*

26. All the following facts about the Fugitive Slave Act of 1850 inspired many Northerners to take an active role in the fight against slavery EXCEPT

    (A) Slaves would carry their slave status with them even when escaping to a free state.
    (B) Thousands of African Americans crossed the border into Canada to avoid being pursued by slave owners.
    (C) Northerners resented being forced to obey the Dred Scott decision without getting something in return.
    (D) Court commissioners would receive more money when they decided a dispute in the slave owner's favor.
    (E) No African American accused of being an escaped slave was permitted to testify in his or her own defense.

27. The Five Civilized Tribes forcibly ejected from the Southeast under the Indian Removal Act included all the following EXCEPT:

    (A) Choctaw
    (B) Creek
    (C) Seminole
    (D) Cherokee
    (E) Osage

28. Malcolm X championed African-American separatism and the use of violence in self-defense in a movement known as

    (A) pan-Africanism
    (B) black nationalism
    (C) civil rights
    (D) black pantheism
    (E) back to Africa

29. What was the main purpose of the naval blockade of the South during the Civil War?

    (A) To capture the capital city of the Confederacy
    (B) To force Jefferson Davis to emancipate all Southern slaves
    (C) To prevent shiploads of imported goods and supplies from reaching the people of the South
    (D) To prevent the Confederate Army from using the Mississippi River to travel north
    (E) To take control of the railroad system

30. The Haymarket Riot of 1886 had all the following effects EXCEPT:

    (A) Eight anarchists were arrested for conspiracy, and four of them were hanged.
    (B) Activism among workers decreased.
    (C) Employers blacklisted people with reputations for organizing their fellow workers.
    (D) Skilled and unskilled workers broke apart into two groups.
    (E) Union membership immediately skyrocketed in protest.

31. All the following are classic novels of U.S. participation in war EXCEPT:

    (A) *One of Ours* by Willa Cather
    (B) *The Red Badge of Courage* by Stephen Crane
    (C) *Slaughterhouse-Five* by Kurt Vonnegut
    (D) *A Farewell to Arms* by Ernest Hemingway
    (E) *Hiroshima* by John Hersey

32. "After being hunted like a dog through swamps, woods . . . till I was forced to return wet, cold, and starving, with every man's hand against me, I am here in despair. And why? For doing what Brutus was honored for. . . ."

    This diary entry most likely was written by which of the following?

    (A) John Wilkes Booth
    (B) Nathan Hale
    (C) Benedict Arnold
    (D) Robert E. Lee
    (E) Frederick Douglass

33. President John F. Kennedy did all the following to oppose the spread of communism in the world EXCEPT:

    (A) establish the Peace Corps
    (B) establish the Alliance for Progress
    (C) continue the buildup of nuclear arms begun under Eisenhower
    (D) work with the cabinet on a plan to invade the Soviet Union
    (E) create the Green Berets

GO ON TO THE NEXT PAGE ▶

PRACTICE TEST—*Continued*

34. Which advantage did the Confederacy have over the Union at the beginning of the Civil War?

 (A) Control over the majority of U.S. industry and material resources

 (B) A larger population and thus larger pool of available soldiers

 (C) The location of major national railroads in Confederate states

 (D) Assurance of support, supplies, and troops from France and Great Britain

 (E) Superior, more experienced military leaders

35. The Freedmen's Bureau accomplished all the following EXCEPT:

 (A) Founded African-American schools throughout the South

 (B) Supervised polling places so that African Americans were ensured of the right to vote

 (C) Helped establish African-American colleges

 (D) Settled contract disputes between planters and African-American wage laborers

 (E) Provided food, clothing, and medical care to Southerners made destitute by the Civil War

36. All the following happened as a direct result of the Boston Massacre EXCEPT:

 (A) Samuel Adams demanded that all British troops immediately leave Boston.

 (B) John Adams agreed to defend the British soldiers arrested after the riot.

 (C) Paul Revere distributed an engraving of the riot that was circulated throughout the colonies.

 (D) Thomas Hutchinson disbanded the Massachusetts legislature.

 (E) John Hancock commissioned a portrait of Samuel Adams that was used for propaganda purposes.

37. "It had been, to say the least, an interesting and challenging situation. The two most powerful nations of the world had squared off against each other, each with its finger on the button."

 The speaker of the above quotation probably is referring to which of the following?

 (A) The Battle of Gettysburg

 (B) The Gulf of Tonkin affair

 (C) The Cuban missile crisis

 (D) The Congress of Versailles

 (E) The fall of Saigon

38. A historian researching the immediate effects of the Intolerable Acts on the American colonies probably would find the most accurate information in a diary written by which of the following?

 (A) Patrick Henry

 (B) Benjamin Franklin

 (C) Abigail Adams

 (D) John Paul Jones

 (E) John Dickinson

39. Which of the following major U.S. enterprises enjoyed an exemption from antitrust legislation?

 (A) Standard Oil of Ohio

 (B) Bethlehem Steel

 (C) Microsoft

 (D) Major league baseball

 (E) Pennsylvania Railroad

40. Which of the following led Congress to reduce immigration quotas in 1921 and again in 1924?

 (A) Racism

 (B) Nationalism

 (C) Nativism

 (D) Communism

 (E) Fascism

41. "This man, although he many not actually have committed the crime attributed to him, is nevertheless morally culpable, because he is an enemy of our existing institutions."

 Which of the following was sent to his death by the judge who spoke these words at his trial?

 (A) Julius Rosenberg

 (B) Bartolomeo Vanzetti

 (C) Charles Guiteau

 (D) Edward Slovik

 (E) Lee Harvey Oswald

42. Which is the correct chronological sequence of these three Revolutionary War battles?

 (A) Brandywine, Brooklyn, Trenton

 (B) Brooklyn, Trenton, Brandywine

 (C) Trenton, Brandywine, Brooklyn

 (D) Brandywine, Trenton, Brooklyn

 (E) Brooklyn, Brandywine, Trenton

GO ON TO THE NEXT PAGE ▶

PRACTICE TEST—*Continued*

43. The political cartoon above refers to the

    (A) Boston Port Act
    (B) Stamp Act
    (C) Embargo Act
    (D) Lend-Lease Act
    (E) Indian Removal Act

44. All the following reforms were enacted during the presidency of Woodrow Wilson EXCEPT:

    (A) the Clayton Antitrust Act
    (B) the Federal Reserve Act
    (C) the Nineteenth Amendment giving women the right to vote
    (D) the Twentieth Amendment shortening the "lame duck" period
    (E) the Keating-Owens Child Labor Act

45. By what name were the Intolerable Acts of 1774 known in Great Britain?

    (A) Townshend Acts
    (B) Stamp Acts
    (C) Coercive Acts
    (D) Boston Port Acts
    (E) Retaliatory Acts

46. All the following were aspects of the Union's military strategy to win the Civil War EXCEPT:

    (A) preventing the Confederacy from using the Mississippi River to travel north or receive supplies in trade
    (B) capturing the Confederate capital city of Richmond, Virginia
    (C) blockading Southern ports to prevent exportation and importation of goods
    (D) controlling the railroad system
    (E) establishing a military alliance with Great Britain and France

47. Which would be the best source material for a historian who wanted to write a biography of John Quincy Adams?

    (A) Adams's personal papers, such as diaries and correspondence
    (B) Acts of Congress passed during Adams's years in the White House and Senate
    (C) Newspaper articles written about Adams during his lifetime
    (D) Other historians' biographies of Adams
    (E) The script of a television miniseries about several generations of the Adams family

48. "Millions of people whose parents or grandparents had never dreamed of going to college saw that they could go. . . . Essentially I think it made us a far more democratic people."

    To which of the following does the above quotation refer?

    (A) The GI Bill of Rights
    (B) The desegregation of the public schools
    (C) The Fair Employment Practices Committee
    (D) The National Defense Education Act
    (E) The Internal Security Act

49. Why did neither John Adams nor Thomas Jefferson take part in the Constitutional Convention of 1787?

    (A) Neither was willing to approve of a design for government that had no bill of rights.
    (B) Both had died by the time the Convention was called.
    (C) Both were representing the United States on diplomatic missions in Europe.
    (D) Both stayed away to protest the excision from the Declaration of Independence of the passage criticizing slavery as a "cruel war against human nature."
    (E) Neither was nominated to attend the Convention by the people of his state.

50. Who was the first African-American to publish a book?

    (A) Phillis Wheatley
    (B) Olaudah Equiano
    (C) Frederick Douglass
    (D) Crispus Attucks
    (E) Venture Smith

GO ON TO THE NEXT PAGE

PRACTICE TEST—*Continued*

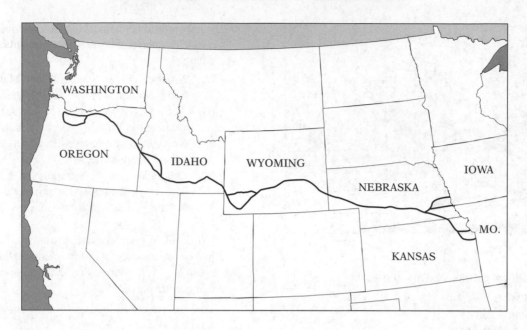

51. Which of the following wrote a multivolume auto-
    biography describing the pioneer experience in the
    Midwest in the 1870s and 1880s?

    (A) Maya Angelou
    (B) Laura Ingalls Wilder
    (C) Willa Cather
    (D) Joseph Conrad
    (E) Stephen Crane

52. Which of the following is shown on the above map?

    (A) Oregon Trail
    (B) Western Road
    (C) Wilderness Road
    (D) California Trail
    (E) Route 66

53. The 1870s and 1880s saw a flood of European immi-
    gration to the American West for all the following
    reasons EXCEPT:

    (A) work for wages building the railroads
    (B) escape from enforced military service at home
    (C) the chance to own land given away by the
        government
    (D) the search for economic opportunity
    (E) the ease of getting rich quickly without effort

54. During the Revolutionary War the U.S. Army had help
    from allies from all the following nations EXCEPT:

    (A) France
    (B) Poland
    (C) Germany
    (D) Spain
    (E) Italy

55. "The thin disguise of 'equal' accommodations for
    passengers in railroad coaches will not mislead
    anyone, nor atone for the wrong this day done."

    Justice John Harlan wrote the dissenting opinion
    quoted above at the conclusion of which Supreme
    Court case?

    (A) *Dred Scott v. Sanford*
    (B) *Plessy v. Ferguson*
    (C) *Powell v. Alabama*
    (D) *Sweatt v. Painter*
    (E) *Brown v. Board of Education*

GO ON TO THE NEXT PAGE ➔

PRACTICE TEST—*Continued*

56. Which of the following is NOT a nonfiction book of the 1950s warning people in the United States to pay attention to pressing issues confronting postwar society?

    (A) *The Affluent Society* by John Kenneth Galbraith
    (B) *The Lonely Crowd* by David Riesman
    (C) *The Organization Man* by William Whyte
    (D) *White Collar* by C. Wright Mills
    (E) *How to Succeed in Business without Really Trying* by Frank Loesser

57. What did the Gulf of Tonkin Resolution state?

    (A) The United States would take military action in response to a supposed Vietnamese attack on a U.S. destroyer.
    (B) Vietnam would be divided politically along the 17th parallel.
    (C) The United States would play an active role in an attempt to overthrow the government of Ngo Dinh Diem.
    (D) The Selective Service would begin drafting men in the United States to fight in Vietnam.
    (E) The U.S. Army would launch a bombing campaign against military targets in North Vietnam.

58. "Stop them pictures. I don't care so much what the papers write about me. My constituents can't read. But they can see pictures."

    Which of the following was William Marcy "Boss" Tweed complaining about in this statement?

    (A) Motion pictures
    (B) Newspaper photographs
    (C) Political cartoons
    (D) Graffiti in public places
    (E) Billboard advertisements

59. All the following were key Southern victories in the Civil War EXCEPT the Battle of

    (A) Chickamauga
    (B) Chancellorsville
    (C) Fredericksburg
    (D) Manassas
    (E) Antietam

60. Which outlined area on the map below represents the Gadsden Purchase?

    (A) I
    (B) II
    (C) III
    (D) IV
    (E) V

GO ON TO THE NEXT PAGE

PRACTICE TEST—*Continued*

61. Which constitutional amendment represented the ultimate goal of the temperance movement?

    (A) Sixteenth, creating the income tax
    (B) Seventeenth, permitting direct popular election of senators
    (C) Eighteenth, banning the manufacture, sale, or transport of alcoholic beverages
    (D) Nineteenth, granting women the right to vote
    (E) Twentieth, changing the first date of a new president's term and setting rules for succession to the presidency

62. In which Supreme Court case did the Court rule against the plaintiff on the grounds that African Americans were "beings of an inferior order" who did not qualify as U.S. citizens?

    (A) *Brown v. Board of Education*
    (B) *Shaw v. Reno*
    (C) *Dred Scott v. Sanford*
    (D) *Wisconsin v. Mitchell*
    (E) *Marbury v. Madison*

63. A government program introduced under President John F. Kennedy that sends U.S. volunteers to work in developing countries for two years is called

    (A) Vista
    (B) the Peace Corps
    (C) Affirmative Action
    (D) the Foreign Service
    (E) National Service

64. Which of the following territories was NOT part of Spain's colonial explorations in the 1500s?

    (A) California
    (B) Arizona
    (C) Texas
    (D) Florida
    (E) Delaware

65. The Twenty-First Amendment to the Constitution is unique among the amendments because it

    (A) repeals another amendment
    (B) was passed when Congress was in recess
    (C) deals with the banking system
    (D) was voted on by women
    (E) deals with foreign policy

66. The Virginia Statute of Religious Freedom of 1779 stated that

    (A) government control over religious beliefs or worship was tyrannical
    (B) the Episcopal Church was the state church of Virginia
    (C) Protestants were free to pray at public governmental functions
    (D) British subjects could worship with Americans
    (E) Christians were finally free to express their religious beliefs in public

67. Matthew Brady is known for

    (A) being a losing presidential candidate in 1896
    (B) leading the abolitionist movement in Ohio
    (C) quoting in a sermon to his congregation, "Go West, young man!"
    (D) writing dime novels about gunfighters
    (E) photographing the dead lying on Civil War battlefields

68. Which of the following measures taken by President Franklin D. Roosevelt's administration brought aid to a rural area plagued by flooding, malnutrition, and poverty?

    (A) National Recovery Act
    (B) Works Progress Administration
    (C) Tennessee Valley Authority
    (D) Public Works Administration
    (E) Federal Deposit Insurance Corporation

69. The Treaty of Ghent was signed in which country?

    (A) Belgium
    (B) Scotland
    (C) Prussia
    (D) Austria
    (E) United States

70. The House Un-American Activities Committee investigated which of the following during the 1950s?

    (A) Feminist groups
    (B) Asian Americans
    (C) The Ku Klux Klan
    (D) Suspected communists
    (E) Beatniks

GO ON TO THE NEXT PAGE

PRACTICE TEST—*Continued*

71. The Constitutional Convention of 1787 met with the goal of strengthening and improving the

    (A) Declaration of Independence
    (B) *Federalist Papers*
    (C) Articles of Confederation
    (D) Virginia Plan
    (E) Albany Plan of Union

72. The Spanish-American War was fought in

    (A) Spain and Portugal
    (B) Mexico and Texas
    (C) Venezuela and Hawaii
    (D) California and Mexico
    (E) the Philippines and Cuba

73. Third-party presidential candidate Ross Perot entered the 1992 presidential race as

    (A) a former governor of Texas
    (B) the leader of the Consumer Party in the United States
    (C) the president of Southern Methodist University
    (D) a billionaire businessman from Texas
    (E) a radio talk-show host from St. Louis

74. Which of the following represents an attempt by the Hoover administration to combat the effects of the Great Depression?

    (A) The McNary-Haugen Farm Relief Bill
    (B) The coining of silver
    (C) The lowering of interest rates
    (D) The encouragement of margin buying on Wall Street
    (E) The public-works construction of the Boulder Dam

75. President Abraham Lincoln was assassinated by John Wilkes Booth, a member of a American family that was prominent in the field of

    (A) firearms
    (B) cotton production
    (C) politics
    (D) rum trade
    (E) theater

76. George Washington chose Christmas night to cross the icy Delaware River and capture Trenton because

    (A) he surmised that the Hessians guarding Trenton would not be prepared for an attack on Christmas morning
    (B) it was the only night his staff officers would agree to attack
    (C) the period for which his troops had enlisted would be over the next morning
    (D) his wife had a dream that he would win a battle before the end of the year
    (E) he was not religious and did not observe Christmas

77. Early explorers such as Columbus, Verrazano, and John Cabot hailed from Italy but sailed under the sponsorship of another European nation. Which of the following best explains this inconsistency?

    (A) The explorers were wanted for piracy in Italy.
    (B) The Italian city-states were the poorest in Europe and could not afford to outfit ships.
    (C) The Italian city-states had no interest in establishing colonies in the New World.
    (D) The explorers refused to ask for or accept Italian sponsorship on religious grounds.
    (E) All European powers cooperated in exploration of the New World.

78. The change in U.S. society in the period between 1820 and 1844 is best explained by which of the following statements?

    (A) The United States changed from a society of peasants to an aristocracy.
    (B) Control of business and government by the well-born gave way to a society based on the economic success of "self-made" men.
    (C) The new social structure was based less on banking and more on Southern plantation life.
    (D) New England's shipping commerce became secondary in the economy to Southern cotton farming.
    (E) Jackson's policies stalled westward expansion of the United States.

GO ON TO THE NEXT PAGE ➡

PRACTICE TEST—*Continued*

79. In *The Grapes of Wrath,* John Steinbeck describes the fortunes of a family forced out of Oklahoma by the ravages of the

    (A) New Deal
    (B) War Department
    (C) Great Society
    (D) Dust Bowl
    (E) Potato famine

80. "Hawks" and "doves" were nicknames given to those who supported and opposed which war?

    (A) Persian Gulf War
    (B) Vietnam War
    (C) War of 1812
    (D) World War I
    (E) Spanish-American War

81. The *Susan Constant,* the *Godspeed,* and the *Discovery* were

    (A) space capsules during the "space race" with the Soviet Union
    (B) ships that brought the English settlers to Jamestown
    (C) ships that sailed across the Atlantic with the *Mayflower*
    (D) steamboats that first piloted up and down the Mississippi River
    (E) covered wagons that carried the first pioneers west of St. Louis

82. Which of the following permitted "any citizen or intended citizen to select any surveyed land up to 160 acres and to gain title to it after five years' residence" if that person cultivated the land?

    (A) Agricultural Advancement Administration
    (B) Lecompton Constitution
    (C) Rush-Bagot Agreement
    (D) Eighteenth Amendment
    (E) Homestead Act

83. The term "political machine" refers to

    (A) the use of balloting machines in elections
    (B) the administration of William McKinley
    (C) a well-organized political party that dominated a city government
    (D) the establishment of policy centers at universities
    (E) the automation of offices in the federal bureaucracy

84. The Twenty-Seventh Amendment to the Constitution which deals with Congressional pay raises was ratified in

    (A) 1892
    (B) 1865
    (C) 1920
    (D) 1956
    (E) 1992

85. Which of the following explains the central role of the Catholic Church in Spanish exploration?

    (A) King Phillip II's *Royal Orders for New Discoveries* commanded the conversion of Native Americans to Catholicism.
    (B) The Pope would not bless ships crossing the Atlantic unless they took Catholic missionaries.
    (C) Native Americans made the establishment of mission schools a condition of peaceful relations with the Europeans.
    (D) Spain competed with France for territory in the New World.
    (E) The Papal Line of Demarcation gave Spain the right to establish mission schools in the Southwest.

86. In 1916, which government organization was established to supervise government-owned nature preserves and monuments?

    (A) City Beautiful movement
    (B) Beautify America
    (C) National Park Service
    (D) Works Progress Administration
    (E) National Guard

87. A large African-American neighborhood in New York City gave its name to an artistic development of the 1920s known as the

    (A) Haight-Ashbury Era
    (B) Battle of Brooklyn
    (C) Harlem Renaissance
    (D) Manhattan Project
    (E) Bronx cheer

GO ON TO THE NEXT PAGE ➤

PRACTICE TEST—*Continued*

88. "You knock over the first one, and what will happen to the last one is a certainty that it will go over very quickly."

    This statement by Dwight D. Eisenhower became known as the

    (A) Red Scare
    (B) domino theory
    (C) fallout theory
    (D) fail-safe theory
    (E) Dr. Strangelove theory

89. "It possesses treasures . . . equal to those of any region of the continent."

    William Seward made this statement to describe which piece of land that he had purchased from which country?

    (A) Louisiana from France
    (B) Florida from Spain
    (C) California from Mexico
    (D) Nevada from Canada
    (E) Alaska from Russia

90. Which of the following was NOT one of the four major labor strikes of 1919?

    (A) Seattle General strike
    (B) Pullman strike
    (C) Boston Police strike
    (D) Pennsylvania Steel strike
    (E) United Mine Workers strike

S T O P

IF YOU FINISH BEFORE TIME RUNS OUT, GO BACK AND CHECK YOUR WORK.

ANSWER KEY

1. B	21. B	41. B	61. C	81. B
2. A	22. D	42. B	62. C	82. E
3. C	23. A	43. C	63. B	83. C
4. A	24. B	44. D	64. E	84. E
5. E	25. A	45. C	65. A	85. A
6. C	26. C	46. E	66. A	86. C
7. A	27. E	47. A	67. E	87. C
8. C	28. B	48. A	68. C	88. B
9. D	29. C	49. C	69. A	89. E
10. C	30. E	50. A	70. D	90. B
11. A	31. E	51. B	71. C	
12. A	32. A	52. A	72. E	
13. B	33. D	53. E	73. D	
14. B	34. E	54. E	74. E	
15. E	35. B	55. B	75. E	
16. E	36. D	56. E	76. A	
17. E	37. C	57. A	77. C	
18. A	38. C	58. C	78. B	
19. E	39. D	59. E	79. D	
20. E	40. D	60. C	80. B	

ANSWERS AND EXPLANATIONS

1. **B** King was a student of the nonviolence that Gandhi had practiced successfully in India.

2. **A** The East India tea, even with the tax, cost less than any other tea available in America.

3. **C** The Pony Express carried mail between St. Joseph and Sacramento.

4. **A** The Missouri Compromise proposed admitting Missouri as a slave state and Maine as a free state, maintaining the even balance.

5. **E** Gambler Arnold Rothstein engineered the fixing of the 1919 World Series, depriving 50 million fans of seeing a fairly contested match.

6. **C** The Great Lakes area lay immediately to the northwest of the Ohio River, hence the name "Northwest Territory."

7. **A** Madison, Hamilton, and Jay were urging their readers to support ratification of the Constitution.

8. **C** Senator Joseph McCarthy made this groundless statement at a press conference, unleashing a flood of anticommunist vitriol and suspicion known as McCarthyism.

9. **D** The principle of judicial review is not specified in the Constitution but has held since *Marbury v. Madison* set the precedent in 1803.

10. **C** All three women fought hard for woman suffrage.

11. **A** They were 10 writers whom no one would hire after they refused to answer the committee's illegal questions.

12. **A** The journalists were figuratively raking through the muck of U.S. business and social institutions to expose what was really going on.

13. **B** President Roosevelt died in office in 1945 and was succeeded by Truman, who hoped to bring the war in the Pacific to a quick conclusion by bombing Japan.

14. **B** The Saturday Night Massacre refers to the resignations of the attorney general and his assistant on refusing to obey Nixon's order and the firing of the special prosecutor by Robert Bork.

15. **E** After the stock market crashed, it became much more difficult to make purchases on credit.

16. **E** This choice does not imply any anti–Native American prejudice on Jackson's part. All the other statements show that whatever his words, Jackson was no friend to the Native Americans in his actions.

17. **E** A strike two years before the fire would not have affected the death rate. The other four choices are all true; if the business had occupied lower floors, workers might have been able to jump to safety, but as it was, most of those who tried were crushed to death.

18. **A** Kennedy spoke of outer space as a new frontier, and that nickname stuck to his programs.

19. **E** Jim Crow was a minstrel-show character from the previous century, not a real person.

20. **E** The railroads met at Promontory Point in the present-day state of Utah.

21. **B** The steamboat enabled planters to ship their cotton upstream to the textile mills.

22. **D** The United States has never set aside valuable land for the Native Americans.

23. **A** The fact that all Puritan ministers were male does not suggest that the church had any authority over the state (the definition of a theocracy).

24. **B** Temperance advocates fought the consumption of alcohol, often by destroying its containers and dumping the contents on the ground.

25. **A** The proslavery faction of Congress passed the gag rule in secret, then confronted the antislavery faction with the accomplished fact.

26. **C** The U.S. Supreme Court handed down the Dred Scott decision in 1857. The Fugitive Slave Act was part of the Compromise of 1850 and in that compromise, the North received the admission of California to the United States as a free state. All of the other choices are true.

27. **E** The fifth tribe was the Chickasaw.

28. **B** Malcolm X supported black nationalism. This was the belief that African Americans should live separately from white society and not work for racial integration. He thought integration represented a rejection of black culture.

29. **C** A naval blockade can only block ships from coming into port or going out. It cannot accomplish any of the other four choices.

30. **E** The Haymarket Riot had the opposite effect. People became afraid to join unions and afraid to encourage others to do so.

31. **E** *Hiroshima* is a piece of nonfiction reporting, not a novel, and it deals not with U.S. participation in the war but with the effect of the atom bomb on Japanese civilians.

32. **A** The reference to Brutus makes it clear that the speaker must have assassinated the head of the government, which is true only of Booth among the five choices.

33. **D** There was no U.S. plan to invade the Soviet Union.

34. **E** The Southern generals were better strategists than the Northern ones in the early years of the Civil War.

35. **B** Supervising polling places was not a major task of the Freedman's Bureau. In addition, the question asks what the Bureau "accomplished," but African Americans in the South quickly lost their right to vote. The other four choices are all true.

36. **D** Royal Governor Hutchinson did not disband the legislature. It was from the legislative assembly that Samuel Adams demanded that the redcoats leave Boston.

37. **C** The speaker (Soviet Premier Nikita Khrushchev) is referring to the fact that either the United States or the Soviet Union might have chosen to end the standoff in Cuba by attacking the other nation with nuclear weapons.

38. **C** The Intolerable Acts were created specifically to punish Massachusetts, and Adams is the only person of the five choices who lived in that colony and thus would be in the best position to write about the effects of the acts from direct observation.

39. **D** To this day major league baseball has been allowed to operate as a monopoly.

40. **D** Nativists did not welcome immigrants because they were afraid they might have revolutionary or socialist tendencies and might organize against the government.

41. **B** There was no question that Oswald and Guiteau committed the crimes of which they were accused; Slovik was executed by the Army after a court-martial; and although Rosenberg denied his guilt, the judge did not suggest that he might not have committed treason.

42. **B** The U.S. Army left Boston, marching south; lost the Battle of Brooklyn (August 27, 1776) and retreated to Pennsylvania; recrossed the Delaware to win at Trenton (December 26, 1776); and later fought the Battle of Brandywine (September 11, 1777).

43. **C** Ograbme is "embargo" spelled backward, providing the necessary clue. The Embargo Act dealt with imports and exports, as the trading ship and barrel in the cartoon imply.

44. **D** The Twentieth Amendment was not ratified until 1933.

45. **C** This was the name Parliament gave to the Intolerable Acts.

46. **E** It was the Confederacy, not the Union, that hoped for the support of Britain and France.

47. **A** A biographer would find Adams's own words to be the most valuable source for writing the story of his life.

48. **A** The GI Bill of Rights provided government assistance to veterans who wanted to go to college.

49. **C** Jefferson and Adams represented the United States in France and England respectively.

50. **A** Phillis Wheatley's volume of poetry was published in England in 1773 and in the United States in 1787. Crispus Attucks, a victim of the Boston Massacre, never wrote a book; the other three are authors of slave narratives that postdate Wheatley's book.

51. **B** Wilder's "Little House" books have been enduringly popular as children's books but are also an important work of social history of her times.

52. **A** The map shows the Oregon Trail.

53. **E** No one would have assumed that staking a claim in the West and making it into a working farm, working on the railroad, or breaking horses and cattle would be an easy way to live.

54. **E** Foreign allies included Lafayette of France, Kosciusko of Poland, Von Steuben of Germany, and leaders in Spanish Florida. On the other hand, Italy did not exist as a unified nation until the middle of the 1800s.

55. **B** *Plessy v. Ferguson* dealt with a claim brought by an African American that the railroad violated his constitutional rights when it enforced segregated seating.

56. **E** This was originally the title of a handbook for those wanting to enter business, used by Loesser as the basis for a hit Broadway musical.

57. **A** The other four choices are all true statements, but they either predate or postdate the Gulf of Tonkin Resolution.

58. **C** Tweed was angry over the fact that cartoonist Thomas Nast continually exposed graft and corruption in Tweed's New York political machine.

59. **E** Antietam was not a decisive victory for either side, but it did halt General Lee's first invasion of the North and force him to retreat.

60. **C** The Gadsden Purchase included parts of the present-day states of Arizona and New Mexico.

61. **C** Temperance advocates wanted to ban alcohol throughout the United States. With the Eighteenth Amendment, they appeared to have succeeded.

62. **C** Chief Justice Roger Taney ruled that no African American had the right to take a case to the U.S. Supreme Court because African Americans were not and could never be U.S. citizens.

63. **B** The Peace Corps continues to send volunteer teachers, farmers, and others to work in foreign nations.

64. **E** Delware was colonized by the Dutch, Swedes, and English, and not until the 1600s.

65. **A** The Twenty-First Amendment repealed the Eighteenth. No other constitutional amendment has ever been repealed.

66. **A** The other four choices are untrue or irrelevant.

67. **E** Brady's hundreds of photographs provide a somber record of the terrible devastation the war brought to the nation.

68. **C** The Tennessee Valley Authority was a specific attempt to bring relief to one of the poorest areas in the country.

69. **A** Ghent is in Belgium.

70. **D** HUAC both created and responded to anticommunist hysteria in the wake of World War II by attacking anyone suspected of membership in the Communist Party.

71. **C** Originally, the Convention intended to revise the Articles of Confederation rather than beginning afresh on a brand-new Constitution.

72. **E** The United States went to war in support of Cuban rebels and to drive Spain out of the Philippines.

73. **D** Despite his great wealth, Perot portrayed himself as a man of the people and persuaded Americans to finance his campaign with individual donations.

74. **E** The McNary-Haugen Farm Relief Bill was passed three times (in 1924, 1926, and 1928) by Congress and vetoed by President Coolidge with the support of Secretary of Commerce Hoover.

75. **E** The three brothers Edwin, Junius Brutus, and John Wilkes Booth were all well-known and popular stage actors.

76. **A** Washington thought that if the Hessians celebrated the holiday, they would be caught completely off guard by an attack at dawn the following morning.

77. **C** The explorers either could not or did not try to interest the rulers of the Italian city-states in sponsoring them because the Italians showed no interest in exploring or colonizing the Americas.

78. **B** The Age of Jackson was notable for the impact of the industrial revolution, westward expansion, lowered suffrage restrictions, and political appeals to the "common man." The other choices are untrue.

79. **D** Thousands of tenant farmers like Steinbeck's fictional Joads were forced off their land because the owners were making nothing from farmland during the sustained and severe droughts of the period.

80. **B** Hawks were in favor of the Vietnam War, and doves preferred peace.

81. **B** The *Mayflower* sailed alone, and the other choices are wrong.

82. **E** The 160 acres were called the "homestead," and the people who claimed homesteads were called "homesteaders."

83. **C** Political machines existed in major cities and controlled many aspects of city services as well as determining who would hold office.

84. **E** The Twenty-Seventh Amendment is the most recent.

85. **A** Converting the "heathens" to Catholicism was an important goal for the Spanish expeditions, at least in theory.

86. **C** The National Park Service was founded in 1916 during Woodrow Wilson's administration.

87. **C** Haight-Ashbury is in San Francisco, the Battle of Brooklyn was fought during the Revolutionary War, the Manhattan Project had to do with atomic science, and the Bronx cheer is a derisive noise.

88. **B** Eisenhower accurately describes what happens to a row of dominoes when the first one is knocked over.

89. **E** Alaska was nicknamed "Seward's Folly" by those who thought he was crazy to insist on acquiring it from Russia.

90. **B** The famous Pullman strike took place in 1894.

PRACTICE TEST 3

▇▇ SCORE SHEET

Number of questions correct: _____

Less: 0.25 × number of questions wrong: _____

(Remember that omitted questions ares not counted as wrong.)

Raw score: _____

Raw Score	Scaled Score	Raw Score	Scaled Score	Raw Score	Scaled Score	Raw Score	Scaled Score	Raw Score	Scaled Score
90	800	65	710	40	550	15	420	−10	300
89	800	64	700	39	550	14	420	−11	290
88	800	63	700	38	540	13	410	−12	290
87	800	62	690	37	540	12	410	−13	280
86	800	61	680	36	530	11	400	−14	280
85	800	60	680	35	530	10	400	−15	270
84	800	59	670	34	520	9	390	−16	260
83	800	58	660	33	520	8	390	−17	260
82	800	57	660	32	510	7	380	−18	250
81	800	56	650	31	510	6	380	−19	240
80	790	55	640	30	500	5	370	−20	230
79	780	54	630	29	500	4	370	−21	230
78	780	53	630	28	490	3	360	−22	230
77	770	52	620	27	480	2	360		
76	760	51	620	26	480	1	350		
75	760	50	610	25	470	0	350		
74	750	49	610	24	470	−1	340		
73	750	48	600	23	460	−2	340		
72	740	47	600	22	460	−3	330		
71	740	46	590	21	450	−4	330		
70	730	45	590	20	450	−5	320		
69	730	44	580	19	440	−6	320		
68	720	43	570	18	440	−7	320		
67	720	42	560	17	430	−8	310		
66	710	41	560	16	430	−9	310		

Note: This is only a sample scoring scale. Scoring scales differ from exam to exam.

PRACTICE TEST 4
U.S. HISTORY

The following Practice Test is designed to be just like the real SAT U.S. History test. It matches the actual test in content coverage and level of difficulty.

When you are finished with the test, determine your score and carefully read the answer explanations for the questions you answered incorrectly. Identify any weak areas by determining the areas in which you made the most errors. Review those chapters of the book first. Then, as time permits, go back and review your stronger areas.

Allow 1 hour to take the test. Time yourself and work uninterrupted. If you run out of time, take note of where you ended when time ran out. Remember that you lose $\frac{1}{4}$ of a point for each incorrect answer. Because of this penalty, do not guess on a question unless you can eliminate one or more of the answers. Your score is calculated by using the following formula:

Number of correct answers $- \frac{1}{4}$(Number of incorrect answers)

This Practice Test will be an accurate reflection of how you'll do on test day if you treat it as the real examination. Here are some hints on how to take the test under conditions similar to those of the actual examination:

- Complete the test in one sitting.
- Time yourself.
- Tear out your Answer Sheet and fill in the ovals just as you would on the actual test day.
- Become familiar with the directions to the test and the reference information provided. You'll save time on the actual test day by already being familiar with this information.

PRACTICE TEST 4

U.S. HISTORY

ANSWER SHEET

Tear out this answer sheet and use it to mark your answers.

There are 100 lines of numbered ovals on this answer sheet. If there are more lines than you need, leave the remainder blank.

1. Ⓐ Ⓑ Ⓒ Ⓓ Ⓔ	26. Ⓐ Ⓑ Ⓒ Ⓓ Ⓔ	51. Ⓐ Ⓑ Ⓒ Ⓓ Ⓔ	76. Ⓐ Ⓑ Ⓒ Ⓓ Ⓔ
2. Ⓐ Ⓑ Ⓒ Ⓓ Ⓔ	27. Ⓐ Ⓑ Ⓒ Ⓓ Ⓔ	52. Ⓐ Ⓑ Ⓒ Ⓓ Ⓔ	77. Ⓐ Ⓑ Ⓒ Ⓓ Ⓔ
3. Ⓐ Ⓑ Ⓒ Ⓓ Ⓔ	28. Ⓐ Ⓑ Ⓒ Ⓓ Ⓔ	53. Ⓐ Ⓑ Ⓒ Ⓓ Ⓔ	78. Ⓐ Ⓑ Ⓒ Ⓓ Ⓔ
4. Ⓐ Ⓑ Ⓒ Ⓓ Ⓔ	29. Ⓐ Ⓑ Ⓒ Ⓓ Ⓔ	54. Ⓐ Ⓑ Ⓒ Ⓓ Ⓔ	79. Ⓐ Ⓑ Ⓒ Ⓓ Ⓔ
5. Ⓐ Ⓑ Ⓒ Ⓓ Ⓔ	30. Ⓐ Ⓑ Ⓒ Ⓓ Ⓔ	55. Ⓐ Ⓑ Ⓒ Ⓓ Ⓔ	80. Ⓐ Ⓑ Ⓒ Ⓓ Ⓔ
6. Ⓐ Ⓑ Ⓒ Ⓓ Ⓔ	31. Ⓐ Ⓑ Ⓒ Ⓓ Ⓔ	56. Ⓐ Ⓑ Ⓒ Ⓓ Ⓔ	81. Ⓐ Ⓑ Ⓒ Ⓓ Ⓔ
7. Ⓐ Ⓑ Ⓒ Ⓓ Ⓔ	32. Ⓐ Ⓑ Ⓒ Ⓓ Ⓔ	57. Ⓐ Ⓑ Ⓒ Ⓓ Ⓔ	82. Ⓐ Ⓑ Ⓒ Ⓓ Ⓔ
8. Ⓐ Ⓑ Ⓒ Ⓓ Ⓔ	33. Ⓐ Ⓑ Ⓒ Ⓓ Ⓔ	58. Ⓐ Ⓑ Ⓒ Ⓓ Ⓔ	83. Ⓐ Ⓑ Ⓒ Ⓓ Ⓔ
9. Ⓐ Ⓑ Ⓒ Ⓓ Ⓔ	34. Ⓐ Ⓑ Ⓒ Ⓓ Ⓔ	59. Ⓐ Ⓑ Ⓒ Ⓓ Ⓔ	84. Ⓐ Ⓑ Ⓒ Ⓓ Ⓔ
10. Ⓐ Ⓑ Ⓒ Ⓓ Ⓔ	35. Ⓐ Ⓑ Ⓒ Ⓓ Ⓔ	60. Ⓐ Ⓑ Ⓒ Ⓓ Ⓔ	85. Ⓐ Ⓑ Ⓒ Ⓓ Ⓔ
11. Ⓐ Ⓑ Ⓒ Ⓓ Ⓔ	36. Ⓐ Ⓑ Ⓒ Ⓓ Ⓔ	61. Ⓐ Ⓑ Ⓒ Ⓓ Ⓔ	86. Ⓐ Ⓑ Ⓒ Ⓓ Ⓔ
12. Ⓐ Ⓑ Ⓒ Ⓓ Ⓔ	37. Ⓐ Ⓑ Ⓒ Ⓓ Ⓔ	62. Ⓐ Ⓑ Ⓒ Ⓓ Ⓔ	87. Ⓐ Ⓑ Ⓒ Ⓓ Ⓔ
13. Ⓐ Ⓑ Ⓒ Ⓓ Ⓔ	38. Ⓐ Ⓑ Ⓒ Ⓓ Ⓔ	63. Ⓐ Ⓑ Ⓒ Ⓓ Ⓔ	88. Ⓐ Ⓑ Ⓒ Ⓓ Ⓔ
14. Ⓐ Ⓑ Ⓒ Ⓓ Ⓔ	39. Ⓐ Ⓑ Ⓒ Ⓓ Ⓔ	64. Ⓐ Ⓑ Ⓒ Ⓓ Ⓔ	89. Ⓐ Ⓑ Ⓒ Ⓓ Ⓔ
15. Ⓐ Ⓑ Ⓒ Ⓓ Ⓔ	40. Ⓐ Ⓑ Ⓒ Ⓓ Ⓔ	65. Ⓐ Ⓑ Ⓒ Ⓓ Ⓔ	90. Ⓐ Ⓑ Ⓒ Ⓓ Ⓔ
16. Ⓐ Ⓑ Ⓒ Ⓓ Ⓔ	41. Ⓐ Ⓑ Ⓒ Ⓓ Ⓔ	66. Ⓐ Ⓑ Ⓒ Ⓓ Ⓔ	91. Ⓐ Ⓑ Ⓒ Ⓓ Ⓔ
17. Ⓐ Ⓑ Ⓒ Ⓓ Ⓔ	42. Ⓐ Ⓑ Ⓒ Ⓓ Ⓔ	67. Ⓐ Ⓑ Ⓒ Ⓓ Ⓔ	92. Ⓐ Ⓑ Ⓒ Ⓓ Ⓔ
18. Ⓐ Ⓑ Ⓒ Ⓓ Ⓔ	43. Ⓐ Ⓑ Ⓒ Ⓓ Ⓔ	68. Ⓐ Ⓑ Ⓒ Ⓓ Ⓔ	93. Ⓐ Ⓑ Ⓒ Ⓓ Ⓔ
19. Ⓐ Ⓑ Ⓒ Ⓓ Ⓔ	44. Ⓐ Ⓑ Ⓒ Ⓓ Ⓔ	69. Ⓐ Ⓑ Ⓒ Ⓓ Ⓔ	94. Ⓐ Ⓑ Ⓒ Ⓓ Ⓔ
20. Ⓐ Ⓑ Ⓒ Ⓓ Ⓔ	45. Ⓐ Ⓑ Ⓒ Ⓓ Ⓔ	70. Ⓐ Ⓑ Ⓒ Ⓓ Ⓔ	95. Ⓐ Ⓑ Ⓒ Ⓓ Ⓔ
21. Ⓐ Ⓑ Ⓒ Ⓓ Ⓔ	46. Ⓐ Ⓑ Ⓒ Ⓓ Ⓔ	71. Ⓐ Ⓑ Ⓒ Ⓓ Ⓔ	96. Ⓐ Ⓑ Ⓒ Ⓓ Ⓔ
22. Ⓐ Ⓑ Ⓒ Ⓓ Ⓔ	47. Ⓐ Ⓑ Ⓒ Ⓓ Ⓔ	72. Ⓐ Ⓑ Ⓒ Ⓓ Ⓔ	97. Ⓐ Ⓑ Ⓒ Ⓓ Ⓔ
23. Ⓐ Ⓑ Ⓒ Ⓓ Ⓔ	48. Ⓐ Ⓑ Ⓒ Ⓓ Ⓔ	73. Ⓐ Ⓑ Ⓒ Ⓓ Ⓔ	98. Ⓐ Ⓑ Ⓒ Ⓓ Ⓔ
24. Ⓐ Ⓑ Ⓒ Ⓓ Ⓔ	49. Ⓐ Ⓑ Ⓒ Ⓓ Ⓔ	74. Ⓐ Ⓑ Ⓒ Ⓓ Ⓔ	99. Ⓐ Ⓑ Ⓒ Ⓓ Ⓔ
25. Ⓐ Ⓑ Ⓒ Ⓓ Ⓔ	50. Ⓐ Ⓑ Ⓒ Ⓓ Ⓔ	75. Ⓐ Ⓑ Ⓒ Ⓓ Ⓔ	100. Ⓐ Ⓑ Ⓒ Ⓓ Ⓔ

PRACTICE TEST 4

Time: 60 Minutes

<u>Directions</u>: Each of the questions or incomplete statements below is followed by five suggested answers or completions. Select the one that is best in each case and then fill in the corresponding oval on the answer sheet.

1. All the following authors wrote about the history and experiences of African-American women EXCEPT:

   (A) Toni Morrison
   (B) Alice Walker
   (C) Maya Angelou
   (D) Jamaica Kincaid
   (E) Nella Larsen

2. The conference held between the U.S. government and the Plains tribes of Native Americans in 1851 resulted in which of the following?

   (A) The tribes agreed not to migrate freely throughout the Plains anymore.
   (B) The United States banished the tribes to present-day Oklahoma.
   (C) The United States agreed to end westward migration through Native American territory.
   (D) The U.S. government outlawed the killing of buffalo.
   (E) The tribes accepted an offer of full U.S. citizenship in exchange for giving up their traditional hunting culture.

3. "It has been done for the sake of political power, in order to bring two new slaveholding senators upon this floor."

   The senator who made the above statement was referring to the passage of the

   (A) Fugitive Slave Act
   (B) Kansas-Nebraska Act
   (C) Dred Scott decision
   (D) Reconstruction Acts
   (E) Thirteenth Amendment

4. Which of the following philosophers had the strongest influence on the framers' decision that the Constitution would require a government with three branches and a balance of power among them?

   (A) Locke
   (B) Montesquieu
   (C) Voltaire
   (D) Franklin
   (E) Hobbes

5. The Supreme Court decision in the case of *Dred Scott v. Sanford* stated all the following EXCEPT:

   (A) A slave could not gain his or her freedom by moving to a free state or territory.
   (B) Slaves had the legal status of property, not people.
   (C) The Founding Fathers had never intended for Africans to become U.S. citizens.
   (D) The Missouri Compromise violated the Fifth Amendment.
   (E) Only individual states could decide whether a slave could become a citizen.

6. The scriptwriters known as the "Hollywood Ten" were blacklisted by the movie industry because they

   (A) failed to win awards for their studio producers
   (B) made public speeches urging people to vote for third-party presidential candidates
   (C) accused several people in the movie industry of being Communist Party members
   (D) refused to answer questions asked by the House Un-American Activities Committee
   (E) tried to organize a screenwriters' union in Hollywood

7. The Triangle Shirtwaist Company fire resulted in all the following EXCEPT:

   (A) The New York legislature enacted a stricter fire code.
   (B) A labor reform commission was created.
   (C) New workplace safety regulations were passed.
   (D) The U.S. congress passed the Elkins Act and the Hepburn Act.
   (E) About 150 workers were burned or crushed to death.

8. Bartolomeo Vanzetti and Nicola Sacco were convicted of the crime of

   (A) murder
   (B) treason
   (C) grand theft
   (D) anarchy
   (E) draft dodging

GO ON TO THE NEXT PAGE ➤

PRACTICE TEST—*Continued*

9. The GI Bill of Rights altered U.S. society by
   (A) admitting women to the U.S. military and naval academies
   (B) making it possible for millions of veterans to attend college
   (C) integrating the armed forces
   (D) guaranteeing civilian employment to all veterans
   (E) creating the U.S. Department of Veterans' Affairs

10. All the following are classic American autobiographies EXCEPT:
   (A) *The Narrative of the Life of Frederick Douglass* by Frederick Douglass
   (B) *I Know Why the Caged Bird Sings* by Maya Angelou
   (C) *Little Town on the Prairie* by Laura Ingalls Wilder
   (D) *The Story of My Life* by Helen Keller
   (E) *The Red Badge of Courage* by Stephen Crane

11. The cattle boom of the late 1800s ended abruptly in part because of the
   (A) severe winter weather of the 1880s
   (B) rise in prices as supply grew far beyond demand
   (C) cooperative agreements among ranchers to allow free access across the plains to all herds
   (D) trend toward larger ranches
   (E) expansion of sheep ranching

12. The bar graph below implies which of the following about U.S. public opinion in the period preceding U.S. entry into World War I?
   (A) Most people in the United States preferred that the country remain neutral in the war.
   (B) There were very few people of German descent in the United States.
   (C) More than half of all people in the United States strongly supported the Allies.
   (D) Most of the people surveyed were women.
   (E) Most people in the United States would support a decision to go to war.

13. Which of the following rights did the Emancipation Proclamation confer on which group of people?
   (A) It freed all Confederate prisoners of war on condition that they not rejoin their army.
   (B) It freed all slaves in the United States.
   (C) It freed all slaves in the states in open rebellion.
   (D) It gave all slaves the right to vote.
   (E) It gave all Confederate citizens the right to move north and settle in Union states without suffering any penalty.

Survey on American Foreign Policy Choices, 1916

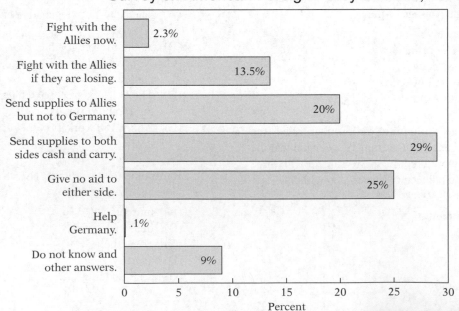

GO ON TO THE NEXT PAGE

PRACTICE TEST—*Continued*

14. Prohibition had all the following effects EXCEPT:

    (A) People formed organizations to lobby for its repeal.
    (B) Organized crime and violence escalated.
    (C) The terms "speakeasy" and "bathtub gin" were added to the language.
    (D) People in the United States stopped buying, selling, and drinking alcoholic beverages.
    (E) The FBI established a department of operatives who investigated only Prohibition-related crimes.

15. Which of the following is the best example of the importance of a free press in a republic?

    (A) The disclosure of high crimes committed by members of the Nixon administration
    (B) The television broadcasts of the destruction of the World Trade Center
    (C) The "fireside chats" given by President Franklin D. Roosevelt over the radio
    (D) The publication in the next day's newspapers of important presidential speeches
    (E) The coverage of the legal battle over Terry Schiavo's right to die

16. Cuba and the Philippines were the primary battle-grounds in which of the following wars?

    (A) Mexican-American War
    (B) War of 1812
    (C) World War I
    (D) Spanish-American War
    (E) World War II

17. Which of the following political parties passed a "gag rule" in 1837 that banned any discussion of abolition in Congress?

    (A) Whig Party
    (B) Democratic Party
    (C) Federalist Party
    (D) Free-Soil Party
    (E) Republican Party

18. The Antifederalists were unwilling to approve the Constitution primarily because

    (A) it did not include a Bill of Rights
    (B) it did not give the central government enough authority over the states
    (C) it made no provision for a judicial branch of government
    (D) it referred to the chief executive of the nation as the "president of the United States"
    (E) it was largely the work of Southern delegates

19. The completion of the transcontinental railroad in 1869 had all the following effects EXCEPT:

    (A) increase in westward migration
    (B) growth in the number of Western towns and cities
    (C) rise in the national employment rate
    (D) growth in the steel industry
    (E) rise in automobile ownership and production

20. Newspaper illustrator—"Everything is quiet. There is no trouble here. There will be no war. I wish to return." Editor—"Please remain. You furnish the pictures and I'll furnish the war."

    The above exchange of telegrams most likely refers to

    (A) the Mexican-American War
    (B) the First Seminole War
    (C) the French and Indian War
    (D) the Spanish-American War
    (E) the Civil War

21. Before the United States gained sovereignty over the Panama Canal, it had been the project of

    (A) a French company led by Ferdinand de Lesseps
    (B) a Spaniard named Vasco da Gama
    (C) a collective South American venture led by Simon Bolivar
    (D) the Dutch West India Company
    (E) the British Empire

22. Puritan authorities banished Roger Williams from the Massachusetts Bay Colony primarily because he

    (A) believed in independence from the British king
    (B) taught his congregation to sing and dance
    (C) believed in strict separation of church and state
    (D) wanted to be the leader of the Puritans
    (E) preached against peace with the Native Americans

23. Which of the following Founding Fathers was never elected president of the United States?

    (A) Thomas Jefferson
    (B) James Madison
    (C) John Adams
    (D) Elbridge Gerry
    (E) James Monroe

GO ON TO THE NEXT PAGE

PRACTICE TEST—*Continued*

24. Confederate leaders hoped for a military alliance with Great Britain and France primarily because

    (A) European nations did not disapprove of slavery
    (B) Britain and France bought the bulk of the Southern cotton crop
    (C) the Confederate industrial base was much smaller than the Union's
    (D) the federal navy had remained loyal to the Union government
    (E) the Civil War was fought largely in Confederate territory

25. Which of the following women was an outspoken critic of the Equal Rights Amendment?

    (A) Bella Abzug
    (B) Phyllis Schlafly
    (C) Shirley Chisholm
    (D) Betty Friedan
    (E) Jane Fonda

26. The Comstock Lode was discovered in 1857 in which of the following present-day states?

    (A) Alaska
    (B) Texas
    (C) New Mexico
    (D) Nevada
    (E) California

27. "Rosie the Riveter" became famous in the 1940s as which of the following?

    (A) A singing star on the radio
    (B) An antiwar film heroine
    (C) A weekly comic radio program
    (D) A symbol of the importance of female workers to the war effort
    (E) A nickname given to President Franklin D. Roosevelt

28. Which of the following statements best defines the economic term "depression"?

    (A) A sharp drop in business activity along with rising unemployment
    (B) A large influx of foreign capital
    (C) An unpredicted increase in exports with a decline in imports
    (D) A lowering of interest rates
    (E) The laws of supply and demand

29. Francis Cabot Lowell's development of the power loom in Massachusetts in the early 1800s gave rise to which of the following?

    (A) Automation
    (B) Socialism
    (C) Assembly-line manufacturing
    (D) The factory system
    (E) Labor strikes

30. New York Governor Alfred Smith's 1928 campaign for the presidency marked the first time that

    (A) a New Yorker was ever on the ballot
    (B) the Democrats nominated the governor of a large state
    (C) a Catholic ran for president
    (D) a career politician was nominated to national office
    (E) the Democratic Convention reached a decision on the first ballot

31. George Rogers Clark made which of the following contributions to the Revolutionary War in the Northwest Territory?

    (A) He captured the traitor Benedict Arnold.
    (B) He led the army that defeated the French.
    (C) He captured Forts Ticonderoga and Crown Point.
    (D) He captured Forts Kaskaskia, Cahokia, and Vincennes.
    (E) He defeated Lord Nelson on Lake Erie.

32. Southern farmers who could not afford slaves supported the institution of slavery primarily because

    (A) slaves allowed poor white farmers to prosper
    (B) slavery gave poor whites status and a stake in society
    (C) slaves needed overseers and Southern whites knew the job was well paid
    (D) slaveowners lent slaves in slow times to poor farmers to help work their land
    (E) farmers knew that competition would help the Southern economy in the long run

GO ON TO THE NEXT PAGE →

PRACTICE TEST—*Continued*

33. The Potsdam Conference was convened in July 1945 so that

    (A) Allied leaders could decide how to handle postwar Germany
    (B) Allied leaders could determine how to handle the occupation of Japan
    (C) the Soviet Union and the United States could decide how to divide China
    (D) plans could be made for the Soviet Union to invade Japan
    (E) Japan and the United States could draw up a peace agreement

34. Secretary of State John Hay called for an Open Door Policy toward China in 1899 primarily because

    (A) Japan threatened to close its ports to the West
    (B) Britain and France were pulling out of Asia
    (C) The United States feared it would be shut out of trade and investment in China
    (D) Russia and France were about to go to war over China
    (E) Russia blocked sea access to Manchuria

35. Article I of the Constitution assigns the vice president the duty of

    (A) signing legislation when the president is out of Washington
    (B) negotiating treaties
    (C) representing the United States at social functions
    (D) presiding over meetings of the Senate
    (E) introducing legislation to Congress

36. Which one of the following women found refuge in Rhode Island after the courts banished her from the Massachusetts Bay Colony in 1638?

    (A) Susan B. Anthony
    (B) Anne Hutchinson
    (C) Anne Bradstreet
    (D) Carrie Nation
    (E) Hester Prynne

37. The Anasazi people constructed dwellings of

    (A) rock and adobe
    (B) sticks and wet sand
    (C) straw and mud
    (D) mud and brick
    (E) wood and stone

38. The success of the automobile industry caused rapid growth in all the following industries EXCEPT:

    (A) communications
    (B) advertising
    (C) credit
    (D) oil refining
    (E) asphalt and paving

39. In 1937 President Franklin D. Roosevelt asked Congress to grant him the power to do which of the following?

    (A) Move the Supreme Court into the White House
    (B) Put the Supreme Court on administrative leave
    (C) Replace every Supreme Court justice who was over 70 years of age
    (D) Appoint nine new Supreme Court justices
    (E) Dissolve the Supreme Court

40. Which of the following was president when the U.S. government acquired the last of the territory that would make up the contiguous United States?

    (A) Abraham Lincoln
    (B) William McKinley
    (C) James Polk
    (D) Woodrow Wilson
    (E) Franklin Pierce

41. Which statement best explains the trickle-down theory of economics?

    (A) Government-sponsored lotteries give people a chance to get rich.
    (B) Lowering the top income tax rates will spur economic growth.
    (C) Government programs that hire the unemployed lower the poverty rates.
    (D) Lowering the bottom income tax rates encourages spending.
    (E) Low-interest government loans spur economic growth.

42. The popular nickname of President Ronald Reagan's space-based missile defense system was

    (A) SALT
    (B) Dune
    (C) Space Shield
    (D) Skylab
    (E) Star Wars

GO ON TO THE NEXT PAGE ➔

PRACTICE TEST—*Continued*

43. From 1863 to 1871, William Marcy Tweed was the powerful political boss of which of the following cities?

    (A) Boston
    (B) New York City
    (C) Washington, D.C.
    (D) Philadelphia
    (E) New Orleans

44. John C. Calhoun's view that the states had the right to refuse to obey any act of Congress they considered unconstitutional became known as the

    (A) doctrine of equal rights
    (B) right of first refusal
    (C) doctrine of nullification
    (D) Carolina Plan
    (E) Calhoun Compromise

45. The Federal Securities Act created which of the following in an effort to reform business and guard against another stock market crash?

    (A) The Agricultural Adjustment Administration
    (B) The Civilian Conservation Corps
    (C) The Federal Emergency Relief Administration
    (D) The Securities and Exchange Commission
    (E) The National Industrial Recovery Act

46. "We fight not to enslave, but to set a country free, and to make room upon the earth for honest men to live in."

    The writer of the above statement was most likely referring to which of the following wars?

    (A) The Civil War
    (B) The Vietnam War
    (C) The War of 1812
    (D) World War II
    (E) The Revolutionary War

47. The Eighteenth Amendment was passed primarily because of a crusade led by the

    (A) National Association for the Advancement of Colored People
    (B) Women's Christian Temperance Movement
    (C) Daughters of the American Revolution
    (D) Mayflower Society
    (E) International Ladies' Garment Workers' Union

48. In 1969, Native American activists occupied the abandoned prison on Alcatraz Island in order to protest all the following EXCEPT:

    (A) refusal of the U.S. and state government to honor treaty obligations
    (B) discrimination against Native Americans by whites
    (C) oppression of Native Americans by whites over three centuries
    (D) refusal of the U.S. government to allow profitable businesses to operate on Native American reservations
    (E) marginalization of Native American culture by U.S. society

49. Which one of the following was NOT an important leader of organized labor?

    (A) George Pullman
    (B) Eugene V. Debs
    (C) Mary Harris Jones
    (D) Samuel Gompers
    (E) Terence V. Powderly

U.S. Higher Education, 1957 and 1997

	1957	1997
Number of Institutions of Higher Education	1,863	4,064
Annual Student Body Enrollment	2,281,000	14,350,000
Annual Number of Bachelor Degrees Conferred	496,874	1,172,000

Student Body

■ Female
□ Male

32% 68% 43% 57%

50. The chart and graphs above lend support to which of the following statements?

    (A) Only wealthy people could afford a college education before 1957.
    (B) About 30 percent of all women in the United States were enrolled in college in 1957.
    (C) The number of male college students declined during the 1950s.
    (D) Thousands of colleges opened between 1957 and 1997.
    (E) More men than women graduated from college in 1957.

GO ON TO THE NEXT PAGE ➤

PRACTICE TEST—*Continued*

51. In defiance of federal orders to desegregate Arkansas public schools, Governor Orval Faubus did all the following EXCEPT:

    (A) post the Arkansas National Guard at Little Rock High School to bar African-American students from entering

    (B) close down the Little Rock public schools for the 1958–1959 school year

    (C) petition the White House to overturn *Brown v. Board of Education*

    (D) work with others to establish private, all-white schools in Little Rock

    (E) speak out publicly against forced integration of Arkansas schools

52. "Our diplomats and their advisers . . . lost sight of our tremendous stake in a non-Communist China. . . . This House must now assume the responsibility of preventing the onrushing tide of communism from engulfing all of Asia."

    The speaker probably issued this statement to the House of Representatives on the eve of which of the following?

    (A) Russo-Japanese War

    (B) Korean War

    (C) Persian Gulf War

    (D) World War II

    (E) Second Sino-Japanese War

53. Which of the following colonial actions provoked the British Parliament to pass the Intolerable Acts?

    (A) Signing of the Declaration of Independence

    (B) Tarring and feathering of British agents sent to the colonies to distribute stamps

    (C) Dumping chests of East India Tea into Boston harbor

    (D) Convening of the Constitutional Convention

    (E) Demanding that the governor of Massachusetts expel all British troops from Boston

54. Which of the following statements supports the theory that the Brooklyn Dodgers played an important role in the struggle for civil rights by hiring Jackie Robinson?

    (A) Negro League players made much less money than white major leaguers.

    (B) Millions of fans saw and heard every day that Robinson played as well as or better than the white players.

    (C) The Dodgers were one of three baseball teams in New York, the largest city in the United States.

    (D) Robinson was named baseball's first rookie of the year in 1947.

    (E) Robinson never responded to taunts, jeers, or death threats from racist baseball fans.

55. Which of the following Broadway musicals was the center of a series of court cases that established the tenet that the content of paid theatrical performances, no matter how offensive some might find it, is fully protected by the First Amendment?

    (A) *Chicago*

    (B) *Hair*

    (C) *The Cradle Will Rock*

    (D) *The Who's Tommy*

    (E) *Oh, Calcutta!*

56. President Abraham Lincoln considered it crucial to prevent Maryland from seceding from the Union primarily because

    (A) it surrounded Washington, D.C., on three sides

    (B) it shared a long border with Pennsylvania

    (C) it was the site of the Battles of Antietam and Fredericksburg

    (D) it was home to John Wilkes Booth, Lincoln's assassin

    (E) it contained the greatest number of factories of any Southern state

57. Which of the following best describes the effect of the Monroe Doctrine on world politics?

    (A) Great Britain became more actively involved in Canadian affairs.

    (B) The United States was determined to take over Central and South America.

    (C) Spain began to play an active role in a series of Latin American wars for independence.

    (D) France began supporting Native Americans in their attempts to retake their ancestral lands from the U.S. government.

    (E) It set the tone for U.S. foreign policy in the future.

58. The American Colonization Society was founded in the early 1800s primarily to

    (A) forcibly expel African Americans from the United States

    (B) establish Native American reservations on good, fertile farming and hunting lands

    (C) encourage residents of the Eastern states to settle the Great Plains and the Southwest

    (D) help free African Americans resettle in northwestern Africa

    (E) achieve immediate and universal abolition of slavery throughout the United States

GO ON TO THE NEXT PAGE

PRACTICE TEST—*Continued*

59. Which of the following was founded in the aftermath of the Haymarket Riot of 1886?

    (A) Congress of Industrial Organizations
    (B) Teamsters' Union
    (C) American Railway Union
    (D) American Federation of Labor
    (E) Knights of Labor

60. Which of the following factors contributed most to California's decision to apply for statehood in 1850?

    (A) Increase in population as a result of the Gold Rush
    (B) Democratic Party success in the California legislature
    (C) Local insistence that California would be a slaveholding state
    (D) Decision of Congress to build a transcontinental railroad
    (E) Realization that the United States would soon be at war with Mexico

61. Many teenagers in the United States in the 1960s demanded that the voting age be lowered to 18 from 21 primarily because

    (A) they wanted the privilege of protesting against government policies
    (B) they supported a political party that intended to overthrow the U.S. government
    (C) they wanted to be able to vote to lower the legal drinking age
    (D) they hoped to vote down a recent increase in income tax rates
    (E) they felt that since they were old enough to fight and die in military service, they were old enough to vote

62. President Andrew Johnson's Reconstruction programs included all the following EXCEPT:

    (A) a blanket pardon to all Confederate soldiers
    (B) the removal of Union troops of occupation from the South
    (C) a requirement that Southern states abolish slavery
    (D) annulment of old debts to the Confederate government
    (E) full civil rights for all African Americans

63. The U.S. government encouraged the growth of settlement on the Great Plains in the mid-nineteenth century primarily by passing the

    (A) Homestead Act
    (B) Pacific Railway Act
    (C) Volstead Act
    (D) Morrill Act
    (E) Kansas-Nebraska Act

64. A "Horatio Alger" hero is a fictional character who symbolized which of the following to readers of the 1860s and 1870s?

    (A) The evil effects of gambling
    (B) The ability to get rich by working one's way up from poor beginnings
    (C) The value of social programs that helped working people
    (D) The importance of acquiring a four-year college degree
    (E) The importance of aristocratic family connections to those who want to succeed

65. Education reform during the late 1800s had all the following effects EXCEPT:

    (A) raising the literacy rate of people in the United States
    (B) changing teaching methods in the public schools
    (C) increasing the enrollment of students in all grade levels
    (D) integrating the public schools by race
    (E) founding more colleges and universities

66. The American Indian movement of the 1970s accomplished which of the following?

    (A) Took permanent control of the federal Bureau of Indian Affairs
    (B) Recovered thousands of acres of ancestral tribal lands in Maine and New Mexico
    (C) Won a lawsuit over an incident at Wounded Knee, South Dakota
    (D) Burned a replica of the Pilgrim ship *Mayflower* in Boston harbor
    (E) Established the National Museum of the American Indian in New York City

67. All the following types of music were fused together to become jazz EXCEPT:

    (A) ragtime
    (B) the blues
    (C) spirituals
    (D) hymns
    (E) work songs

GO ON TO THE NEXT PAGE

PRACTICE TEST—*Continued*

68. During the late 1800s newly arrived immigrants supported political machines primarily because

    (A) political machines offered them jobs and essential city services in exchange for their votes
    (B) political machines committed fraud to get their candidates elected when necessary
    (C) political machines received kickbacks from businesses
    (D) political bosses were fellow immigrants
    (E) political bosses supported the settlement-house movement and public education reform

69. The first shiploads of British colonists who settled on the Atlantic coast faced all the following problems EXCEPT:

    (A) hunger
    (B) disease
    (C) difficult winter weather
    (D) implacable hostility of the Native Americans
    (E) lack of essential supplies

NO COMMUNION WITH SLAVEHOLDERS.

70. The main point of the political cartoon above is that

    (A) the United States was founded by slaveholders such as George Washington
    (B) Abraham Lincoln was a deeply religious man
    (C) churches in the United States were hypocritical because seating was segregated by race
    (D) Abraham Lincoln did not have a prayer of winning a series of debates with Stephen Douglas
    (E) no slaveholder could ever expect absolution for any sins he had committed

71. The British were the first Europeans to settle all the following colonies EXCEPT:

    (A) Rhode Island
    (B) Connecticut
    (C) New York
    (D) Pennsylvania
    (E) Virginia

72. The colonists took all the following actions in opposition to the Stamp Act EXCEPT:

    (A) tarring and feathering the stamp agents
    (B) convening the Stamp Act Congress in New York City
    (C) passing resolutions declaring the Stamp Act illegitimate
    (D) boycotting British imports
    (E) sending the Olive Branch Petition to Parliament

73. Which one of the following men spearheaded the religious revival known as the Great Awakening of the mid-1700s?

    (A) Benjamin Franklin
    (B) William Penn
    (C) Jonathan Edwards
    (D) Edmund Andros
    (E) Oliver Cromwell

74. Congress passed the National Recovery Act in 1933 to do all the following EXCEPT:

    (A) stabilize prices
    (B) create jobs through public-works projects
    (C) allow industries to regulate themselves
    (D) raise wages
    (E) enforce antitrust laws

75. "Who pays the big election expenses of your congressman? . . . Do you imagine those who foot those huge bills are fools? Don't you know that they make sure of getting their money back, with interest?"

    The speaker of the above quotation most likely supported which of the following?

    (A) Progressivism
    (B) Prohibition
    (C) Segregation
    (D) Reconstruction
    (E) Cronyism

76. All the following contributed to the decline of the Colored Farmers' Alliance EXCEPT:

    (A) racial divisions within the Alliance movement
    (B) declining membership
    (C) use of violence by white farmers against black workers
    (D) failure of a cotton pickers' strike in 1891
    (E) expansion of the national money supply

GO ON TO THE NEXT PAGE

PRACTICE TEST—*Continued*

77. All the following photographers created important visual records of aspects of U.S. history EXCEPT:

    (A) Jacob Riis
    (B) Matthew Brady
    (C) Dorothea Lange
    (D) Jessie Tarbox Beals
    (E) Ansel Adams

78. The Articles of Confederation did not provide a good basis for government primarily because

    (A) they established no legislative branch for the national government
    (B) they gave the federal government no power to raise money from the states
    (C) they put too much power in the hands of the federal judiciary
    (D) they reserved no individual rights to the states of the Union
    (E) they required a unanimous vote of all the states to pass any legislation

79. The Populist Party of the 1890s supported all the following EXCEPT:

    (A) a graduated income tax
    (B) maintaining the gold standard
    (C) bank regulation
    (D) voting reform
    (E) limits on immigration

80. Which of the following novelists wrote mainly about the social class whose lifestyle Thorstein Veblen described in 1899 as the embodiment of "conspicuous consumption"?

    (A) Mark Twain
    (B) J. D. Salinger
    (C) Edith Wharton
    (D) Jack London
    (E) Ernest Hemingway

81. The Armory Show of 1913 was significant primarily because

    (A) it displayed the results of an explosion in a shingle factory
    (B) it was the first major exhibition of modern art in the United States
    (C) it was entirely under the control of the American Museum Association
    (D) it convinced the public that European painters were better than U.S. painters
    (E) it was a huge success with the critics and the public

82. President Lyndon B. Johnson became the national leader most responsible for ending racial segregation by taking all the following actions EXCEPT:

    (A) integrating the armed forces
    (B) appointing Thurgood Marshall to the Supreme Court
    (C) signing into law the Civil Rights Act of 1964
    (D) creating the Office of Economic Opportunity
    (E) signing into law the Voting Rights Act of 1965

83. The French and Indian War resulted in all the following EXCEPT:

    (A) Colonists gained their first experience of organized military action.
    (B) France ceded all territory east of the Mississippi River, except New Orleans, to Britain.
    (C) Seeds of distrust and resentment were sown between the British Army and the colonial volunteers.
    (D) Britain accumulated an enormous war debt.
    (E) Colonial legislatures voted to approve Ben Franklin's Albany Plan of Union.

84. The above cartoon urges the American colonies to support which of the following?

    (A) The Albany Plan of Union
    (B) The Articles of Confederation
    (C) The Declaration of Independence
    (D) The Treaty of Paris
    (E) The Constitution of the United States

GO ON TO THE NEXT PAGE

PRACTICE TEST—*Continued*

85. Which of the following is a classic American novel of adolescent rebellion?

 (A) *Moby-Dick* by Herman Melville
 (B) *The Catcher in the Rye* by J. D. Salinger
 (C) *To Kill a Mockingbird* by Harper Lee
 (D) *My Ántonia* by Willa Cather
 (E) *The Moon Is Down* by John Steinbeck

86. All the following combined to help form the Free-Soil Party in 1848 EXCEPT:

 (A) farmers
 (B) land reformers
 (C) industrial workers
 (D) abolitionists
 (E) Southern conservatives

87. Which of the following resulted when the workers at the Carnegie Steel Company of Homestead, PA, went on strike in 1892?

 (A) Eugene Debs made a public speech expressing support for the strikers.
 (B) The company had the union leaders arrested for theft.
 (C) Strikers achieved their goal of higher wages.
 (D) Andrew Carnegie resigned as chairman of U.S. Steel.
 (E) Management locked the workers out of the plant.

88. "Rather than trying to climb the economic ladder, people are becoming more concerned with relationships and family and community involvement."

 The speaker of the above quotation is most likely commenting on the passage into law of which of the following?

 (A) Family and Medical Leave Act
 (B) North American Free Trade Agreement
 (C) Immigration Act
 (D) Operation Restore Hope
 (E) Contract with America

89. "Mr. Rockefeller has systematically played with loaded dice. . . . Business played in this way loses all its sportsmanlike qualities. It is fit only for tricksters."

 The above statement most likely was made by which of the following muckraking journalists in which exposé?

 (A) Ida M. Tarbell, *History of the Standard Oil Company*
 (B) Lincoln Steffens, *Tweed Days in St. Louis*
 (C) Theodore Dreiser, *The Financier*
 (D) Ray Stannard Baker, *Following the Color Line*
 (E) Jacob Riis, *How the Other Half Lives*

90. Which of the following African-American leaders wrote *Up From Slavery?*

 (A) Malcolm X
 (B) Frederick Douglass
 (C) Ida B. Wells-Barnett
 (D) Booker T. Washington
 (E) Medgar Evers

STOP

IF YOU FINISH BEFORE TIME RUNS OUT, GO BACK AND CHECK YOUR WORK.

ANSWER KEY

1. D	21. A	41. B	61. E	81. B
2. A	22. C	42. E	62. E	82. A
3. B	23. D	43. B	63. A	83. E
4. B	24. C	44. C	64. B	84. A
5. E	25. B	45. D	65. D	85. B
6. D	26. D	46. E	66. B	86. E
7. D	27. D	47. B	67. D	87. E
8. A	28. A	48. D	68. A	88. A
9. B	29. D	49. A	69. D	89. A
10. E	30. C	50. D	70. A	90. D
11. A	31. D	51. C	71. C	
12. A	32. B	52. B	72. E	
13. C	33. A	53. C	73. C	
14. D	34. C	54. B	74. E	
15. A	35. D	55. B	75. A	
16. D	36. B	56. A	76. E	
17. B	37. A	57. E	77. E	
18. A	38. A	58. D	78. B	
19. E	39. C	59. D	79. B	
20. D	40. E	60. A	80. C	

ANSWERS AND EXPLANATIONS

1. **D** Jamaica Kincaid's novels are based on her life experiences in her native Caribbean Islands.

2. **A** The Plains tribes' agreement to define their territorial borders and remain within them was a key provision of this conference.

3. **B** The Kansas-Nebraska Act is the only one of the five choices that affected the number and likely political bias of incoming senators.

4. **B** Montesquieu's *Spirit of the Laws* included his ideal design for a government, with the powers divided among different branches, each of which could check the powers of the others in some way.

5. **E** The Court expressly stated that a slave's status could not be changed by any power except that of the person who owned him or her.

6. **D** No one in Hollywood would hire the writers because their refusal to testify implied to many that they were in fact communists. Hollywood producers were worried that if they hired suspected communists, people would boycott their films and they would lose money.

7. **D** The Elkins Act (1903) and the Hepburn Act (1906) were important examples of railroad legislation passed before the Triangle fire (1911).

8. **A** Sacco and Vanzetti were convicted of murder but in fact were executed because the authorities did not like their radical political views.

9. **B** The GI Bill meant that millions of veterans could attend college, thus substantially raising the educational level of people in the United States.

10. **E** *The Red Badge of Courage* is a classic historical novel of Civil War combat. The other four choices are all well-known autobiographical works that deal with various aspects of the American experience.

11. **A** Severe droughts and then severe blizzards killed up to 90 percent of the cattle herds in the late 1880s.

12. **A** The graph shows that 54 percent of all people in the United States preferred either to aid both sides in the war or to aid neither side. A further 9 percent gave "other answers" that did not include support for the Allies or Germany.

13. **C** The Emancipation Proclamation went into effect on January 1, 1863, and freed all slaves in states then in rebellion against the United States.

14. **D** Prohibition had many effects, but it never succeeded in its intended effect of stopping people in the United States from buying, selling, or drinking alcoholic beverages. It simply made their behavior illegal. However, Prohibition did reduce alcohol consumption in the United States.

15. **A** A free press is important primarily because it reports accurately on activities within the government. Only choice A describes a situation in which the press revealed damaging information that the government certainly would have kept secret if there had not been a free press to reveal it.

16. **D** The world wars were fought in Europe, North Africa, and the Pacific; the Mexican-American War was fought in the Southwest and in Mexico; and the War of 1812 was fought in the United States and its territories and in Canada.

17. **B** The Democratic Party was the proslavery party.

18. **A** The Antifederalists were concerned primarily with the issues of states' rights and individual rights.

19. **E** The rise of the automobile throughout the twentieth century spelled disaster for the railroads.

20. **D** The newspapers of William Randolph Hearst published propaganda that aroused public opinion against Spain to such a degree that Washington felt it had no choice but to declare war on Spain. Historians have always credited—or discredited—Hearst with forcing this war to happen in order to boost his newspaper's circulation.

21. **A** Ferdinand de Lesseps had just finished overseeing the design and building of the Suez Canal and hoped to repeat his success in Panama, but the French project ran out of money before he could finish the job.

22. **C** Puritan authorities did not believe in freedom of religion for anyone but themselves, and they did not believe in the separation of church and state.

23. **D** Elbridge Gerry of Massachusetts was never elected president.

24. **C** The Confederacy wanted a military alliance with England and France, not to provide European soldiers, but to acquire weapons and gunpowder, supplies, money in the form of loans, and naval assistance in breaking the blockade.

25. **B** Schlafly was the main spokesperson for the "Stop the ERA" movement. She said that, "The ERA would lead to women being drafted by the military and to public unisex bathrooms."

26. **D** The Comstock Lode was located in the western region of present-day Nevada about 15 miles from Carson City and 25 miles from Reno.

27. **D** Rosie the Riveter was featured on a popular wartime poster, wearing a coverall with her hair tied back in a scarf and proclaiming, "We Can Do It!"

28. **A** An economic depression occurs when prices and wages fall and businesses cut back on the number of employees.

29. **D** The power loom led directly to the factory system, in which workers were brought to the workplace to manufacture goods rather than working artisan-style in their homes.

30. **C** Smith lost the election in rural districts for various reasons, including the fact that he was a Catholic big-city politician.

31. **D** Clark and his troops captured the three forts in the summer of 1778.

32. **B** Only about one-third of Southern whites owned slaves yet poor whites without slaves willingly died for the Confederacy in the Civil War. Slavery (and racism) gave status to poor whites and was sufficient to compensate them for their lack of political or economic power in the South.

33. **A** In July 1945 the war in Europe was over. World leaders were divided on how best to take charge of a defeated Germany so that nation never again would rearm and try to conquer all of Europe.

34. **C** The Open Door Policy called for fair trade access to China for all nations.

35. **D** Article I, which describes the functions of the Senate, notes that the vice president will preside over it but not vote unless the Senate is tied.

36. **B** Anne Hutchinson had been a popular independent religious leader in Massachusetts, banished because she disagreed publicly with the church authorities.

37. **A** The Anasazi lived in the Southwest in an area known today as the Four Corners. They constructed apartment building–type structures of adobe on the sides of cliffs.

38. **A** The rise of automobile ownership meant a rise in paving the roads on which cars drove, refining the oil used to fuel cars, advertising that sold cars, and credit with which people bought cars.

39. **C** Congress rejected Roosevelt's request, since the Constitution specified that judges would serve "during good behavior," meaning that they served for life unless they committed crimes or misdemeanors.

40. **E** The United States acquired the Southwestern land known as the Gadsden Purchase in 1854 during Franklin Pierce's presidency. This was six years after the Mexican Cession that the U.S. acquired at the end of the Mexican-American War under James Polk.

41. **B** According to this theory, if wealthy businesses owners spend less on taxes, they can spend more on hiring employees and perhaps lower the prices of goods and services. Therefore, the poorer classes will benefit from tax cuts for the wealthy.

42. **E** This program was called the Strategic Defense Initiative, but the public nicknamed it "Star Wars" after the name of a popular science-fiction/fantasy movie.

43. **B** Tweed was famous for running New York City from Tammany Hall.

44. **C** Calhoun contended that the states had the right to nullify unconstitutional acts of Congress; hence, this is referred to as the doctrine of nullification.

45. **D** The purpose of the Securities and Exchange Commission is to regulate companies that sell stocks and bonds.

46. **E** The phrase "set a country free" makes it clear that the writer (Thomas Paine) must be speaking of the Revolutionary War, in which the colonists saw themselves as slaves fighting for their freedom from the tyranny of Great Britain.

47. **B** The Eighteenth Amendment, popularly known as Prohibition, was the longtime goal of the temperance movement.

48. **D** Native Americans had accrued many serious grievances against the U.S. government for over 200 years, but the United States had not barred Native Americans from operating businesses on their reservations.

49. **A** As a business owner, George Pullman was an opponent of organized labor

50. **D** Choice D is the only statement supported by the information and the graphs.

51. **C** Faubus did not appeal to the federal government, which he knew would oppose his requests.

52. **B** China became a communist nation after World War II; Congress did not want the Chinese to spread communism to any of the neighboring nations, such as Korea.

53. **C** Parliament felt that it had to take stern measures against the colonists because during the Boston Tea Party, they destroyed valuable property.

54. **B** Every time he came to bat, Jackie Robinson proved to millions of people that African Americans clearly deserved the same opportunities as whites. The other choices are all true but not relevant to the question.

55. **B** *Hair* offended many with its nudity, strong language, and criticism of mainstream American society. Nevertheless, the courts ruled that it was clearly protected under the First Amendment right to free speech.

56. **A** If Maryland had seceded, the U.S. capital city would have been surrounded on all four sides by the Confederacy. That was clearly untenable.

57. **E** The Monroe Doctrine threatened any nation with colonial ambitions in the western hemisphere. The threat set the tone for U.S. foreign policy into the 21st century.

58. **D** The Colonization Society hoped that the issue of abolition could be settled peacefully by persuading and helping Africans leave North America altogether.

59. **D** The Haymarket Riot caused skilled workers to break ranks with unskilled workers and form their own union, the American Federation of Labor.

60. **A** California's population had become so enormous during the Gold Rush that it needed to organize its government and apply for statehood.

61. **E** Teenagers in the United States felt that if they were old enough to be drafted at 18, they ought to be allowed at the same age to vote for the leaders who would decide whether to draft them.

62. **E** Johnson did not believe, personally or politically, in full civil rights for African Americans.

63. **A** The Homestead Act encouraged settlement by giving away land to anyone who would settle on it and farm it for five years.

64. **B** The novels of Horatio Alger, Jr., were rags-to-riches stories featuring heroes who began life in poverty and patiently and honestly worked their way up to great wealth.

65. **D** Education reformers in this era did not tackle the issue of integration.

66. **B** The American Indian movement helped tribes initiate lawsuits in which they eventually recovered huge tracts of their ancestral lands from the U.S. government.

67. **D** Jazz is a musical tradition that combines four other African-American musical traditions: spirituals, the blues, ragtime, and work songs. Although jazz combines African musical elements such as the "blue note" and the call-and-response motif with European elements such as melody and harmony, it is least influenced by hymns.

68. **A** The primary reason for immigrants to support bosses was because the bosses saw to it that important social and public services that directly benefited immigrants were provided.

69. **D** In the first years of British colonization there were friendly relations between Native Americans and colonists. Colonists probably would not have survived the first few years in North America without the help of Native Americans such as Squanto.

70. **A** The cartoon suggests that the Union position against slaveholding is hypocritical because Washington and others who founded the United States were slaveholders.

71. **C** The first Europeans to settle New York were the Dutch.

72. **E** Colonists sent the Olive Branch Petition to Great Britain long after the Stamp Act was repealed.

73. **C** Jonathan Edwards of Connecticut generally is credited with starting the Great Awakening by preaching salvation through intense faith rather than predestination.

74. **E** The NRA allowed industries to regulate themselves by establishing a code system of fair competition. Those industry-created codes had the force of law and were exempt from antitrust laws.

75. **A** Progressivism was a movement that included political reform: Progressives tried to eliminate the political habit of kowtowing to the special-interest lobbies that the speaker describes in the quotation.

76. **E** The expansion of the money supply would have helped, not hurt, the Colored Farmers' Alliance.

77. **E** Ansel Adams was not a photojournalist but an artistic photographer. The other four published their photographs with the purpose of informing the public about current events rather than creating art.

78. **B** The lack of any strength at all in the central government, especially its lack of the power to raise money, was the primary reason the framers wrote a new governing document, the Constitution.

79. **B** The Populist Party did not support maintaining the gold standard.

80. **C** Thorstein Veblen was referring to the idle, wealthy class at the top of the social pyramid. Edith Wharton, born into that social class, wrote about it in novels such as *The House of Mirth* and *The Age of Innocence*.

81. **B** The Armory Show provided most of the U.S. public with its first look at modern European and American art.

82. **A** The armed forces had been integrated under President Harry S. Truman.

83. **E** The Albany Plan (1754), proposed by Ben Franklin, would have placed the American colonies under a more centralized government. The plan predated the French and Indian War and was never carried out.

84. **A** Franklin designed this cartoon to show how powerless the colonies were separately and how strong and dangerous they could be if they united. He proposed the Albany Plan of Union long before the other four choices existed.

85. **B** *My Ántonia* and *To Kill a Mockingbird* both have important adolescent characters, but only *The Catcher in the Rye*'s Holden Caulfield spends the entire book rebelling against society and authority.

86. **E** Southern conservatives wanted to maintain the slave system; this made them directly opposed to the goals of the Free-Soilers.

87. **E** None of the first four choices happened as a result of the Homestead Strike. As soon as the workers struck, management locked them out and hired guards to protect the plant.

88. **A** The Family and Medical Leave Act ensured that U.S. workers would be paid during long-term absences from work taken for their own illnesses or disabilities or because a family member, such as a new baby, needed full-time care.

89. **A** The Rockefellers owned the Standard Oil Company, and Ida Tarbell is famous for exposing its shady business dealings in print.

90. **D** Booker T. Washington (1856–1915), the great African American leader, published his autobiography, *Up From Slavery*, in 1901.

PRACTICE TEST 4

▮▮ SCORE SHEET

Number of questions correct: _____

Less: 0.25 × number of questions wrong: _____

(Remember that omitted questions ares not counted as wrong.)

Raw score: _____

Raw Score	Scaled Score	Raw Score	Scaled Score	Raw Score	Scaled Score	Raw Score	Scaled Score	Raw Score	Scaled Score
90	800	65	710	40	550	15	420	−10	300
89	800	64	700	39	550	14	420	−11	290
88	800	63	700	38	540	13	410	−12	290
87	800	62	690	37	540	12	410	−13	280
86	800	61	680	36	530	11	400	−14	280
85	800	60	680	35	530	10	400	−15	270
84	800	59	670	34	520	9	390	−16	260
83	800	58	660	33	520	8	390	−17	260
82	800	57	660	32	510	7	380	−18	250
81	800	56	650	31	510	6	380	−19	240
80	790	55	640	30	500	5	370	−20	230
79	780	54	630	29	500	4	370	−21	230
78	780	53	630	28	490	3	360	−22	230
77	770	52	620	27	480	2	360		
76	760	51	620	26	480	1	350		
75	760	50	610	25	470	0	350		
74	750	49	610	24	470	−1	340		
73	750	48	600	23	460	−2	340		
72	740	47	600	22	460	−3	330		
71	740	46	590	21	450	−4	330		
70	730	45	590	20	450	−5	320		
69	730	44	580	19	440	−6	320		
68	720	43	570	18	440	−7	320		
67	720	42	560	17	430	−8	310		
66	710	41	560	16	430	−9	310		

Note: This is only a sample scoring scale. Scoring scales differ from exam to exam.

PRACTICE TEST 5

U.S. HISTORY

The following Practice Test is designed to be just like the real SAT U.S. History test. It matches the actual test in content coverage and level of difficulty.

When you are finished with the test, determine your score and carefully read the answer explanations for the questions you answered incorrectly. Identify any weak areas by determining the areas in which you made the most errors. Review those chapters of the book first. Then, as time permits, go back and review your stronger areas.

Allow 1 hour to take the test. Time yourself and work uninterrupted. If you run out of time, take note of where you ended when time ran out. Remember that you lose $\frac{1}{4}$ of a point for each incorrect answer. Because of this penalty, do not guess on a question unless you can eliminate one or more of the answers. Your score is calculated by using the following formula:

Number of correct answers $- \frac{1}{4}$(Number of incorrect answers)

This Practice Test will be an accurate reflection of how you'll do on test day if you treat it as the real examination. Here are some hints on how to take the test under conditions similar to those of the actual examination:

- Complete the test in one sitting.
- Time yourself.
- Tear out your Answer Sheet and fill in the ovals just as you would on the actual test day.
- Become familiar with the directions to the test and the reference information provided. You'll save time on the actual test day by already being familiar with this information.

PRACTICE TEST 5

U.S. HISTORY

ANSWER SHEET

Tear out this answer sheet and use it to mark your answers.

There are 100 lines of numbered ovals on this answer sheet. If there are more lines than you need, leave the remainder blank.

1. Ⓐ Ⓑ Ⓒ Ⓓ Ⓔ	26. Ⓐ Ⓑ Ⓒ Ⓓ Ⓔ	51. Ⓐ Ⓑ Ⓒ Ⓓ Ⓔ	76. Ⓐ Ⓑ Ⓒ Ⓓ Ⓔ
2. Ⓐ Ⓑ Ⓒ Ⓓ Ⓔ	27. Ⓐ Ⓑ Ⓒ Ⓓ Ⓔ	52. Ⓐ Ⓑ Ⓒ Ⓓ Ⓔ	77. Ⓐ Ⓑ Ⓒ Ⓓ Ⓔ
3. Ⓐ Ⓑ Ⓒ Ⓓ Ⓔ	28. Ⓐ Ⓑ Ⓒ Ⓓ Ⓔ	53. Ⓐ Ⓑ Ⓒ Ⓓ Ⓔ	78. Ⓐ Ⓑ Ⓒ Ⓓ Ⓔ
4. Ⓐ Ⓑ Ⓒ Ⓓ Ⓔ	29. Ⓐ Ⓑ Ⓒ Ⓓ Ⓔ	54. Ⓐ Ⓑ Ⓒ Ⓓ Ⓔ	79. Ⓐ Ⓑ Ⓒ Ⓓ Ⓔ
5. Ⓐ Ⓑ Ⓒ Ⓓ Ⓔ	30. Ⓐ Ⓑ Ⓒ Ⓓ Ⓔ	55. Ⓐ Ⓑ Ⓒ Ⓓ Ⓔ	80. Ⓐ Ⓑ Ⓒ Ⓓ Ⓔ
6. Ⓐ Ⓑ Ⓒ Ⓓ Ⓔ	31. Ⓐ Ⓑ Ⓒ Ⓓ Ⓔ	56. Ⓐ Ⓑ Ⓒ Ⓓ Ⓔ	81. Ⓐ Ⓑ Ⓒ Ⓓ Ⓔ
7. Ⓐ Ⓑ Ⓒ Ⓓ Ⓔ	32. Ⓐ Ⓑ Ⓒ Ⓓ Ⓔ	57. Ⓐ Ⓑ Ⓒ Ⓓ Ⓔ	82. Ⓐ Ⓑ Ⓒ Ⓓ Ⓔ
8. Ⓐ Ⓑ Ⓒ Ⓓ Ⓔ	33. Ⓐ Ⓑ Ⓒ Ⓓ Ⓔ	58. Ⓐ Ⓑ Ⓒ Ⓓ Ⓔ	83. Ⓐ Ⓑ Ⓒ Ⓓ Ⓔ
9. Ⓐ Ⓑ Ⓒ Ⓓ Ⓔ	34. Ⓐ Ⓑ Ⓒ Ⓓ Ⓔ	59. Ⓐ Ⓑ Ⓒ Ⓓ Ⓔ	84. Ⓐ Ⓑ Ⓒ Ⓓ Ⓔ
10. Ⓐ Ⓑ Ⓒ Ⓓ Ⓔ	35. Ⓐ Ⓑ Ⓒ Ⓓ Ⓔ	60. Ⓐ Ⓑ Ⓒ Ⓓ Ⓔ	85. Ⓐ Ⓑ Ⓒ Ⓓ Ⓔ
11. Ⓐ Ⓑ Ⓒ Ⓓ Ⓔ	36. Ⓐ Ⓑ Ⓒ Ⓓ Ⓔ	61. Ⓐ Ⓑ Ⓒ Ⓓ Ⓔ	86. Ⓐ Ⓑ Ⓒ Ⓓ Ⓔ
12. Ⓐ Ⓑ Ⓒ Ⓓ Ⓔ	37. Ⓐ Ⓑ Ⓒ Ⓓ Ⓔ	62. Ⓐ Ⓑ Ⓒ Ⓓ Ⓔ	87. Ⓐ Ⓑ Ⓒ Ⓓ Ⓔ
13. Ⓐ Ⓑ Ⓒ Ⓓ Ⓔ	38. Ⓐ Ⓑ Ⓒ Ⓓ Ⓔ	63. Ⓐ Ⓑ Ⓒ Ⓓ Ⓔ	88. Ⓐ Ⓑ Ⓒ Ⓓ Ⓔ
14. Ⓐ Ⓑ Ⓒ Ⓓ Ⓔ	39. Ⓐ Ⓑ Ⓒ Ⓓ Ⓔ	64. Ⓐ Ⓑ Ⓒ Ⓓ Ⓔ	89. Ⓐ Ⓑ Ⓒ Ⓓ Ⓔ
15. Ⓐ Ⓑ Ⓒ Ⓓ Ⓔ	40. Ⓐ Ⓑ Ⓒ Ⓓ Ⓔ	65. Ⓐ Ⓑ Ⓒ Ⓓ Ⓔ	90. Ⓐ Ⓑ Ⓒ Ⓓ Ⓔ
16. Ⓐ Ⓑ Ⓒ Ⓓ Ⓔ	41. Ⓐ Ⓑ Ⓒ Ⓓ Ⓔ	66. Ⓐ Ⓑ Ⓒ Ⓓ Ⓔ	91. Ⓐ Ⓑ Ⓒ Ⓓ Ⓔ
17. Ⓐ Ⓑ Ⓒ Ⓓ Ⓔ	42. Ⓐ Ⓑ Ⓒ Ⓓ Ⓔ	67. Ⓐ Ⓑ Ⓒ Ⓓ Ⓔ	92. Ⓐ Ⓑ Ⓒ Ⓓ Ⓔ
18. Ⓐ Ⓑ Ⓒ Ⓓ Ⓔ	43. Ⓐ Ⓑ Ⓒ Ⓓ Ⓔ	68. Ⓐ Ⓑ Ⓒ Ⓓ Ⓔ	93. Ⓐ Ⓑ Ⓒ Ⓓ Ⓔ
19. Ⓐ Ⓑ Ⓒ Ⓓ Ⓔ	44. Ⓐ Ⓑ Ⓒ Ⓓ Ⓔ	69. Ⓐ Ⓑ Ⓒ Ⓓ Ⓔ	94. Ⓐ Ⓑ Ⓒ Ⓓ Ⓔ
20. Ⓐ Ⓑ Ⓒ Ⓓ Ⓔ	45. Ⓐ Ⓑ Ⓒ Ⓓ Ⓔ	70. Ⓐ Ⓑ Ⓒ Ⓓ Ⓔ	95. Ⓐ Ⓑ Ⓒ Ⓓ Ⓔ
21. Ⓐ Ⓑ Ⓒ Ⓓ Ⓔ	46. Ⓐ Ⓑ Ⓒ Ⓓ Ⓔ	71. Ⓐ Ⓑ Ⓒ Ⓓ Ⓔ	96. Ⓐ Ⓑ Ⓒ Ⓓ Ⓔ
22. Ⓐ Ⓑ Ⓒ Ⓓ Ⓔ	47. Ⓐ Ⓑ Ⓒ Ⓓ Ⓔ	72. Ⓐ Ⓑ Ⓒ Ⓓ Ⓔ	97. Ⓐ Ⓑ Ⓒ Ⓓ Ⓔ
23. Ⓐ Ⓑ Ⓒ Ⓓ Ⓔ	48. Ⓐ Ⓑ Ⓒ Ⓓ Ⓔ	73. Ⓐ Ⓑ Ⓒ Ⓓ Ⓔ	98. Ⓐ Ⓑ Ⓒ Ⓓ Ⓔ
24. Ⓐ Ⓑ Ⓒ Ⓓ Ⓔ	49. Ⓐ Ⓑ Ⓒ Ⓓ Ⓔ	74. Ⓐ Ⓑ Ⓒ Ⓓ Ⓔ	99. Ⓐ Ⓑ Ⓒ Ⓓ Ⓔ
25. Ⓐ Ⓑ Ⓒ Ⓓ Ⓔ	50. Ⓐ Ⓑ Ⓒ Ⓓ Ⓔ	75. Ⓐ Ⓑ Ⓒ Ⓓ Ⓔ	100. Ⓐ Ⓑ Ⓒ Ⓓ Ⓔ

PRACTICE TEST 5
Time: 60 Minutes

<u>Directions</u>: Each of the questions or incomplete statements below is followed by five suggested answers or completions. Select the one that is best in each case and then fill in the corresponding oval on the answer sheet.

1. Women who opposed passage of the Equal Rights Amendment did so primarily because

    (A) they believed that women do not deserve the same rights as men
    (B) they did not want to lose certain privileges, such as exemption from the military draft
    (C) they felt that it would destroy women's role in the home
    (D) they thought it was best to fight for equality on a local level
    (E) they did not want to lose any of the rights for which they had fought for so many decades

2. Which of the following granted all African-American men the right to vote?

    (A) The Emancipation Proclamation
    (B) The Reconstruction Acts
    (C) The Freedmen's Bureau
    (D) The Fifteenth Amendment
    (E) The Enforcement Acts

3. Which of the following administrations authorized continued financial aid to the Nicaraguan Contras in defiance of congressional laws against it?

    (A) Gerald Ford
    (B) Jimmy Carter
    (C) Ronald Reagan
    (D) George H. W. Bush
    (E) George W. Bush

4. The Northwest Ordinance of 1787 specified which of the following?

    (A) The federal government would sell land in the Northwest Territory on credit.
    (B) The Northwest Territory was divided into townships and lots that were sold to the public.
    (C) Any precious metals discovered in the Northwest Territory were the property of the federal government.
    (D) Only Native Americans were entitled to live in the Northwest Territory.
    (E) When a section of the Northwest Territory had a large enough population, it could draft a constitution and apply for statehood.

5. Eleanor Roosevelt accomplished all the following EXCEPT:

    (A) writing a daily newspaper column
    (B) holding the post of special ambassador to the United Nations
    (C) visiting soldiers in dangerous combat zones such as Guadalcanal
    (D) taking a public stand in favor of civil rights for African Americans
    (E) founding the National Organization for Women

6. In the aftermath of World War I, President Woodrow Wilson

    (A) urged U.S. neutrality toward European nations
    (B) fought for the establishment of the League of Nations
    (C) signed the Balfour Declaration with Great Britain
    (D) participated in a peace conference in Berlin
    (E) vetoed the Espionage and Sedition Acts

7. Hillary Rodham Clinton is the first first lady to do which of the following?

    (A) Hold elected political office
    (B) Publish an autobiography
    (C) Fight for education and health-care reform
    (D) Get a college education
    (E) Restore and redecorate public rooms in the White House

8. The Black Codes of the late 1860s had which of the following purposes?

    (A) To restore the status quo of Southern society before the Civil War
    (B) To enforce freedmen's right to vote
    (C) To allow African Americans to hold elected office
    (D) To intimidate Democrats into staying away from the polls
    (E) To nullify the Secession Acts of 1860 and 1861

GO ON TO THE NEXT PAGE

PRACTICE TEST—*Continued*

9. During the mid-1800s farmers faced all the following problems EXCEPT:

   (A) The supply of crops exceeded the demand for them.
   (B) They incurred debt from purchases of land or equipment.
   (C) The prices of crops had fallen.
   (D) There were no protective tariffs on imported crops.
   (E) The Grange and Alliance movements prevented them from organizing.

10. Strikes led by members of the International Ladies' Garment Workers' Union had all the following effects EXCEPT:

    (A) Employers agreed to raise wages.
    (B) Employers agreed to shorten the workweek.
    (C) Employers agreed to a closed shop.
    (D) Union membership rose by the tens of thousands.
    (E) Many African American women joined the strikers.

11. Theodore Roosevelt began his presidency with all the following goals EXCEPT:

    (A) fighting rigid class distinctions in U.S. society
    (B) speaking his mind on important issues of the day
    (C) forcing corporations to serve the public good
    (D) overseeing ratification of the Nineteenth Amendment on woman suffrage
    (E) fighting unethical and illegal conduct in big businesses

12. Which of the following does NOT characterize the Clinton administrations of the 1990s?

    (A) Economic prosperity
    (B) Federal budget surpluses
    (C) Low unemployment rates
    (D) Passage of important social legislation
    (E) Strained relations with foreign allies

13. American Tories remained loyal to Great Britain during the Revolutionary War for all the following reasons EXCEPT:

    (A) belief that it was immoral to turn against a hereditary monarch
    (B) desire to protect the power and wealth they enjoyed as British subjects
    (C) personal loyalty to King George III
    (D) unwillingness to commit what they believed was treason by taking up arms against Britain
    (E) belief that the various acts of Parliament were neither onerous nor oppressive

14. All the following factors led to the decline and fall of the Industrial Workers of the World EXCEPT:

    (A) the failure of several labor strikes
    (B) people's fear of the IWW's methods and goals
    (C) refusal of employers to accept an open shop
    (D) a government crackdown on union activity
    (E) conflict within the IWW leadership

15. Europeans explored and colonized the "New World" for all the following motives EXCEPT:

    (A) desire for religious and political freedom
    (B) expansion of European-based empires
    (C) discovery of the Northwest Passage
    (D) greed for gold, treasure, and natural resources
    (E) assimilation into New World cultures

16. Which of the following was NOT a prominent protest group during the civil rights era?

    (A) Southern Christian Leadership Conference
    (B) Fair Employment Practices Committee
    (C) Montgomery Improvement Association
    (D) Student Nonviolent Coordinating Committee
    (E) Congress of Racial Equality

17. American pop music of the 1960s was characterized by all the following EXCEPT:

    (A) song lyrics with political messages
    (B) use of electrically amplified instruments
    (C) a new link between rock and folk music
    (D) a rise in the popularity of big bands
    (E) song lyrics that protested against "the establishment"

GO ON TO THE NEXT PAGE

PRACTICE TEST—*Continued*

18. "We are people of this generation, bred in at least modest comfort, housed now in universities, looking uncomfortably to the world we inherit."

    The author of the above quotation most likely would have supported which of the following movements?

    (A) Counterculture
    (B) Labor
    (C) Temperance
    (D) Religious revival
    (E) Feminist

19. The Seneca Falls Convention of 1848 was called primarily to

    (A) integrate U.S. society along race, gender, and class lines
    (B) declare that women and men should have equal rights
    (C) revise the Declaration of Independence
    (D) force the president of the United States to grant women the right to vote
    (E) do away with the economic system based on owning private property

20. All the following authors were considered members of the nineteenth-century Transcendentalist community EXCEPT:

    (A) Bronson Alcott
    (B) Ralph Waldo Emerson
    (C) Margaret Fuller
    (D) Henry David Thoreau
    (E) Emily Dickinson

21. Henry Clay's American System called for all the following EXCEPT:

    (A) a national bank
    (B) protective tariffs
    (C) a national transportation system
    (D) a sound national currency
    (E) a free-trade agreement with Great Britain

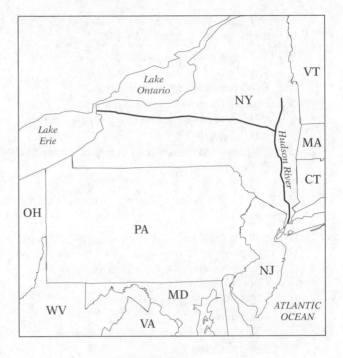

22. The heavy line on the map shows

    (A) the Pony Express
    (B) the Erie Canal
    (C) the Cumberland Road
    (D) the Trail of Tears
    (E) the Appalachian Trail

23. Which one of the following men did NOT play a key role in the U.S. military during the Revolutionary War?

    (A) Benedict Arnold
    (B) Ethan Allen
    (C) Samuel Adams
    (D) George Rogers Clark
    (E) Nathaniel Greene

24. The Japanese Internment of World War II was focused primarily on Japanese-Americans who resided in the following state:

    (A) Florida
    (B) California
    (C) New York
    (D) Illinois
    (E) Michigan

GO ON TO THE NEXT PAGE →

PRACTICE TEST—*Continued*

25. Demobilization after World War I had all the following effects on the economy EXCEPT:

    (A) Factories cut back production and dismissed workers.
    (B) Crop prices fell to new lows.
    (C) Prices of consumer goods went up.
    (D) Women were pressured into giving up their jobs to men.
    (E) Employment rates rose as veterans returned to the workforce.

26. During the 1920s African Americans migrated to the North primarily to

    (A) join the NAACP
    (B) escape violence and oppression
    (C) organize unions for African-American laborers
    (D) take jobs on cattle ranches or acquire homesteads
    (E) take part in major protests against racial discrimination

27. "This bill will destroy our common life and will rob us of everything which we hold dear—our lands, our customs, our traditions."

    The speaker of the above quotation most likely was referring to which of the following?

    (A) The Bursum Bill
    (B) The Taft-Hartley Act
    (C) The Sherman Antitrust Act
    (D) The Immigration Act
    (E) The Equal Rights Amendment

28. All the following were Union generals during the Civil War EXCEPT:

    (A) William Tecumseh Sherman
    (B) Ambrose Burnside
    (C) Thomas "Stonewall" Jackson
    (D) Ulysses S. Grant
    (E) George McClellan

29. The GI Bill of Rights gave millions of veterans the opportunity to

    (A) get a college education
    (B) join a branch of the armed forces
    (C) refuse combat duty
    (D) move to Canada
    (E) be given a fair trial if court-martialed

30. All the following were parts of the Anaconda Plan in the Civil War EXCEPT:

    (A) a Union blockade of Confederate ports
    (B) a siege of Richmond by federal troops
    (C) a campaign to destroy Southern railroads and industries
    (D) cutting the South in half by seizing the Mississippi
    (E) assaulting coastal ports to seize trading vessels

31. Theodore Roosevelt's "Square Deal" called for all the following EXCEPT:

    (A) limiting the power of trusts
    (B) enacting cuts in personal income taxes
    (C) promoting public health and safety
    (D) improving working conditions for the laboring class
    (E) balancing the interests of big business, consumers, and labor

32. Which of the following novels is a literary icon of the Jazz Age?

    (A) *The Troll Garden* by Willa Cather
    (B) *The Great Gatsby* by F. Scott Fitzgerald
    (C) *The House of Mirth* by Edith Wharton
    (D) *Of Mice and Men* by John Steinbeck
    (E) *The Portrait of a Lady* by Henry James

33. In *Powell v. Alabama,* the Supreme Court revoked the death sentences of the "Scottsboro boys" on the grounds that

    (A) the police had forced the defendants to confess their guilt
    (B) the defendants had been denied the right to a trial by jury
    (C) the defendants had alibis from eyewitnesses who had not been allowed to testify
    (D) the defendants had been denied the right to due process
    (E) the defendants had been framed for crimes committed by other people

GO ON TO THE NEXT PAGE

PRACTICE TEST—*Continued*

34. "For what did you throw off the yoke of Britain and call yourselves independent? Was it from a disposition fond of change, or to procure new masters? . . . This new form of national government . . . will be dangerous to your liberty and happiness."

    The speaker of the above quotation was most likely a member of which group?

    (A) Federalists
    (B) Sons of Liberty
    (C) Democrats
    (D) Antifederalists
    (E) Tories

35. All the following were New Deal programs EXCEPT:

    (A) Civil Works Administration
    (B) Reconstruction Finance Corporation
    (C) National Labor Relations Act
    (D) Farm Security Administration
    (E) Federal Housing Administration

36. Which of the following was a leader of Sioux resistance in the 1870s?

    (A) Chief Joseph
    (B) Geronimo
    (C) Squanto
    (D) Sitting Bull
    (E) Powhatan

37. The eastern half of which present-day state was called "Indian Territory" until 1907?

    (A) Nebraska
    (B) Kansas
    (C) Oklahoma
    (D) Colorado
    (E) Arizona

38. Nativists took all the following steps to protest immigration EXCEPT:

    (A) committing violence against immigrants
    (B) vandalizing Catholic churches because they were centers of immigrant neighborhoods
    (C) forming a political party to support restrictions on immigration
    (D) lynching immigrants and blaming African Americans for the crimes
    (E) electing many state and local officials who discriminated against immigrants

39. Before 1800, most immigrants to the United States were

    (A) Mexican
    (B) British
    (C) Dutch
    (D) German
    (E) Chinese

40. The United States acquired the last of the territory that would make up the contiguous United States during which decade?

    (A) 1770s
    (B) 1800s
    (C) 1840s
    (D) 1850s
    (E) 1950s

41. Between 1830 and 1860, the majority of European immigrants to the United States were from

    (A) France and Hungary
    (B) Belgium and Switzerland
    (C) Italy and Spain
    (D) Ireland and Germany
    (E) Russia and Greece

42. Which section of Article VI of the Constitution states that when federal and state laws come into conflict with each other, ultimate authority is given to federal laws?

    (A) Eminent domain
    (B) Supremacy clause
    (C) Public domain
    (D) Sovereignty clause
    (E) Elastic clause

43. The Indian Removal Act of 1830 stated that

    (A) all East Indian immigrants were to be deported
    (B) burial grounds would be established for Native Americans killed in conflict with federal troops
    (C) all Native American images would be removed from public display
    (D) Native American tribes living east of the Mississippi River would be relocated
    (E) all government officials of Native American ancestry would be dismissed from their posts

GO ON TO THE NEXT PAGE ➤

PRACTICE TEST—*Continued*

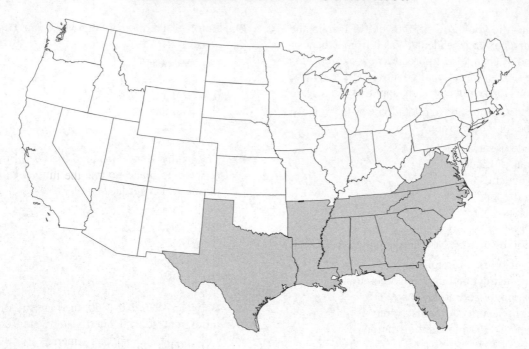

44. The shaded area on the map above represents

    (A) the Gadsden Purchase
    (B) the Louisiana Purchase
    (C) the Confederate States of America
    (D) the Mexican Cession
    (E) Indian Territory

45. William Jennings Bryan's "Cross of Gold" speech at the Democratic Convention of 1896 proposed which of the following?

    (A) That the United States maintain the gold standard
    (B) That a cross of gold be erected on the White House lawn
    (C) That silver be coined to inflate the U.S. currency
    (D) That churches pay income taxes to aid the poor
    (E) That the United States sell gold to foreign investors

46. Cesar Chavez became prominent in the 1960s as

    (A) the speaker of the house in Texas
    (B) a bilingual television host in California
    (C) the head of an organization that promoted Hispanic boxers
    (D) the leader of the United Farm Workers
    (E) the first Hispanic mayor of a U.S. city

47. The first President of the Independent Republic of Texas was

    (A) Sam Houston
    (B) Walter Dallas
    (C) Stephen F. Austin
    (D) Jim Bowie
    (E) Dallas Green

48. All the following innovations were a direct result of the growth of U.S. cities from 1865 to 1900 EXCEPT:

    (A) the elevator
    (B) the skyscraper
    (C) the automobile
    (D) trolley cars
    (E) steel frame construction

GO ON TO THE NEXT PAGE →

PRACTICE TEST—*Continued*

49. "One of the best ways to cope with (fear), is to turn it around and put it out to others . . . if you are afraid of the dark, you put the audience in a dark theater. I had a great fear of the ocean."

    This quotation most likely describes which of the following blockbuster American films?

    (A) *Gone With the Wind*
    (B) *Star Wars*
    (C) *Jaws*
    (D) *The Sound of Music*
    (E) *The Wizard of Oz*

50. Which of the following made New York the first state to grant women the right to own property?

    (A) The Nineteenth Amendment, 1920
    (B) The Married Women's Property Act, 1848
    (C) The Emancipation Proclamation, 1863
    (D) The Seneca Falls Declaration of Sentiments, 1848
    (E) The Fourteenth Amendment, 1868

51. Which of the following helped make the Second Great Awakening a success?

    (A) The growth of Lutheranism
    (B) Early German immigration
    (C) The preaching of Jonathan Edwards
    (D) A decline in Protestant denominations
    (E) Circuit riders, or itinerant ministers

52. Which of the following is a nickname for the generation born between 1945 and 1965?

    (A) The lost generation
    (B) The beat generation
    (C) The baby boom generation
    (D) The peace generation
    (E) Generation X

53. Which of the following is a broad program created by Martin Luther King, Jr., to confront the issues of U.S. economic inequalilty and poverty regardless of race.

    (A) The Poor People's Campaign
    (B) The March on Washington
    (C) Affirmative action
    (D) Black power
    (E) War on Poverty

54. Which of the 13 British colonies was founded on the southern frontier of British North America to provide a fresh start for debtors?

    (A) South Carolina
    (B) Virginia
    (C) Florida
    (D) Georgia
    (E) North Carolina

55. Pickett's Charge became the turning point for the Union against the Confederacy in which of the following Civil War battles?

    (A) Chancellorsville
    (B) Gettysburg
    (C) Antietam
    (D) Vicksburg
    (E) Second Bull Run

56. During the 1860s and 1870s federal troops repeatedly clashed with Native Americans in which of the following regions?

    (A) Northeast
    (B) Great Lakes
    (C) Southeast
    (D) Mississippi Valley
    (E) Great Plains

57. Which of the following proposed a 1930s relief program in which money would be taken from the wealthy and given to the poor?

    (A) Harold Ickes
    (B) Huey Long
    (C) John Nance Garner
    (D) Alf Landon
    (E) Father Charles Coughlin

58. Mary Boykin Chesnut is best known for which of the following?

    (A) Writing a diary that documents home life on the plantation during the Civil War
    (B) Acting as a spy, passing secret troop placements to the Union
    (C) Writing newspaper editorials opposing the Confederacy
    (D) Running for the Senate in 1864
    (E) Harboring runaway slaves in South Carolina

GO ON TO THE NEXT PAGE

PRACTICE TEST—*Continued*

59. Which group opposed ratification of the Constitution because its members feared a powerful national government?

    (A) Whigs
    (B) Continentalists
    (C) Tories
    (D) Democratic-Republicans
    (E) Antifederalists

60. Which of the following leaders did NOT sign the Treaty of Versailles, ending World War I?

    (A) Woodrow Wilson
    (B) Georges Clemenceau
    (C) Vittorio Orlando
    (D) Henry Cabot Lodge
    (E) David Lloyd George

61. The active colonial protest group called Sons of Liberty first organized in which of the following cities?

    (A) Philadelphia
    (B) New York
    (C) Boston
    (D) Williamsburg
    (E) Charleston

62. Powers shared by the federal and state governments are called

    (A) concurrent powers
    (B) sovereign powers
    (C) bicameral powers
    (D) reduced powers
    (E) federal powers

63. The first election in which the Twenty-Sixth Amendment (allowing 18-year olds to vote) was in effect was held in

    (A) 1948
    (B) 1964
    (C) 1972
    (D) 1976
    (E) 1980

64. The term "planned obsolescence" refers to which of the following?

    (A) The practice of letting a contract expire
    (B) An urban planning strategy designed to rebuild neighborhoods on a timed schedule
    (C) The business practice of manufacturing products specifically designed to go out of style and be replaced by new models
    (D) A temporary construction site
    (E) The government system for maturing savings bonds

65. The skyscraper boom in U.S. cities was facilitated by Elisha Otis's development of

    (A) the revolving door
    (B) the elevator
    (C) the telephone
    (D) refrigeration
    (E) the lightbulb

66. Which of the following Eastern tribes was NOT a member of the Iroquois League?

    (A) Seneca
    (B) Mohawk
    (C) Onondaga
    (D) Delaware
    (E) Cayuga

67. Which prominent U.S. inventor was known as "the Wizard of Menlo Park"?

    (A) Albert Einstein
    (B) Alexander Graham Bell
    (C) Henry Ford
    (D) Tobias Fuller
    (E) Thomas Edison

68. All the following statements support the theory that the West was developed by big business, big government, and technology EXCEPT:

    (A) The government gave away land to anyone who would claim it, live on it, and farm it.
    (B) The railroad companies brought thousands of Chinese immigrants to the West.
    (C) The U.S. Army protected the settlers and evicted Native Americans.
    (D) The railroad made it possible to transport necessary supplies to pioneer farmers in rural areas.
    (E) Farmers had no national association to which they could apply for help.

GO ON TO THE NEXT PAGE ▶

PRACTICE TEST—*Continued*

69. The phrase "Great White Hope" refers to which of the following?

   (A) Babe Ruth, whose home run hitting restored faith in baseball after the Black Sox scandal of 1919
   (B) Boston Celtics basketball star Larry Bird
   (C) The women's gymnastics team at the 1980 Olympic Games
   (D) A white boxer good enough to defeat Jack Johnson, world heavyweight champion in 1908
   (E) Swedish tennis champion Bjorn Borg

70. All the following factors combined to cause the United States to declare war on Great Britain in 1812 EXCEPT:

   (A) U.S. desire to acquire Canada and Florida
   (B) bumbling policies of President James Madison
   (C) impressment of U.S. sailors into the British Navy
   (D) British alliance with and support of Native American tribes
   (E) U.S. purchase of New France, later called the Louisiana Territory

71. In 1837 Horace Mann worked for all the following public-school reforms in Massachusetts EXCEPT:

   (A) raising teacher salaries
   (B) pressuring the legislature to increase funding for schools
   (C) opening the nation's first public high schools
   (D) starting teacher training schools
   (E) updating the curriculum

72. Some historians date the start of the Civil War to April 1861 when

   (A) John Brown led a raid on the federal arsenal at Harpers Ferry
   (B) South Carolina seceded from the United States
   (C) Confederate forces fired on Fort Sumter, South Carolina
   (D) President Lincoln issued the Emancipation Proclamation
   (E) Union troops laid siege to Richmond, Virginia

73. The primary cause of the market revolution of the early 1800s was

   (A) the creation of a national bank
   (B) the building of national roads and canals
   (C) the abandonment of the gold standard
   (D) the development of refrigeration
   (E) the signing of an international trade agreement

74. The Voting Rights Act of 1975 stated which of the following?

   (A) Young people between the ages of 18 and 21 had the right to vote.
   (B) People must register with a political party in order to vote.
   (C) Resident aliens could vote in local elections.
   (D) People did not have to reveal which candidates they voted for.
   (E) Voting materials must be made available in a variety of languages.

75. "The party reached out mostly to men, to young, black urban men who were on the streets, who knew that there were no options somewhere in their lives."

   The speaker of the above quotation most likely is referring to which of the following?

   (A) The Black Panther Party
   (B) The civil rights movement
   (C) The Reform Party
   (D) The Urban League
   (E) The Socialist Party

76. Which of the following was NOT a U.S. victory in the Pacific in World War II?

   (A) The attack on Guadalcanal
   (B) The Battle of the Coral Sea
   (C) The Battle of the Bulge
   (D) The Battle of Midway
   (E) The Battle of Leyte Gulf

GO ON TO THE NEXT PAGE

PRACTICE TEST—*Continued*

77. Congress passed the War Powers Act primarily because

    (A) Presidents Johnson and Nixon had usurped congressional authority in making war on Vietnam
    (B) the United States had not achieved a clear victory in Vietnam
    (C) the Vietnam War had been unpopular with the voters from the beginning
    (D) Congress believed that only the president should have the power to declare war
    (E) the public wanted to end the military draft and replace it with an all-volunteer army

78. The U.S. Department of Agriculture was created primarily to assist which of the following?

    (A) tenant farmers who were forced off their land during the Dust Bowl era
    (B) former slaves who wanted to acquire homesteads in the West
    (C) miners who fought against unsafe working conditions
    (D) struggling farmers on the Great Plains
    (E) ranchers who wanted to import a healthier breed of cattle

79. The Atlantic Charter, signed by the United States and Great Britain in 1941, stated all the following EXCEPT:

    (A) Aggressor nations would be disarmed after the end of the war.
    (B) All nations had the right to choose their own form of government.
    (C) All nations should have equal and free access to international trade.
    (D) The United States and Great Britain would not expand their territory.
    (E) Germany would be split into two nations at the end of the war.

80. "I didn't want to believe it at first—people protesting against us when we were putting our lives on the line for our country."

    The speaker of the above quotation is most likely a veteran of the

    (A) Korean War
    (B) Vietnam War
    (C) Persian Gulf War
    (D) invasion of Afghanistan
    (E) war in Iraq

81. All the following are major photojournalists of the Great Depression EXCEPT:

    (A) Margaret Bourke-White
    (B) Walker Evans
    (C) Althea Gibson
    (D) Dorothea Lange
    (E) Gordon Parks

82. The first U.S. school where women and African Americans, as well as men, could earn a four-year college degree was

    (A) Oberlin College, Oberlin, Ohio
    (B) Bryn Mawr College, Bryn Mawr, Pennsylvania
    (C) Harvard University, Cambridge, Massachusetts
    (D) Yale University, New Haven, Connecticut
    (E) The University of Pennsylvania, Philadelphia, Pennsylvania

83. Which of the following works of the American theater explicitly compares McCarthyism to the Puritan "witch hunts" of Salem, Massachusetts?

    (A) *A Man for All Seasons* by Robert Bolt
    (B) *The Crucible* by Arthur Miller
    (C) *Strange Interlude* by Eugene O'Neill
    (D) *Angels in America* by Tony Kushner
    (E) *Assassins* by Stephen Sondheim

84. Samuel Colt's revolver, which was patented in the United States in 1836, revolutionized armed combat because of which of the following innovations?

    (A) It did not have to be taken apart during reloading.
    (B) It could be used as either a firing weapon or a bayonet.
    (C) It had sights along the barrel that improved accuracy.
    (D) It could be fired six times before being reloaded.
    (E) It enabled the soldier to shoot from a greater distance.

85. Which of the following machines, invented in 1793, was primarily responsible for an economic boom in the South?

    (A) Eli Whitney's cotton gin
    (B) Robert Fulton's steam engine
    (C) Henry Bessemer's steel converter
    (D) John Deere's tractor
    (E) Edwin L. Drake's oil drill

GO ON TO THE NEXT PAGE ➔

PRACTICE TEST—*Continued*

86. The Great Migration took place during which of the following decades?

    (A) 1920s
    (B) 1850s
    (C) 1890s
    (D) 1960s
    (E) 1990s

87. The growth of the railroad industry in the 1870s stimulated all the following EXCEPT:

    (A) settlement of Western states
    (B) growth in the steel industry
    (C) expansion of markets for trade and sales
    (D) high employment rates
    (E) development of the automobile

88. James Madison, Alexander Hamilton, and John Jay were all

    (A) members of President George Washington's cabinet
    (B) signers of the Declaration of Independence
    (C) authors of the *Federalist Papers*
    (D) prominent Antifederalists
    (E) heroes of Revolutionary War battles

89. All the following characterize the Native American literary tradition EXCEPT:

    (A) trickster tales
    (B) creation stories
    (C) fables featuring animal characters
    (D) tales based on the sacred books of Native American religion
    (E) stories passed down orally over generations

90. During the 1770s punitive Acts of Parliament were aimed primarily at Massachusetts because

    (A) Massachusetts's governor was a member of the Sons of Liberty
    (B) Bostonians had provoked the Boston Massacre and had held the Boston Tea Party
    (C) the stamp agent for Massachusetts had been attacked and thrown out of town
    (D) the Massachusetts legislature had abolished slavery throughout the colony
    (E) the people of Massachusetts did not believe in the separation of church and state

STOP

IF YOU FINISH BEFORE TIME RUNS OUT, GO BACK AND CHECK YOUR WORK.

ANSWER KEY

1. B	21. E	41. D	61. C	81. C
2. D	22. B	42. B	62. A	82. A
3. C	23. C	43. D	63. C	83. B
4. E	24. E	44. C	64. C	84. D
5. E	25. E	45. C	65. B	85. A
6. B	26. B	46. D	66. D	86. A
7. A	27. A	47. A	67. E	87. E
8. A	28. C	48. C	68. E	88. C
9. E	29. A	49. C	69. D	89. D
10. C	30. B	50. B	70. E	90. B
11. D	31. B	51. E	71. C	
12. E	32. B	52. C	72. C	
13. E	33. D	53. A	73. B	
14. C	34. D	54. D	74. E	
15. E	35. B	55. B	75. A	
16. B	36. D	56. E	76. C	
17. D	37. C	57. B	77. A	
18. A	38. D	58. A	78. D	
19. B	39. B	59. E	79. E	
20. E	40. D	60. D	80. B	

ANSWERS AND EXPLANATIONS

1. **B** Women have certain privileges in U.S. society, such as exemption from the military draft. Women who opposed the ERA preferred to retain those privileges.

2. **D** The Fifteenth Amendment states that no one can be banned from voting because of "race, color, or previous condition of servitude."

3. **C** Reagan was exonerated from any wrongdoing, but it was his administration that aided the Nicaraguan Contras in defiance of congressional laws.

4. **E** The Northwest Ordinance of 1787 set forth the rules for how the sections of the Northwest Territory could become states.

5. **E** Eleanor Roosevelt's daily column was called "My Day"; she was instrumental in passing the UN Declaration of Human Rights; she frequently traveled abroad to visit U.S. servicemen in hospitals; and she is famous for having resigned from an organization that would not allow the African-American contralto Marian Anderson to sing in its hall, and then helping to arrange Anderson's concert at the Lincoln Memorial.

6. **B** Wilson fought an uphill battle against the U.S. Congress to establish the League of Nations, which he lost; the League was founded, but the United States did not play any part in it.

7. **A** Clinton was elected to the U.S. Senate from New York after she left the White House.

8. **A** The Black Codes varied from state to state, but they all abridged the rights of African Americans. Southern legislatures could not restore slavery, but they insisted on continuing a system of racial segregation and oppression.

9. **E** The Grange and Alliance movements did the opposite; they were national organizations that helped farmers band together to achieve common goals.

10. **C** Employers continued to fight the idea of a closed shop; they insisted that they would not require any workers to join unions.

11. **D** The Nineteenth Amendment was passed during the presidency of Woodrow Wilson.

12. **E** President Clinton had exceptionally good relations with traditional U.S. allies.

13. **E** Most Tories did not like the acts of Parliament any better than other colonists, but they did not see independence as a viable solution.

14. **C** An open shop is one in which workers are not required to join a union. The IWW and other labor organizations always fought for a closed shop because they knew that unions were most effective when all the employees belonged.

15. **E** Europeans never even considered assimilating themselves into whatever culture they might find in the Americas.

16. **B** The Fair Employment Practices Committee was established in 1941 to ensure that there would be no discrimination in hiring by the defense industry.

17. **D** Big bands were popular during the late 1930s and through the 1940s.

18. **A** The speaker is clearly ill at ease with being financially and socially secure; this points to someone who would become a supporter of and a participant in the counterculture.

19. **B** The Seneca Falls Convention was convened primarily to raise awareness and to be the springboard to a fight for women's legal rights, such as the right to own property.

20. **E** Emily Dickinson did not belong to any literary movement or school; she lived as a recluse and wrote highly individual and idiosyncratic poetry.

21. **E** Protective tariffs and a free-trade agreement are mutually exclusive.

22. **B** The Erie Canal stretched from the Great Lakes to the Hudson River.

23. **C** Samuel Adams was a political activist who took no part in armed combat during the Revolution.

24. **E** Albright and Kissinger were both secretaries of state; one was born in Czechoslovakia, the other in Germany. Paine was the Englishman who wrote *Common Sense*. Jones was a labor organizer who was born in Ireland.

25. **E** Veterans were ready to return to the workforce, but there were not always jobs for them. Overall, employment rates fell.

26. **B** When African Americans left the South it was always for the same reason: to escape the all-pervasive discrimination and segregation.

27. **A** The Bursum Bill would have made it possible for non–Native Americans to claim Pueblo land.

28. **C** "Stonewall" Jackson was one of the wiliest generals of the Confederate Army.

29. **A** The GI Bill made it possible for veterans— many of whom were from poor families—to go to college in an era when most people who attended college were children of the wealthy.

30. **B** The Anaconda Plan refers specifically to the blockade, which was meant to crush the life out of the South as an anaconda squeezes the life out of its prey. General Winfield Scott, who proposed the plan, warned against trying to capture Richmond.

31. **B** There were no personal income taxes in the United States until the ratification of the Sixteenth Amendment in 1913, well after Roosevelt left office.

32. **B** F. Scott and Zelda Fitzgerald were to many people the embodiment of the Jazz Age, and *The Great Gatsby* captures the era in which it was written.

33. **D** The Supreme Court found that the defendants were not assigned attorneys until the morning of the trial; thus, they had no opportunity to speak with their counsel or prepare a defense. This violated their Fourteenth Amendment right to due process and a fair trial.

34. **D** The reference to "the yoke of Britain" and the objection to the "new form of national government" make it clear that the speaker must have been an Antifederalist objecting to the Constitution.

35. **B** The Reconstruction Finance Corporation predated Roosevelt's presidency.

36. **D** Chief Joseph was a Nez Percé, Geronimo was an Apache, and Squanto and Powhatan were from East Coast nations. The Sioux were a tribe from the Great Plains.

37. **C** When Oklahoma was granted statehood in 1907, the eastern half, called Indian Territory, was included within the borders of the new state.

38. **D** Nativists did not lynch immigrants. They committed acts of violence against them, but those acts usually were intended to intimidate, not to murder.

39. **B** In the decade after the Revolution the majority of immigrants to the United States were British.

40. **D** The United States acquired the Southwestern land known as the Gadsden Purchase in 1854 during Franklin Pierce's presidency. This was six years after the Mexican-American War.

41. **D** The huge influx into the United States of Italian, Eastern European, and Chinese immigrants did not begin until after the Civil War.

42. **B** The Constitution states that it is "the supreme law of the land . . . laws of any state to the contrary notwithstanding."

43. **D** The Indian Removal Act, like most laws of the 1800s relating to Native Americans, had to do with their forced relocation.

44. **C** The Confederacy included the group of 11 states shaded on the map.

45. **C** Bryan opposed the gold standard and supported the notion of coining silver.

46. **D** Cesar Chavez was a successful Mexican-American labor leader.

47. **A** Sam Houston, who played a major role in the capture of Santa Anna, became the first president of Texas.

48. **C** The automobile was not the result of the growth of cities; millions of people who lived in cities could not afford a car and had no use for one.

49. **C** Only *Jaws* has a plot that is related to fear of monsters (sharks) lurking under the water.

50. **B** Only the Married Women's Property Act relates to ownership of property.

51. **E** Ministers who traveled and held revival meetings in outlying areas were largely responsible for the widespread success of the Second Great Awakening.

52. **C** The post–World War II generation is called the "baby boom generation" because so many babies were born during those years.

53. **A** In 1968, King organized the Poor People's Campaign to focus the nation on economic inequality. King's campaign demanded that the U.S. government aid the poor with a large jobs program that would rebuild U.S. inner cities. He was angry that money for social programs was being used instead to fight the Vietnam War.

54. **D** British debtors could win release from debtor's prison if they agreed to go to Georgia and start anew.

55. **B** Gettysburg was the turning point of the Civil War for the Union.

56. **E** The other areas of the nation were already settled, and Native Americans had been driven out or agreements had been made with them. The clashes in the Great Plains occurred while those areas were being settled during the 1860s and 1870s.

57. **B** Huey Long was the author of this Robin Hood–style idea.

58. **A** Mary Chesnut's diary of the Civil War is an important primary source for historians.

59. **E** The Antifederalists got their name from their opposition to a strong federal government.

60. **D** Wilson, Clemenceau, Lloyd George, and Orlando were the chief executives of the Big Four nations that signed the treaty.

61. **C** The first group of Sons of Liberty was organized in Boston in the mid-1760s. Other colonies soon copied that organization.

62. **A** These powers are called concurrent precisely because they are held jointly by two authorities.

63. **C** The Twenty-Sixth Amendment lowered the voting age to 18; this was largely a response to protests against the Vietnam War. Young people felt that if they were old enough to fight and die, they were old enough to vote.

64. **C** "Obsolescence" means that something passes into a state of uselessness. Businesses employ this practice so that consumers will have to spend more money to buy the new model.

65. **B** People would not walk up more than about six flights of steps; skyscrapers would never have been practical without elevators and escalators.

66. **D** The Iroquois lived in New York State; the Delaware are from somewhat farther south, near the Delaware River.

67. **E** Edison's laboratory was in Menlo Park, New Jersey.

68. **E** The first four choices all describe direct action taken by the government, big business, and technology to settle the West.

69. **D** When Jack Johnson became world heavyweight champion, almost every white sports journalist in the country expressed the desire for a "great white hope" to come along and defeat him.

70. **E** The Louisiana Purchase had happened in 1803, well before war was declared; it was not a factor in the war.

71. **C** The first public high schools were already open before Mann began his crusade.

72. **C** The official start of the war was the attack on Fort Sumter.

73. **B** The market revolution refers to the expansion of local markets into regional and national ones. The transportation system was what made this possible.

74. **E** The Voting Rights Act of 1975 ordered communities with a large foreign-born population to provide bilingual ballots and oral assistance for people who spoke Spanish, Chinese, Japanese, Korean, Native American languages, and Eskimo languages.

75. **A** The Black Panther Party urged African Americans to carry guns and take an active role in defending themselves against white oppression. That message spoke powerfully to urban young black men.

76. **C** The Battle of the Bulge took place in Europe.

77. **A** Johnson and Nixon had gone to war without Congress having declared war; that robbed Congress of one of its most important constitutional powers. The War Powers Act stated that the president could commit troops to a conflict for only 60 days without congressional authorization.

78. **D** The Department of Agriculture was created in 1862 to help farmers on the Great Plains who were not used to farming terrain with a small water supply and no trees to use for timber.

79. **E** Germany was split into two nations after the war because of Cold War tensions between the United States and the Soviet Union, not because of anything in the Atlantic Charter.

80. **B** Especially during the later years of the Vietnam War, antiwar protests were common.

81. **C** Althea Gibson was a famous tennis player, not a photojournalist.

82. **A** Oberlin accepted female and black students in the 1830s. Bryn Mawr was not founded until the 1880s; the other three schools are older than Oberlin but did not welcome female students until well into the twentieth century.

83. **B** *The Crucible* is a historical play based on Miller's reading of the Salem witch trial transcripts. Miller drew a deliberate and explicit analogy between those times in U.S. history and the period of McCarthyism during which he was living; both were times when an accusation was enough to ruin a person's reputation and deprive him or her of a livelihood.

84. **D** Before the Colt revolver, a weapon could be fired only once before the soldier had to stop and reload. The Colt was much more efficient. Later models did not have to be taken apart for reloading, but this was not true of the original 1836 Colt.

85. **A** The cotton gin could process more cotton than hundreds of slaves could process by hand in the same amount of time.

86. **A** The Great Migration usually refers to the movement of about 1.5 million African Americans from the South to the North from about 1910 to 1930. African Americans migrated to escape racism, get a better education, and find work in northern cities. Between 1910 and 1930, the black population of the north rose about 207 percent; Chicago's black population grew by 148 percent, and Detroit's by 611 percent.

87. **E** The growth of the railroad had no effect on the development of the automobile.

88. **C** The Federalists Madison, Hamilton, and Jay strongly supported ratification of the Constitution and wrote the *Federalist Papers* to persuade voters to support it too.

89. **D** The Native American literary tradition is an oral, not a written, one. There are no sacred books of Native American religion; religion is preserved in stories, customs, and artifacts.

90. **B** Conflict with soldiers and the deliberate destruction of valuable property made Boston the target of Parliament's anger.

PRACTICE TEST 5

▉ SCORE SHEET

Number of questions correct: _____

Less: 0.25 × number of questions wrong: _____

(Remember that omitted questions ares not counted as wrong.)

Raw score: _____

Raw Score	Scaled Score	Raw Score	Scaled Score	Raw Score	Scaled Score	Raw Score	Scaled Score	Raw Score	Scaled Score
90	800	65	710	40	550	15	420	−10	300
89	800	64	700	39	550	14	420	−11	290
88	800	63	700	38	540	13	410	−12	290
87	800	62	690	37	540	12	410	−13	280
86	800	61	680	36	530	11	400	−14	280
85	800	60	680	35	530	10	400	−15	270
84	800	59	670	34	520	9	390	−16	260
83	800	58	660	33	520	8	390	−17	260
82	800	57	660	32	510	7	380	−18	250
81	800	56	650	31	510	6	380	−19	240
80	790	55	640	30	500	5	370	−20	230
79	780	54	630	29	500	4	370	−21	230
78	780	53	630	28	490	3	360	−22	230
77	770	52	620	27	480	2	360		
76	760	51	620	26	480	1	350		
75	760	50	610	25	470	0	350		
74	750	49	610	24	470	−1	340		
73	750	48	600	23	460	−2	340		
72	740	47	600	22	460	−3	330		
71	740	46	590	21	450	−4	330		
70	730	45	590	20	450	−5	320		
69	730	44	580	19	440	−6	320		
68	720	43	570	18	440	−7	320		
67	720	42	560	17	430	−8	310		
66	710	41	560	16	430	−9	310		

Note: This is only a sample scoring scale. Scoring scales differ from exam to exam.

PRACTICE TEST 6
U.S. HISTORY

The following Practice Test is designed to be just like the real SAT U.S. History test. It matches the actual test in content coverage and level of difficulty.

When you are finished with the test, determine your score and carefully read the answer explanations for the questions you answered incorrectly. Identify any weak areas by determining the areas in which you made the most errors. Review those chapters of the book first. Then, as time permits, go back and review your stronger areas.

Allow 1 hour to take the test. Time yourself and work uninterrupted. If you run out of time, take note of where you ended when time ran out. Remember that you lose $\frac{1}{4}$ of a point for each incorrect answer. Because of this penalty, do not guess on a question unless you can eliminate one or more of the answers. Your score is calculated by using the following formula:

Number of correct answers $- \frac{1}{4}$(Number of incorrect answers)

This Practice Test will be an accurate reflection of how you'll do on test day if you treat it as the real examination. Here are some hints on how to take the test under conditions similar to those of the actual examination:

- Complete the test in one sitting.
- Time yourself.
- Tear out your Answer Sheet and fill in the ovals just as you would on the actual test day.
- Become familiar with the directions to the test and the reference information provided. You'll save time on the actual test day by already being familiar with this information.

PRACTICE TEST 6
U.S. HISTORY

ANSWER SHEET

Tear out this answer sheet and use it to mark your answers.

There are 100 lines of numbered ovals on this answer sheet. If there are more lines than you need, leave the remainder blank.

1. (A) (B) (C) (D) (E)	26. (A) (B) (C) (D) (E)	51. (A) (B) (C) (D) (E)	76. (A) (B) (C) (D) (E)
2. (A) (B) (C) (D) (E)	27. (A) (B) (C) (D) (E)	52. (A) (B) (C) (D) (E)	77. (A) (B) (C) (D) (E)
3. (A) (B) (C) (D) (E)	28. (A) (B) (C) (D) (E)	53. (A) (B) (C) (D) (E)	78. (A) (B) (C) (D) (E)
4. (A) (B) (C) (D) (E)	29. (A) (B) (C) (D) (E)	54. (A) (B) (C) (D) (E)	79. (A) (B) (C) (D) (E)
5. (A) (B) (C) (D) (E)	30. (A) (B) (C) (D) (E)	55. (A) (B) (C) (D) (E)	80. (A) (B) (C) (D) (E)
6. (A) (B) (C) (D) (E)	31. (A) (B) (C) (D) (E)	56. (A) (B) (C) (D) (E)	81. (A) (B) (C) (D) (E)
7. (A) (B) (C) (D) (E)	32. (A) (B) (C) (D) (E)	57. (A) (B) (C) (D) (E)	82. (A) (B) (C) (D) (E)
8. (A) (B) (C) (D) (E)	33. (A) (B) (C) (D) (E)	58. (A) (B) (C) (D) (E)	83. (A) (B) (C) (D) (E)
9. (A) (B) (C) (D) (E)	34. (A) (B) (C) (D) (E)	59. (A) (B) (C) (D) (E)	84. (A) (B) (C) (D) (E)
10. (A) (B) (C) (D) (E)	35. (A) (B) (C) (D) (E)	60. (A) (B) (C) (D) (E)	85. (A) (B) (C) (D) (E)
11. (A) (B) (C) (D) (E)	36. (A) (B) (C) (D) (E)	61. (A) (B) (C) (D) (E)	86. (A) (B) (C) (D) (E)
12. (A) (B) (C) (D) (E)	37. (A) (B) (C) (D) (E)	62. (A) (B) (C) (D) (E)	87. (A) (B) (C) (D) (E)
13. (A) (B) (C) (D) (E)	38. (A) (B) (C) (D) (E)	63. (A) (B) (C) (D) (E)	88. (A) (B) (C) (D) (E)
14. (A) (B) (C) (D) (E)	39. (A) (B) (C) (D) (E)	64. (A) (B) (C) (D) (E)	89. (A) (B) (C) (D) (E)
15. (A) (B) (C) (D) (E)	40. (A) (B) (C) (D) (E)	65. (A) (B) (C) (D) (E)	90. (A) (B) (C) (D) (E)
16. (A) (B) (C) (D) (E)	41. (A) (B) (C) (D) (E)	66. (A) (B) (C) (D) (E)	91. (A) (B) (C) (D) (E)
17. (A) (B) (C) (D) (E)	42. (A) (B) (C) (D) (E)	67. (A) (B) (C) (D) (E)	92. (A) (B) (C) (D) (E)
18. (A) (B) (C) (D) (E)	43. (A) (B) (C) (D) (E)	68. (A) (B) (C) (D) (E)	93. (A) (B) (C) (D) (E)
19. (A) (B) (C) (D) (E)	44. (A) (B) (C) (D) (E)	69. (A) (B) (C) (D) (E)	94. (A) (B) (C) (D) (E)
20. (A) (B) (C) (D) (E)	45. (A) (B) (C) (D) (E)	70. (A) (B) (C) (D) (E)	95. (A) (B) (C) (D) (E)
21. (A) (B) (C) (D) (E)	46. (A) (B) (C) (D) (E)	71. (A) (B) (C) (D) (E)	96. (A) (B) (C) (D) (E)
22. (A) (B) (C) (D) (E)	47. (A) (B) (C) (D) (E)	72. (A) (B) (C) (D) (E)	97. (A) (B) (C) (D) (E)
23. (A) (B) (C) (D) (E)	48. (A) (B) (C) (D) (E)	73. (A) (B) (C) (D) (E)	98. (A) (B) (C) (D) (E)
24. (A) (B) (C) (D) (E)	49. (A) (B) (C) (D) (E)	74. (A) (B) (C) (D) (E)	99. (A) (B) (C) (D) (E)
25. (A) (B) (C) (D) (E)	50. (A) (B) (C) (D) (E)	75. (A) (B) (C) (D) (E)	100. (A) (B) (C) (D) (E)

PRACTICE TEST 6

Time: 60 Minutes

Directions: Each of the questions or incomplete statements below is followed by five suggested answers or completions. Select the one that is best in each case and then fill in the corresponding oval on the answer sheet.

1. The main components of Henry Clay's American System were

   (A) a canal, railroads, and lower taxes
   (B) low tariffs, public education, military spending, and agriculture
   (C) a national bank, a protective tariff, and a national transportation system
   (D) trade with Europe, income taxes, and deficit spending
   (E) states' rights, local transportation, and a tax on Southern farmers

2. All the following were possible motives for President Harry S. Truman using the atomic bomb against Japan EXCEPT:

   (A) Japan refused to surrender.
   (B) Truman wanted to dismantle Japan's nuclear facilities.
   (C) the bombing could prevent a costly U.S. land invasion of Japan.
   (D) Truman wished to demonstrate the power of the bomb to the Soviet Union.
   (E) The United States wanted revenge for Japan's attack on Pearl Harbor.

3. As the automobile industry developed, it promoted the growth of all the following EXCEPT:

   (A) the asphalt and road-paving industries
   (B) the advertising business
   (C) the oil-refining industry
   (D) the telephone and telegraph industries
   (E) the importation of rubber

4. The nickname "Star Wars" refers to which of the following?

   (A) Public arguments among cabinet members during the Ford administration
   (B) The race to be the first nation to land an astronaut on the moon
   (C) A missile-based defense system conceived by President Ronald Reagan
   (D) The race for the top ratings for the evening network news broadcasts in the 1990s
   (E) Special Prosecutor Kenneth Starr's tactics during his investigation of allegations against President Bill Clinton

5. Jazz is a blend of all the following musical influences EXCEPT:

   (A) spirituals
   (B) the blues
   (C) hymns
   (D) work songs
   (E) ragtime

6. "It was a pleasure to live in those good old days, when a Federalist could knock a Republican down in the streets and not be questioned about it."

   The speaker of the above quotation most likely was referring to which decade in history?

   (A) 1800s
   (B) 1850s
   (C) 1870s
   (D) 1920s
   (E) 1960s

7. Which political party was formed during the 1890s to address the concerns of U.S. farmers?

   (A) Democratic Party
   (B) Republican Party
   (C) Progressive Party
   (D) Populist Party
   (E) Socialist Party

8. African Americans and women first served in combat duty in which of the following wars?

   (A) Revolutionary War
   (B) World War I
   (C) Vietnam War
   (D) Persian Gulf War
   (E) War in Iraq

9. Which of the following groups did NOT help form the Free-Soil Party in 1848?

   (A) Abolitionists
   (B) Farmers
   (C) Industrial workers
   (D) Land reformers
   (E) Southern conservatives

GO ON TO THE NEXT PAGE

PRACTICE TEST—*Continued*

10. Which of the following works would be most useful to a historian researching the living conditions of immigrants in New York City in the 1890s?

    (A) *The House of Mirth* by Edith Wharton
    (B) *How the Other Half Lives* by Jacob Riis
    (C) *Theory of the Leisure Class* by Thorstein Veblen
    (D) *The Bloodhounds of Broadway* by Damon Runyon
    (E) *The Gangs of New York* by Herbert Asbury

11. Civil rights groups opposed the Vietnam War primarily because

    (A) they supported the North Vietnamese and the communists
    (B) the media had stopped covering the civil rights movement in order to cover the war news
    (C) money that had been earmarked for social programs was diverted to military use
    (D) they objected to the war on religious and pacifist grounds
    (E) they wanted to prevent the reelection of President Lyndon Johnson

12. Accusations of improper conduct in the personal life of a candidate for high office are an example of which of the following?

    (A) Muckraking
    (B) Mudslinging
    (C) Gerrymandering
    (D) Grandstanding
    (E) Posturing

13. "Whenever I hear anyone arguing for slavery, I feel a strong impulse to see it tried on him personally."

    The speaker of the above quotation is probably which of the following?

    (A) Jefferson Davis
    (B) Abraham Lincoln
    (C) Theodore Roosevelt
    (D) Stephen Douglas
    (E) Robert E. Lee

14. The precedent for a free press in the United States was set by a trial involving which of the following?

    (A) Thomas Paine
    (B) John Peter Zenger
    (C) Samuel Adams
    (D) Phillis Wheatley
    (E) Frederick Douglass

15. In 1837, Democratic Party members of Congress passed a "gag rule" forbidding any discussion or debate of

    (A) corruption
    (B) sedition
    (C) abolition
    (D) expansion
    (E) imperialism

16. Which of the following established a court system in the United States?

    (A) The Articles of Confederation
    (B) The Bill of Rights
    (C) The Fifth Amendment
    (D) The Sixth Amendment
    (E) The Judiciary Act of 1789

17. "A man who is good enough to shed his blood for his country is good enough to be given a square deal afterwards. More than that no man is entitled to, and less than that no man shall have."

    Which of the following is most likely true of the speaker of the above quotation?

    (A) He believed in equal opportunities for people of all social classes.
    (B) He approved of U.S. involvement in foreign wars.
    (C) He felt that veterans were entitled to special benefits.
    (D) He was likely to side with owners rather than workers in labor disputes.
    (E) He supported an all-volunteer military rather than a military draft.

18. All of the following were proposals of Alexander Hamilton EXCEPT:

    (A) a national bank
    (B) repeal of the whiskey tax
    (C) protective tariffs
    (D) the federal government should assume state debts incurred during the Revolution
    (E) direct support to industry by government subsidies

GO ON TO THE NEXT PAGE

PRACTICE TEST—*Continued*

19. Which of the following did President Abraham Lincoln quote from in his Gettysburg Address?

    (A) The Constitution
    (B) The Declaration of Independence
    (C) *Common Sense*
    (D) The *Federalist Papers*
    (E) The Emancipation Proclamation

20. The American Federation of Labor was founded in 1886 as a result of

    (A) the Haymarket Riot
    (B) the election of President Grover Cleveland
    (C) a severe financial panic
    (D) federal legislation
    (E) negotiations between owners and workers

21. Which of the following spurred young people in the United States to push for the ratification of the Twenty-Sixth Amendment?

    (A) Opposition to the Vietnam War
    (B) Support for a Republican administration
    (C) Concern for veterans' rights
    (D) Commitment to civil rights for all Americans
    (E) Determination to ensure equal rights for men and women

22. Which of the following was designed to enforce the provisions of the Eighteenth [Prohibition] Amendment?

    (A) Kansas-Nebraska Act
    (B) War Powers Act
    (C) Voting Rights Act
    (D) Volstead Act
    (E) Pure Food and Drug Act

23. A supporter of the Niagara Movement of 1905 probably would applaud all the following EXCEPT:

    (A) civil rights
    (B) federal antilynching legislation
    (C) integration of the public schools
    (D) the African Colonization Society
    (E) the founding of the NAACP

24. To show their opposition to the Stamp Act, colonists took all the following actions EXCEPT:

    (A) holding a meeting of colonial leaders in New York City
    (B) calling up the members of the various colonial militias to active duty
    (C) passing local legislation that declared the Stamp Act illegal
    (D) refusing to purchase any products imported from Great Britain
    (E) tarring and feathering the stamp agents

25. All the following are major African-American literary figures EXCEPT:

    (A) Frederick Douglass
    (B) Richard Wright
    (C) Ralph Ellison
    (D) James Weldon Johnson
    (E) Harriet Beecher Stowe

26. The Erie Canal connected the Great Lakes with which of the following?

    (A) The Pacific Ocean
    (B) The Mississippi River
    (C) The Hudson River
    (D) The Cumberland Road
    (E) The Chesapeake Bay

27. All the following contributed to President Franklin D. Roosevelt's election to an unprecedented third term EXCEPT:

    (A) his skill at conducting the war in Europe
    (B) his outstanding skill as a political campaigner
    (C) his success in creating jobs
    (D) his opponent's failure to offer attractive alternatives to Roosevelt's policies
    (E) his enormous personal popularity and ability to inspire people with his courage and optimism

28. W. E. B. DuBois disagreed with Booker T. Washington's argument against African-American political activism primarily because

    (A) DuBois felt that African Americans' political activism would force the white majority to correct racial injustice
    (B) DuBois felt that only African Americans had any right to speak about racial issues
    (C) DuBois felt that Washington was a tool of the white majority
    (D) DuBois had no faith in African Americans' ability to help themselves
    (E) DuBois supported the African Colonization Society

GO ON TO THE NEXT PAGE ➡

PRACTICE TEST—*Continued*

29. President Harry S. Truman ordered the dropping of atomic bombs on Japanese cities primarily because

    (A) he wanted to save U.S. lives by forcing the Japanese to surrender
    (B) he wanted to intimidate the German Army into surrendering
    (C) he wanted the United States to be in the strongest possible position during peace negotiations with the other Allied Powers
    (D) he wanted Japan to shut down its own nuclear facilities
    (E) he wanted to destroy the capital city of Japan

30. The resignations of which two men made Gerald R. Ford president of the United States?

    (A) Bob Haldeman and John Erlichman
    (B) Spiro Agnew and Richard Nixon
    (C) Jimmy Carter and Ronald Reagan
    (D) Robert Kennedy and Lyndon Johnson
    (E) Henry Morgenthau and Harold Ickes

31. Which of the following most accurately defines Transcendentalism?

    (A) The belief that people can rise above material things in life to reach a higher understanding
    (B) The belief that one religion could transcend denominationalism
    (C) The belief that the Puritan faith could be combined with Unitarianism
    (D) The belief that Native Americans could never attain heaven
    (E) The belief in predestination and God's assignment at birth of people to their fate

32. The Sixteenth Amendment, passed in 1913, did which of the following?

    (A) Made the sale of alcoholic beverages illegal
    (B) Gave women the right to vote
    (C) Allowed for direct election of U.S. senators
    (D) Enabled Congress to levy taxes on income
    (E) Raised the voting age to 21

33. The Lincoln-Douglas debates took place during

    (A) the presidential election of 1860
    (B) the presidential election of 1864
    (C) the congressional debate over secession
    (D) the House of Representatives elections of 1854
    (E) the Senate elections of 1858

34. The Wright Brothers developed an airplane using experience gained from

    (A) working with locomotives and large engines
    (B) operating a bicycle shop and experimenting with small engines
    (C) repairing tractors and farm equipment
    (D) designing steam engines
    (E) manufacturing sewing machines

35. Which of the following describes one major effect of President Warren G. Harding's economic policies?

    (A) The elimination of tariffs on imported goods
    (B) A rise in union membership
    (C) Increased profits for business owners
    (D) Increased profits for farmers
    (E) Strict enforcement of antitrust legislation

36. Which of the following took its name from a British political party that opposed the power of the monarch?

    (A) The Know-Nothings
    (B) The Mugwumps
    (C) The Republicans
    (D) The Bull Moose Party
    (E) The Whigs

37. The Native American literary tradition can be best described as which of the following?

    (A) Classical poetry
    (B) Folk songs
    (C) Sermons
    (D) Creation myths and legends
    (E) Oral history

38. Which of the following commanded the United States Expeditionary Forces during World War I?

    (A) John J. Pershing
    (B) George S. Patton
    (C) Douglas MacArthur
    (D) Nathanael Greene
    (E) Dwight D. Eisenhower

GO ON TO THE NEXT PAGE ➡

PRACTICE TEST—*Continued*

39. The remains of one of the most sophisticated prehistoric native civilizations north of Mexico are preserved at Cahokia, Illinois. The people who lived at this site were called:

(A) the Toltec
(B) the Choctaw
(C) the Mound Builders
(D) the Creek Nation
(E) the Anasazi

40. ". . . government of the people, by the people, for the people, shall not perish from the earth."

This statement was first made in which of the following?

(A) The Preamble to the Constitution
(B) The Declaration of Independence
(C) The Magna Carta
(D) The Fifteenth Amendment
(E) The Gettysburg Address

41. The total value of all goods and services produced in a nation during a given year is referred to as

(A) the federal deficit
(B) the import-export ratio
(C) the federal budget
(D) the gross national product
(E) the distribution of wealth

42. The Iran hostage crisis had an impact on which presidential election?

(A) 1972
(B) 1976
(C) 1980
(D) 1984
(E) 1988

43. Spirituals were of great importance to which of the following?

(A) The Methodist Church
(B) Occult groups in New Orleans
(C) Slaves on plantations
(D) Catholic missions in the Southwest
(E) Immigrant funerals

44. Which of the following best describes Andrew Carnegie's practice of acquiring companies that provided raw materials and services for his steel business?

(A) Vertical integration
(B) Lateral growth
(C) Cross-disciplinary exploitation
(D) Venture capitalism
(E) Horizontal integration

45. "The ability to get to the verge without getting into war is the necessary art."

The speaker is describing which of the following?

(A) Brinksmanship
(B) Appeasement
(C) Imperialism
(D) Dollar diplomacy
(E) Containment

46. Which of the following was NOT an action authorized by the Federal Trade Commission (FTC) in 1914?

(A) The investigation of corporations
(B) A ban on fraudulent or unfair business practices
(C) The use of the courts to enforce FTC rulings
(D) The levying of taxes on interstate commerce
(E) The targeting of abuses such as mislabeling and false claims

47. Which of the following constituted the most significant international impact of the War of 1812?

(A) It caused diplomatic tensions between the United States and Spain.
(B) It forced France to nullify the Louisiana Purchase.
(C) It lessened shipping commerce on the Great Lakes.
(D) It forced the United States to police the Atlantic Ocean.
(E) It removed the British from the Northwest Territories

48. George Washington's first cabinet consisted of

(A) secretaries of war, state, commerce, and treasury
(B) attorney and postmaster generals and secretaries of state, treasury, and war
(C) secretaries of war, state, labor, and commerce
(D) secretaries of war, state, treasury, commerce, and Indian affairs
(E) chief justice, attorney general, and secretaries of state, war, and treasury

49. Congressional Republicans challenged President Clinton's domestic agenda in 1994 with their own proposals, popularly known as

(A) the Reform Act
(B) the Economic Initiative
(C) the Contract with America
(D) the McCain-Feingold Bill
(E) Operation Restore Hope

GO ON TO THE NEXT PAGE

PRACTICE TEST—*Continued*

50. The Zapruder film, which was shot with a hand-held camera in 1963, depicts which of the following?

    (A) The invention of the hula hoop
    (B) The construction of the *Pioneer 6* spacecraft
    (C) The development of the measles vaccine
    (D) The assassination of President John F. Kennedy
    (E) The Watergate hearings

51. All or parts of the following present-day states were part of the Mexican Cession EXCEPT:

    (A) California
    (B) Nevada
    (C) Utah
    (D) Colorado
    (E) Oklahoma

52. The first 10 constitutional amendments are known as

    (A) the Bill of Rights
    (B) Article VIII of the Constitution
    (C) the Civil Rights amendments
    (D) the elastic clause
    (E) the Federalist amendments

53. "There never has yet existed a wealthy and a civilized society in which one portion of the community did not . . . live on the labor of another."

    The speaker of the above quotation was defending which of the following?

    (A) The establishment of the Confederacy
    (B) South Carolina's right to secede from the United States
    (C) the creation of the National Bank
    (D) The institution of slavery
    (E) The doctrine of nullification

54. The two-party political system emerged in part because of which of the following?

    (A) Progressivism
    (B) Civil unrest
    (C) Sectionalism
    (D) Republicanism
    (E) Nationalism

55. Which one of the following people became the first female pilot to complete a solo transatlantic flight?

    (A) Charles Lindbergh
    (B) Harriet Quimby
    (C) Bessie Coleman
    (D) Gertrude Ederle
    (E) Amelia Earhart

56. The government's policy of allowing cattle ranchers to let their herds graze on public land was called

    (A) the roundup
    (B) range riding
    (C) the long drive
    (D) rustling
    (E) open range

57. Which of the following best describes the purpose of the Seneca Falls Convention of 1848?

    (A) To unite the Native American tribes of New York State
    (B) To discuss agricultural problems for farmers in the Eastern states
    (C) To form a society to advance the rights of women
    (D) To discuss antislavery strategies
    (E) To select a leader for a group of evangelist congregations

58. The turning point of the Revolutionary War was a battle fought at

    (A) Bunker Hill, Massachusetts
    (B) Saratoga, New York
    (C) Brandywine, Pennsylvania
    (D) Cowpens, South Carolina
    (E) Ticonderoga, Vermont

59. Which of the following was a marketing innovation of General Motors in the 1920s to help consumers buy more expensive cars?

    (A) Subliminal advertising
    (B) Rebates
    (C) Discounts for trading in an old car
    (D) Bargaining
    (E) The installment plan

60. Which of the following was most likely NOT a goal of George W. Bush in creating the Department of Homeland Security?

    (A) Improving airport security
    (B) Protecting transportation systems from attack
    (C) Expanding law-enforcement powers to combat terrorism
    (D) Building impenetrable walls along the Mexican and Canadian borders
    (E) Protecting vital power networks from attack

GO ON TO THE NEXT PAGE

PRACTICE TEST—*Continued*

61. Which faction formed in opposition to President Rutherford B. Hayes's support of civil-service reform?

    (A) Progressives
    (B) National Grangers
    (C) Populists
    (D) Half-Breeds
    (E) Stalwarts

62. *Uncle Tom's Cabin* provoked strong reactions in the South because

    (A) it justified Southerners' view that slavery was morally permissible
    (B) it depicted slavery as wrong and slaveholders as corrupt
    (C) it depicted romantic relations between African Americans and whites
    (D) it predicted that the South would lose the Civil War
    (E) it had no white characters

63. Which of the following helped the Pilgrims survive their first year in Plymouth by showing them how to grow crops?

    (A) Pocahontas
    (B) Sacagawea
    (C) Squanto
    (D) Powhatan
    (E) Sequoya

64. Which of the following geographical markings established the boundary between the United States and Spanish Florida in 1795?

    (A) The 38th parallel
    (B) Fifty-four/forty
    (C) Seventy-six degrees longitude, forty degrees latitude
    (D) The 31st parallel
    (E) The Tropic of Cancer

65. Which of the following most aptly describes Booker T. Washington's belief about the key to social and political equality for African Americans?

    (A) Economic independence through training and education
    (B) Protesting against discrimination
    (C) Overthrowing the U.S. government
    (D) Militant opposition to U.S. policies
    (E) Activist religious organizations

66. During Prohibition people drank alcohol at places called

    (A) back-room pubs
    (B) bathtub gin mills
    (C) stills
    (D) speakeasies
    (E) fraternity clubs

67. Which of the following congressional actions gave the president authority to take "all necessary measures to repel any attack against forces of the United States"?

    (A) The Bursum Bill
    (B) The Dawes Act
    (C) The Tonkin Gulf Resolution
    (D) The Smoot-Hawley Tariff
    (E) The War Powers Act

68. Sitting Bull was an important spiritual leader of the

    (A) Apache
    (B) Comanche
    (C) Navajo
    (D) Sioux
    (E) Creek

69. Shays' Rebellion in 1786 is significant because it

    (A) gave the U.S. militia a chance to demonstrate its efficiency
    (B) raised doubts about the ability of a decentralized government to deal with civil unrest
    (C) opened the door to westward expansion
    (D) united farmers against Native Americans
    (E) allowed former Revolutionary War officers to take up arms again

70. All the following were major crops in the antebellum South EXCEPT:

    (A) cotton
    (B) tobacco
    (C) maple syrup
    (D) rice
    (E) sugarcane

GO ON TO THE NEXT PAGE ➤

PRACTICE TEST—*Continued*

71. Nearly 600,000 U.S. lives were claimed in 1918–1919 by

    (A) an epidemic of influenza
    (B) World War I
    (C) an outbreak of polio
    (D) violent labor strikes
    (E) border violence with Mexico

72. President Richard Nixon and Secretary of State Henry Kissinger shared a belief in "realpolitik," which is best described as

    (A) a realistic belief in the ideal of democracy over any other interests
    (B) a foreign policy that puts human rights first
    (C) a foreign policy patterned after that of Germany
    (D) diplomacy guided by the writings of Immanuel Kant
    (E) a foreign policy guided by national interests rather than ideals

73. Which of the following was the first major farmers' organization, founded in 1867?

    (A) The 4-H Club
    (B) The National Grange
    (C) The Alliance
    (D) The American Federation of Labor
    (E) FarmAid

74. Which of the following was a severe low point for the Continental Army in the Revolutionary War?

    (A) The siege of Boston
    (B) The Battle of Brandywine
    (C) The Battle of Trenton
    (D) The winter at Valley Forge
    (E) The surrender at Yorktown

75. Balboa's sighting of the Pacific Ocean and Magellan's voyage around the tip of South America motivated other European explorers to seek which of the following?

    (A) A land route to India
    (B) Spanish permission to sail the Pacific
    (C) A caravan route to the Indies
    (D) A Northwest Passage to the Pacific and Asia
    (E) The Middle Passage to the Americas

76. Which of the following five Republicans who ran for president in 1824 won the election?

    (A) William Crawford of Georgia
    (B) John C. Calhoun of South Carolina
    (C) John Quincy Adams of Massachusetts
    (D) Henry Clay of Kentucky
    (E) Andrew Jackson of Tennessee

77. During President Theodore Roosevelt's administration, the federal government first began making damaged land productive again in a process called

    (A) reclamation
    (B) rejuvenation
    (C) progressivism
    (D) conservation
    (E) preservation

78. Which of the following generals did President Harry S. Truman fire for interfering with peace negotiations with Korea?

    (A) Dwight D. Eisenhower
    (B) Omar Bradley
    (C) Douglas MacArthur
    (D) James Stewart
    (E) Mark Clark

79. A second Industrial Revolution in the late 1800s was generated by innovations in which industries?

    (A) Automobile and railroad
    (B) Steel and oil refining
    (C) Telephone and telegraph
    (D) Advertising and radio
    (E) Agriculture and livestock

80. The Twenty-Third Amendment gave residents of the District of Columbia

    (A) exemption from the income tax
    (B) the right to sue the federal government
    (C) the right to vote in presidential elections
    (D) exemption from property taxes
    (E) the right to elect their own Congress

81. The Fundamental Orders of Connecticut of 1639 can be described as which of the following?

    (A) A set of strict religious guidelines
    (B) Precepts of the Puritans
    (C) A royal charter that established a hierarchy of authority
    (D) A peace treaty with the local Native Americans
    (E) The first written constitution in the colonies

GO ON TO THE NEXT PAGE →

PRACTICE TEST—*Continued*

82. Which of the following names the typical shelters built by the first white settlers on the Great Plains?

    (A) Adobe houses
    (B) Tepees
    (C) Sod houses
    (D) Log cabins
    (E) Prairie schooners

83. Which of the following explains the original purpose of the Federal Deposit Insurance Corporation (FDIC)?

    (A) To force poor people to deposit their income tax returns
    (B) To force employers to insure workers against injury
    (C) To insure corporations exploring for mineral deposits
    (D) To insure bank deposits up to $5,000
    (E) To protect banks against securities fraud

84. The attack launched by North Vietnamese troops on January 30, 1968, is called the Tet Offensive because

    (A) January 30 is Tet, the Vietnamese New Year
    (B) Tet is the province where fighting was launched
    (C) General Tet and his staff advisors planned the attack
    (D) the fighting began with the troops crossed the Tet River
    (E) Tet was a Vietnamese code name for the operation

85. Which of the following describes the most popular form of stage entertainment during the late 1800s?

    (A) Opera
    (B) Ballet
    (C) Vaudeville
    (D) Musical comedy
    (E) Tableaux

86. Which of the following describes General William T. Sherman's strategy of total war against the Confederacy?

    (A) Using both navy and army troops
    (B) Employing all the troops all the time
    (C) Destroying everything that would allow the Confederacy to keep fighting
    (D) Killing all enemies rather than taking them prisoner
    (E) Enlisting civilians to fight

87. The power of the courts to declare an act of Congress unconstitutional was established in the landmark Supreme Court case

    (A) *Roe v. Wade*
    (B) *Marbury v. Madison*
    (C) *McCulloch v. Maryland*
    (D) *Plessy v. Ferguson*
    (E) *Dred Scott v. Sandford*

88. The Americans with Disabilities Act of 1990 includes all the following EXCEPT:

    (A) prohibition of discrimination in employment against qualified individuals with disabilities
    (B) requirement of access for the physically disabled to all public buildings
    (C) prohibition of discrimination against the mentally handicapped in transportation
    (D) guarantee of fair and easy access to telephone services
    (E) guarantee of scholarship opportunities for people with learning disabilities

89. Madame C. J. Walker became a millionaire in the early 1900s by marketing

    (A) canned peas and greens
    (B) Walker's sweet potato pies
    (C) a bottled tonic for digestion
    (D) a hair-conditioning treatment for African-American women
    (E) the Walker bicycle for girls

90. The Pilgrims were called Separatists because they had broken with

    (A) the king of England
    (B) the Catholics
    (C) the Anglican Church
    (D) the New England Way
    (E) the Jamestown Colony

S T O P

IF YOU FINISH BEFORE TIME RUNS OUT, GO BACK AND CHECK YOUR WORK.

ANSWER KEY

1. C	21. A	41. D	61. E	81. E
2. B	22. D	42. C	62. B	82. C
3. D	23. D	43. C	63. C	83. D
4. C	24. B	44. A	64. D	84. A
5. C	25. E	45. A	65. A	85. C
6. A	26. C	46. D	66. D	86. C
7. D	27. A	47. E	67. C	87. B
8. A	28. A	48. B	68. D	88. E
9. E	29. A	49. C	69. B	89. D
10. B	30. B	50. D	70. C	90. C
11. C	31. A	51. E	71. A	
12. B	32. D	52. A	72. E	
13. B	33. E	53. D	73. B	
14. B	34. B	54. C	74. D	
15. C	35. C	55. E	75. D	
16. E	36. E	56. E	76. C	
17. A	37. D	57. C	77. A	
18. B	38. A	58. B	78. C	
19. B	39. C	59. E	79. B	
20. A	40. E	60. D	80. C	

ANSWERS AND EXPLANATIONS

1. **C** The American System advocated a national bank with a sound national currency, protective tariffs that would encourage people to buy U.S.-made goods, and a national transportation system that would open new markets and make trade easier within the United States.

2. **B** Japan had no nuclear facilities of its own in 1945.

3. **D** The rise in auto ownership meant a rise in paved roads on which to drive; auto makers increased advertising so that people would buy their cars and not those of their rivals; oil refining was necessary for fuel for cars; and more rubber had to be imported to meet the need for tires.

4. **C** The missile defense system was nicknamed for a popular fantasy movie of the era.

5. **C** Jazz music was developed from African-American religious and popular music, which did not include hymns.

6. **A** The Federalist Party had disappeared by 1810, and so choice A is the only possible answer.

7. **D** The Populist Party was created specifically to address the concerns of rural dwellers.

8. **A** African Americans have served with distinction in combat in every war the United States has ever fought, although the armed forces were segregated from 1812 until after World War II. Women fought in combat in the Revolutionary War, some in disguise, such as Deborah Sampson, and others openly in an emergency, such as Mary Ludwig Hayes.

9. **E** The Free Soil Party consisted of those people who wanted slavery barred from the Mexican Cession. As their name suggests, the Free Soil Party opposed any expansion of slavery into the American west. Therefore, the party did not include Southern conservatives.

10. **B** *How the Other Half Lives* specifically addresses the living conditions of poor immigrants in New York City tenements. *The Gangs of New York* also deals with this subject, but in an earlier era.

11. **C** Civil rights groups did not approve of spending money to fight a dubious foreign war when that money could be better spent fighting a war on poverty and discrimination at home.

12. **B** Mudslinging is the process of trying to turn voters against a candidate by spreading ugly personal rumors, whether true or untrue, about him or her.

13. **B** The speaker of the quotation is clearly against the institution of slavery, and among the choices, only Abraham Lincoln falls into this category. It is not likely that Theodore Roosevelt (choice C) is the speaker since slavery had been abolished by the time he became an adult.

14. **B** In 1735, Zenger was put on trial and was found innocent of slander because his paper had printed the truth.

15. **C** The Democratic Party was the proslavery party; therefore, Democrats did not want to discuss the issue of abolition.

16. **E** The Constitution gave Congress the authority to set up a court system; Congress fulfilled that obligation by passing the Judiciary Act of 1789.

17. **A** The term "square deal" is associated with Theodore Roosevelt. Although the reference seems to apply to soldiers, Roosevelt makes no reference to special benefits. Instead, he seems to believe that men of all social classes should have the same opportunities and benefits.

18. **B** Hamilton helped push the excise tax on whiskey through Congress as a way to raise revenue. When opposition to the tax developed in western Pennsylvania in 1794, Hamilton accompanied President Washington and a large U.S. Army to put down the so-called Whiskey Rebellion. The other choices are all actual proposals of Hamilton.

19. **B** Lincoln began his Gettysburg Address with a direct allusion to and quotation from the Declaration of Independence. "Fourscore and seven years ago" refers to 1776, and "all men are created equal" is a quotation from the document.

20. **A** The Haymarket Riot led skilled workers to break away from unskilled workers and join the AFL, which was founded by Samuel Gompers in 1886.

21. **A** The Twenty-Sixth Amendment lowered the voting age from 21 to 18, largely in response to protests by young people that if they were old enough to fight in a war and die for their country, they were old enough to vote for or against leaders who might send them to war.

22. **D** The Volstead Act enforced the Eighteenth Amendment's ban on the sale, production, and transport of liquor.

23. **D** The Niagara Movement protested discrimination against African Americans. The Colonization Society was an example of discrimination, although many people associated with it claimed it was well intentioned.

24. **B** The colonial militias were not called up for duty until long after the repeal of the Stamp Act.

25. **E** Harriet Beecher Stowe's novel *Uncle Tom's Cabin* certainly supported the cause of African Americans, but Stowe was not African American.

26. **C** The Erie Canal connected Lake Erie and the Hudson River.

27. **A** The United States was not yet involved in World War II, except to provide financial and material support to the Allies, when Roosevelt ran for reelection in 1940.

28. **A** DuBois believed that African Americans must be politically active and force the white majority to correct racial injustice. He felt that Washington's attitude would never achieve that goal.

29. **A** The Germans already had surrendered; Japan had no nuclear facilities; Japan's capital city, Tokyo, was not attacked with an atomic bomb; and peace negotiations with the other Allies already had taken place, although more were to follow. Truman simply wanted to end the fighting as soon as possible.

30. **B** Spiro Agnew resigned as vice president and was replaced by Gerald Ford. Ford became president when Richard Nixon resigned in order to avoid impeachment.

31. **A** Transcendentalists were influenced by Kant and by Romantic poets. They believed that the way to perfection was through the acquisition of knowledge.

32. **D** Progressives believed that a graduated income tax based on the amount of money a person earned was a fair means of funding necessary government programs and services.

33. **E** Abraham Lincoln and Stephen Douglas held their famous series of debates when both were candidates for the Illinois Senate seat that Douglas already held. Douglas won the election; two years later, Lincoln became president.

34. **B** In their home town of Dayton the Wright brothers ran a bicycle shop together. They and their sister Kate had been fascinated by the idea of flight since they were small children.

35. **C** Harding was unapologetically probusiness, and his policies meant increased profits for owners but not for workers.

36. **E** Whigs and Tories were the two major British political parties during the late 1700s.

37. **D** The Native American literary tradition is an oral tradition of stories, legends, and myths, many of which account for the creation of the world.

38. **A** Pershing was a veteran of the Spanish-American War who was appointed commander of the American Expeditionary Force in 1917. Patton and Eisenhower became famous during World War II; MacArthur is best known for his role in helping Japan recover after World War II; Greene fought during the Revolutionary War.

39. **C** The Mound Builders' culture developed in the Mississippi Valley of the American Southeast. Cahokia was inhabited from about 700 to 1400 C.E. At its peak, the city covered nearly six square miles and possibly 10,000 people lived there. More than 120 mounds were built there.

40. **E** Abraham Lincoln made this statement in the final sentence of the Gettysburg Address.

41. **D** The gross national product includes all the goods and services a nation produces.

42. **C** Many people held President Jimmy Carter responsible for failing to resolve the Iran hostage crisis; Ronald Reagan made this a centerpiece of his victorious campaign against Carter.

43. **C** Slaves sang spirituals because of the comfort they brought. Slaves likened their situation to that of the Jews in the Bible who were led to the Promised Land by Moses.

44. **A** Carnegie integrated his business vertically by owning all aspects of production and service related to it, from bottom to top.

45. **A** John Foster Dulles was speaking of getting to the brink, or edge, of war without actually having to fight.

46. **D** There have never been any taxes imposed on interstate commerce in the United States.

47. **E** Driving the British away from the Northwest Territories for good was an important step toward the United States gaining control of the central portion of the North American continent.

48. **B** Washington's first cabinet had only five officers, as specified in choice B.

49. **C** The Contract with America pledged that Congress would reform itself by implementing a series of new rules.

50. **D** Abraham Zapruder's home movie of the Dallas motorcade and the assassination was used by members of the Warren Commission who investigated the crime. It has appeared repeatedly ever since on television and in documentaries on the president's assassination.

51. **E** The Mexican Cession included all or part of the following states: California, Nevada, Utah, Arizona, Colorado, New Mexico, and Wyoming.

52. **A** The Bill of Rights was added to the Constitution soon after it was ratified.

53. **D** The speaker clearly is defending slavery by stating that there are historical precedents for it.

54. **C** Sectionalism divided the nation in half along regional lines, and each region came to be identified with a political party. In the presidential election of 1796, the Democratic-Republicans controlled the South (and Pennsylvania) while the Federalists controlled the northeast (and Maryland and Delaware).

55. **E** Charles Lindbergh was not a female pilot. Quimby and Coleman were famous female pilots but in 1932, Earhart was the first woman to fly solo across the Atlantic. Ederle was the first woman to swim the English Channel (1926).

56. **E** The open range was called "open" because it was land free to all, with none of it closed off by fences.

57. **C** The Seneca Falls Convention was called to bring the issue of women's rights to public notice.

58. **B** Saratoga was a turning point because it was after that victory that the French agreed to support the American colonists in their fight against Britain.

59. **E** General Motors allowed customers to make a down payment on a car and then pay a certain mount each month, including interest, until the full price was paid.

60. **D** No official of the Bush administration ever suggested building walls along the Mexican or Canadian border.

61. **E** The Half-Breeds supported civil service reform. The other three groups were not primarily concerned with the issue of civil service reform.

62. **B** Choices A, C, D, and E are inaccurate descriptions of the novel. Southerners did not like it because it portrayed slavery in a bad light.

63. **C** Squanto is the name of the Indian who befriended the Pilgrims and without whose help they probably would not have survived.

64. **D** The 31st Parallel marks the border of Spanish Florida.

65. **A** Washington believed that African Americans eventually would win full civil rights and independence once they achieved education and economic independence.

66. **D** "Speakeasy" was coined in the 1920s to describe a club that served alcoholic beverages.

67. **C** With the Tonkin Gulf Resolution, Congress ceded to the president its constitutional power to declare war.

68. **D** Sitting Bull was a leader of the Sioux.

69. **B** Shays' Rebellion made it clear that the Articles of Confederation did not give the central government enough authority to hold the nation together.

70. **C** Maple syrup is harvested in the United States in northern locations such as Wisconsin, Vermont, New York, and Maine.

71. **A** The worldwide epidemic of influenza killed millions; the world war that was going on at the time helped the virus spread. Far more Americans died of the flu than of bullet wounds.

72. **E** Realpolitik first was practiced by Otto von Bismarck in Germany in the nineteenth century. It involves dealing with realities rather than ideals.

73. **B** The National Grange was the first major farmers' movement.

74. **D** The Army of the United States made camp at Valley Forge in what one soldier described as "a truly forlorn condition," with almost no food, dressed in rags, and with little hope of victory. The soldiers had only their determination to hold them together.

75. **D** The famous "Northwest Passage" never existed; until the Panama Canal was completed, there was no water route from the Atlantic to the Pacific without going all the way around South America or somehow negotiating the frigid waters of the chain of islands north of mainland Canada.

76. **C** Adams became president in 1824; in 1828 Jackson defeated him to become president.

77. **A** The conversion of damaged land to productive land is called reclamation.

78. **C** MacArthur had defied orders from his superior, which is the worst sin a soldier can commit; other generals agreed that he should be fired for that offense.

79. **B** Steel and oil refining made possible the rest of the innovations of the second Industrial Revolution.

80. **C** Until the Twenty-Third Amendment was ratified in 1961, residents of Washington, D.C., could not vote for president.

81. **E** The Fundamental Orders set out how the colony would be governed.

82. **C** People built sod houses because there was almost no timber on the Great Plains; there also were no large rocks or any factories that made bricks.

83. **D** The original purpose of the FDIC was to make sure that if there was another widespread bank failure, people would not lose everything they had saved. The federal government would guarantee that up to $5,000 of their money would be safe.

84. **A** "Tet" is the Vietnamese name for the New Year's holiday.

85. **C** Vaudeville, with its variety of acts—juggling, dramatic scenes, tumbling, child performers, song-and-dance numbers, knockabout comedy acts, and trained animal acts—offered something for everybody.

86. **C** Sherman wanted to defeat the South as quickly as possible; therefore, his troops were ordered to destroy anything they came across that might conceivably help the South. The Union troops set fire to cotton fields, burned down houses, stole livestock, and so on.

87. **B** This principle is known as judicial review.

88. **E** The Americans with Disabilities Act forbids any school to discriminate against a disabled student but does not offer disabled students any financial aid.

89. **D** Walker made a fortune on her line of hair-care products.

90. **C** The Puritans had broken with the Anglican Church, and the Pilgrims were a radical sect of Puritans.

■ SCORE SHEET

Number of questions correct: _____

Less: 0.25 × number of questions wrong: _____

(Remember that omitted questions ares not counted as wrong.)

Raw score: _____

Raw Score	Scaled Score	Raw Score	Scaled Score	Raw Score	Scaled Score	Raw Score	Scaled Score	Raw Score	Scaled Score
90	800	65	710	40	550	15	420	−10	300
89	800	64	700	39	550	14	420	−11	290
88	800	63	700	38	540	13	410	−12	290
87	800	62	690	37	540	12	410	−13	280
86	800	61	680	36	530	11	400	−14	280
85	800	60	680	35	530	10	400	−15	270
84	800	59	670	34	520	9	390	−16	260
83	800	58	660	33	520	8	390	−17	260
82	800	57	660	32	510	7	380	−18	250
81	800	56	650	31	510	6	380	−19	240
80	790	55	640	30	500	5	370	−20	230
79	780	54	630	29	500	4	370	−21	230
78	780	53	630	28	490	3	360	−22	230
77	770	52	620	27	480	2	360		
76	760	51	620	26	480	1	350		
75	760	50	610	25	470	0	350		
74	750	49	610	24	470	−1	340		
73	750	48	600	23	460	−2	340		
72	740	47	600	22	460	−3	330		
71	740	46	590	21	450	−4	330		
70	730	45	590	20	450	−5	320		
69	730	44	580	19	440	−6	320		
68	720	43	570	18	440	−7	320		
67	720	42	560	17	430	−8	310		
66	710	41	560	16	430	−9	310		

Note: This is only a sample scoring scale. Scoring scales differ from exam to exam.

18.00   7/18/16.